CASES AND MATERIALS

LAND LAW

CASES AND MATERIALS

LAND LAW

Third Edition

Gary Watt, MA (Oxon), Solicitor
Senior Lecturer in Law, Nottingham Law School

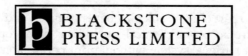

BLACKSTONE PRESS LIMITED

First published in Great Britain 1996 by Blackstone Press Limited,
Aldine Place, London W12 8AA.   Telephone 0181–740 2277

© Nottingham Law School, Nottingham Trent University, 1996

First edition 1996
Second edition 1997
Third edition 1998

ISBN: 1 85431 825 X

British Library Cataloguing in Publication Data
A CIP catalogue record for this book is available from the British Library.

Typeset by Style Photosetting Limited, Mayfield, East Sussex
Printed by Livesey Limited, Shrewsbury, Shropshire

FOREWORD

The books in the LLB series have been written for students studying law at undergraduate level. There are two books for each subject. The first is the *Learning Text* which is designed to teach you about the particular subject in question. However, it does much more than that. By means of Activities, Self Assessment, and End of Chapter Questions, the *Learning Text* allows you to test your knowledge and understanding as you work. Each chapter starts with 'Objectives' which indicate what you should be able to do by the end of it. You should use these Objectives in your learning — check them frequently and ask yourself whether you have attained them.

The second book is a volume of *Cases and Materials*. This is cross-referenced from the *Learning Text*. It contains the primary sources of law such as statutes and cases plus subsidiary sources such as extracts from journals, law reform papers and textbooks. This is your portable library. Although each volume can stand alone, they are designed to be complementary.

The two-volume combination aims to support your learning by challenging you to demonstrate your mastery of the principles and application of the law. They are appropriate whatever your mode of study — full-time or part-time.

CONTENTS

PREFACE

Land law is like chess. The pieces are for the most part simple to identify and the characteristics of each piece are basically straightforward, but when the game is played the pieces combine in complex and difficult forms. The aim of this volume is to identify the pieces and the rules in the clearest possible way using selected statutes and cases, extracts from journal articles, law reform proposals, scholarly texts and illustrative questions and answers. The student will see that land law has thrown up some fascinating games.

Primarily, of course, this volume is intended to accompany the *Distance Learning Text* on *Land Law*. The author of the Learning Text is Dr Roger Sexton, a 'Grandmaster' of land law, to whom I am grateful for providing the structural basis for the present volume. It is an extensive resource which should assist students of any land law degree course to approach the subject with the confidence and authority that comes from using primary source materials.

This volume is to be your portable library, and as such I have extracted for your use that which is relevant from a typical University Law Library. The extracts, wherever possible, are of sufficient length to encourage independent reflection. Distance learning students will do well to make their own connections and discoveries and it is hoped that the present volume will provide scope for this.

This edition has been fully revised to take into account the changes introduced by the Trusts of Land and Appointment of Trustees Act 1996, the Family Law Act 1996 and the Land Registration Act 1997.

You may never be a criminal, you may never commit a tort, but you will invariably have some right or interest in land. I hope that this volume will encourage interest in this area of law.

Gary Watt
Nottingham Law School

ACKNOWLEDGMENTS

Nottingham Law School and the publishers would like to thank the following for permission to reproduce copyright material:

Butterworths & Co. (Publishers) Ltd for extracts from the All England Law Reports, *New Law Journal* and Radcliffe and Cross, *The English Legal System*.

Cambridge University Press for extracts from *Cambridge Law Journal*.

Clarendon Press, Oxford, for extracts from Lawson and Rudden, *The Law of Property* and B. Nicholls, *Introduction to Roman Law*.

The Estates Gazette for extracts from The Estates Gazette Law Reports.

Her Majesty's Stationery Office for extracts from the Law Commission and Scottish Law Commission Reports and Law Commission Working Papers and the Land Registry Certificate.

The Incorporated Council of Law Reporting for England & Wales for extracts from the Law Reports and the Weekly Law Reports.

Law Book Company of Australia for extracts from the Australian Law Journal Reports.

Times Newspapers Ltd for extracts from The Times Law Reports.

Sweet & Maxwell for extracts from *Modern Law Review*, the English Reports, *The Conveyancer and Property Lawyer*, B. Harvey, *Settlements of Land* and Megarry & Wade 'The Law of Real Property'.

TABLE OF CASES

Cases reported in full are shown in heavy type. The page at which the report is printed is shown in heavy type.

TABLE OF STATUTES

Statutes, and sections thereof, which are set out in full or in part are shown in heavy type. The page at which the statute or section is printed is shown in heavy type.

CHAPTER ONE

INTRODUCTION TO THE TYPES OF PROPERTY RIGHTS IN LAND

1.1 Introduction

Lawson, F.H. and Rudden, B., The Law of Property 2nd edn,
Oxford: Clarendon Press, 1982, pp. 6–9

REAL RELATIONS

Having sketched in outline the sort of persons that can have legal relations with things and the kind of things subject to those relations, it is time to consider the relations themselves. The obvious ones are *possession* and *ownership* and they are easy to illustrate. If there is a library book on my desk then I have possession of it but not ownership. If I ask a friend to lend me a jug of milk and he does so then I acquire possession of the jug and he remains owner; but I acquire ownership of the milk and *owe him* its value, and he owns the abstract thing which is my debt to him.

Ownership would seem to the layman to be a simple notion. It is merely a question of *meum* and *tuum*. If the thing is mine, I own it; if it is not, I do not. Often the law conforms to this simple way of looking at ownership. Thus for example, a person may live alone in a house which he has bought and paid for, no one else has any rights over it, and his title is registered in the Land Registry; and he may have in his garage a car which he has bought direct from the manufacturer. In both cases he can correctly say, without qualification, that the thing is his. Or he may reasonably say that he is an absolute owner.

But even in such simple cases it is evident that the words absolute owner are being used to express two quite different ideas: that his ownership is both *indisputable* and that it is *unshared*. The ownership is asserting at the same moment that he and no one else is entitled to the house and car, and that his interest in them is exclusive and complete; or, in negative terms, that no other person can regard the things as his and that no other person can do anything which cuts down their use or reduces their value. The one assertion relates to what lawyers call 'title', the other to the content of ownership. In English law, as we shall see, it is perfectly possible to have one without the other.

Title

Some ways of acquiring title are original in the sense that a person is the first ever owner of a thing: if I write a song I own the copyright. Usually, however, things are acquired from someone else. A person buying a thing wants to be sure that it is the seller's to sell. With movable objects there are few problems—the seller's *possession* of the thing is normally good enough evidence of his *ownership*.

In the case of land, however, the matter is rather more complex. The word 'title' belongs to the vocabulary of a purchaser's solicitor who is trying to ensure that his client will be safe in buying the house and cannot be turned out by anyone else. He is concerned to see that his client gets what is called a good title. In the event of dispute the question of who is *entitled* to it—the issue of title—may have to be tested by a lawsuit in which, although the plaintiff's object would be to obtain possession of the thing, he must try to prove that element of ownership which is the right to immediate possession. . . .

The content of ownership

. . . The main elements are (a) the right to make physical use of a thing; (b) the right to the income from it, in money, in kind, or in services; and (c) the power of management, including that of alienation. Thus the owner of a car may drive it, hire it out, or sell it. And of course within these areas he may do the same things more generously: take the children for a drive, lend it to a friend, give it away. The owner of a house may live there, lease it, or sell it; and so on.

There are certain advantages to be obtained by keeping in the same hands the right or power to do all these things. A buyer normally wants them all and it is inconvenient if the seller cannot give him them. On the other hand, there has always been a need to detach some elements of ownership from others and to vest them in different persons, a need felt most strongly in regard to land. One of the main tasks of the law of property is to reconcile this need with the advantages of simplicity. . . .

Gray, K., Property in Thin Air,
[1991] *Cambridge Law Journal* 252–307 at 292–294

. . . The classic common law criteria of 'property' have tended to rest a twin emphasis on the assignability of the benefits inherent in a resource and on the relative permanence of those benefits if unassigned. Before a right can be admitted within the category of 'property' it must, according to Lord Wilberforce in *National Provincial Bank Ltd* v *Ainsworth* [1965] AC 1175, be 'definable' identifiable by third parties, capable in its nature of assumption by third parties, and have some degree of permanence or stability. This preoccupation with assignability of benefit and enforceability of burden doubtless owes much to the fact that the formative phases of the common law concept of property coincided with a remarkable culture of bargain and exchange. Non-transferable rights or rights which failed on transfer were simply not 'property'. Within the crucible of transfer lawyers affected to demarcate rights of 'property' from rights founded in contract and tort or, for that matter, from human rights and civil liberties. Only brief reflection is required in order to perceive the horrible circularity of such hallmarks of 'property'. If naively we ask which rights are proprietary, we are told that they are those rights which are assignable to and enforceable against third parties. When we then ask which rights these may be, we are told that they comprise, of course, the rights which are traditionally identified as 'proprietary'. 'Property' is 'property because it is 'property': property status and proprietary consequence confuse each other in a deadening embrace of cause and effect. . . .
. . . In their respective preoccupations with resource allocation and institutional justification, lawyers and philosophers alike have largely failed to identify the characteristic hallmark of the common law notion of 'property'. If our own travels in search of 'property' have indicated one thing, it is that the criterion of 'excludability' gets us much closer to the core of 'property' than does the conventional legal emphasis on the assignability or enforceability of benefits. For 'property' resides not in consumption of benefits but in control over benefits. 'Property' is not about *enjoyment of access* but about *control over access*. 'Property' is the power-relation constituted by the state's endorsement of private claims to regulate the access of strangers to the benefits of particular resources. If, in respect of a given claimant and a given resource, the exercise of such regulatory control is physically impracticable or legally abortive or morally or socially undesirable, we say that such a claimant can assert no 'property' in that resource and for that matter can lose no 'property' in it either. Herein lies an important key to the 'propertiness' of property . . . .

Nicholls, Barry, An Introduction To Roman Law,
Oxford: Clarendon Press, 1962, p. 153

OWNERSHIP

. . . It can indeed be said that ownership is either so simple as to need no explanation or so elusive as to defy definition. At its simplest it is the difference between mine and thine, at its most sophisticated it is the ultimate right, the right behind all other rights. The elusive character of ownership can be appreciated if one attempts to give a precise meaning to the often-repeated statement that Roman ownership is markedly, and to some of its critics excessively, 'absolute'.

The most obvious sense in which ownership may be 'absolute' is that of enjoyment. Though there is no Roman definition of ownership, there is no lack of Romanistic ones, and these are usually in terms of enjoyment. Thus, the commentators adapted the definition of usufruct by adding to the rights of use and enjoyment the right of abuse—*ius utendi fruendi abutendi*. The adaptation is a little forced, since 'abuse' has to include alienation, but it is also, in its emphasis on the plenitude of enjoyment conferred by ownership, misleading. In the first place, no enjoyment can ever be absolute in the sense that it is free from any restrictions whatever. At the very least the use, enjoyment, and abuse of his property by one owner must be reconciled with the equal use, enjoyment, and abuse by all other owners of their property. In a simple sense this is one of the functions of law. Moreover, in all but the crudest system of law there will be other restrictions which, in the general interest, are imposed on the enjoyment of the owner, and the extent of these restrictions will depend very largely on the political and economic ideas of the time. The enjoyment of the modern English owner is far less absolute than that of his Roman predecessor, but this difference in the content of ownership derives from a difference not in the technical legal character of ownership but in the extent to which the public law restricts the rights of the owner in the general interest. For this reason the French Civil Code, thought it declares that ownership is 'the right to enjoy and dispose of things in the most absolute way', adds the proviso that such enjoyment must not contravene the general law. . . .

ELITESTONE LTD v *MORRIS* [1997] 1 WLR 687, House of Lords

FACTS: The plaintiffs were the freehold owners of land on which a number of wooden bungalows were erected, one of which was occupied by the defendants pursuant to an agreement described as a 'licence' and in return for an annual payment; the terms of the agreement permitted the defendants to enter upon the piece of land and 'to keep thereon a bungalow and to reside' in it. The main structure of the bungalow rested on concrete pillars which were attached to the ground. The bungalow could only be removed by being demolished. In 1991 the plaintiffs issued proceedings in the county court seeking possession from the occupiers of the land, including the defendants. The assistant recorder held that the defendants were protected tenants within section 1 of the Rent Act 1977. The Court of Appeal allowed the plaintiffs' appeal, holding that the ownership of the land was vested in the plaintiffs but that the bungalow was a chattel, ownership of which vested in the defendants, and that the plaintiffs were entitled to possession.

HELD: Allowing the appeal, that the answer to the question whether a structure became part and parcel of the land itself depended on the degree and the object of annexation to the land; that, assessed objectively, a house built in such a way that it could not be removed except by destruction could not have been intended to remain a chattel and must have been intended to form part of the realty.

LORD LLOYD OF BERWICK: . . . The nature of the structure is such that it could not be taken down and re-erected elsewhere. It could only be removed by a process of demolition. This, as will appear later, is a factor of great importance in the present case. If a structure can only be enjoyed in situ, and is such that it cannot be removed in whole or in sections to another site, there is at least a strong inference that the purpose of placing the structure on the original site was that it should form part of the realty at that site, and therefore cease to be a chattel.

There were a number of other issues in the Court of Appeal. I need only mention one. This was an argument by the plaintiffs that Mr Morris was estopped by convention from denying that the bungalow was a chattel. There was, so it was said, a common assumption that the chalets were owned separately from the land, since each occupier purchased his own chalet from the previous occupier (Mr Morris paid £250 for No. 6 in 1971), and each occupier paid an annual licence fee to the freeholders. Since the Court of Appeal held that the bungalow was a chattel, they did not find it necessary to deal with the estoppel argument. The plaintiffs might have renewed the argument before your Lordships. But in the meantime the House had given judgment in *Melluish* v *BMI (No. 3) Ltd* [1996] AC 454. In that case Lord Browne-Wilkinson said, at p. 473:

The terms expressly or implicitly agreed between the fixer of the chattel and the owner of the land cannot affect the determination of the question whether, in law, the chattel has become a fixture and therefore in law belongs to the owner of the soil: . . . The terms of such agreement will regulate the contractual rights to sever the chattel from the land as between the parties to that contract and, where an equitable right is conferred by the contract, as against certain third parties. But such agreement cannot prevent the chattel, once fixed, becoming in law part of the land and as such owned by the owner of the land so long as it remains fixed.

If an express agreement cannot prevent a chattel from becoming part of the land, so long as it is fixed to the land, it is obvious that a common assumption cannot have that effect. It is not surprising, therefore, that Mr Thom abandoned his estoppel argument.

Thus the sole remaining issue for your Lordships is whether Mr Morris's bungalow did indeed become part of the land, or whether it has remained a chattel ever since it was first constructed before 1945.

It will be noticed that in framing the issue for decision I have avoided the use of the word 'fixture'. There are two reasons for this. The first is that 'fixture', though a hallowed term in this branch of the law, does not always bear the same meaning in law as it does in everyday life. In ordinary language one thinks of a fixture as being something fixed to a building. One would not ordinarily think of the building itself as a fixture. Thus in *Boswell v Crucible Steel Co.* [1925] 1 KB 119 the question was whether plate glass windows which formed part of the wall of a warehouse were landlord's fixtures within the meaning of a repairing covenant. Atkin LJ said, at p. 123:

> . . . I am quite satisfied that they are not landlord's fixtures, and for the simple reason that they are not fixtures at all in the sense in which that term is generally understood. A fixture, as that term is used in connection with the house, means something which has been affixed to the freehold as accessory to the house. It does not include things which were made part of the house itself in the course of its construction.

Yet in *Billing v Pill* [1954] 1 QB 70, 75 Lord Goddard CJ said:

> What is a fixture? The commonest fixture is a house which is built into the land, so that in law it is regarded as part of the land. The house and the land are one thing.

There is another reason. The term fixture is apt to be a source of misunderstanding owing to the existence of the category of so called 'tenants' fixtures' (a term used to cover both trade fixtures and ornamental fixtures), which are fixtures in the full sense of the word (and therefore part of the realty) but which may nevertheless be removed by the tenant in the course of or at the end of his tenancy. Such fixtures are sometimes confused with chattels which have never become fixtures at all. . . .

For my part I find it better in the present case to avoid the traditional twofold distinction between chattels and fixtures, and to adopt the threefold classification set out in *Woodfall, Landlord and Tenant* (looseleaf ed.), vol. 1, para. 13.131:

> An object which is brought onto land may be classified under one of three broad heads. It may be (a) a chattel; (b) a fixture; or (c) part and parcel of the land itself. Objects in categories (b) and (c) are treated as being part of the land.

So the question in the present appeal is whether, when the bungalow was built, it became part and parcel of the land itself. The materials out of which the bungalow was constructed, that is to say, the timber frame walls, the feather boarding, the suspended timber floors, the chipboard ceilings, and so on, were all, of course, chattels when they were brought onto the site. Did they cease to be chattels when they were built into the composite structure? The answer to the question, as Blackburn J pointed out in *Holland v Hodgson* (1872) LR 7 CP 328, depends on the circumstances of each case, but mainly on two factors, the degree of annexation to the land, and the object of the annexation.

Degree of annexation

The importance of the degree of annexation will vary from object to object. In the case of a large object, such as a house, the question does not often arise. Annexation goes without saying. So there is little recent authority on the point, and I do not get much help from the early cases in which wooden structures have been held not to form part of the realty, such as the wooden mill in *Rex* v *Otley* (1830) 1 B & Ad 161, the wooden barn in *Wansbrough* v *Maton* (1836) 4 A & E 884 and the granary in *Wiltshear* v *Cottrell* (1853) 1 E & B 674. But there is a more recent decision of the High Court of Australia which is of greater assistance. In *Reid* v *Smith* (1905) 3 CLR 656, 659 Griffith CJ stated the question as follows:

> The short point raised in this case is whether an ordinary dwelling-house, erected upon an ordinary town allotment in a large town, but not fastened to the soil, remains a chattel or becomes part of the freehold.

The Supreme Court of Queensland had held that the house remained a chattel. But the High Court reversed this decision, treating the answer as being almost a matter of common sense. The house in that case was made of wood, and rested by its own weight on brick piers. The house was not attached to the brick piers in any way. It was separated by iron plates placed on top of the piers, in order to prevent an invasion of white ants. There was an extensive citation of English and American authorities. It was held that the absence of any attachment did not prevent the house forming part of the realty. Two quotations, at p. 667, from the American authorities may suffice. In *Snedeker* v *Warring* (1854) 12 NY 170, 175 Parker J said: 'A thing may be as firmly affixed to the land by gravitation as by clamps or cement. Its character may depend upon the object of its erection.' In *Goff* v *O'Conner* (1855) 16 Ill 421, 423, the court said:

> Houses, in common intendment of the law, are not fixtures to, but part of, the land. . . . This does not depend, in the case of houses, so much upon the particular mode of attaching, or fixing and connecting them with the land upon which they stand or rest, as it does upon the uses and purposes for which they were erected and designed.

Purpose of annexation
Many different tests have been suggested, such as whether the object which has been fixed to the property has been so fixed for the better enjoyment of the object as a chattel, or whether it has been fixed with a view to effecting a permanent improvement of the freehold. This and similar tests are useful when one is considering an object such as a tapestry, which may or may not be fixed to a house so as to become part of the freehold: see *Leigh* v *Taylor* [1902] AC 157. These tests are less useful when one is considering the house itself. In the case of the house the answer is as much a matter of common sense as precise analysis. A house which is constructed in such a way so as to be removable, whether as a unit, or in sections, may well remain a chattel, even though it is connected temporarily to mains services such as water and electricity. But a house which is constructed in such a way that it cannot be removed at all, save by destruction, cannot have been intended to remain as a chattel. It must have been intended to form part of the realty. I know of no better analogy than the example given by Blackburn J in *Holland* v *Hodgson* (1872) LR 7 CP 328, 335:

> Thus blocks of stone placed one on the top of another without any mortar or cement for the purpose of forming a dry stone wall would become part of the land, though the same stones, if deposited in a builder's yard and for convenience sake stacked on the top of each other in the form of a wall, would remain chattels.

Applying that analogy to the present case, I do not doubt that when Mr Morris's bungalow was built, and as each of the timber frame walls were placed in position, they all became part of the structure, which was itself part and parcel of the land. The object of bringing the individual bits of wood onto the site seems to be so clear that the absence of any attachment to the soil (save by gravity) becomes an irrelevance.

Finally I return to the judgment of the Court of Appeal. I need say no more about the absence of attachment, which was the first of the reasons given by the Court of Appeal for reversing the assistant recorder. The second reason was the intention which the court inferred from the previous course of dealing between the parties, and in particular the uncertainty of Mr Morris's tenure. The third reason was the analogy with the shed in *Webb* v *Frank Bevis Ltd* [1940] 1 All ER 247, and the greenhouse in *Deen* v *Andrews* [1986] 1 EGLR 262.

As to the second reason the Court of Appeal may have been misled by Blackburn J's use of the word 'intention' in *Holland* v *Hodgson* (1872) LR 7 CP 328. But as the subsequent decision of the Court of Appeal in *Hobson* v *Gorringe* [1897] 1 Ch 182 made clear, and as the decision of the House in *Melluish* v *BMI (No. 3) Ltd* [1996] AC 454 put beyond question, the intention of the parties is only relevant to the extent that it can be derived from the degree and object of the annexation. The subjective intention of the parties cannot affect the question whether the chattel has, in law, become part of the freehold, any more than the subjective intention of the parties can prevent what they have called a licence from taking effect as a tenancy, if that is what in law it is: see *Street* v *Mountford* [1985] 1 AC 809.

As for the third of the reasons, I have already pointed out that *Webb* v *Frank Bevis Ltd* does not support the Court of Appeal's conclusion, because the shed in that case was held to be a fixture, albeit a fixture which the tenant was entitled to remove.

In *Deen* v *Andrews* the question was whether a greenhouse was a building so as to pass to the purchaser under a contract for the sale of land 'together with the farmhouses and other buildings'. Hirst J held that it was not. He followed an earlier decision in H. E. *Dibble Ltd* v *Moore* [1970] 2 QB 181 in which the Court of Appeal, reversing the trial judge, held that a greenhouse was not an 'erection' within s. 62(1) of the Law of Property Act 1925. I note that in the latter case Megaw LJ, at p. 187G, drew attention to some evidence 'that it was customary to move such greenhouses every few years to a fresh site'. It is obvious that a greenhouse which can be moved from site to site is a long way removed from a two bedroom bungalow which cannot be moved at all without being demolished.

LORD CLYDE: . . . As the law has developed it has become easy to neglect the original principle from which the consequences of attachment of a chattel to realty derive. That is the principle of accession, from which the more particular example has been formulated, inaedificatum solo solo cedit. A clear distinction has to be draw between the principle of accession and the rules of removability.

My Lords, the distinction between these two matters was pointed out long ago by Lord Cairns LC in *Bain* v *Brand* (1876) 1 App Cas 762. In that case it was declared that the law as to fixtures is the same in Scotland as in England. His Lordship stated, at p. 767, that there were two general rules under the comprehensive term of fixtures:

> one of these rules is the general well-known rule that whatever is fixed to the freehold of land becomes part of the freehold or inheritance. The other is quite a different and separate rule;—whatever once becomes part of the inheritance cannot be severed by a limited owner, whether he be owner for life or for years, without the commission of that which, in the law of England, is called waste, and which, according to the law of both England and Scotland, is undoubtedly an offence which can be restrained. Those, my Lords, are two rules, not one by way of exception to the other, but two rules standing consistently together. My Lords, an exception indeed, and a very important exception, has been made, not to the first of these rules, but to the second. To the first rule which I have stated to your Lordships there is, so far as I am aware, no exception whatever. That which is fixed to the inheritance becomes a part of the inheritance at the present day as much as it did in the earliest times. But to the second rule, namely, the irremovability of things fixed to the inheritance, there is undoubtedly ground for a very important exception. That exception has been established in favour of fixtures which have been attached to the inheritance for the purposes of trade, and perhaps in a minor degree for the purpose of agriculture. Under that exception a tenant who has fixed to the inheritance things for the purpose of trade has a certain power of severance and removal during the tenancy.

It would be right to add that the exception has been developed so as to extend beyond the purposes of trade. By the end of the 19th century it was clearly established that the exception included objects which had been affixed to the freehold by way of ornament: *In re De Falbe; Ward* v *Taylor* [1901] 1 Ch 523, 539. This reflected not a change in the law but, as Lord Macnaghten put it in *Leigh* v *Taylor* [1902] AC 157, 162, a change 'in our habits and mode of life'. No doubt the category of exceptions may continue to change.

The present case, however, is concerned with the first of the two rules and not the second. But it is not altogether clear that the distinction between the two rules was clearly put before the Court of Appeal in the present case. If the distinction is not noticed there is a danger that the true issue may become confused by questions truly relating to removability. The Court of Appeal found assistance in the decision in *Webb v Frank Bevis Ltd* [1940] 1 All ER 247, regarding the bungalow as no more annexed to the land and just as much a chattel as the large shed in that case. But the court in the *Webb* case held that the large shed was a fixture but was removable by the tenant. I should add that the second rule may involve particular consideration of the various relationships between the interested parties which may play a part in the matter of removability, such as landlord and tenant, or mortgagor and mortgagee. But those differences play only a subordinate role in relation to the first rule.

The answer to that question is to be found by a consideration of the particular facts and circumstances. In the generality there are a number of considerations to which resort may be had to solve the problem. But each case in this matter has to turn on its own facts. Comparable cases are useful for guidance in respect of the considerations employed but can only rarely provide conclusive answers. It has not been suggested that if the bungalow is real property it can be regarded as distinct from the site so as to be excluded from the property let to Mr Morris. The question then can be simply asked whether the bungalow is a chattel or realty. On that wider approach a useful starting point can be found in the words of the old commentator Heineccius (Elementa Iuris Civilis secundum ordinem Pandectarum, Lib.I. Tit. VIII, Sec.199) where, in classifying things as moveable or immoveable he describes the latter as being things 'quae vel salvae moveri nequeunt, ut fundus, aedes, ager . . . vel usus perpetui causa iunguntur immobilibus, aut horum usui destinantur'.

The first of these factors may serve both to identify an item as being real property in its own right and to indicate a case of accession. But account has also to be taken of the degree of physical attachment and the possibility or impossibility of restoring the article from its constituent parts after dissolution. In one early Scottish case large leaden vessels which were not fastened to the building in any way but simply rested by their own weight were held to be heritable since they had had to be taken to pieces in order to be removed and had then been sold as old lead: *Niven v Pitcairn* (1823) 2 S 239. In *Hellawell v Eastwood* (1851) 6 Exch 295, 312, Parke B, in considering the mode and extent of annexation of the articles in that case, referred to the consideration whether the object in question 'can easily be removed, integré, salvé, et commodé, or not, without injury to itself or the fabric of the building'. It is agreed in the present case that as matter of fact that 'the bungalow is not removable in one piece; nor is it demountable for re-erection elsewhere'. That agreed finding is in my view one powerful indication that it is not of the nature of a chattel.

In many cases the problem of accession arises in relation to some article or articles which have been placed in or affixed to a building. An unusual, although by no means unique, feature of the present case is that the alleged chattel is the building itself. This invites the approach of simply asking whether it is real property in its own right. Apart from the considerations which I already mentioned it seems to me that it is proper to have regard to the genus of the alleged chattel. That approach was adopted in the Australian case, *Reid v Smith* (1905) 3 CLR 656. At p. 668 Griffith CJ said under reference to the decision in the lower court:

> I differ from the learned judge in thinking that it is not sufficient to show that the thing in question is a dwelling-house—an ordinary dwelling-house, on a town allotment, in an inhabited town. In the case of a similar building in another part of the country, erected under entirely different circumstances, a different conclusion might be drawn.

O'Connor J put the point more strongly, at p. 679:

> It would I think be stretching the rules of the common law to a point at which they cease to be rules of common sense, if it were to be laid down as a general rule that, except in very exceptional cases, wooden houses, resting by their own weight on land, could ever be regarded as mere chattels, removable at the will of the owner of the timber of which they are built.

In several cases before the Lands Valuation Appeal Court in Scotland where the issue has arisen whether particular subjects are heritable or moveable for the purposes of valuation for local taxation the test has been applied by asking the question whether the particular subjects belong to a genus which is prima facie of a heritable character and, if they are, whether there are any special facts to deprive them of that character. This approach was recognised in *Assessor for the City of Glasgow* v *Gilmartin* 1920 SC 488 and in *John Menzies & Co. Ltd* v *Assessor for Edinburgh* 1937 SC 784. It was later applied to such subjects as residential chalets: *Assessor for Renfrewshire* v *Mitchell* 1966 SLT 53, contractors' huts: *Assessor for Dunbarton* v *L. K McKenzie and Partners* 1968 SLT 82 and static caravans: *Redgates Caravan Parks Ltd* v *Assessor for Ayrshire* 1973 SLT 52. Beyond question Mr Morris's bungalow is of the genus 'dwelling-house' and dwelling houses are generally of the nature of real property. While it is situated in a rural setting it evidently forms part of a development of a number of other houses whose positions are even noted on the ordnance survey map. I find no factors which would justify taking it out of the category of dwelling houses. On the contrary there are powerful indications that it and its constituent parts do not possess the character of a chattel. It seems to me to be real property.

If the problem is approached as one of accession it has to be noted that in the present case the bungalow is not attached or secured to any realty. It is not joined by any physical link which would require to be severed for it to be detached. But accession can operate even where there is only a juxtaposition without any physical bond between the article and the freehold. Thus the sculptures in *D'Eyncourt* v *Gregory* (1866) LR 3 Eq 382 which simply rested by their own weight were held to form part of the architectural design for the hall in which they were placed and so fell to be treated as part of the freehold. The reasoning in such a case where there is no physical attachment was identified by Blackburn J in *Holland* v *Hodgson* (1872) LR 7 CP 328, 335: 'But even in such a case, if the intention is apparent to make the articles part of the land, they do become part of the land'. He continued with the following instructive observations:

> Thus blocks of stone placed one on the top of another without any mortar or cement for the purpose of forming a dry stone wall would become part of the land, though the same stones, if deposited in a builder's yard and for convenience sake stacked on the top of each other in the form of a wall, would remain chattels. On the other hand, an article may be very firmly fixed to the land, and yet the circumstances may be such as to show that it was never intended to be part of the land, and then it does not become part of the land. The anchor of a large ship must be very firmly fixed in the ground in order to bear the strain of the cable, yet no one could suppose that it became part of the land, even though it should chance that shipowner was also the owner of the fee of the spot where the anchor was dropped. An anchor similarly fixed in the soil for the purpose of bearing the strain of the chain of a suspension bridge would be part of the land. Perhaps the true rule is, that articles not otherwise attached to the land than by their own weight are not to be considered as part of the land, unless the circumstances are such as to show that they were intended to be part of the land, the onus of showing that they were so intended lying on those who assert that they have ceased to be chattels, and that, on the contrary, an article which is affixed to the land even slightly is to be considered as part of the land, unless the circumstances are such as to show that it was intended all along to continue a chattel, the onus lying on those who contend that it is a chattel.

It is important to observe that intention in this context is to be assessed objectively and not subjectively. Indeed it may be that the use of the word intention is misleading. It is the purpose which the object is serving which has to be regarded, not the purpose of the person who put it there. The question is whether the object is designed for the use or enjoyment of the land or for the more complete or convenient use or enjoyment of the thing itself. As the foregoing passage from the judgment of Blackburn J makes clear, the intention has to be shown from the circumstances. That point was taken up by A. L. Smith LJ in *Hobson* v *Goringe* [1897] 1 Ch 182, 193, a decision approved by this House in *Reynolds* v *Ashby & Son* [1904] AC 466, where he observes that Blackburn J,

> was contemplating and referring to circumstances which showed the degree of annexation and the object of such annexation which were patent for all to see, and not to

the circumstances of a chance agreement that might or might not exist between the owner of a chattel and a hirer thereof.

Regard may not be paid to the actual intention of the person who has caused the annexation to be made. In *In re De Falbe; Ward* v *Taylor* [1901] 1 Ch 523, 535, Vaughan Williams LJ said that there was not to be an inquiry into the motive of the person who annexed the articles, 'but a consideration of the object and purpose of the annexation as it is to be inferred from the circumstances of the case'. As Lord Cockburn put it in *Dixon* v *Fisher* (1843) 5 D 775, 793 'no man can make his property real or personal by merely thinking it so'. The matter has to be viewed objectively.

If one considers the object or purpose which the structure serves by being placed where it is, it was clearly placed there to enable the amenity of Holt's Field to be enjoyed through the establishment of a residence. The bungalow was built there in order that people could live in what is represented as being an idyllic rural environment. The Court of Appeal, however, had regard to the belief of Mr Morris that he owned the bungalow as evidence of his intention. But his belief cannot control the operation of the law in relation to accession and the matter of intention has to be judged objectively. Indeed the fact that the freeholders may have believed and reminded the occupants that their rights to remain could be terminated, which was also a factor on which the Court of Appeal relied, cannot affect the operation of the law.

Accession also involves a degree of permanence, as opposed to some merely temporary provision. This is not simply a matter of counting the years for which the structure has stood where it is, but again of appraising the whole circumstances. The bungalow has been standing on its site for about half a century and has been used for many years as the residence of Mr Morris and his family. That the bungalow was constructed where it is for the purpose of a residence and that it cannot be removed and re-erected elsewhere point in my view to the conclusion that it is intended to serve a permanent purpose. If it was designed and constructed in a way that would enable it to be taken down and rebuilt elsewhere, that might well point to the possibility that it still retained its character of a chattel. That the integrity of this chalet depends upon it remaining where it is provides that element of permanence which points to its having acceded to the ground. The Court of Appeal took the view that the bungalow was no more annexed to the land and just as much a chattel as the greenhouse in *Deen* v *Andrews* [1986] 1 EGLR 262 (or, as I have already mentioned, the large shed in *Webb* v *Frank Bevis Ltd* [1940] 1 All ER 247). But there is a critical distinction between *Deen* v *Andrews* and the present case in the fact that the greenhouse was demountable while the bungalow is not. I prefer the conclusion reached by the assistant recorder after hearing the evidence and visiting the site to form his own impression of the situation. As he observed towards the end of his judgment, a judgment which deserves commendation for the detail and care which has gone into it:

> it seems to me clear that at least by 1985 and probably before, it would have been clear to anybody that this was a structure which was not meant to be enjoyed as a chattel to be picked up and moved in due course but that it should be a long-term feature of the realty albeit that, because of its construction, it would plainly need more regular maintenance.

In my view the conclusion reached on this matter by the assistant recorder was correct. The appeal should be allowed. . . .

1.2   Property Rights which Give Immediate Use and Enjoyment of Land

1.2.1   FEE SIMPLE ESTATE

See **4.1**.

1.2.2 LEASES

See **Chapters 17** to **20.**

1.3 Property Rights Against Land Owned by Other People

1.3.1 MORTGAGES

See **Chapter 29** to **33.**

1.3.2 RESTRICTIVE COVENANTS

See **Chapters 26** to **28.**

1.3.3 EASEMENTS

See **Chapters 23** to **25.**

1.3.4 PROFITS À PRENDRE

See **Chapters 23** to **25.**

1.3.5 RENTCHARGES

RENTCHARGES ACT 1977
as amended by the Trusts of Land etc. Act 1996

1.   Meaning of 'rentcharge'
For the purposes of this Act 'rentcharge' means any annual or other periodic sum charged
on or issuing out of land, except—
    (a)   rent reserved by a lease or tenancy, or
    (b)   any sum payable by way of interest.

2.   Creation of rentcharges prohibited
   (1)   Subject to this section, no rentcharge may be created whether at law or in equity
after the coming into force of this section.
   (2)   Any instrument made after the coming into force of this section shall, to the extent that
it purports to create a rentcharge the creation of which is prohibited by this section, be void.
   (3)   This section does not prohibit the creation of a rentcharge—
    [(a)   in the case of which paragraph 3 of Schedule 1 to the Trusts of Land and
Appointment of Trustees Act 1996 (trust in case of family charge) applies to the land on
which the rent is charged;
    (b)   in the case of which paragraph (a) above would have effect but for the fact that
the land on which the rent is charged is settled land or subject to a trust of land;]
    (c)   which is an estate rentcharge;
    (d)   under any Act of Parliament providing for the creation of rentcharges in
connection with the execution of works on land (whether by way of improvements, repairs
or otherwise) or the commutation of any obligation to do such work; or
    (e)   by, or in accordance with the requirements of, any order of a court.

3.   Extinguishment of rentcharges
   (1)   Subject to this section, every rentcharge shall (if it has not then ceased to have effect)
be extinguished at the expiry of the period of 60 years beginning—

(a) with the passing of this Act, or

(b) with the date on which the rentcharge first became payable, whichever is the later; and accordingly the land on which it was charged or out of which it issued shall, at the expiration of that period, be discharged and freed from the rentcharge. . . .

1.3.6 RIGHTS OF OCCUPATION UNDER THE MATRIMONIAL HOMES ACTS, NOW RENAMED MATRIMONIAL HOME RIGHTS

FAMILY LAW ACT 1996

30. Rights concerning matrimonial home where one spouse has no estate, etc

(1)   This section applies if—

(a)   one spouse is entitled to occupy a dwelling-house by virtue of—

(i)   a beneficial estate or interest or contract; or

(ii)   any enactment giving that spouse the right to remain in occupation; and

(b)   the other spouse is not so entitled.

(2)   Subject to the provisions of this Part, the spouse not so entitled has the following rights ('matrimonial home rights')—

(a)   if in occupation, a right not to be evicted or excluded from the dwelling-house or any part of it by the other spouse except with the leave of the court given by an order under section 33;

(b)   if not in occupation, a right with the leave of the court so given to enter into and occupy the dwelling-house.

(3)   If a spouse is entitled under this section to occupy a dwelling-house or any part of a dwelling-house, any payment or tender made or other thing done by that spouse in or towards satisfaction of any liability of the other spouse in respect of rent, mortgage payments or other outgoings affecting the dwelling-house is, whether or not it is made or done in pursuance of an order under section 40, as good as if made or done by the other spouse.

(4)   A spouse's occupation by virtue of this section—

(a)   is to be treated, for the purposes of the Rent (Agriculture) Act 1976 and the Rent Act 1977 (other than Part V and sections 103 to 106 of that Act), as occupation by the other spouse as the other spouse's residence, and

(b)   if the spouse occupies the dwelling-house as that spouse's only or principal home, is to be treated, for the purposes of the Housing Act 1985 and Part I of the Housing Act 1988, as occupation by the other spouse as the other spouse's only or principal home.

(5)   If a spouse ('the first spouse')—

(a)   is entitled under this section to occupy a dwelling-house or any part of a dwelling-house, and

(b)   makes any payment in or towards satisfaction of any liability of the other spouse ('the second spouse') in respect of mortgage payments affecting the dwelling-house, the person to whom the payment is made may treat it as having been made by the second spouse, but the fact that that person has treated any such payment as having been so made does not affect any claim of the first spouse against the second spouse to an interest in the dwelling-house by virtue of the payment.

(6)   If a spouse is entitled under this section to occupy a dwelling-house or part of a dwelling-house by reason of an interest of the other spouse under a trust, all the provisions of subsections (3) to (5) apply in relation to the trustees as they apply in relation to the other spouse.

(7)   This section does not apply to a dwelling-house which has at no time been, and which was at no time intended by the spouses to be, a matrimonial home of theirs.

(8)   A spouse's matrimonial home rights continue—

(a)   only so long as the marriage subsists, except to the extent that an order under section 33(5) otherwise provides; and

(b)   only so long as the other spouse is entitled as mentioned in subsection (1) to occupy the dwelling-house, except where provision is made by section 31 for those rights to be a charge on an estate or interest in the dwelling-house.

(9)   It is hereby declared that a spouse—

(a)   who has an equitable interest in a dwelling-house or in its proceeds of sale, but

(b)   is not a spouse in whom there is vested (whether solely or as joint tenant) a legal estate in fee simple or a legal term of years absolute in the dwelling-house,

is to be treated, only for the purpose of determining whether he has matrimonial home rights, as not being entitled to occupy the dwelling-house by virtue of that interest.

31.   Effect of matrimonial home rights as charge on dwelling-house

(1)   Subsections (2) and (3) apply if, at any time during a marriage, one spouse is entitled to occupy a dwelling-house by virtue of a beneficial estate or interest.

(2)   The other spouse's matrimonial home rights are a charge on the estate or interest.

(3)   The charge created by subsection (2) has the same priority as if it were an equitable interest created at whichever is the latest of the following dates—

(a)   the date on which the spouse so entitled acquires the estate or interest;

(b)   the date of the marriage; and

(c)   1st January 1968 (the commencement date of the Matrimonial Homes Act 1967).

(4)   Subsections (5) and (6) apply if, at any time when a spouse's matrimonial home rights are a charge on an interest of the other spouse under a trust, there are, apart from either of the spouses, no persons, living or unborn, who are or could become beneficiaries under the trust.

(5)   The rights are a charge also on the estate or interest of the trustees for the other spouse.

(6)   The charge created by subsection (5) has the same priority as if it were an equitable interest created (under powers overriding the trusts) on the date when it arises.

(7)   In determining for the purposes of subsection (4) whether there are any persons who are not, but could become, beneficiaries under the trust, there is to be disregarded any potential exercise of a general power of appointment exercisable by either or both of the spouses alone (whether or not the exercise of it requires the consent of another person).

(8)   Even though a spouse's matrimonial home rights are a charge on an estate or interest in the dwelling-house, those rights are brought to an end by—

(a)   the death of the other spouse, or

(b)   the termination (otherwise than by death) of the marriage,

unless the court directs otherwise by an order made under section 33(5).

(9)   If—

(a)   a spouse's matrimonial home rights are a charge on an estate or interest in the dwelling-house, and

(b)   that estate or interest is surrendered to merge in some other estate or interest expectant on it in such circumstances that, but for the merger, the person taking the estate or interest would be bound by the charge,

the surrender has effect subject to the charge and the persons thereafter entitled to the other estate or interest are, for so long as the estate or interest surrendered would have endured if not so surrendered, to be treated for all purposes of this Part as deriving title to the other estate or interest under the other spouse or, as the case may be, under the trustees for the other spouse, by virtue of the surrender.

(10)   If the title to the legal estate by virtue of which a spouse is entitled to occupy a dwelling-house (including any legal estate held by trustees for that spouse) is registered under the Land Registration Act 1925 or any enactment replaced by that Act—

(a)   registration of a land charge affecting the dwelling-house by virtue of this Part is to be effected by registering a notice under that Act; and

(b)   a spouse's matrimonial home rights are not an overriding interest within the meaning of that Act affecting the dwelling-house even though the spouse is in actual occupation of the dwelling-house.

(11)   A spouse's matrimonial home rights (whether or not constituting a charge) do not entitle that spouse to lodge a caution under section 54 of the Land Registration Act 1925.

(12)   If—

(a)   a spouse's matrimonial home rights are a charge on the estate of the other spouse or of trustees of the other spouse, and

(b)   that estate is the subject of a mortgage,

then if, after the date of the creation of the mortgage ('the first mortgage'), the charge is registered under section 2 of the Land Charges Act 1972, the charge is, for the purposes of section 94 of the Law of Property Act 1925 (which regulates the rights of mortgagees to make further advances ranking in priority to subsequent mortgages), to be deemed to be a mortgage subsequent in date to the first mortgage.

(13) It is hereby declared that a charge under subsection (2) or (5) is not registrable under subsection (10) or under section 2 of the Land Charges Act 1972 unless it is a charge on a legal estate.

32. Further provisions relating to matrimonial home rights
Schedule 4 re-enacts with consequential amendments and minor modifications provisions of the Matrimonial Homes Act 1983.

33. Occupation orders where applicant has estate or interest etc or has matrimonial home rights
(1) If—
    (a) a person ('the person entitled')—
        (i)   is entitled to occupy a dwelling-house by virtue of a beneficial estate or interest or contract or by virtue of any enactment giving him the right to remain in occupation, or
        (ii)   has matrimonial home rights in relation to a dwelling-house, and
    (b) the dwelling-house—
        (i)   is or at any time has been the home of the person entitled and of another person with whom he is associated, or
        (ii)   was at any time intended by the person entitled and any such other person to be their home,
the person entitled may apply to the court for an order containing any of the provisions specified in subsections (3), (4) and (5).

(2) If an agreement to marry is terminated, no application under this section may be made by virtue of section 62(3)(e) by reference to that agreement after the end of the period of three years beginning with the day on which it is terminated.

(3) An order under this section may—
    (a) enforce the applicant's entitlement to remain in occupation as against the other person ('the respondent');
    (b) require the respondent to permit the applicant to enter and remain in the dwelling-house or part of the dwelling-house;
    (c) regulate the occupation of the dwelling-house by either or both parties;
    (d) if the respondent is entitled as mentioned in subsection (1)(a)(i), prohibit, suspend or restrict the exercise by him of his right to occupy the dwelling-house;
    (e) if the respondent has matrimonial home rights in relation to the dwelling-house and the applicant is the other spouse, restrict or terminate those rights;
    (f) require the respondent to leave the dwelling-house or part of the dwelling-house; or
    (g) exclude the respondent from a defined area in which the dwelling-house is included.

(4) An order under this section may declare that the applicant is entitled as mentioned in subsection (1)(a)(i) or has matrimonial home rights.

(5) If the applicant has matrimonial home rights and the respondent is the other spouse, an order under this section made during the marriage may provide that those rights are not brought to an end by—
    (a) the death of the other spouse; or
    (b) the termination (otherwise than by death) of the marriage.

(6) In deciding whether to exercise its powers under subsection (3) and (if so) in what manner, the court shall have regard to all the circumstances including—
    (a) the housing needs and housing resources of each of the parties and of any relevant child;
    (b) the financial resources of each of the parties;
    (c) the likely effect of any order, or of any decision by the court not to exercise its powers under subsection (3), on the health, safety or well-being of the parties and of any relevant child; and
    (d) the conduct of the parties in relation to each other and otherwise.

(7)   If it appears to the court that the applicant or any relevant child is likely to suffer significant harm attributable to conduct of the respondent if an order under this section containing one or more of the provisions mentioned in subsection (3) is not made, the court shall make the order unless it appears to it that—

(a)   the respondent or any relevant child is likely to suffer significant harm if the order is made; and

(b)   the harm likely to be suffered by the respondent or child in that event is as great as, or greater than, the harm attributable to conduct of the respondent which is likely to be suffered by the applicant or child if the order is not made.

(8)   The court may exercise its powers under subsection (5) in any case where it considers that in all the circumstances it is just and reasonable to do so.

(9)   An order under this section—

(a)   may not be made after the death of either of the parties mentioned in subsection (1); and

(b)   except in the case of an order made by virtue of subsection (5)(a), ceases to have effect on the death of either party.

(10)   An order under this section may, in so far as it has continuing effect, be made for a specified period, until the occurrence of a specified event or until further order.

34.   Effect of order under s. 33 where rights are charge on dwelling-house

(1)   If a spouse's matrimonial home rights are a charge on the estate or interest of the other spouse or of trustees for the other spouse—

(a)   an order under section 33 against the other spouse has, except so far as a contrary intention appears, the same effect against persons deriving title under the other spouse or under the trustees and affected by the charge, and

(b)   sections 33(1), (3), (4) and (10) and 30(3) to (6) apply in relation to any person deriving title under the other spouse or under the trustees and affected by the charge as they apply in relation to the other spouse.

(2)   The court may make an order under section 33 by virtue of subsection (1)(b) if it considers that in all the circumstances it is just and reasonable to do so.

1.3.7   INTEREST UNDER A CONSTRUCTIVE TRUST

LLOYDS BANK PLC v ROSSET [1991] 1 AC 107, House of Lords

FACTS: Mr Rosset had received a loan to buy a derelict house on the understanding that the house should be in his name alone. Mrs Rosset did a limited amount of work helping the renovation of the house, in particular she helped with the interior decorations. However, the vast bulk of the work was carried out by contractors employed and paid for by the husband.

Following matrimonial problems the husband left home, leaving his wife and children in the premises. The loan which the husband had taken out was not, in the event, repaid. Consequently, the bank brought proceedings for possession. The husband raised no defence to that action, but the wife did resist. She claimed to have a beneficial interest in the house under a constructive trust. She also claimed to have been in actual occupation of the property at the time of the completion of the loan (mortgage) from the bank. Accordingly, she claimed to have an interest in the land which would override the bank's right to enforce its security. (Section 70(1)(g) of the Land Registration Act 1925 provides that the rights of any person in actual occupation of land shall be 'overriding'.) The judge at first instance held in favour of the bank, but the Court of Appeal allowed the wife's appeal. The bank appealed to the House of Lords.

HELD: The appeal was allowed.

LORD BRIDGE OF HARWICH: . . . the judge based his inference of a common intention that Mrs Rosset should have a beneficial interest in the property under a constructive trust essentially on what Mrs Rosset did in and about assisting in the renovation of the property between the beginning of November 1982 and the date of completion on 17 December 1982. Yet by itself this activity, it seems to me, could not possibly justify any such inference. It was common ground that Mrs Rosset was extremely anxious that the new matrimonial home should be ready for occupation before Christmas if possible. In these circumstances it would seem the most natural thing in the world for any wife, in the absence of her husband abroad, to spend all the time she could spare and to employ any skills she might have, such as the ability to decorate a room, in doing all she could to accelerate progress of the work quite irrespective of any expectation she might have of enjoying a beneficial interest in the property. The judge's view that some of this work was work 'upon which she could not reasonably have been expected to embark unless she was to have an interest in the house' seems to me, with respect, quite untenable. The impression that the judge may have thought that the share of the equity to which he held Mrs Rosset to be entitled had been 'earned' by her work in connection with the renovation is emphasised by his reference in the concluding sentence of his judgment to the extent to which her 'qualifying contribution' reduced the cost of the renovation.

On any view the monetary value of Mrs Rosset's work expressed as a contribution to a property acquired at a cost exceeding £70,000 must have been so trifling as to be almost *de minimis*. I should myself have had considerable doubt whether Mrs Rosset's contribution to the work of renovation was sufficient to support a claim to a constructive trust in the absence of writing to satisfy the requirements of section 51 of the Law of Property Act 1925 even if her husband's intention to make a gift to her of half or any other share in the equity of the property had been clearly established or if he had clearly represented to her that that was what he intended. But here the conversations with her husband on which Mrs Rosset relied, all of which took place before November 1982, were incapable of lending support to the conclusion of a constructive trust in the light of the judge's finding that by that date there had been no decision that she was to have any interest in the property. The finding that the discussion 'did not exclude the possibility' that she should have an interest does not seem to me to add anything of significance.

These considerations lead me to the conclusion that the judge's finding that Mr Rosset held the property as constructive trustee for himself and his wife cannot be supported and it is on this short ground that I would allow the appeal. . . .

The first and fundamental question which must always be resolved is whether, independently of any inference to be drawn from the conduct of the parties in the course of sharing the house as their home and managing their joint affairs, there has at any time prior to acquisition, or exceptionally at some later date, been any agreement, arrangement or understanding reached between them that the property is to be shared beneficially. The finding of an agreement or arrangement to share in this sense can only, I think, be based on evidence of express discussions between the partners, however imperfectly remembered and however imprecise their terms may have been. Once a finding to this effect is made it will only be necessary for the partner asserting a claim to a beneficial interest against the partner entitled to the legal estate to show that he or she acted to his or her detriment or significantly altered his or her position in reliance on the agreement in order to give rise to a constructive trust or a proprietary estoppel.

In sharp contrast with this situation is the very different one where there is no evidence to support a finding of an agreement or arrangement to share, however reasonable it might have been for the parties to reach such an arrangement if they had applied their minds to the question, and where the court must rely entirely on the conduct of the parties both as the basis from which to infer a common intention to share the property beneficially and as the conduct relied on to give rise to a constructive trust. In this situation direct contributions to the purchase price by the partner who is not the legal owner, whether initially or by payment of mortgage instalments, will readily justify the inference necessary to the creation of a constructive trust. But, as I read the authorities, it is at least extremely doubtful whether anything less will do.

The leading cases in your Lordships' House are *Pettitt* v *Pettitt* [1970] AC 777 and *Gissing* v *Gissing* [1971] AC 866. Both demonstrate situations in the second category to which I have referred and their Lordships discuss at great length the difficulties to which these situations give rise. The effect of these two decisions is very helpfully analysed in the judgment of Lord MacDermott LCJ in *McFarlane* v *McFarlane* [1972] NI 59.

Outstanding examples on the other hand of cases giving rise to situations in the first category are *Eves* v *Eves* [1975] 1 WLR 1338 and *Grant* v *Edwards* [1986] Ch 638. In both these cases, where the parties who had cohabited were unmarried, the female partner had been clearly led by the male partner to believe, when they set up home together, that the property would belong to them jointly. In *Eves* v *Eves* the male partner had told the female partner that the only reason why the property was to be acquired in his name alone was because she was under 21 and that, but for her age, he would have had the house put into their joint names. He admitted in evidence that this was simply an 'excuse.' Similarly in *Grant* v *Edwards* the female partner was told by the male partner that the only reason for not acquiring the property in joint names was because she was involved in divorce proceedings and that, if the property were acquired jointly, this might operate to her prejudice in those proceedings. As Nourse LJ put it, at p. 649:

> Just as in *Eves* v *Eves* [1975] 1 WLR 1338, these facts appear to me to raise a clear inference that there was an understanding between the plaintiff and the defendant, or a common intention, that the plaintiff was to have some sort of proprietary interest in the house; otherwise no excuse for not putting her name on to the title would have been needed.

The subsequent conduct of the female partner in each of these cases, which the court rightly held sufficient to give rise to a constructive trust or proprietary estoppel supporting her claim to an interest in the property, fell far short of such conduct as would by itself have supported the claim in the absence of an express representation by the male partner that she was to have such an interest. It is significant to note that the share to which the female partners in *Eves* v *Eves* and *Grant* v *Edwards* were held entitled were one quarter and one half respectively. In no sense could these shares have been regarded as proportionate to what the judge in the instant case described as a 'qualifying contribution' in terms of the indirect contributions to the acquisition or enhancement of the value of the houses made by the female partners.

I cannot help thinking that the judge in the instant case would not have fallen into error if he had kept clearly in mind the distinction between the effect of evidence on the one hand which was capable of establishing an express agreement or an express representation that Mrs Rosset was to have an interest in the property and evidence on the other hand of conduct alone as a basis for an inference of the necessary common intention. . . .

For the reasons I have indicated I would allow the appeal. . . .

BURNS v *BURNS* [1984] 1 Ch 317, Court of Appeal

FACTS: The plaintiff and the defendant set up home together in 1961 in rented accommodation where their first child was born. In 1963 when the plaintiff was expecting their second child, the defendant decided that it would be a better use of his money to buy a house. The house was purchased and conveyed in the sole name of the defendant who financed the purchase price out of his own money and by way of a mortgage. The plaintiff did not directly contribute to the purchase price or to the mortgage payments. She remained at home to look after the children and to perform domestic duties and was thus unable to earn until 1975 when she started working as a driving instructor. Although the defendant continued to give her a generous housekeeping allowance and did not ask her to contribute to the household expenses, she used her earnings to pay the rates and the telephone bills and to buy fixtures, fittings and certain domestic chattels for the house. She also redecorated the interior of the house. The plaintiff left the defendant in 1980 and brought proceedings against him claiming that she was entitled to a beneficial interest in the house by reason of her contributions to the household over the 17 years they had lived there. The judge dismissed the plaintiff's claim.

HELD: Dismissing the appeal, that since the plaintiff had not made a substantial financial contribution to the acquisition of the house the court could not impute a common intention that she should acquire a beneficial interest in it; that the plaintiff's contribution to the welfare of the family by performing the domestic duties of the household and bringing up the children were not factors which could be taken into account in determining whether or not she had acquired a beneficial interest in the house; and that, accordingly, the plaintiff had failed to demonstrate the existence of any trust in her favour.

FOX LJ: The house with which we are concerned in this case was purchased in the name of the defendant and the freehold was conveyed to him absolutely. That was in 1963. If, therefore, the plaintiff is to establish that she has a beneficial interest in the property she must establish that the defendant holds the legal estate upon trust to give effect to that interest. That follows from *Gissing* v *Gissing* [1971] AC 886. For present purposes I think that such a trust could only arise (a) by express declaration or agreement *or* (b) by way of a resulting trust where the claimant has directly provided part of the purchase price *or* (c) from the common intention of the parties.

In the present case (a) and (b) can be ruled out. There was no express trust of an interest in the property for the benefit of the plaintiff; and there was no express agreement to create such an interest. And the plaintiff made no direct contribution to the purchase price. Her case, therefore, must depend upon showing a common intention that she should have a beneficial interest in the property. Whether the trust which would arise in such circumstances is described as implied, constructive or resulting does not greatly matter. If the intention is inferred from the fact that some indirect contribution is made to the purchase price, the term 'resulting trust' is probably not inappropriate. Be that as it may, the basis of such a claim, in any case, is that it would be inequitable for the holder of the legal estate to deny the claimant's right to a beneficial interest.

In determining whether such common intention exists it is, normally, the intention of the parties when the property was purchased that is important. As to that I agree with the observations of Griffiths LJ in *Bernard* v *Josephs* [1982] Ch 391, 404. As I understand it, that does not mean that for the purpose of determining the ultimate shares in the property one looks simply at the factual position as it was at the date of acquisition. It is necessary for the court to consider all the evidence, including the contributions of the parties, down to the date of separation (which in the case of man and mistress will generally, though not always, be the relevant date). Thus the law proceeds on the basis that there is nothing inherently improbable in the parties acting on the understanding that the woman

> should be entitled to a share which was not to be quantified immediately upon the acquisition of the home but should be left to be determined when the mortgage was repaid or the property disposed of, on the basis of what would be fair having regard to the total contributions, direct or indirect, which each spouse had made by that date (see *Gissing* v *Gissing* [1971] AC 886, 909, *per* Lord Diplock).

That approach does not, however, in my view preclude the possibility that while, initially, there was no intention that the claimant should have any interest in the property, circumstances may subsequently arise from which the intention to confer an equitable interest upon the claimant may arise (e.g., the discharge of a mortgage or the effecting of capital improvements to the house at his or her expense). Further, subsequent events may throw light on the initial intention.

Looking at the position at the time of the acquisition of the house in 1963, I see nothing at all to indicate any intention by the parties that the plaintiff should have an interest in it.

. . . It seems to me that at the time of the acquisition of the house nothing occurred between the parties to raise an equity which would prevent the defendant denying the plaintiff's claim. She provided no money for the purchase; she assumed no liability in respect of the mortgage; there was no understanding or arrangement that the plaintiff would go out to work to assist with the family finances; the defendant did nothing to lead her to change her position in the belief that she would have an interest in the house. It is true that she contemplated living with the defendant in the house and, no doubt, that she would do housekeeping and look after the children. But those facts do not carry with them any implication of a common intention that the plaintiff should have an interest in the house. Taken by themselves they are simply not strong enough to bear such an implication.

I come then to the position in the year after the house was purchased. I will deal with them under three heads, namely financial contributions, work on the house and finally housekeeping. There is some overlapping in these categories. . . .

The judge's findings as to expenditure by the plaintiff were as follows. (i) She made gifts of clothing and other things to the defendant and the children. (ii) She paid for the housekeeping. The defendant allowed her, latterly, £60 per week for housekeeping. It seems to be accepted that the defendant was generous with money and the plaintiff was not kept short as regards housekeeping money. (iii) She paid the rates. The housekeeping payments made by the defendant were, however, fixed at an amount which took account of this. (iv) She paid the telephone bills. That was a matter of agreement between her and the defendant because she spent a lot of time on the telephone talking to her friends. (v) She bought a number of chattels for domestic use: a dishwasher, a washing machine, a tumble dryer and either a drawing room suite or three armchairs and a bed for her separate room. The bed, the dishwasher and the chairs she took with her when she left in 1980. (vi) She provided some doorknobs and door furnishings of no great value.

None of this expenditure, in my opinion, indicates the existence of the common intention which the plaintiff has to prove. What is needed, I think, is evidence of a payment or payments by the plaintiff which it can be inferred was referable to the acquisition of the house. Lord Denning MR in *Hazell* v *Hazell* [1972] 1 WLR 301, 304 thought that expression, which appears in the speech of Lord Diplock in *Gissing* v *Gissing* [1971] AC 886, 909 was being over-used. He said quoting from *Falconer* v *Falconer* [1970] 1 WLR 1333, 1336, that if there was a substantial financial contribution towards the family expenses that would raise an inference of a trust. I do not think that formulation alters the essence of the matter for present purposes. If there is a substantial contribution by the woman to family expenses, and the house was purchased on a mortgage, her contribution is, indirectly, referable to the acquisition of the house since, in one way or another, it enables the family to pay the mortgage instalments. Thus, a payment could be said to be referable to the acquisition of the house if, for example, the payer either (a) pays part of the purchase price or (b) contributes regularly to the mortgage instalments or (c) pays off part of the mortgage or (d) makes a substantial financial contribution to the family expenses so as to enable the mortgage instalments to be paid.

But if a payment cannot be said to be, in a real sense, referable to the acquisition of the house it is difficult to see how, in such a case as the present, it can base a claim for an interest in the house. Looking at the items which I have listed above, and leaving aside, for the present, the housekeeping which I will deal with separately, none of the items can be said to be referable to the acquisition of the house. The making of ordinary gifts between members of a family certainly is not. Nor, in the circumstances as found by the judge, are the payments of rates or of the telephone bills. The provision of the door knobs etc. is of very small consequence. As regards the purchase of chattels for domestic use, the plaintiff must, I think, have regarded at any rate some of these as her own property since she took them away with her when she left. But quite apart from that I do not think that the provision of chattels, by itself, is evidence of any common intention that the plaintiff should have a beneficial interest in the house. In *Gissing* v *Gissing* [1971] AC 886 Viscount Dilhorne, after referring to the requirement of a common intention that the wife should have an interest in the house, said, at p. 900:

> To establish this intention there must be some evidence which points to its existence. It would not, for instance, suffice if the wife just made a mortgage payment while her husband was abroad. Payment for a lawn and provision of some furniture and equipment for the house does not itself point to the conclusion that there was such an intention.

Lord Diplock said, at p. 910: 'The court is not entitled to infer a common intention . . . from the mere fact that she provided chattels for joint use in the new matrimonial home; . . .'.

As regard work on the house, in 1971 a fairly substantial improvement was made to the house; the attic was converted into a bedroom with a bathroom en suite. That was paid for wholly by the defendant.

In 1977 or 1978 the plaintiff decorated the house throughout internally because she wished the house to be wallpapered and not painted. I do not think that carries her case any further. Thus in *Pettitt* v *Pettitt* [1970] AC 777, 826 Lord Diplock said:

> If the husband likes to occupy his leisure by laying a new lawn in the garden or building a fitted wardrobe in the bedroom while the wife does the shopping, cooks the family dinner and bathes the children, I, for my part, find it quite impossible to impute to them as reasonable husband and wife any common intention that these domestic activities or any of them are to have any effect upon the existing proprietary rights in the family home . . .

Accordingly I think that the decoration undertaken by the plaintiff gives no indication of any such common intention as she must assert.

There remains the question of housekeeping and domestic duties. So far as housekeeping expenses are concerned, I do not doubt that (the house being bought in the man's name) if the woman goes out to work in order to provide money for the family expenses, as a result of which she spends her earnings on the housekeeping and the man is thus able to pay the mortgage instalments and other expenses out of his earnings, it can be inferred that there was a common intention that the woman should have an interest in the house—since she will have made an indirect financial contribution to the mortgage instalments. But that is not this case. . . .

For the reasons which I have given I think that the appeal must be dismissed. I only add this. The plaintiff entered upon her relationship with the defendant knowing that there was no prospect of him marrying her. And it is evident that in a number of respects he treated her very well. He was generous to her, in terms of money, while the relationship continued. And, what in the long term is probably more important he encouraged her to develop her abilities in a number of ways, with the result that she built up the successful driving instruction business. Nevertheless, she lived with him for 18 years as man and wife, and, at the end of it, has no rights against him. But the unfairness of that is not a matter which the courts can control. It is a matter for Parliament.

MAY LJ: This appeal raises a question which arises nowadays with increasing frequency. If a man and a woman marry, acquire a home, live in it together, bring up children, but sadly sooner or later separate and divorce, the courts have a wide discretion to adjust their subsequent respective financial situations under the provisions of the Matrimonial Causes Act 1973. In particular the court has power to determine the spouses' respective rights to the matrimonial home, which is usually the family's main asset, and by virtue of s. 25(1) of the Act of 1973 is given a wide discretion to exercise its powers to place the parties, so far as it is practicable and just to do so, in the financial position in which they would have been if the marriage had not broken down and each had properly discharged his or her financial obligations and responsibilities towards the other.

However, it is becoming increasingly frequent that couples live together without being married, but just as if they were so. They acquire a home for themselves and their children whom they bring up in the same way as the family next door. Nevertheless it also happens, just like their married friends, that differences do arise between the couple and they separate. In some cases the man and the woman can agree what is to happen in those circumstances, for instance, to their erstwhile joint home. But if they do not agree, they come to the courts for the resolution of their dispute. In the case of an unmarried couple in these circumstances there is no statute which gives a court similar powers to those which it has as between husband and wife. In these cases the question therefore arises what principles is the court to apply?

For my part, I agree that the principles which the courts must apply are those laid down in *Pettitt v Pettitt* [1970] AC 777 and *Gissing v Gissing* [1971] AC 886. . . .

The speeches in *Pettitt's* case [1970] AC 777 and *Gissing's* case [1971] AC 886 . . . make it clear that there is no general concept in English law of 'family property' or 'family assets': see Lord Reid, at p. 795, Lord Hodson, at p. 810, and Lord Upjohn, at p. 817, in *Pettitt's* case [1970] AC 777 and Viscount Dilhorne in *Gissing's* case [1971] AC 886, 900. Lord Diplock recognised in his speech in the later of the two cases that the view which he had expressed to the contrary in *Pettitt's* case [1970] AC 777 had been disapproved by the majority.

I think that one therefore reaches the position that the resolution of these disputes must depend upon the ascertainment according to normal principles of the respective property rights between the man and the woman. Further, two similar factors militate against and indeed prevent any application of general principles of contract law to the problem. First, it is seldom if ever that the man and the woman in these circumstances in fact come to any agreement between themselves about what should happen to the matrimonial home if they were to part. As Lord Morris of Borth-y-Gest said in *Pettitt's* case [1970] AC 777, 799–800:

In the lengthening line of cases in which questions between spouses have called for adjudication under s. 17, the nature of the difficulties which arise is constantly and recurringly made manifest. When two people are about to be married and when they are arranging to have a home in which to live they do not make arrangements in the contemplation of future discord or separation. As a married couple they do not, when a house is being purchased or when the contents of a house are being acquired, contemplate that a time might come when [a] decision would have to be made as to who owned what. It would be unnatural if at the times of acquisition there was always precise statement or understanding as to where ownership rested. So, if at a later date questions arise as to the ownership of a house or of various things in it, though as to some matters no honest difference of view will arise, as to others there can be such honest difference because previously the parties might never really have applied their minds to the question as to where ownership lay.

Second, even if it be shown in any particular case that the parties had reached some agreement themselves, there is I think real doubt whether this can be said to have been intended to create enforceable legal relations between them: cf. *Balfour* v *Balfour* [1919] 2 KB 571. There is in any event a very real evidentiary difficulty. . . .

Further, as their Lordships pointed out in the two leading cases, if the only realistic conclusion on the material before the court is that the parties in fact never made any agreement binding at law between them, then it necessarily follows that it is impossible to imply such agreement or, which comes to much the same thing, to imply more precise terms where any existing arrangement is imprecise.

In the result, my opinion is that the correct and general approach to these cases should be that summed up in a passage from Lord Pearson's speech in *Gissing's* case [1971] AC 886, 902 where he said:

I think it must often be artificial to search for an agreement made between husband and wife as to their respective ownership rights in property used by both of them while they are living together. In most cases they are unlikely to enter into negotiations or conclude contracts or even make agreements. The arrangements which they make are likely to be lacking in the precision and finality which an agreement would be expected to have. On the other hand, an intention can be imputed: it can be inferred from the evidence of their conduct and the surrounding circumstances. The starting point, in a case where substantial contributions are proved to have been made, is the presumption of a resulting trust, though it may be displaced by rebutting evidence. It may be said that the imputed intent does not differ very much from an implied agreement. Accepting that, I still think it is better to approach the question through the doctrine of resulting trusts rather than through contract law. Of course, if an agreement can be proved it is the best evidence of intention.

Where the legal estate to the family home had been taken in joint names then generally the beneficial interests will depend on the respective contributions of the parties to the acquisition of the property: see *Crisp* v *Mullings* (1976) 239 EG 119 and the recent decision in this court in *Walker* v *Hall* (unreported), 30 June 1983; Court of Appeal (Civil Division) Transcript No. 300 of 1983.

Where the legal estate in the family home has, however, been taken in the name of one of the parties only, then prima facie it will carry with it the whole of the beneficial interest. But for the reasons to which I have briefly referred, a claim to a beneficial interest in land made by a person in whom the legal estate is not vested can in certain circumstances be made by resorting to the doctrine of resulting trusts. Where the legal estate to the family home is in one name only, which is usually the male member of the couple, and the parties to the acquisition of the house have not expressed their common intention that the beneficial interest should be shared between them it may nevertheless be possible to infer that common intention from their conduct and thus give rise to a resulting trust to which the courts will give effect. It may be demonstrably inequitable to permit the legal title holder to retain the whole of the beneficial interest in the property. The inference about the parties' common intention to which the court will give effect in this way is that which objectively a reasonable man would draw from their words and conduct at the relevant time. . . .

. . . in some of the earlier decisions before *Pettitt* v *Pettitt* [1970] AC 777 and *Gissing* v *Gissing* [1971] AC 886, Lord Denning MR had held that the court did have a power 'to do what is fair and reasonable in all the circumstances'. In both *Pettitt's* case and *Gissing's* case the House of Lords made it quite clear, in my view, that no such general power exists. In all the decisions prior to *Hall's* case (1982) 3 FLR 379 in which the wife or woman was held to be entitled to a share in the family home, on the evidence she had made a 'real' or 'substantial' contribution either to the deposit paid for the acquisition of the family home or to the instalments of the mortgage with whose assistance it was bought. In *Pettitt's* case [1970] AC 777 Lord Diplock, whose speech was the most favourable to the applicant's case, said, at p. 826:

> It is common enough nowadays for husbands and wives to decorate and to make improvements in the family home themselves, with no other intention than to indulge in what is now a popular hobby, and to make the home pleasanter for their common use and enjoyment. If the husband likes to occupy his leisure by laying a new lawn in the garden or building a fitted wardrobe in the bedroom while the wife does the shopping, cooks the family dinner or bathes the children, I, for my part, find it quite impossible to impute to them as reasonable husband and wife any common intention that these domestic activities or any of them are to have any effect upon the existing proprietary rights in the family home on which they are undertaken. It is only the bitterness engendered by the break-up of the marriage that so bizarre a notion would enter their heads.

In these circumstances, I respectfully think that the dictum of Lord Denning MR that the woman's contribution to the family well-being by keeping the house and looking after the children can be taken into account in assessing the extent to which a resulting trust has arisen in her favour was wrong.

On the other hand it would appear from a passage from the judgment of the judge in the county court quoted by Dunn LJ in the Court of Appeal in *Hall's* case (1982) 3 FLR 379, 384 that the woman had been working and had been applying substantially all her earnings towards the housekeeping. In these circumstances it may have been argued that the woman had made an actual financial contribution to the acquisition of the family home, in that her pooled earnings had at the least made it easier for the man to pay the mortgage instalments. . . .

In the light of all these cases, I think that the approach which the courts should follow, be the couples married or unmarried, is now clear. What is difficult, however, is to apply it to the facts and circumstances of any given case. Where the family home is taken in the joint names, then unless the facts are very unusual I think that both the man and the woman are entitled to a share in the beneficial interest. Where the house is bought outright and not on mortgage, then the extent of their respective shares will depend upon a more or less precise arithmetical calculation of the extent of their contributions to the purchase price. Where, on the other hand, and as is more usual nowadays, the house is bought with the aid of a mortgage, then the court has to assess each of the parties' respective contributions in a broad sense; nevertheless the court is only entitled to look at the financial contributions or their real or substantial equivalent, to the acquisition of the house; that the husband may spend his weekends redecorating or laying a patio is neither here nor there, nor is the fact the woman has spent so much of her time looking after the house, doing the cooking and bringing up the family.

The inquiry becomes even more difficult when the home is taken in only one of the two names. For present purposes I will assume that it is the man, although the same approach will be followed if it is taken in the name of the woman. Where a matrimonial or family home is bought in the man's name alone on mortgage by the mechanism of deposit and instalments, then if the woman pays or contributes to the initial deposit this points to a common intention that she should have *some* beneficial interest in the house. If thereafter she makes direct contributions to the instalments, then the case is a fortiori and her rightful share is likely to be greater. If the woman, having contributed to the deposit, but although not making direct contributions to the instalments, nevertheless uses her own money for other joint household expenses so as to enable the man the more easily to pay the mortgage instalments out of his money, then her position is the same. Where a woman has made no contribution to the initial deposit, but makes regular and substantial contributions to the mortgage instalments, it may still be reasonable to infer a common intention that she should share the beneficial interest from the outset or a fresh agreement after the original conveyance that she should acquire such a share. It is only when there is no evidence upon which a court can reasonably draw an inference about the extent of the share of the contributing woman, that it should fall back on the maxim 'equality is equity'. Finally, when the house is taken in the man's name alone, if the woman makes no 'real' or 'substantial' financial contribution towards either the purchase price, deposit or mortgage instalments by the means of which the family home was acquired, then she is not entitled to any share in the beneficial interest in that home even though over a very substantial number of years she may have worked just as hard as the man in maintaining the family in the sense of keeping the house, giving birth to and looking after and helping to bring up the children of the union.

On the facts of the instant case, which Waller LJ has outlined, I think that it is clear that the plaintiff falls into the last of the categories to which I have just referred and accordingly I too would dismiss this appeal. When one compares this ultimate result with what it would have been had she been married to the defendant, and taken appropriate steps under the Matrimonial Causes Act 1973, I think that she can justifiably say that fate has not been kind to her. In my opinion, however, the remedy for any inequity she may have sustained is a matter for Parliament and not for this court.

NOTE: The Appeal Committee of the House of Lords (Lord Diplock, Lord Scarman and Lord Brightman) dismissed a petition by the plaintiff for leave to appeal.

SPRINGETTE v *DEFOE* [1992] 2 FCR 561, Court of Appeal

FACTS: The parties met in 1979. The appellant was the tenant of a council flat in the London Borough of Ealing. The respondent moved in and paid half the rent. They lived together as husband and wife. Early in 1982 they moved and became joint tenants of 49 St. Andrews Road, another council property. On June 30, 1982 the property was offered to them by the council at a price of £14,445. This give a discount of 41% on the estimated market value because the appellant had been a tenant of the council for over 11 years. The parties arranged to buy the property jointly. At that stage they intended to marry.

The total purchase price was £14,706.35. £12,000 of that was raised by way of a mortgage to the Nationwide Building Society in joint names. It was agreed that each would contribute half of the mortgage instalments. Of the balance, the respondent contributed £180 and the rest came out of the appellant's savings. The parties were registered as joint proprietors but the registered transfer was silent as to the beneficial interests.

The relationship broke down in 1985. Proceedings started in January 1987. It was common ground that the parties were each intended to have some beneficial interest in the property. The appellant claimed that she was entitled to a 75% share and the respondent to a 25% share on the basis that those were the proportions in which they provided the purchase money.

The recorder found that the parties never had any discussion at or before the time of the purchase about what their respective beneficial interests were to be. He concluded, however, that they were to share equally on the ground that each had in his or her own mind an uncommunicated belief or intention to that effect. He found that upon looking at the surrounding facts at the time of the acquisition there was sufficient evidence to infer a common intention that the property should be owned in equal shares.

The appellant appealed.

HELD: Allowing the appeal: The principle of law invoked on behalf of the appellant was that if two or more persons purchased property in their joint names and there had been no declaration of the trusts upon which it was to be held, in the absence of evidence to the contrary they would hold that property on a resulting trust for the persons who provided the purchase money in the proportions in which they provided it: *Dyer* v *Dyer* (1788) 2 Cox Eq Cas 92; *Pettitt* v *Pettitt* [1970] AC 777 *per* Lord Upjohn at p. 814. The question was whether the recorder was right in concluding that an actual common intention to acquire the property in equal beneficial shares had been established on the evidence. It was established that there had been no discussion at all regarding the shares. It made no difference that both parties thought that they were acquiring equal shares if they did not say so to each other. The law had to concentrate on external signs of common intention rather than on what was privately thought or speculated. Inference of common intention might be drawn from circumstantial evidence. But those inferences would be drawn from the *words or conduct* of the parties. It was not capable of arising by virtue of any subjective intention or absence of intention which was not made manifest at the time of the transaction: *Gissing* v *Gissing* [1971] AC 886 at p. 906 *per* Lord Diplock. It followed that it was not enough to establish common intention to found a trust of land that each party happened to be thinking the same thing at the same time while neither had any knowledge of the thinking of the other. No authority was put before the court to support a contrary proposition. Further, the evidence of surrounding facts before the recorder could not support the inference of common intention that he sought to draw. Accordingly, the appeal would be allowed and the recorder's decision varied to apportion the beneficial interest as 75% to the appellant and 25% to the respondent.

DILLON LJ: This is yet another case in which it falls to the court to decide the proportions of the beneficial interests of a man and a woman, who are not married to each other, in the proceeds of the sale of a house which they have acquired in their joint names for the purpose of living together in it. . . .

. . . The common intention must be founded on evidence such as would support a finding that there is an implied or constructive trust for the parties in proportions to the purchase price. The court does not as yet sit, as under a palm tree, to exercise a general discretion to do what the man in the street, on a general overview of the case, might regard as fair.

But the common intention of the parties must, in my judgment, mean a shared intention communicated between them. It cannot mean an intention which each happened to have in his or her own mind but had never communicated to the other. I find some assistance in this respect in the observation of Lord Bridge of Harwich in *Lloyds Bank plc* v *Rosset* [1991] AC 107 where he said at p. 132 in relation to the question whether there had been any agreement, arrangement or understanding reached between the parties to the effect that a property was to be shared beneficially:

> This finding of an agreement or arrangement to share in this sense can only, I think, be based on evidence in express discussions between the partners, however imperfectly remembered and however imprecise their terms may have been.

It is not enough to establish a common intention which is sufficient to found an implied or constructive trust of land that each of them happened at the same time to have been thinking on the same lines in his or her uncommunicated thoughts, while neither had any knowledge of the thinking of the other.

Since, therefore, it is clear in the present case that there never was any discussion between the parties about what their respective beneficial interests were to be, they cannot, in my judgment, have had in any relevant sense any common intention to the beneficial ownership of 49 St Andrews Road. I cannot, therefore, support the conclusion of the recorder that the beneficial interest was held by Miss Springette and Mr Defoe in equal shares. The presumption of a resulting trust is not displaced. Accordingly, I would allow this appeal and would declare instead that they are beneficially entitled in the proportions of 75% to Miss Springette and 25% to Mr Defoe.

STEYN LJ: . . . Our trust law does not allow property rights to be affected by telepathy. *Prima facie*, therefore, the alleged actual common intention was not established.

Can it make any difference that both the man and the woman thought that they were acquiring equal shares albeit that they did not say so to each other? No authority in favour of an affirmative answer was cited. In my judgment, the answer must be a decisive no. The law must perforce concentrate on external signs of common intention. It must concentrate on what was said or done, rather than on what was privately thought or speculated. If any authority for this proposition is needed, it is to be found in the decision of the House of Lords in *Lloyds Bank Plc* v *Rosset and Another* [1991] 1 AC 107 at p. 132. See also *Gissing* v *Gissing* [1971] AC 886 and p. 906.

I readily accept that an inference of actual common intention may be warranted by circumstantial evidence. But the inference sought to be drawn in such a case would have to be that the parties had at the time of the acquisition communicated to one another a common intention to acquire the property in equal shares. . . .

SIR CHRISTOPHER SLADE: . . . All too frequently the courts of this country still have to consider cases where, despite many prior judicial warnings given to their legal advisers, the parties to a transfer of the legal estate in property into joint names have failed either to include in the form of transfer a declaration of trust, stating the shares in which they are to hold the property beneficially, or to reach any explicit agreement defining such shares, prior to the transfer.

On the particular facts of some such cases, the court may think it right to infer that the common intention of the parties as at the date of the original acquisition was

　(a)　that their respective shares in the property should not crystallize as at that date, but should instead be assessed only when the property subsequently comes to be sold;

　(b)　that such assessment should be made having regard to the respective contributions which each of them had by *that date* (the date of the sale) made towards the acquisition, whether in the form of cash paid on the initial purchase or the discharge of all or part of a mortgage debt taken to assist the purchase or in some other form: (see for example *Passee v Passee* [1988] 1 FLR 263, particularly at pp. 270–272 per Nicholls LJ).

The case before us, however, is not of the latter class. Four points have, I think, been common ground on this appeal:

　(1)　As from the date of the transfer, the two parties took the property as beneficial tenants in common, rather than beneficial joint tenants.

　(2)　Their respective shares in the property were intended to crystallize, and did crystallize, as at the date of the transfer.

　(3)　Save in cases of the type exemplified by *Passee v Passee* (above), the presumption of equity, commonly known as the presumption of resulting trust, (albeit rebuttable by evidence of an inconsistent intention), is that, where the purchase money for property acquired by two or more persons in their joint names has been contributed by them in unequal amounts, they will be beneficially entitled as between themselves in the proportions in which they contributed the purchase money.

　(4)　The application of the contribution basis referred to in (3) above would leave the plaintiff in the present case with a 75% interest and the defendant with a 25% interest in the property. [The relevant figures producing these percentages are set out in the judgment of Dillon LJ.]

In my judgment, therefore, the issue on this appeal is ultimately a short one: Was there sufficient evidence to justify the Judge (or would there be sufficient evidence to justify this court) in holding that the presumption of resulting trust is rebutted, and that the arrangement between the parties was that each of them should have a 50% interest.

The defendant has consistently said that such was his intention at the time of the purchase. Miss Brann, who no doubt conducted the defendant's case in the court below with the same skill as in this court, elicited from the plaintiff in cross-examination statements to the effect that at the time of the purchase, she too intended or contemplated that the property would be owned in equal shares. These statements formed the basis of Miss Brann's argument before us. However, while she suggested that the plaintiff's understanding of the situation and the similar understanding of the defendant would have been communicated to the other before completion of the purchase, there is absolutely no evidence that it was. There is no evidence or finding by the Judge of any agreement or discussion concerning the shares which the parties were to have in the property; on the contrary, there seems to have been no such discussion.

Many of the reported cases dealing with implied and resulting trusts refer to the 'common intention' of the parties as at the date of the purchase as being the relevant factor. It has to be borne in mind, however, that in the absence of writing as provided for by s. 53(1) of the Law of Property Act 1925, a party claiming a beneficial interest under an asserted trust in a case such as this has to rely on the provisions of s. 53(2), which exempt 'resulting, implied or constructive' trusts from the operation of s. 53(1).

In my judgment, while a trust of any of these three last-mentioned categories is capable of arising by giving effect to 'the inferences as to the intentions of parties to a transaction which a reasonable man would draw from their *words or conduct*' (emphasis added), it is not capable of arising by virtue of 'any subjective intention or absence of intention which was not made manifest at the time of the transaction itself': (see *Gissing v Gissing* [1971] AC 886 at p. 906 *per* Lord Diplock). This short point of law is, in my judgment, conclusive in relation to this appeal. I think that no authority has been cited to us which supports a contrary proposition. . . .

For these reasons, and for the further reasons given by Dillon and Steyn LJJ, I too would allow this appeal.

MIDLAND BANK PLC v COOKE AND ANOTHER [1995] 4 All ER 562,
Court of Appeal

FACTS: The husband and wife married in 1971 and moved into a house purchased for £8,500 in the husband's sole name. The purchase was financed by a mortgage of £6,450, with the balance provided from the husband's savings and a wedding gift of £1,100 from his parents. In 1978 the mortgage was replaced by a general mortgage in favour of the respondent bank granted to the husband to secure repayment of his company's business overdraft. In 1979, at the bank's request, the wife signed a form of consent to any present or future right or interest which she might have in the property being postponed to the bank's security under the mortgage. The property was subsequently transferred into the joint names of the husband and wife as tenants in common, following proceedings brought by the wife under the Married Women's Property Act 1964. In 1987 the bank commenced county court proceedings against the husband and wife, claiming payment of £52,491 as the sum due under the mortgage, and possession in default of payment. The wife filed a defence, asserting that her signature to the consent form had been procured to the knowledge of the bank by her husband's undue influence, and counterclaimed for declarations that she was the joint legal owner of the property and entitled to a beneficial half interest in the property overriding any interests of the bank under the mortgage. The judge held, on the undue influence issue, that the consent form was not binding on the wife and that her equitable interest took priority over the bank's claims. He further held that the wife's beneficial interest depended on her monetary contribution and that, since her maintenance and improvement contribution did not amount to a contribution to the purchase price, she was entitled to a beneficial interest of 6.74% in the property, being the proportion represented by her half share of the wedding gift from the husband's parents (£550) to the total purchase price of the property (£8,500). The wife appealed, contending that the judge had adopted the wrong approach to the quantification of her beneficial interest. The bank cross-appealed.

HELD: (1) Where a partner in a matrimonial home without legal title had established an equitable interest through direct contribution, the court would assess (in the absence of express evidence of intention) the proportions the parties were to be assumed to have intended for their beneficial ownership by undertaking a survey of the whole course of dealing between the parties relevant to their ownership and occupation of the property and their sharing of its burdens and advantages and would take into consideration all conduct which threw light on the question what shares were intended. In particular, the court was not bound to deal with the matter on the strict basis of the trust resulting from the cash contribution to the purchase price, and was free to attribute to the parties an intention to share the beneficial interest in some different proportions; and the fact that the parties had neither discussed nor intended any agreement as to the proportions of their beneficial interest did not preclude the court from inferring one on general equitable principles . . .

(2) It followed that the judge had erred in treating the wife's cash contribution to the purchase price as wholly determinative of the issue of the current proportion of beneficial entitlement without regard to the other factors emerging from the whole course of dealing between the husband and wife. Applying the proper approach to the facts, it was clear that the couple's presumed intention was to share the beneficial interest in the property in equal shares and that intention was reinforced by the subsequent terms of their compromise of the Married Women's Property Act proceedings. The wife was therefore entitled to a beneficial half interest in the matrimonial home and a declaration would be granted to that effect. The appeal would therefore be allowed and the cross-appeal would be dismissed . . .

WAITE LJ: This appeal, concerning the disputed beneficial interests in a matrimonial home, was heard during the week in which the Law Commission published its *Sixth Programme of Law Reform* (Law Com No. 234). Item 8 of the programme recommends an examination of the property rights of home sharers. The report comments (p. 34): 'The present legal rules are uncertain and difficult to apply and can lead to serious injustice.'

Though that was a reference to the problems of unmarried home-owners, the rights of married occupiers can be equally problematic—as the present case shows—when the claims of third parties such as creditors or mortgagees become involved. The economic and social significance of home-ownership in modern society, and the frequency with which cases involving disputes as to the property rights of home-sharers (married or unmarried) are coming before the courts, suggest that the Law Commission's intervention is well-timed and has the potential to save a lot of human heartache as well as public expense.
. . .

(A) *Was there a gift by Mr Cooke's parents to both spouses?*
The judge was in my view (rejecting Mr Bergin's first submission) fully entitled, on the evidence which I have quoted, to hold that there was. In a case where the bride's parents were paying for the wedding and reception and the bridegroom's parents were providing a contribution to the purchase price of the matrimonial home, it would not only be sensible to draw the inference that the bridegroom's parents intended to make a present to them both of the moneys which were to be applied in the purchase, but highly artificial to draw any other inference.

(B) *Is the proportion of Mrs Cooke's beneficial interest to be fixed solely by reference to the percentage of the purchase price which she contributed directly, so as to make all other conduct irrelevant?*
In contending that it is, Mr Bergin submits as follows.

   (a) It is now well settled that in determining (in the absence of evidence of express agreement) whether a party unnamed in the deeds has any beneficial interest in the property at all the test is the stringent one stated by Lord Bridge of Harwich in *Lloyds Bank plc v Rosset* [1990] 1 All ER 1111 at 1119:

   In this situation direct contributions to the purchase price by the partner who is not the legal owner, whether initially or by payment of mortgage instalments, will readily justify the inference necessary to the creation of a constructive trust. But, as I read the authorities, it is at least extremely doubtful whether anything less will do.

   (b) By parity of reasoning, in cases where a direct contribution has been duly proved by the partner who is not the legal owner (thus establishing a resulting trust in his or her favour of *some* part of the beneficial interest) the proportion of that share will be fixed at the proportion it bears to the overall price of the property. Although the proportion may be enlarged by subsequent contribution to the purchase price, such contributions must be direct—ie further cash payments or contribution to the capital element in instalment repayments of any mortgage under which the unpaid proportion of the purchase remains secured. Nothing less will do. . . .
[His Lordship then referred to the judgment of Dillon LJ in *Springette* v *Defoe* [1992] 2 FCR 561 (see above).]

   That decision has to be compared with *McHardy & Sons (a firm)* v *Warren* [1994] 2 FLR 338, a case in which (as here) it became necessary to quantify the interests of husband and wife on a strict equitable basis because of third party claims against the property. The purchase of the first matrimonial home was (again, as in this case) partly financed by a contribution from the husband's parents, but with the difference that in that instance the husband's parents paid the whole of the deposit (using that term in the sense of the net purchase price not covered by a mortgage) for the property, which was registered in the husband's sole name. The two subsequent homes successively purchased by the parties out of the net proceeds of sale of the former home were similarly taken in his name alone. The husband then executed a charge on the current home to secure his indebtedness to the plaintiffs, who were trade creditors. In proceedings by the plaintiffs against both husband and wife to enforce their charge, the plaintiffs asserted that the wife either had no beneficial interest or at most an interest equivalent to 8.97%, representing the proportion that half the initial deposit of £650 bore to the total purchase price of the first home. The judge rejected that claim, holding that the parties were beneficially entitled in equal shares. He was upheld on appeal. It does not appear from the law report that *Springette* v *Defoe* was cited, but the presiding Lord Justice was again Dillon LJ, who said (at 340):

To my mind it is the irresistible conclusion that where a parent pays the deposit, either directly or to the solicitors or to the bride and groom, it matters not which, on the purchase of their first matrimonial home, it is the intention of all three of them that the bride and groom should have equal interests in the matrimonial home, not interests measured by reference to the percentage half the deposit [bears] to the full price . . .

I confess that I find the differences of approach in those two cases mystifying. In the one a strict resulting trust geared to mathematical calculation of the proportion of the purchase price provided by cash contribution is treated as virtually immutable in the absence of express agreement: in the other a displacement of the cash-related trust by inferred agreement is not only permitted but treated as obligatory. Guidance out of this difficulty is to be found, fortunately, in the passage in the speech of Lord Diplock in *Gissing* v *Gissing* [1970] 2 All ER 780 at 792–793, where he is dealing with the approach to be adopted by the court when evaluating the proportionate shares of the parties, once it has been duly established through the direct contributions of the party without legal title, that *some* beneficial interest was intended for both. He said:

Where in any of the circumstances described above contributions, direct or indirect, have been made to the mortgage instalments by the spouse into whose name the matrimonial home has not been conveyed, and the court can infer from their conduct a common intention that the contributing spouse should be entitled to *some* beneficial interest in the matrimonial home, what effect is to be given to that intention if there is no evidence that they in fact reached any express agreement as to what the respective share of each spouse should be? I take it to be clear that if the court is satisfied that it was the common intention of both spouses that the contributing wife should have a share in the beneficial interest and that her contributions were made on this understanding, the court in the exercise of its equitable jurisdiction would not permit the husband in whom the legal estate was vested and who had accepted the benefit of the contributions to take the whole beneficial interest merely because at the time the wife made her contributions there had been no express agreement as to how her share in it was to be quantified. In such a case the court must first do its best to discover from the conduct of the spouses whether any inference can reasonably be drawn as to the probable common understanding about the amount of the share of the contributing spouse on which each must have acted in doing what each did, even though that understanding was never expressly stated by one spouse to the other or even consciously formulated in words by either of them independently. It is only if no such inference can be drawn that the court is driven to apply as a rule of law, and not as an inference of fact, the maxim 'equality is equity', and to hold that the beneficial interest belongs to the spouses in equal shares. The same result however may often be reached as an inference of fact. The instalments of a mortgage to a building society are generally repayable over a period of many years. During that period, as both must be aware, the ability of each spouse to contribute to the instalments out of their separate earnings is likely to alter, particularly in the case of the wife if any children are born of the marriage. If the contribution of the wife in the early part of the period of repayment is substantial but is not an identifiable and uniform proportion of each instalment, because her contributions are indirect or, if direct, are made irregularly, it may well be a reasonable inference that their common intention at the time of acquisition of the matrimonial home was that the beneficial interest should be held by them in equal shares and that each should contribute to the cost of its acquisition whatever amounts each could afford in the varying exigencies of family life to be expected during the period of repayment. In the social conditions of today this would be a natural enough common intention of a young couple who were both earning when the house was acquired but who contemplated having children whose birth and rearing in their infancy would necessarily affect the future earning capacity of the wife. The relative size of their respective contributions to the instalments in the early part of the period of repayment, or later if a subsequent reduction in the wife's contribution is not to be accounted for by a reduction in her earnings due to motherhood or some other cause from which the husband benefits as well, may make it a more probable inference that the wife's share in the beneficial interest was intended to be in some proportion other than one-half. And there is nothing inherently improbable in their acting on the understanding that the wife should be entitled to a share which was not to be quantified immediately on the acquisition of the home but should be left to be determined when the mortgage was repaid or the property disposed of, on the basis of what would be fair having regard to the total contributions, direct or indirect, which each spouse had made by that date. Where this was the most likely inference from their conduct it would be for the court to give effect to that common intention of the parties by determining what in all the circumstances was a fair share. Difficult as they are to solve, however, these problems as to the amount of the share of a spouse in the beneficial interest in a matrimonial home where the legal estate is vested solely in the other spouse, only arise in cases where the court is satisfied by the words or conduct of the parties that it was their common intention that the beneficial interest was not to belong solely to the spouse in whom the legal estate was vested but was to be shared between them in some proportion or other. (Lord Diplock's emphasis.)

The decision of this court in *Grant* v *Edwards* [1986] 2 All ER 426 also affords helpful guidance. The context was different, in that the court was there dealing with a legal owner who has made representations to the occupier on which the latter has relied to her detriment so as to introduce equities in the nature of estoppel. Once a beneficial interest had been established by that route, however, the court then proceeded—as I read the judgments—to fix the proportions of the beneficial interests on general grounds which were regarded as applying in all cases. That appears from the judgments of Nourse LJ ([1986] 2 All ER 426 at 434) and of Browne-Wilkinson V-C, where (after citing the passage I have quoted from Lord Diplock in *Gissing* v *Gissing*) he says:

Where, as in this case, the existence of some beneficial interest in the claimant has been shown, prima facie the interest of the claimant will be that which the parties intended: see *Gissing* v *Gissing* [1970] 2 All ER 780 at 792. In *Eves* v *Eves* [1975] 3 All ER 768 at 775 Brightman LJ plainly felt that a common intention that there should be a joint interest pointed to the beneficial interests being equal. However, he felt able to find a lesser beneficial interest in that case without explaining the legal basis on which he did so. With diffidence, I suggest that the law of proprietary estoppel may again provide useful guidance. If proprietary estoppel is established, the court gives effect to it by giving effect to the common intention so far as may fairly be done between the parties. For that purpose, equity is displayed at its most flexible: see *Crabb* v *Arun DC* [1975] 3 All ER 865. Identifiable contributions to the purchase of the house will of course be an important factor in many cases. But in other cases, contributions by way of the labour or other unquantifiable actions of the claimant will also be relevant. Taking into account the fact that the house was intended to be the joint property, the contributions to the common expenditure and the payment of the fire insurance moneys into the joint account, I agree that the plaintiff is entitled to a half interest in the house. (See [1986] 2 All ER 426 at 439–440.)

The general principle to be derived from *Gissing* v *Gissing* and *Grant* v *Edwards* can in my judgment be summarised in this way. When the court is proceeding, in cases like the present where the partner without legal title has successfully asserted an equitable interest through direct contribution, to determine (in the absence of express evidence of intention) what proportions the parties must be assumed to have intended for their beneficial ownership, the duty of the judge is to undertake a survey of the whole course of dealing between the parties relevant to their ownership and occupation of the property and their sharing of its burdens and advantages. That scrutiny will not confine itself to the limited range of acts of direct contribution of the sort that are needed to found a beneficial interest in the first place. It will take into consideration all conduct which throws light on the question what shares were intended. Only if that search proves inconclusive does the court fall back on the maxim that 'equality is equity'.

My answer to question B would therefore be No. The court is not bound to deal with the matter on the strict basis of the trust resulting from the cash contribution to the purchase price, and is free to attribute to the parties an intention to share the beneficial interest in some different proportions.

Mr Bergin submits, however, that in the particular circumstances of this case, that is an approach which the court is precluded from following by the evidence of actual intention given by the spouses themselves. That brings me to his last submission.

(C) *Can an agreement be attributed by inference of law to parties who have expressly stated that they reached no agreement?*

Mr Bergin begins by pointing out (rightly) that this is an area of the law in which there is no scope for discretion. The entire jurisdiction rests upon the very limited exception provided by Parliament to the general requirement in s. 53 of the Law of Property Act 1925 that trusts must be evidenced in writing. It is an exception in favour of trusts that are 'resulting, implied or constructive'. Mr Bergin then submits that the resulting trust is that which results from a contribution to the purchase price, and prima facie that fixes the proportion of the beneficial interest. Any implied or constructive trust relied on to alter or enlarge that prima facie entitlement must rest upon an imputed agreement inferred from conduct by equity. If the parties themselves testify on oath that they made no agreement, there is no scope for equity to make one for them. . . .

I would reject instinctively on the ground that it runs counter to the very system of law—equity—on which it seeks to rely. Equity has traditionally been a system which matches established principle to the demands of social change. The mass diffusion of home ownership has been one of the most striking social changes of our own time. The present case is typical of hundreds, perhaps even thousands, of others. When people, especially young people, agree to share their lives in joint homes they do so on a basis of mutual trust and in the expectation that their relationship will endure. Despite the efforts that have been made by many responsible bodies to counsel prospective cohabitants as to the risks of taking shared interests in property without legal advice, it is unrealistic to expect that advice to be followed on a universal scale. For a couple embarking on a serious relationship, discussion of the terms to apply at parting is almost a contradiction of the shared hopes that have brought them together. There will inevitably be numerous couples, married or unmarried, who have no discussion about ownership and who, perhaps advisedly, make no agreement about it. It would be anomalous, against that background, to create a range of home-buyers who were beyond the pale of equity's assistance in formulating a fair presumed basis for the sharing of beneficial title, simply because they had been honest enough to admit that they never gave ownership a thought or reached any agreement about it. . . .

1.3.8 LICENCES BY ESTOPPEL

INWARDS v *BAKER* [1965] 1 All ER 446, Court of Appeal

FACTS: Baker junior was keen to build himself a bungalow, but he could not afford the price of an empty site. His father had some spare land. Baker senior said to his son, 'Why not put the bungalow on my land and make the bungalow a little bigger?'. Baker junior did exactly that, and made the bungalow his permanent home.

Baker senior retained ownership of the fee simple to the land, and so the house also became **Baker senior's** property. All was well while both senior and junior were still alive, but when Baker senior died his will (made long before the bungalow was built) left the land in question not to Baker junior but to Inwards. Inwards brought proceedings to recover possession of the bungalow. These proceedings failed.

HELD: The Court of Appeal found that where a landowner (L) encourages a third party (T) to expend money and/or effort on L's land, and T reasonably assumes that he will have some degree of permanence on the land, T acquires some sort of right with respect to the land. This right is (in principle) binding on third parties.

LORD DENNING MR: . . . We have had the advantage of cases which were not cited to the county court judge—cases in the last century, notably *Dillwyn* v *Llewelyn* (1862) 4 De GF & J 517 and *Plimmer* v *Wellington Corporation* (1884) 9 App Cas 699. This latter was a decision of the Privy Council which expressly affirmed and approved the statement of the law made by Lord Kingsdown in *Ramsden* v *Dyson* (1866) LR 1 HL 129. It is quite plain from those authorities that if the owner of land requests another, or indeed allows another, to expend money on the land under an expectation created or encouraged by the landlord that he will be able to remain there, that raises an equity in the licensee such as to entitle him to stay. He has a licence coupled with an equity. Mr Goodhart urged before us that the licensee could not stay indefinitely. The principle only applied, he said, when there was an expectation of some precise legal term. But it seems to me, from *Plimmer's* case in particular, that the equity arising from the expenditure on land need not fail 'merely on the ground that the interest to be secured has not been expressly indicated . . . the court must look at the circumstances in each case to decide in what way the equity can be satisfied.'

So in this case, even though there is no binding contract to grant any particular interest to the licensee, nevertheless the court can look at the circumstances and see whether there is an equity arising out of the expenditure of money. All that is necessary is that the licensee should, at the request or with the encouragement of the landlord, have spent the money in the expectation of being allowed to stay there. If so, the court will not allow that expectation to be defeated where it would be inequitable so to do. In this case it is quite plain that the father allowed an expectation to be created in the son's mind that this bungalow was to be his home. It was to be his home for his life or, at all events, his home as long as he wished it to remain his home. It seems to me, in the light of that equity, that the father could not in 1932 have turned to his son and said: 'You are to go. It is my land and my house'. Nor could he at any time thereafter so long as the son wanted it as his home.

Mr Goodhart put the case of a purchaser. He suggested that the father could sell the land to a purchaser who could get the son out. But I think that any purchaser who took with notice would clearly be bound by the equity. So here, too, the present plaintiffs, the successors in title of the father, are clearly themselves bound by this equity. It is an equity well recognised in law. It arises from the expenditure of money by a person in actual occupation of land when he is led to believe that, as the result of that expenditure, he will be allowed to remain there. It is for the court to say in what way the equity can be satisfied. I am quite clear in this case it can be satisfied by holding that the defendant can remain there as long as he desires to as his home.

I would allow the appeal accordingly and enter judgment for the defendant.

DANCKWERTS LJ: . . . It is not necessary, I think, to imply a promise. It seems to me that this is one of the cases of an equity created by estoppel, or equitable estoppel, as it is sometimes called, by which the person who has made the expenditure is induced by the expectation of obtaining protection, and equity protects him so that an injustice may not be perpetrated.

I am clearly of opinion that the appeal should be allowed and judgment should be entered for the defendant.

CRABB v ARUN DISTRICT COUNCIL [1976] 1 Ch 179, Court of Appeal

FACTS: The plaintiff owned a piece of land which had access at point A on to a road owned by the defendants and a right of way from A along the road. To enable him to sell his land in two parts the plaintiff sought from the defendants a second point of access, at point B, and a further right of way along the road. At a site meeting in July 1967 between the plaintiff, his architect and a representative of the defendants the additional access point, B, was agreed. Subsequently, the defendants fenced the boundary between their road and the plaintiff's land, erecting gates at both A and B. After the plaintiff had sold part of his land, in October 1968, together with the right of access at A and easement over the road, without reserving any right in favour of the land retained, the defendants removed the gates at B and fenced the gap, leaving the retained part of the plaintiff's land landlocked. The plaintiff brought an action for a declaration and injunction, claiming that the defendants were estopped by their conduct from denying him a right of access at B and a right of way along the road. Pennycuick VC held that in the absence of a definite assurance by the defendants' representative no question of estoppel could arise and dismissed the action.

On appeal by the plaintiff:

HELD: Allowing the appeal, that the defendants, knowing of the plaintiff's intention to sell his land in separate portions, by their representative led the plaintiff to believe that he would be granted a right of access at B and, by erecting the gates and failing to disabuse him of his belief, encouraged the plaintiff to act to his detriment in selling part of his land without reservation over it of any right of way, thereby giving rise to an equity in the plaintiff's favour . . .; that that equity should be satisfied by granting the plaintiff a right of access at B and a right of way along the road; and in view of the sterilisation of the plaintiff's land for a considerable period resulting from the defendants' action, the right should be granted without any payment by the plaintiff. . . .

Decision of Pennycuick V-C reversed.

LORD DENNING MR : . . . The basis of this proprietary estoppel—as indeed of promissory estoppel—is the interposition of equity. Equity comes in, true to form, to mitigate the rigours of strict law. The early cases did not speak of it as 'estoppel'. They spoke of it as 'raising an equity'. If I may expand what Lord Cairns LC said in *Hughes* v *Metropolitan Railway Co.* (1877) 2 App Cas 439, 448: 'it is the first principle upon which all courts of equity proceed', that it will prevent a person from insisting on his strict legal rights—whether arising under a contract, or on his title deeds, or by statute—when it would be inequitable for him to do so having regard to the dealings which have taken place between the parties.

What then are the dealings which will preclude him from insisting on his strict legal rights? If he makes a binding contract that he will not insist on the strict legal position, a court of equity will hold him to his contract. Short of a binding contract, if he makes a promise that he will not insist upon his strict legal rights—then, even though that promise may be unenforceable in point of law for want of consideration or want of writing—then, if he makes the promise knowing or intending that the other will act upon it, and he does act upon it, then again a court of equity will not allow him to go back on that promise: see *Central London Property Trust Ltd* v *High Trees House Ltd* [1947] KB 130 and *Charles Rickards Ltd* v *Oppenhaim* [1950] 1 KB 616, 623. Short of an actual promise, if he, by his words or conduct, so behaves as to lead another to believe that he will not insist on his strict legal rights—knowing or intending that the other will act on that belief—and he does so act, that again will raise an equity in favour of the other; and it is for a court of equity to say in what way the equity may be satisfied. The cases show that this equity does not depend on agreement but on words or conduct. In *Ramsden* v *Dyson* (1866) LR 1 HL 129, 170 Lord Kingsdown spoke of a verbal agreement 'or what amounts to the same thing, an expectation, created or encouraged'. In *Birmingham and District Land Co.* v *London and North Western Railway Co.* (1888) 40 ChD 268, 277, Cotton LJ said that '. . . what passed did not make a new agreement, but . . . what took place . . . raised an equity against him'. And it was the Privy Council in *Plimmer* v *Wellington Corporation* (1884) 9 App Cas 699, 713–714 who said that '. . . the court must look at the circumstances in each case to decide in what way the equity can be satisfied' giving instances.

Recent cases afford illustrations of the principle. In *Inwards* v *Baker* [1965] 2 QB 29 it was held that, despite the legal title being in the plaintiffs, the son had an equity to remain in the bungalow 'as long as he desired to use it as his home'. Danckwerts LJ said, at p. 38: 'equity protects him so that an injustice may not be perpetrated'. In *E R Ives Investment Ltd* v *High* [1967] 2 QB 379, it was held that Mr High and his successors had an equity which could only be satisfied by allowing him to have a right of access over the yard, 'so long as the block of flats has its foundations on his land'. In *Siew Soon Wah* v *Yong Tong Hong* [1973] AC 836 the Privy Council held that there was an 'equity or equitable estoppel protecting the defendant in his occupation for 30 years'. In *Bank Negara Indonesia* v *Hoalim* [1973] 2 MLJ 3 the Privy Council held that, despite the fact that the defendant had no protection under the Rent Acts, he had an equity to remain 'so long as he continued to practise his profession'.

The question then is: were the circumstances here such as to raise an equity in favour of the plaintiff? True the defendants on the deeds had the title to their land, free of any access at point B. But they led the plaintiff to believe that he had or would be granted a right of access a point B. At the meeting of July 26, 1967, Mr Alford and the plaintiff told the defendants' representative that the plaintiff intended to split the two acres into two portions and wanted to have an access at point B for the back portion; and the defendants' representative agreed that he should have this access. I do not think the defendants can avoid responsibility by saying that their representative had no authority to agree this. They entrusted him with the task of setting out the line of the fence and the gates, and they must be answerable for his conduct in the course of it: see *Attorney-General to the Prince of Wales* v *Collom* [1916] 2 KB 193, 207; and *Moorgate Mercantile Co. Ltd* v *Twitchings* [1976] QB 225, 243.

The judge found that there was 'no definite assurance' by the defendants' representative, and 'no firm commitment', but only an 'agreement in principle', meaning I suppose that, as Mr Alford said there were 'some further processes' to be gone through before it would become binding. But if there were any such processes in the mind of the parties, the subsequent conduct of the defendants was such as to dispense with them. The defendants actually put up the gates at point B at considerable expense. That certainly led the plaintiff to believe that they agreed that he should have the right of access through point B without more ado.

The judge also said that, to establish this equity or estoppel, the defendants must have known that the plaintiff was selling the front portion without reserving a right of access for the back portion. I do not think this was necessary. The defendants knew that the plaintiff *intended* to sell the two portions separately and that he would need an access at point B as well as point A. Seeing that they knew of his intention—and they did nothing to disabuse him but rather confirmed it by erecting gates at point B—it was their conduct which led him to act as he did: and this raises an equity in his favour against them.

In the circumstances it seems to me inequitable that the council should insist on their strict title as they did; and to take the high-handed action of pulling down the gates without a word of warning: and to demand of the plaintiff £3,000 as the price for the easement. If he had moved at once for an injunction in aid of his equity—to prevent them removing the gates—I think he should have been granted it. But he did not do so. He tried to negotiate terms, but these failing, the action has come for trial. And we have the question: in what way now should the equity be satisfied?

Here equity is displayed at its most flexible, see *Snell's Principles of Equity*, 27th ed. (1973), p. 568, and the illustrations there given. If the matter had been finally settled in 1967, I should have thought that, although nothing was said at the meeting in July 1967, nevertheless it would be quite reasonable for the defendants to ask the plaintiff to pay something for the access at point B, perhaps—and I am guessing—some hundreds of pounds. But, as Mr Millett pointed out in the course of the argument, because of the defendants' conduct, the back land has been landlocked. It has been sterile and rendered useless for five or six years: and the plaintiff has been unable to deal with it during that time. This loss to him can be taken into account. And at the present time, it seems to me that, in order to satisfy the equity, the plaintiff should have the right of access at point B without paying anything for it.

I would, therefore, hold that the plaintiff, as the owner of the back portion, has a right of access at point B over the verge on to Mill Park Road and a right of way along that road to Hook Lane without paying compensation. I would allow the appeal and declare that he has an easement, accordingly.

1.3.9 ESTATE CONTRACTS

See **5.2.2** and **5.2.2.2**.

1.3.10 OPTIONS

See **5.2.2.2**.

CHAPTER TWO

SOME BASIC CONCEPTS OF PROPERTY LAW

2.1 The Trust

See **Chapters 11** to **13**.

2.2 Real Property and Personal Property

**Megarry, Sir R, and Wade, H.W.R., The Law of Real Property, 5th edn,
London: Stevens & Sons Limited, 1984, p. 10**

Meaning of 'Real Property'

As is the case with so many expressions in English law, the explanation of the term 'real property' is historical.

In early law, property was deemed 'real' if the courts would restore to a dispossessed owner the thing itself, the '*res*,' and not merely give compensation for the loss. Thus If X forcibly evicted Y from his freehold land, Y could bring a 'real' action whereby he could obtain an order from the court that X should return the land to him. But if X took Y's sword or glove from him, he could bring only a personal action which gave X the choice of either returning the article or paying the value thereof. Consequently a distinction was made between real property (or 'realty'), which could be specifically recovered, and personal property (or 'personalty'), which was not thus recoverable. Nature has provided one division of property, namely into immovables (i.e. land) and movables; the English division into real and personal property is similar with one important exception. In general, all interests in land are real property, with the exception of leaseholds (or 'terms of years'), which are classified as personalty.

This peculiar exception was first of all due to the fact that leases were foreign to the feudal system of landholding by tenure, under which, in its earliest form, the social and economic status of every member of society was fixed. Originally leases were rather regarded as personal business arrangements under which one party allowed the other the use of his land in return for a rent. They were, in other words, personal contracts, operating *in personam* between the parties and not creating or transferring any rights *in rem*, i.e. rights in the land itself which could affect feudal status. Leases helped to supply a useful form of investment for a society which knew nothing of stocks and shares. Money might be employed in buying land and letting it out on lease in order to obtain an income from the capital, or in buying a lease for a lump sum which would be recovered with interest out of the produce of the land. These were commercial transactions, more in the sphere of money than of land, as land-owning was then understood. Once leaseholds were classed with personal property it was discovered that the position was not without its advantages. Not only were leases then immune from feudal burdens and the intricate legal procedure required for freeholds: they could be bequeathed by will in times when wills of other land were still not allowed. Thus the illogical position continued until it became too well settled to alter.

Leaseholds are still, therefore, personalty in law. But having now for so long been recognised as interests in land and not merely contractual rights, they have been classed under the paradoxical heading of chattels real. The first word indicates their personal nature (cattle were the most important chattels in early days, hence the name), the second shows their connection with land. The three types of property may, therefore, be classified thus:

Land   { (i)   Realty.
Personality { (ii)   Chattels real.
              { (iii) Pure personalty.

. . . The legislation of 1925 abolished many of the remaining differences between the law governing realty and that governing personalty. For example, before 1926, if a person died intestate (i.e. without a will), all his realty passed to his heir, while his personalty was divided between certain of his relatives; again, realty could be entailed and personalty could not. After 1925, however, realty and personalty both pass on intestacy to certain relatives, and both kinds of property can be entailed. Nevertheless, the distinction still remains of importance.

Real property itself comprises two distinct genera, called corporeal and incorporeal hereditaments. 'Hereditament' indicates property which descended to the heir on intestacy before 1926, i.e. realty as opposed to personalty. Corporeal hereditaments are lands, buildings, minerals, trees and all other things which are part of or affixed to land – in other words, the physical matter over which ownership is exercised. Incorporeal hereditaments, on the other hand, are not things at all, but rights. Certain rights were classified as real property, so that on intestacy before 1926 they also descended to the heir, rather than to the relatives entitled to personalty. The most important incorporeal hereditaments are easements, profits and rentcharges, but there are others also. . . .

CHAPTER THREE

TENURES

3.1 Feudal Tenures

Simpson, A.W.B., An Introduction to the History of the Land Law,
1st edn, Oxford: Oxford University Press, 1961, p. 2

. . . The doctrine of tenure has its origin in the state of social organization known as 'feudalism'. 'Feudalism' is undoubtedly a vague and imprecise term, with a number of connotations. For our immediate purpose it is sufficient to note that the feudal structure of society, which was firmly established in England after the Norman Conquest, involved dependent land holding—the holding of land in return for the rendering of sevices, typically military sevice. Even before the Conquest land tenure of a sort was known; the *loan* of land created a relationship between lender and holder which closely resembles the feudal relationship between lord and tenant of post-Conquest times, and the relationship between the Saxon lord and the village community where he held sway could be described in tenurial terms. How widespread tenure was in Anglo-Saxon England is a moot point, and a somewhat artificial one; until there was a theory of tenure the question can hardly be asked. What is clear is that the Norman administrators did have a theory of tenure, and applied it universally; all land whatsoever was held of some lord, and ultimately of the Crown. This is fully recognized in Domesday Book (1086) and certainly no such rigid doctrine could possibly have existed before 1066; indeed, in England alone was feudalism so universalized. On the Continent feudal land-holding did not engulf all land; some tracts of land—called allodial lands—escaped the net. In Domesday Book the compilers sometimes seem puzzled by a landholder who seems to have no lord, but such puzzlement is assumed to arise rather from ignorance of the facts than from any exception to the universal application of the concept of tenure. The consequence of this was that feudal law did not become the law of the knightly, aristocratic class, nor the law of some parts of the country alone; it became the common law of England.

This triumph of order was made possible by the Conquest, and by the high degree of administrative efficiency attained by King William's staff. The invasion of England by a band of military adventurers made it necessary to quarter this military aristocracy on the conquered land; William had to reward his followers and preserve his military strength for the future. He was able to achieve both these ends by parcelling up the land of the country amongst his followers, who became his tenants for their land, holding by his grant. In return he bargained for services; and most of his tenants were bound to serve in the Royal army and bring with them a specified number of knights. The tenure thus created was knight-service, the typical feudal tenure, and it was wholly Norman. The tenant who owed the service of ten knights was said to hold ten *knight's fees*, and so on; there is some evidence to show that the quota of knights due was fixed in multiples of five or ten knights. The immediate tenants of the Crown were called his tenants in chief, and there were probably about fifteen hundred of these tenants by 1086.

Now when it is said that the country was granted out by the King to his tenants in chief it must not be imagined that any process of wholesale eviction took place. At the bottom of the social scale were those humble peasants who actually wrested the agricultural wealth of the country from the soil; it was their labour which made the whole paraphernalia of knights and castles possible. At the time of the Conquest many were slaves, the property of some Saxon lord; some were free men who had a lord, but who did not hold their lands of their lord, for their personal relationship of dependence was unconnected with their enjoyment of land. Others perhaps could be regarded as tenants, who held of their lords. The greater part of these peasants would be bound by custom to perform various duties of a public nature, such as to repair bridges, and also other duties which were of personal benefit to the Saxon lord of the village community in which they lived—for example they might be bound to provide him with a food rent, or to labour on the land of their lord. The tendency before the Conquest had been for the peasants of a village community to become increasingly dependent upon the local lord, and it has been suggested that it may have often happened that the peasants surrendered their lands into the local lord's hands and received them back again in return for an obligation to labour on their lord's land; in return for a greater degree of subservience the peasants received the protection of a powerful man. In general the effect of the Norman Conquest was only to substitute a new, alien, lord for his Saxon predecessor. What a tenant in chief acquired by the enjoyment of rights over land and services due from peasants who cultivated that land; to the peasant it may not have seemed that anything very momentous had occurred. . . .

The King's immediate grantee—the tenant in chief *ut de corona*—could retain his land and provide knights by paying for them, and keeping them in his household, but more frequently he provided his quota by subinfeudation. This took the form of a grant by the tenant in chief of one parcel of land to some lesser man, X, the land to be held of the grantor in return for the service of one or more knights in the Royal army. The grantee, X, in his turn could again subinfeudate to another, Y, a part or the whole of his parcel of land, and in this way any number of rungs in the ladder could be created. Upon such a subinfeudation the grantor and grantee could reach any bargain they wished as to the services, but this in no way concerned the lord of whom the grantor held, for the service due to him remained burdened on the land, unaffected by subinfeudation. . . .

The provision of an army was but one of the requirements of medieval society. By the creation of tenures involving other forms of service the land, which was the major source of wealth, could be made to yield to lords whatever goods or labour they required. It is important to realise that no fixed rules governed the type or nature of the services which could be stipulated for upon a grant of land. The result was the creation of tenures which range from the ludicrous to the obscene and from the onerous to the nominal. A few examples will illustrate this diversity. In the reign of John we find that William, Earl Warren granted lands in Stamford to be held for the service of finding annually a mad bull to divert his lordship, whilst there are several grants of land for the service of holding the seasick King's head on his trips across the channel. Straw for the royal privy had to be found by one unfortunate landholder, and the tenant of lands in Suffolk, one Rolland, was obliged upon Christmas Day to make a leap, a whistle and a fart *coram domino rege*, a service subseqently commuted for a less embarrassing money payment. At the other end of the scale come really heavy burdens—tenants in chief who owe the service of forty or more knights, those who hold at substantial rents in kind, and those who hold in return for onerous services, such as the duty of caring for falcons and hounds. Upon this diversity of social relationships the medieval lawyers imposed a deceptively simple classification of tenures. The basis for this classification—which was only achieved by degrees—was the nature of the service due. . . .

MABO v *QUEENSLAND* (1992) 66 ALJR 408, High Court of Australia

FACTS: In this case the High Court of Australia had to consider whether certain islands were subject to the native title of the indigenous inhabitants, or whether they were lands held by the Crown.

HELD: Native title should be preserved.

BRENNAN J:

The feudal basis of the proposition of absolute Crown ownership

The land law of England is based on the doctrine of tenure. In English legal theory, every parcel of land in England is held either mediately or immediately of the King who is the Lord Paramount; the term 'tenure' is used to signify the relationship between tenant and lord (*Attorney-General of Ontario* v *Mercer* (1883) LR 8 App Cas 767 at 771–772), not the relationship between tenant and land. The characteristic of feudalism 'is not tenere terram, but tenere terram de X' (Pollock and Maitland, *The History of English Law* (2nd edn, 1898, reprinted 1952), vol. 1, p. 234n). It is implicit in the relationship of tenure that both lord and tenant have an interest in the land; 'The King had *"dominium directum"*, the subject *"dominium utile"*' (at p. 773; Co Litt 16). Absent a *'dominium directum'* in the Crown, there would be no foundation for a tenure arising on the making of a grant of land. When the Crown acquired territory outside England which was to be subject to the common law, there was a natural assumption that the doctrine of tenure should be the basis of the land law. Perhaps the assumption did not have to be made. After all, as Holdsworth observed . . . the universal application of the doctrine of tenure is a purely English phenomenon.

(QUIA EMPTORES) (1289–90)

A Statute of Our Lord The King, Concerning the Selling and Buying of Land

Chapter 1   Freeholders may sell their lands; so that the feoffee do hold of the chieflord
. . . Our lord the King, in his Parliament at Westminster after Easter, the eighteenth year of his reign, that is to wit, in the quinzime of Saint John Baptist, at the instance of the great men of the realm, granted, provided, and ordained, that from henceforth it shall be lawful to every freeman to sell at his own pleasure his lands and tenements, or part of them; so that the feoffee shall hold the same lands or tenements of the chief lord of the same fee, by such service and customs as his feoffor held before.

TENURES ABOLITION ACT 1660

An Act takeing away the Court of Wards and Liveries and Tenures in Capite and by Knights Service and Purveyance, and for setling a Revenue upon his Majesty in Lieu thereof

4.   All tenures to be created by the King hereafter to be in free and common socage
And . . . that all tenures hereafter to be created by the King Majestic his heires or successors upon any gifts or grants of any mannours landes tenements or hereditaments of any estate of inheritance at the common law shall be in free and common soccage, and shall be adjudged to be in free and common soccage onely, and not by knight service or in capite, and shall be discharged of all wardship value and forfeiture of marriage livery primer-seizin ouster le main aide pur faier fitz chivalier & pur file marrier, any law statute or reservation to the contrary thereof any wise notwithstanding.

3.2   Leasehold Tenures

See **2.2** and **Chapters 17 to 22**.

CHAPTER FOUR

ESTATES

4.1   Fee Simple

4.1.1   MODIFIED FEES SIMPLE

4.1.1.1   Public policy

BLATHWAYT v CAWLEY (BARON) AND OTHERS [1976] AC 397, House of Lords

FACTS: A clause of a testator's will provided that, in the event that one of the beneficiaries under his will should 'be or become a Roman Catholic . . . the estate hereby limited to him shall cease and determine and be utterly void'. It later transpired that a life tenant did indeed become a Roman Catholic. The judge at first instance held that his estate should be forfeit.

HELD: The House of Lords unanimously upheld the condition subsequent.

LORD WILBERFORCE: . . . as to public policy. The argument under this heading was put in two alternative ways. First, it was said that the law of England was now set against discrimination on a number of grounds including religious grounds, and appeal was made to the Race Relations Act 1968 which does not refer to religion and to the European Convention of Human Rights of 1950 which refers to freedom of religion and to enjoyment of that freedom and other freedoms without discrimination on ground of religion. My Lords, I do not doubt that conceptions of public policy should move with the times and that widely accepted treaties and statutes may point the direction in which such conceptions, as applied by the courts, ought to move. It may well be that conditions such as this are, or at least are becoming, inconsistent with standards now widely accepted. But acceptance of this does not persuade me that we are justified, particularly in relation to a will which came into effect as long ago as 1936 and which has twice been the subject of judicial consideration, in introducing for the first time a rule of law which would go far beyond the mere avoidance of discrimination on religious grounds. To do so would bring about a substantial reduction of another freedom, firmly rooted in our law, namely that of testamentary disposition. Discrimination is not the same thing as choice: it operates over a larger and less personal area, and neither by express provision nor by implication has private selection yet become a matter of public policy.

4.2   Fee Tail

FINES AND RECOVERIES ACT 1833

15.   Power of actual tenants in tail, after 31st December, 1833, to dispose of entailed lands in fee simple or for less estate, saving the rights of certain persons.

. . . After the thirty-first day of December one thousand eight hundred and thirty-three every actual tenant in tail, whether in possession, remainder, contingency or otherwise, shall have full power to dispose of for an estate in fee simple absolute or for any less estate the lands entailed, as against all persons claiming the lands entailed by force of any estate tail which shall be vested in or might be claimed by, or which but for some previous act would have been vested in or might have been claimed by, the person making the disposition at the time of his making the same, and also as against all persons, including the King's most excellent Majesty, whose estates are to take effect after the determination or in defeasance of any such estate tail; saving always the rights of all persons in respect of estates prior to the estate tail in respect of which such disposition shall be made, and the rights of all other persons, except those against whom such disposition is by this Act authorised to be made.

4.3 Life Estates

See **Chapter 11**.

4.4 Reform

**The Law Commission (Law Com. No. 181) Transfer of Land: Trusts of Land
8 June 1989**

Entailed Interests

16.1 In the working paper we proposed that the creation of new entailed interests should be prevented. This proposal met with strong approval from several consultees. At present, entailed interests can only be constituted behind a strict settlement. Given that our recommendations are designed to minimise use of the Settled Land Act 1925, it seems logical to suggest that there should be no new entails, particularly as the latter would have little purpose outwith the framework of a strict settlement. We recommend that an attempt to create an entailed interest in land should operate as a grant of a fee simple absolute, unless the grantor has an equitable interest only. In this latter case, the attempt to create an entail will take effect as a declaration of trust on the part of the settlor or the personal representative that the land is held on trust (under the new system) for the grantee absolutely. It is at present possible to create entailed interests in personalty. Given that we are concerned to approximate the positions of trusts of real and personal property, we further recommend that it should no longer be possible to create entailed interests in personal property. . . .

TRUSTS OF LAND AND APPOINTMENT OF TRUSTEES ACT 1996

SCHEDULE 1

Entailed interests

5.—(1) Where a person purports by an instrument coming into operation after the commencement of this Act to grant to another person an entailed interest in real or personal property, the instrument—

(a) is not effective to grant an entailed interest, but

(b) operates instead as a declaration that the property is held in trust absolutely for the person to whom an entailed interest in the property was purportedly granted.

(2) Where a person purports by an instrument coming into operation after the commencement of this Act to declare himself a tenant in tail of real or personal property, the instrument is not effective to create an entailed interest.

**Sexton, R., 'The Law Commission's report on trusts of land, at last a law
for contemporary society?' *Trust Law and Practice*, January 1989, p. 66**

The continued existence of outmoded rights in land

As every law student knows, land law is still cluttered up with strange devices such as fees tail, determinable fees and fees upon condition subsequent. The Commission does propose (cl. 16 of the Bill) that no new entails should be created; any attempt to create an entail would in future result in a fee simple being transferred. This proposal does not, however, go far enough.

In its working paper, the Commission proposed to convert all existing fees tail into fees simple, but this is another proposal which has disappeared (without any explanation) from the final report. The Commission should have stuck by its original proposal. Indeed it should have gone further. Modified fees should also be banned, and any existing ones converted into absolute fees simple (many modified fees where the 'modification' relates to marriage or religion must surely infringe the European Convention on Human Rights). . . .

4.5 End of Chapter Assessment Question

'As every law student knows, land law is cluttered up with strange devices such as fees tail, determinable fees and fees upon condition subsequent. In 1989, the Law Commission merely proposed that no new entails should be created. This proposal, now enacted as part of the Trusts of Land and Appointment of Trustees Act 1996, does not go far enough.'

Critically examine this statement.

4.6 End of Chapter Assessment Outline Answer

On 8 June 1989 the Law Commission published a Report titled 'Transfer of Land: Trusts of Land' (Law Com. No. 181). The Report considered entailed interests and modified fees simple. It recommended that no new entailed interests should be created, but it did not recommend the prohibition of new modified fees. Although fees tail are now very few in number, and modified fees are virtually non-existent, it can still be argued that the Law Commission did not go far enough in its proposals for reform of these estates.

The fee tail is a strange legal relic which has somehow survived into the late twentieth century. Fees tail were first recognised as estates in land in 1285. Until the nineteenth century land (particularly the large country estate) was often subject to a fee tail. Very few exist today. A fee tail is an estate of inheritance, i.e. it can pass from generation to generation within the same family and lasts as long as the original grantee or any of his lineal descendants are alive. However, there are strict rules governing which of the descendants may inherit the fee tail. When an owner of the fee tail dies the rules ensure that the land must pass to the 'heir' of the deceased owner. Thus the land will pass first to the eldest male descendant and only if there is no male descendant will the land pass to the eldest female descendant. A fee simple is different. As the word 'simple' informs us, it may be left to anybody, whether or not they are the 'heir'.

Before 1833 the fee tail was a useful device for keeping land within the family, but since the Fines and Recoveries Act 1833 the person who owns the fee tail estate in possession (known as the 'tenant in tail') may, if they are of full age, 'bar' the entail by a relatively cheap and simple process. Barring the entail converts the fee tail into a fee simple. The result is that the fee tail, once it has been transformed into a fee simple, may be sold or given away to persons outside the family. Consequently, there can be no good reason for creating a fee tail today.

In its 1989 Report the Law Commission acknowledged the irrelevance of fees tail to modern land ownership by recommending legislation to prevent the creation of any new fees tail (para. 16.1) and this proposal has now been enacted in the Trusts of Land and Appointment of Trustees Act 1996 (Schedule 1, para. 5). However, in making this recommendation, the Law Commission did not go far enough. The Working Paper which preceded the Report had recommended that existing fees tail should be converted into fees simple. It is regrettable that this recommendation did not appear in the final report, it could have saved future tenants in tail the expense of having to bar the entail. Further, the very concept of inheritance by the 'heir' might be thought of as unsuitable to a modern statute, providing as it does for inheritance by males in preference to females. It sits uneasily in the statute books with the Sex Discrimination Act 1975. There are not many tenants in tail nowadays, but any that do exist will necessarily incur the expense of executing a disentailing assurance (barring the entail) before being able to leave the land to, say, a daughter in preference to a son.

The vast majority of fees in existence today are 'absolute', which means that, in principle, they will last for ever. An almost negligible minority of fees are said to be 'modified'.

The determinable fee simple is a fee simple which is modified in such a way that it will terminate automatically upon the occurrence of a specified event. The specified event must be such that it may never occur. Examples include: 'to John Smith in fee simple until he marries Fanny Bloggs' and 'to Ann Green in fee simple during the time that she remains a faithful protestant'. The essence of the modification is that it is of a temporal nature, using words such as 'until', 'while' and 'during'.

The fee simple upon condition subsequent can be defined as a fee simple where the grantee is given an apparently absolute fee simple to which a clause is added to the effect that if a stated condition is broken, the estate shall be forfeit. For example: 'To John Smith in fee simple provided that he never marries Fanny Bloggs' and 'to Ann Green in fee simple unless she forsakes the Protestant religion'. The essence of the modification is that it is of a conditional nature, using words such as 'provided that', 'on condition', 'unless' and 'but not if'.

In its 1989 Report the Law Commission considered modified fees (para. 17.1) and had the opportunity to recommend their abolition. The Commission did not take this opportunity and today it is still possible to create modified fees simple.

One argument in favour of their abolition is that they are out of line with modern ideas of freedom, particularly religious freedom. As things presently stand modified fees limiting freedom to marry and freedom of religion are valid. Indeed, as recently as 1975, the House of Lords unanimously upheld a condition subsequent which provided for forfeiture on the grantee becoming a Roman Catholic (*Blathwayt* v *Lord Cawley* [1975] 3 All ER 625). Lord Wilberforce, delivering the leading speech, acknowledged that 'conditions such as this are, or at least are becoming, inconsistent with standards now widely accepted' but upheld the condition because in 1936, when the fee had been granted, the condition had been added through the exercise, not of discrimination, but of choice. His Lordship did tacitly acknowledge, however, that the condition might infringe the European Convention on Human Rights of 1950 which protects the enjoyment of freedoms without discrimination on ground of religion. In coming to the conclusion it did, the House of Lords side-stepped a dilemma. It is not actually the dilemma between the grantor's freedom of disposition and the grantee's freedom of religion. Nothing ever prevented the grantee from becoming a Roman Catholic! It is the dilemma between the grantor's freedom of disposition and the grantee's freedom as a property owner to hold a valuable estate without the threat that it might be lost through the exercise of freedom of religion. The Law Commission also side-stepped this dilemma in failing to recommend the abolition of modified fees. This is also regrettable, for it is a dilemma that only Parliament can resolve.

Fees tail, determinable fees and fees upon condition subsequent are 'strange devices' indeed. The creation of new ones should be prohibited, and those that already exist should be converted to fees simple.

CHAPTER FIVE

LEGAL AND EQUITABLE RIGHTS IN LAND

5.1 Creation and Transfer of Legal Property Rights

SMITH v BUSH [1990] 1 AC 849, House of Lords

This case is included because of a useful summary of conveyancing procedure provided by Lord Templeman. The decision in the case itself is of more direct relevance to the tort of negligence.

LORD TEMPLEMAN: Each year one million houses may be bought and sold. Apart from exceptional cases the procedure is always the same. The vendor and the purchaser agree a price but the purchaser cannot enter into a contract unless and until a mortgagee, typically a building society, offers to advance the whole or part of the purchase price. A mortgage of 80 per cent or more of the purchase price is not unusal. Thus, if the vendor and the purchaser agree a price of £50,000 and the purchaser can find £10,000, the purchaser then applies to a building society for a loan of £40,000. The purchaser pays the building society a valuation fee and the building society instructs a valuer who is paid by the building society. If the valuer reports to the building society that the house is good security for £40,000, the building society offers to advance £40,000 and the purchaser contracts to purchase the house for £50,000. The purchaser, who is offered £40,000 on the security of the house, rightly assumes that a qualified valuer had valued the house at not less than £40,000.

At the date when the purchaser pays the valuation fee, the date when the valuation is made and at the date when the purchaser is offered an advance, the sale may never take place. The amount offered by way of advance may not be enough, the purchaser may change his mind, or the vendor may increase his price and sell elsewhere. For many reasons a sale may go off, and in that case, the purchaser has paid his valuation fee without result and must pay a second valuation fee when he finds another house and goes through the same procedure. The building society which is anxious to attract borrowers and the purchaser who has no money to waste on valuation fees, do not encourage or pay for detailed surveys. Moreover, the vendor may not be willing to suffer the inconvenience of a detailed survey on behalf of a purchaser who has not contracted to purchase and may exploit minor items of disrepair disclosed by a detailed survey in order to obtain a reduction in the price.

The Law Commission Working Paper No. 92, Transfer of Land: Formalities for Contracts for Sale etc. of Land, London: HMSO, 1985, p. 9

General principles

5.2 We consider that there are three general principles which must be taken into account so far as possible in any reform in this area.

(i)   No reform should increase the likelihood of contracts for the sale (or other disposition) of land becoming binding before the parties have been able to obtain legal advice. This is not to say, however, that any reform should itself result in formalities which can only be undertaken by lawyers and not, for example, by the parties themselves if they so decide.

(ii)   Any reform if unable to reduce the risk of injustice should at least not increase it. In particular, the imposition of any formal requirements should not be so inflexible that hardship or unfairness is perceived in cases of minor non-compliance.

(iii)   Any reform should simplify or at least not complicate conveyancing. Although this is an argument for reducing formalities, so containing professionals' fees and assisting 'do-it-yourself' conveyancers, certainty and reliability are often essential in dealings with land and may call for extra formalities.

Is land different?

5.3   The question of whether land should be treated differently from other property is important, and one which deserves serious consideration. There are many other forms of property which may be worth far more than a piece of land, yet no formalities are required for contracts relating to them. If one can contract to buy or sell £1 million pounds' worth of shares without formality, why should even the smallest interest in land require any contractual formality? One reason conventionally given is that land has the particular characteristic that many people may acquire interests in or over one piece of land. For this reason, it is said, some formality must be required in dealings with land if confusion is not to arise as to whom owns what. From this point of view section 40(1) is obviously linked with the other sections of the Law of Property Act 1925 which require formalities for dealings with land. While we find this argument persuasive in relation to the completion of contracts, i.e., the actual creation of interests in land, even then it may not be totally compelling, because some third party interests can be created in other forms of property. More persuasive is the point that in principle each particular piece of land is unique, so that for contracts relating to land the important remedy of specific performance is much more likely to be available.

5.4   Another convincing argument, in our view, is that while there are other forms of property as valuable as land, for example, a Rolls Royce motorcar, most people do not deal in such property. For most people, the most significant transaction they will ever enter into is one relating to land, in particular the sale or purchase of a dwelling house. From this point of view, insisting on some formalities for the sale or purchase of land can be seen as a form of consumer protection for ordinary people who are engaged in a transaction which they will enter into only a few times in their lifetime, and which will often involve them in major financial commitments. However, the consumer protection approach is obviously not so appropriate for business transactions, for example, contracts for the grant of leases of commercial premises.

5.5   On balance, it is our provisional view that contracts for the sale of land should still be treated differently. . . .

5.1.1   FORMALITIES FOR A DEED: THE MODERN RULE

LAW OF PROPERTY (MISCELLANEOUS PROVISIONS) ACT 1989

1.   Deeds and their execution

(1)   Any rule of law which —

(a)   restricts the substances on which a deed may be written;

(b)   requires a seal for the valid execution of an instrument as a deed by an individual; or

(c)   requires authority by one person to another to deliver an instrument as a deed on his behalf to be given by deed,

is abolished.

(2)   An instrument shall not be a deed unless —

(a)   it makes it clear on its face that it is intended to be a deed by the person making it or, as the case may be, by the parties to it (whether by describing itself as a deed or expressing itself to be executed or signed as a deed or otherwise); and

(b)   it is validly executed as a deed by that person or, as the case may be, one or more of those parties.

(3)   An intrument is validly executed as a deed by an individual if, and only if—
   (a)   it is signed —
      (i)   by him in the presence of a witness who attests the signature; or
      (ii)   at his direction and in his presence and the presence of two witnesses who each attest the signature; and
   (b)   it is delivered as a deed by him or a person authorised to do so on his behalf. . . .

LAW OF PROPERTY ACT 1925

52.   Conveyances to be by deed
   (1)   All conveyances of land or of any interest therein are void for the purpose of conveying or creating a legal estate unless made by deed.
   (2)   This section does not apply to —
   (a)   assents by a personal representative;
   (b)   disclaimers made in accordance with [sections 178 to 180 or sections 315 to 319 of the Insolvency Act 1986], or not required to be evidenced in writing;
   (c)   surrenders by operation of law, including surrenders which may, by law, be effected without writing;
   (d)   leases or tenancies or other assurances not required by law to be made in writing;
   (e)   receipts not required by law to be under seal;
   (f)   vesting orders of the court or other competent authority;
   (g)   conveyances taking effect by operation of law.

5.2   Creation of Equitable Interests in Land

5.2.1   CREATION OF EQUITABLE INTERESTS IN LAND BY EXPRESS TRUST

LAW OF PROPERTY ACT 1925

53.   Instruments required to be in writing
   (1)   Subject to the provisions hereinafter contained with respect to the creation of interests in land by parol—
   (a)   no interest in land can be created or disposed of except by writing signed by the person creating or conveying the same, or by his agent thereunto lawfully authorised in writing, or by will, or by operation of law;
   (b)   a declaration of trust respecting any land or any interest therein must be manifested and proved by some writing signed by some person who is able to declare such trust or by his will;
   (c)   a disposition of an equitable interest or trust subsisting at the time of the disposition, must be in writing signed by the person disposing of the same, or by his agent thereunto lawfully authorised in writing or by will.
   (2)   This section does not affect the creation or operation of resulting, implied or constructive trusts.

5.2.2   CREATION OF EQUITABLE INTERESTS BY A CONTRACT TO CONVEY OR CREATE A LEGAL ESTATE OR INTEREST

5.2.2.1   Formalities for contracts to sell estates or interests in land

See also **5.1.**

(Note that s. 40 (below) has been repealed by s. 2 of the Law of Property (Miscellaneous Provisions) Act 1989. *Steadman* v *Steadman* has also been superseded by s. 2 of the 1989 Act.)

LAW OF PROPERTY ACT 1925

40.   Contracts for sale, etc, of land to be in writing

(1)   No action may be brought upon any contract for the sale or other disposition of land or any interest in land, unless the agreement upon which such action is brought, or some memorandum or note thereof, is in writing, and signed by the party to be charged or by some other person thereunto by him lawfully authorised.

(2)   This section applies to contracts whether made before or after the commencement of this Act and does not affect the law relating to part performance, or sales by the court.

STEADMAN v *STEADMAN* [1976] AC 536, House of Lords

FACTS: Mr and Mrs Steadman were divorced, but the property side of the break-up had not been concluded. During the course of negotiating a settlement of the wife's disputed claim to joint ownership of the matrimonial home, the husband made an oral offer to pay to Mrs Steadman lump sums of £1,500 (in return for which she would surrender her interest in the matrimonial home) and £100 (by way of child maintenance). They reached an oral agreement on these terms. Accordingly, he paid the £100 as agreed, but she refused to sign the land transfer when it was presented to her. The registrar who first heard the case held that preparing the transfer document was an act of part performance by the husband. On appeal to a county court judge, the judge held that there had been no act of part performance. In the Court of Appeal the judgment was again reversed. That court held that the payment of the £100 was an act of part performance, even though it had been made by way of child maintenance and was therefore not directly referable to the matrimonial home. The wife appealed to the House of Lords.

HELD: The appeal was dismissed. On the balance of probabilities, and taking into account all the facts of the case, there had been acts of part performance of the oral agreement to transfer the wife's interest in the matrimonial home.

LORD REID: . . . In my view, unless the law is to be divorced from reason and principle: the rule must be that you take the whole circumstances, leaving aside evidence about the oral contract, to see whether it is proved that the acts relied on were done in reliance on a contract: that will be proved if it is shown to be more probable than not.

Authorities which seem to require more than that appear to be based on an idea, never clearly defined, to the effect that the law of part performance is a rule of evidence rather than an application of an equitable principle. . . .

The Law Commission (Law Com. No. 164), Formalities for Contract for Sale, etc., of Land

1.   Part performance and equitable estoppel

5.4   We have already pointed out that it is implicit in our recommendation that a contract will no longer be enforceable simply because one party has performed some or all of his obligations under it. We believe this not to be a consequence to be regretted. The doctrine of part performance has, as explained in the working paper, become very confused: it is not clear to what extent the act of part performance must relate to the contract, nor is it clear whether the act can be unilateral, without the consent or even the knowledge of the other party. Nevertheless there are clearly circumstances in which injustice could be caused through the inability to plead part performance. For example, if a person genuinely believes he has a contract to buy a piece of land and does work on it, to the knowledge of the owner, it seems wrong that the owner should be allowed to retain the improved land and the 'purchaser' receive nothing. It could be argued that the would-be purchaser should be taken to know the law and therefore should have known that writing was necessary for a valid contract. However, the principles of equity have never allowed English law to be so harsh. Are there other solutions than that which might have been provided by part performance? We believe that there are, and that the courts would use doctrines of estoppel to achieve very similar results where appropriate to those of part performance.

5.5   Where the doctrine of part performance is applicable the result is that the contract for sale itself is enforced which may be by an order for specific performance or by an award of damages for breach. Where doctrines of estoppel apply, the relief available is not restricted to enforcement of a contract but is flexible and will vary with the circumstances. Nevertheless it cannot today be doubted that the equitable doctrines are already sufficiently strong and developed to enable the court to require that land be transferred. . . .

LAW OF PROPERTY (MISCELLANEOUS PROVISIONS) ACT 1989
as amended by the Trusts of Land etc. Act 1996

2.   Contracts for sale etc of land to be made by signed writing
   (1)   A contract for the sale or other disposition of an interest in land can only be made in writing and only by incorporating all the terms which the parties have expressly agreed in one document or, where contracts are exchanged, in each.
   (2)   The terms may be incorporated in a document either by being set out in it or by reference to some other document.
   (3)   The document incorporating the terms or, where contracts are exchanged, one of the documents incorporating them (but not necessarily the same one) must be signed by or on behalf of each party to the contract.
   (4)   Where a contract for the sale or other disposition of an interest in land satisfies the conditions of this section by reason only of the rectification of one or more documents in pursuance of an order of a court, the contract shall come into being, or be deemed to have come into being, at such time as may be specified in the order.
   (5)   This section does not apply in relation to—
      (a)   a contract to grant such a lease as is mentioned in section 54(2) of the Law of Property Act 1926 (short leases);
      (b)   a contract made in the course of a public auction; or
      (c)   a contract regulated under the Financial Services Act 1986;
and nothing in this section affects the creation or operation of resulting, implied or constructive trusts.
   (6)   In this section—
      'disposition' has the same meaning as in the Law of Property Act 1925;
      'interest in land' means any estate, interest or charge in or over land [. . .]
   (7)   Nothing in this section shall apply in relation to contracts made before this section comes into force.
   (8)   Section 40 of the Law of Property Act 1925 (which is superseded by this section) shall cease to have effect.

5.2.2.2   Estate contracts

SPIRO v GLENCROWN PROPERTIES LTD AND ANOTHER
[1991] 1 All ER 600, Chancery Division

FACTS: The vendor granted the purchaser an option to buy certain property. The central question was whether the option itself was a 'contract for sale' in accordance with section 2 of the Law of Property Miscellaneous Provisions Act 1989, or whether the option was merely an irrevocable offer of sale which did not become a contract until a notice exercising the option had been served.
HELD: The reason for the formality requirements laid down in section 2 of the LP(MP)A 1989 was to ensure an adequate evidential record of the consent of the contracting parties to the terms of their contract. Accordingly, the formality requirements of section 2 would only apply to the original grant of the option, as this was the document which enshrined the bi-lateral agreement of the parties. The notice exercising the option was exercised unilaterally and would therefore not have to comply with section 2.

HOFFMANN J: Apart from authority, it seems to me plain enough that s. 2 was intended to apply to the agreement which created the option and not to the notice by which it was exercised. Section 2, which replaced s. 40 of the Law of Property Act 1925, was intended to prevent disputes over whether the parties had entered into a binding agreement or over what terms they had agreed. It prescribes the formalities for recording their mutual consent. But only the grant of the option depends upon consent. The exercise of the option is a unilateral act. It would destroy the very purpose of the option if the purchaser had to obtain the vendor's counter-signature to the notice by which it was exercised. The only way in which the concept of an option to buy land could survive s. 2 would be if the purchaser ensured that the vendor not only signed the agreement by which the option was granted but also at the same time provided him with a counter-signed form to use if he decided to exercise it. There seems to be no conceivable reason why the legislature should have required this additional formality.

. . . the underlyiing principles are clear enough. The granting of the option imposes no obligation upon the purchaser and an obligation upon the vendor which is contingent upon the exercise of the option. When the option is exercised, vendor and purchaser come under obligations to perform as if they had concluded an ordinary contract of sale. And the analogy of an irrevocable offer is, as I have said, a useful way of describing the position of the purchaser between the grant and exercise of the option. Thus in the recent case of *J Sainsbury plc v O'Connor (Inspector of Taxes)* [1990] STC 516 at 532 Millett J used it to explain why the grantee of an option to buy shares did not become the beneficial owner until he had exercised the option.

But the irrevocable offer metaphor has much less explanatory power in relation to the position of the vendor. The effect of the 'offer' which the vendor has made is, from his point of view, so different from that of an offer in its primary sense that the metaphor is of little assistance. Thus in the famous passage in *London and South Western Rly Co v Gomm* (1882) 20 ChD 562 at 581, [1881–5] All ER Rep 1190 at 1193 Jessel MR had no use for it in explaining why the grant of an option to buy land confers an interest in the land upon the grantee:

> The right to call for a conveyance of the land is an equitable interest or equitable estate. In the ordinary case of a contract for purchase there is no doubt about this, and an option for repurchase is not different in its nature. A person exercising the option has to do two things, he has to give notice of his intention to purchase, and to pay the purchase-money; but as far as the man who is liable to convey is concerned, his estate or interest is taken away from him without his consent, and the right to take it away being vested in another, the covenant giving the option must give that other an interest in the land. . . .

The purchaser's argument requires me to say that 'irrevocable offer' and 'conditional contract' are mutually inconsistent concepts and that I must range myself under one or other banner and declare the other to be heretical. I hope that I have demonstrated this to be a misconception about the nature of legal reasoning. An option is not strictly speaking either an offer of a conditional contract. It does not have *all* the incidents of the standard form of either of these concepts. To that extent it is a relationship *sui generis*. But there are ways in which it resembles each of them. Each analogy is in the proper context a valid way of characterising the situation created by an option. The question in this case is not whether one analogy is true and the other false, but which is appropriate to be used in the construction of s. 2 of the Law of Property (Miscellaneous Provisions) Act 1989. . . .

Perhaps the most helpful case for present purposes is *Re Mulholland's Will Trusts, Bryan v Westminster Bank Ltd* [1949] 1 All ER 460. A testator had let premises to the Westminster Bank on a lease which included an option to purchase. He appointed the bank his executor and trustee and after his death the bank exercised the option. It was argued for his widow and children that the bank was precluded from exercising the option by the rule that a trustee cannot contract with himself. Wynn-Parry J was pressed with the irrevocable offer metaphor, which, it was said, led inexorably to the conclusion that when the bank exercised the option, it was indeed entering into a contract with itself. But the judge held that if one considered the purpose of the self-dealing rule, which was to prevent a trustee from being subjected to a conflict of interest and duty, the only relevant contract was the grant of the option. The rule could only sensibly be applied to a consensual transaction. While for some purposes it might be true to say that the exercise of the option brought the contract into existence, there could be no rational ground for applying the self-dealing rule to the unilateral exercise of a right granted before the trusteeship came into existence. The judge quoted the passage I have cited from Jessel MR in *Gomm's* case and said ([1949] 1 All ER 460 at 464):

As I understand that passage, it amounts to this, that, as regards this option, there was between the parties only one contract, namely the contract constituted by the provisions in the lease which I have read creating the option. The notice exercising the option did not lead, in my opinion, to the creation of any fresh contractual relationship between the parties, making them for the first time vendors and purchasers, nor did it bring into existence any right in addition to the right conferred by the option. . . .

In my judgment there is nothing in the authorities which prevents me from giving s. 2 the meaning which I consider to have been the clear intention of the legislature. On the contrary, the purposive approach taken in cases like *Mulholland* encourages me to adopt a similar approach to s. 2. And the plain purpose of s. 2 was, as I have said, to prescribe the formalities for recording the consent of the parties. It follows that in my view the grant of the option was the only 'contract for the sale or other disposition of an interest in land' within the meaning of the section and the contract duty complied with the statutory requirements. There must be judgment for the plaintiff against both defendants with costs.

(a)   The vendor must take good care of the property and consult the purchaser before taking managerial decisons regarding the property.

MOHAMED HAJI ABDULLAH AND ANOTHER v GHELA MANEK SHAH [1959] AC 124, Privy Council

FACTS: The vendor owned a row of three shops. At the time the contract of sale for the shops was signed all three of them were leased to tenants. Between contract and completion one of the tenants (unexpectedly) terminated his tenancy. The vendor, without asking the purchaser, immediately relet the shop. The premises would have been more valuable to the purchaser had they remained unlet. The purchaser claimed specific performance of the contract of sale and also claimed compensation for the financial loss arising out of the sub-letting.
HELD: Both under the Indian Transfer of Property Act 1882 and under English law the vendor should have consulted the purchaser about the proposed reletting. Consequently, the purchaser was entitled to a reduction in the agreed completion price, by way of compensation.

LORD SOMERVELL OF HARROW: The obligations imposed by section 55(1)(e) are substantially those imposed on a vendor under English law.
   The Court of Appeal cited with approval the opinion of Mulla and Gour in their textbooks on the Indian Act that the vendor's duties to a purchaser under paragraph (e), although he is not a trustee, are the same as they would be if section 15 of the Indian Trusts Act, 1882, were applicable. That section reads as follows:

15.   A trustee is bound to deal with the trust property as carefully as a man of ordinary prudence would deal with such property if it were his own; and in the absence of a contract to the contrary a trustee so dealing is not responsible for the loss, destruction, or deterioration of the trust property.

This is substantially the position of a trustee in relation to property under English law. Their Lordships therefore agree with the courts below that English principles and authorities are relevant and of assistance.
   On this basis it seems plain that the vendors had no right without consultation with the purchasers to diminish the value of the property as it was after the surrender by reletting. . . .
   The purchasers sought alternatively to support the decision of the Court of Appeal on the terms of the contract, and on a general proposition that a purchaser ought always to be consulted with regard to a new letting. It is unnecessary to consider circumstances other than the present, which are in their Lordships' opinion covered by section 55(1)(e).
   Their Lordships will therefore humbly advise Her Majesty that the appeal be dismissed and the order of the Court of Appeal confirmed. The appellants must pay the costs of the appeal.

(b) The risk of anything untoward happening to the property passes to the purchaser when the contract is signed.

HILLINGDON ESTATES CO. v STONEFIELD ESTATES LTD
[1952] 1 Ch 62, Chancery Division

FACTS: In this case the parties having already contracted to sell and purchase certain freehold land, and the purchaser having already paid a deposit in accordance with the contract, the local authority made a compulsory purchase order affecting some of the freehold land. As a result the purchase of that land was never completed. The purchasers brought the present action, alleging that they should be entitled to be discharged from the contract, and should be able to claim a refund of their deposit together with interest thereon. The defendants counterclaimed for specific performance of the contract upon the original terms, including the original price, despite the fact that the purchasers could no longer build on the land as they had intended.

HELD: The vendor was entitled to insist upon the completion of the sale, even though the purchaser would subsequently have to convey the land to the local authority.

VAISEY J: . . . I should have thought that the situation must have arisen in a great many cases, and, in the large majority of them, must have been a most important point for consideration in the position of the parties (that is to say, vendors and purchasers) as between themselves; and the complete absence of authority rather suggests to my mind that, although this doctrine of frustration may operate in some circumstances, it does not operate normally in the case of contracts for the sale of land.

What is the effect of the compulsory purchase order on the rights and position of, first, the purchasers, and, secondly, the vendors? Undoubtedly the position of the vendors in an unperformed contract for the sale of land is radically different, in quality and in nature, from that of the purchasers. I have always understood (and indeed it is a common-place) that when there is a contract by A to sell land to B at a certain price, B becomes the owner in equity of the land, subject, of course, to his obligation to perform his part of the contract by paying the purchase-money; but subject to that, the land is the land of B, the purchaser. What is the position of A, the vendor? He has, it is true, the legal estate in the land, but, for many purposes, from the moment the contract is entered into he holds it as trustee for B, the purchaser. True, he has certain rights in the land remaining, but all those rights are conditioned and limited by the circumstance that they are all referable to his right to recover and receive the purchase-money. His interest in the land when he has entered into a contract for sale is not an interest in land; it is an interest in personal estate, in a sum of money; and it seems to me that in a case such as this, when the date for completion is long past, the purchasers, subject to the payment of that purchase-money, are to be regarded as the owners of the land. So I think they are; and the effect of this notice to treat and this compulsory purchase process is merely to place an obligation on those who are already the owners of the land in question. The compulsory purchase order does not affect the vendors; they have no interest in the matter save in respect of the purchase-money which they are entitled to be paid. The persons who are affected by the compulsory purchase order are the owners of the land, namely, the plaintiffs, i.e., the purchasers.

AMALGAMATED INVESTMENT & PROPERTY CO. LTD v
JOHN WALKER & SONS LTD [1976] 3 All ER 509, Court of Appeal

FACTS: The defendants (the well-known whisky firm) contracted to buy an old building which they planned to demolish and replace with modern offices. The local authority then 'listed' the building as one of 'special architectural or historic interest', thus effectively preventing the development. The purchasers claimed rescission of the contract on the ground of 'mutual mistake', which is to say that both parties had thought, at the time of the contract, that the land would be suitable for development and would not be subject to a listing. On the other side, the vendors sought specific performance of the contract.

LAWTON LJ: . . . Anybody who buys property knows, and certainly those who buy property as property developers know, that there are all kinds of hazards which have to be taken into consideration. There is the obvious hazard of planning permission. There is the hazard of fiscal and legislative changes. There is the hazard of existing legislation being applied to the property under consideration—compulsory purchase, for example. Amongst the hazards are the provisions of section 54 of the Town and Country Planning Act 1971. That seems now to be a well-known hazard, as is shown by the form of inquiry before contract which was made by the purchasers in this case. They used a printed form. The printed form asked whether the property had been listed. Similarly, when they came to make a search in the local registry of land charges, once again they made specific inquiries as to whether there had been any listing of the premises. All that adds up, in my judgment, to indicating that those who deal in property nowadays appreciate the existence of these kind of risks. At common law anyone entering into a contract for the purchase of real property had to accept the risk of damage to the property after the contract had been made. Damage to the property nowadays can arise from causes other than fire and tempest. Financial loss can arise from government intervention. This is a risk which people have to suffer. . . .

SIR JOHN PENNYCUICK: In the present case, the contract was one of which, upon the date of its signature, specific performance would have been ordered. Consequently, the purchasers became in equity the owners of the property, subject , of course, to vendor's lien: see *Williams on Vendor and Purchasers*, 4th edn. (1936), p. 547. The listing struck down the value of the property as might a fire or a compulsory purchase order or a number of other events. It seems to me, however, that the listing did not in any respect prevent the contract from being carried to completion according to its terms; that is to say, by payment of the balance of the purchase price and by conveyance of the property. The property is none the less the same property by reason that listing imposed a fetter upon its use. . . . One cannot say that the circumstances in which performance, i.e., completion, will be called for would render that performance a thing radically different from that which was undertaken by the contract. On the contrary, completion, according to the terms of the contract, would be exactly what the purchasers promised to do, and of course the vendors.

For those reasons, I would dismiss the appeal.

Thompson M. P., Must a Purchaser buy a Charred Ruin? (1984) 48 Conv 43

In 1876, Sir George Jessel MR said that 'if anything happens to the estate between the time of the sale and the time of completion of purchase it is at the risk of the purchaser. If it is a house that is sold, and the house is burnt down, the purchaser loses the house.' [*Lysaght* v *Edwards* (1876) 2 ChD 499 at p. 507]. The purpose of this article is to examine this statement with a view to showing that, although it has long been taken as representing the conventional wisdom in this area, it is possible that if directly challenged today, it may not remain as an accurate statement of the law, so that if the house is burnt down between contract and conveyance, the loss falls on the vendor, irrespective of whether or not it was his fault that the damage occurred.

THE EFFECT OF A CONTRACT OF SALE

To explain why it is the purchaser who is said to have to bear the risk of disasters befalling the property between contract and conveyance, it is necessary to examine the effect on the parties' position of an enforceable contract coming into existence. From very early days, it has been said that the effect of a contract for the sale of land is that the vendor becomes a trustee of the property; a doctrine which is now well-settled. Because it is a trust which arises irrespective of the intentions of the parties, it has been classified as being a constructive trust. While it is too late to argue against the view that some sort of trust arises, it is contended that it is misleading to describe it as a constructive trust and that it is better to regard it as *sui generis*.

Why does a trust of any sort arise due to the existence of a valid contract for the sale of land? The answer was provided by Lord Parker, delivering the opinion of the Privy Council, who said:

It is sometimes said that under a contract for the sale of an interest in land the vendor becomes a constructive trustee for the purchaser of the interest contracted to be sold subject to a lien for the purchase money; but however useful such a statement may be as illustrating a general principle of equity, it is only true *if and so far as* a Court of Equity would under all the circumstances grant specific performance of the contract.

This is an important statement of principle, in that it emphasises that the creation of the trust is dependent on the availability of specific performance. The trust that arises does so because of the operation of the maxim: equity looks on that which ought to be done as done; a principle best illustrated by the doctrine of *Walsh v Lonsdale* (1882) 21 ChD 9, CA. . . .

Normally constructive trusts require no written evidence. In the case of a contract for the sale of land, however, this is not so. In the absence of part performance, an oral contract is now enforceable by action, with the consequence that specific performance is unavailable and the doctrine of conversion does not operate. A trust is not, therefore, created. So, although if there is an enforceable contract, the vendor is recognised as the owner at law and the purchaser as the owner in equity—the paradigm trust—it is more helpful to view the situation as very much an individual type of trust. One should not forget that its existence depends on the availability of specific performance. . . . The trust that arises on the formation of an enforceable contract for sale is what lies behind the notion that from that date the risk of damage to the property rests with the purchaser. Subject to the duty on the vendor to take reasonable care of the property, the purchaser is the owner in equity and is, therefore, the one to bear the risk of damage not caused by the vendor's default. This result could have been achieved by the use of implied contractual terms and, indeed, the law would probably have been easier to explain if this had been the case. Nevertheless, the explanation of the risk passing to the purchaser lies in the utilisation of the law of trusts, although . . . the type of trust involved is an inappropriate method by which to achieve this.

5.2.2.3   A contract to create rights in land itself create an equitable interest in the land

WALSH v LONSDALE (1882) 21 ChD 9, Court of Appeal

FACTS: A landlord and tenant had entered into a contract for a seven year lease and the tenant had gone into possession, but the parties had forgotten to execute the formal deed needed for a valid legal lease. The rent clause in the contract provided that under the lease the rent should be per year payable in advance at the beginning of each year (the precise figure would depend upon the number of looms run by the tenant for his business). Despite the absence of a deed granting a legal lease, the landlord demanded the rent in advance in accordance with the contractual term. Indeed, he attempted to recover the rent due by exercising his right of distress. The tenant claimed that as there was no deed and therefore no proper lease, any rent should be payable in arrear. He therefore claimed an injunction against the action for distress.
HELD: The landlord could claim rent in advance. The contract had created an equitable lease enforceable between the parties. The terms of this lease would correspond to the terms of the contract.

JESSEL MR: . . . The question is one of some nicety. There is an agreement for a lease under which possession has been given. Now since the *Judicature Act* the possession is held under the agreement. There are not two estates as there were formerly, one estate at common law by reason of the payment of the rent from year to year, and an estate in equity under the agreement. There is only one Court, and the equity rules prevail in it. The tenant holds under an agreement for a lease. He holds, therefore, under the same terms in equity as if a lease had been granted, it being a case in which both parties admit that relief is capable of being given by specific performance. That being so, he cannot complain of the exercise by the landlord of the same rights as the landlord would have had if a lease had been granted. On the other hand, he is protected in the same way as if a lease had been granted; he cannot be turned out by six months' notice as a tenant from year to year. He has a right to say, 'I have a lease in equity, and you can only re-enter if I have committed such a breach of covenant as would if a lease had been granted have entitled you to re-enter according to the terms of a proper proviso for re-entry.' That being so, it appears to me that being a lessee in equity he cannot complain of the exercise of the right of distress merely because the actual parchment has not been signed and sealed.

5.2.3 AN INFORMAL GRANT OF RIGHTS IN LAND IS TREATED AS A CONTRACT AND SO CREATES AN EQUITABLE INTEREST IN LAND

(Note that the cases in this section must now be read subject to s. 2 of the Law of Property (Miscellaneous Provisions) Act 1989.)

PARKER v TASWELL (1858) 2 De G & J 559, Lord Chancellor's Court

FACTS: A landlord and tenant signed a document which purported to grant a lease to the tenant. The document did not bear a seal, and therefore could not constitute the grant of a legal lease by deed.
HELD: A purported grant of land which lacked the necessary formality should be deemed to be a contract which could be enforced by a decree of specific performance. The discretionary remedy of specific performance was awarded in this case.

THE LORD CHANCELLOR: . . . the instrument now in question could not amount to a lease, because it was not signed by an agent lawfully authorized by writing, nor was it signed in the name of the principal, so as to render it a lease binding upon the lessor. Assuming, however, that it had been signed in the name of the lessor, and would therefore have amounted to a lease, as containing words of present demise, yet there is nothing, in the Act to prevent its being used as an agreement, though void as a lease because not under seal.

The Legislature appears to have been very cautious and guarded in language, for it uses the expression 'shall be void at law' — that is as a lease. If the Legislature had intended to deprive such a document of all efficacy, it would have said that the instrument should be 'void to all intents and purposes.' There are no such words in the Act. I think it would be too strong to say that because it is void at law as a lease, it cannot be used as an agreement enforceable in equity, the intention of the parties having been that there should be a lease, and the aid of equity being only invoked to carry that intention into effect. . . .

5.2.3.1 Limits on the principle that a contract or informal grant creates an equitable interest

COATSWORTH v JOHNSON [1886–90] All ER Rep 547, Court of Appeal

FACTS: Johnson entered into an agreement to lease a farm to Coatsworth for twenty-one years. The agreement contained a clause to farm 'in good and husband-like manner'. Coatsworth took possession of the farm without a formal deed being executed in his favour. Within a few months of his taking possession he had allowed the condition of the land to deteriorate very badly. Johnson took the rather drastic step of evicting Coatsworth from the farm. Coatsworth sued for wrongful eviction, contending that the agreement created an equitable lease lasting 21 years.
HELD: Coatsworth's failure to take good care of the farm was a substantial breach of the contract which meant that he had 'unclean hands' in the sight of equity. He would therefore be denied the discretionary remedy of specific performance of the contract. He was evicted.

LORD ESHER MR: . . . If there is a tenancy at will, how is the landlord to put an end to it? By giving notice to quit, and that is all. He has not to assign any reasons for giving that notice. Supposing there had been no breach of any covenant, he could have given that notice to quit so far as it is a tenancy at will. If it is a tenancy at will, the question of whether there is a breach of covenant or not is immaterial. But it is argued that it was not a tenancy at will, because, under the circumstances, the court of equity would have decreed specific performance of the lease; and it is said that now both sides of the court would consider that as done which the court of equity would have decreed to be done. That proposition is not to be denied.

That raises this question: Would the court of equity in this case have decreed specific performance? If it would, then that is to be considered as done, and then there is a lease. But if it would not, then, there being no lease at common law, it being in the position that the court of equity would not decree specific performance for a lease, then it is no lease at common law. But the proposition is this: It is admitted that, before the Conveyancing Act 1881, if there had been a breach of the contract as to cultivation, the court of equity would not have decreed specific performance. But it is said that, although the tenant has declined or neglected to cultivate in the way mentioned in the agreement, nevertheless the court of equity would decree specific performance, because it is said that the Conveyancing Act 1881, by s. 14, has altered the contract; and that now there is no breach of the contract to cultivate in a particular way, unless, besides the non-cultivation, there has been a demand by the landlord, or a notice by the landlord, not properly observed by the tenant. In other words, that s. 14 of the Conveyancing Act 1881, has altered the contract, and that it is not confined merely to relief in the case of breach of the contract.

It is clear to my mind that s. 14 of the Conveyancing Act 1881, has not altered the contract at all. It has merely dealt with relief, or non-relief, on the assumption that that particular stipulation of the contract has been broken. If the contract is not altered, then by the non-cultivation there is a breach of the contract. Would the court of equity then decree specific performance, there being in existence at the time this state of facts? The moment the plaintiff went into equity, and asked for specific performance, and it was proved that he himself was guilty of the breach of contract, which the defendant says he is by not cultivating, the court of equity would refuse to grant specific performance, and would leave the parties to their other rights. Then, if the court of equity would not grant specific performance, we are not to consider specific performance as granted. Then the case is at an end. It is a lease at will. . . .

5.3 End of Chapter Assessment Question

(a) Norma owns the legal fee simple estate (unregistered title) in 'Ramsey House'. Two months ago she entered into a written agreement (not in the form of a deed) to let Ramsey House to Matthew for five years. The agreement specifically stated that the house should be used for residential purposes only.

Matthew has just been made redundant, and is now considering using Ramsey House for a business repairing bicycles. He has heard rumours that Norma is about to sell the house.

Advise Matthew, who is concerned that, as his lease is not in the form of a deed, he might be evicted by Norma.

And

(b) Last week, by a written contract, Teresa agreed to sell 'Taylor Cottage' to Henry, the sale to be completed in six weeks time.

Unfortunately yesterday, a bus crashed into Taylor Cottage causing considerable damage.

This morning Teresa demolished a small outhouse which stood at the bottom of the garden of Taylor Cottage.

Advise Henry, who wants either to rescind the contract or at least obtain a reduction in the previously agreed price.

5.4 End of Chapter Assessment Outline Answer

PART A

Section 52 of the LPA 1925 requires, subject to certain exceptions not applicable here, that grants (and transfers) of legal rights be made by deed. The agreement of two months ago is not in the form of a deed, and therefore cannot be a legal lease.

Matthew has however, almost certainly got an equitable lease. A line of nineteenth century cases, culminating in *Walsh* v *Lonsdale* (1882) 21 ChD 9 (decided just after the Judicature Acts) held that any contract for a lease (or informal grant of a lease) is regarded by Equity as creating an equitable lease. In Equity the parties to the contract or informal transaction have the same rights and duties they would have had, had a deed been executed.

Subject to certain points raised below, Matthew will be able to invoke the principle in *Walsh* v *Lonsdale* and claim that the written agreement confers on him an equitable lease.

One possible initial stumbling block for Matthew is that for an agreement to create an equitable lease, it must be a legally valid contract. Contracts for the sale or transfer of rights in land (unlike most contracts) are subject to special requirements as to form. Section two of the 1989 Law of Property Miscellaneous Provisions Act requires land contracts to be in a written document signed by both parties, including all the agreed terms. Thus if (say) Matthew did not sign the agreement, or some of the agreed terms did not appear in the document, the agreement would be VOID. Consequently Matthew would not have an equitable lease.

Assuming that the agreement did comply with section two, then Matthew has an equitable lease, but the continued existence of that lease is under threat from another direction.

Matthew's right to an equitable lease depends upon his right to claim the equitable remedy of specific performance of the agreement. If Matthew is in substantial breach of his agreement he will lose the right to specific performance ('He who comes to Equity must have clean hands') and thus destroy his equitable lease. Matthew does not want to suffer the fate of the tenant farmer in *Coatsworth* v *Johnson* [1886–90] All ER Rep 547, who lost his equitable lease because he failed to comply with the obligation to farm 'in a husbandlike manner'. Matthew must abandon his plan to run a bike-repair business from the house.

PART B

The first point to make is that if the 'contract' between Henry and Teresa does not comply with Section 2 of the 1989 Act, then the contract is void, and Henry can repudiate the 'arrangement' without fear of being sued by Teresa.

Assuming the contract complies with section two, then in principle an ancient rule of Equity will operate on that contract. Applying the maxim 'Equity looks on as done that which ought to be done', somebody who has contracted to buy a piece of land is regarded in Equity as owner of that land even though the legal estate has not yet been conveyed to him. That in particular means that the 'risk' of anything untoward happening to a property passes to a purchaser when the contract is signed, not (at the later stage) when the legal estate is conveyed to the purchaser.

Thus if a building is destroyed by fire or other calamity between contract and completion, the (unfortunate) purchaser must complete the deal. Applied to Taylor Cottage, this principle would mean that Henry would have to accept a conveyance of the badly damaged building and pay the full price.

The principle that 'the risk passees on contract not completion' has been heavily criticised in recent years, and in 1990 the Law Society drew up a new set of standard conditions for the sale of land, clause five of which is crucial. Clause five provides that the seller of land must 'transfer the property in the same state as it was at the date of the contract', and also that if between contract and completion 'the physical state of the property makes it unusable for its purpose' the buyer can rescind the contract.

Thus, provided the contract signed last week incorporated clause five, Henry can certainly claim compensation from Teresa, and (alternatively) if the property is uninhabitable, rescind the contract.

If the contract did not include clause five, then Henry must complete the deal. He will have to hope that his solicitor arranged insurance for the cottage from the date of the contract.

The point regarding the outhouse is only relevant if Henry cannot rescind the contract because of the bus damage. Another consequence (more beneficial to purchasers) of the theory that a purchaser becomes owner in Equity on contract not completion is the rule that the vendor must take managerial decisions with respect to the land only in consultation with the purchaser. In *Abdullah* v *Shah* [1959] AC 124 the vendor immediately relet part of the property which had fallen vacant between contract and completion. The purchaser, who would have preferred the property empty, was awarded a reduction in price by the Judicial Committee of the Privy Council.

In the same way Henry (if forced to complete the deal despite the bus damage), can claim a reduction in price to compensate for the demolition of the outhouse.

CHAPTER SIX

DIFFERENCE IN VALIDITY BETWEEN LEGAL PROPERTY RIGHTS AND EQUITABLE PROPERTY RIGHTS

6.1 The Elements of the Doctrine of Notice

A bona fide purchaser for value of a legal estate or legal interest without notice of equitable interests burdening the legal estate or interest will take free of those equitable interests provided that those equitable interests are subject to 'the doctrine of notice'. We will now consider each element of the doctrine in turn.

6.1.1 BONA FIDE

PILCHER v RAWLINS (1872) 7 Ch App 259

The following dictum should be noted, knowledge of the facts of the case is not essential.

SIR W. M. JAMES LJ: I propose simply to apply myself to the case of a purchaser for valuable consideration, without notice, obtaining, upon the occasion of his purchase, and by means of his purchase deed, some legal estate, some legal right, some legal advantage; and, according to my view of the established law of this Court, such a purchaser's plea of a purchase for valuable consideration without notice is an absolute, unqualified, unanswerable defence, and an unanswerable plea to the jurisdiction of this Court. Such a purchaser, when he has once put in that plea, may be interrogated and tested to any extent as to the valuable consideration which he has given in order to show the *bona fides* or *mala fides* of his purchase, and also the presence or the absence of notice; but when once he has gone through that ordeal, and has satisfied the terms of the plea of purchase for valuable consideration without notice, then, according to my judgment, this Court has no jurisdiction whatever to do anything more than to let him depart in possession of that legal estate, that legal right, that legal advantage which he has obtained, whatever it may be. In such a case a purchaser is entitled to hold that which, without breach of duty, he has had conveyed to him.

6.1.2 PURCHASER FOR VALUE

6.1.2.1 The meaning of value

See *Midland Bank Trust Co. Ltd v Green* [1981] AC 513 (**8.1.3**).

6.1.2.2   Marriage as 'value'

Until the passing of the Law Reform (Miscellaneous Provisions) Act 1970 an engagement to marry was a legally enforceable contract and the promise to marry was, accordingly, 'value' for the purposes of the doctrine of notice.

6.1.3   OF A LEGAL ESTATE OR LEGAL INTEREST

See *Pilcher* v *Rawlins* (above at **6.1.1**).

6.1.4   WITHOUT NOTICE

6.1.4.1   Actual notice

A purchaser has actual notice of documents in his possession, even if he has not read them. 'Notice' is not the same as 'knowledge'.

6.1.4.2   Constuctive notice

HUNT v *LUCK* [1902] 1 Ch 428, Court of Appeal

The following dictum should be noted, the facts of the case are not essential. Vaughan Williams LJ affirmed the judgment of Farwell J in the court below.

VAUGHAN WILLIAMS LJ: In my opinion, the judgment of Farwell J was quite right. . . .

In his judgment he, after quoting the older authorities, said: 'The rule established by these two cases may be stated thus: (1) A tenant's occupation is notice of all that tenant's rights, but not of his lessor's title or rights; (2) actual knowledge that the rents are paid by the tenants to some person whose receipt is inconsistent with the title of the vendor is notice of that person's rights.' In the present case I do not understand that any one suggests, and, if it is suggested, in my opinion the suggestion is ill-founded, that there was actual knowledge that the rents were paid by the tenants to some person whose receipt would be inconsistent with the title of the mortgagor, Gilbert. We have, therefore, to apply the first of the rules stated by the learned judge. Now, what does that mean? It means that, if a purchaser or a mortgagee has notice that the vendor or mortgagor is not in possession of the property, he must make inquiries of the person in possession—of the tenant who is in possession—and find out from him what his rights are, and, if he does not choose to do that, then whatever title he acquires as purchaser or mortgagee will be subject to the title or right of the tenant in possession.

That, I believe, is a true statement of the law . . .

BARCLAYS BANK PLC v *O'BRIEN* [1993] 4 All ER 417, House of Lords

FACTS: Mrs O'Brien, the claimant, was surety for a loan made by the bank to her husband. Mr O'Brien's business had been struggling and the loan was taken out to resolve some of its financial problems. The loan was secured by a mortgage on the matrimonial home, in which Mrs O'Brien had an equitable interest. Mrs O'Brien signed the mortgage documents at the bank without reading them and without taking independent legal advice. In due course Mr O'Brien defaulted in repayment of the loan and the bank sought to enforce its security by taking possession of the matrimonial home. Mrs O'Brien claimed that the mortgage should be set aside, alleging that Mr O'Brien had assured her that the loan was of £60,000 only. It was, in fact, a loan of £135,000.

HELD: A wife who has been induced to stand as a surety for her husband's debts by his undue influence, misrepresentation or other legal wrong has an equity as against him to set aside the transaction. The bank took with constructive notice of Mrs O'Brien's equity and therefore would be unable to enforce its later equity by taking possession of the matrimonial home.

LORD BROWNE-WILKINSON: . . . The large number of cases of this type coming before the courts in recent years reflects the rapid changes in social attitudes and the distribution of wealth which have recently occurred. Wealth is now more widely spread. Moreover a high proportion of privately owned wealth is invested in the matrimonial home. Because of the recognition by society of the equality of the sexes, the majority of matrimonial homes are now in the joint names of both spouses. Therefore in order to raise finance for the business enterprises of one or other of the spouses, the jointly owned home has become a main source of security. The provision of such security requires the consent of both spouses.

In parallel with these financial developments, society's recognition of the equality of the sexes has led to a rejection of the concept that the wife is subservient to the husband in the management of the family's finances. A number of the authorities reflect an unwillingness in the court to perpetuate law based on this outmoded concept. Yet, as Scott LJ in the Court of Appeal rightly points out, although the concept of the ignorant wife leaving all financial decisions to the husband is outmoded, the practice does not yet coincide with the ideal. . . . In a substantial proportion of marriages it is still the husband who has the business experience and the wife is willing to follow his advice without bringing a truly independent mind and will to bear on financial decisions. The number of recent cases in this field shows that in practice many wives are still subjected to, and yield to, undue influence by their husbands. Such wives can reasonably look to the law for some protection when their husbands have abused the trust and confidence reposed in them.

On the other hand, it is important to keep a sense of balance in approaching these cases. It is easy to allow sympathy for the wife who is threatened with the loss of her home at the suit of a rich bank to obscure an important public interest, viz the need to ensure that the wealth currently tied up in the matrimonial home does not become economically sterile. If the rights secured to wives by the law renders vulnerable loans granted on the security of matrimonial homes, institutions will be unwilling to accept such security, thereby reducing the flow of loan capital to business enterprises. It is therefore essential that a law designed to protect the vulnerable does not render the matrimonial home unacceptable as security to financial institutions.

With these policy considerations in mind I turn to consider the existing state of the law. . . .

In my judgment, if the doctrine of notice is properly applied, there is no need for the introduction of a special equity in these types of cases. A wife who has been induced to stand as a surety for her husband's debts by his undue influence, misrepresentation or some other legal wrong has an equity as against him to set aside that transaction. Under the ordinary principles of equity, her right to set aside that transaction will be enforceable against third parties (eg against a creditor) if either the husband was acting as the third party's agent or the third party had actual or constructive notice of the facts giving rise to her equity. Although there may be cases where, without artificiality, it can properly be held that the husband was acting as the agent of the creditor in procuring the wife to stand as surety, such cases will be of very rare occurrence. The key to the problem is to identify the circumstances in which the creditor will be taken to have had notice of the wife's equity to set aside the transaction.

The doctrine of notice lies at the heart of equity. Given that there are two innocent parties, each enjoying rights, the earlier right prevails against the later right if the acquirer of the later right knows of the earlier right (actual notice) or would have discovered it had he taken proper steps (constructive notice). In particular, if the party asserting that he takes free of the earlier rights of another knows of certain facts which put him on inquiry as to the possible existence of the rights of that other and he fails to make such inquiry or take such other steps as are reasonable to verify whether such earlier right does or does not exist, he will have constructive notice of the earlier right and take subject to it. Therefore where a wife has agreed to stand surety for her husband's debts as a result of undue influence or misrepresentation, the creditor will take subject to the wife's equity to set aside the transaction if the circumstances are such as to put the creditor on inquiry as to the circumstances in which she agreed to stand surety.

It is at this stage that, in my view, the 'invalidating tendency' or the law's 'tender treatment' of married women, becomes relevant. As I have said above in dealing with undue influence, this tenderness of the law towards married women is due to the fact that, even today, many wives repose confidence and trust in their husbands in relation to their financial affairs. This tenderness of the law is reflected by the fact that voluntary dispositions by the wife in favour of her husband are more likely to be set aside than other dispositions by her: a wife is more likely to establish presumed undue influence of class 2B by her husband than by others because, in practice, many wives do repose in their husbands trust and confidence in relation to their financial affairs. Moreover the informality of business dealings between spouses raises a substantial risk that the husband has not accurately stated to the wife the nature of the liability she is undertaking, ie he has misrepresented the position, albeit negligently.

Therefore, in my judgment a creditor is put on inquiry when a wife offers to stand surety for her husband's debts by the combination of two factors: (a) the transaction is on its face not to the financial advantage of the wife; and (b) there is a substantial risk in transactions of that kind that, in procuring the wife to act as surety, the husband has committed a legal or equitable wrong that entitles the wife to set aside the transaction.

It follows that, unless the creditor who is put on inquiry takes reasonable steps to satisfy himself that the wife's agreement to stand surety has been properly obtained, the creditor will have constructive notice of the wife's rights. . . .

BARCLAYS BANK PLC v BOULTER AND ANOTHER [1997] 2 All ER 100, Court of Appeal

FACTS: In September 1979 the husband and wife executed an 'all moneys or liabilities' charge over a property which they jointly owned in favour of the plaintiff bank. In March 1993 the bank demanded payment by the husband of £122,881.46 alleged to be owed by him on three home mortgage accounts and a current account together with interest. The husband did not comply with the demand and subsequently the bank commenced proceedings against the husband and wife for possession of the house. The wife served a separate defence counterclaim, asserting that she had been induced to sign the charge by her husband's misrepresentation that the charge only secured the amount borrowed for the purposes of purchasing the house, which she knew to be about £36,000, and that the charge should therefore be set aside as against her. At the opening of the trial, before any evidence was called, the bank contended that the wife was not entitled to argue that the bank had constructive notice of the alleged misrepresentation as that had not been pleaded. The judge upheld the bank's contention and the wife appealed. HELD: Where a bank, as mortgagee of a property jointly owned by a husband and wife, brought proceedings for possession on the husband's default, and the wife alleged that her half share of the property was free of the bank's legal charge on the ground that her husband had induced her to sign the charge by misrepresentation, the burden was on the bank to plead and prove that it did not have constructive notice of the misrepresentation, and not on the wife to prove that it did. It followed, in the instant case, that as the wife had pleaded the necessary material facts in support of her claim in her defence and counterclaim, she was entitled to argue the issue of constructive notice at the trial and did not need to amend her pleading. The appeal would accordingly be allowed.

MUMMERY LJ: . . . Neither *O'Brien's* case [[1993] 4 All ER 417, see above] nor the ensuing clutch of cases decided in this court raised a specific issue on the pleading and proof of constructive notice (see *Banco Exterior Internacional v Mann* [1995] 1 All ER 936, *Massey v Midland Bank plc* [1995] 1 All ER 929, *TSB Bank plc v Camfield* [1995] 1 All ER 951 and *Banco Exterior Internacional SA v Thomas* [1997] 1 All ER 46). The question of notice usually arises in county court proceedings brought by a bank or other creditor for possession of the matrimonial home. In those circumstances pleading points taken, as here, before evidence is called, are rightly given short shrift in most cases: the objection is either rejected and not pursued to appeal or it is upheld and an application for leave to amend is then made and granted on terms. The present case is exceptional. The critical point is whether it is (a) for the defendant wife to plead that the plaintiff bank had constructive notice of her equity against her husband; or (b) for the plaintiff bank or other creditor to plead, by way of reply to the wife's challenge to the validity of the legal charge, that it had no constructive notice of the matters relied on by her in support of her challenge.

The judge accepted the bank's contention that it was necessary for Mrs Boulter to plead constructive notice by the bank and that Mrs Boulter could not succeed on this part of her case without making an amendment, which she was unwilling to make. . . .

In my judgment, this appeal should be allowed. The facts and matters which should be pleaded in any particular case, either by way of claim or defence, are determined partly by the rules of procedure and practice and partly by the substantive law relevant to the cause of action and the available defences to it.

Procedure and practice require that all material facts should be pleaded. In general, *only* facts should be pleaded: not evidence relied on to prove the facts; not points of law; not argument.

As only material facts have to be pleaded, Mrs Boulter is entitled at the trial to argue, on the basis of the facts already set out in her defence and counterclaim, the issue of constructive notice. It is not necessary for her to add another paragraph expressly alleging constructive notice. At trial Mrs Boulter will be limited to adducing evidence and advancing arguments on the basis of the facts pleaded. It will then be open to the bank to submit that those facts have not been established on the evidence or that, even if those facts are established, the bank is not, in fact or in law, fixed with constructive notice.

The relevant substantive law confirms this conclusion. On the authority of Lord Browne-Wilkinson's speech in *O'Brien's* case and on well-established equitable principles, the burden is not on Mrs Boulter to plead and prove that the bank had constructive notice: it is on the bank to plead and prove that it did *not* have constructive notice. This has not been highlighted in any of the previous decisions and the point merits elaboration, as a matter of principle and of authority.

It is well established at this level of decision that the doctrine of bona fide purchaser for value without actual or constructive notice is a defence which can be raised to defeat a claim of an equitable right or interest and that the burden is on the person raising that defence to plead and prove *all* its elements: it is a 'single defence'. In *Pilcher* v *Rawlins* (1872) LR 7 Ch App 259 at 268–269 James LJ said:

> . . . a purchaser's plea of a purchase for valuable consideration without notice is an absolute, unqualified, unanswerable defence, and an unanswerable plea to the jurisdiction of this Court.

In his Lectures on Equity (2nd edn), F W Maitland wrote (p. 119):

> Against a person who acquires a legal right bona fide, for value, without notice express or constructive of the existence of equitable rights those rights are of no avail.

Thesiger LJ, in giving the judgment of the court in *A-G* v *Biphosphated Guano Co.* (1878) 11 Ch D 327 at 337, said: 'The defence of a purchase without notice is one which ought to be specifically alleged as well as proved by those who rely upon it.' This view was shared by Farewell J in *Re Nisbet and Potts' Contract* [1905] 1 Ch 351 at 402, by the Court of Appeal in that case [1906] 1 Ch 386 at 403, 404, 409, 410 and by Farwell LJ in *Wilkes* v *Spooner* [1911] 2 KB 473 at 486. See the valuable discussion of this topic in Meagher, Gummow and Lehane *Equity: Doctrines and Remedies* (3rd edn, 1992) para. 860, pp. 257–259.

The speech of Lord Browne-Wilkinson in *O'Brien's* case supports the view that the same approach to pleading and proof of constructive notice applies in *O'Brien* cases as in the standard case of the bona fide purchaser for value of the legal estate without notice of an equitable estate or interest. There are three relevant passages in Lord Browne-Wilkinson's speech. He said ([1993] 4 All ER 417 at 424–425):

> But in surety cases the decisive question is whether the claimant wife can set aside the transaction, not against the wrongdoing husband, but against the creditor bank. Of course, if the wrongdoing husband is acting as agent for the creditor bank in obtaining the surety from the wife, the creditor will be fixed with the wrongdoing of its own agent and the surety contract can be set aside as against the creditor. Apart from this, if the creditor bank has notice, actual or constructive, of the undue influence exercised by the husband (and consequentially of the wife's equity to set aside the transaction) the creditor will take subject to that equity and the wife can set aside the transaction against the creditor (albeit a purchaser for value) as well as against the husband . . . Similarly, in cases such as the present where the wife has been induced to enter into the transaction by the husband's misrepresentation, her equity to set aside the transaction will be

enforceable against the creditor if either the husband was acting as the creditor's agent or the creditor had actual or constructive notice.

Lord Browne-Wilkinson, having rejected the Court of Appeal's notion of a 'special equity' in this type of case, said ([1993] 4 All ER 417 at 428–429):

> Under the ordinary principles of equity, her right to set aside that transaction will be enforceable against third parties (e.g. against a creditor) if either the husband was acting as the third party's agent or the third party had actual or constructive notice of the facts giving rise to her equity . . . The key to the problem is to identify the circumstances in which the creditor will be taken to have had notice of the wife's equity to set aside the transaction. The doctrine of notice lies at the heart of equity. Given that there are two innocent parties, each enjoying rights, the earlier right prevails against the later right if the acquirer of the later right knows of the earlier right (actual notice) or would have discovered it had he taken proper steps (constructive notice). In particular, if the party asserting that he takes free of the earlier rights of another knows of certain facts which put him on inquiry as to the possible existence of the rights of that other and he fails to make such inquiry or take such other steps as are reasonable to verify whether such earlier right does or does not exist, he will have constructive notice of the earlier right and take subject to it. Therefore where a wife has agreed to stand surety for her husband's debts as a result of undue influence or misrepresentation, the creditor will take subject to the wife's equity to set aside the transaction if the circumstances are such as to put the creditor on inquiry as to the circumstances in which she agreed to stand surety.

Later, Lord Browne-Wilkinson said ([1993] 4 All ER 417 at 429):

> Therefore, in my judgment a creditor is put on inquiry when a wife offers to stand surety for her husband's debts by the combination of two factors: (a) the transaction is on its face not to the financial advantage of the wife; and (b) there is a substantial risk in transactions of that kind that, in procuring the wife to act as surety, the husband has committed a legal or equitable wrong that entitles the wife to set aside the transaction . . . It follows that, unless the creditor who is put on inquiry takes reasonable steps to satisfy himself that the wife's agreement to stand surety has been properly obtained, the creditor will have constructive notice of the wife's rights. What, then are the reasonable steps which the creditor should take to ensure that it does not have constructive notice of the wife's rights, if any? Normally the reasonable steps necessary to avoid being fixed with constructive notice consist of making inquiry of the person who may have the earlier right (i.e. the wife) to see if whether such right is asserted.

Lord Browne-Wilkinson described those steps which a creditor can reasonably be expected to take 'in order to avoid being fixed with constructive notice'. In my judgment, these passages, the summary at the end of Lord Browne-Wilkinson's speech already quoted and his reasoning on the facts leading to a conclusion in favour of Mrs O'Brien (see [1993] 4 All ER 417 at 432), support the submission that it is for the bank or other creditor to prove (and to plead) that it did not have constructive notice of the equity asserted by the wife. The bank, in addition to arguing that there is no case made out against the husband, may contend that it is not fixed with constructive notice, (1) because, in all the circumstances, there was nothing to put it on inquiry as to the potential existence of the claim, and (2) if there was, it has taken reasonable steps necessary to avoid being fixed with such notice. Both being put on inquiry and taking reasonable steps are aspects of constructive notice. I would reject the submission of Mr Sullivan, on behalf of the bank, that the burden of proof and the pleading is split and that it is for Mrs Boulter to plead that the bank is put on inquiry and that then, and only then, is it for the bank to plead that it took reasonable steps to avoid being fixed with constructive notice.

In *CIBC Mortgages plc v Pitt* [1993] 4 All ER 433 at 440 Lord Browne-Wilkinson said:

> Even though, in my view, Mrs Pitt is entitled to set aside the transaction as against Mr Pitt, she has to establish that in some way the plaintiff is affected by the wrongdoing of Mr Pitt so as to be entitled to set aside the legal charge as against the plaintiff.

Taken out of context, that passage might lend support to the proposition that it is for the wife to plead and prove constructive notice. However, I am of the view that Lord Browne-Wilkinson was not addressing the pleading issue in that part of his speech.

The judgment of Hobhouse LJ in *Banco Exterior Internacional* v *Mann* [1995] 1 All ER 936 at 946 supports Mrs Boulter's submission. Although Hobhouse LJ dissented from Morritt LJ and Bingham MR on the result in that case, his helpful analysis of Lord Browne-Wilkinson's speech was not the point of dissent. In the course of identifying the three steps to be followed in *O'Brien* cases, Hobhouse LJ stated that the third stage was:

> Has the third party proved that he did not have constructive notice of the undue influence that is presumed to have occurred or did in fact occur? This is the critical question on the present appeal.

I agree with Hobhouse LJ that the correct question on notice is whether the third party has proved that it did not have constructive notice. This places the burden of proof on the bank which should plead that it does not have constructive notice. Mrs Boulter does not have to plead and prove that the bank had constructive notice.

At a late stage in the argument, counsel, prompted by the production by Mr Sullivan of copies of M P Thompson 'The Enforceability of Mortgages' [1994] Conv 140 and Dixon and Harpum 'Fraud, Undue Influence and Mortgages of Registered Land' [1994] Conv 421, raised the question whether there was a difference between registered land and unregistered land in this recent development of equitable doctrine. Although it is true that the doctrine of purchaser for value without notice has no application to registered land, no one has seriously argued on this appeal that *O'Brien* is inapplicable to registered land. No distinction between unregistered and registered land was drawn by Lord Browne-Wilkinson. Indeed, it appears from the relevant documents in *O'Brien's* case shown to us by Mr Coney that the O'Briens' matrimonial home was registered land. It is unnecessary to consider the application of the doctrine of notice to registered land or the registered conveyancing doctrines of overriding interests and actual occupation. In *O'Brien* cases it is irrelevant whether the land is registered or unregistered: the question is whether the third party creditor has actual or constructive notice of the facts on which the equity to set aside the transaction is founded.

For all those reasons I would allow the appeal. . . .

LAW OF PROPERTY ACT 1925

199. Restrictions on constructive notice

(1) A purchaser shall not be prejudicially affected by notice of—

(i) any instrument or matter capable of registration under the provisions of the Land Charges Act 1925, or any enactment which it replaces, which is void or not enforecable as against him under that Act or enactment, by reason of the non-registration thereof;

(ii) any other instrument or matter or any fact or thing unless—

(a) it is within his own knowledge, or would have come to his knowledge if such inquiries and inspection had been made as ought reasonably to have been made by him; or

(b) in the same transaction with respect to which a question of notice to the purchaser arises, it has come to the knowledge of his counsel, as such, or of his solicitor or other agent, as such or would have come to the knowledge of his solicitor or other agent, as such, if such inquiries and inspections had been made as ought reasonably to have been made by the solicitor or other agent.

(2) Paragraph (ii) of the last subsection shall not exempt a purchaser from any liability under, or any obligation to perform or observe, any covenant, condition, provision, or restriction contained in any instrument under which his title is derived, mediately or immediately; and such liability or obligation may be enforced in the same manner and to the same extent as if that paragraph had not been enacted.

(3) A purchaser shall not by reason of anything in this section be affected by notice in any case where he would not have been so affected if this section had not been enacted.

(4) This section applies to purchases made either before or after the commencement of this Act.

LAW OF PROPERTY ACT 1969

23. Reduction of statutory period of title

Section 44(1) of the Law of Property Act 1925 (under which the period of commencement of title which may be required under a contract expressing no contrary intention is thirty years except in certain cases) shall have effect, in its application to contracts made after the commencement of this Act, as if it specified fifteen years instead of thirty years as the period of commencement of title which may be so required.

6.1.4.3 Imputed notice

KINGSNORTH FINANCE CO. LTD v *TIZARD AND ANOTHER* [1986] 1 WLR 783,
High Court

FACTS: Mr and Mrs Tizard lived in the matrimonial home, Willowden, which had been built using funds to which they had made roughly equal contributions. Only Mr Tizard's name appeared on the title deeds. The marriage later broke down and Mrs Tizard moved out. However, she occasionally slept at Willowden in her husband's absence, and often spent time there looking after the children of the marriage. Mr Tizard wished to mortgage the property to Kingsnorth. They instructed brokers to investigate the property, who in turn appointed a surveyor. Kingsnorth believed that Mr Tizard was unmarried, on account of his application form, but the surveyor's searches revealed that he was 'recently separated'. In the event the mortgage was completed on the basis of the survey and application form, with Kingsnorth never having had actual notice of the fact that Mr Tizard was married.

HELD: The surveyor should have communicated to his principals the fact that Mr Tizard had recently separated from his wife. This should have prompted further searches which should then have led to Mrs Tizard. Mrs Tizard had not truly ceased to be in actual occupation, as her occupation had only temporarily been disturbed. Following *Hunt* v *Luck*, the surveyor had constructive notice of Mrs Tizard's interest. This notice would be imputed to Kingsnorth.

JUDGE JOHN FINLAY QC: The house Willowdown was the matrimonial home of Mr Tizard and his wife, the second defendant. The property was vested in Mr Tizard alone. Mrs Tizard claims an equitable interest in it. The plaintiffs are seeking to enforce their legal charge. The question in this action is whether that legal charge is subject to or overrides the equitable interest, if any, which Mrs Tizard has. That is the question between the plaintiffs and Mrs Tizard. Between Mr and Mrs Tizard there is also the question whether Mrs Tizard has an equitable interest and if so what it is. . . .

In 1982 the marriage broke down. Mr and Mrs Tizard agreed that Willowdown and the adjoining land should be sold and the net proceeds divided between them in equal shares. This was not done before Mr Tizard emigrated and it has not been done since.

Mrs Tizard moved into the spare bedroom when the marriage broke down. Willowdown had four bedrooms: the master bedroom, which until then the spouses had used and which continued to be used by Mr Tizard; two bedrooms occupied by the two children respectively, and the spare bedroom which was a room with a double bed. In November 1982 Mrs Tizard began to sleep not always but sometimes at her sister's house, about four miles away. She would sleep at Willowdown when Mr Tizard was not spending the night there. He was away quite often, and kept her informed when he would not be there. If she slept at her sister's, Mrs Tizard would drive over early in the morning, give the children breakfast and get them ready for school, and then make herself ready to go to work at 9 am. She returned to give the children and herself an evening meal. She would leave if Mr Tizard returned in the evening, but stay the night, sleeping in the spare bedroom, if he was not to be there. Sometimes he was away for several nights, occasionally even weeks. Mrs Tizard formed a relationship with a Mr Mead; and instead of going to her sister's when she was not sleeping at Willowdown, Mrs Tizard began to go to Mr Mead's cottage, which also was not far away. Most of her wardrobe she kept at Willowdown: her clothes were in three of the four wardrobe compartments in the master bedroom. Her toiletries, her dressing gown, her nightwear and so forth were also at Willowdown. These arrangements I find continued until the time in mid-1983 when Mrs Tizard found a note from Mr Tizard saying that he was going on holiday abroad with the boy twin. Neither he nor the boy has returned.

I find that Mrs Tizard contributed substantially to the successive property ventures by putting up money for the first deposit, by contributing through the earnings of hers which went into the common pool out of which mortgage instalments and building costs were paid, and by her labour. No accounts were kept of the spouses' respective contributions whether in money or in labour either before or after they were married. I find that they contributed substantially equally. Mrs Tizard is entitled to half of the equity. Furthermore, I find that Mrs Tizard remained at all material times in occupation of Willowdown House. Mr Tizard, the owner of the legal estate, was in occupation, until he departed for the Americas in about June 1983. That circumstance does not however prevent Mrs Tizard also being in occupation. . . .

The brokers whose fee was to be £1,240 were Bradshaws. They instructed a chartered surveyor, Mr Marshall, to carry out an inspection. He did so on 13 March 1983, and made a report dated 15 March. Mr Wigmore, for the plaintiffs, accepts that Mr Marshall must be treated as the agent of the plaintiffs. . . .

In his evidence Mr Marshall made it clear that he was suspicious; he was on the lookout for signs of female occupation; not the occupation of a wife, but that of a girl friend. He found no such signs, but his evidence made it clear that he regarded it as his duty to look for them. He drew the line however at opening cupboards and drawers. Mr Marshall's understanding of his duty to look for signs of occupation by anyone else accords with mine. That being the scope of his duty, I consider that he should have enlarged on his answer to the question, 'Who occupies the property?' The answer that he gave was. 'Applicant, son and daughter.' That was founded in part on his own observation; in part on what Mr Tizard told him. He should, in my view, have added, either in the 'Occupation' or in the 'General observations' section, 'Applicant states that he is separated from wife who lives nearby,' or something to that effect.

My reason for that view is this. It is common ground that Mr Marshall was acting as agent of the plaintiffs. He was not instructed by the plaintiffs. He was instructed by Bradshaws. Before Mr Marshall inspected the property, Bradshaws had the document dated 12 March 1983 which Mr Tizard signed. What Mr Tizard told Bradshaws about his material status at that stage can be inferred from what he told them later when he signed the plaintiffs' form, namely, that he was 'single.' In a document which gives only one alternative to 'single,' namely, 'married,' 'single' must signify either bachelor or spinster as the case may be, or a widow or widower, or a person whose marriage has been dissolved. It cannot mean 'married but separated.' As Bradshaws were instructing Mr Marshall to make an inspection on behalf of the plaintiffs, they were acting as the plaintiffs' agents for that purpose. The fact that Mr Marshall was looking for evidence of the occupation of a female cohabitee coupled with what I infer from the two documents signed by Mr Tizard was Bradshaw's understanding of Mr Tizard's marital status, implies that Mr Marshall approached his inspection on the footing that Mr Tizard was not married; when it appeared that he was, I consider that he had a duty to communicate this new information to his principals. It follows in my judgment that the knowledge of the agent, Mr Marshall, that Mr Tizard had a wife is to be taken to be the knowledge of the principal, the plaintiffs.

The plaintiffs received Mr Tizard's application in which he described himself as single; and received Mr Marshall's report in which there was mention of a son and daughter. The application mentioned two 'children or other dependants' who were stated to be both aged 15. The application had a space in which there fell to be inserted 'Age of spouse next birthday.' It was left blank. It also contained spaces for insertion of the spouse's name, and the name and address of the spouse's employers: and in these spaces there appeared 'N/A', not applicable. The application left it in doubt whether the two 15-year old dependants were children or others, but Mr Marshall's report made it clear that they were son and daugter of the applicant. Had Mr Marshall's report indicated that Mr Tizard was married, it seems to me to be clear that bearing in mind that the application stated over Mr Tizard's signature that he was single, the plaintiffs would have been put on notice that further investigation was required. Indeed, even if I am wrong in my view that Mr Marshall should have reported what Mr Tizard said about his wife, the reference to 'son and daughter' in the report should have alerted the plaintiffs to the need to make further inquiries. Primarily, the plaintiffs are to be taken to have been aware that Mr Tizard was married and had described himself as single; and in these circumstances their further inquiries should have led them to Mrs Tizard.

Section 199(1) of the Law of Property Act 1925 provides:

A purchaser shall not be prejudicially affected by notice of—(i) any instrument or matter capable of registration under the provisions of the Land Charges Act 1925, or any enactment which it replaces, which is void or not enforceable as against him under that Act or enactment, by reason of the non-registration thereof; (ii) any other instrument or matter or any fact or thing unless—(a) it is within his own knowledge, or would have come to his knowledge if such inquiries and inspections had been made as ought reasonably to have been made by him; or (b) in the same transaction with respect to which a question of notice to the purchaser arises, it has come to the knowledge of his counsel, as such, or of his solicitor or other agent, as such, or would have come to the knowledge of his solicitor or other agent, as such, if such inquiries and inspections had been made as ought reasonably to have been made by the solicitor or other agent.

'Purchaser' in that provision, includes a mortgagee: see section 205(1) of the Act.

Although a spouse's statutory rights of occupation under section 1 of the Matrimonial Homes Act 1983, and the statutory provisions replaced by that Act are capable of protection by registration as a Class F land charge, by virtue of the Land Charges Act 1972, the equitable interest of such a spouse in the matrimonial home is not capable of being so protected. The plaintiffs were prejudicially affected by the knowledge of their agent, Mr Marshall, that Mr Tizard, contrary to what he had said in his application, was married: see section 199(1)(ii)(b). That put them on notice that further inquiries were necessary; the inquiries which in these circumstances ought reasonably to have been made by the plaintiffs would, in my judgment, have been such as to have apprised them of the fact that Mrs Tizard claimed a beneficial interest in the property; and accordingly, they would have had notice of such equitable rights as she had and the mortgage in these circumstances takes effect subject to these rights: see Section 199(1)(ii)(a).

I arrive at that conclusion without having considered the question: does the occupation of Mrs Tizard affect the mortgagees with notice of her rights, or are they only so affected if, as Mr Wigmore submits, they are aware of her occupation, that is, if they find her in occupation?

On the balance of probabilities, I find that the reason Mr Marshall did not find Mrs Tizard in the house was that Mr Tizard had arranged matters to achieve that result. He told Mrs Tizard that on a particular Sunday, and I find in fact that it was the Sunday that Mr Marshall did inspect, he was going to entertain friends to lunch and would she take the children out for the day. She did; and having regard to the manner in which I find that the signs of he occupation were temporarily eliminated by Mr Tizard, the reasonable inference is that he made this request so that Mr Marshall could inspect and find no evidence of Mrs Tizard's occupation.

In *Caunce v Caunce* [1969] 1 WLR 286 Stamp J held that where a wife who had an equitable interest in a property being mortgaged to the bank by he husband was resident with him in the property, that circumstance did not result in the bank taking the property fixed with notice of her rights because, finding her in occupation, the bank made no inquiry of her. Stamp J said, at p. 293:

Here it is said that the plaintiff was in possession or occupation. No inquiry was made of her and therefore the bank is fixed with notice of her equitable interest. In my judgment, it is here that the fallacy arises, for the plaintiff, unlike the deserted wife, was not in apparent occupation or possession. She was there, ostensibly, because she was the wife, and her presence was wholly consistent with the title offered by the husband to the bank.

In *Williams & Glyn's Bank Ltd v Boland* [1981] AC 487, 505, Lord Wilberforce said in the passage I have already read: 'But the presence of the vendor, with occupation, does not exclude the possibility of occupation of others.' He went on to say there were observations suggesting the contrary in *Caunce v Caunce* [1969] 1 WLR 286 but he agreed with the disapproval of those and with the assertion expressed by Russell LJ in *Hodgson* v *Marks* [1971] Ch 892, 934. Russell LJ there stated:

> I would only add that I do not consider it necessary to this decision to pronounce on the decision in *Caunce* v *Caunce* [1969] 1 WLR 286. In that case the occupation of the wife may have been rightly taken to be not her occupation but that of her husband. In so far, however, as some phrases in the judgment might appear to lay down a general proposition that inquiry need not be made of any person on the premises if the proposed vendor himself appears to be in occupation, I would not accept them.

I have already stated my finding that the wife was in occupation. In the circumstances in which she was, I find that her occupation was not that of her husband. Guided by the high authority of the two passages I have just cited, Lord Wilberforce in *Williams & Glyn's Bank Ltd* v *Boland* [1981] AC 487, 505, and Russell LJ in *Hodgson* v *Marks* [1971] Ch 892, 934, I conclude that had Mrs Tizard been found to be in occupation by the plaintiffs or their agent and so found in the context of what had been said by Mr Tizard to Mr Marshall and stated or implied in the forms he had signed, they, the plaintiffs, would clearly either have learned of her rights by inquiry of her or been fixed with notice of those rights had not inquiry of her been made.

In the light of my finding that Mr Marshall's information about Mr Tizard's wife is to be imputed to the plaintiffs and my conclusion that further inquiries should have been made by the plaintiffs because of that imputed knowledge, do I ask myself whether such an inspection as would have disclosed that Mrs Tizard was in the premises is one which ought reasonably to have been made by them, or is the proper question: can the plaintiffs show that no such inspection was reasonably necessary? The latter appears to me to be the proper way to put it. The plaintiffs did not make any further inquiries or inspections; had they done so it would have been open to them to contend that they had done all that was reasonably required and if they still had no knowledge of Mrs Tizard's rights or claims, that they were not fixed with notice of them. But in the absence of further inquiries or inspections, I do not think that it is open to the plaintiffs to say that if they had made a further inspection they would still not have found Mrs Tizard in occupation.

I would put it briefly thus. Mr Tizard appears to have been minded to conceal the true facts; he did not do so completely; the plaintiffs had, or are to be taken to have had, information which should have alerted them to the fact that the full facts were not in their possession and that they should make further inspections or inquiries; they did not do so; and in these circumstances I find that they are fixed with notice of the equitable interest of Mrs Tizard. . . .

Thompson, M. P., The Purchaser as Private Detective
Kingsnorth Trust Ltd v *Tizard* (1986) 50 Conv 283

. . . While the position of a first mortgagee, who acquires his interest at the time the property is bought, has been substantially eased, the position of purchasers and other mortgagees has become extremely parlous. They are faced with invidious choices. They can further alter their conduct to resemble that of an enthusiastic private investigator and accept the need to behave in a potentially offensive manner towards a householder. Unfortunately they could not even then be sure of safeguarding their position. So far as mortgagees are concened, they can simply accept that the security for a number of mortgages will inevitably be lost, regarding that as an ordinary business hazard or finally insurance could be taken out against the risk of each mortgage being rendered substantially worthless. Any of these options will, of course, inevitably increase the transaction cost of conveyancing. . . .

CHAPTER SEVEN

THE IMPACT OF THE 1925 LEGISLATION

7.1 Legal Estates and Interests and the 1925 Legislation

LAW OF PROPERTY ACT 1925

1. Legal estates and equitable interests

(1) The only estates in land which are capable of subsisting or of being conveyed or created at law are—

    (a) An estate in fee simple absolute in possession;

    (b) A term of years absolute.

(2) The only interests or charges in or over land which are capable of subsisting or of being conveyed or created at law are—

    (a) An easement, right, or privilege in or over land for an interest equivalent to an estate in fee simple absolute in possession or a term of years absolute;

    (b) A rentcharge in possession issuing out of or charged on land being either perpetual or for a term of years absolute;

    (c) A charge by way of legal mortgage;

    (d) ... and any other similar charge on land which is not created by an instrument;

    (e) Rights of entry exercisable over or in respect of a legal term of years absolute, or annexed, for any purpose, to a legal rentcharge.

(3) All other estates, interests, and charges in or over land take effect as equitable interests.

(4) The estates, interests, and charges which under this section are authorised to subsist or to be conveyed or created at law are (when subsisting or conveyed or created at law) in this Act referred to as 'legal estates,' and have the same incidents as legal estates subsisting at the commencement of this Act; and the owner of a legal estate is referred to as 'an estate owner' and his legal estate is referred to as his estate.

(5) A legal estate may subsist concurrently with or subject to any other legal estate in the same land in like manner as it could have done before the commencement of this Act.

(6) A legal estate is not capable of subsisting or of being created in an undivided share in land or of being held by an infant.

(7) Every power of appointment over, or power to convey or charge land or any interest therein, whether created by a statute or other instrument or implied by law, and whether created before or after the commencement of this Act (not being a power vested in a legal mortgagee or an estate owner in right of his estate and exercisable by him or by another person in his name and on his behalf), operates only in equity.

(8) Estates, interests, and charges in or over land which are not legal estates are in this Act referred to as 'equitable interests', and powers which by this Act are to operate in equity only are in this Act referred to as 'equitable powers'.

7.2 Legal Estates Existing After 1925

7.2.1 TERM OF YEARS ABSOLUTE

See **Chapter 17**.

LAW OF PROPERTY ACT 1925

205. General definitions

(1) (xxvii) 'Term of years absolute' means a term of years (taking effect either in possession or in reversion whether or not at a rent) with or without impeachment for waste, subject or not to another legal estate, and either certain or liable to determination by notice, re-entry, operation of law, or by a provision for cesser on redemption, or in any other event (other than the dropping of a life, or the determination of a determinable life interest); but does not include any term of years determinable with life or lives or with the cesser of a determinable life interest, nor, if created after the commencement of this Act, a term of years which is not expressed to take effect in possession within twenty-one years after the creation thereof where required by this Act to take effect within that period; and in this definition the expression 'term of years' includes a term for less than a year, or for a year or years and a fraction of a year or from year to year.

7.2.2 FEE SIMPLE ABSOLUTE IN POSSESSION

7.2.2.1 'Absolute'

LAW OF PROPERTY (AMENDMENT) ACT 1926

1. Conveyances of legal estates subject to certain interests

(1) Nothing in the Settled Land Act 1925 shall prevent a person on whom the powers of a tenant for life are conferred by paragraph (ix) of subsection (1) of section twenty of that Act from conveying or creating a legal estate subject to a prior interest as if the land had not been settled land.

(2) In any of the following cases, namely—

(a) where a legal estate has been conveyed or created under subsection one of this section, or under section sixteen of the Settled Land Act 1925, subject to any prior interest, or

(b) where before the first day of January, nineteen hundred and twenty-six, land has been conveyed to a purchaser for money or money's worth subject to any prior interest whether or not on the purchase the land was expressed to be exonerated from, or the grantor agreed to indemnify the purchaser against, such prior interest,

the estate owner for the time being of the land subject to such prior interest may, notwithstanding any provision contained in the Settled Land Act 1925, but without prejudice to any power whereby such prior interest is capable of being overreached, convey or create a legal estate subject to such prior interest as if the instrument creating the prior interest was not an instrument or one of the instruments constituting a settlement of the land.

(3) In this section 'interest' means an estate, interest, charge or power of charging subsisting, or capable of arising or of being exercised, under a settlement, and, where a prior interest arises under the exercise of a power, 'instrument' includes both the instrument conferring the power and the instrument exercising it.

LAW OF PROPERTY ACT 1925
as amended by the Trusts of Land etc. Act 1996

7. Saving of certain legal estates and statutory powers

(1) A fee simple which, by virtue of the Lands Clauses Acts . . . or any similar statute, is liable to be divested, is for the purposes of this Act a fee simple absolute, and remains

liable to be divested as if this Act had not been passed [and a fee simple subject to a legal or equitable right of entry or re-entry is for the purposes of this Act a fee simple absolute].

(2) A fee simple vested in a corporation which is liable to determine by reason of the dissolution of the corporation is, for the purposes of this Act, a fee simple absolute.

(3) The provisions of—

(a) ... ;

(b) [...]

(c) any other statutes conferring special facilities or prescribing special modes (whether by way of registered memorial or otherwise) for disposing of or acquiring land, or providing for the vesting (by conveyance or otherwise) of the land in trustees or any person, or the holder for the time being of an office or any corporation sole or aggregate (including the Crown);

shall remain in full force.

This subsection does not authorise an entailed interest to take effect otherwise than as in equitable interest.

CHAPTER EIGHT

STATUS OF EQUITABLE INTERESTS AFTER 1925

8.1 Registration of Land Charges

LAW OF PROPERTY ACT 1925

198. Registration under the Land Charges Act 1925 to be notice

(1) The registration of any instrument or matter [in any register kept under the Land Charges Act 1972 or any local land charges register] shall be deemed to constitute actual notice of such instrument or matter, and of the fact of such registration, to all persons and for all purposes connected with the land affected, as from the date of registration or other prescribed date and so long as the registration continues in force.

LAND CHARGES ACT 1972
as amended by the Trusts of Land etc. Act 1996

1. The registers and the index

(1) The registrar shall continue to keep at the registry in the prescribed manner the following registers, namely—

 (a) a register of land charges;
 (b) a register of pending actions;
 (c) a register of writs and orders affecting land;
 (d) a register of deeds of arrangement affecting land;
 (e) a register of annuities,

and shall also continue to keep there an index whereby all entries made in any of those registers can readily be traced.

(2) Every application to register shall be in the prescribed form and shall contain the prescribed particulars.

(3) Where any charge or other matter is registrable in more than one of the registers kept under this Act, it shall be sufficient if it is registered in one such register, and if it is so registered the person entitled to the benefit of it shall not be prejudicially affected by any provision of this Act as to the effect of non-registration in any such register. . . .

2. The register of land charges

(1) If a charge on or obligation affecting land falls into one of the classes described in this section, it may be registered in the register of land charges as a land charge of that class.

(2) A class A land charge is—

 (a) a rent or annuity or principal money payable by instalments or otherwise, with or without interest, which is not a charge created by deed but is a charge upon land (other than a rate) created pursuant to the application of some person under the provisions of any Act of Parliament, for securing to any person either the money spent by him or the costs, charges and expenses incurred by him under such Act, or the money advanced by him for repaying the money spent or the costs, charges and expenses incurred by another person under the authority of an Act of Parliament; or

(b)   a rent or annuity or principal money payable as mentioned in paragraph (a) above which is not a charge created by deed but is a charge upon land (other than a rate) created pursuant to the application of some person under any of the enactments mentioned in Schedule 2 to this Act.

(3)   A Class B land charge is a charge on land (not being a local land charge . . .) of any kind described in paragraph (a) of subsection (2) above, created otherwise than pursuant to the application of any person.

(4)   A Class C land charge is any of the following (not being a local land charge), namely—

(i)   a puisne mortgage;

(ii)   a limited owner's charge;

(iii)   a general equitable charge;

(iv)   an estate contract;

and for this purpose—

(i)   a puisne mortgage is a legal mortgage which is not protected by a deposit of documents relating to the legal estate affected;

(ii)   a limited owner's charge is an equitable charge aquired by a tenant for life or statutory owner under the Capital Transfer Tax Act 1984 or under any other statute by reason of the discharge by him of any capital transfer tax or other liabilities and to which special priority is given by the statute;

(iii)   a general equitable charge is any equitable charge which—

(a)   is not secured by a deposit of documents relating to the legal estate affected; and

(b)   does not arise or affect an interest arising under a [trust of land] or a settlement; and

(c)   is not a charge given by way of idemnity against rents equitable apportioned or charged exclusively on land in exoneration of other land and against the breach or non-observance of covenants or conditions; and

(d)   is not included in any other class of land charge;

(iv)   an estate contract is a contract by an estate owner or by a person entitled at the date of the contract to have a legal estate conveyed to him to convey or create a legal estate, including a contract conferring either expressly or by statutory implication a valid option to purchase, a right of pre-emption or any other like right.

(5)   A Class D land charge is any of the following (not being a local land charge), namely—

(i)   an Inland Revenue Charge;

(ii)   a restrictive covenant;

(iii)   an equitable easement;

and for this purpose—

(i)   an Inland Revenue charge is a charge on land, being a charge acquired by the Board under the Capital Transfer Tax Act 1984;

(ii)   a restrictive covenant is a covenant or agreement (other than a covenant or agreement between a lessor and a lessee) restrictive of the user of land and entered into on or after 1st January 1926;

(iii)   an equitable easement is an easement, right or privilege over or affecting land created or arising on or after 1st January 1926, and being merely an equitable interest.

(6)   A Class E land charge is an annuity created before 1st January 1926 and not registered in the register of annuities.

(7)   A Class F land charge is a charge affecting any land by virtue of the Matrimonial Homes Act 1983.

(8)   A charge or obligation created before 1st January 1926 can only be registered as a Class B land charge or a Class C land charge if it is acquired under a conveyance made on or after that date.

(9)   . . .

3.   Registration of land charges

(1)   A land charge shall be registered in the name of the estate owner whose estate is intended to be affected. . . .

4. Effect of land charges and protection of purchasers

(1)   A land charge of Class A (other than a land improvement charge registered after 31st December 1969) or of Class B shall, when registered, take effect as if it had been created by a deed of charge by way of legal mortgage, but without prejudice to the priority of the charge.

(2)   A land charge of Class A created after 31st December 1888 shall be void as against a purchaser of the land charged with it or of any interest in such land, unless the land charge is registered in the register of land charges before the completion of the purchase.

(3)   After the expiration of one year from the first conveyance occurring on or after 1st January 1889 of a land charge of Class A created before that date the person entitled to the land charge shall not be able to recover the land charge or any part of it as against a purchaser of the land charged with it or of any interest in the land, unless the land charge is registered in the register of land charges before the completion of the purchase.

(4)   If a land improvement charge was registered as a land charge of Class A before 1st January 1970, any body corporate which, but for the charge, would have power to advance money on the security of the estate or interest affected by it shall have that power notwithstanding the charge.

(5)   A land charge of Class B and a land charge of Class C (other than an estate contract) created or arising on or after 1st January 1926 shall be void as against a purchaser of the land charged with it, or of any interest in such land, unless the land charge is registered in the appropriate register before the completion of the purchase.

(6)   An estate contract and a land charge of Class D created or entered into on or after 1st January 1926 shall be void as against a purchaser for money or money's worth (or, in the case of an Inland Revenue charge, a purchaser within the meaning of the Capital Transfer Tax Act 1984) of a legal estate in the land charged with it, unless the land charge is registered in the appropriate register before the completion of the purchase.

(7)   After the expiration of one year from the first conveyance occurring on or after 1st January 1926 of a land charge of Class B or Class C created before that date the person entitled to the land charge shall not be able to enforce or recover the land charge or any part of it as against a purchaser of the land charged with it, or of any interest in the land, unless the land charge is registered in the appropriate register before the completion of the purchase.

(8)   A land charge of Class F shall be void as against a purchaser of the land charged with it, or of any interest in such land, unless the land charge is registered in the appropriate register before the completion of the purchase.

11.   Date of effective registration and priority notices

(1)   Any person intending to make an application for the registration of any contemplated charge, instrument or other matter in pursuance of this Act or any rule made under this Act may give a priority notice in the prescribed form at least the relevant number of days before the registration is to take effect.

(2)   Where a notice is given under subsection (1) above, it shall be entered in the register to which the intended application when made will relate.

(3)   If the application is presented within the relevant number of days thereafter and refers in the prescribed manner to the notice, the registration shall take effect as if the registration had been made at the time when the charge, instrument or matter was created, entered into, made or arose, and the date at which the registration so takes effect shall be deemed to be the date of registration.

(4)   Where—

(a)   any two charges, instruments or matters are contemporaneous; and

(b)   one of them (whether or not protected by a priority notice) is subject to or dependent on the other; and

(c)   the latter is protected by a priority notice,

the subsequent or dependent charge, instrument or matter shall be deemed to have been created, entered into or made, or to have arisen, after the registration of the other.

(5)   Where a purchaser has obtained a certificate under section 10 above, any entry which is made in the register after the date of the certificate and before the completion of the purchase, and is not made pursuant to a priority notice entered on the register on or before the date of the certificate, shall not affect the purchaser if the purchase is completed before the expiration of the relevant number of days after the date of the certificate.

(6)   The relevant number of days is—
   (a)   for the purposes of subsections (1) and (5) above, fifteen;
   (b)   for the purposes of subsection (3) above, thirty;

or such other numbers as may be prescribed; but in reckoning the relevant number of days for any of the purposes of this section any days when the registry is not open to the public shall be excluded.

13.   Saving for overreaching powers

(1)   The registration of any charge, annuity or other interest under this Act shall not prevent the charge, annuity or interest being overreached under any other Act, except where otherwise provided by that other Act.

(2)   The registration as a land charge of a puisne mortgage or charge shall not operate to prevent that mortgage or charge being overreached in favour of a prior mortgagee or a person deriving title under him where, by reason of a sale or foreclosure, or otherwise, the right of the puisne mortgagee or subsequent chargee to redeem is barred.

HOLLINGTON BROTHERS LTD v RHODES AND ANOTHER [1951] 2 All ER 578, Chancery Division

FACTS: H 'leased' some offices to R for seven years by a document which was not a deed. R therefore acquired only an equitable lease. R took possession of the premises but failed to register his lease as a land charge (equitable leases are registrable as Class C(iv) Land Charges under the Land Charges Act 1972—the successor statute to the Land Charges Act 1925 which was then in force). H later sold his reversion to D, the sale being expressly 'subject to and with the benefit of such tenancies as may affect the premises'.

HELD: The equitable lease was valid against H, but not against D, despite the fact that D undoubtedly had notice of the existence of the tenancy.

HARMAN J: . . . held that there was no contract between the plaintiffs and the defendants as alleged by the plaintiffs and continued: If I am right, the action fails and I need go no further, but it may be useful that I should express a view on two further points which were fully argued before me:—(i) assuming that there was a contract such as the plaintiffs alleged, was there a breach by the defendants; and (ii) if so, what is the proper measure of damages? After 1925 by virtue of the Land Charges Act 1925, s. 10(1), this contract came within class C(iv) as a 'charge or obligation affecting land,' and, therefore, might be registered as a land charge in the register of land charges. Accordingly, by virtue of s. 13 (2), this being a land charge of class C, it is void '. . . against a purchaser of the land charged therewith, or of any interest in such land, unless the land charge is registered in the appropriate register before the completion of the purchase . . .'. Moreover, by the Law of Property Act 1925, s. 199(1)(i), a purchaser is not to be prejudicially affected by notice of any instrument or matter capable of registration under the Land Charges Act 1925, which is void against him by reason of non-registration. This land charge was not registered, and, accordingly, it is said that it was void against Daymar Estates Ltd., notwithstanding their notice or knowledge, and, moreover, that there was no duty lying on the plaintiffs to register the contract to prevent this result.

    . . . The defendants' answer to this point was that Daymar Estates Ltd, did not contract to obtain, and did not by the assignment get, any estate in the land expressed to override the plaintiffs' rights, and that, consequently, they took subject to those rights, which are expressly mentioned, and that the land which they purchased was, in fact, only an interest in the land subject to the rights of the plaintiffs in it. This argument seemed to me attractive because it appears at first glance wrong that a purchaser, who knows perfectly well of rights and is expressed to take subject to them, should be able to ignore them.

    . . . It seems to me, however, that this argument cannot prevail having regard to the words in s. 13(2) of the Land Charges Act 1925, coupled with the definition of 'land' in s. 20(6) of the Act. The fact is that it was the policy of the framers of the legislation of 1925 to get rid of equitable rights of this kind unless registered. . . .

    . . . Finally, as under the Land Charges Act 1925, s. 13(2), an unregistered estate contract is void as against a purchaser of the land, and under the Law of Property Act 1925, s. 199(1), the purchaser is not to be prejudicially affected by it, I do not see how that which is void and which is not to prejudice the purchaser can be validated by some equitable doctrine. There is, after all, no great hardship in this. The plaintiffs could, at any time until the completion of the assignment to Daymar Estates Ltd, have preserved their rights by registration, just as the defendants could have protected their obligations by completing the underlease, of which Daymar Estates Ltd, could not have complained as they knew all about it. . . .

8.1.1 SEARCHES OF THE LAND CHARGES REGISTER

OAK CO-OPERATIVE BUILDING SOCIETY v BLACKBURN AND OTHERS
[1968] 1 Ch 730, Court of Appeal

FACTS: The defendant, Francis David Blackburn, had granted a mortgage of his land. This mortgage was registered in the Land Charges register against the name 'Francis David Blackburn'. Later Mr Blackburn agreed to sell his land to a Ms Caines. She registered this agreement (an estate contract) as a class C(iv) Land Charge against the name 'Frank David Blackburn'. She entered into possession of the land on the strength of the agreement. Still later Mr Blackburn granted the second mortgage on his land to a building society. Before making the loan the building society searched the Land Charges register against the name 'Francis Davis Blackburn'. This search revealed the first mortgage, but not the estate contract. On the strength of the results of the search, the building society made a loan to Mr Blackburn secured by a second mortgage on his land. In due course Mr Blackburn fell behind on his mortgage repayments and was declared bankrupt. The building society brought the present action for, *inter alia*, a possession order against Ms Caines. The judge at first instance granted the building society possession of the property on grounds that although the building society's search was not carried out accurately, the more important fact was that Ms Caines had failed to register her interest correctly. Ms Caines appealed to the Court of Appeal.

HELD: The appeal was allowed. Ms Caines had registered her interest against a legitimate variation of the estate owner's name. Such a registration would have been ineffective against the building society had it searched the estate owner's correct names, but it would be effective against a building society (or other 'purchaser'), as here, which had failed to make a proper search.

RUSSELL LJ: . . . The question is whether her estate contract is valid against the subsequent legal charge to the plaintiffs as being effectively registered as an estate contract, or whether the use of the name 'Frank' rather than 'Francis' invalidates it.

. . . The application for an official search certificate was against the name 'Francis Davis Blackburn'.

. . . Section 17 [Land Charges Act 1925] provides for an official search. A proposing purchaser (for example) may lodge a requisition for such a search and thereupon the registrar shall 'make the search required, and shall issue a certificate setting forth the result thereof'. Subsection (3) provides that in favour of the intending purchaser as against the person interested under the instrument (here the estate contract) 'the certificate, according to the tenor thereof, shall be conclusive, affirmatively or negatively, as the case may be.' Subsection (4) provides that every such requisition shall be in writing *specifying the name against which* he desires search to be made, or in relation to which he requires a certificate of result of search, and other sufficient particulars.'

. . . The real problem is, what is meant by the name or the names of the estate owner in this legislation?

As a matter of theoretical approach it is obvious that it is intended or hoped by the legislation that every registered land charge will be safeguarded by registration because due diligence in search will reveal it: and correspondingly that every duly diligent search will reveal every registered land charge affecting the land to be purchased. It is realised that if an official search certificate is issued there may be a blunder for which some innocent person must suffer, and s. 17(3) provides, for example, that if a nil certificate is given the owner of the land charge suffers, however valid his registration. But it would be supposed that it would be intended to reduce error to a minimum. What then is meant by the requirement that the name—surname and Christian names—of the estate owner be given when requisitioning a search? People use different names at different times and for different purposes. But the matter now under consideration relates to two things: first, the investigation into the soundness of the paper title of a proposed vendor by a proposed purchaser: second, the attempt to prevent by registration the disposal by the owner of that paper title of the legal estate in a manner which will override the interest of the owner of the land charge.

In the case of a request for an official search, which of course takes place before completion after the title examined, we can only think that the name or names referred to in the request should be that or those appearing on the title. A nil certificate here as to Francis Davis *Blackburn* would not have served to override the third defendants land charge had it been registered in the name of Francis Davi*d Blackburn*, though it *could* have been issued. . . .

. . . If a proposing purchaser here had requested a search in the correct full names he would have got a clean certificate and a clear title under s. 17(3) of the Land Charges Act 1925, and would have suffered no harm from the fact that the registration was not in such names: and a person registering who is not in a position to satisfy himself what are the correct full names runs that risk. But if there be registration in what may be fairly described as a version of the full names of the vendor, albeit not a version which is bound to be discovered on a search in the correct names, we would not hold it a nullity against someone who does not search at all, or who (as here) searches in the wrong name.

There is one objection to this approach, and that is that provision is made for personal as distinct from official search: . . .

. . . But we think that anyone who nowadays is foolish enough to search personally deserves what he gets: and if the aim of the statute is to arrive at a sensible working system that aim is better furthered by upholding a registration such as this than protecting a personal searcher from his folly. . . .

DILIGENT FINANCE CO. LTD v *ALLEYNE AND ANOTHER* (1972) 23 P&CR 346, Chancery Division

FACTS: Diligent Finance Co. Ltd brought this action for possession of a matrimonial home currently occupied by the second defendant, Cynthia Alleyne. She had been deserted by her husband, Erskine Owen Alleyne, the first defendant to the action. The plaintiff was the holder of a mortgage against the matrimonial home which had been executed in the name of the first defendant only. The second defendant had registered her matrimonial rights of occupation as a 'Class F' land charge against the name Erskine Alleyne. She should have registered her charge against her husband's full name, Erskine Owen Alleyne, for that was the name appearing on the conveyance to him and on the mortgage to the plaintiff.
HELD: The Class F land charge did not rank ahead of the legal charge of the plaintiff. The plaintiff was awarded possession.

FOSTER J: . . . Valiant efforts have been made by the second defendant to discover what the true names are of her husband—who in fact went back to Barbados the day after he had obtained the new charge, i.e. on February 19 1970—but a certificate of registration of birth which is forthcoming and which is dated March 2 1972, shows a certificate of registration of birth but under the column 'Baptismal name if added after registration of birth' there is given no name at all, and counsel for the second defendant told me that he had tried to get a baptismal certificate but that it had not been forthcoming.

The question therefore is whether the court is entitled to assume from the conveyancing documents which I have mentioned that the first defendant's name Erskine Owen Alleyne is in fact his real and full name. It was pointed out on behalf of the plaintiff that no one was in a better position to know what the full name of her husband was than his wife, and further it was pointed out that the second defendant must have known that the freehold property was mortgaged to the Greater London Council where one could find the name Erskine Owen Alleyne.

In my judgment, in the absence of any other evidence— and there is none— it is right for the court, following Ungoed-Thomas J's statement in the court below and Russell L J, in the Court of Appeal, to assume in the absence of evidence to the contrary that the proper name of a person is that in which the conveyancing documents have been taken. It is unfortunate, to say the least, that the Class F registration was not made against the proper name Erskine Owen Alleyne but only against Erskine Alleyne, but that is a mistake which I for my part cannot unfortunately rectify. If follows that the official certificate granted to the plaintiff on February 13 1970, under s. 17(3) of the Land Charges Act 1925 is conclusive and that the Class F charge does not rank ahead of the legal charge of the plaintiff.

8.1.2 EQUITABLE INTERESTS REGISTRABLE AS LAND CHARGES

SHILOH SPINNERS LTD v *HARDING* [1973] AC 691, House of Lords

FACTS: The plaintiffs had assigned their leasehold interest to a company, T Ltd., which promised to meet certain leasehold obligations. Upon a failure by T Ltd. to meet any of those obligations, the plaintiffs were to be entitled to exercise a right of re-entry. This right of re-entry was not registered as a Land Charge. The question therefore arose whether it was binding on a purchaser from T Ltd.
HELD: The equitable right of re-entry did not fall within any of the categories of Land Charges. Accordingly, it did not need to be protected by registration as a Land Charge, and would be binding on the purchaser.

LORD WILBERFORCE: The right of entry, it is said, is unenforceable against the respondent, although he took with actual notice of it, because it was not registered as a charge under the Land Charges Act 1925. There is no doubt that if it was capable of registration under that Act, it is unenforceable if not registered: the appellants deny that it was so capable either (i) because it was a legal right, not an equitable right, or (ii) because if equitable, it does not fall within any of the classes or descriptions of charges registration of which is required.

I consider first whether the right of entry is legal in character or equitable, using these adjectives in the technical sense in which they are used in the 1925 property legislation. The question is purely one of statutory definition, the ingredients of which are found in ss. 1 and 205(1)(x) of the Law of Property Act 1925. The contention that the right is legal was not accepted by Burgess V-C or advanced in the Court of Appeal below, nor was it contained in the printed case signed by eminent counsel, though if it were upheld it would be decisive of the case. The appellants were, however, permitted to lodge an amended case raising the point. I set out for convenience s. 1(1), (2) and (3) of the Act. The definition s. 205(1)(x) uses the same verbiage and adds nothing to the argument.

(1) The only estates in land which are capable of subsisting or of being conveyed or created at law are—(a) An estate in fee simple absolute in possession; (b) A term of years absolute. (2) The only interests or charges in or over land which are capable of subsisting or of being conveyed or created at law are—(a) An easement, right, or privilege in or over land for an interest equivalent to an estate in fee simple absolute in possession or a term of years absolute; (b) A rentcharge in possession issuing out of or charged on land being either perpetual or for a term of years absolute; (c) A charge by way of legal mortgage; (d) Land tax, tithe rentcharge, and any other similar charge on land which is not created by an instrument; (e) Rights of entry exercisable over or in respect of a legal term of years absolute, or annexed, for any purpose, to a legal rentcharge. (3) All other estates, interests, and charges on or over land take effect as equitable interests.

The right of entry in this case is not contained in a lease, so as to be annexed to a reversion, nor is it exercisable for a term of years, or (comparably with a fee simple) indefinitely. Its duration is limited by a perpetuity period. Whether it can be said to be 'exercisable over or in respect of a legal term of years absolute' appears obscure. It is not exercisable for a legal term of years (whether that granted by the lease or any other term): it is not so exercisable as to determine a legal term of years. To say that a right of entry is exercisable in respect of a legal term of years appears to me, with respect, to be without discernible meaning. The effect of this right of entry is to cause a legal term of years to be divested from one person to another upon an event which may occur over a perpetuity period. It would, I think, be contrary to the whole scheme of the Act, which requires the limiting and vesting of legal estates and interests to be by reference to a fee simple or a term of years absolute, to allow this to rank as a legal interest. In my opinion it is clearly equitable.

. . . There is certainly nothing exhaustive about the expression 'equitable interests'—just as certainly it has no clear boundaries. The debate whether such rights as equity, over the centuries, has conferred against the holder of the legal estate are truly proprietary in character, or merely *in personam*, or a hybrid between the two, may have lost some of its vitality in the statutory context but the question inevitably rises to mind whether the 'curtain' or 'overreaching' provisions of the 1925 legislation extend to what are still conveniently called 'equities' or 'mere equities' such as rights to rectification, or to set aside a conveyance. There is good authority, which I do not presume to doubt, for a sharp distinction between the two—I instance Lord Upjohn in *National Provincial Bank Ltd* v *Hastings Car Mart Ltd* [1965] AC 1175, 1238 and *Snell's Principles of Equity*, 25th edn. (1960) p. 38. I am impressed by the decision in *E. R. Ives Investment Ltd* v *High* [1967] 2 QB 379 in which the Court of Appeal held that a right by estoppel—producing an effect similar to an easement—was not registrable under Class D(iii). Lord Denning MR referred to the right as subsisting only in equity. Danckwerts LJ thought it was an equity created by estoppel or a proprietary estoppel: plainly this was not an equitable interest capable of being overreached, yet no member of the court considered that the right—so like an easement—could be brought within Class D(iii). The conclusion followed, and the court accepted it, that whether it was binding on a purchaser depended on notice. All this seems to show that there may well be rights, of an equitable character, outside the provisions as to registration and which are incapable of being overreached.

That equitable rights of entry should be among them is not in principle unacceptable. First, rights of entry, before 1925, were not considered to confer an interest in the land. They were described as bare possibilities (*Challis's Real Property*, 3rd edn. (1911), p. 76) so that it is not anomalous that equitable rights of entry should not be treated as equitable interests. Secondly, it is important that s. 10 of the Land Charges Act 1925 should be given a plain and ordinary interpretation. It is a section which involves day to day operation by solicitors doing conveyancing work: they should be able to take decisions and advise their clients upon a straightforward interpretation of the registration classes, not upon one depending upon a sophisticated, not to say dsiputable, analysis of other statutes. Thirdly, the consequence of equitable rights of entry not being registrable is that they are subject to the doctrine of notice, preserved by s. 199 of the Law of Property Act. This may not give complete protection, but neither is it demonstrable that it is likely to be less effective than the present system of registration against names. I am therefore of opinion that Class D(iii) should be given its plain prima facie meaning and that so read it does not comprise equitable rights of entry. It follows that non-registration does not make the appellants' rights unenforceable in this case.

8.1.3   CONSEQUENCES OF FAILURE TO REGISTER A LAND CHARGE

MIDLAND BANK TRUST CO. LTD v *GREEN* [1981] AC 513, House of Lords

FACTS: In this case a father owned a farm. He granted his son an option to purchase the farm at any time in the next ten years. The son should have registered this option (technically a form of 'estate contract') as a Class C(iv) Land Charge, but he omitted to do so. Father and son later fell out. In order to deprive the son, the father sold the farm (worth about £40,000) to his wife for just £500. The wife, of course knew all about the option. After the wife's death, her son brought an action against her estate to establish that his option was binding on the land. The Court of Appeal held that the wife's estate was bound by the option. That court held that 'money or money's worth' meant a fair price, which clearly £500 was not. The executors of the wife's estate appealed to the House of Lords.
HELD: The wife's estate was not bound by her son's option.

LORD WILBERFORCE: My Lords, this appeal relates to a 300-acre farm in Lincolnshire called 'Gravel Hill Farm.' It was owned by Walter Stanley Green ('Walter') and since 1954, let to his son Thomas Geoffrey Green ('Geoffrey') who farmed it as tenant. Walter owned another larger farm which he farmed jointly with another son Robert Derek Green ('Robert'), the appellant. In 1960 Walter sold this other farm to Robert at £75 per acre.

On March 24, 1961, Walter granted to Geoffrey an option to purchase Gravel Hill Farm, also at £75 per acre. The option was granted for the consideration of £1, and so was contractually binding upon Walter. It was to remain open for ten years. It seems that the reason why this transaction was entered into, rather than one of sale to Geoffrey, was to save estate duty on Walter's death.

This option was, in legal terms, an estate contract and so a legal charge, Class C, within the meaning of the Land Charges Act 1925. The correct and statutory method for protection of such an option is by means of entering it in the Register of Land Charges maintained under the Act. If so registered, the option would have been enforceable, not only (contractually) against Walter, but against any purchaser of the farm.

The option was not registered, a failure which inevitably called in question the responsibility of Geoffrey's solicitor. . . .

. . . the case appears to be a plain one. The 'estate contract,' which by definition (s. 11) includes an option of purchase, was entered into after January 1 1926: Evelyne took an interest (in fee simple) in the land 'for valuable consideration'—so was a 'purchaser': she was a purchaser for money—namely £500: the option was not registered before the completion of the purchase. It is therefore void as against her.

In my opinion this appearance is also the reality. The case is plain: the Act is clear and definite. Intended as it was to provide a simple and understandable system for the protection of title to land, it should not be read down or glossed: to do so would destroy the usefulness of the Act. Any temptation to remould the Act to meet the facts of the present case, on the supposition that it is a hard one and that justice requires it, is, for me at least, removed by the consideration that the Act itself provides a simple and effective protection for persons in Geoffrey's position—*viz*—by registration.

The respondents submitted two arguments as to the interpretation of s. 13(2): the one sought to introduce into it a requirement that the purchaser should be 'in good faith': the other related to the words 'in money or money's worth.'. . .

As to the requirement of 'good faith' we are faced with a situation of some perplexity. The expression 'good faith' appears in the Law of Property Act 1925 definition of 'purchaser' ('a purchaser in good faith for valuable consideration'), s. 205(1)(xxi); in the Settled Land Act 1925, s. 117(1)(xxi) (ditto); in the Administration of Estates Act 1925, s. 55(1)(xviii) ('"Purchaser" means a lessee, mortagee or other person who in good faith acquires an interest in property for valuable consideration') and in the Land Registration Act 1925, s. 3(xxi) which does not however, as the other Acts do, include a reference to nominal consideration. So there is certainly some indication of an intention to carry the concept of 'good faith' into much of the 1925 code. What then do we find in the Land Charges Act 1925? We were taken along a scholarly peregrination through the numerous Acts antecedent to the final codification and consolidation in 1925. . . .

My Lords, I recognise that the inquiring mind may put the question: why should there be an omission of the requirement of good faith in this particular context? I do not think there should be much doubt about the answer. Addition of a requirement that the purchaser should be in good faith would bring with it the necessity of inquiring into the purchaser's motives and state of mind. The present case is a good example of the difficulties which would exist. If the position was simply that the purchaser had notice of the option, and decided nevertheless to buy the land, relying on the absence of notification, nobody could contend that she would be lacking in good faith. She would merely be taking advantage of a situation, which the law has provided, and the addition of a profit motive could not create an absence of good faith. But suppose, and this is the respondents' argument, the purchaser's motive is to defeat the option, does this make any difference? Any advantage to oneself seems necessarily to involve a disadvantage for another: to make the validity of the purchase depend upon which aspect of the transaction was prevalent in the purchaser's mind seems to create distinctions equally difficult to analyse in law as to establish in fact: avarice and malice may be distinct sins, but in human conduct they are liable to be intertwined. The problem becomes even more acute if one supposes a mixture of motives. Suppose—and this may not be far from the truth—that the purchaser's motives were in part to take the farm from Geoffrey, and in part to distribute it between Geoffrey and his brothers and sisters, but not at all to obtain any benefit for herself, is this acting in 'good faith' or not? Should family feeling be denied a protection afforded to simple greed? To eliminate the necessity for inquiries of this kind may well have been part of the legislative intention. Certainly there is here no argument for departing—violently—from the wording of the Act. . . .

My Lords, I can deal more shortly with the respondents' second argument. It relates to the consideration for the purchase. The argument is that the protection of s. 13(2) of the Land Charges Act 1925 does not extend to a purchaser who has provided only a nominal consideration and that £500 is nominal. A variation of this was the argument accepted by the Court of Appeal that the consideration must be 'adequate'—an expression of transparent difficulty. The answer to both contentions lies in the language of the subsection. The word 'purchaser,' by definition (s. 20(8)), means one who provides valuable consideration—a term of art which precludes any inquiry as to adequacy. This definition is, of course, subject to the context. Section 13(2), proviso, requires money or money's worth to be provided: the purpose of this being to exclude the consideration of marriage. There is nothing here which suggests, or admits of, the introduction of a further requirement that the money must not be nominal.

The argument for this requirement is based upon the Law of Property Act 1925 which, in s. 205(1)(xxi) defining 'purchaser' provides that 'valuable consideration' includes marriage but does not include a 'nominal consideration in money.' The Land Charges Act 1925 contains no definition of 'valuable consideration,' so it is said to be necessary to have resort to the Law of Property Act definition: thus 'nominal consideration in money,' is excluded. An indication that this is intended is said to be provided by s. 199(1)(i). I cannot accept this. The fallacy lies in supposing that the Acts—either of them—set out to define 'valuable consideration'; they do not: they define 'purchaser,' and they define the word differently (see the first part of the argument). 'Valuable consideration' requires no definition: it is an expression denoting an advantage conferred or detriment suffered. What each Act does is, for its own purposes, to exclude some things from this general expression: the Law of Property Act includes marriage but not a nominal sum in money; the Land Charges Act excludes marriage but allows 'money or money's worth.' There is no coincidence between these two; no link by reference or necessary logic between them. Section 199(1)(i) by referring to the Land Charges Act 1925, necessarily incorporates—for the purposes of this provision—the definition of 'purchaser' in the latter Act, for it is only against such a 'purchaser' that an instrument is void under this Act. It cannot be read as incorporating the Law of Property Act definition into the Land Charges Act. As I have pointed out the land charges legislation has contained its own definition since 1888, carried through, with the addition of the reference to 'money or money's worth' into 1925. To exclude a nominal sum of money from s. 13(2) of the Land Charges Act would be to rewrite the section.

This conclusion makes it unnecessary to determine whether £500 is a nominal sum of money or not. But I must say that for my part I should have great difficulty in so holding. 'Nominal consideration' and a 'nominal sum' in the law appear to me, as terms of art, to refer to a sum or consideration which can be mentioned as consideration but is not necessarily paid. To equate 'nominal' with 'inadequate' or even 'grossly inadequate' would embark the law upon inquiries which I cannot think were contemplated by Parliament.

I would allow the appeal.

LLOYDS BANK v CARRICK (1996) 146 NLJ 405, Court of Appeal

FACTS: B contracted to sell a long lease of a maisonette to S. A deed transferring the lease was never executed. However, S paid the price, took possession and (it appears) spent a lot of money upon the property. B later mortgaged the lease to the Bank. S had never registered her 'estate contract' to purchase the lease as a class C(iv) Land Charge. Her estate contract was therefore void as against the Bank. However, S claimed that, in addition to her estate contract, she also had a constructive trust or proprietary estoppel interest which would be binding on the Bank under the doctrine of notice as it had not made adequate enquiries.

HELD: The Court of Appeal rejected S's claim. If a person acquires an estate contract to purchase a property, that person cannot in addition claim a constructive trust or proprietary estoppel interest however much money and/or effort she/he has expended.

MORRITT LJ: [In] this case as Mrs Carrick had paid the whole of the purchase price at the time the contract became enforceable Mr Carrick as the vendor had no beneficial interest. Thus he may properly be described as a bare trustee . . . It follows that at all times after November 1982 Mrs Carrick was the absolute beneficial owner of the maisonette and Mr Carrick was a trustee of it without any beneficial interest in it. The argument for Mrs Carrick relied on the relative position at law and in equity . . . to found the argument that such an absolute equitable interest was not itself registrable but bound the bank as they had constructive notice of it . . . For my part I am unable to accept this analysis. The payment of £19,000 by Mrs Carrick to Mr Carrick did not as such and without more give her any interest in the maisonette. Nor, prior to the conclusion of the contract, were the circumstances such that Mrs Carrick could assert that her brother-in-law held the maisonette on any trust for her benefit. The source and origin of the trust was the contract; the payment of the price by Mrs Carrick served only to make it a bare trust by removing any beneficial interest of Mr Carrick. Section 4(6) of the Land Charges Act 1972 avoids that contract as against the bank. The result, in my judgment, must be that Mrs Carrick is unable to establish the bare trust as against the bank for it has no existence except as the equitable consequence of the contract. Accordingly, I reject the contention founded on the bare trust.

The second contention for Mrs Carrick was to the effect that she was entitled to the whole beneficial interest in the maisonette arising under a constructive trust and that that interest was not registrable so that the bank having had constructive notice of it took subject to it. For this proposition her counsel relied on the speech of Lord Bridge in *Lloyds Bank plc* v *Rosset* [1990] 1 All ER 1111 . . . counsel recognised that in this case the contract between Mr Carrick and Mrs Carrick was entered into after Mr Carrick had taken an assignment of the lease into his own name. But he submitted that the same principle applied and for that purpose relied on the statement of Lord Oliver of Aylmerton in giving the opinion of the Privy Council in *Austin* v *Keele* (1987) 61 ALJR 605 at 609 . . . counsel for Mrs Carrick submitted that if there had been no contract then on the proper application of these principles there would have been a constructive trust in favour of Mrs Carrick. From this he argued that Mrs Carrick should not be in any worse position just because there was a contract.

In this case there was a trust of the maisonette for the benefit of Mrs Carrick precisely because there had been an agreement between her and Mr Carrick which, for her part, she had substantially if not wholly performed. As between her and Mr Carrick such trust subsisted at all times after November 1982.

I agree with counsel for the bank that there is no room in those circumstances for the implication or imposition of any further trust of the maisonette for the benefit of Mrs Carrick. In *Lloyds Bank plc* v *Rosset* there was no contract which conferred any interest in the house on the wife [and] there is nothing in [the case] to suggest that where there is a specifically enforceable contract the court is entitled to superimpose a further constructive trust on the vendor in favour of the purchaser over that which already exists in consequence of the contractual relationship.

It is true that on this footing the ultimate position of Mrs Carrick with the benefit of a specifically enforceable contract may be worse than it would have been if there had been no contract. But that is because she failed to do that which Parliament has ordained must be done if her interest is to prevail over that of the bank, namely register the estate contract. Her failure in that respect cannot, in my view, justify the implication or imposition of a trust after the execution of the charge when the dealings between Mr Carrick and Mrs Carrick before such execution did not. For these reasons I would reject the second point on which Mrs Carrick relied.

The third contention was that Mrs Carrick is entitled to the benefit of a proprietary estoppel . . . Reliance was placed on the decisions of this court in *Inwards* v *Baker* [1965] 1 All ER 446 and *Ives Investments Ltd* v *High* [1967] 1 All ER 504 as establishing that such an estoppel gives rise to an interest in land capable of binding a successor in title with notice. This was disputed by counsel for the bank . . . she relied on *Western Fish Products Ltd* v *Penwith DC* [1981] 2 All ER 204. Further she submitted that the facts did not warrant such an estoppel as they did not cover all the elements referred to as 'probanda' in *Willmott* v *Barber* (1880) 15 Ch D 96 and were otherwise insufficient. In addition she submitted that such an estoppel cannot give rise to an interest in land capable of binding successors in title with notice . . . With regard to the second submission of counsel for the bank I think that it is now clear that to constitute the requisite estoppel it is not necessary to establish all of the five elements or 'probanda' referred to by Fry J in *Willmot v Barber*. In his judgment in *Taylor Fashions Ltd v Liverpool Victoria Trustees Co. Ltd* [1981] 1 All ER 897 Oliver J traced through the subsequent cases [and I] would respectfully agree with [his] conclusion . . . that proof of all those elements or 'probanda' is not necessary to found an estoppel . . .

In my judgment the claim of Mrs Carrick fails on a number of grounds. First, as in the case of the constructive trust, I do not see how there is any room for the application of the principles of proprietary estoppel when at the time of the relevant expenditure there was already a bare trust arising in consequence of an enforceable contract to the same effect as the interest sought pursuant to the proprietary estoppel . . . Thus at the time that she paid the price and committed herself to the expenditure on the subsequent improvements she believed, rightly, that she was spending the money in respect of her own property albeit under an uncompleted contract. In this respect I see no relevant distinction between this case and that of *Western Fish Products Ltd v Penwith DC*.

Second, this is not a case in which the expectations of Mrs Carrick have been defeated by Mr Carrick seeking to resile from the position he had encouraged her to expect . . . Mrs Carrick's expectations have been defeated because the contract was not registered at any time before the charge was granted and Parliament has decreed that in those circumstances the contract is void against the bank.

Third, it was common ground that the right arising from a proprietary estoppel cannot exceed that which the party sought to be estopped encouraged the other to believe that she had or would acquire. The party sought to be estopped is Mr Carrick. In so far as he encouraged Mrs Carrick to believe that she was or would become the beneficial owner of the maisonette there is no further right to be obtained for she was, and, subject to the charge, still is . . . Section 4(6) of the 1972 Act invalidates, as against the bank, any unregistered contract by the estate owner for the conveyance of the legal estate. It cannot be unconscionable for the bank to rely on the non-registration of the contract. I do not see how it could be right to confer on Mrs Carrick indirectly and by means of a proprietary estoppel binding on the bank that which Parliament prevented her from obtaining directly by the contract it has declared to be void. To avoid any future misunderstanding I would emphasise that there was and is a valid and enforceable contract as against the vendor. Accordingly this case is quite unlike those which may become more prevalent where there is no contract at all not because there was no agreement but because the agreement was not in writing as now required by s. 2, Law of Property (Miscellaneous Provisions) Act 1989.

In my judgment the claim based on proprietary estoppel fails . . . For all these reasons . . . I would allow this appeal. This result seems to me to be inevitable in the light of the provisions of the 1972 Act and of the Law of Property Act 1925 I quoted earlier. However it should be noted that the result would have been different if the title to the maisonette had been registered. In such a case the interest of Mrs Carrick who was in possession of the maisonette and of whom no enquiry had been made, would have been an overriding interest under s. 70(1)(g) of the Land Registration Act 1925. As such it would have been binding on the bank.

8.1.4 OTHER REGISTERS ASSOCIATED WITH THE LAND CHARGES REGISTER

8.1.4.1 The register of pending actions

PEREZ-ADAMSON v PEREZ-RIVAS [1987] 2 WLR 500, Court of Appeal

FACTS: A wife included in her divorce petition a plea for ancillary relief by way of, *inter alia*, a property adjustment order. She registered this claim against the former matrimonial home as a pending land action. Later, the husband took out a loan with a bank and granted the bank a mortgage over the matrimonial home as security. The bank had failed to make a search of the Land Charges registery and so was unaware of the wife's claim. The husband realised all his assets and left the country without paying off the loan with the bank. The judge at first instance set aside the bank's charge on the matrimonial home. The bank appealed.
HELD: The appeal was dismissed. The wife's pending land action took priority over all subsequent charges on the property.

DILLON LJ: . . . It is common ground in these proceedings, in so far as it is material, that the legal charge in favour of the bank was made for valuable consideration and that the bank acted in relation to it in good faith. It is also clear that the bank had no express notice of any intention on the part of the husband to defeat the wife's claim for financial relief. The case turns on the effect of the registration under s. 5 of the Act of 1972. . . .

The position therefore is that the long-established procedure for the registration of a lis pendens has to be married with the code under the Matrimonial Causes Act 1973 for property adjustment as between spouses. The Land Charges Act 1972 also includes provisions for the registration of various other property rights or interests which have in some cases been previously the subject of registration under quite different statutes.

Taking the whole together, I would accept the view of Stamp LJ that the code, as we now have it, has the effect that the registration of the lis pendens in respect of the wife's claim for property adjustment gives her priority over any subsequent conveyance or mortgage of the property executed by the husband. Mr Lightman urges that that is only so if the other party to the transaction, being supposed to know of the claim for ancillary relief and the property adjustment order, is to be held to have had notice of intention on the part of the husband to defeat the wife's claim for financial relief. If the bank or other third party, not having actual knowledge of the registration and of the existence of the claim for ancillary relief, did not ask any questions, it might be difficult to establish that it had notice of an intention on the part of the husband to defeat the claim for ancillary relief. If the bank or third party did ask but was given a specious but untruthful answer, it would be well nigh impossible for a court to hold that the bank or other third party had the requisite notice of the husband's intention. There would be a very serious lacuna in the protection for the wife which Stamp LJ thought so desirable.

In my judgment there is no such lacuna, and so, for these reasons which are substantially the same as those which the judge in the court below gave, I would dismiss the appeal because the wife's claim for a property adjustment order has priority to the bank's charge and the wife has obtained, from the order of the judge now under appeal an order for the transfer of the proceeds of the property to her. The property was sold pending the hearing, it being common ground that neither spouse was then occupying it.

I would dismiss the appeal.

NICHOLLS LJ: I agree. . . .

The effect of registration of a pending land action in the register of pending actions is, as provided in s. 198(1) of the Law of Property Act 1925, that the registration is 'deemed to constitute actual notice of [the] . . . matter . . . to all persons and for all purposes connected with the land affected . . .' In this case the 'matter' consists of the proceedings in which the property transfer order is being claimed. . . .

MATRIMONIAL CAUSES ACT 1973

24. Property adjustment orders in connection with divorce proceedings, etc

(1) On granting a decree of divorce, a decree of nullity of marriage or a decree of judicial separation or at any time thereafter (whether, in the case of a decree of divorce or of nullity of marriage, before or after the decree is made absolute), the court may make any one or more of the following orders, that is to say—

(a)   an order that a party to the marriage shall transfer to the other party, to any child of the family or to such person as may be specified in the order for the benefit of such a child such property as may be so specified, being property to which the first-mentioned party is entitled, either in possession or reversion;

(b)   an order that a settlement of such property as may be so specified, being property to which a party to the marriage is so entitled, be made to the satisfaction of the court for the benefit of the other party to the marriage and of the children of the family or either or any of them;

(c)   an order varying for the benefit of the parties to the marriage and of the children of the family or either or any of them any ante-nuptial or post-nuptial settlement (including such a settlement made by will or codicil) made on the parties to the marriage;

(d)   an order extinguishing or reducing the interests of either of the parties to the marriage under any such settlement;

subject, however, in the case of an order under paragraph (a) above, to the restrictions imposed by section 29(1) and (3) below on the making of orders for a transfer of property in favour of children who have attained the age of eighteen.

(2)   The court may make an order under subsection (1)(c) above notwithstanding that there are no children of the family.

(3)   Without prejudice to the power to give a direction under section 30 below for the settlement of an instrument by conveyancing counsel, where an order is made under this section on or after granting a decree of divorce or nullity of marriage, neither the order nor any settlement made in pursuance of the order shall take effect unless the decree has been made absolute.

(Note: The Family Law Act 1996, this part of which has not yet come into force, will replace s. 24, Matrimonial Causes Act 1973 with new sections which will preserve the court's power to make property adjustment orders in cases of divorce. It is anticipated under the new scheme, however, that divorcing couples will be responsible for reaching their own negotiated settlement.)

8.2   End of Chapter Assessment Question

In 1960 Ruth purchased the fee simple in Grand Villa, a large country house with two acres of grounds. The title was unregistered in an area which did not become an area of compulsory registration until 1988. Grand Villa was conveyed to Ruth in her sole name.

Four weeks ago William purchased Grand Villa from Ruth. Since the execution of the conveyance, the following matters have come to light.

(a)   Martin, Ruth's husband, has returned from an extended business trip to Malaysia, and is alarmed to discover that Ruth has sold Grand Villa to William. Martin claims that, since in 1980 he paid £200,000 for a total reconstruction of Grand Villa, he has 'rights' which bind William.

(b)   David has arrived at Grand Villa and has produced a document (not in the form of a deed) which Ruth and David signed six months ago. The document is a lease for fifteen years of part of the grounds of Grand Villa.

(c)   Harry, owner of neighbouring Blackview, has arrived at Grand Villa and produced a deed executed some time in the 1920s. (The exact date is difficult to read.) This deed was executed by the then owner of Grand Villa, and contains a restrictive covenant in favour of the owners of Blackview to the effect that Grand Villa is to be used for residential purposes only. William plans to convert Grand Villa into a conference centre.

Advise William as to whether any of these matters will affect him.

8.3   End of Chapter Assessment Outline Answer

(a)   There are TWO types of right which Martin can claim against Grand Villa. The first is his 'Rights of Occupation' granted by the Matrimonial Homes Acts. These rights automatically arise from the fact that he is Ruth's spouse and she had sole title to the matrimonial home.

The 'Rights of Occupation' are classed as an equitable interest, but are not subject to the doctrine of notice; they are registrable as a Land Charge 'Class F'. Almost certainly Martin did not know that he needed to register his Class F charge, and thus it is almost certain that his rights of occupation will not bind William.

Martin's second right is the constructive trust interest which he obtained in Grand Villa through paying £200,000 for a total reconstruction. Cases such as *Lloyds Bank* v *Rosset* (see **1.3.7**) hold that substantial contributions to the cost of purchasing or reconstructing a property will give rise to a constructive trust interest in the contributor's favour.

A constructive trust interest is subject to the equitable Doctrine of Notice. Thus Martin's interest will bind William unless William can prove that he is a bona fide purchaser for value of a legal estate (or interest) without notice of Martin's interest. It is reasonably clear that William is a bona fide purchaser for value of a legal estate. Thus William will take Grand Villa free from Martin's interest if he can prove that at the time of the conveyance he was without notice of Martin's claim.

'Notice' comes in three forms, actual, constructive and imputed. It would appear that at the time of the purchase William had no actual knowledge (i.e. actual notice) of Martin's constructive trust interest. However Martin will probably contend that William had constructive notice of Martin's interest.

Under the constructive notice rule a purchaser of land must make all those enquiries which a reasonable purchaser makes. In particular he must inspect the land for signs of occupiers other than the vendor and investigate the title deeds. If a purchaser fails to make a reasonable enquiry which would have revealed an equitable interest, he will be stuck with constructive notice of that interest.

Martin's interest is not the sort which is revealed in title deeds. But it is the sort which may gain protection from the rule in *Hunt* v *Luck* [1902] 1 Ch 428. If on inspecting the land the (potential) purchaser sees signs of a person other than the vendor occupying the land, then the purchaser must seek out that other person and enquire of him what claim he has to the land.

We must hope that William made a proper inspection of Grand Villa, and that when he made that inspection there were no signs that Martin lived there. . . . Only if that is the case will William be without notice of Martin's interest.

If William employed a surveyor to inspect the land, we must hope that there were no signs of Martin when the surveyor called to inspect. This is because of the imputed notice rule. If a purchaser employs an agent then any (actual or constructive) notice which comes to that agent is automatically attributed to the purchaser with the result that he is bound by the relevant equitable interest.

(b)   As the document granting the lease is not a deed, David has only got an equitable lease. Post-1925 such a lease is not subject to the doctrine of notice. It is registrable as an 'Estate Contract' land charge. It is unlikely that David (who probably did not take legal advice) will have registered. If he has not registered then his equitable lease will be void against William, as William is (apparently) a purchaser for money or money's worth of a legal estate. Moreover it will be void against William even if he actually knew of the equitable lease. (See *Hollington Brothers* v *Rhodes* [1951] 2 All ER 578.)

(c)   Whether the restrictive covenant benefiting Blackview binds William may well depend upon the date it was entered into. The deed produced by Harry must be carefully examined to see whether or not it was executed after 1925.

If it transpires that the 'residential purposes' only covenant was entered into after 1925, then it will be registrable as a land charge. It will only bind William if it was correctly registered as a land charge against the name of the owner of Grand Villa who (back in the 'twenties') entered into the restrictive covenant. If the covenant was not correctly registered it will be void against William, even if he knew about the covenant through looking at the title deeds.

If the covenant was entered into before 1926 then it will not be registrable as a land charge; it will be subject to the old doctrine of notice.

As mentioned earlier, the purchaser of land is expected to investigate the title deeds. If William inspected the deeds and saw the restrictive covenant mentioned, he would have actual notice. If his solicitor inspected the deeds and saw the covenant, William would have imputed notice.

If William (or his solicitor) failed to investigate title properly, with the result that the covenant ought to have been discovered from the deeds but wasn't, then William will have constructive (or constructive imputed) notice.

The duty to investigate deeds is not however a duty to investigate documents back to the time immemorial. It is a duty to go back to the 'root of title'; the root is the most recent conveyance which is at least fifteen years old. When William purchased Grand Villa the root would have been the conveyance to Ruth in 1960. If (as is possible) the 'residential only' covenant is not mentioned in that conveyance (nor in any later document such as a mortgage of Grand Villa produced by Ruth to William or his solicitor), then William will not have notice of the covenant and will not be bound by it.

CHAPTER NINE

REGISTRATION OF TITLE — THE BASIC PRINCIPLES

9.1 Introduction

Lawson, F. H. and Rudden, B., *The Law of Property*, **2nd edn, Oxford: Clarendon Press, 1982, Chapter XVI**

REGISTRATION

. . . Registration has been accepted wholeheartedly for ships, for bills of sale, and for various kinds of companies; and there has been no difficulty in insisting on companies keeping registers of shares and shareholders. Moreover, the practice of proving wills has always carried with it registration.

With land the story has been very different. The obvious advantages attaching to registration have had to fight against many adverse forces, of which the most important have been the desire of landowners and their lawyers to keep transactions secret and the difficulty of placing all the immensely complicated mass of interests that may coexist in land on a single register. During the latter half of the nineteenth century there were among reformers of real property law two opposing schools of thought, the one insisting that registration should be pushed forward as rapidly as possible, the other insisting on its difficulty without a preliminary simplification of the law and on the probability that it would be found unnecessary once the law was simplified. The dispute between the two schools helped to prevent anything being done on either side, but eventually the simplifiers won. Registration has been extended greatly in many ways, but perhaps not so much as if the movement in favour of it had alone held the field. . . .

9.2 Register of Estates not Register of Plots

LAND REGISTRATION ACT 1925

1. Registers to be continued

(1) The Chief Land Registrar shall continue to keep a register of title to freehold land and leasehold land.

(2) The register need not be kept in documentary form.

2. What estates may be registered

(1) After the commencement of this Act, estates capable of subsisting as legal estates shall be the only interests in land in repect of which a proprietor can be registered and all other interests in registered land (except overriding interests and interests entered on the register at or before such commencement) shall take effect in equity, as minor interests, but all interests (except undivided shares in land) entered on the register at such commencement which are not legal estates shall be capable of being dealt with under this Act:

Provided that, on the occasion of the first dealing with any such interest, the register shall be rectified in such manner as may be provided by rules made to secure that the entries therein shall be similar to those which would have been made if the title to the land had been registered after the commencement of this Act.

LAND REGISTRATION ACT 1997

1. Compulsory first registration

The following sections shall be substituted for section 123 of the Land Registration Act 1925—

'123. Compulsory registration: dispositions to which requirement to register applies

(1) The requirement of compulsory registration applies in relation to the following dispositions of unregistered land—

(a) any qualifying conveyance of the freehold estate;

(b) any qualifying grant of a term of years absolute of more than 21 years from the date of the grant;

(c) any qualifying assignment of a term of years absolute which on the date of the assignment has more than 21 years to run; and

(d) any disposition effected by an assent (including a vesting assent) or by a vesting deed which is a disposition of—

(i) the freehold estate, or

(ii) a term of years absolute which on the date of the disposition has more than 21 years to run.

(2) The requirement of compulsory registration also applies in relation to any disposition by the estate owner of unregistered land which is a legal mortgage of—

(a) the freehold estate, or

(b) a term of years absolute which on the date of the mortgage has more than 21 years to run,

where, on its creation, the mortgage takes effect as a mortgage to be protected by the deposit of documents relating to that estate or term of years, and ranks in priority ahead of all other mortgages (if any) then affecting that estate or term of years.

(3) Without prejudice to the power to make an order under subsection (4) below, nothing in this section or section 123A of this Act has the effect of requiring the registration of title to—

(a) an incorporeal hereditament;

(b) mines and minerals apart from the surface; or

(c) corporeal hereditaments which are part of a manor and included in the sale of a manor as such.

(4) The Lord Chancellor may by order—

(a) amend this section so as to add to the dispositions in relation to which the requirement of compulsory registration applies any such disposition of, or otherwise affecting, a legal estate in unregistered land as is specified in the order; and

(b) make such consequential amendments of any provision of, or having effect under, any Act as he thinks appropriate.

(5) Any order under subsection (4) above shall be made by statutory instrument subject to annulment in pursuance of a resolution of either House of Parliament.

(6) For the purposes of this section—

(a) a conveyance, grant or assignment is a 'qualifying' conveyance, grant or assignment if it is made—

(i) for valuable or other consideration,

(ii) by way of gift, or

(iii) in pursuance of an order of any court;

(b) a conveyance, grant or assignment of property with a negative value is to be regarded (without prejudice to the generality of paragraph (a)(i) above) as made for valuable or other consideration; and

(c) 'assignment' does not include an assignment or surrender of a lease to the owner of the immediate reversion where the term is to merge in that reversion.

123A. Compulsory registration: effect of requirement to register

(1)   This section applies to any disposition which, by virtue of any provision of section 123 of this Act, is one in relation to which the requirement of compulsory registration applies.

(2)   Where any such disposition is effected, then—

(a)   if it is a disposition falling within section 123(1), the person who under the disposition is entitled to the legal estate transferred or created by it, or

(b)   if it is a disposition falling within section 123(2), the estate owner of the legal estate charged by the mortgage, or

(c)   (in either case) that person's successor in title or assign,

must before the end of the applicable period apply to the registrar to be registered (or alternatively, where he is not a person in a fiduciary position, to have any nominee registered) as the first proprietor of that estate.

(3)   In this section 'the applicable period' means in the first instance the period of two months beginning with the date of the disposition, but—

(a)   the registrar may, if satisfied on the application of any interested person that there is good reason for doing so, make an order extending or further extending that period; and

(b)   if he does so, 'the applicable period' means that period as for the time being extended under this subsection.

(4)   Pending compliance with subsection (2) above the disposition shall operate to transfer or grant a legal estate, or (as the case may be) create a legal mortgage, in accordance with its terms.

(5)   If subsection (2) above is not complied with, the disposition shall at the end of the applicable period become void as regards any such transfer, grant or creation of a legal estate; and—

(a)   if it is a disposition purporting to transfer a legal estate, the tide to that estate shall thereupon revert to the transferor who shall hold that estate on a bare trust for the transferee;

(b)   if it is a disposition purporting to grant a legal estate or create a legal mortgage, the disposition shall thereupon take effect as if it were a contract to grant or create that estate or mortgage made for valuable consideration (whether or not it was so made or satisfies any of the formal requirements of such a contract).

(6)   If an order extending the applicable period under subsection (3) above is made at a time when the disposition has become void in accordance with subsection (5) above, then as from the making of the order—

(a)   subsection (5) shall cease to apply to the disposition, and

(b)   subsection (4) above shall apply to it instead,

and similarly in the case of any further order so made.

(7)   If any disposition is subsequently effected by way of replacement for a disposition which has become void in accordance with subsection (5) above, the requirement of compulsory registration shall apply in relation to it under section 123 in the same way as it applied in relation to the void disposition, and the provisions of this section shall have effect accordingly.

(8)   Except to the extent to which the parties to any such replacement disposition agree otherwise, the transferee or grantee (as the case may be) shall—

(a)   bear all the proper costs of and incidental to that disposition, and

(b)   indemnify the transferor or grantor (as the case may be) in respect of any other liability reasonably incurred by him in consequence of the failure to comply with subsection (2) above.

(9)   Where any such replacement disposition is a mortgage falling within section 123(2) of this Act, subsection (8) above shall apply as if the reference to the grantee were a reference to the mortgagor and the reference to the grantor were a reference to the mortgagee.

(10)   Rules under this Act may make provision—

(a)   applying the provisions of this Act to any dealings which take place between—

(i)   the date of any disposition to which this section applies, and

(ii)   the date of the application for first registration,

as if the dealings had taken place after the date of the registration, and for the registration to be effective as of the date of the application;

(b) enabling the mortgagee under any mortgage falling within section 123(2) of this Act to require the legal estate charged by the mortgage to be registered whether or not the mortgagor consents.'

2. Indemnity for errors or omissions in the register
[Section 2 substitutes a new s. 83 of the Land Registration Act 1925 (see **22.2**).]

3. Registration fees
The following subsections shall be substituted for subsection (3) of section 145 of the Land Registration Act 1925 (registration fees)—

'(3) Notwithstanding the provisions of subsection (1)(a) to (c) above, an order under this section may provide for reduced fees to be charged on the first registration of title to freehold or leasehold land in cases where such registration is not effected on an application made in pursuance of section 123A(2) of this Act.

(3A) An order under this section may make different provision for different cases, and may in particular provide that no fees are payable in certain cases.'

9.3   Grades of Title

LAND REGISTRATION ACT 1925
(as amended by the Trusts of Land etc. Act 1996 and the Land Registration Act 1997
(in italics)

5. Effect of first registration with absolute title
Where the registered land is a freehold estate, the registration of any person as first proprietor thereof with an absolute title shall vest in the person so registered an estate in fee simple in possession in the land, together with all rights, privileges, and appurtenances belonging or appurtenant thereto, subject to the following rights and interests, that is to say,—
    (a) Subject to the incumbrances, and other entries, if any, appearing on the register; and
    (b) Unless the contrary is expressed on the register, subject to such overriding interest, if any, as affect the registered land; and
    (c) Where the first proprietor is not entitled for his own benefit to the registered land subject, as between himself and the persons entitled to minor interests, to any minor interests of such persons of which he has notice,
but free from all other estates and interests whatsoever, including estates and interests of His Majesty.

6. Effect of first registration with possessory title
Where the registered land is a freehold estate, the registration of any person as first proprietor thereof with a possessory title only shall not affect or prejudice the enforcement of any estate, right or interest adverse to or in derogation of the title of the first proprietor, and subsisting or capable of arising at the time of registration of that proprietor; but save as aforesaid, shall have the same effect as registration of a person with an absolute title.

7. Qualified title
    (1) Where an absolute title is required, and on the examination of the title it appears to the registrar that the title can be established only for a limited period, or only subject to certain reservations, the registrar may, on the application of the party applying to be registered, by an entry made in the register, except from the effect of registration any estate, right, or interest—
    (a) arising before a specified date; or
    (b) arising under a specified instrument or otherwise particularly described in the register,
and a title registered subject to such excepted estate, right, or interest shall be called a qualified title.

8. Application for registration of leasehold land

(1) Where the title to be registered is a title to a leasehold interest in land—

(a) any estate owner (including a tenant for life, statutory owner, personal representative, or [trustee of land], but not including a mortgagee where there is a subsisting right of redemption), holding under a lease for a term of years absolute of which more than twenty-one are unexpired, whether subject or not to incumbrances; or

(b) any other person (not being a mortgagee as aforesaid and not being a person who has merely contracted to buy the leasehold interest) who is entitled to require a legal leasehold estate held under such a lease as aforesaid (whether subject or not to incumbrances) to be vested in him,

may apply to the registrar to be registered in respect of such estate, or in the case of a person not being in a fiduciary position to have registered in his stead any nominee, as proprietor with an absolute title, with a good leasehold title or with a possessory title:

Provided that—

(i) Where an absolute title is required, the applicant or his nominee shall not be registered as proprietor until and unless the title both to the leasehold and to the freehold, and to any intermediate leasehold that may exist, is approved by the registrar;

(ii) Where a good leasehold title is required, the applicant or his nominee shall not be registered as proprietor until and unless the title to the leasehold interest is approved by the registrar;

(iii) Where a possessory title is required, the applicant or his nominee may be registered as proprietor on giving such evidence of title and serving such notices, if any, as may for the time being be precsribed;

(iv) If on an application for registration with a possessory title the registrar is satisfied as to the title to the leasehold interest, he may register it as good leasehold, whether the applicant consents to such registration or not, but in that case no higher fee shall be charged than would have been charged for registration with possessory title. . . .

9. Effect of first registration with absolute title

Where the registered land is a leasehold interest, the registration under this Act of any person as first proprietor thereof with an absolute title shall be deemed to vest in such person the possession of the leasehold interest described, with all implied or expressed rights, privileges, and appurtenances attached to such interest, subject to the following obligations, rights, and interests, that is to say—

(a) Subject to all implied and express covenants, obligations, and liabilities incident to the registered land; and

(b) Subject to the incumbrances and other entries (if any) appearing on the register; and

(c) Unless the contrary is expressed on the register, subject to such overriding interests, if any, as affect the registered land; and

(d) Where such first proprietor is not entitled for his own benefit to the registered land subject, as between himself and the persons entitled to minor interest, to any minor interests of such persons of which he has notice;

but free from all other estates and interests whatsoever, including estates and interests of His Majesty.

10. Effect of first registration with good leasehold title

Where the registered land is a leasehold interest, the registration of a person as first proprietor thereof with a good leasehold title shall not affect or prejudice the enforcement of any estate, right or interest affecting or in derogation of the title of the lessor to grant the lease, but, save as aforesaid, shall have the same effect as registration with an absolute title.

11. Effect of first registration with possessory title

Where the registered land is a leasehold interest, the registration of a person as first proprietor thereof with a possessory title shall not affect or prejudice the enforcement of any estate, right, or interest (whether in respect of the lessor's title or otherewise) adverse to or in derogation of the title of such first registered proprietor, and subsisting or capable of arising at the time of the registration of such proprietor; but, save as aforesaid, shall have the same effect as registration with an absolute title.

12. Qualified title

(1)   Where on examination it appears to the registrar that the title, either of the lessor to the reversion or of the lessee to the leasehold interest, can be established only for a limited period, or subject to certain reservations, the registrar may, upon the request in writing of the person applying to be registered, by an entry made in the register, except from the effect of registration any estate, right or interest—

(a)   arising before a specified date, or

(b)   arising under a specified instrument, or otherwise particularly described in the register,

and a title registered subject to any such exception shall be called a qualified title.

(2)   Where the registered land is a leasehold interest, the registration of a person as first proprietor thereof with a qualified title shall not affect or prejudice the enforcement of any estate, right, or interest appearing by the register to be excepted, but save as aforesaid, shall have the same effect as registration with a good leasehold title or an absolute title, as the case may be.

20. Effect of registration and dispositions of freeholds

(1)   In the case of a freehold estate registered with an absolute title, a diposition of the registered land or of a legal estate therein, including a lease thereof, for valuable consideration shall, when registered, confer on the transferee or grantee an estate in fee simple or the term of years absolute or other legal estate expressed to be created in the land dealt with, together with all rights, privileges, and appurtenances belonging or appurtenant thereto including (subject to any entry to the contrary in the register) the appropriate rights and interests which would, under the Law of Property Act 1925, have been transferred if the land had not been registered, subject—

(a)   to the incumbrances and other entries, if any, appearing on the register [and any charge for capital transfer tax subject to which the disposition takes effect under section 73 of this Act]; and

(b)   unless the contrary is expressed on the register, to the overrriding interests, if any, affecting the estate transferred or created,

but free from all other estates and interests whatsoever, including estates and interests of His Majesty, and the disposition shall operate in like manner as if the registered transferor or grantor were (subject to any entry to the contrary in the register) entitled to registered land in fee simple in possession for his own benefit.

(2)   . . .

(3)   . . .

(4)   Where any such disposition is made without valuable consideration, it shall, so far as the transferee or grantee is concerned, be subject to any minor interests subject to which the transferor or grantor held the same, but, save as aforesaid, shall, when registered, in all respects, and in particular as respects any registered dealings on the part of the transferee or grantee, have the same effect as if the disposition had been made for valuable consideration.

69. Effect of registration on the legal estate

(1)   The proprietor of land (whether he was registered before or after the commencement of this Act) shall be deemed to have vested in him without any conveyance, where the registered land is freehold, the legal estate in fee simple in possession, and where the registered land is leasehold the legal term created by the registered lease, but subject ot the overriding interests, if any, including any mortgage term or charge by way of legal mortgage created by or under the Law of Property Act 1925, or this Act or otherwise which has priority to the registered estate.

(2)   Where any legal estate or term left outstanding at the date of first registration (whether before or after the commencement of this Act), or disposed of or created under section forty-nine of the Land Transfer Act 1875, before the commencement of this Act, becomes satisfied, or the proprietor of the land becomes entitled to require the same to be vested in or surrendered to him, and the entry, if any, for protecting the same on the register has been cancelled, the same shall thereupon, without any conveyance, vest in the proprietor of the land, as if the same had been conveyed or surrendered to him as the case may be.

(3)   If and when any person is registered as first proprietor of *any land*, the provisions of the Law of Property Act 1925 for getting in legal estates shall apply to any legal estate in

the land which was expressed to be conveyed or created in favour of a purchaser or lessee before the commencement of this Act but which failed to pass or to be created by reason of the omission of such purchaser or lessee to be registered as proprietor of the land under the Land Transfer Acts 1875 and 1897, and shall operate to vest that legal estate in the person so registered as proprietor on his registration, but subject to any mortgage term or charge by way of legal mortgage having priority thereto.

(4)   The estate for the time being vested in the proprietor shall only be capable of being disposed of or dealt with by him in manner authorised by this Act.

(5)   Nothing in this section operates to render valid a lease registered with possessory or good leasehold title.

77.   Conversion of title

(1)   Where land is registered with a good leasehold title, or satisfies the conditions for such registration under this section, the registrar may, and on application by the proprietor shall, if he is satisfied as to the title to the freehold and the title to any intermediate leasehold, enter the title as absolute.

(2)   Where land is registered with a possessory title, the registrar may, and on application by the proprietor shall—

(a)   if he is satisfied as to the title, or

(b)   if the land has been so registered for at least twelve years and he is satisfied that the proprietor is in possession,

enter the title in the case of freehold land as absolute and in the case of leasehold land as good leasehold.

(3)   Where land is registered with a qualified title, the registrar may, and on application by the proprietor shall, if he is satisfied as to title, enter it in the case of freehold land as absolute and in the case of leasehold land as good leasehold.

(4)   If any claim adverse to the title of the proprietor has been made, an entry shall not be made in the register under this section unless and until the claim has been disposed of.

(5)   No fee shall be charged for the making of an entry in the register under this section at the instance of the registrar or on an application by the proprietor made in connection with a transfer for valuable consideration of the land to which the application relates.

(6)   Any person, other than the proprietor, who suffers loss by reason of any entry on the register made by virtue of this section shall be entitled to be indemnified under this Act as if a mistake had been made in the register.

9.3.1   UPGRADING OF TITLE

LAND REGISTRATION ACT 1986

1.   Conversion of title

(1)   . . .

(2)   In the case of land registered with a possessory title before the commencement of this Act—

(a)   subsection (2)(b) of section 77 of the 1925 Act as substituted by this section applies only where the land has been so registered for a period of at least 12 years after that commencement, but

(b)   nothing in this section affects the operation of subsection (3)(b) of section 77 of the 1925 Act as originally enacted (which provides for conversion of a possessory title after 15 years' registration in the case of freehold land and 10 years' registration in the case of leasehold land) in relation to a period of registration beginning before that commencement.

9.4   The Form of the Register

(See specimen register on page 94.)

Specimen Register

HM Land Registry

TITLE NUMBER: CS72510

Edition date: 2 April 1996

Entry No.	**A. PROPERTY REGISTER** containing the description of the registered land and the estate comprised in the Title
	CORNSHIRE : MARADON
1.	(19 December 1989) The Freehold land shown edged with red on the plan of the above Title filed at the Registry and being 13 Augustine Way, Kerwick, (PL14 3JP).
2.	(19 December 1989) The land has the benefit of a right of way on foot only over the passageway at the rear leading into Monks Mead.

Entry No.	**B. PROPRIETORSHIP REGISTER** stating nature of the Title, name, address and description of the proprietor of the land and any entries affecting the right of disposing thereof **TITLE ABSOLUTE**
1.	(31 August 1990) Proprietor: PAUL JOHN DAWKINS and ANGELA MARY DAWKINS both of 13 Augustine Way, Kerwick, Maradon, Cornshire PL14 3JP.
2.	(2 April 1996) RESTRICTION: Except under an order of the registrar no disposition by the proprietor(s) of the land is to be registered without the consent of the proprietor(s) of the Charge dated 23 March 1996 in favour of Weyford Building Society referred to in the Charges Register.

Entry No.	**C. CHARGES REGISTER** containing charges, incumbrances etc adversely affecting the land and registered dealings therewith
1.	(19 December 1989) The passageway at the side included in the title is subject to rights of way on foot only.
2.	(31 August 1990) A Transfer of the land in this title dated 29 July 1990 made between (1) JOHN EDWARD CHARLES BROWN and (2) PAUL JOHN DAWKINS and ANGELA MARY DAWKINS contains restrictive covenants. *NOTE:– Copy in Certificate*
3.	(2 April 1996) REGISTERED CHARGE dated 23 March 1996 to secure the moneys including the further advances therein mentioned.
4.	(2 April 1996) Proprietor(s): WEYFORD BUILDING SOCIETY of Society House, The Avenue, Weyford, Cornshire

***** END OF REGISTER *****

NOTE A: A date at the beginning of an entry is the date on which the entry was made in the Register.
NOTE B: This certificate was officially examined with the register on **2 April 1996**.

LAND REGISTRATION ACT 1925

110. Provisions as between vendor and purchaser

On a sale or other disposition of registered land to a purchaser other than a lessee or chargee—

(1) The vendor shall, notwithstanding any stipulation to the contrary, at his own expense furnish the purchaser with an authority to inspect the register, and, if required, with a copy of the subsisting entries in the register and of any filed plans and copies or abstracts of any documents or any part thereof noted on the register so far as they respectively affect the land to be dealt with (except charges or incumbrances registered or protected on the register which are to be disharged or overrridden at or prior to completion):

Provided that—

(a) unless the purchase money exceeds one thousand pounds the costs of the copies and abstracts of the said entries plans and documents shall, in the absence of any stipulation to the contrary, be borne by the purchaser requiring the same; . . .

9.4.1 THE PROPERTY PART

The Law Commission (Law Com. No. 125) Property Law: Land Registration, London: HMSO, 26 October 1983

Boundaries

2.17 It has long been an accepted principle that the boundaries indicated by the register are *general boundaries* only. This is known as the 'general boundaries rule' and is now expressed in rule 278, which is in the following terms:—

278.—(1) Except in cases in which it is noted in the Property Register that the boundaries have been fixed, the filed plan or General Map shall be deemed to indicate the general boundaries only.

(2) In such cases the exact line of the boundary will be left undetermined—as, for instance, whether it includes a hedge or wall and ditch, or runs within or beyond it; or whether or not the land registered includes the whole or any portion of an adjoining road or stream.

(3) When a general boundary only is desired to be entered in the register, notice to the owners of the adjoining lands need not be given.

(4) This rule shall apply notwithstanding that a part or the whole of a ditch, wall, fence, road, stream or other boundary is expressly included in or excluded from the title or that it forms the whole of the land comprised in the title.

The effect of this rule is that no guarantee is given by the Land Registry that the legal boundary is the centre of a fence, hedge or ditch or on one side of it or the other; and if the boundary is a road or stream, there will usually be no guidance as to whether the title includes the whole or any part of that road or stream.

2.18 A procedure does however remain whereby applications may be made for the boundaries of registered land to be fixed; if they are so fixed the filed plan is then 'deemed to define accurately the fixed boundaries'. This procedure is rarely used: of some 8.3 million titles now registered only about 20 are registered with fixed boundaries, and since 1970 only four applications to fix boundaries have been made, of which only one was pursued to completion.

Criticisms of the present law and practice . . .

2.20 . . . Boundary disputes are both a source and a product of ill-feeling between neighbours; and we have no doubt that the vagueness with which boundaries have traditionally been defined is an important contributory factor to these disputes. . . .

Merits of the General Boundaries Rule . . .

2.25 If boundaries are to be fixed, notice clearly has to be served on all neighbouring owners and their titles have to be investigated. The fixing of boundaries, not only on all first registrations but also on many dealings with registered land, would involve an enormous amount of work for the Registry, but without commensurate return because the existence of the general boundaries rule means that land can be brought onto the Register without costly surveys or any elaborate investigative procedure. The rule also facilitates the work of mapping in the Registry; a return to a system of registration with precise and accurate boundaries would seriously hamper the work of bringing new land onto the Register. We regard that as being far too high a price to pay for the somewhat nebulous benefits to be derived from a reversion to the system of fixed boundaries. There are clear advantages in getting land onto the Register as soon as possible, not only to facilitate and simplify conveyancing, but also to secure the real advantages of superior identification which the registered system provides. . . .

Conclusion

2.28   We recommend that the general boundaries rule should be retained. We consider that the likelihood of boundary disputes can best be reduced by improvements in conveyancing practice.

9.5   The Effect of the 1997 Act

Wilkinson, H. W., 'Title registration and the new Act' (1997) 147 NLJ 925

It is not long since the land registration system was creaking under the strain of work generated by the property boom of the 1980s. The Chief Land Registrar's Annual Report for 1986–7 said that an average of over 28 weeks (143 working days) was being taken to process first registrations where no requisitions arose and 131 days were needed for transfers of part. Record volumes of business were reported from 1983–4 onwards, generating record fee income despite increasing stockpiles of applications—what the *Estates Gazette* called at the time, 'a paradox of ample fees generated by indifferent performance'. The number of registered titles passed 10 million in 1986–7. By 1991 the housing market had slumped and, with increases in staff and productivity and the introduction of computerisation, a backlog of 1.1 m applications in November 1988 shrank to 500,900 at March 31, 1991 (Review of Performance 1991). Then the average wait for registration was less than eight weeks and it is now four weeks (quarterly table to March 31, 1997). On December 1, 1990 compulsory registration applied throughout England and Wales and the system was potentially complete.

The Chief Land Registrar then considered the extension of registration to bring onto the register the remaining unregistered titles and issued in 1992 a Discussion and Consultation Paper on whether (and if so how) the remaining land could be dealt with. Should big sticks, carrots or an appeal to better natures be employed? Or as the Paper put it, should there be wider use of triggering events, or voluntary registration, or targeting of types of owner, or time limits and sanctions for compulsory registration or a combination of them? In August 1995 a Joint Working Group reported and presented a draft Bill with its recommendations. The suggestions were threefold: the circumstances which attracted compulsory registration should be enlarged; voluntary registration should be encouraged by a new fee structure, and there should be fairer provision for those who suffered loss from an error or omission on the register. The 1997 Act implements these proposals. It came into force largely on April 27, 1997 but the registration requirements of s. 1 will only be effective as the Lord Chancellor appoints, possibly on January 1, 1998.

The Act

Section 1 substitutes a new s. 123 of the Land Registration Act 1925 ('the 1925 Act') and adds a s. 123A which deals with the effect of the requirement to register. By s. 123 a 'qualifying' conveyance, grant or assignment of unregistered land attracts registration. That means, by s. 123(6)(a) and (b), a transaction for valuable or other consideration, or by way of gift, or under a court order, or with a negative value.

'Assignment' does not include an assignment or surrender of the lease to the owner of the immediate reversion where the term is to merge in that reversion (s. 123(6)(c)).

Section 123 has been widened and added to so that the following transactions come within the requirement to register (the list is not exclusive).

- Conveyance on sale or gift of freehold.
- Qualifying grant of a term of years absolute with more than 21 years from the date of the grant.
- Qualifying assignment of a term of years absolute with more than 21 years to run at the date of the assignment.
- Disposition effected by an assent (including a vesting assent) or by vesting deed which is a disposition of the freehold or a leasehold with more than 21 years to run.
- A first legal mortgage of the freehold or a leasehold with at least 21 years to run protected by deposit of documents.
- Any category added by order of the Lord Chancellor which affects a legal estate, for example a second and subsequent legal mortgage.
- Purchase under the right to buy under a secure tenancy attracts registration, even if the lease does not exceed 21 years, s. 154 Housing Act 1985.
- There is expressly stated to be no requirement to register an incorporeal hereditament (such as a legal easement), mines and minerals apart from the surface, or corporeal hereditaments which are part of a manor and are included in the sale of the manor as such, s. 123(3).

Comment on s. 1

- The Joint Working Group suggested that registration should be attracted by conveyances giving effect to the appointment of new trustees but the matter was not pursued after it attracted objections from 'the larger private landowners'.

However, the effect will be that many large landholdings remain outside the registration system unless their owners decide to effect registration voluntarily. The position is to be reviewed in, say, five years' time.

- Although assents on death attract registration, there is no need for an assent to be made in the course of administration. Personal representatives can give good title on a sale in their representative capacity (s. 36(6), Administration of Estates Act 1925); the purchaser will then need to register. Where there is an assent to a beneficiary, for example, registration will be attracted.
- Anyone making even a short-term loan by way of legal mortgage on property and holding the deeds as security must be alert to the need to register; an equitable mortgage will not attract registration but must comply with the Law of Property (Miscellaneous Provisions) Act 1989 if it is to be enforceable.
- Settlements are usually made with legal advice and due formality so the additional requirement to register will not be overlooked. Informal settlements have always been hazardous and will be more so.
- An exchange of a freehold or lease with 21 years to run, with or without equality money being paid, seems now to attract registration of both plots. The partition of land previously held in undivided shares seems not to, though it may be 'convenient and proper' in *Ruoff and Roper's* words (1991 edn, para. 32–14) to make some entry on the register of the dealing.
- The view is expressed by *Ruoff and Roper* (para. 11–06) that there is no requirement to register where property is acquired by a general vesting declaration but acquisition by deed poll does attract registration (because there is the notional relationship of vendor and purchaser and the purchase price/compensation money has already been assessed). That still appears the case.

Section 123A: failure to register

By s. 123(1) of the 1925 Act, as amended by s. 2 of the Land Registration Act 1986, failure to effect first registration within two months of the date of the conveyance, lease or assignment, meant that the transaction became void as regards the grant or conveyance of the legal estate. There could be an extension of time allowed if there was 'accident or other sufficient cause' but late applications seemed never to be refused for whatever cause. It was not clear who held the legal estate if the transaction became void, or on what terms, it was even possible that a strict settlement was created (Professor DG Barnsley, (1968) 32 *Conveyancer* 391). Section 123A seeks to clarify the matter. It says in summary:

- where a registrable disposition is made, the person entitled to the legal estate (or, as the case may be, the mortgagor) or those person's successors or assignees, must apply to be registered as proprietor within two months of the disposition;

- pending compliance with (1), the disposition 'shall operate to transfer or grant a legal estate (or, as the case may be) a legal mortgage';
- if registration is not effected within two months the transaction becomes void as regards any transfer of a legal estate and shall revert to the transferor 'who shall hold that estate on a bare trust for the transferee'. In the case of a mortgage 'the disposition shall take effect as if it were a contract to grant or create that estate or mortgage made for valuable consideration';
- if a disposition is later effected by way of replacement for a disposition which has become void, there is a duty to register that disposition within two months of its creation.

Comment on s. 123A

- It is suggested in the annotations to *Current Law Statutes* (Professor PH Kenny) on the Act that after the two month period has elapsed without registration the transferor will have the large powers of a trustee under the Trusts of Land and Appointment of Trustees Act 1996 and can sell the land to a third party, who will take good title even if he knows of the earlier transaction. The first transferee will be overreached by ss. 1 and 16 of the 1996 Act. The suggestion is unlikely to be tested in practice, for the transferee has only to apply for registration for the Registrar (on past practice) to accept the application or he could register a caution against first registration of the third party; moreover the transferor/seller will have no documents to prove title as the transferee will have taken them on completion.

  The further suggestion is made that the transferor may alternatively conceal the disposition and sell to an innocent third party who will be a *bona fide* purchaser for value without notice. Again, without deeds, the transferor will be unable to proceed in this way.
- In *Pinekerry Ltd v Needs (Kenneth) (Contractors) Ltd* (1992) 64 P & CR 245 it was held that a person who had not procured his own registration of title was in default in his contractual obligations and could not serve an effective notice to complete.

  Current Law (above) suggests that the position would now be different because 'the seller under s. 123A(5) will hold on bare trust for the first purchaser . . . [who] is therefore in a position to be able to force the seller to complete and can, therefore, make out a good title'. *Re Baker & Selmon's Contract* [1907] 1 Ch 238 is rightly cited as authority. *Emmett on Title* looseleaf issue, para. 5.002, states the rule as being that 'although the contract states that title shall be made in a particular way or particular capacity, the purchaser cannot object to a good title made otherwise unless there was a warranty as to how it would be made'. However, delay experienced whilst the bare trustee is being approached to agree to make a transfer may result in the completion date going by.

Section 2: indemnity

A new s. 83 replaces the existing one. It provides in summary that:

- Any person suffering loss by reason of the rectification of the register shall be entitled to an indemnity;
- If a person still suffers loss even though the register is rectified in his favour he can have indemnity. This provision corrects a potential injustice identified in *Freer v Unwins Ltd* [1976] Ch 288 where notice of a restrictive covenant had been omitted from a title on first registration. The owner of the land entitled to the benefit of the covenant got it entered on the register but was held unable to enforce it against the holder of a leasehold interest granted before rectification.
- Where there has been an error or omission in the register but the register is not rectified, any person so suffering loss may be indemnified.
- Indemnity is available where a person suffers loss from destruction or loss of any document lodged at the registry.
- A person who claims in good faith under a forged disposition is entitled to indemnity when the register is rectified.
- No indemnity is payable for a loss suffered by a claimant wholly or partly as a result of his own fraud, or wholly from his own lack of proper care; or for any mines and minerals unless the register is noted that they are included in the title; or for costs or expenses incurred without the consent of the registrar unless there was urgency and they were subsequently approved.
- Where the loss is suffered partly as a result of the claimant's lack of proper care, the indemnity is to be reduced to such an extent as is just and equitable, having regard to his share of responsibility.

• Fraud or lack of proper care on the part of a person from whom the claimant derives title (except by registered disposition for valuable consideration) shall be regarded as that of the claimant. A donor and donee or a devisee under a will are examples.

• Where indemnity is paid to a claimant, the registrar has rights to recover the amount paid from any person who caused or substantially contributed to the loss by his fraud and to enforce any right of action which the claimant would have had.

Voluntary registration and concessionary fees

The first comprehensive Act was the Land Registry Act 1862. Under it registration of title was voluntary and because the registrar insisted on strict proof of title there was no incentive for owners to put themselves to the expense of having the validity of their landholdings called into question. Only 410 titles were registered between 1863 and 1877. The system was made less strict but still proved unsatisfactory.

Between 1889 and 1905 there were 401 absolute titles granted and 89,147 possessory ones. That position has now been reversed, possessory titles are rare and absolute ones are the norm. Three major disincentives to register nonetheless remain. They are that if there is no transaction which attracts compulsory registration, there is no need to go to the trouble and expense of doing so; that the fees on registering a large area with many titles could be very large; and that an attempt to register may raise disputes, such as over boundaries and other third party rights, 'and a dispute is forced upon neighbours whose only desire is to live at peace', as the Royal Commissioners put it in 1870. So far the system has fought shy of requiring everyone to register within, say, five years of a stated date, it being impossible to devise an appropriate sanction for failure to comply. A large amount of land is never likely to change hands in a registrable transaction, for example that of hospital trusts, local authorities, service providers such as gas, water and electricity, universities, ecclesiastical buildings, wealthy landowners, that needed for defence and training, National Trust and English Heritage. By s. 145(3) of the 1925 Act, reduced fees could be charged on the registration of title where land was acquired, not for re-sale, by government departments, local authorities or other statutory bodies. This provision has been replaced by s. 3 of the 1997 Act. It allows for an order to allow reduced fees 'where registration is not effected on an application made in pursuance of s. 123A(2)', that means where the application is voluntary. An order 'may make different provision for different cases and may in particular provide that no fees are payable in certain cases'. One hesitates to suggest that the registry will come up with special offers, 'register one, get one free, only available to 31 March'; 'thinking of making a voluntary settlement? See us first.' The 1992 Discussion Paper said that in 1981 there were 7.2 million titles on the register, in 1991 there were 13.9m; on then current procedures there would be 19m by 2011 but that would leave 2m unregistered. Hence the need for the 1997 Act to enlarge the scope of registrable transactions. Within perhaps three years it will be seen what impact the Act has had—more drastic action may yet be needed.

CHAPTER TEN

OVERRIDING INTERESTS AND MINOR INTERESTS

10.1 Overriding Interests

LAND REGISTRATION ACT 1925

70. Liability of registered land to overriding interests

(1) All registered land shall, unless under the provisions of this Act the contrary is expressed on the register, be deemed to be subject to such of the following overriding interests as may be for the time being subsisting in reference thereto, and such interests shall not be treated as incumbrances within the meaning of this Act, (that is to say):—

(a) Rights of common, drainage rights, customary rights (until extinguished), public rights, profits à prendre, rights of sheepwalk, rights of way, watercourses, rights of water, and other easements not being equitable easements required to be protected by notice on the register;

(b) Liability to repair highways by reason of tenure, quit-rents, crown rents, heriots, nd other rents and charges (until extinguished) having their origin in tenure;

(c) Liability to repair the chancel of any church;

(d) Liability in respect of embankments, and sea and river walls;

(e) ..., payments in lieu of tithe, and charges of annuities payable for the redemption of tithe rentcharges;

(f) Subject to the provisions of this Act, rights acquired or in course of being acquired under the Limitation Acts;

(g) The rights of every person in actual occupation of the land or in receipt of the rents and profits thereof, save where enquiry is made of such person and the rights are not disclosed;

(h) In the case of a possessory, qualified, or good leasehold title, all estates, rights, interests, and powers excepted from the effect of registration;

(i) Rights under local land charges unless and until registered or protected on the register in the prescribed manner;

(j) Rights of fishing and sporting, seignorial and manorial rights of all descriptions (until extinguished), and franchises;

(k) Leases granted for a term not exceeding twenty-one years;

(l) In respect of land registered before the commencement of this Act, rights to mines and minerals, and rights of entry, search, and user, and other rights and reservations incidental to or required for the purpose of giving full effect to the enjoyment of rights to mines and minerals or of property in mines or minerals, being rights which, where the title was first registered before the first day of January, eighteen hundred and ninety-eight, were created before that date, and where the title was first registered after the thirty-first day of December, eighteen hundred and ninety-seven, were created before the date of first registration:

Provided that, where it is proved to the satisfaction of the registrar that any land registered or about to be registered is exempt from land tax, or tithe rentcharge or payments in lieu of tithe, or from charges or annuities payable for the redemption of tithe rentcharge, the registrar may notify the fact on the register in the prescribed manner.

(2)   Where at the time of first registration any easement, right, privilege, or benefit created by an instrument and appearing on the title adversely affects the land, the registrar shall enter a note thereof on the register.

(3)   Where the existence of any overriding interest mentioned in this section is proved to the satisfaction of the registrar or admitted, he may (subject to any prescribed exceptions) enter notice of the same or of a claim thereto on the register, but no claim to an easement, right, or privilege not created by an instrument shall be noted against the title to the servient land if the proprietor of such land (after the prescribed notice is given to him) shows sufficient cause to the contrary.

(See s. 31(10)(b) of the Family Law Act 1996 at **1.3.6**.)

10.1.1   S. 70(1)(a) . . . PROFITS À PRENDRE, . . . AND EASEMENTS NOT BEING EQUITABLE EASEMENTS REQUIRED TO BE PROTECTED BY NOTICE ON THE REGISTER

THATCHER v *DOUGLAS* (1996) 146 NLJ 282, Court of Appeal

FACTS: The plaintiff, T, purchased a property in 1966 and agreed with the adjoining landowner, W, to share the use of a slipway leading down to tidal mudflats. The slipway had been built in the general area of their common boundary and intruded partly onto T's land. Thereafter W's property changed hands several times, and T continued to use the slipway for the launching, recovery and repair of boats. However, in 1989 W's successors in title, Mr and Mrs D, objected to his further use. T brought proceedings against Mr and Mrs D to establish his right to use the slipway. The recorder upheld T's claim that the agreement between T and W gave rise to an equitable easement, binding on W's successors in title as an overriding interest under s. 70 of the Land Registration Act 1925, and granted an injunction and awarded damages against Mr and Mrs D, who appealed.
HELD: *inter alia*, an equitable easement is an overriding interest within s. 70(1)(a).

NOURSE LJ: . . . Although there are cases in which it has been held that a valid equitable easement can be created by an oral agreement for value supported by a sufficient act of part performance (see *Duke of Devonshire* v *Eglin* (1851) 14 Beav 530, and *McManus* v *Cooke* (1887) 35 Ch D 681), the natural inference to be drawn from an informal agreement between friendly neighbours such as we have here, is that it is intended to be personal to them. However, two features of the present case have brought us to the contrary conclusion.

First, Mr Thatcher's evidence appears to have supported the view that the agreement was intended to enure for the benefit of and to bind the successors in title of himself and Mr Williams . . . Secondly, it is clear from Mr Thatcher's answers both in chief and in cross-examination that the quid pro quo for his use of the slipway was his permission for the trespass to continue. Since the trespass was inherently likely to continue indefinitely, so, it must be assumed, was the common intention of the parties in regard to the user. In this respect the facts of the case are closely comparable to those of *E R Ives Investments Ltd* v *High* [1967] 1 All ER 504 where the defendant had orally agreed with his neighbour, a predecessor in title of the plaintiff, that the neighbour should be allowed to retain the foundations of a block of flats which encroached on the defendant's land, and that the defendant should have a right of way from his land across the yard of the block of flats so as to give access to a side road. The plaintiff having purchased the neighbouring property with notice of the defendant's right, this court held that it was enforceable against the plaintiff . . . [The] significance [of the *Ives* case] for present purposes is that both Lord Denning MR and Danckwerts LJ thought that an agreement between neighbours entered into in closely comparable circumstances enured for the benefit of and bound the parties' respective successors in title.

For these reasons, we are of the view that the recorder's decision as to the nature of the agreement was correct. It was intended to enure for the benefit of and to bind the successors in title of Mr Thatcher and Mr Williams respectively and it did and continues to do so . . . The effect of our holdings thus far is that the oral agreement between Mr Thatcher and Mr Williams, being one made for value and supported by sufficient acts of part performance, created equitable easements in favour of No. 33 over No. 35 and vice versa. The remaining question is whether the easement in favour of No. 33 is enforceable against Mr and Mrs Douglas, the factual position being that it was not protected by any entry on the register when they purchased No. 35 in 1976; nor did they have notice of it in any other way.

No. 35 having at all material times been registered land, it is agreed that this question depends on whether the easement was an overriding interest within s. 70(1) of the Land Registration Act 1925, a question which in turn depends on whether the decision of Scott J at first instance in *Celsteel Ltd* v *Alton House Holdings Ltd* [1985] 2 All ER 562 is, as Mr Lyons submitted, distinguishable or, if it is not, was as he further submitted, wrong . . . no ground has been shown on which the decision in the *Celsteel* case is distinguishable [and since] no other ground [was] put forward for saying that the decision in the *Celsteel* case was wrong, we see no reason for not following and applying it in this case. The recorder's decision was correct on this point also.

10.1.2   SECTION 70(1)(g) A VERY DIFFERENT AND IMPORTANT OVERRIDING INTEREST

WILLIAMS & GLYN'S BANK LIMITED v *BOLAND AND ANOTHER*
[1981] AC 487, House of Lords

FACTS: The title to the land was registered. Mr Boland ('H') bought a house, registered title, in his sole name. His wife ('W') made substantial contributions to the cost of acquisition, and therefore acquired a constructive trust interest in the house. While H and W were living happily together in the house, H decided to borrow some more money. Without telling his wife, he borrowed it from the bank. He granted the bank a mortgage by registered charge. The bank did not go to the trouble of sending an employee to the house, and certaiinly did not ask W any questions. H defaulted in repaying the loan, and the bank now wished to enforce their mortgage by taking possession of the house and selling. The issue was as follows: Was W's interest binding on the bank? If it was, the bank would effectively be prevented from enforcing its security.
HELD: the wife's equitable interest was binding on the bank as an 'overriding interest' due to the fact that the wife was in 'actual occupation' of the land (Land Registration Act 1925, s. 70(1)(g)).

LORD WILBERFORCE: . . . The system of land registration, as it exists in England, which long antedates the Land Registration Act 1925, is designed to simplify and to cheapen conveyancing. It is intended to replace the often complicated and voluminous title deeds of property by a single land certificate, on the strength of which land can be dealt with. In place of the lengthy and often technical investigation of title to which a purchaser was committed, all he has to do is to consult the register; from any burden not entered on the register, with one exception, he takes free. Above all, the system is designed to free the purchaser from the hazards of notice—real or constructive—which, in the case of unregistered land, involved him in enquiries, often quite elaborate, failing which he might be bound by equities. The Law of Property Act 1925 contains provisions limiting the effect of the doctrine of notice, but it still remains a potential source of danger to purchasers. By contrast, the only provisions in the Land Registration Act 1925 with regard to notice are provisions which enable a purchaser to take the estate free from equitable interests or equities whether he has notice or not. (See, for example, s. 3(xv) s.v. 'minor interests'). The only kind of notice recognised is by entry on the register.

The exception just mentioned consists of 'overriding interests' listed in s. 70. As to these, all registered land is stated to be deemed to be subject to such of them as may be subsisting in reference to the land, unless the contrary is expressed on the register. The land is so subject regardless of notice actual or constructive. In my opinion therefore, the law as to notice as it may affect purchasers of unregistered land, whether contained in decided cases, or in a statute (the Conveyancing Act 1882, s. 3, Law of Property Act, s. 199) has no application even by analogy to registered land. Whether a particular right is an overriding interest, and whether it affects a purchaser, is to be decided upon the terms of s. 70, and other relevant provisions of the Land Registration Act 1925, and upon nothing else.

In relation to rights connected with occupation, it has been said that the purpose and effect of s. 70(1)(g) of the Land Registration Act 1925 was to make applicable to registered land the same rule as previously had been held to apply to unregistered land: see *per* Lord Denning MR in *National Provincial Bank Ltd v Hastings Car Mart Ltd* [1964] Ch 665, 689, and in this House [1965] AC 1175, 1259.

I adhere to this, but I do not accept the argument which learned counsel for the appellant sought to draw from it. His submission was that, in applying s. 70(1)(g), we should have regard to and limit the application of the paragraph in the light of the doctrine of notice. But this would run counter to the whole purpose of the Act. The purpose, in each system, is the same, namely, to safeguard the rights of persons in occupation, but the method used differs. In the case of unregistered land, the purchaser's obligation depends upon what he has notice of—notice actual or constructive. In the case of registered land, it is the fact of occupation that matters. If there is actual occupation, and the occupier has rights, the purchaser takes subject to them. If not, he does not. No further element is material.

I now deal with the first question. Were the wives here in 'actual occupation'? These words are ordinary words of plain English, and should, in my opinion, be interpreted as such. Historically they appear to have emerged in the judgment of Lord Loughborough LC in *Taylor v Stibbert* (1794) 2 Ves Jun 437, 439–440, in a passage which repays quotation:

> . . . whoever purchases an estate from the owner, knowing it to be in possession of tenants, is bound to inquire into the estates, those tenants have. It has been determined, that a purchaser being told, particular parts of the estate were in possession of a tenant, without any information as to his interest, and taking it for granted it was only from year to year, was bound by a lease, that tenant had, which was a surprise upon him. That was rightly determined; for it was sufficient to put the purchaser upon inquiry, that he was informed, the estate was not in the *actual possession* of the person, with whom he contracted; that he could not transfer the ownership and possession at the same time; that there were interests, as to the extent and terms of which it was his duty to inquire.

They were taken up in the judgment of the Privy Council in *Barnhart v Greenshields* (1853) 9 Moo PCC 18. The purpose for which they were used, in that case, was evidently to distinguish the case of a person who was in some kind of legal possession, as by receipt of the rents and profits, from that of a person actually in occupation as tenant. Given occupation, i.e., presence on the land, I do not think that the word 'actual' was intended to introduce any additional qualification, certainly not to suggest that possession must be 'adverse': it merely emphasises that what is required is physical presence, not some entitlement in law. So even if it were necessary to look behind these plain words into history, I would find no reason for denying them their plain meaning.

Then, were the wives in actual occupation? I ask: why not? There was physical presence, with all the rights that occupiers have, including the right to exclude all others except those having similar rights. The house was a matrimonial home, intended to be occupied, and in fact occupied by both spouses, both of whom have an interest in it: it would require some special doctrine of law to avoid the result that each is in occupation. . . . There are observations which suggest the contrary in the unregistered land case of *Caunce v Caunce* [1969] 1 WLR 286, but I agree with the disapproval of these, and with the assertion of the proposition I have just stated by Russell LJ in *Hodgson v Marks* [1971] Ch 892, 934. Then it was suggested that the wife's occupation was nothing but the shadow of the husband's—a version I suppose of the doctrine of unity of husband and wife. This expression and the argument flowing from it was used by Templeman J in *Bird v Syme-Thomson* [1979] 1 WLR 440, 444, a decision preceding and which he followed in the present case. The argument was also inherent in the judgment in *Caunce v Caunce* [1969] 1 WLR 286 which influenced the decisions of Templeman J. It somewhat faded from the arguments in the present case and appears to me to be heavily obsolete. . . .

This brings me to the second question which is whether such rights as a spouse has under a trust for sale are capable of recognition as overriding interests—a question to my mind of some difficulty. The argument against this is based upon the structure of the Land Registration Act 1925 and upon specific provisions in it.

As to structure, it is said that the Act recognises three things: (a) legal estates, (b) minor interests, which take effect in equity, (c) overriding interests. These are mutually exclusive: an equitable interest, which is a minor interest, is incapable of being at the same time an overriding interest. The wife's interest, existing under or behind a trust for sale, is an equitable interest and nothing more. To give it the protection of an overriding interest would, moreover, contradict the principle according to which such an equitable interest can be overreached by an exercise of the trust for sale. As to the provisions of the Act, particular emphasis is placed on s. 3(xv) which, in defining 'minor interests' specifically includes in the case of land held on trust for sale 'all interests and powers which are under the Law of Property Act 1925 capable of being overriden by the trustees for sale 'and excludes, expressly, overriding interests. Reliance is also placed on s. 86, which, dealing analogously, so it is said, with settled land, prescribes that successive or other interests created by or arising under a settlement take effect as minor interests and not otherwise, and on s. 101 which, it is argued, recognises the exclusive character of minor interests, which in all cases can be overridden.

My Lords, I find this argument formidable. To reach a conclusion upon it involves some further consideration of the nature of trusts for sale, in relation to undivided shares. The trust upon which, in this case, the land is to be held are defined—as 'statutory trusts'—in s. 35 of the Law of Property Act 1925, i.e.:

> . . . upon trust to sell the same and to stand possessed of the net proceeds of sale, after payment of costs, and of the net rents and profits until sale after payment of rates, taxes, cost of insurance, repairs, and other outgoings, upon such trusts, and subject to such powers and provisions, as may be requisite for giving effect to the rights of the persons . . . interested in the land.

In addition to this specific disposition, the general provisions as to trusts for sale in ss. 23 to 31, where not inconsistent, appear to apply. The right of occupation of the land pending sale is not explicitly dealt with in these sections and the position as to it is obscure. Before the Act the position was that owners of undivided shares (which could exist at law) had concurrent rights of occupation. In *Bull v Bull* [1955] 1 QB 234, it was held by the Court of Appeal, applying *In Re Warren* [1932] 1 Ch 42, that the conversion of these legal estates into equitable interests by the Law of Property Act 1925 should not affect the mutual rights of the owners. Denning LJ, in a judgment which I find most illuminating, there held, at p. 238 in a factual situation similar to that of the instant cases, that 'when there are two equitable tenants in common, then, until the place is sold, each of them is entitled concurrently with the other to the possession of the land and to the use and enjoyment of it in a proper manner.' And he referred to s. 14 of the Law of Property Act 1925 which provides that the Act 'shall not prejudicially affect the interest of any person in possession or in actual occupation of land to which he may be entitled in right of such possession or occupation'.

How then are these various rights to be fitted into the scheme of the Land Registration Act 1925? It is clear, at least, that the interests of the co-owners under the 'statutory trusts' are minor interests—this fits with the definition in s. 3(xv), But I can see no reason why, if these interests, or that of any one of them, are or is protected by 'actual occupation' they should remain merely as 'minor interests.' On the contrary, I see every reason why, in that event, they should acquire the status of overriding interests. And, moreover, I find it easy to accept that they satisfy the opening, and governing, words of s. 70, namely, interests subsisting in reference to the land. As Lord Denning MR points out, to describe the interests of spouses in a house jointly bought to be lived in as a matrimonial home as merely an interest in proceeds of sale, or rents and profits until sale, is just a little unreal: see also *Elias v Mitchell* [1972] Ch 652, *per* Pennycuick V-C with whose analysis I agree, and contrast, *Cedar Holdings Ltd v Green* [1981] Ch 129 (which I consider to have been wrongly decided). . . .

. . . I would only add, in conclusion, on the appeal as it concerns the wives a brief observation on the conveyancing consequences of dismissing the appeal. These were alarming to Templeman J, and I can agree with him to the extent that whereas the object of a land registration system is to reduce the risks to purchasers from anything not on the register, to extend (if it be an extension) the area of risk so as to include possible interests of spouses, and indeed, in theory, of other members of the family or even outside it, may add to the burdens of purchasers, and involve them in enquiries which in some cases may be troublesome.

But conceded, as it must be, that the Act, following established practice, gives protection to occupation, the extension of the risk area follows necessarily from the extension, beyond the paterfamilias, of rights of ownership, itself following from the diffusion of property and earning capacity. What is involved is a departure from an easy-going practice of dispensing with enquiries as to occupation beyond that of the vendor and accepting the risks of doing so. To substitute for this a practice of more careful enquiry as to the fact of occupation, and if necessary, as to the rights of occupiers can not, in my view of the matter, be considered as unacceptable except at the price of overlooking the widespread development of shared interests of ownership. In the light of s. 70 of the Act, I cannot believe that Parliament intended this, though it may be true that in 1925 it did not foresee the full extent of this development. . . .

The Law Commission (Law Com. No. 115) Property Law: the Implications of *Williams & Glyn's Bank Ltd* v *Boland*, London: HMSO, August 1982, Cmnd. 8636

70. We are now in a position to point to those aspects of the law affected by *Boland* which we consider to be in need of reform, and to suggest what the aims of that reform should be. The consistency of *Boland* with current social policy which favours the protection of the wife in the matrimonial home is in contrast to its inconsistency with the policy of property law which upholds the security of titles, the marketability of land and the simplification of conveyancing. Whilst the law as developed in *Boland* confers a measure of protection on the wife's interest in the matrimonial home, areas of uncerainty as to the existence of that protection remain. First, there is the uncertainty about the *fact of occupation*, the purchaser not knowing whether he has discovered all the occupiers and the co-owner not knowing whether he or she will be in actual occupation at the relevant time. Secondly, there is the uncertainty as to the *right of occupation*, which may be lost through the co-owner's interest being converted into money. Thirdly, there is the uncertainty as to *co-ownership* itself, that is to say whether or not on particular facts it exists at all, and if so what is its extent. In our view the aims of law reform in this field should be to uphold social policy in the protection of the matrimonial home, to remove unnecessary complications in property law and conveyancing, and, in accordance with these general aims, to remove or reduce these areas of uncertainty. . . .

The conveyancing problem: how may a co-owner ensure that his interest is protected against a purchaser and the purchaser ensure that he takes free of co-ownersip interests of which he is unaware?
73. The simplest and most effective way to deal with this problem would be for co-ownership interests not to be enforceable as overriding interests, or through the operation of the doctrine of constructive notice, but to be recorded on the appropriate register under the Land Registration Act 1925 (registered land) or the Land Charges Act 1972 (unregistered land). These Acts provide for the registration of certain interests and contain machinery by which purchasers take subject to these interests if they appear on the register and free of them if they do not.

HODGSON v MARKS AND ANOTHER [1971] 1 Ch 892, Court of Appeal

FACTS: The plaintiff transferred her legal title in certain land to her lodger on the understanding, orally agreed, that the plaintiff would remain equitable owner of the property. In course of time the lodger sold the house to the first defendant. The first defendant then raised a mortgage on the security of the house, the mortgagee being the second defendant to this action. The plaintiff commenced the present proceedings for a declaration that the house should be transferred to her and that the second defendant's mortgage should not be binding on her. The judge at first instance found against the plaintiff and she appealed.
HELD: The plaintiff's rights, being the rights of a person 'in actual occupation' of the land, had the status of overriding interests and were therefore binding upon the defendants.

RUSSELL LJ: . . . It is a principle of law (and of the Land Registration Act 1925) that a person in occupation is protected in his rights by that occupation, unless, of course, the rights are such that they require registration if they are to be protected. A purchaser must pay heed to anyone in occupation if he is to be sure of getting a good title. It was argued, on the basis of a quotation from the judgment of Vaughan Williams LJ in *Hunt* v *Luck* [1902] 1 Ch 428,

432 that this does not apply when the vendor is in occupation, and that (as is the fact) there is no reported case of unregistered land where a purchaser was fixed with constructive notice of the rights of any other occupier when the vendor was in occupation, and that any other view would lead to an impossible burden of inquiry on a purchaser and more particularly on a lender of money on mortgage such as the building society. (As to the defendant building society it is plain that it made no inquiries on the spot save as to repairs; it relied on Mr Marks, who lied to it: and I waste no tears on it.) I do not think this is a real problem. Conveyancing is conducted generally upon a basis of good faith, with something of a long stop in the shape of covenants for title. Moreover, I do not consider that it is correct in law to say that any rights of a person who is in occupation will be overridden whenever the vendor is, or appears to be, also in occupation.

I do not think it desirable to attempt to lay down a code or catalogue of situations in which a person other than the vendor should be held to be in occupation of unregistered land for the purpose of constructive notice of his rights, or in actual occupation of registered land for the purposes of s. 70(1)(g). It must depend on the circumstances, and a wise purchaser or lender will take no risks. Indeed, however wise he may be he may have no ready opportunity of finding out; but, nevertheless, the law will protect the occupier. Reliance upon the untrue ipse dixit of the vendor will not suffice. Take the present case—though the test of occupation must be objective. Mr Evans was only a lodger, and whether in law he was in occupation at all is at least doubtful. But the plaintiff was there for Mr Marks to see and he saw her on two occasions. He did not introduce himself to her as an intending purchaser. He made no inquiry of her. He assumed her to be Mr Evans' wife who knew all about the proposed purchase. This assumption may well have stemmed from a lie told by Mr Evans, though neither Mr Marks nor Mrs Marks actually said so. Nonetheless, there was the plaintiff de facto living in the house as her house, and, if the judge's gloss were to be accepted, I should say just as much in apparent actual occupation of it as before the transfer to Mr Evans; and, indeed, if Mr Evans had stopped lodging there before the registration in Mr Marks' name she would unquestionably have been in actual occupation. In short, unless it can be established in law that a person is not to be regarded as in actual occupation for the purposes of s. 70(1)(g) merely because the vendor appears also to be occupying the property, it seems to me that the judge's decision on this point cannot be supported. (I observe that it was necessary for the defendants' argument on actual occupation to contend that if the plaintiff had said in conversation to Mr Marks that it was her house and Mr Evans her lodger, and Mr Marks had believed Mr Evans when he said, 'The old lady has a bee in her bonnet and is talking rubbish,' her interest would not have been enforceable against Mr Marks because she was not in actual occupation and, accordingly, without an overriding interest.) I do not accept that proposition of law. Accordingly, I would hold that the plaintiff was at all material times a person in actual occupation of the property. . . .

To the whole of this, I venture to think, somewhat amorphous approach to the problem, the answer seems to me to be that an overriding interest is just that. A registered proprietor cannot transfer free from an overriding interest. Registration itself is subject to overriding interests. Moreover, a person who remains in actual occupation does not do anything to abandon the rights which her actual occupation protects, unless on inquiry she does not reveal them: that is what s. 70(1)(g) enacts. The plaintiff did not arm Mr Evans with the apparent ability or power to deal with the property free from any overriding interest.

I would only add that I do not consider it necessary to this decision to pronounce on the decision in *Caunce* v *Caunce* [1969] 1 WLR 286. In that case the occupation of the wife may have been rightly taken to be not her occupation but that of her husband. In so far, however, as some phrases in the judgment might appear to lay down a general proposition that enquiry need not be made of any person on the premises if the proposed vendor himself appears to be in occupation, I would not accept them.

Accordingly, I would allow the appeal with such order as may be consequential on the establishment by the plaintiff of her overriding beneficial entitlement to the premises.

ABBEY NATIONAL BUILDING SOCIETY v *CANN AND ANOTHER*
[1991] AC 56, House of Lords

FACTS: George Cann purchased a maisonette in his sole name. His mother (who lived with him) made a substantial contribution to the cost of the acquisition and thus was entitled to

a constructive trust interest. At about 11.45 on the 13 August ('the date of completion') furniture removers acting on behalf of Mrs Cann started laying carpets and bringing in her furniture. (She herself was on holiday in the Netherlands.) At 12.20 the same day, a land transfer was executed in favour of George. As is normal in these situations, he immediately executed a mortgage in favour of the building society. The society were, of course, lending a substantial proportion of the purchase price, and were taking the mortgage as security for the loan. Both the land transfer and the mortgage were registered on the 13 September ('the date of registration') by which time Mrs Cann was living in the maisonette with her son. After some time, George defaulted in repaying the loan. Mrs Cann then claimed that her constructive trust interest was an overriding interest under s. 70(1)(g), binding on the building society.
HELD: Her claim failed.

LORD OLIVER OF AYLMERTON: In the Court of Appeal Mrs Cann's claim failed because, in the view of all members of the court, she was aware that the balance of the purchase price of 7, Hillview, over and above the net amount to be produced by the sale of 30, Island Road, was going to be raised by George Cann by mortgage of the premises. Having thus impliedly authorised him to raise this amount on mortgage she must necessarily have authorised him to that extent to create a charge to the society having priority to her interest and could not, as against the society, complain that George had exceeded a limitation on his authority of which the society was unaware. Dillon LJ, however, took the view that the events which took place between 11.45 a.m. and 12.20 p.m on 13 August did constitute actual occupation of the property by Mrs Cann sufficient to enable her to claim an overriding interest, a proposition which was doubted by Ralph Gibson and Woolf LJJ. . . .
    . . . the relevant date for determining the existence of overriding interests which will 'affect the estate transferred or created' is the date of registration. This does, of course, give rise to the theoretical difficulty that since a transferor remains the registered proprietor until registration of the transfer, it would be possible for him, in breach of trust, to create overriding interests, for instance, by grant of an easement or of a lease, which would be binding on the transferee and against which the transferee would not be protected by an official search. That would, of course, equally be the case in a purchase of unregistered land where the purchaser pays the price in advance of receiving a conveyance. I cannot, however, find in the theoretical possibility of so improbable an event a context for preferring the judge's construction.
    The question remains, however, whether the date of registration is also the relevant date for determining whether a claimant to a right is in actual occupation. It is to be noted that it is not the actual occupation which gives rise to the right or determines its existence. Actual occupation merely operates as the trigger, as it were, for the treatment of the right, whatever it may be, as an overriding interest. Nor does the additional quality of the right as an overriding interest alter the nature or quality of the right itself. If it is an equitable right it remains an equitable right. As was observed in *Williams & Glyn's Bank Ltd* v *Boland* [1981] AC 487, 504, the purpose of s. 70(1)(g) was to make applicable to registered land the same rule for the protection of persons in actual occupation as had been applied in the case of unregistered land in, for instance, *Hunt* v *Luck* [1902] 1 Ch 428. In relation to legal rights it does nothing, for it is not easy to conceive of a legal right in the land which would not already be an overriding interest under some other head, as, for instance, paragraphs (a) or (k). Again, as regards equitable rights in an occupier which arise before completion and are supported by occupation at that date there is no difficulty. A chargee who advances money and so acquires an equitable charge prior to the creation of the occupier's right does not lose his priority because the occupier's right becomes an overriding interest. That interest remains what it always was, an interest subject to the prior equity of the chargee which, on registration, is fortified by the legal estate. Equally, a chargee advancing his money after the creation of the occupier's equitable right is, as one would expect, subject to such right.
    The case which does give rise to difficulty if the date of registration is the relevant date for determining whether there is a claimant in actual occupation is one in which the sequence of events is that the right, unaccompanied by occupation, is created before completion and before the chargee has advanced his money and then subsequently the claimant enters into actual occupation after completion and remains in occupation up to

the date when the registration of the charge is effected. The chargee in that event would have no possibility of discovering the existence of the claimant's interest before advancing his money and taking his charge, but would nevertheless, be subject, on registration, to the claimant's prior equitable interest which, *ex hypothesi*, would not have been subject to the charge at its creation.

This does indeed produce a conveyancing absurdity and there is, as Nicholls LJ observed [1989] Ch 350, 374B–C, an internal context for supposing that the legislature, in enacting paragraph (g), must have been contemplating an occupation which preceded and existed at completion of a transfer or disposition. Not only was the paragraph clearly intended to reflect the rule discussed in *Hunt* v *Luck* with regard to unregistered conveyancing, but the reference to inquiry and failure to disclose cannot make any sense unless it is related to a period in which such inquiry could be other than otiose. That absurdity can, I think, be avoided only by the route which the Court of Appeal adopted and by referring the 'actual occupation' in paragraph (g) to the date of completion of the transaction by transfer and payment of the purchase money. Section 70(1) refers to such interests 'as may be for the time being subsisting' and in order to affect 'the estate transferred or created' on registration such interests would no doubt require to be subsisting on that date. But I see no insuperable difficulty in holding that the actual occupation required to support such an interest as a subsisting interest must exist at the date of completion of the transaction giving rise to the right to be registered, for that is the only date at which the inquiry referred to in paragraph (g) could, in practice, be made and be relevant. I agree, therefore, with the conclusion of the Court of Appeal in *Rosset* [1989] Ch 350 that it is at that moment that it falls to be determined whether there is an actual occupation for the purposes of paragraph (g). I do not think that I can improve upon Nicholls LJ's analysis when he said, in the course of his judgment in Rosset, at p. 374:

> If this is right, the pieces of the jigsaw fit together reasonably well. A purchaser or mortgagee inspects and inquires before completion, in the established fashion. Or he fails to do so, at this own risk. He then completes the transaction, taking an executed transfer or mortgage. Whether or not an overriding interest under paragraph (g) subsists so far as his freehold or mortgage is concerned falls to be determined at that moment. If an overriding interest does subsist, then his estate when registered takes subject to that interest. If it does not, then subsequently entry of a person into occupation before the transfer or mortgage has been registered, and 'completed' for the purposes of section 19, does not have the consequence of creating an overriding interest under paragraph (g) in relation to that freehold or mortgage. . . .

I have, up to this point, been content to assume that the facts of the instant case justify the proposition which found favour with Dillon LJ, that she was in actual occupation of the property at the material time. This is, of course, essentially a question of fact, but there is the serious question of what, in law, can amount to 'actual occupation' for the purposes of s. 70(1)(g). In *Williams & Glyn's Bank Ltd* v *Boland* [1981] AC 487, 504. Lord Wilberforce observed that these words should be interpreted for what they are, that is to say, ordinary words of plain English. But even plain English may contain a variety of shades of meaning. At the date of completion Mrs Cann was not personally even in England, leave alone in personal occupation of the property, and the trial judge held that the acts done by Mr Abraham Cann and Mr George Cann amounted to

> no more than the taking of preparatory steps leading to the assumption of actual residential occupation on or after completion, whatever the moment of the day when completion took place . . .

For my part, I am content to accept this as a finding of fact which was amply justified by the evidence before him, and I share the reservations expressed by Ralph Gibson and Woolf LJJ in the Court of Appeal. It is, perhaps, dangerous to suggest any test for what is essentially a question of fact, for 'occupation' is a concept which may have different connotations according to the nature and purpose of the property which is claimed to be occupied. It does not necessarily, I think, involve the personal presence of the person claiming to occupy. A caretaker or the representative of a company can occupy. I should have thought, on behalf of his employer. On the other hand, it does, in my judgment, involve some degree of permanence and continuity which would rule out mere fleeting presence. A prospective tenant or purchaser who is allowed, as a matter of indulgence, to go into property in order to plan decorations or measure for furnishing would not, in ordinary parlance, be said to be occupying it, even though he might be there for hours at a time. Of course, in the instant case, there was, no doubt, on the part of the persons involved in moving Mrs Cann's belongings, an intention that they would remain there and would render the premises suitable for her ultimate use as a residential occupier. Like the trial judge, however, I am unable to accept that acts of this preparatory character carried out by courtesy of the vendor prior to completion can constitute 'actual occupation' for the purposes of s. 70(1)(g). Accordingly, all other considerations apart, Mrs Cann fails, in my judgment, to establish the necessary condition for the assertion of an overriding interest.

Baughen, S., 'Some Lessons of *Cann*' (1991) 55 Conv 116

At first glance *Cann* seems so uniformly in favour of the mortgagee that it would be tempting to believe that it had removed nearly all the uncertainties that have surrounded s. 70(1)(g). Persons such as Mrs Cann can no longer establish an equitable interest prior to completion. All they can obtain at this stage is a potential equitable interest. They will find it extremely difficult to establish 'actual occupation' at the date of completion. Assuming they can clear these hurdles, they will always lose out to a mortgagee, even if their potential equitable interest came first in time, if the property could not have been purchased 'but for' the mortgage. Finally, even if they succeed on all these points, they will be taken to have postponed their interest to that of the mortgagee if they knew a mortgage *might* have to be taken out. However, several uncertainties still remain.

First, there is the application of the 'but for' test. *Cann* illustrates the difficulty in applying such a test in cases of dishonesty. What *actually* happened was that £25,000 was taken out on mortgage. What *should have* happened was that only £4,000 was taken out. In the latter situation 'but for' Mrs Cann vacating Island Road it could not have been sold and the greater part of the purchase price could not have been released. Their Lordships did not need to consider the problem of conflicting 'but for' interests because they resolved the dilemma posed by the dishonesty by focusing on what actually happened. But what if there had been a mortgage for only £4,000? The financial scales would not be substantially tilted towards Mrs Cann, but could the mortgagee still prevail by arguing that 'but for' its lending the final £4,000 Hillview could not have been purchased? The matter could be resolved by applying the 'consent' principles of *Henning,* but suppose George had fraudulently told his mother he would make up the shortfall by his savings, and she had no reasonable grounds to disbelieve him?

Secondly, there is the issue of re-mortgages. A distinction must be drawn between further advances which have no relevance to the initial purchase, as in *Boland,* and re-mortgages which discharge the initial mortgage. The former will not take priority over the rights of those in 'actual occupation' unless they can be taken to have consented to this. The 'but for' argument is inapplicable. However, it will apply to straight re-mortgages. 'But for' the first mortgage there would be no purchase. Therefore, 'but for' the second mortgage there would be no discharge from the first mortgage. There will never be a time when the legal estate is held free from encumbrances. However, if the re-mortgage is for an amount greater than that required to discharge the first mortgage, the surplus will be treated on the same principles as *Boland.* It, therefore, follows that mortgagees must still continue to exercise the greatest care in surveying the property on which they propose to lend money.

Thirdly, a question mark still hangs over what acts can constitute 'actual occupation.' *Cann* leaves open the question of whether acts taking place prior ro the acquisition of the equitable interest which gives the *right* to occupation, are still relevant to this issue. Until this point is clarified, mortgagees need to remember that those in 'actual occupation' may not only be those claiming title through the vendor but may extend to those whose title will, on completion derive from the intending purchaser. The former's rights will usually be revealed by a thorough survey before exchange. However, the latter's can only be revealed between exchange and completion. If there is a significant delay in completion, mortgagees would be advised to make a second survey during this period and to make such a survey a condition of the advance.

Fourthly, there is the possibility that overriding interests under s. 70(1)(a) and s. 70(1)(k) may be created by a fraudulent vendor in the gap between transfer and registration. This is an extension of a problem that was already latent in that such interests would have been created by the vendor prior to completion without anyone being able to discover them. They will only lose priority if those claiming under them knew of the vendor's fraud. The purchaser can protect itself against such interests being created *after* completion by immediately going into 'actual occupation' then, so as to become protected by s. 70(1)(g). However, there is nothing a mortgagee can do to protect itself against such a situation.

STRAND SECURITIES v CASWELL AND ANOTHER [1965] 1 Ch 958, Court of Appeal

FACTS: Caswell took a 39 year lease of a London flat. As the lease was for over 21 years, it should have been registered. Caswell did not register the lease. The practical effect of this failure to register the lease was that it only took effect as an equitable lease. The reversion was sold to Strand. They would only be bound by Caswell's lease if it was an overriding interest within the Land Registration Act 1925, s. 70(1)(g). Caswell did not personally live in the flat, but was an occasional visitor. The permanent occupant of the flat was his step-daughter. He let her live there rent-free, as her marriage had broken down.
HELD: Caswell was not in actual occupation of the premises and therefore could not claim to have an overriding interest under s. 70(1)(g).

LORD DENNING MR: . . . Even if the first defendant did not apply in time to register his sublease, he is not necessarily defeated. He may have an 'overriding interest' within s. 70(1)(g). This subsection expressly preserves 'the rights of every person in actual occupation of the land or in receipt of 'the rents and profits thereof.' [His Lordship stated the facts and continued]: Section 70(1)(g) as an important provision. Fundamentally its object is to protect a person in actual occupation of land from having his rights lost in the welter of registration. He can stay there and do nothing. Yet he will be protected. No one can buy the land over his head and thereby take away or diminish his rights. It is up to every purchaser before he buys to make inquiry on the premises. If he fails to do so, it is at his own risk. He must take subject to whatever rights the occupier may have. Such is the doctrine of *Hunt v Luck* [1902] 1 Ch 428 for unregistered land. Section 70(1)(g) carries the same doctrine forward into registered land but with this difference. Not only is the actual occupier protected, but also the person from whom he holds. It is up to the purchaser to inquire of the occupier, not only about the occupier's own rights, but also about the rights of his immediate superior. The purchaser must ask the occupier: 'To whom do you pay your rent?' And the purchaser must inquire what the rights of that person are. If he fails to do so, it is at his own risk for he takes subject to 'the rights of every person in actual occupation of the land or in receipt of the rents and profits thereof.'

In this case it is clear that the second defendant was in actual occupation of the flat. The plaintiffs, therefore, took subject to her rights, whatever they were; see *National Provincial Bank Ltd v Hastings Car Mart Ltd* [1964] Ch 665. She was not a tenant but only a licensee; see *Foster v Robinson* [1951] 1 KB 149; *Cobb v Lane* [1952] 1 All ER 1199. She had no contractual right to stay there. Her licence could be determined at any time and she would have to go in a reasonable time thereafter; see *Minister of Health v Bellotti* [1944] KB 298. So the plaintiffs could get her out, provided always that they could get rid of the first defendant's sublease.

But although the second defendant was in actual occupation, it is said that the first defendant was also in actual occupation. We have had several cases lately in which we have held that 'possession in law is, of course, single and exclusive but occupation may be shared with others or had on behalf of others'; see *Hills (Patents) Ltd v University College Hospital Board of Governors* [1956] 1 QB 90, and *Willis v Association of Universities of the British Commonwealth* [1965] 1 QB 140. In this case it is said that the first defendant did share the actual occupation of the flat with the second defendant.

I would like to hold that the first defendant was sharing the occupation of the flat with the second defendant. But I cannot bring myself to this conclusion. The truth is that he allowed her to be in actual occupation, and that is all there is to it. She was a licensee rent free and I fear that it does not give him protection. It seems to be a very rare case—a case which the legislature did not think of. For it is quite clear that if the second defendant had paid a token sum as rent, or for use and occupation, to the first defendant, he would be 'in receipt of the rents and profits' and his rights would be protected under s. 70(1)(g). Again if the first defendant put his servant or caretaker into the flat, rent free, he would be protected because his agent would have actual occupation on his behalf. It is odd that the first defendant is not protected simply because he let his stepdaughter in rent free. Odd as it is, however, I fear the words of the statute do not cover this case and the first defendant does not succeed on this point. . . .

WEBB v POLLMOUNT [1966] 1 Ch 584, Chancery Division

FACTS: L granted to Webb a legal lease to last for seven years, the lease was overriding under s. 70(1)(k). The lease also granted to Webb an option to purchase the fee simple reversion. No notice or caution was entered on the register to protect Webb's option. The fee simple was sold to Pollmount Ltd, who claimed that the option was not binding on it. HELD: Section 70(1)(g) would assist Webb. He was actually occupying the leased property at the time of the sale. Therefore his option was an overriding interest within s. 70(1)(g).

UNGOED-THOMAS . . . As a matter of first impression, 'land' in s. 70(1)(g) does not appear to me to refer to an estate in land, but to the physical land. The references which are contained in the subparagraph to 'actual occupation' and 'receipt of the rents and profits thereof' indicate this conclusion: and (g) is not limited to the rights of every tenant or estate owner, but extends to the rights of every person in actual occupation. 'Registered land' and 'land' are by definition not limited to estates in land, but include physical land. In this case, the only registered land is land comprised in the title mentioned in the pleadings, namely, 'the freehold property, No. 139, High Street, Plumstead.' In the Property Register under the heading 'The Freehold Land Shown and Numbered as below on H.M. Land Registry General Map' and sub-heading 'Short Description' the entry is '139, High Street, Plumstead.' It is the Proprietorship Register which shows the title and the proprietor. The registered land as appearing from the register is the physical land, 139, High Street, Plumstead. . . .

In s. 70(1)(g) itself, notice is covered by the concluding words 'save where inquiry is made of such person and the rights are not disclosed.' Thus, in this very subsection, 'the rights' are contrasted with and therefore are not defined or ascertained by reference to what constitutes notice of these rights. Notice, before the Act, is replaced by the express provision relating to notice in sub-paragraph (g) itself. So, it seems to me, that the question whether an option to purchase is a right within s. 70(1)(g) has to be decided independently of what constitutes notice of those rights. But, were it necessary, for the purposes of this case, to decide what has not hitherto been decided, whether before 1926 occupation by the lessee gave constructive notice of an option to purchase contained in his lease, I would decide that it did so (in accordance with the statement in Williams on Vendor and Purchaser, 4th edn. (1936), vol. 1, p. 636, and the judgments in Hunt v Luck [1902] 1 Ch 428 and Barnhart v Greenshields (1853) 9 Moo PCC 18).

It was suggested for the defendant that 'the right of every person in actual occupation of the land' should be construed as the rights by virtue of which a person is in actual occupation of the land. The short answer to this, it seems to me, is that it does not say so; and the wording is in marked contrast with the wording in s. 14 of the Law of Property Act 1925, where reference is made to the interest of a person in possession or occupation of land 'to which he may be entitled in right of such possession or occupation.' It is neither, in my view, consistent with the wording of s. 70(1)(g) of the Land Registration Act 1925, nor with the authorities from which I have quoted.

Although an option to purchase does not, like an option to renew, 'touch,' 'concern' or 'affect' 'the land demised and regarded as the subject-matter of the lease ' (so as, e.g., to bind the reversion under the Grantees of Reversions Act 1540), what we are concerned with here is not whether it so 'affects' 'the land demised' and is within the relationship of landlord and tenant as considered in the judgment of the Court of Appeal in Woodall v Clifton [1905] 2 Ch 257, but whether within s. 20(1)(b) it is an interest 'affecting the estate transferred' to the defendant. That it is capable of affecting the estate transferred to the defendant is not disputed; e.g., if the defendant had notice of it before transfer to him. So, it seems to me to fall within Russell LJ's test in *National Provincial Bank Ltd* v *Hastings Car Mart Ltd* [1964] Ch 665 of 'being capable of enduring through different ownerships of the land according to normal conceptions of title to real property.' And if it, thus, in the circumstances of this case, is a right 'affecting the estate transferred,' within the requirement of s. 20(1)(b), it seems to me that it is 'for the time being subsisting in reference to 'registered land within the requirement of s. 70(1). My conclusion, therefore, is that subject to deciding the question as to the effect of s. 59, the option to purchase appears to be an overriding interest. . . .

10.2   Minor Interests

10.2.1   PROTECTION OF MINOR INTERESTS

LAND REGISTRATION ACT 1925

20.   Effect of registration of dispositions of freeholds

(1)   In the case of a freehold estate registered with an absolute title, a disposition of the registered land or of a legal estate therein, including a lease thereof, for valuable consideration shall, when registered, confer on the transferee or grantee an estate in fee simple or the terms of years absolute or other legal estate expressed to be created in the land dealt with, together with all rights, privileges, and appurtenances belonging or appurtenant thereto, including (subject to any entry to the contrary in the register) the appropriate rights and interests which would, under the Law of Property Act 1925, have been transferred if the land had not been registered, subject—

(a)   to the incumbrances and other entries, if any, appearing on the register [and any charge for [inheritance tax] subject to which the disposition takes effect under section 73 of this Act]; and

(b)   unless the contrary is expressed on the register, to the overriding interests, if any, affecting the estate transferred or created,

but free from all other estates and interests whatsoever, including estates and interests of His Majesty, and the disposition shall operate in like manner as if the registered transferor or grantor were (subject to any entry to the contrary in the register) entitled to the registered land in fee simple in possession for his own benefit.

LYUS v *PROWSA DEVELOPMENTS* [1982] 1 WLR 1044, Chancery Division

FACTS: The land was registered. A land transfer was executed, expressly subject to a minor interest which had not been protected by entry on the register.
HELD: The purchaser was bound by the minor interest.

DILLON J: . . . It has been pointed out by Lord Wilberforce in *Midland Bank Trust Co. Ltd* v *Green* [1981] AC 513, 531, that it is not fraud to rely on legal rights conferred by Act of Parliament. Under s. 20, the effect of the registration of the transferee of a freehold title is to confer an absolute title subject to entries on the register and overriding interests, but, 'free from all other estates and interests whatsoever, including estates and interests of His Majesty . . .' In *Miles* v *Bull* (*No. 2*) [1969] 3 All ER 1585, Bridge J expressed the view that the words which I have quoted embraced, *prima facie*, not only all kinds of legal interests, but all kinds of equitable interests: see p. 1589. He therefore held, at p. 1590, as I read his judgment, that actual or constructive notice on the part of a purchaser of an unregistered interest would not have the effect of imposing a constructive trust on him. The interest in *Miles* v *Bull* (*No. 2*) was the interest in the matrimonial home of a deserted wife who had failed to protect her interest by registration under the Matrimonial Homes Act 1967. The contract for sale between the husband, who was the registered proprietor, and the purchaser provided that the house concerned was sold, subject to such rights of occupation as might subsist in favour of the wife, with a proviso that this was not to imply that the wife had, or would after completion have any such rights as against the purchaser. Plainly, therefore, the clause was only included in the contract for the protection of the husband who was the vendor. The wife was to get no fresh rights, and it was not in *Miles* v *Bull* (*No. 2*) a stipulation of the bargain between the vendor and the purchaser that the purchaser should give effect to the rights as against the vendor of the deserted wife. *Miles* v *Bull* (*No. 2*) is thus distinguishable from the facts of the present case as I interpret those facts.

It seems to me that the fraud on the part of the defendants in the present case lies not just in relying on the legal rights conferred by an Act of Parliament, but in the first defendant reneging on a positive stipulation in favour of the plaintiffs in the bargain under which the first defendant acquired the land. That makes, as it seems to me, all the difference. It has long since been held, for instance, in *Rochefoucauld* v *Boustead* [1897] 1 Ch 196, that the provisions of the Statute of Frauds 1677 (29 Car, 2 c. 3), now incorporated in certain sections of the Law of Property Act 1925, cannot be used as an instrument of fraud, and that it is fraud for a person to whom land is agreed to be conveyed as trustee for another to deny the trust and relying on the terms of the statute to claim the land for himself. *Rochefoucauld* v *Boustead* was one of the authorities on which the judgment in *Bannister* v *Bannister* [1948] 2 All ER 133 was founded.

It seems to me that the same considerations are applicable in relation to the Land Registration Act 1925. If, for instance, the agreement of October 18, 1979, between the bank and the first defendant had expressly stated that the first defendant would hold Plot 29 upon trust to give effect for the benefit of the plaintiffs to the plaintiffs' agreement with the vendor company, it would be difficult to say that that express trust was overreached and rendered nugatory by the Land Registration Act 1925. The Land Registration Act 1925 does not, therefore affect the conclusion which I would otherwise have reached in reliance on *Bannister* v *Bannister* and the judgment of Lord Denning MR in *Binions* v *Evans* [1972] Ch 359 had Plot 29 been unregistered land.

The plaintiffs are, therefore, entitled to succeed in this action. The appropriate relief in that event is that specific performance should be ordered as against the second defendants of the sale to the plaintiffs of Plot 29, with the completed house thereon, on the terms of the agreement of January 30, 1978, made between the plaintiffs and the vendor company.

Kenny, P.H., Constructive Trusts of Registered Land (1983) 46 MLR 96

Lyus v *Prowsa* [1982] 1 WLR 1044 concerned the enforceability of an unregistered third-party interest which was not an overriding interest against a transferee of registered land. The question was whether a purchaser was bound by a previous contract to sell part of the land to the plaintiff. The court held that the principle that a statute cannot be used as an instrument of fraud applied to the Land Registration Act 1925 and that in this case the purchaser was bound by a constructive trust ot the unregistered estate contract. . . .

The case is as important for what was omitted as for what was decided. Key sections of the Land Registration Act were not referred to: s. 74 which states that no 'person dealing with a registered estate or charge shall be affected with notice of a trust express implied or constructive' was ignored. Similarly, s. 59(1) providing that matters registerable in the case of unregistered land under the Land Charges Act 1972 are to be 'protected only by lodging a creditor's notice, a bankruptcy inhibition or a caution against dealings with the land or charge' was ignored. Presumably, the same sweeping principles of equity would have sidestepped these provisions.

The court here showed the usual judicial reluctance to grapple firmly with the mechanics of land registration. This arm's-length approach to the registration system led it not to give effect to the prescriptive system of registration in the Land Registration Act 1925. In the same way that the effect of non-registration of an estate contract is prescribed by s. 4 of the Land Charges Act 1972 and had to be given effect to in *Midland Bank Trust Co. Ltd* v *Green* [1981] AC 513 so the need to register an equivalent interest in registered land is prescribed by s. 59(1) of the Land Registration Act 1925 which, with s. 20 and s. 34(4), should have been given effect to by the court. The legislation for both registered and unregistered land makes mandatory provision for registration and is specific on the effect of non-registration. The estate contract could, under the Land Registration Act, have been protected against the charge only by registration giving priority over the charge with the bank's consent. If there is a principle of equity which allows such transparently clear provisions to be sidestepped it should at least be described with greater precision and result from a less cavalier treatment of the relevant legislation.

Harpum, C., 'Constructive Trusts and Registered Land'
[1983] *Cambridge Law Journal* 54

The decision of Dillon J in *Lyus* v *Prowsa Developments Ltd* [1982] 1 WLR 1044 is another example of judicial unwillingness to come to terms with the Land Registration Act 1925. . . .

The consequences of the decision are far-reaching. A novel method has been found of assigning the burden of a contract that relates to property. The property is simply sold subject to those contractual rights and by the medium of a constructive trust the purchaser becomes bound by them even though he could not otherwise have been. The equitable obligation arises from the undertaking in the contract to sell the property and no mention of the liability need appear on the title. In this way, the burden of positive covenants may be transferred to a purchaser, the vendor thereby escaping liability. It also means that unregistered equitable encumbrances may be made to bind purchasers. For example, A contracts to grant a lease of unregistered land to B. B neglects to register the agreement as a Class C(iv) land charge. A then sells the land to C 'subject to' B's contract. Although by reason of s. 4(6) of the Land Charges Act 1972, C should take free of B's unregistered charge: *Hollington Brothers Ltd* v *Rhodes* [1951] 2 All ER 578 *Lyus* suggests that he will not, because a constructive trust will be imposed upon him. What then if C sells the land to D without any reservation in favour of B's rights, but where D is fully aware of them and perhaps pays less for the land as a result? If the basis of the imposition of the constructive trust in *Lyus* was to prevent unconscionable conduct, then D too should be a constructive trustee. If that is correct, what has become of *Midland Bank Trust Co Ltd* v *Green* [1981] AC 513? The *Lyus* constructive trust looks to be 'remedial' rather than 'substantive' and as such without much precedent in English law, which has tended to treat constructive trusts as part of the law of property, preferring to develop the remedial possibilities of estoppel instead. It remains to be seen whether the *Lyus* constructive trust is a one-case mutant or the progenitor of a new species. . . .

PEFFER v *RIGG AND ANOTHER* [1977] 1 WLR 285, Chancery Division

FACTS: Title to the land was registered. Mr Peffer and Mr Rigg purchased a house as an investment and in order to accommodate a relative. The house was registered in Mr Rigg's sole name, but it was agreed that he would hold the legal title on trust for himself and Mr Peffer as tenants in common in equal shares. This arrangement was confirmed by an express deed of trust at a later date. On their divorce Mr Rigg transferred the house to Mrs Rigg for £1, as part of the divorce settlement. Mrs Rigg was, accordingly, registered as sole legal proprietor. She was fully aware, throughout of the trust in favour of Mr Peffer. Unfortunately Mr Peffer had failed to protect his interest on the register and so the question arose whether Mrs Rigg was bound by his interest.

HELD: Even if the £1 consideration could be treated as valuable consideration, it was still necessary for the purchaser to show that she had purchased in good faith. This she had failed to do. Consequently, she could not take advantage of the Land Registration Act, s. 59(6) which provides that 'a purchaser aquiring title under a registered disposition' shall not be concerned with unprotected minor interests, apart from overriding interests. Her lack of 'good faith' meant that she wasn't to be regarded as a 'purchaser', at all, for the purposes of this section.

In any event, the purchaser had known that the property she had received was trust property. She would therefore be liable as a constructive trustee, under normal trust principles, to account to the plaintiff for his share of the property.

GRAHAM J: . . . was the letting to Mr and Mrs Lewis by the defendants a breach of trust *qua* the plaintiff? I do not think so. . . .

The purported transfer, however, of the whole of the beneficial interest in the property by the first defendant to the second defendant on the occasion of the divorce agreement in the light of their knowledge of the true facts as I have found them, seems to me to be in a very different position. It was argued by Mr Banks, for the second defendant, that the property was transferred to her for valuable consideration as part of the divorce agreement and that, therefore, the combined effect of ss. 20 and 59 of the Land Registration Act 1925 protected the second defendant against any claim or interest of the plaintiff because there is no entry on the register in his favour prior to the transfer to the second defendant. This argument would be convincing if it were not for my finding that the second defendant at the time knew perfectly well that the first defendant could not transfer to her more than a half share of the property. It is this knowledge which seems to me to cause great difficulty to her and prevents her argument succeeding for a number of different reasons put forward by Mr Poulton for the plaintiff at the second hearing. He argues first that the purported transfer from the first defendant to the second defendant of the beneficial interest of the whole of the property of 103, Leighton Road was expressed to be for the consideration of £1. This is a nominal consideration and not valuable consideration and it follows that the second defendant is not protected by s. 20 of the Land Registration Act 1925. In accordance with the provisions of s. 20(4) she can only take subject to any minor interests subject to which the first defendant held the same. He was party to the trust deed of May 30, 1968, and clearly had notice of the plaintiff's half interest in the property. The second defendant can therefore only take subject to the minor interest of the plaintiff in the property subject to which the first defendant held it.

The argument to the contrary is that the transfer was only part of the whole agreement entered into by the first and second defendants on the occasion of the divorce and it is not therefore right to limit the consideration for the transfer to the £1 expressed to be therefor. The consideration, there, was a great deal more and included all the obligations undertaken by the second defendant. Such consideration was therefore not nominal but valuable within s. 20 and the second defendant received the protection of the section. I do not see why, when the parties have chosen to express a transfer as being for a nominal consideration, the court should seek to hold that the consideration was in fact otherwise than as agreed and stated. If, however, the proper view is that there was valuable consideration for the transfer here, then it is argued as follows. There is a contrast between ss. 20 and 59 of the Act. Section 20(1) protects any 'transferee' for valuable consideration. By s. 18(5) 'transfer' and 'transferee' in relation to freehold land have very wide meanings but are not specifically defined in s. 3. It is to be noted, however, that s. 20, though it mentions valuable consideration, does not mention 'good faith' as being necessary on the part of the transferee, nor does it mention notice. It can be argued therefore that the section seems to be saying that a transferee whether he has good faith or not, and whether he has notice or not, takes free of all interests (other than overriding interests) provided he has given valuable consideration.

This at first sight seems a remarkable proposition and though undoubtedly the property legislation of 1925 was intended to simplify such matters of title as far as possible, I find it difficult to think that s. 20 of this Act can have been intended to be as broad in scope as this. Similar doubt is expressed in *Brickdale & Stewart-Wallace's Land Registration Act 1925*, 4th edn. (1939), p. 107, note (1). The provisions for rectification in s. 82 as against a proprietor in possession who has been a party to a fraud, mistake or an omission in consequence of which rectification of the register is sought also seems to me to show that s. 20 must be read with some limitations: see also *Ruoff & Roper*.

Registered Conveyancing, 3rd edn. (1972), p. 417. Section 59(6) on the other hand speaks of a 'purchaser' not being affected by matters which are not protected by a caution or other entry on the register. By definition, however (see s. 3(xxi)), 'purchaser' means a purchaser in good faith for valuable consideration. It seems clear therefore that as a matter of construction a purchaser who is not in fact one 'in good faith' will be concerned with matters not protected by a caution or other entry on the register, at any rate, as I hold, if he has notice thereof. If these sections 20 and 59 are read together in the context of the Act they can be reconciled by holding that if the 'transferee' spoken of in s. 20 is in fact a 'purchaser' he will only be protected if he has given valuable consideration and is in good faith. He cannot in my judgment be in good faith if he has in fact notice of something which affects his title as in the present case. Of course if he and, *a fortiori*, if a purchaser from him has given valuable consideration and in fact has no notice he is under no obligation to go behind the register, and will in such a case be fully protected. This view of the matter seems to me to enable the two sections to be construed consistently together without producing the unreasonable result of permitting a transferee purchaser to take advantage of the Act, and divest himself of knowledge of defects in his own title, and secure to himself a flawless title which he ought not in justice to be allowed to obtain. This view of the Act produces a result which is also produced by applying the principles applicable in the case of a constructive trust, which I will now consider.

On the evidence in this case I have found that the second defendant knew quite well that the first defendant held the property on trust for himself and the plaintiff in equal shares. The second defendant knew this was so and that the property was trust property when the transfer was made to her, and therefore she took the property on a constructive trust in accordance with general equitable principles: see *Snell's Principles of Equity*, 27th edn. (1973), pp. 98–99. This is a new trust imposed by equity and is distinct from the trust which bound the first defendant. Even if, therefore, I am wrong as to the proper construction of ss. 20 and 59, when read together, and even if section 20 strikes off the shackles of the express trust which bound the first defendant, this cannot invalidate the new trust imposed on the second defendant. . . .

CLARK v *CHIEF LAND REGISTRAR* [1993] 2 WLR 141, Chancery Division, Ferris J; [1994] 3 WLR 593, Court of Appeal, Nourse LJ

FACTS: The Jarvises, the owners of 'Spinner's Corner', owed the Clarks money under a judgment debt. The Clarks, in an effort to enforce their judgment, obtained a 'charging order' against Spinners Corner. This gave them an interest in Spinners Corner similar to that of an equitable mortgagee. They perfectly correctly 'protected' their interest by lodging a Caution.

The Jarvises then executed a legal mortgage of Spinners Corner to Jones. When Jones presented his mortgage for registration as a mortgage by registered charge, the Land Registry made a mistake. They omitted to send a warning of the proposed transaction to the Clarks. Thus the Clarks did not object to Jones registering his mortgage by registered charge.

HELD: Jones was not bound by the Clarks charging order, (even though Jones presumably knew of the Caution). However, the Clarks were entitled to claim compensation from the Land registry, whose negligence had effectively destroyed their rights.

FERRIS J: . . . On the footing that, as I have now held, the charging order obtained by the plaintiffs charges the land, the registrar contends that the plaintiffs have nevertheless suffered no loss as the result of the failure to give notice pursuant to their caution. (By 'their caution' I mean the caution lodged on 29 November 1990 in respect of their charging order absolute. Although the caution in respect of the charging order nisi remained on the register for some time it had no substantive effect after 29 November 1990). The caution remains on the register and it is said that it has the effect that, if the second defendant were to obtain the surplus proceeds of sale not required to satisfy the charge in favour of Barclays Bank Plc, he would have to satisfy the interests of the plaintiffs as cautioners before he could take anything in satisfaction of his own charge. This contention, if it were right, would be advantageous to the plaintiffs, who would not then need to seek an indemnity from the registrar. The plaintiffs do not, however, support it. On their behalf Mr Nugee submits that it is manifestly wrong. . . .

. . . The effect of a caution was considered by the Court of Appeal in *Barclays Bank Ltd* v *Taylor* [1974] Ch 137. In this case the land certificate of registered land had been deposited with the bank by way of security and the bank had registered at the Land Registry a notice of deposit which, under the rules, had effect as a caution under s. 54 of the Land Registration Act 1925. Subsequently the bank was granted a legal mortgage but before this had been registered the registered proprietors entered into a contract to sell the land to purchasers who lodged a caution to protect their interest as purchasers under the contract. The bank subsequently took steps to register its legal charge and notice of this application was given to the purchasers as cautioners. The purchasers claimed that the bank's charge should be registered only subject to their contract. The Court of Appeal held that the bank's unregistered mortgage and the purchasers' contract were both minor interests which took effect in equity only and that the priority beween them was governed by the normal rules, the interest which was first in time having priority. In giving the judgment of the court, Russell LJ made a number of observations which bear upon the effect of a caution, at p. 147:

The caution lodged on behalf of the purchasers had no effect whatever by itself on priorities: it simply conferred on the cautioners the right to be given notice of any dealing proposed to be registered . . . so that they might have the opportunity of contending that it would be a dealing which would infringe their rights and to which the applicants for the registration were not as against them entitled: . . . [The purchasers'] caution did not and could not confer on their equitable entitlement or interest any priority over the bank's equitable charge . . .

Later he observed:

counsel for [the purchasers] was quite unable to point to any provision in the statute which stated that their caution as such gave them priority in respect of their equitable interest over the earlier equitable interest of the bank under its mortgage. If such had been the intention of the legislature, it would not have been difficult for the statute to have so provided: see the express provision in section 29 on priorities between registered charges . . .

The argument on behalf of the plaintiffs was that the registrar's contention concerning the plaintiffs' caution seeks to give to that caution precisely the effect on priorities which the Court of Appeal said that a caution does not and cannot have. Moreover the suggestion that the plaintiffs have priority over the second defendant is contrary to s. 29 of the Act of 1925 under which

Subject to any entry on the contrary on the register, registered charges on the same land shall as between themselves rank according to the order in which they are entered on the register, and not according to the order in which they are created.

Looking at the register immediately after the second defendant's charge was registered, that charge ranked, it is said, subject only to the prior charge of Barclays Bank Plc. It cannot rank subject to the plaintiffs' charging order, because that charging order has not been entered on the register.

The registrar's answer to this argument is based upon s. 59 of the Act of 1925 and *Parkash* v *Irani Finance Ltd* [1970] Ch 101. Section 59(1) provides:

A writ, order, deed of arrangement, pending action, or other interest which in the case of unregistered land may be protected by registration under the Land Charges Act 1925 shall, where the land affected or the charge securing the debt affected is registered, be protected only by lodging a creditor's notice, a bankruptcy inhibition or a caution against dealings with the land or the charge.

As I have mentioned, s. 3(3) of the Charging Orders Act 1979 now expressly permits a charging order to be protected by a notice and even before that Act was passed the registrar allowed this as a matter of discretion. However these facts do not affect the submission of the registrar, which was based on s. 59(6) which provides that, subject to certain immaterial exceptions,

a purchaser acquiring title under a registered disposition, shall not be concerned with any . . . order . . . or other document, matter, or claim (not being an overriding interest) which is not protected by a caution or other entry on the register, whether he has or has not notice thereof, express, implied, or constructive.

The argument is that where a charging order *is* protected by a caution or other entry on the register a purchaser *is* 'affected by it' and that, in the context, 'affected by it' means that he takes subject to it. It was submitted that this had been held to be so in *Parkash* v *Irani Finance Ltd* and that this view was endorsed in *Megarry and Wade, The Law of Real Property*, 5th edn. (1984), p. 213, footnote 88.

In *Parkash* v *Irani Finance Ltd* [1970] Ch 101 the defendant obtained a charging order on registered land which it protected by lodging a caution. The plaintiff entered into a contract to purchase the land and his solicitors obtained an official search which, by an error, did not disclose the caution. The plaintiff then completed his purchase and executed a legal charge over the property. When the transfer in favour of the plaintiff and the charge executed by him were presented for registration, notice was given to the defendant as cautioner. The defendant objected to these instruments being registered until its charge had been redeemed. The registrar, in accordance with the rules, ordered that the following questions be referred to the court: (a) whether the caution should continue to have effect or be cancelled; and (b) if the caution was to continue to have effect the order of priority in which the charging order to Irani, the transfer to the plaintiff and the charge to the plaintiff's mortgagee should be entered on the register. The report of the argument shows that it was accepted on behalf of the plaintiff that, unless there was something to give priority to the transfer in his favour (which at that stage took effect in equity only by virtue of s. 106 of the Land Registration Act 1925) the prior equity of Irani must prevail. It was contended that the plaintiff's transfer should have priority because the plaintiff had no notice of the interest protected by the caution and, if it were not for the caution, would have become a purchaser for value without notice. The main argument for Irani was that the ordinary doctrine of notice had no application to registered land. If it were applicable it would be in conflict with s. 59. The plaintiff's mortgagee supported the plaintiff's argument and raised other arguments which do not matter for present purposes.

Plowman J rejected the plaintiff's argument based on the absence of notice. In doing so he referred to s. 59(6) and said [1970] Ch 101, 110:

> It is true, as was stressed in the argument before me, that what the subsection says is that a purchaser is *not* affected by notice, express, implied or constructive, of matters capable of protection by a caution and not so protected and that (unlike the case of a notice of lease under s. 48(1) of the Act) it does not say in terms that a purchaser *is* affected by a notice of matters capable of protection by caution, which *are* so protected, but that, in my judgment, is implicit in the scheme of the Act and in the subsection.

He went on to hold first that the appropriate form of protection for a charging order is a caution (this may, it seems, have been before the registrar began to allow protection by notice); secondly that once the caution is registered the cautioner could only lose his protection in various specific ways which were not applicable to that case; and thirdly, at p. 111:

> that therefore he does not lose it merely because a purchaser of the property does not know of its existence, even if the purchaser's ignorance is the result of a mistake of the Land Registry, short of a failure to act on an application to register the caution in the first place.

His ultimate conclusion, at p. 112, was that 'Irani's caution should continue to have effect and that it takes priority over the transfer of 10 August 1967 and the charge of the same date.'

I have thought it necessary to summarise *Parkash* v *Irani Finance Ltd* [1970] Ch 101 in some detail because Mr Nugee contended, on behalf of the plaintiffs, that although the reasoning of Plowman J might appear to support the registrar's argument, this was not in fact the case. Mr Nugee supported that part of the reasoning which rejected the argument that the principles of notice applicable to unregistered land were also applicable to registered land, in so far as this reasoning did not depend on s. 59(6). That was all that was necessary to decide the case. The plaintiff could not establish that he was a purchaser of a legal estate because, at the time when the matter came before the court, he did not have the legal estate. Accordingly the contest was between two equitable interests and, in accordance with the principles subsequently applied in *Barclays Bank Ltd* v *Taylor* [1974] Ch 137, the interest of Irani prevailed because it was first in time. When, at the end of his judgment, Plowman J said that Irani's caution took priority over the transfer in favour of the plaintiff and the charge executed by him, he should be taken as meaning that the charging order protected by the caution took priority. That was, in substance the answer to the second question which had been referred to the court by the registrar. I note that Mrs Crampin sought instructions as to what entries had been made in the register pursuant to the order of Plowman J, but the answer was unhelpful as it appears that the registrar indemnified Irani and cancelled the caution, so leaving the field open for registration of the plaintiff and his mortgagee.

Mr Nugee contended that the observations of Plowman J on s. 59(6) were unnecessary to his decision and, in so far as they suggest that a caution has, in some respects at least, an effect similar to that of a notice, they were inconsistent with s. 56(2) and with the emphatic statements of the Court of Appeal in *Barclays Bank Ltd* v *Taylor* and ought not to be followed. *Parkash* v *Irani Finance Ltd* [1970] Ch 101 was cited in argument in *Barclays Bank Ltd* v *Taylor* [1974] Ch 137 but was not commented upon in the judgment. In my judgment Mr Nugee's submissions concerning *Parkash* v *Irani Finance Ltd* [1970] Ch 101 are correct. I doubt whether Plowman J intended to suggest that a caution had much the same effect as a notice. In so far as his language, may suggest otherwise I must, I think, decline to apply it. If I were to do so I would, it appears to me, ignore the binding reasoning of *Barclays Bank Ltd* v *Taylor* [1974] Ch 137.

NOURSE LJ: . . . The views expressed by . . . this court in *Barclays Bank Limited* v *Taylor* are decisive of the caution point. They have the very great merit of having been based essentially on those provisions—ss. 54 to 56 of the Act of 1925—which were clearly intended to describe and declare the nature and effect of cautions against dealings. They show that it is for that purpose unnecessary to look beyond those provisions. The deletion of Sir George Curtis's and Mr Ruoff's original firm opinion that cautions do not confer any kind of priority, an opinion which is as correct now as it was then, is of no significance. The lack of priority remains implicit in the revised version. Moreover, the attempts made in argument to depreciate the manifest value of the views expressed in *Barclays Bank Ltd* v *Taylor* were unsuccessful.

The principal consequence of the arguments advanced on behalf of the Chief Land Registrar and Mr Ketteringham was to demonstrate the unwisdom of straying from ss. 54 to 56 to other provisions of the Act of 1925. It is hardly surprising that counsel were able to extract from legislation 'of exceptionally low quality' provisions which, on a myopic view, give some semblance of support for those arguments. None of those provisions can prevail over the clear effect of ss. 54 to 56.

In this court, as in the courts below, the Chief Land Registrar relied principally on s. 59(1) and (6) of the Act of 1925 and *Parkash* v *Irani Finance Ltd* [1970] Ch 101. For the reasons given by Ferris J [1993] Ch 294, 311F to 313H, I agree with him that those provisions and that decision do not assist them. For myself, I am certain that Plowman J a judge of great experience in conveyancing matters, did not intend to suggest that a caution had much the same effect as a notice. . . .

10.3   End of Chapter Assessment Question

George is currently setting himself up as a farmer. In the last month he has acquired the following property rights.

(a)   A freehold title to Broad Field acquired from Harry. The title is unregistered, and Harry was only able to produce one title deed, the conveyance to him when he bought the land 11 years ago.

(b)   The grant of a new lease for 30 years over Wide Field.

(c)   The grant of a new lease over Low Field for 8 years.

(d)   The grant of a profit to graze 100 sheep on East Moor. The profit is to last for George's lifetime.

(e)   An agreement for a right of way across West Meadow to get to Broad Field.

Advise George as to:

(i)   which of these property rights will acquire substantive registration;

(ii)   the effects of such registration;

(iii)   the consequences of failure to register a title which should have been registered;

(iv)   whether any of the rights which are not capable of substantive registration should be protected by an entry on the Register of Title or on the Land Charges Register.

10.4   End of Chapter Assessment Outline Answer

(a)(i)   When George buys Harry's freehold title to Broad Field there will be clearly a 'conveyance on sale' which will oblige George to register that title. (Since 1990 the whole country has been a compulsory area of registration of title.)

(b)(i)   When George applies for the first registration of his freehold title to Blue Field, there will be the problem that he will only be able to produce a 'root of title' which is ten years old, rather than the requisite fifteen. As things stand at the moment somebody (call him X) might still come along and (1) produce documents proving that X was originally owner of Broad Field and (2) prove that X's rights have not yet been 'time-barred' by adverse possession.

The Land Registry are thus unlikely to grant George an 'absolute title' guaranteeing that he is outright owner of the land. They might conceivably grant George a 'Qualified Title' guaranteeing that, except for claims arising more than ten years ago which are not time-barred, he is owner of the land. However, it is not the general practice for the registry to grant qualified titles.

Almost certainly the Registry will grant George a possessory title. This will not guarantee George against any competing claims to Broad Field which arise before the date of registration. The value of this possessory title to George will initially be limited. But if he remains in undisputed control of Broad Field for twelve years his title will be upgraded to absolute. (Assuming George registers in early 1996, he will get an absolute title in 2008.)

(c)(i)   If George fails to register within two months of the conveyance, the legal title to Broad Field will revest in Harry in trust for George. George will thus only have an equitable fee simple.

This 'sanction' is not a severe one. George can always apply for late registration, which will revest the legal title in himself. The registry could charge him a 'late fee', but in practice the registry only rarely require the payment of such a fee.

(a)(ii)   As the lease of Wide Field is over twenty-one years, it will also require registration.

(b)(ii)   If the freehold reversion to Wide Field is registered with absolute title, then George will be granted an absolute leasehold title to the field, giving him a firm guarantee that he has a thirty year lease.

If the reversion is unregistered then George will only get a good leasehold title (unless he can persuade his landlord to produce his deeds to the registry). Good leasehold guarantees George's lease only on the assumption that the landlord's title is sound. (I.e., if somebody came along and proved that he had a better title to Wide Field than George's 'landlord', George will lose his lease and will have no claim against the registry.)

(c)(ii)   If George fails to register within two months he will cease to have a legal lease and will (in effect) only have an equitable lease. George can always apply for late registration, which will revest a legal lease in himself. Again, the registry might possibly charge him a 'late fee'.

(a)(iii)   A lease for not more than twenty-one years is not capable of substantive registration.

(d)(iii)   Provided the lease of Low Field is by deed, there is no further action which George need take to protect his right to Low Field. If the reversion to Low Field is unregistered, then George has a legal lease which is automatically binding on the whole world. If the reversion to the lease is registered then George will have an overriding interest within the Land Registration Act 1925, s. 70(1)(k) which will be binding on the purchaser of the reversion. (George need not worry about whether he is an 'actual occupation'.)

(d)(iv)   A profit is not capable of substantive registration. As this profit only lasts for George's lifetime, it is outside the scope of the Law of Property Act 1925, s. 1(2) and is purely equitable. Thus if the title to East Moor is unregistered, George should register his profit as a class D(iii) landcharge. If he fails to do so, his profit would be void against a purchaser for money or money's worth of East Moor.

If the title to East Moor is registered, George need do nothing to protect his profit. He has an overriding interest within the Land Registration Act 1925, s. 70(1)(a), a provision which extends to both legal and equitable profits.

(d)(v)   This right is clearly an equitable easement (there is no deed) and it is not capable of substantive registration. If the title to West Meadow is unregistered, George should register his easement as a class D(iii) landcharge. If he fails to do so, his easement will be void against a purchaser for money or money's worth of West Meadow.

If the title to West Meadow is registered, then it is debatable whether George's easement is an overriding or minor interest. The wording of section 70(1)(a) suggests that an equitable easement can only be a minor interest. However in *Alton House* Scott J held that an equitable easement was an overriding interest which bound a purchaser of the servient land even though it had not been protected by an entry on the register.

This is a very questionable decision, and George should act on the assumption that it is wrong. He should protect his interest by entry of a Notice or Caution. A 'Notice' is preferable, but to enter one against West Meadow he will need to produce the Land Certificate to the registry.

If the owner of West Meadow will not agree to the production of the Land Certificate, then George should lodge a 'Caution'. In theory this only entitles him to fourteen days warning of proposed transactions with West Meadow, though in practice all but foolhardy purchasers will be put off by the presence of the Caution.

CHAPTER ELEVEN

OLD-STYLE TRUSTS OF LAND

11.1 Historical Introduction

Harvey, B.W., *Settlements of Land,* **London: Sweet & Maxwell, 1973, p. 3**

. . . It is now comparatively rare to find large tracts of land in England still the subject of the traditional family settlement. There are in essence two reasons, one economic and one fiscal.

The economic reason is that from about the middle of the nineteenth century onwards it became plain that there was no inherent superiority in land as an investment for wealth. Investment in land which had been in the family for many years had, it is true, a strong sentimental attraction, but at this time the growth of the joint stock company combined with readily available facilities for lending money at interest, whether privately or to the government, provided alternative uses for wealth. England was becoming more of a trading than of an agricultural nation and the demand for coal and other minerals made it more desirable for mineral leases to be granted for exploitation of the underground wealth of the land. The growth of the population also put pressure on land for housing development. Land subject to the traditional family settlements was ill-suited for these purposes. Large tracts were vested in limited owners with inadequate powers of disposition, the land itself being burdened with charges in favour of other members of the family. Agricultural depression, too, became an issue in 1879 when the government appointed a Royal Commission to investigate the condition of farmers. The depression was caused basically by the repeal of the Corn Laws which after a time resulted in the cheap importation of foreign grain. Farming tended to be inefficient and unscientific and tenant farmers suffered particularly badly. Landlords were forced to lower rents, but the fixed charges payable out of their land, if settled, remained. The result in their case too was a decline in standards of living . . . so that it became much less easy for any settlor to ordain whether the family wealth should be held in the form of land or personalty.

The fiscal reason stems from the drastic steepening of the rates of income tax, surtax and estate duty since the early 1900s. . . . The impact of taxation, which bears on the nominal value of money, has been increased by a steady decline in the real value (or purchasing power) of the currency. Apart from a period between the wars, the average loss in value of the pound since 1900 has been about 4 per cent per annum. This reduces the value of £1 to 1/4d. (7p.) over seventy years. These taxes are adverse to large landholdings in that as far as taxes on income are concerned, in order to retain spending power it is necessary to keep raising rents (where not controlled by statute) or otherwise make the land yield money, and owners were often either unable or unwilling to do this. . . .

11.2 Criticisms of the Trust for Sale

(Note: The Settled Land Act 1925 has been superseded in the case of all new trusts by the Trusts of Land and Appointment of Trustees Act 1996. The following extract is included to illustrate the complexity of the law affecting strict settlements which were in existence before 1 January 1997.)

SETTLED LAND ACT 1925

1. What constitutes a settlement

(1) Any deed, will, agreement for a settlement or other agreement, Act of Parliament, or other instrument, or any number of instruments, whether made or passed before or after, or partly before and partly after, the commencement of this Act, under or by virtue of which instrument or instruments any land, after the commencement of this Act, stands for the time being—

    (i)   limited in trust for any persons by way of succession; or

    (ii)   limited in trust for any person in possession—

        (a)   for an entailed interest whether or not capable of being barred or defeated;

        (b)   for an estate in fee simple or for a term of years absolute subject to an executory limitation, gift, or disposition over on failure of his issue or in any other event;

        (c)   for a base or determinable fee or any corresponding interest in leasehold land;

        (d)   being an infant, for an estate in fee simple or for a term of years absolute; or

    (iii)   limited in trust for any person for an estate in fee simple or for a term of years absolute contingently on the happening of any event; or

    (iv)   . . .

    (v)   charged, whether voluntary or in consideration of marriage or by way of family arrangement, and whether immediately or after an interval, with the payment of any rentcharge for the life of any person, or any less period, or of any capital, annual, or periodical sums for the portions, advancement, maintenance, or otherwise for the benefit of any persons, with or without any term of years for securing or raising the same;

creates or is for the purposes of this Act a settlement and is in this Act referred to as a settlement, or as the settlement, as the case requires:

Provided that, where land is the subject of a compound settlement, references in this Act to the settlement shall be construed as meaning such compound settlement, unless the context otherwise requires.

(2) Where an infant is beneficially entitled to land for an estate in fee simple or for a term of years absolute and by reason of an intestacy or otherwise there is no instrument under which the interest of the infant arises or is acquired, a settlement shall be deemed to have been made by the intestate, or by the person whose interest the infant has acquired.

(3) . . .

(4) An estate or interest not disposed of by a settlement and remaining in or reverting to the settlor, or any person deriving title under him, is for the purposes of this Act an estate or interest comprised in the subject of the settlement and coming to the settlor or such person under or by virtue of the settlement.

(5) Where—

    (a)   a settlement creates an entailed interest which is incapable of being barred or defeated, or a base or determinable fee, whether or not the reversion or right of reverter is in the Crown, or any corresponding interest in leasehold land; or

    (b)   the subject of a settlement is an entailed interest, or a base or determinable fee, whether or not the reversion or right of reverter is in the Crown, or any corresponding interest in leasehold land;

the reversion or right of reverter upon the cesser of the interests so created or settled shall be deemed to be an interest comprised in the subject of the settlement, and limited by the settlement.

(6) Subsections (4) and (5) of this section bind the Crown.

(7) This section does not apply to land held upon trust for sale.

11.3 Criticisms of Strict Settlements and the Settled Land Act 1925

11.3.1 LIMITED POWERS OF DISPOSITION OF LIFE TENANTS

The thinking in 1925 was *not* to give the life tenant under a strict settlement unrestricted powers over the settled land. Rather it was to give him only the powers which a 'reasonable landowner' would want. Unfortunately, in the light of changed economic conditions, some of these powers are today inadequate.

11.3.1.1   The statutory powers

(Note: After 1 January 1997 and the Trusts of Land and Appointment of Trustees Act 1996 the following powers apply only to pre-1997 trusts.)

SETTLED LAND ACT 1925

38.   Powers of sale and exchange
A tenant for life—

(i)   May sell the settled land, or any part thereof, or any easement, right or privilege of any kind over or in relation to the land; and

(ii)   . . .

(iii)   May make an exchange of the settled land, or any part thereof, or of any easement, right, or privilege of any kind, whether or not newly created, over or in relation to the settled land, or any part thereof, for other land, or for any easement, right or privilege of any kind, whether or not newly created, over or in relation to other land, including an exchange in consideration of money paid for equality of exchange.

41.   Power to lease for ordinary or building or mining or forestry purposes
A tenant for life may lease the settled land, or any part thereof, or any easement, right, or privilege of any kind over or in relation to the land, for any purpose whatever, whether involving waste or not, for any term not exceeding—

(i)   In case of a building lease, nine hundred and ninety-nine years;

(ii)   In case of a mining lease, one hundred years;

(iii)   In case of a forestry lease, nine hundred and ninety-nine years;

(iv)   In case of any other lease, fifty years.

51.   Power to grant options

(1)   A tenant for life may at any time, either with or without consideration, grant by writing an option to purchase or take a lease of the settled land, or any part thereof, or any easement, right, or privilege over or in relation to the same at a price or rent fixed at the time of the granting of the option.

(2)   Every such option shall be made exercisable within an agreed number of years not exceeding ten.

(3)   The price or rent shall be the best which, having regard to all the circumstances, can reasonably be obtained and either—

(a)   may be a specified sum of money or rent, or at a specified rate according to the superficial area of the land with respect to which the option is exercised, or the frontage thereof or otherwise; or

(b)   in the case of an option to purchase contained in a lease or agreement for a lease, may be a stated number of years' purchase of the highest rent reserved by the lease or agreement; or

(c)   if the option is exercisable as regards part of the land comprised in the lease or agreement, may be a proportionate part of such highest rent;
and any aggregate price or rent may be made to be apportionable in any manner, or according to any system, or by reference to arbitration.

(4)   An option to take a mining lease may be coupled with the grant of a licence to search for and prove any mines or minerals under the settled land, or any part thereof, pending the exercise of the option.

(5)   The consideration for the grant of the option shall be capital money arising under this Act.

71.   Power to raise money by mortgage

(1)   Where money is required for any of the following purposes namely:—

(i)   Discharging an incumbrance on the settled land or part thereof;

(ii)   Paying for any improvement authorised by this Act or by the settlement;

(iii)   Equality of exchange;

(iv)   (v)...;

(vi)   *Redeeming a compensation rentcharge in respect of the extinguishment of manorial incidents and affecting the settled land;*

(vii)   Commuting any additional rent made payable on the conversion of a perpetually renewable leasehold interest into a long term;

(viii)   Satisfying any claims for compensation on the conversion of a perpetually renewable leasehold interest into a long term by any officer, solicitor, or other agent of the lessor in repect of fees or remuneration which would have been payable by the lessee or under-lessee on any renewal;

(ix)   Payment of the costs of any transaction authorised by this section or either of the two last preceding sections;

the tenant for life may raise the money so required, on the security of the settled land, or of any part thereof, by a legal mortgage, and the money so raised shall be capital money for that purpose, and may be paid or applied accordingly....

11.3.1.2   Invalidation of all restrictions on a life tenant's powers

SETTLED LAND ACT 1925

106.   Prohibition or limitation against exercise of powers void, and provision against forfeiture

(1)   If in a settlement, will, assurance, or other instrument executed or made before or after, or partly before and partly after, the commencement of this Act a provision is inserted—

(a)   purporting or attempting, by way of direction, declaration, or otherwise, to forbid a tenant for life or statutory owner to exercise any power under this Act, or his right to require the settled land to be vested in him; or

(b)   attempting, or tending, or intended, by a limitation, gift, or dispositon over of settled land, or by a limitation, gift, or disposition of other real or any personal property, or by the imposition of any condition, or by forfeiture, or in any other manner whatever, to prohibit or prevent him from exercising, or to induce him to abstain from exercising, or to put him into a position inconsistent with his exercising any power under this Act, or his right to require the settled land to be vested in him;

that provision, as far as it purports, or attempt, or tends, or is intended to have, or would or might have, the operation aforesaid, shall be deemed to be void....

(Note: Contrast s. 106 with s. 8 of the Trusts of Land and Appointment of Trustees Act 1996.)

11.3.2   ACCIDENTAL STRICT SETTLEMENTS

BINIONS v EVANS [1972] 1 Ch 359, Court of Appeal

FACTS: The trustees of the Tredegar Estate owned a cottage in which there resided rent-free Mrs Evans, the widow of an employee of the Estate. The trustees sold the cottage to Binions, expressly on the condition that Mrs Evans should be allowed to live there for the rest of her life. Binions paid a reduced price because of this condition. Binions nevertheless tried to evict Mrs Evans; he claimed that she had no proprietary interest in the land.

HELD: Not surprisingly, Binions found no sympathy in the Court of Appeal. The majority of the Court of Appeal (Megaw and John Stephenson LJJ) held that the conveyance to Binions created a life interest in favour of Mrs Evans. Therefore the land was 'settled land' within the meaning of the 1925 Act, with Mrs Evans as life tenant.

(Note: under the new Trusts of Land and Appointment of Trustees Act 1996 there would now be a new-style trust, with Tredegar Estates as the (sole) trustee and Mrs Evans and Binions as the beneficaries.)

LORD DENNING MR: . . . Seeing that the defendant has no legal estate or interest in the land, the question is what right has she? At any rate, she has a contractual right to reside in the house for the remainder of her life or as long as she pleases to stay. I know that in the agreement it is described as a tenancy: but that does not matter. The question is: What is it in reality? To my mind it is a licence, and no tenancy. It is a privilege which is personal to her. On all the modern cases, which are legion, it ranks as a contractual licence, and not a tenancy: see *Shell-Mex and BP Ltd* v *Manchester Garages Ltd* [1971] 1 WLR 612.

What is the status of such a licence as this? There are a number of cases in the books in which a similar right has been given. They show that a right to occupy for life, arising by contract, gives to the occupier an equitable interest in the land: just as it does when it arises under a settlement: see *In re Carne's Settled Estates* [1899] 1 Ch 324 and *In re Boyer's Settled Estates* [1916] 2 Ch 404. The courts of equity will not allow the landlord to turn the occupier out in breach of the contract: see *Foster* v *Robinson* [1951] 1 KB 149, 156; nor will they allow a purchaser to turn her out if he bought with knowledge of her right—*Errington* v *Errington and Woods* [1952] 1 KB 290, 299.

It is instructive to go back to the cases before the Supreme Court Judicature Act 1873. They show that, if a landlord, by a memorandum in writing, let a house to someone, let us say to a widow, at a rent, for her life or as long as she pleased to stay, the courts of equity would not allow the landlord to turn her out in breach of his contract. If the landlord were to go to the courts of law and obtain an order in ejectment against her, as in *Doe d Warner* v *Browne*, 8 East 165, the courts of equity would grant an injunction to restrain the landlord from enforcing his rights at law, as in *Browne* v *Warner* (1808) 14 Ves 409. The courts of equity would give the agreement a construction, which Lord Eldon LC called an 'equitable construction,' and construe it as if it were an agreement to execute a deed granting her a lease of the house for her life—*Browne* v *Warner*, 14 Ves 156, 158. They would order the landlord specifically to perform the contract, so construed, by executing such a deed. This court did so in *Zimbler* v *Abraham* [1903] 1 KB 577. This means that she had an equitable interest in the land. So much so that if a purchaser wished to buy her interest from her, he had to pay her its full value as such. Matins V-C so held in *In re King's Leasehold Estates* (1873) LR 16 Eq 521, 527, where he described it as an 'equitable interest.' It follows that, if the owner sold his reversion to another, who took with notice of the widow's interest, his successor could not turn her out any more than he could. She would have, I should have thought, at least as strong a case as the occupier in *Webb* v *Paternoster* (1619) Poph 151, which received the blessing of Lord Upjohn in *National Provincial Bank Ltd* v *Hastings Car Mart Ltd* [1965] AC 1175, 1239.

Suppose, however, that the defendant did not have an equitable interest at the outset, nevertheless it is quite plain that she obtained one afterwards when the Tredegar Estate sold the cottage. They stipulated with the plaintiffs that they were to take the house 'subject to' the defendant's rights under the agreement. They supplied the plaintiffs with a copy of the contract: and the plaintiffs paid less because of her right to stay there. In these circumstances, this court will impose on the plaintiffs a constructive trust for her benefit: for the simple reason that it would be utterly inequitable for the plaintiffs to turn the defendant out contrary to the stipulation subject to which they took the premises. That seems to me clear from the important decision *Bannister* v *Bannister* [1948] 2 All ER 133, which was applied by the judge, and which I gladly follow.

This imposing of a constructive trust is entirely in accord with the precepts of equity. As Cardozo J once put it: 'A constructive trust is the formula through which the conscience of equity finds expression,' see *Beatty* v *Guggenheim Exploration Co.* (1919) 225 NY 380, 386: or, as Lord Diplock put it quite recently in *Gissing* v *Gissing* [1971] AC 886, 905, a constructive trust is created 'whenever the trustee has so conducted himself that it would be inequitable to allow him to deny to the cestui que trust a beneficial interest in the land acquired.'

. . . At any rate when the licensee is in actual occupation of the land, so that the purchaser must know he is there, and of the rights which he has: see *Hodgson* v *Marks* [1971] Ch 892. Whenever the purchaser takes the land impliedly subject to the rights of the contractual licensee, a court of equity will impose a constructive trust for the beneficiary. So I still adhere to the proposition I stated in *Errington* v *Errington and Woods* [1952] 1 KB 290, 299; and elaborated in *National Provincial Bank Ltd* v *Hastings Car Mart Ltd* [1964] Ch 665, 686–689, namely, that when the licensee is in actual occupation, neither the licensor nor anyone who claims through him can disregard the contract except a purchaser for value without notice.

... In my opinion the defendant, by virtue of the agreement, had an equitable interest in the cottage which the court would protect by granting an injunction against the landlords restraining them from turning her out. When the landlords sold the cottage to a purchaser 'subject to' her rights under the agreement, the purchaser took the cottage on a constructive trust to permit the defendant to reside there during her life, or as long as she might desire. The courts will not allow the purchaser to go back on that trust. I entirely agree with the judgment of Judge Bulger. I would dismiss this appeal.

MEGAW LJ: ... What was the effect in law of that agreement, as between the trustees and the defendant? In my view, Judge Bulger was right in holding that the effect was the same as the effect of the agreement considered by this court in *Bannister* v *Bannister* [1948] 2 All ER 133. In that case the defendant had orally agreed to sell two cottages to her brother-in-law, the plaintiff, in reliance on his statement: 'I do not want to take any rent, but will let you stay' in one of the cottages 'as long as you like rent free.' Troubles arose between the parties a few years later and the plaintiff sought to turn the defendant out, claiming that she was a mere tenant at will. The court (Scott LJ, Asquith LJ and Jenkins J) held, at p. 137:

> ... the plaintiff holds no. 30 in trust during the life of the defendant to permit the defendant to occupy the same for so long as she may desire to do so and subject thereto in trust for the plaintiff. A trust in this form has the effect of making the beneficiary a tenant for life within the meaning of the Settled Land Act 1925, and, consequently, there is a very little practical difference between such a trust and a trust for life simpliciter.

As was said by the court, at p. 136:

> Similar words in deeds and wills have frequently been held to create a life interest determinable (apart from the special considerations introduced by the Settled Land Act 1925) on the beneficiary ceasing to occupy the premises: ...

I confess that I have had difficulty in seeing precisely how the Settled Land Act of 1925 was applicable. But the court in *Bannister* v *Bannister* [1948] 2 All ER 133 so held, and I am certainly content, and we are probably bound, to follow that authority. I see no relevant distinction. The fact that the transaction—the creation of the trust—was there effected orally, whereas here there is an agreement in writing, surely cannot be a ground for saying that the principle is not here applicable. The fact that there is here express provision for determination by the beneficiary cannot provide a relevant distinction. The defendant in *Bannister* v *Bannister* [1948] 2 All ER 133 was free to give up occupation whenever she wished. The fact and nature of the obligations imposed upon the defendant by the agreement in the present case must tend in favour of, rather than adversely to, the creation of an interest in land, as compared with *Bannister's* case.

I realise that the application of the Settled Land Act 1925 may produce some odd consequences; but no odder than those which were inherent in the decision in *Bannister* v *Bannister* [1948] 2 All ER 133. I do not find anything in the possible, theoretical, consequences to lead me to the conclusion that *Bannister's* case should not be followed.

The plaintiffs took with express notice of the agreement which constitutes, or gives rise to, the trust. They cannot turn the defendant out of the house against her will; for that would be a breach of the trust which binds them. ...

STEPHENSON LJ: ... The words 'tenant for life' are not used, but that in one sense is what the landlords are agreeing that this widow should become. If, however, these words were in the agreement they would be used like 'tenant at will' in the context of the whole agreement as conferring a life interest, whatever called or however described, which was determinable by the so-called tenant for life on four weeks' notice or by ceasing permanently to live in the cottage.

Apart from authority, I would not have thought that such an interest could be understood to amount to a tenancy for life within the meaning of the Settled Land Act 1925, and I would have thought that the other terms of her tenancy (as I think it ought properly to be called) are inconsistent with a power to ask for the legal estate to be settled on her or to sell the cottage. But *Bannister* v *Bannister* [1948] 2 All ER 133 is a clear decision of this court that such words as have been used in this agreement (excepting, I must concede, the words 'as tenant at will of them') create a life interest determinable (apart from the special considerations introduced by the Settled Land Act 1925) on the beneficiary ceasing to occupy the premises and the landlords hold the cottage on trust to permit her to occupy it 'during her life or as long as she lives' as Judge Bulger held and subject thereto in trust for them.

I therefore find it unnecessary to consider or decide the vexed questions (1) whether this agreement is or creates an irrevocable contractual licence to occupy; and (2) whether such a licence has been elevated to a status equivalent to an estate or interest in land. . . .

UNGURIAN v *LESNOFF AND OTHERS* [1989] 3 WLR 840, Chancery Division

FACTS: Ms Lesnoff gave up her Polish nationality, secure home and academic career, in order to take up residence with Mr Ungurian in Muswell Hill, London. They lived at No. 136, Muswell Hill Road as *de facto* husband and wife. Ms Lesnoff made substantial improvements to the premises throughout the four years of their relationship and she remained in the premises after their separation. The home was registered in Mr Ungurian's sole name. He brought this present action to recover possession of the premises.
HELD: Ms Lesnoff would be entitled to a life interest in the property, with the result that she became the tenant for life under a strict settlement.

(Note: Under the new Trusts of Land and Appointment of Trustees Act 1996 there would be a new-style trust, with Ungurian (he created the trust) as (sole) trustee of the legal estate, holding the house in trust for Lesnoff for life and then on resulting trust for himself.)

VINELOTT J: . . . In summary . . ., I am not satisfied that the house was bought by Mr Ungurian with the intention that it would belong to Mrs Lesnoff, either immediately or when she gave up her flat in Poland and obtained permission to live permanently abroad; but I am satisfied that it was bought with the common intention that Mrs Lesnoff would be entitled to live there with her children, sharing it with Mr Ungurian when he was in England, and with any of his children who were here for the purpose of being educated. I am satisfied that Mrs Lesnoff went through with this plan, initiated in Beirut and later elaborated, in the expectation that Mr Ungurian would provide her with a secure home and that she burnt her boats by giving up her flat in Wraclow in the belief that he had done so. The question is whether these facts, and the work subsequently done by Mrs Lesnoff, give rise, either to a constructive trust under which Mrs Lesnoff became entitled to a beneficial interest in the house, or to a licence to reside, or to an estoppel preventing Mr Ungurian from denying her right to reside in the house.

Mr Pascoe submitted that these facts found the inference that there was a bargain or common intention that Mrs Lesnoff was to have a beneficial interest, and that the interest should be commensurate with the extent to which the value of the house was improved by her labours. I accept that Mrs Lesnoff and her sons did do a great deal of work to the house, though I think that in retrospect Mrs Lesnoff has probably come to exaggerate both the extent of the work she did, and in particular the skilled work. Mrs Lesnoff gave a graphic account of wielding a pickaxe. No doubt her solicitors had retailed to her the facts in *Eves* v *Eves* [1975] 1 WLR 1338 which they drew to the attention of Mr Ungurian's solicitors. In the course of her evidence this was reduced to a claim that she used a pickaxe to lever doorframes away from the brickwork where they needed to be replaced. I doubt whether Mrs Lesnoff used a tool as clumsy as a pickaxe at all, unless possibly she picked up one that had been left lying around by workmen and put it to some temporary, and possibly inappropriate, use. I am not persuaded that, as she claimed, she mastered the art of plastering walls. As I have said, I am satisfied that she and her sons did a substantial amount of work, but I think she did the work on the understanding that she had the right to reside in the house and because she wanted to make it more comfortable for her and Mr Ungurian, and for her growing sons. Mr Ungurian in particular wanted some privacy and the alterations to the ground floor were designed to that end.

In my judgment, the inference to be drawn from the circumstances in which the property was purchased and the subsequent conduct of the parties—the intention to be attributed to them—is that Mrs Lesnoff was to have the right to reside in the house during her life. It would be to that extent her house, and although the expectation was that Mr Ungurian would live there with her when he was in England, and that Paul, and possibly in due course his younger son also, would be accommodated there while they were being educated, that result would flow from the continued relationship between Mrs Lesnoff and Mr Ungarian and would be dependent on it. It must be borne in mind that Mr Ungurian was a man of considerable means with flats in Beirut, Amman and Switzerland. He was providing a house as a home for a woman much younger than himself who would be likely to survive him. I do not think that full effect would be given to this common intention by inferring no more than an irrevocable licence to occupy the house. I think the legal consequences which flow from the intention to be imputed to the parties was that Mr Ungurian held the house on trust to permit Mrs Lesnoff to reside in it during her life unless and until Mr Ungurian, with her consent, sold the property and bought another residence for her in substitution for it.

If that is the right conclusion, then the house became settled land within the Settled Land Act 1925 and Mrs Lesnoff is tenant for life and entitled to call for the execution of a vesting deed and for the appointment of trustees. Any understanding that Mr Ungurian was not to be entitled with her consent to sell the house and apply the proceeds, in whole or in part, towards the purchase of another house would be avoided by section 106 of the Settled Land Act 1925. . . .

11.4   Criticisms of the Trust for Sale

11.4.1   THE ARTIFICIAL NATURE OF THE *DUTY* TO SELL

LAW OF PROPERTY ACT 1925
as amended by the Trusts of Land etc. Act 1996

205.   General definitions

(1)(xxix)   'Trust for sale', in relation to land, means an immediate [. . .] trust for sale, whether or not exercisable at the request or with the consent of any person [. . .]; 'trustees for sale' mean the persons (including a personal representative) holding land on trust for sale; and 'power to postpone a sale' means power to postpone in the exercise of a discretion.

LAW OF PROPERTY ACT 1925

25.   Power to postpone sale

(1)   A power to postpone sale shall, in the case of every trust for sale of land, be implied unless a contrary intention appears.

(2)   Where there is a power to postpone the sale, then (subject to any express direction to the contrary in the instrument, if any, creating the trust for sale) the trustees for sale shall not be liable in any way for postponing the sale, in the exercise of their discretion, for any indefinite period; nor shall a purchaser of a legal estate be concerned in any case with any direction respecting the postponement of a sale.

(3)   The foregoing provisions of this section apply whether the trust for sale is created before or after the commencement or by virtue of this Act.

(4)   Where a disposition or settlement coming into operation after the commencement of this Act contains a trust either to retain or sell land the same shall be construed as a trust to sell the land with power to postpone the sale.

(Note: Section 25 is now repealed by the Trusts of Land and Appointment of Trustees Act 1996.)

11.4.2   LIMITED POWERS OF TRUSTEES OF SALE

11.4.2.1   Dispositions other than sale

LAW OF PROPERTY ACT 1925

28.   Powers of management, etc. conferred on trustees for sale

(1)   Trustees for sale shall, in relation to land or to manorial incidents and to the proceeds of sale, have all the powers of a tenant for life and the trustees of a settlement

under the Settled Land Act 1925 including in relation to the land the powers of management conferred by that Act during a minority: and where by statute settled land is or becomes vested in the trustees of the settlement upon the statutory trusts, such trustees and their successors in office shall also have all the additional or larger powers (if any) conferred by the settlement on the tenant for life, statutory owner, or trustees of the settlement, and (subject to any express to the contrary) all capital money arising under the said powers shall, unless paid or applied for any purpose authorised by the Settled Land Act 1925 be applicable in the same manner as if the money represented proceeds of sale arising under the trust for sale.

(Note: Compare s. 28 to ss. 6 and 7(1) of the Trusts of Land and Appointment of Trustees Act 1996. Section 28 has been repealed by the 1996 Act.)

11.4.2.2   Delegation of management and leasing powers

LAW OF PROPERTY ACT 1925

29.   Delegation of powers of management by trustees for sale

(1)   The powers of an incidental to leasing, accepting surrenders of leases and management, conferred on trustees for sale whether by this Act or otherwise, may, until sale of the land, be revocably delegated from time to time, by writing, signed by them, to any person of full age (not being merely an annuitant) for the time being beneficially entitled in possession to the net rents and profits of the land during his life or for any less period: and in favour of a lessee such writing shall, unless the contrary appears, be sufficient evidence that the person named therein is a person to whom the powers may be delegated, and the production of such writing shall, unless the contrary appears, be sufficient evidence that the delegation has not been revoked.

(2)   Any power so delegated shall be exercised only in the names and on behalf of the trustees delegating the power.

(3)   The persons delegating any power under this section shall not, in relation to the exercise or purported exercise of the power, be liable for the acts or defaults of the person to whom the power is delegated, but that person shall, in relation to the exercise of the power by him, be deemed to be in the position and to have the duties and liabilities of a trustee.

(Note: Compare s. 29 to s. 9 of the Trusts of Land and Appointment of Trustees Act 1996. Section 29 has been repealed.)

11.4.3   THE ANOMALOUS CONCEPT OF A TRUST FOR SALE SUBJECT TO CONSENTS

LAW OF PROPERTY ACT 1925

26.   Consents to the execution of a trust for sale

(1)   If the consent of more than two persons is by the disposition made requisite to the execution of a trust for sale of land, then, in favour of a purchaser, the consent of any two such persons to the execution of the trust or to the exercise of any statutory or other powers vested in the trustees for sale shall be deemed sufficient.

(2)   Where the person whose consent to the execution of any such trust or power is expressed to be required in a disposition is not *sui juris* or becomes subject to disability, his consent shall not, in favour of a purchaser, be deemed to be requisite to the execution of the trust or the exercise of the power; but the trustees shall, in any such case, obtain the separate consent of the parent or testamentary or other guardian of an infant or of the . . . receiver (if any) of a person suffering from mental disorder. . . .

(Note: Compare s. 26 to s. 10(1) of the Trusts of Land and Appointment of Trustees Act 1996. Section 26 has been repealed.)

CHAPTER TWELVE

NEW-STYLE TRUSTS OF LAND DEFINED

12.1 Introduction

The Trusts of Land and Appointment of Trustees Act 1996 simply talks of 'trusts of land'. I have added the words 'new-style' to emphasise the fact that we are dealing with a new (all-embracing) concept very different from what has gone before.

12.2 The Definition in Section 1

TRUSTS OF LAND AND APPOINTMENT OF TRUSTEES ACT 1996

1. Meaning of 'trust of land'
   (1)   In this Act—
      (a)   'trust of land' means (subject to subsection (3)) any trust of property which consists of or includes land, and
      (b)   'trustees of land' means trustees of a trust of land.
   (2)   The reference in subsection (1)(a) to a trust—
      (a)   is to any description of trust (whether express, implied, resulting or constructive), including a trust for sale and a bare trust, and
      (b)   includes a trust created, or arising, before the commencement of this Act.
   (3)   The reference to land in subsection (1)(a) does not include land which (despite section 2) is settled land or which is land to which the Universities and College Estates Act 1925 applies.

12.2.1 EXISTING TRUSTS FOR SALE

TRUSTS OF LAND AND APPOINTMENT OF TRUSTEES ACT 1996

2. Trusts in place of settlements
   (1)   No settlement created after the commencement of this Act is a settlement for the purposes of the Settled Land Act 1925; and no settlement shall be deemed to be made under that Act after that commencement.
   (2)   Subsection (1) does not apply to a settlement created on the occasion of an alteration in any interest in, or of a person becoming entitled under, a settlement which—
      (a)   is in existence at the commencement of this Act, or
      (b)   derives from a settlement within paragraph (a) or this paragraph.
   (3)   But a settlement created as mentioned in subsection (2) is not a settlement for the purposes of the Settled Land Act 1925 if provision to the effect that it is not is made in the instrument, or any of the instruments, by which it is created.
   (4)   Where at any time after the commencement of this Act there is in the case of any settlement which is a settlement for the purposes of the Settled Land Act 1925 no relevant

property which is, or is deemed to be, subject to the settlement, the settlement permanently ceases at that time to be a settlement for the purposes of that Act.

In this subsection 'relevant property' means land and personal chattels to which section 67(1) of the Settled Land Act 1925 (heirlooms) applies.

(5)   No land held on charitable, ecclesiastical or public trusts shall be or be deemed to be settled land after the commencement of this Act, even if it was or was deemed to be settled land before that commencement.

(6)   Schedule 1 has effect to make provision consequential on this section (including provision to impose a trust in circumstances in which, apart from this section, there would be a settlement for the purposes of the Settled Land Act 1925 (and there would not otherwise be a trust)).

4.   Express trusts for sale as trusts of land

(1)   In the case of every trust for sale of land created by a disposition there is to be implied, despite any provision to the contrary made by the disposition, a power for the trustees to postpone sale of the land; and the trustees are not liable in any way for postponing sale of the land, in the exercise of their discretion, for an indefinite period.

(2)   Subsection (1) applies to a trust whether it is created, or arises before or after the commencement of this Act.

(3)   Subsection (1) does not affect any liability incurred by trustees before that commencement.

12.2.1.1   Doctrine of conversion abolished

TRUSTS OF LAND AND APPOINTMENT OF TRUSTEES ACT 1996

3.   Abolition of doctrine of conversion

(1)   Where land is held by trustees subject to a trust for sale, the land is not to be regarded as personal property; and where personal property is subject to a trust for sale in order that the trustees may acquire land, the personal property is not to be regarded as land.

(2)   Subsection (1) does not apply to a trust created by a will if the testator died before the commencement of this Act.

(3)   Subject to that, subsection (1) applies to a trust whether it is created, or arises, before or after that commencement.

12.2.1.2   Conveyance to a minor

A minor (a person under 18) cannot own a legal estate in land. What then happens if someone purported to convey a legal estate to a minor(s)? Under the old law (a) the minor acquired an equitable interest; **and** (b) the land became settled land subject to all the complexities of the Settled Land Act 1925.

Schedule 1, para. 1(1) of the Trusts of Land and Appointment of Trustees Act 1996 will in future govern an attempted conveyance to a minor.

TRUSTS OF LAND AND APPOINTMENT OF TRUSTEES ACT 1996

SCHEDULE 1

Minors

1.—(1)   Where after the commencement of this Act a person purports to convey a legal estate in land to a minor, or two or more minors, alone, the conveyance—

(a)   is not effective to pass the legal estate, but

(b)   operates as a declaration that the land is held in trust for the minor or minors (or if he purports to convey it to the minor or minors in trust for any persons, for those persons).

12.3   Appointment, Retirement and Removal of Trustees

12.3.1   METHOD OF APPOINTMENT OF TRUSTEES

TRUSTEE ACT 1925
as amended by the Trusts of Land etc. Act 1996

40.   Vesting of trust property in new or continuing trustees

(1)   Where by a deed a new trustee is appointed to perform any trust, then—

(a)   if the deed contains a declaration by the appointor to the effect that any estate or interest in any land subject to the trust, or in any chattel so subject, or the right to recover or receive any debt or other thing in action so subject, shall vest in the persons who by virtue of the deed become or are the trustees for performing the trust, the deed shall operate, without any conveyance or assignment, to vest in those persons as joint tenants and for the purposes of the trust the estate interest or right to which the declaration relates; and

(b)   if the deed is made after the commencement of this Act and does not contain such a declaration, the deed shall, subject to any express provision to the contrary therein contained, operate as if it had contained such a declaration by the appointor extending to all the estates interests and rights with respect to which a declaration could have been made.

(2)   Where by a deed a retiring trustee is discharged under [section 39 of this Act or section 19 of the Trusts of Land and Appointment of Trustees Act 1996] without a new trustee being appointed, then—

(a)   if the deed contains such a declaration as aforesaid by the retiring and continuing trustees, and by the other person, if any, empowered to appoint trustees, the deed shall, without any conveyance or assignment, operate to vest in the continuing trustees alone, as joint tenants, and for the purposes of the trust, the estate, interest, or right to which the declaration relates; and

(b)   if the deed is made after the commencement of this Act and does not contain such a declaration, the deed shall, subject to any express provision to the contrary therein contained, operate as if it had contained such a declaration by such persons as aforesaid extending to all the estates, interests and rights with respect to which a declaration could have been made.

(3)   An express vesting declaration, whether made before or after the commencement of this Act, shall, notwithstanding that the estate, interest or right to be vested is not expressly referred to, and provided that the other statutory requirements were or are complied with, operate and be deemed always to have operated (but without prejudice to any express provision to the contrary contained in the deed of appointment or discharge) to vest in the persons respectively referred to in subsections (1) and (2) of this section, as the case may require, such estates, interests and rights as are capable and ought to be vested in those persons. . . .

TRUSTS OF LAND AND APPOINTMENT OF TRUSTEES ACT 1996

19.   Appointment and retirement of trustee at instance of beneficiaries

(1)   This section applies in the case of a trust where—

(a)   there is no person nominated for the purpose of appointing new trustees by the instrument, if any, creating the trust, and

(b)   the beneficiaries under the trust are of full age and capacity and (taken together) are absolutely entitled to the property subject to the trust.

(2)   The beneficiaries may give a direction or directions of either or both of the following descriptions—

(a)   a written direction to a trustee or trustees to retire from the trust, and

(b)   a written direction to the trustees or trustee for the time being (or, if there are none, to the personal representative of the last person who was a trustee) to appoint by writing to be a trustee or trustees the person or persons specified in the direction.

(3)   Where—

(a)   a trustee has been given a direction under subsection (2)(a),

(b)   reasonable arrangements have been made for the protection of any rights of his in connection with the trust,

(c)   after he has retired there will be either a trust corporation or at least two persons to act as trustees to perform the trust, and

(d)   either another person is to be appointed to be a new trustee on his retirement (whether in compliance with a direction under subsection (2)(b) or otherwise) or the continuing trustees by deed consent to his retirement,

he shall make a deed declaring his retirement and shall be deemed to have retired and be discharged from the trust.

(4)   Where a trustee retires under subsection (3) he and the continuing trustees (together with any new trustee) shall (subject to any arrangements for the protection of his rights) do anything necessary to vest the trust property in the continuing trustees (or the continuing and new trustees).

(5)   This section has effect subject to the restrictions imposed by the Trustee Act 1925 on the number of trustees.

20.   Appointment of substitute for incapable trustee

(1)   This section applies where—

(a)   a trustee is incapable by reason of mental disorder of exercising his functions as trustee,

(b)   there is no person who is both entitled and willing and able to appoint a trustee in place of him under section 36(1) of the Trustee Act 1925, and

(c)   the beneficiaries under the trust are of full age and capacity and (taken together) are absolutely entitled to the property subject to the trust.

(2)   The beneficiaries may give to—

(a)   a receiver of the trustee,

(b)   an attorney acting for him under the authority of a power of attorney created by an instrument which is registered under section 6 of the Enduring Powers of Attorney Act 1985, or

(c)   a person authorised for the purpose by the authority having jurisdiction under Part VII of the Mental Health Act 1983,

a written direction to appoint by writing the person or persons specified in the direction to be a trustee or trustees in place of the incapable trustee.

CHAPTER THIRTEEN

THE POWERS OF NEW-STYLE TRUSTEES OF LAND

13.1 The Powers of Disposition of 'New-style' Trustees of Land

TRUSTS OF LAND AND APPOINTMENT OF TRUSTEES ACT 1996

6. General powers of trustees

(1) For the purpose of exercising their functions as trustees, the trustees of land have in relation to the land subject to the trust all the powers of an absolute owner.

(2) Where in the case of any land subject to a trust of land each of the beneficiaries interested in the land is a person of full age and capacity who is absolutely entitled to the land, the powers conferred on the trustees by subsection (1) include the power to convey the land to the beneficiaries even though they have not required the trustees to do so; and where land is conveyed by virtue of this subsection—

    (a) the beneficiaries shall do whatever is necessary to secure that it vests in them, and

    (b) if they fail to do so, the court may make an order requiring them to do so.

(3) The trustees of land have power to purchase a legal estate in any land in England or Wales.

(4) The power conferred by subsection (3) may be exercised by trustees to purchase land—

    (a) by way of investment,

    (b) for occupation by any beneficiary, or

    (c) for any other reason.

(5) In exercising the powers conferred by this section trustees shall have regard to the rights of the beneficiaries.

(6) The powers conferred by this section shall not be exercised in contravention of, or of any order made in pursuance of, any other enactment or any rule of law or equity.

(7) The reference in subsection (6) to an order includes an order of any court or of the Charity Commissioners.

(8) Where any enactment other than this section confers on trustees authority to act subject to any restriction, limitation or condition, trustees of land may not exercise the powers conferred by this section to do any act which they are prevented from doing under the other enactment by reason of the restriction, limitation or condition.

7. Partition by trustees

(1) The trustees of land may, where beneficiaries of full age are absolutely entitled in undivided shares to land subject to the trust, partition the land, or any part of it, and provide (by way of mortgage or otherwise) for the payment of any equality money.

(2) The trustees shall give effect to any such partition by conveying the partitioned land in severalty (whether or not subject to any legal mortgage created for raising equality money), either absolutely or in trust, in accordance with the rights of those beneficiaries.

(3) Before exercising their powers under subsection (2) the trustees shall obtain the consent of each of those beneficiaries.

(4) Where a share in the land is affected by an incumbrance, the trustees may either give effect to it or provide for its discharge from the property allotted to that share as they think fit.

(5) If a share in the land is absolutely vested in a minor, subsections (1) to (4) apply as if he were of full age, except that the trustees may act on his behalf and retain land or other property representing his share in trust for him.

17.   Applications of provisions to trusts of proceeds of sale

(1)   Section 6(3) applies in relation to trustees of a trust of proceeds of sale of land as in relation to trustees of land.

13.2   The Trustees' Duties on Exercising their Powers

13.2.1   PLACING TRUSTEES OF LAND UNDER A DUTY TO CONSULT THE BENEFICIARIES

TRUSTS OF LAND AND APPOINTMENT OF TRUSTEES ACT 1996

11.   Consultation with beneficiaries

(1)   The trustees of land shall in the exercise of any function relating to land subject to the trust—

(a)   so far as practicable, consult the beneficiaries of full age and beneficially entitled to an interest in possession in the land, and

(b)   so far as consistent with the general interest of the trust, give effect to the wishes of those beneficiaries, or (in case of dispute) of the majority (according to the value of their combined interests).

(2)   Subsection (1) does not apply—

(a)   in relation to a trust created by a disposition in so far as provision that it does not apply is made by the disposition,

(b)   in relation to a trust created or arising under a will made before the commencement of this Act, or

(c)   in relation to the exercise of the power mentioned in section 6(2).

(3)   Subsection (1) does not apply to a trust created before the commencement of this Act by a disposition, or a trust created after that commencement by reference to such a trust, unless provision to the effect that it is to apply is made by a deed executed—

(a)   in a case in which the trust was created by one person and he is of full capacity, by that person, or

(b)   in a case in which the trust was created by more than one person by such of the persons who created the trust as are alive and of full capacity.

(4)   A deed executed for the purposes of subsection (3) is irrevocable.

13.2.2   PERSONAL OCCUPATION OF TRUST LAND BY BENEFICIARIES

TRUSTS OF LAND AND APPOINTMENT OF TRUSTEES ACT 1996

12.   Right of beneficiaries to occupy trust land

(1)   A beneficiary who is beneficially entitled to an interest in possession in land subject to a trust of land is entitled by reason of his interest to occupy the land at any time if at that time—

(a)   the purposes of the trust include making the land available for his occupation (or for the occupation of beneficiaries of a class of which he is a member or of beneficiaries in general), or

(b)   the land is held by the trustees so as to be so available.

(2)   Subsection (1) does not confer on a beneficiary a right to occupy land if it is either unavailable or unsuitable for occupation by him.

(3)   This section is subject to section 13.

13.3 Restrictions on Trustees of Land Powers of Disposition

13.3.1 TAKEAWAY CLAUSES

TRUSTS OF LAND AND APPOINTMENT OF TRUSTEES ACT 1996

8. Exclusion and restriction of powers

(1) Sections 6 and 7 do not apply in the case of a trust of land created by a disposition in so far as provision to the effect that they do not apply is made by the disposition.

(2) If the disposition creating such a trust makes provision requiring any consent to be obtained to the exercise of any power conferred by section 6 or 7, the power may not be exercised without that consent.

(3) Subsection (1) does not apply in the case of charitable, ecclesiastical or public trusts.

(4) Subsections (1) and (2) have effect subject to any enactment which prohibits or restricts the effect of provision of the description mentioned in them.

Watt, G., 'Escaping Section 8(1) Provisions in "New Style" Trusts of Land' (1997) 61 Conv 263

Until the latter part of the last century much of the land in England and Wales was held under traditional family settlements by limited owners with restricted rights of disposition. The 'dead hand' of the settlor of the trust rested heavily upon such owners, excluding or curtailing their powers of sale, mortgage and lease. Eventually economic and fiscal imperatives led to the enactment of the Settled Land Acts of 1882 and 1925, as a result of which the grip of the dead hand was almost utterly cast off. However, with the passing of those historical factors, we might not be surprised to find a modern parliament more tolerant of the settlor's grip. This paper will suggest, first, that the Trusts of Land and Appointment of Trustees Act 1996 (in this article referred to as 'the 1996 Act') has indeed permitted the dead hand once more to take hold; and suggests, secondly, a number of ways in which trustees of 'new style' trusts might nevertheless wrest themselves free of it.

The express words of s. 6(1) of the 1996 Act, when read in isolation, appear to run directly contrary to the first of the above suggestions. Section 6(1) provides that, '[f]or the purpose of exercising their functions as trustees, trustees of land shall have in relation to the land subject to the trust all the powers of an absolute owner'. Accordingly, the effect of this section is *prima facie* to extend the trustees' powers even further beyond those granted to life tenants of Settled Land Act strict settlements and trustees of 'old style' trusts for sale.

Interpreting s. 6(1) in a vacuum, the dead hand of the settlor appears, at last, to have lost its grip entirely. However, when s. 6(1) is read in the light of the whole Act, a quite different picture emerges. This is particularly true when s. 6(1) is read alongside s. 8(1). The text of s. 8(1) reads as follows 'Sections 6 and 7 do not apply in the case of a trust for land created by a disposition in so far as provision to the effect that they do not apply is made by the disposition.' It follows from s. 8(1) that, whereas the powers of a life tenant under a Settled Land Act strict settlement could not be restricted by the settlor of the trust, and the powers of 'old style' trustees for sale could only be restricted indirectly and in part, trustees of 'new style' trusts of land might have their powers of disposition entirely removed. This will occur if the settlor of the trust makes provision to that effect by means of a s. 8(1) clause. . . .

Escaping the Grip of the Dead Hand

One might expect the 1996 Act itself to provide some means of escape from the effect of s. 8(1) clauses. In fact, a detailed reading of the Act reveals no such hope for the constrained trustee. It is true that s. 14 of the Act authorises trustees (and indeed beneficiaries) to apply to court for any order 'relating to the exercise by the trustees of any of their functions (including an order relieving them of any obligation to obtain the consent of, or to consult, any person in connection with the exercise of any of their functions) . . . as the court thinks fit'. Nevertheless, this does not appear to authorise the court to make an order relating to the exercise by trustees of functions which have been removed by a s. 8(1) clause, for surely such functions would thereby fail to qualify as 'their functions', as those words are used in s. 14.

The express inclusion of orders freeing trustees from s. 8(2) consent clauses within the ambit of s. 14 could be read as authorising the court generally to make orders relating to functions which have been taken away by the settlor. However, it is submitted that the more logical and natural statutory interpretation, by extension of the rule *expressio unius exclusio alterius*, is to read the express inclusion of orders relating to s. 8(2) clauses as implicitly excluding the court's authority to make orders relating to the potentially far more inhibiting (from the applicant's point of view) s. 8(1) clauses.

Section 14 having failed to assist, by what other means might trustees and beneficiaries escape the effect of a s. 8(1) provision? There appear to be at least seven possible options, albeit, as will be seen, some are of very limited application.

(1)   *By pleading that the Trust of Land has been rendered void ab initio under the rule against inalienability of capital.* . . .

(2)   *By court order sanctioning a compromise of disputed rights.* . . .

(3)   *By court order under s. 53 of the Trustee Act 1925.*

The relevant part of s. 53 of the Trustee Act 1925 provides as follows:

Where an infant is beneficially entitled to any property the courts may, with a view to the application of the capital or income thereof for the maintenance, education, or benefit of the infant, make an order—

(a)   appointing a person to convey such property . . .

. . .

(4)   *Under the rule in Saunders* v *Vautier (1841) 4 Beav 115.*

This rule applies to all private trusts so as to allow the beneficiaries to bring the trust to an end provided that all the beneficiaries are *sui juris* and all agree to that course of action.

(5)   *Variation under the Variation of Trusts Act 1958.* . . .

(6)   *By court order under the court's inherent jurisdiction to vary trusts in cases of emergency.*

This jurisdiction survives s. 57 Trustee Act 1925 (see (7), below) and the 1996 Act. In the leading case, *Re New* [1901] 2 Ch 534, Romer LJ (after stating the general rule that 'the Court has no jurisdiction to give, and will not give, its sanction to the performance by trustees of acts . . . which are not, on the face of the instrument creating the trust, authorised by its terms') noted the important exception where circumstances have arisen which the settlor had not foreseen. It is a moot point whether the express inclusion of a s. 8(1) clause indicates foresight for all purposes of all circumstances which might necessitate the exercise by the trustees of the powers removed by the clause. Could it not be that circumstances might yet develop 'where the trustees are embarrassed by the emergency that has arisen'?

Romer LJ provided an interesting illustration of the sort of emergency with which the court would be competent to deal under its inherent jurisdiction. The illustrative emergency was a case where a testator had expressly provided that trust property should be sold on a certain date, but in the event sale at that date would have proved ruinous to the trust property. His Lordship would have been quite happy in those circumstances to postpone a sale, contrary to the settlor's expressed intentions. By analogy, it could be argued that where a trustee is required by a settlor to postpone sale (or even to sell not at all), a court may be prepared (if necessary to prevent calamity to the trust land) to order a sale against the expressed intentions of the settlor. It could, of course, be argued that every case of an 'emergency' of this sort must be a case where it is also 'expedient' to vary the administration of the trust under s. 57 of the Trustee Act 1925 (see (7), below). If that argument is correct it may be that a court would have no need to look beyond s. 57 of the Trustee Act 1925 and to rely instead upon its inherent jurisdiction.

(7)   *By court order under s. 57 of the Trustee Act 1925.*

Section 57(1) of the Trustee Act 1925 provides that:

Where in the management or administration of any property vested in trustees, any sale, lease, mortgage, surrender, release, or other disposition, or any purchase, investment, acquisition, expenditure, or other transaction, is in the opinion of the court expedient, but the same cannot be effected by reason of the absence of any power for that purpose vested in the trustees by the trust instrument, if any, or by law, the court may by order confer upon the trustees, either generally or in any particular instance, the necessary power for the purpose, on such terms, and subject to such provisions and conditions, if any, as the court may think fit . . .

The initial point to be made is that s. 8(1) should (according to s. 8(4)) be read as taking subject to s. 57(1). That being so, s. 57(1) appears to provide the court with the opportunity to authorise a sale, mortgage, lease etc. of the trust land, even in the face of a s. 8(1) clause to the contrary, if in the opinion of the court such disposition is 'expedient'. However, at least two objections might be raised against a court taking such an approach. The first, is that s. 57 applies only in the 'absence' of a power, and the word 'absence' admits of some ambiguity. Does it mean 'absence' where the particular power was passively omitted (which interpretation would attribute to s. 57 the perfectly proper role of remedying the settlor's oversight), or does it mean 'absence' where, in the particular trust, a power has been deliberately excluded or restricted (as would be the case where a settlor had inserted a s. 8(1) clause)? The point is not merely semantic. According to one view, s. 57 is in essence a statutory codification of the court's inherent jurisdiction to deal with 'emergencies'. An 'emergency' being a set of circumstances which the settlor *had not foreseen*, it follows, on that view, that 'absence' in s. 57 ought to be interpreted as denoting the absence of powers due to the settlor's failure to provide them. From that interpretation it would follow that s. 57 should have no application to revoke or vary s. 8(1) provisions. This is precisely because such provisions arise not from the settlor's neglect, but arise rather from his deliberate choice.

The logic of the above line of reasoning is seductive, but perhaps ultimately not compelling because the mere inclusion of a s. 8(1) clause cannot necessarily be interpreted as showing an intention, on the settlor's part, that the trust should suffer the consequences of genuinely unforeseen emergencies. The second, and somewhat related, objection which might be raised to the use of s. 57 is that it is a section designed to facilitate the settlor's implicit dispositive intentions; it is not designed to militate against his express intentions.

Despite these objections it may in practice be a relatively undaunting task to convince a court of first instance, desirous of restricting the settlor's control, that a straightforward reading of s. 57 permits the variation of a trust so as to include any powers which, *for whatever reason*, are in fact absent. The lower courts have already shown a willingness to adopt an expansive interpretation of s. 57, which acknowledges its effect beyond the limit of those cases already covered under the court's inherent jurisdiction to respond to emergencies.

Conclusion

Every conveyancer and property lawyer has been taught at some point that the great reforms enacted by the statutory scheme of 1925 facilitated the more liberal use and disposition of land. One means by which this liberalisation was achieved was to limit the extent to which settlors of trusts of land could restrict the alienation of the land by their trustees. It should now be noted that as a result of s. 8(1) of the Trusts of Land and Appointment of Trustees Act 1996, the settlor is under no such limitation. By an appropriate provision in the trust instrument the settlor is able to restrict or exclude the trustees' exercise, by means of their statutory powers, of their functions as trustees. The dead hand of the settlor has once again taken hold. Nevertheless, it should still be possible to escape a s. 8(1) provision by one or more of a variety of means.

In the majority of cases, the means of escape most likely to succeed is to seek a court order under s. 57 of the Trustee Act 1925 conferring on the trustees the power (either generally or in a particular case) to enable the trustees to carry out any disposition or transaction where expedient.

13.3.2 THE CONSENT REQUIREMENTS

TRUSTS OF LAND AND APPOINTMENT OF TRUSTEES ACT 1996

10. Consents

(1) If a disposition creating a trust of land requires the consent of more than two persons to the exercise by the trustees of any function relating to the land, the consent of any two of them to the exercise of the function is sufficient in favour of a purchaser.

(2) Subsection (1) does not apply to the exercise of a function by trustees of land held on charitable, ecclesiastical or public trusts.

(3)   Where at any time a person whose consent is expressed by a disposition creating a trust of land to be required to the exercise by the trustees of any function relating to the land is not of full age—

(a)   his consent is not, in favour of a purchaser, required to the exercise of the function, but

(b)   the trustees shall obtain the consent of a parent who has parental responsibility for him (within the meaning of the Children Act 1989) or of a guardian of his.

13.4   Protection of Purchasers

TRUSTS OF LAND AND APPOINTMENT OF TRUSTEES ACT 1996

16.   Protection of purchasers

(1)   A purchaser of land which is or has been subject to a trust need not be concerned to see that any requirement imposed on the trustees by section 6(5), 7(3) or 11(1) has been complied with.

(2)   Where—

(a)   trustees of land who convey land which (immediately before it is conveyed) is subject to the trust contravene section 6(6) or (8), but

(b)   the purchaser of the land from the trustees has no actual notice of the contravention,

the contravention does not invalidate the conveyance.

(3)   Where the powers of trustees of land are limited by virtue of section 8—

(a)   the trustees shall take all reasonable steps to bring the limitation to the notice of any purchaser of the land from them, but

(b)   the limitation does not invalidate any conveyance by the trustees to a purchaser who has no actual notice of the limitation.

(4)   Where trustees of land convey land which (immediately before it is conveyed) is subject to the trust to persons believed by them to be beneficiaries absolutely entitled to the land under the trust and of full age and capacity—

(a)   the trustees shall execute a deed declaring that they are discharged from the trust in relation to that land, and

(b)   if they fail to do so, the court may make an order requiring them to do so.

(5)   A purchaser of land to which a deed under subsection (4) relates is entitled to assume that, as from the date of the deed, the land is not subject to the trust unless he has actual notice that the trustees were mistaken in their belief that the land was conveyed to beneficiaries absolutely entitled to the land under the trust and of full age and capacity.

(6)   Subsections (2) and (3) do not apply to land held on charitable, ecclesiastical or public trusts.

(7)   This section does not apply to registered land.

13.5   Delegation of Trustees' Powers to Beneficiaries

TRUSTS OF LAND AND APPOINTMENT OF TRUSTEES ACT 1996

9.   Delegation by trustees

(1)   The trustees of land may, by power of attorney, delegate to any beneficiary or beneficiaries of full age and beneficially entitled to an interest in possession in land subject to the trust any of their functions as trustees which relate to the land.

(2)   Where trustees purport to delegate to a person by a power of attorney under subsection (1) functions relating to any land and another person in good faith deals with him in relation to the land, he shall be presumed in favour of that other person to have been a person to whom the functions could be delegated unless that other person has knowledge at the time of the transaction that he was not such a person.

And it shall be conclusively presumed in favour of any purchaser whose interest depends on the validity of that transaction that that other person dealt in good faith and did not have such knowledge if that other person makes a statutory declaration to that effect before or within three months after the completion of the purchase.

(3)   A power of attorney under subsection (1) shall be given by all the trustees jointly and (unless expressed to be irrevocable and to be given by way of security) may be revoked by any one or more of them; and such a power is revoked by the appointment as a trustee of a person other than those by whom it is given (though not by any of those persons dying or otherwise ceasing to be a trustee).

(4)   Where a beneficiary to whom functions are delegated by a power of attorney under subsection (1) ceases to be a person beneficially entitled to an interest in possession in land subject to the trust—

(a)   if the functions are delegated to him alone, the power is revoked,

(b)   if the functions are delegated to him and to other beneficiaries to be exercised by them jointly (but not separately), the power is revoked if each of the other beneficiaries ceases to be so entitled (but otherwise functions exercisable in accordance with the power are so exercisable by the remaining beneficiary or beneficiaries), and

(c)   if the functions are delegated to him and to other beneficiaries to be exercised by them separately (or either separately or jointly), the power is revoked in so far as it relates to him.

(5)   A delegation under subsection (1) may be for any period or indefinite.

(6)   A power of attorney under subsection (1) cannot be an enduring power within the meaning of the Enduring Powers of Attorney Act 1985.

(7)   Beneficiaries to whom functions have been delegated under subsection (1) are, in relation to the exercise of the functions, in the same position as trustees (with the same duties and liabilities); but such beneficiaries shall not be regarded as trustees for any other purposes (including, in particular, the purposes of any enactment permitting the delegation of functions by trustees or imposing requirements relating to the payment of capital money).

(8)   Where any function has been delegated to a beneficiary or beneficiaries under subsection (1), the trustees are jointly and severally liable for any act or default of the beneficiary, or any of the beneficiaries, in the exercise of the function if, and only if, the trustees did not exercise reasonable care in deciding to delegate the function to the beneficiary or beneficiaries.

(9)   Neither this section nor the repeal by this Act of section 29 of the Law of Property Act 1925 (which is superseded by this section) affects the operation after the commencement of this Act of any delegation effected before that commencement.

13.6   End of Chapter Assessment Question

Samantha owns two houses, Black House and White House. She is critically ill, and wishes to make a new will.

With respect to Black House, she wants to leave it to her son Thomas for life, remainder in fee simple to her grandsons Luke and John. 'I am very keen that Luke and John should inherit Black House after Thomas' death. I don't want the house disposed of during Thomas' lifetime.'

With respect to White House, she wants to leave it to her cousin Norman for life, remainder in fee simple to Norman's two children Philip and Philippa. 'White House is rather large and a long way from the shops. It may prove unsuitable for Norman. If that proves to be the case, would it be possible for him, or somebody on his behalf, to sell White House and buy (say) a lease of a smaller house on the edge of the town centre?'

Advise Samantha as to the drafting of her will.

13.7   End of Chapter Assessment Outline Answer

Black House

Samantha desires to create successive interests in Black House by the terms of her will. Her son Thomas is to be the life beneficiary, and after his death her grandsons Luke and John are to take the fee simple. She is also eager to keep the house in the family, and to that end wishes to prevent any disposition of the house during Thomas' lifetime.

Successive ownership of the sort envisaged by Samantha can only be effected by means of a trust, and according to the Trusts of Land and Appointment of Trustees Act 1996 (which came into force on 1 January 1997) the trust must take the form of a new-style 'trust of land'.

The trustees of a new-style trust of land are expressly granted, in relation to the land subject to the trust, all the powers of an absolute owner of land (s. 6(1)). It follows that, *prima facie*, the trustees' power of sale cannot be qualified to take effect only after Thomas' death. In fact, the picture is not that simple, for a number of reasons.

First, s. 8(1) permits Samantha to expressly provide that the trustees shall have no power of sale during Thomas' lifetime. Samantha should be advised, however, that such an absolute restriction could have potentially disastrous economic consequences. In the future the value of the property might fall or threaten to fall, and in such an event the trustees might wish to sell Black House and invest the proceeds in other land. This they would be unable to do if their power to sell has been removed under s. 8(1).

Secondly, s. 8(2) provides for another means of limiting the trustees' power of sale, but one that is significantly less rigid in its result than the power contained in s. 8(1). Section 8(2) provides that the exercise of the trustees' power of sale and the exercise of the trustees' other powers can be made expressly subject to the consent of any person or persons. Samantha should be advised, therefore, to put a clause in her will trust which will prevent a sale by the trustees without the consent of certain named individuals. She might, for instance, wish to make any sale subject to Thomas' consent, with a view to keeping Black House unsold during Thomas' lifetime. However, if she is concerned that Thomas might consent to a sale, she could make the trustees' power of sale subject to the consent of another trusted friend. She should choose a friend whom she is confident will not consent to a sale in Thomas' lifetime unless circumstances are such that a sale becomes necessary for the welfare of the beneficiaries. If a sale is necessary in order to avoid economic catastrophe the trusted friend will no doubt consent to a sale.

Where the power to sell is restricted by s. 8(1) this flexibility to respond to changing economic circumstances *prima facie* does not exist. Samantha should be advised, however, that if she stipulates for the consents of more than two persons to be obtained before any sale can proceed, the trustees are only obliged to obtain the consents of any *two* of those persons before exercising their power of sale (s. 10(1)).

Thirdly, if Samantha includes a clause expressly making Thomas' occupation of Black House a purpose of the trust, he will be entitled to occupy the house unless the land becomes unsuitable for him or unavailable to him (s. 12). However, if Thomas occupies the land by reason of his entitlement under s. 12 the trustees can subject him to certain reasonable conditions of occupation (s. 13(3)). He might, for example, be required to keep the premises in a good state of repair.

Fourthly, if the trustees intend to sell the house against the wishes of Thomas and/or any other person with an interest under the trust, s. 14 of the 1996 Act provides that any such person may apply to court for an order relating to the exercise by the trustees of any of their functions. Having heard such an application the court may make such order as it thinks fit. According to s. 15 the court must consider, *inter alia*, the wishes of Samantha when considering the appropriate order to be made.

Finally, in advising Samantha, one crucial general point should be made. Namely, that if Thomas, Luke and John are all adults and have capacity (that is, do not suffer from a legally relevant disability) and together agree, they can bring the trust to an end under the rule in *Saunders* v *Vautier* [1825–42] 1 All ER Rep 58. In such a case neither Samantha nor her trustees would have any power to prevent a sale of the house during Thomas' lifetime.

White House
As before, Samantha should be advised that her proposed disposition can only be effected by a new-style trust of land. The issues are whether Samantha can ensure that the house will be sold at Norman's request, and whether the proceeds will be reinvested according to Norman's wishes.

As to the first issue, it is worth noting that under the traditional Settled Land Act 'strict settlement' Norman, as tenant for life, would have had the power to sell the land. After the Trusts of Land etc. Act 1996 it is no longer possible to create a trust of this type. Section 6(1) of the 1996 Act vests the power of sale in the trustees of the new-style 'trust of land' and s. 4(1) grants the trustees the power to postpone sale of the land indefinately, the length of postponement lying entirely within the trustees' discretion (s. 4(1)). This statutory power cannot be excluded by contrary expression in the trust instrument. Thus, the trustees cannot be placed under a duty to sell, and consequently Samantha cannot ensure that the house will be sold at Norman's request. Accordingly, Samantha should be advised to choose trustees who are likely to respond favourably to Norman's request. To this end she could, of course, appoint Norman himself to be one of the trustees if she so wishes (members of our firm of solicitors could be appointed to be the other trustees).

As to the second issue, Samantha should be advised that the trustees are authorised to reinvest the proceeds of sale in new land (ss. 6(3) and 17(1)), the old rule in *Re Wakeman* has been abolished which required trustees to retain *some* land unsold at all times in order to be entitled to reinvest the proceeds of a sale in new land. Samantha should also be informed that, before reinvesting the proceeds of sale, the trustees will be obliged to consult Norman, as the beneficiary in possession, and to give effect to his wishes so far as his wishes are deemed by them to be consistent with the general interests of the trust (s. 11(1)).

For completeness we should also advise Samantha that if her trustees refuse to accede to Norman's reasonable request for a sale and/or reinvestment in appropriate property, all is not lost. Norman could apply under s. 14 for a court order requiring the trustees to reinvest the proceeds of sale in, say, a smaller house nearer to the shops! According to s. 15 the court must have regard to, *inter alia*, the intentions of Samantha, the purposes for which the trust land is held and the welfare of any minors (in this case Philippa and Philip may be minors).

CHAPTER FOURTEEN

CO-OWNERSHIP OF LAND —
THE BASIC CONCEPTS

14.1 Introduction

Lawson, F. H. and Rudden, B., The Law of Property, 2nd edn,
Oxford: Clarendon Press, 1982, p. 82

CO-OWNERSHIP

Ownership of the same thing at the same time and in the same way by a number of persons has been general from early times. Indeed, some students of primitive law think that ownership by communities such as families, tribes, and clans everywhere preceded ownership by individuals. Roman law admitted common ownership and it has survived everywhere in one form or another.

Even in the modern world there are many occasions on which this may happen. A man may, for instance, die intestate leaving two unmarried sons who go on living together in his house; they do not choose to divide it into two self-contained flats but use most of the rooms in common. In many countries marriage usually makes some at least of what was hitherto the separate property of each of the spouses their common property; and in England it is common for husband and wife to operate a joint banking account. Or two men may run a business in partnership, which involves using the same factory or office in common.

English law has always known two kinds of co-ownership, in accordance with which several persons enjoy what are called concurrent interests. They are called respectively joint ownership and ownership in common. In speaking of land the terms joint tenancy and tenancy in common are used, but this is used of freehold owners and has nothing to do with the law of leases. The difference between them is that whereas if one owner or tenant in common dies, his share passes to his successors, whether by will or on an intestacy, one joint tenant's share accrues on his death to the other joint tenants, so that when all the joint tenants but one are dead the last survivor becomes sole owner tenant.

Lawyers have tried to explain this right of survivorship in a thoroughly artificial way by saying that whereas tenants in common are regarded as holding undivided shares in the land, each share being capable of being alienated, joint tenants do not own shares, but each joint tenant owns the whole, subject to the concurrent ownership of the other joint tenants. When one dies the others do not in theory acquire anything that they had not already, but are merely relieved of the presence of a competing tenant.

The phrase 'undivided shares' has a long history and is much used in modern statutes, so it is a burden we must accept. But it would be meaningless to call a share 'undivided' if by that were meant not separate from the other shares. The simplest way to grasp the position of tenants in common is to think of shares in a company. The shareholders each have a separate thing which they can alienate or leave to pass on their death. It is the property in which the share subsists—the company—which is undivided. So two tenants in common of a house each have a separate, though intagible, asset; it is the house which is not divided into distinct 'shares'. . . .

14.2 Joint Tenancy

14.2.1 RIGHT OF SURVIVORSHIP

The Law Commission, Working Paper No. 105, Transfer of Land: Title on Death, London: HMSO, 1987, p. 47

Co-ownership

2.43 Modern English co-ownership of land is built on the concept of the trust for sale. On the death of a legal co-owner (who has to be a joint tenant since 1925) his surviving co-owner or co-owners take by the *jus accrescendi* (right of survivorship). If co-ownership remains in existence, then there must be at least two trustees (unless the sole one is a trust corporation) before any disposition involving capital money can be effected. If co-ownership has ceased and the sole survivor is beneficially entitled, the position will differ according as the title is registered or unregistered. It will also differ according as the beneficial entitlement in the sole survivor has come about by the operation of the *jus accrescendi* on the end of a beneficial joint tenancy or by the inheritance of the undivided beneficial joint tenancy or by the inheritance or the undivided beneficial share of the deceased by his surviving co-tenant in common. If the title is registered and there was a beneficial joint tenancy before the death, there should be no restriction relating to the co-ownership on the register and the Registrar will merely delete the deceased's name from the proprietorship register, leaving the survivor as unrestricted sole proprietor, unless the Registrar has reason to believe that a severance of the joint tenancy had occurred by or at the date of death. If the title is registered and there was restriction on the register at death because the co-owners were not then joint owners, the Registrar will need to have evidence of the vesting in the survivor of the whole beneficial interest before he removes the restricton from the register. If the title is unregistered and the co-owners appeared as beneficial joint tenants on the title deeds at the death, then the Law of Property (Joint Tenants) Act 1964 seems to provide purchasers from the survivor with full protection so long as the provisions of that Act are fulfilled. If, however, the title is unregistered and the 1964 Act does not apply, the survivor will either have to appoint a new trustee to act with him or (uniquely if the transaction is one such as a sale at an under value which trustes do not have authority to make) show the passage to him of the deceased's equitable share by assent or assignment. . . .

14.3 The Reform of Co-ownership in 1925 — the Main Objective

LAW OF PROPERTY ACT 1925
as amended by the Trusts of Land etc. Act 1996

34. Effect of future dispositions to tenants in common

(1) An undivided share in land shall not be capable of being created except as provided by the Settled Land Act 1925 or as hereinafter mentioned.

(2) Where, after the commencement of this Act, land is expressed to be conveyed to any persons in undivided shares and those persons are of full age, the conveyance shall (notwithstanding anything to the contrary in this Act) operate as if the land had been expressed to be conveyed to the grantees, or, if there are more than four grantees, to the four first named in the conveyance, as joint tenants [in trust for the persons interested in the land]:

Provided that, where the conveyance is made by way of mortgage the land shall vest in the grantees or such four of them as aforesaid for a term of years absolute (as provided by this Act) as joint tenants subject to cesser on redemption in like manner as if the mortgage money had belonged to them on a joint account, but without prejudice to the beneficial interests in the mortage money and interest. . . .

14.4   The Modern Conveyancing Practice to create an Express Trust (for Sale)

WALKER v *HALL* (1984) 5 FLR 126, Court of Appeal

FACTS: An unmarried couple had been living together as *de facto* man and wife and had purchased a house in joint names as a family home. During the relationship they pooled their earnings to pay various expenses, and to repay the mortgage by instalments. A short while later the couple separated, Mrs Walker leaving Mr Hall in the family home. He continued to pay off the mortgage instalments from his own funds, with the result that his contributions to the price of the property far outweighed hers. Mrs Walker claimed a beneficial share in the property.

HELD: In the absence of an express declaration as to the extent of her beneficial interest, Mrs Walker's share would be determined, according to normal trust principles, with reference only to the extent of her financial contribution to the value of the property. *Per curiam*: solicitors acting for joint purchasers of land should ascertain, and declare by express deed of trust, the parties' intentions as to the extent of their respective beneficial shares in the land.

DILLON LJ: . . . The transfer of 33 Foxberry Road to Mr Hall and Mrs Walker is in the common form of a Land Registry Transfer. It transfers the property to Mr Hall and Mrs Walker as joint tenants but contains no statement of what their respective beneficial interests are to be. Ten years ago Bagnall J in *Cowcher* v *Cowcher* [1972] 1 WLR 425 at p. 442 drew attention to the desirability that solicitors should take steps to find out and declare what the beneficial interests are to be, when the legal estate in a house is acquired by two persons in their joint names. The difficulties which otherwise arise, and which can so easily be avoided by a little care on the part of the solicitors, were emphasized recently by Griffiths LJ in *Bernard* v *Josephs* (1983) 4 FLR 178. I would wish to underline the point as strongly as I can and to suggest that the courts may soon have to consider whether a solicitor acting for joint purchasers is not guilty of negligence if he fails to find out and record what the joint purhasers' beneficial interests in the relevant property are to be. . . .

If there is evidence that both parties were to have beneficial interests in the house, and there is no further evidence at all to indicate the extent of those interests, the conclusion would be that equity follows the law, and the parties holding the legal estate as joint tenants, are entitled beneficially as joint tenants also. As Lord Upjohn pointed out in *Pettitt* v *Pettitt* [1970] AC 777 at pp. 813–14:

> . . . in the absence of all other evidence, if the property is conveyed . . . to the spouses jointly that operates to convey the beneficial interest to the spouses jointly, i.e. with benefit of survivorship, but it is seldom that this will be determinative.

In particular, the law of trusts has concentrated on how the purchase money has been provided and it has been consistently held that where the purchase money for property acquired by two or more persons in their joint names has been provided by those persons in unequal amounts, they will be beneficially entitled as between themselves in the proportions in which they provided the purchase money. This is the basic doctrine of the resulting trust.

GOODMAN v *GALLANT* [1986] 2 WLR 236, Court of Appeal

FACTS: A married couple purchased a house in their joint names and held it as beneficial joint tenants in equity. The husband left his wife (the plaintiff) and the defendant moved in with her. They purchased the husband's interest from him, the conveyance providing that the plaintiff and defendant were to hold the property on trust for sale as joint tenants in equity. The defendant left and the plaintiff served a notice severing the tenancy. She then issued a summons for a declaration as to their respective shares in the property. She claimed to be entitled to a three-quarters share. The registrar held that the express

declaration of the joint tenancy in equity had established their respective beneficial shares, upon severance, as half and half. The judge at first instance upheld the registrar's conclusion and the plaintiff appealed to the Court of Appeal.
HELD: The appeal was dismissed.

SLADE LJ: . . . ss. 34 to 36, while importing a trust for sale in certain cases where it would not otherwise have arisen, are designed merely to simplify the mechanics of conveyancing. They have no effect whatever on the nature and extent of the respective beneficial interest in the proceeds of sale of the several persons interested. Accordingly, in our judgment, the provisions of clause 2(a) of the conveyance, by which *express trusts* are declared concerning the beneficial interests in the property or its proceeds of sale, cannot be regarded as otiose. The position is quite the contrary.

In a case where the legal estate in property is conveyed to two or more persons as joint tenants, but neither the conveyance nor any other written document contains any express declaration of trust concerning the beneficial interests in the property (as would be required for an express declaration of this nature by virtue of s. 53(1)(b) of the Law of Property Act 1925), the way is open for persons claiming a beneficial interest in it or its proceeds of sale to rely on the doctrine of 'resulting, implied or constructive trusts': see s. 53(2) of the Law of Property Act 1925. In particular, in a case such as that, a person who claims to have contributed to the purchase price of property which stands in the name of himself and another can rely on the well known presumption of equity that a person who has contributed a share of the purchase price of property is entitled to a corresponding proportionate beneficial interest in the property by way of implied or resulting trust: see, for example, *Pettitt* v *Pettitt* [1970] AC 777, 813–814, *per* Lord Upjohn. If, however, the relevant conveyance contains an express declaration of trust which comprehensively declares the beneficial interests in the property or its proceed of sale, there is no room for the application of the doctrine of resulting implied or constructive trusts unless and until the conveyance is set aside or rectified; until that event the declaration contained in the document speaks for itself.

. . . in the absence of any claim for rectification or rescission, the provision in the conveyance declaring that the plaintiff and the defendant were to hold the proceeds of sale of the property 'upon trust for themselves as joint tenants' concludes the question of the respective beneficial interests of the two parties in so far as that declaration of trust, on its true construction, exhaustively declares the beneficial interests.

CHAPTER FIFTEEN

SEVERANCE OF JOINT TENANCIES

15.1   Methods of Severance

Since 1925, a legal tenancy cannot be severed. Any severance affects only the equitable interests under the trust for sale. In this section we shall consider the various methods of severance of the equitable joint tenancy.

15.1.1   TOTAL ALIENATION

If a joint tenant sells (or gives away inter vivos) his equitable interest, that effects a severance.

15.1.2   BANKRUPTCY

RE DENNIS (A BANKRUPT) [1992] 3 WLR 204, Chancery Division

FACTS: A husband and wife were beneficial joint tenants of certain freehold properties. On 21 September 1982 the husband failed to comply with a bankruptcy notice and as a consequence of this failure a bankruptcy petition was served on him. Before he was actually declared bankrupt his wife died, having devised her estate on her children. The trustee in bankruptcy applied for a declaration that the two freeholds were vested in him. HELD: The joint tenancy had been severed by the final adjudication of bankruptcy, and not by the failure to comply with the notice, nor by service of the petition. Accordingly, the joint tenancy had not been severed before the wife's death and the two properties could not devolve as part of her estate. They had vested in her husband by right of survivorship and were now vested in the trustee in bankruptcy.

SIR DONALD NICHOLLS V-C: A joint tenancy is severed if a joint tenant disposes of his interest *inter vivos*. Such a disposition may be voluntary, for example a gift or a sale; it may be involuntary, as occurs upon bankruptcy when the bankrupt's property vests in his trustee. In the present case the position when Mrs Dennis died was that her husband had not yet been adjudicated bankrupt. He had committed an act of bankruptcy and a petition had been presented. The petition had been followed by a receiving order. This was after Mrs Dennis' death, but in any event a receiving order does not operate to divest a debtor of his property. If authority is needed for that proposition, it can be found in the decision of the Court of Appeal in *Rhodes* v *Dawson* (1886) 16 QBD 548. Thus, by the moment of Mrs Dennis' death on 24 February 1983, there had been no alienation by her husband of his interest in the joint tenancy.

Subsequently he became bankrupt. At that moment he was divested of his property. At that moment there was therefore an involuntary alienation by him of his property. The concluding words of s. 18(1) of the Bankruptcy Act 1914 provide for the consequence of an adjudication in these terms: 'and thereupon the property of the bankrupt shall become divisible among his creditors and shall vest in a trustee.' To the like effect is s. 53 which provides:

(1) Until a trustee is appointed, the official receiver shall be the trustee for the purposes of this Act, and, immediately on a debtor being adjusted bankrupt, the property of the bankrupt shall vest in the trustee. (2) On the appointment of a trustee, the property shall forthwith pass to and vest in the trustee appointed. . . .

15.1.3 PARTIAL ALIENATION

A partial alienation would occur where a joint tenant mortgaged or leased his or her interest.

15.1.4 CONTRACT TO ALIENATE

If a joint tenant contracts to sell, lease, or mortgage his interest that will effect a severance.

15.1.5 WRITTEN NOTICE AND INFORMAL SEVERANCE UNDER THE LAW OF PROPERTY ACT 1925

LAW OF PROPERTY ACT 1925

36. Joint tenancies

(1)   Where a legal estate (not being settled land) is beneficially limited to or held in trust for any persons as joint tenants, the same shall be held on trust for sale, in like manner as if the persons beneficially entitled were tenants in common, but not so as to sever their joint tenancy in equity.

(2)   No severance of a joint tenancy of a legal estate, so as to create a tenancy in common land, shall be permissible, whether by operation of law or otherwise, but this subsection does not affect the right of a joint tenant to release his interest to the other joint tenants, or the right to sever a joint tenancy in an equitable interest whether or not the legal estate is vested in the joint tenants:

Provided that, where a legal estate (not being settled land) is vested in joint tenants beneficially, and any tenant desires to sever the joint tenancy in equity, he shall give to the other joint tenants a notice in writing of such desire or do such other acts or things as would, in the case of personal estate, have been effectual to sever the tenancy in equity, and thereupon under the trust for sale affecting the land the net proceeds of sale, and the net rents and profits until sale, shall be held upon the trusts which would have been requisite for giving effect to the beneficial interests if there had been an actual severance.

Nothing in this Act affects the right of a survivor of joint tenants, who is solely and beneficially interested, to deal with his legal estate as if it were not held on trust for sale.

(3)   Without prejudice to the right of a joint tenant to release his interest to the other joint tenants no severance of a mortgage term or trust estate, so as to create a tenancy in common, shall be permissible.

15.1.5.1 Severance by written notice

LAW OF PROPERTY ACT 1925

196. Regulations respecting notices

(1)   Any notice required or authorised to be served or given by this Act shall be in writing.

(2)   Any notice required or authorised by this Act to be served on a lessee or mortgagor shall be sufficient, although only addressed to the lessee or mortgagor by that designation, without his name, or generally to the persons interested, without any name, and

notwithstanding that any person to be affected by the notice is absent, under disability, unborn, or unascertained.

(3) Any notice required or authorised by this Act to be served shall be sufficiently served if it is left at the last-known place of abode or business in the United Kingdom of the lessee, lessor, mortgagee, mortgagor, or other person to be served, or, in case of a notice required or authorised to be served on a lessee or mortgagor, is affixed or left for him on the land or any house or building comprised in the lease or mortgage, or, in case of a mining lease, is left for the lessee at the office or counting-house of the mine.

(4) Any notice required or authorised by this Act to be served shall also be sufficiently served, if it is sent by post in a registered letter addressed to the lessee, lessor, mortgagee, mortgagor, or other person to be served, by name, at the aforesaid place of abode or business, office, or counting-house, and if that letter is not returned through the post office undelivered; and that service shall be deemed to be made at the time at which the registered letter would in the ordinary course be delivered. . . .

RE 88 BERKELEY ROAD, N.W.9. [1971] 1 All ER 254, Chancery Division

FACTS: Two unmarried ladies, Miss Eldridge and Miss Goodwin, were joint tenants of their home, 88 Berkeley Road. Eldridge announced that she was getting married. Goodwin consulted solicitors, who advised her to sever the joint tenancy. The solicitors drafted a notice of severance and this was sent by recorded delivery to Eldridge at her 'residence', 88 Berkeley Road. When the postman called, Eldridge had already gone to work. Goodwin signed for the letter. Goodwin died soon afterwards. In the ensuing proceedings, Eldridge swore that she had never seen the letter. The question was whether there had been an effective severance of the joint tenancy.

HELD: There had been a severance, because the letter had not been 'returned undelivered' and was therefore notice of severance was deemed to have been properly served.

PLOWMAN J: Mr Bramall's second submission was, if he will allow me to say so, an ingenious one. He pointed to the words in s. 196(4)—and I quote: '. . . if that letter is not returned through the post office undelivered'—and he submitted that the facts of the present case showed that the letter was delivered into the hand of Miss Goodwin: in other words, it was really delivered to the sender, because the solicitors who sent it were Miss Goodwin's solicitors and her agents for this purpose, and that, since the letter was delivered into the hands of the sender, it was in effect returned through the Post Office undelivered.

Again, I do not feel able to accept that submission. In my view, the words '. . . if that letter is not returned through the post office undelivered' refer to the ordinary case of the Post Office being unable to effect delivery at the address on the letter for some reason or other, such as that the addressee has gone away or the house is shut or empty. It does not, in my judgment, apply to a case like the present where the letter has in fact been delivered by the postman at the address to which it was sent.

The third submission which Mr Bramall made was to this effect, that where a section in an Act of Parliament is potentially creating an unjust situation, as would be the case here if the notice is to be taken as having been received by the plaintiff although she never received it, then the Act ought to be construed strictly, and that that involves strict proof that the relevant document—the letter containing the notice of severance, in this case—was in fact served. And Mr Bramall pointed out that Mr Bender, who was an assistant solicitor in the firm of solicitors who were Miss Goodwin's solicitors at this time and who was responsible for dealing with this matter, could not actually prove putting the notice of severance in the envelope with the covering letter before it was sent. In my judgment, the onus of proof on the defendants here is no higher than proof that, on the balance of probabilities, that was done; and I feel no difficulty in reaching the conclusion that, on the balance of probabilities, it was in fact done.

For those reasons, I cannot accept Mr Bramall's submissions on s. 196(4). . . .

In those circumstances, and with some regret having regard to my findings of fact, I feel bound to conclude that the notice of severance, even though never received by the plaintiff, was in fact sufficiently served for the purposes of s. 36(2) of the Law of Property Act 1925 with the consequence that the joint tenancy was severed during the lifetime of Miss Goodwin.

HARRIS v *GODDARD* [1983] 1 WLR 1203, Court of Appeal

FACTS: A husband and wife were beneficial joint tenants of the matrimonial home, from which the husband ran his retail business. After some time, the wife left and served a divorce petition. Paragraph 3 of the petition prayed that 'such order may be made by way of transfer or property and/or settlement of property and/or variation of settlement in respect of the former matrimonial home . . . and otherwise as may be just'. Three days before the hearing of the petition the husband was involved in a car crash, resulting in a coma from which he never recovered. The husband's executors sought a declaration that the joint tenancy of the former matrimonial home had been effectively severed before the husband's death. They pointed to paragraph 3 of the divorce petition as constituting a valid notice of severance within the proviso to s. 36(2) of the Law of Property Act 1925.

HELD: Severance had not been effected before the husband's death. A notice of severance within s. 36(2) had to evince an intention to sever immediately. The paragraph in the petition had merely expressed the wife's desire to invite the court to exercise its jurisdiction to apportion property entitlements according to justice. She could not have known the precise course that the court might take.

LAWTON LJ: I start with s. 36. It dealt with beneficial tenancies, which must mean all joint tenancies, including those held by husbands and wives. The section makes no special provisions by way of giving extra rights or raising presumptions in favour of spouses. When severance is said to arise under s. 36(2), not from the giving of a notice in writing, but from '[doing] . . . other acts or things' which would, in the case of personal estate, have been effectual to sever a joint tenancy in equity, the fact that the parties were married may make the drawing of inferences easier. It is, in my judgment, only in this limited evidential context that the existence of the married state has any relevance. In reaching this conclusion I have followed what Russell LJ said in *Bedson* v *Bedson* [1965] 2 QB 666, 689–690 rather than the obiter statement of Lord Denning MR in the same case at p. 678. Lord Denning MR said that spouses holding as beneficial joint tenants cannot sever their interests so as to convert them into tenancies in common. The trial judge seems to have been influenced to some extent by what Lord Denning MR said. Since in this case severance is said to have come about by a notice in writing the sole question is whether that which is said to be the notice did show that Mrs Harris desired to sever the joint tenancy.

In *Williams* v *Hensman* (1861) 1 Johns & Hem 546, 557, Page-Wood V-C said that a joint tenancy could be severed in three ways, that is, by disposal of one of the interests, by mutual agreement and 'by any course of dealing sufficient to intimate that the interests of all were mutually treated as constituting a tenancy in common.' The words in s. 36(2) 'do such other acts or things as would . . . have been effectual to sever the tenancy' put into statutory language the other ways of effecting severance to which Page Wood V-C referred in *Williams* v *Hensman*. The words 'and any tenant desires to sever the joint tenancy in equity, he shall give to the other joint tenants a notice in writing of such desire' operate to extend the mutual agreement concept of severance referred to in *Williams* v *Hensman*. Unilateral action to sever a joint tenancy is now possible. Before 1925 severance by unilateral action was only possible when one joint tenant disposed of his interest to a third party. When a notice in writing of a desire to sever is served pursuant to s. 36(2) it takes effect forthwith. It follows that a desire to sever must evince an intention to bring about the wanted result immediately. A notice in writing which expresses a desire to bring about the wanted result at some time in the future is not, in my judgment, a notice in writing within s. 36(2). Further the notice must be one which allows an intent to bring about the consequences set out in s. 36(2), namely, that the net proceeds of the statutory trust for sale 'shall be held upon the trusts which would have been requisite for giving effect to the beneficial interests if there had been an actual severance.' I am unable to accept Mr Berry's submission that a notice in writing which shows no more than a desire to bring the existing interest to an end is a good notice. It must be a desire to sever which is intended to have the statutory consequences. . . .

Perhaps this case should be a cautionary tale for those who draft divorce petitions when the spouses hold property as joint tenants in equity. The decision of Plowman J in *In re Draper's Conveyance* [1969] 1 Ch 486 is an example of how starting legal proceedings can sever a joint tenancy. In that case a wife, after a decree nisi but before a decree absolute, issued a summons under s. 17 of the Married Women's Property Act 1882 asking for an order that a house in the joint names of herself and her husband be sold and the proceeds of sale distributed in accordance with the parties' respective interests therein. An affidavit sworn by the wife in support of the summons contained this paragraph:

> In the premises I humbly ask that the said property may be sold and that the proceeds of sale thereof may be distributed equally; alternatively that the respondent pay me one half of the value of the said property with vacant possession. . . .

Plowman J adjudged that the summons and the affidavit together effected a severance during the lifetime of the husband. I agree that it did; but it is not clear from the judgment whether the judge regarded the summons or the affidavit or both as notices in writing or whether the service of the summons and the filing of the affidavit were acts which were effectual to sever the joint tenancy. I do not share the doubts about the correctness of this judgment on this point which Walton J expressed in *Nielson-Jones* v *Fedden* [1975] Ch 222, 236 relying on *In re Wilks* [1981] 3 Ch 59. The fact that the wife in *In re Draper's Conveyance* [1969] 1 Ch 486 could have withdrawn the summons is a factor which could have been taken into account in deciding whether what was done was effectual to sever the joint tenancy in equity. The weight of that factor would have depended upon all the other circumstances and was in that case clearly negligible.

I would dismiss the appeal.

RE DRAPER'S CONVEYANCE [1969] 1 Ch 486, Chancery Division

FACTS: A husband and wife held the matrimonial home as joint tenants in equity. Some time later the wife served a divorce petition. Between decree nisi and decree absolute of the divorce, the wife sought an order under the Married Women's Property Act 1882 in terms that the house be sold and the proceeds apportioned according to the parties respective interests therein.

The registrar granted the wife an order for possession but the husband died shortly afterwards and the house was not sold. The wife issued a summons to determine the basis on which she currently held title to the matrimonial home.

HELD: The wife's summons and supporting affidavit under the Married Women's Property Act 1882 evinced an intention to sever the joint tenancy.

PLOWMAN J: . . . Mr Cooke, . . . puts it in two ways; first, he submits that the wife's conduct was such as to effect a severance of the joint tenancy, and in relation to that matter he relies on the summons of February 11 1966, in the Probate, Divorce and Admiralty Division, coupled with the orders which were made by that court, coupled with the plaintiff's solicitor's letter of June 7 1966. And he says, either as a result of those three matters or as a result of any of them, the joint tenancy became severed by conduct, and he referred me to the decision of Havers J in *Hawkesley* v *May* [1956] 1 QB 304. The part of that case which is relevant for present purposes depends upon these facts, which I read from the headnote: 'A settled fund was held by trustees upon trusts under which on attaining the age 21 the plaintiff and his younger sister became absolutely entitled as joint tenants.' The question was whether that joint tenancy had become severed, and Havers J. said:

> The joint tenancy was capable of being severed by the plaintiff on attaining the age of 21. There are a number of ways by which a joint tenancy may be servered. In *Williams* v *Hensman* (1861) 1 Johns & Hem 546 Page-Wood V-C in the course of his judgment, said: 'A joint-tenancy may be severed in three ways: in the first place, an act of any one of the persons interested operating upon his own share may create a severance as to that share. The right of each joint-tenant is a right by survivorship only in the event of no severance having taken place of the share which is claimed under the jus accrescendi. Each one is at liberty to dispose of his own interest in such manner as to sever it from the joint fund—losing, of course, at the same time, his own right of survivorship. Secondly, a joint-tenancy may be severed by mutual agreement. And, in the third place, there may be a severance by any course of dealing sufficient to intimate that the interests of all were mutually treated as constituting a tenancy in common. When the severance depends on

an inference of this kind without any express act of severance, it will not suffice to rely on an intention, with respect to the particular share, declared only behind the backs of the other persons interested.'

Havers J continued:

The first method indicated, namely, an act of any one of the persons interested operating upon his own share, obviously includes a declaration of intention to sever by one party.' . . .

So from that case I derive this; a declaration by one of a number of joint tenants of his intention to sever operates as a severance. Mr Cooke also, as I have said, relied upon the notice in writing which under s. 36(2) of the Law of Property Act, 1925, is allowed in the case of a joint tenancy in land, although not in personalty, and he submits that the summons to which I have already referred, although not signed, amounted to a notice in writing on the part of the wife that she desired to sever the joint tenancy in equity. I say 'although not signed by the wife or by anybody on her behalf' because there is no requirement in the subsection of a signature.

. . . I feel little doubt that in one way or the other this joint tenancy was severed in equity before the end of February 1966, as a result of the summons which was served on the husband and as a result of what the wife stated in her affidavit in support of the summons. . . .

15.1.6 INFORMAL SEVERANCE

BURGESS v RAWNSLEY [1975] 1 Ch 429, Court of Appeal

FACTS: Mr Honick (a widower) and Mrs Rawnsley (a widow) met at a scripture rally in Trafalgar Square. They became close friends and bought as joint tenants the fee simple to the house of which Mr Honick had hitherto been a tenant. However, they later fell out. It was orally agreed that Honick should buy out Mrs Rawnsley's interest for £750. Before matters could finally be resolved, Honick died. The issue before the court was whether there had or had not been a severance.
HELD: The oral agreement (though not an enforceable contract) had been sufficient to sever the joint tenancy.

LORD DENNING MR: . . . Nowadays everyone starts with the judgment of Sir William Page Wood V-C in *Williams* v *Hensman* (1861) 1 Johns & Hem 546, 557, where he said:

A joint tenancy may be severed in three ways: in the first place, an act of any one of the persons interested operating upon his own share may create a severance as to that share. . . . Secondly, a joint tenancy may be severed by mutual agreement. And, in the third place, there may a severance by any course of dealing sufficient to intimate that the interests of all were mutually treated as constituting a tenancy in common. When the severance depends on an inference of this kind without any express act of severance, it will not suffice to rely on an intention, with respect to the particular share, declared only behind the backs of the other persons interested. You must find in this class of cases a course of dealing by which the shares of all the parties to the contest have been effected, as happened in the cases of *Wilson* v *Bell* (1843) 5 IrEqR 501 and *Jackson* v *Jackson* (1804) 9 Ves Jun 591.

In that passage Page Wood V-C distinguished between severance 'by mutual agreement' and severance by a 'course of dealing.' That shows that a 'course of dealing' need not amount to an agreement, expressed or implied, for severance. It is sufficient if there is a course of dealing in which one party makes clear to the other that he desires that their shares should no longer he held jointly but be held in common. I emphasise that it must be made clear to the other party. That is implicit in the sentence in which Page Wood V-C says:

it will not suffice to rely on an intention, with respect to the particular share, declared only behind the backs of the other persons interested.

Similarly it is sufficient if both parties enter on a course of dealing which evinces an intention by both of them that their shares shall henceforth be held in common and not jointly. As appears from the two cases to which Page Wood V-C referred of *Wilson* v *Bell* 5 IrEqR 501 and *Jackson* v *Jackson* 9 Ves Jun 591.

I come now to the question of notice. Suppose that one party gives a notice in writing to the other saying that he desires to sever the joint tenancy. Is that sufficient to effect a severance? I think it is. It was certainly the view of Sir Benjamin Cherry when he drafted s. 36(2) of the Law of Property Act 1925. It says in relation to real estates:

> ... where a legal estate (not being settled land) is vested in joint tenants beneficially, and any tenant desires to sever the joint tenancy in equity, he shall give to the other joint tenants a notice in writing of such desire or do such other acts or things as would, in the case of personal estate, have been effectual to sever the tenancy in equity, and thereupon under the trust for sale affecting the land the net proceeds of sale, and the net rents and profits until sale, shall be held upon the trusts which would have been requisite for giving effect to the beneficial interests if there had been an actual severance.

I have underlined the important words. The word 'other' is most illuminating. It shows quite plainly that, in the case of personal estate one of the things which is effective in equity to sever a joint tenancy is 'a notice in writing' of a desire to sever. So also in regard to real estate.

Taking this view, I find myself in agreement with Havers J in *Hawkesley* v *May* [1956] 1 QB 304, 313–314, and of Plowman J in *In re Draper's Conveyance* [1969] 1 Ch 486. I cannot agree with Walton J [1975] Ch 222, 234–235, that those cases were wrongly decided. It would be absurd that there should be a difference between real estate and personal estate in this respect. Suppose real estate is held on a joint tenancy on a trust for sale and is sold and converted into personal property. Before sale, it is severable by notice in writing. It would be ridiculous if it could not be severed afterwards in like manner. I look upon s. 36(2) as declaratory of the law as to severance by notice and not a a new provision confined to real estate. A joint tenancy in personal estate can be severed by notice just as a joint tenancy in real estate. . . .

It remains to apply these principles to the present case. I think there was evidence that Mr Honick and Mrs Rawnsley did come to an agreement that he would buy her share for £750. That agreement was not in writing and it was not specifically enforceable. Yet it was sufficient to effect a severance. Even if there was not any firm agreement but only a course of dealing, it clearly evinced an intention by both parties that the property should henceforth be held in common and not jointly.

On these grounds I would dismiss the appeal.

SIR JOHN PENNYCUICK: . . . I think it may be helpful to state very shortly certain views which I have formed in the light of the authorities.

(1) I do not think rule 3 in Page Wood V-C's statement, 1 John & Hem 546, 557, is a mere sub-heading of rule 2. It covers only acts of the parties, including, it seems to me, negotiations which, although not otherwise resulting in any agreement, indicate a common intention that the joint tenancy should be regarded as severed.

I do not overlook the words which I have read from Page Wood V-C's statement, namely, that you must find a course of dealing by which the shares of all the parties to the contract have been affected. But I do not think those words are sufficient to import a binding agreement.

(2) Section 36(2) of the Law of Property Act 1925 has radically altered the law in respect of severance by introducing an entirely new method of severance as regards land, namely, notice in writing given by one joint tenant to the other.

(3) Pre-1925 judicial statements, in particular that of Stirling J in *In re Wilks, Child* v *Bulmer* [1891] 3 Ch 59, must be read in the light of this alteration in the law; and, in particular, I do not see why the commencement of legal proceedings by writ or originating summons or the swearing of an affidavit in those proceedings, should not in appropriate circumstances

constitute notice in writing within the meaning of s. 36(2). The fact that the plaintiff is not obliged to prosecute the proceedings is I think irrelevant in regard to notice.

(4)   Perhaps in parenthesis because the point does not arise, the language of s. 36(2) appears to contemplate that even under the existing law notice in writing would be effective to sever a joint tenancy in personalty; see the words 'such other act or thing.' The authorities to the contrary are rather meagre and I am not sure how far this point was ever really considered in relation to personalty before 1925. If this anomaly does exist, and I am afraid I am not prepared to say positively that it does not exist, the anomaly is quite indefensible and should be put right as soon as possible.

(6)   An uncommunicated declaration by one party to the other or indeed a mere verbal notice by one party to another clearly cannot operate as a severance.

(7)   The policy of the law as it stands today, having regard particularly to s. 36(2), is to facilitate severance at the instance of either party, and I do not think the court should be over zealous in drawing a fine distinction from the pre-1925 authorities.

(8)   The foregoing statement of principles involves criticism of certain passages in the judgments of Plowman J and Walton J in the two cases cited. Those cases, like all other cases, depend on their own particular facts, and I do not myself wish to go on to apply these *obiter* statements of principle to the actual decisions in these cases.

Finally, I would say that if, contrary to my view, there was a resulting trust in this case, I should have no doubt that, on the particular facts in the case, the resulting trust would be for Mr Honick and for Mrs Rawnsley in equal shares. I was referred to *Robinson v Preston* (1858) 4 Kay & J 505. The circumstances of the present case are I think plainly such as to take this case out of the general principle laid down in that case as applicable apart from particular circumstances.

I would dismiss the appeal.

15.2   Matters which are Not a Severance

15.2.1   UNILATERAL ORAL STATEMENTS

Lord Denning in *Burgess* v *Rawnsley* (15.1.6 above) took the view that even a unilateral oral statement by one joint tenant to the other(s) could amount to severance. This view is not shared by any other judge (ancient or modern) and is clearly wrong.

15.2.2   SUBSEQUENT USE OF PROPERTY FOR BUSINESS PURPOSES

BARTON v *MORRIS* [1985] 2 All ER 1032, Chancery Division

FACTS: A farm was conveyed to two cohabitees on express trust for themselves as joint tenants in equity. 'The property was run as a guest house and small farm on a partnership basis and Miss Barton kept partnership accounts which showed the farm as a partnership asset'.
HELD: The use of the property for the purpose of a partnership did not, on the facts of the present case, sever the joint tenancy.

NICHOLLS J: In this action it is common ground that Miss Barton and Mr Morris carried on their business as a partnership at will, with profits and losses being shared equally. There was no written partnership agreement. . . .

Counsel for the plaintiff advanced the case in favour of severance in two ways. He accepted that the onus of establishing severance lay on the plaintiff, but he pointed out that equity leans in favour of tenancies in common. He observed, and I accept, that in a case such as this, the evidence of Mr Morris as the survivor must be viewed with caution. He drew my attention, amongst other authorities, to the judgment of Lord Denning MR in *Burgess* v *Rawnsley* [1975] 3 All ER 142 at 146–147, [1975] Ch 429 at 438–439. Lord Denning MR referred to Page Wood V-C's well-known classification in *Williams* v *Hensman* (1861) 1 John & H 546 at 557–558, 70 ER 862 at 867, of the three ways in which a joint tenancy may be severed. In short the third of these three modes of severance is by any course of dealing sufficient to intimate that the interests of the joint tenants were mutually treated as constituting a tenancy in common. . . .

. . . Here, submitted counsel for the plaintiff, there was such a course of dealing. The property was made subject to a joint tenancy declared in August 1979, but at that stage Miss Barton and Mr Morris did not want a formal partnership agreement. They wanted to see how the business went. By the autumn of 1980 Miss Barton had paid off the whole of the bank loan from her own money and the way ahead had become clearer. It was submitted that in this manner there had been a change in the situation. Further funds had been injected by Miss Barton as a matter of necessity, and thereafter the property and the partnership became inextricably interwoven. What happened, and this is the course of dealing relied on, was that Miss Barton prepared draft accounts to the knowledge of Mr Morris, showing the property as a partnership asset. The two of them then visited Mr Howells, and without dissent from Mr Morris Miss Barton indicated that the property was to be included for the sake of completeness. Matters then proceeded on that footing.

. . . To my mind the evidence establishes clearly that when the express declaration of joint tenancy in the conveyance was executed by the parties in about mid-August 1979, they both knew what the effect of that joint tenancy would be, and they both intended that the property should automatically accrue to the survivor on the death of the first to die. I accept the evidence of Miss Malthouse, the solicitor who acted for the parties on their purchase, concerning what passed between her and Miss Barton and Mr Morris on this topic prior to completion. In particular, beneficial joint tenancy was Miss Barton's intention, even though she was providing the lion's share of the purchase price. Again, it is plain from the evidence that from the outset the parties hoped and intended that the farmhouse would be used by them as a guest-house, and indeed, they took over one booking from their vendor. They planned to carry on such a business there together, with the house also being their home. Improvements and decorations would be necessary and Mr Morris was to carry out the heavy physical work. . . .

In those circumstances I am wholly unable to accept that the events relied on by counsel for the plaintiff as constituting the course of dealing he submits do in fact do so. . . .

15.2.3 'SEVERANCE BY WILL'

A joint tenancy cannot be severed by will.

CHAPTER SIXTEEN

CO-OWNERSHIP — THE PROBLEMS WHEN CO-OWNERS FALL OUT

16.1 Tenancy in Common Arising Because There is a Constructive Trust

16.1.1 DISPOSITIONS BY A SINGLE TRUSTEE

16.1.1.1 Registered title

ELIAS v *MITCHELL AND ANOTHER* **[1972] 1 Ch 652, Chancery Division**

FACTS: Two business partners had fallen out. One was the sole registered proprietor of their business premises, but both had 'shares' (as tenants in common) in the premises. The partner who was not the registered proprietor had left those premises.
HELD: The interest of the 'departed' partner was a minor interest which could be protected by lodging a caution.

PENNYCUICK V-C: . . . Then one comes to s. 54(1): 'Any person interested . . . howsoever, in any land . . . may lodge a caution . . .' If it is right to say that an interest in the proceeds of sale being by definition a minor interest is, within the intendment of this Act, an interest in land, then there is no doubt that a person interested in the proceeds of sale is a person interested in land for the purpose of s. 54(1) and can accordingly lodge a caution. If there were any doubt on this point, it would, I think, be set at rest by s. 101(3) which provides that minor interests may be protected by entry on the register of cautions. So that subsection in terms provides that minor interests, which by definition include interests under a trust for sale, may be protected by entry on the register, and that means that such interests are interests in land within the scope of s. 54. . . .

16.1.2 DISPOSITIONS BY MORE THAN ONE TRUSTEE

LAW OF PROPERTY ACT 1925
as amended by the Trusts of Land etc. Act 1996

2. Conveyances overreaching certain equitable interests and powers
   (1)   A conveyance to a purchaser of a legal estate in land shall overreach any equitable interest or power affecting that estate, whether or not he has notice thereof, if—
      (i)   the conveyance is made under the powers conferred by the Settled Land Act 1925 or any additional powers conferred by a settlement, and the equitable interest or power is capable of being overreached thereby, and the statutory requirements respecting the payment of capital money arising under the settlement are complied with;

(ii)   the conveyance is made by [trustees of land] and the equitable interest or power is at the date of the conveyance capable of being overreached by such trustees under the provisions of sub-section (2) of this section or independently of that sub-section, and [the requirements of section 27 of this Act respecting the payment of capital money arising on such a conveyance] are complied with;

(iii)   the conveyance is made by a mortgagee or personal representative in the exercise of his paramount powers, and the equitable interest or power is capable of being overreached by such conveyance, and any capital money arising from the transaction is paid to the mortgagee or personal representative;

(iv)   the conveyance is made under an order of the court and the equitable interest or power is bound by such order, and any capital money arising from the transaction is paid into, or in accordance with the order of, the court.

[(1A)   An equitable interest in land subject to a trust of land which remains in, or is to revert to, the settlor shall (subject to any contrary intention) be overreached by the conveyance if it would be so overreached were it an interest under the trust.]

(2)   Where the legal estate affected is subject to a [trust of land], then if at the date of a conveyance made after the commencement of this Act [by the trustees], the trustees (whether original or substituted) are either—

(a)   two or more individuals approved or appointed by the court or the successors in office of the individuals so approved or appointed; or

(b)   a trust corporation,

any equitable interest or power having priority [to the trust] shall, notwithstanding any stipulation to the contrary, be overreached by the conveyance, and shall, according to its priority, take effect as if created or arising by means of a primary trust affecting the proceeds of sale and the income of the land until sale.

(3)   The following equitable interests and powers are excepted from the operation of subsection (2) of this section, namely—

(i)   Any equitable interest protected by a deposit of documents relating to the legal estate affected;

(ii)   The benefit of any covenant or agreement restrictive of the user of land;

(iii)   Any easement, liberty, or privilege over or affecting land and being merely an equitable interest (in this Act referred to as an 'equitable easement');

(iv)   The benefit of any contract (in this Act referred to as an 'estate contract') to convey or create a legal estate, including a contract conferring either expressly or by statutory implication a valid option to purchase, a right of pre-emption, or any other like right;

(v)   Any equitable interest protected by registration under the Land Charges Act 1925 other than—

(a)   an annuity within the meaning of Part II of that Act;

(b)   a limited owner's charge or a general equitable charge within the meaning of that Act.

(4)   Subject to the protection afforded by this section to the purchaser of a legal estate, nothing contained in this section shall deprive a person entitled to an equitable charge of any of his rights or remedies for enforcing the same.

27.   Purchaser not to be concerned with the trusts of the proceeds of sale which are to be paid to two trustees or to a trust corporation

[(1)   A purchaser of a legal estate from trustees of land shall not be concerned with the trusts affecting the land, the net income of the land or the proceeds of sale of the land whether or not those trusts are declared by the same instrument as that by which the trust of land is created.]

(2)   Notwithstanding anything to the contrary in the instrument (if any) creating a [trust] of land or in [any trust affecting the net proceeds of sale of the land if it is sold], the proceeds for sale or other capital money shall not be paid to or applied by the direction of fewer than two persons as [trustees], except where the trustee is a trust corporation, but this subsection does not affect the right of a sole personal representative as such to give valid receipts for, or direct the application of, proceeds of sale or other capital money, nor, except where capital money arises on the transaction, render it necessary to have more than one trustee.

CITY OF LONDON BUILDING SOCIETY v *FLEGG* **[1988] 1 AC 54, House of Lords**

(Note: This case appears to survive the Trusts of Land etc. Act 1996.)

FACTS: Mr and Mrs Flegg had both contributed to the purchase of a house; the title to the house was registered in the names of their daughter and son-in-law (the Maxwell-Browns). The Fleggs, as a consequence of their contributions, each had an interest as a tenant in common under a resulting trust. All four lived in the house, and were therefore in 'actual occupation'. The house was subsequently mortgaged to the building society by the Maxwell-Browns. The building society argued that the mortgage, being executed by two trustees, overreached the rights of Mr and Mrs Flegg and that, as a result, they could sell the house 'over the heads' of the Fleggs.
HELD: The argument of the building society succeeded.

LORD TEMPLEMAN: . . . The respondents claim to be entitled to overriding interests because they were in actual occupation of Bleak House on the date of the legal charge. But the interests of the respondents cannot at one and the same time be overreached and overridden and at the same time be overriding interests. The appellants cannot at one and the same time take free from all the interests of the respondents yet at the same time be subject to some of those interests. The right of the respondents to be and remain in actual occupation of Bleak House ceased when the respondents' interests were overreached by the legal charge save in so far as their rights were transferred to the equity of redemption. As persons interested under the trust for sale the respondents had no right to possession as against the appellants and the fact that the respondents were in actual occupation at the date of the legal charge did not create a new right or transfer an old right so as to make the right enforceable against the appellants.

One of the main objects of the legislation of 1925 was to effect a compromise between on the one hand the interests of the public in securing that land held in trust is freely marketable and, on the other hand, the interests of the beneficiaries in preserving their rights under the trusts. By the Settled Land Act 1925 a tenant for life may convey the settled land discharged from all the trusts powers and provisions of the settlement. By the Law of Property Act 1925 trustees for sale may convey land held on trust for sale discharged from the trusts affecting the proceeds of sale and rents and profits until sale. Under both forms of trust the protection and the only protection of the beneficiaries is that capital money must be paid to at least two trustees or a trust corporation. . . .

For these reasons and for the reasons to be given by my noble and learned friend, Lord Oliver of Aylmerton, I would allow this appeal and restore the order of Judge Thomas who ordered the respondents to deliver up Bleak House to the appellants.

LORD OLIVER OF AYLMERTON: . . . I turn to consider whether, in fact, the decision of this House in *Boland* [1981] AC 487 does lead to the conclusion that the occupying co-owner's interest unde the statutory trusts is, by reason of his occupation, one which is incapable of being overreached. It has, I think, to be borne in mind when reading both the judgments in the Court of Appeal in that case and the speeches in the House that they were prepared and delivered against a background of fact which precluded any argument that the interests of Mrs Boland and Mrs Brown had been overreached under the provisions of the Law of Property Act 1925. . . .

Considered in the context of a transaction complying with the statutory requirements of the Law of Property Act 1925 the question of the effect of s. 70(1)(g) of the Land Registration Act 1925 must, in my judgment, be approached by asking first what are the 'rights' of the person in occupation and whether they are, at the material time, subsisting in reference to the land. In the instant case the exercise by the registered proprietors of the powers conferred on trustees for sale by s. 28(1) of the Law of Property Act 1925 had the effect of overreaching the interests of the respondents under the statutory trusts upon which depended their right to continue in occupation of the land. The appellants took free from those trusts (s. 27) and were not, in any event, concerned to see that the respondents' consent to the transaction was obtained (s. 26). If, then, one asks what were the subsisting rights of the respondents referable to their occupation, the answer must, in my judgment, be that they were rights which, vis-à-vis the appellants, were, *eo instante* with the creation of the charge, overreached and therefore subsisted only in relation to the equity of redemption. I do not, for my part, find in *Boland's* case [1981] AC 487 anything which compels a contrary conclusion. Granted that the interest of a co-owner pending the execution of the statutory trust for sale is, despite the equitable doctrine of conversion, an interest subsisting in reference to the land the subject matter of the trust and granted also that *Boland's* case establishes that such an interest, although falling within the definition of minor interest and so liable to be overriden by a registered disposition, will, so long as it subsists, be elevated to the status of an overriding interest if there exists also the additional element of occupation by the co-owner, I cannot for my part accept that, once what I may call the parent interest, by which alone the occupation can be justified, has been overreached and thus subordinated to a legal estate properly created by the trustees under their statutory powers, it can, in relation to the proprietor of the legal estate so created, be any longer said to be a right 'for the time being subsisting.' Section 70(1)(g) protects only the rights in reference to the land of the occupier whatever they are at the material time—in the instant case the right to enjoy in specie the rents and profits of the land held in trust for him. Once the beneficiary's rights have been shifted from the land to capital moneys in the hands of the trustees, there is no longer an interest in the land to which the occupation can be referred or which it can protect. If the trustees sell in accordance with the statutory provisions and so overreach the beneficial interests in reference to the land, nothing remains to which a right of occupation can attach and the same result must, in my judgment, follow vis-à-vis a chargee by way of legal mortgage so long as the transaction is carried out in the manner prescribed by the Law of Property Act 1925, overreaching the beneficial interests by subordinating them to the estate of the chargee which is no longer 'affected' by them so as to become subject to them on registration pursuant to s. 20(1) of the Land Registration Act 1925. In the instant case, therefore, I would, for my part, hold that the charge created in favour of the appellants overreached the beneficial interests of the respondents and that there is nothing in s. 70(1)(g) of the Land Registration Act 1925 or in *Boland's* case which has the effect of preserving against the appellants any rights of the respondents to occupy the land by virtue of their beneficial interests in the equity of redemption which remains vested in the trustees. . . .

Swadling, W.J., 'The Conveyancer's Revenge, *City of London Building Society* v *Flegg* [1987] 2 WLR 1266' (1987) 51 Conv 451 at 454

. . . In *Flegg* it was assumed that overreaching was effected by the Law of Property Act 1925 itself. Lord Templeman thought that the relevant statutory provisions were contained in ss. 27 and 28 whilst Lord Oliver preferred to think that it was an amalgam of ss. 2, 26, 27 and 28 of the Law of Property Act and s. 17 of the Trustee Act 1925 which triggered the process. It is submitted, however, that this approach is incorrect. Overreaching . . . occurs through the exercise of a trustee's powers and is dependent on the purchaser taking without notice of a breach of trust. All the statutory provisions do is to relieve the purchaser from making inquiries where certain procedures are followed. They do not facilitate the overreaching of the beneficial interests themselves which is dependent on the powers conferred by the trust instrument or statutory trust for sale.

On either view, however, it is important that the beneficial interests exist behind a trust for sale since only a purchaser from trustees for sale can claim the protection given by the legislation. Here the House of Lords held that such a trust was imposed by statute. Lord Oliver, however, did find some difficulty with the point. This was because he acknowledged that the way in which the equitable interest of the parents arose, i.e. under a resulting trust, is not specifically dealt with by that part of the 1925 legislation which imposes trusts for sale in certain situations.

> Nevertheless, section 34(1) [Law of Property Act 1925] provides that an undivided share shall not be capable of being created except as provided by the Settled Land Act 1925 or as thereinafter mentioned and section 36(4) of the Settled Land Act 1925 provides in terms that an undivided share in land shall not be capable of being created except under a trust instrument or under the Law of Property Act 1925, and shall then only take effect behind a trust for sale.

This, his Lordship reasoned, established the trust for sale as the conveyancing machinery for ownership of undivided shares. With respect, the result is nothing of the sort. What it means is that if an interest behind a resulting trust is to arise at all then it must do so *despite* the statute using the maxim that equity will not allow a statute to be used as an engine of fraud. If the legislation on the one hand prevents the interest from coming into being it is difficult to see how on the other it turns what would otherwise be a bare trust into a trust for sale. How can it apply to something it forbids? Lord Templeman did not feel that the point even merited discussion. With the drastic consequences such a finding can have on equitable co-owners it is a pity that the whole question was not more fully ventilated. . . .

The Law Commission, Working Paper No. 106, Trusts of Land: Overreaching, London: HMSO, 1988

7.   Provisional conclusion
7.1   It is our present view that there is a case for reforming the law on 'overreaching' for private trusts (i.e. when interests in land become instead interests in money). We are also at the moment of the opinion that, in principle, the law would better balance the practical concerns of purchasers and mortgagees against the special needs of beneficiaries for the land itself if it prevented their interests being 'overreached' without their consent where they are in actual occupation and of full age. In other words, we tentatively favour Proposal II [see below]. In addition, we would repeat the suggestion that the 'overreaching' machinery should be available for the protection of purchasers and mortgagees in respect of interests under bare trusts too.

Proposal II: no overreaching without consent of occupying beneficiaries
6.5   . . . it could be suggested that no overreaching should be possible without every beneficiary's consent. It may be argued that the duty to consult is far too limited and that the only way to protect beneficiaries adequately is to involve them directly in every sale or mortgage. However, this wide proposal would be impracticable. The purchaser/mortgagee could have no acceptable means of ascertaining who all the beneficiaries are, and they might not be of full age.
6.6   However, requiring consent of those beneficiaries in occupation may well strike the right balance between beneficiaries and purchasers. Accordingly this Proposal actually is that the interest of an occupying beneficiary should only be capable of being overreached with his or her consent, irrespective of whether the beneficiary has sought to protect himself by an entry on the register. The proposal is consistent with the approach to the rights of occupiers seen in *Boland*. . . . In cases of a sole registered proprietor or sole estate owner it appears inconsistent to protect benficiaries in actual occupation only until a second trustee is appointed. Further if interests in actual occupation are worth protecting, they ought to be protected whether or not the property was originally conveyed to or subsequently vested in joint owners at law. . . .

Harpum, C., 'Overreaching, Trustees' Powers and the Reform of the 1925 Legislation' [1990] *Cambridge Law Journal* 277–333

A number of misconceptions exist about overreaching. The first is that overreaching is something that occurs only in relation to land. It is undoubtedly true that the expression 'overreaching' gained currency during the 19th century and appears always to have been used in connection with dispositions of land. That association has been firmly cemented by the provisions of the Law of Property Act 1925, s. 2, which set out the circumstances in which a conveyance of a legal estate in land will overreach any equitable interest or power affecting that land. But overreaching must take place in relation to other forms of property. A trustee who sells trust investments must necessarily hold the proceeds of sale on the same trusts as the original investment. It must also follow from this that the basis of overreaching does not lie in the statutory provisions of section 2 of the Law of Property Act 1925. It must have a common law basis if it applies to personalty, and there are clear accounts of the effects of overreaching that pre-date the 1925 property legislation.

The second misconception is that overreaching is connected with the doctrine of conversion, at least in relation to trusts for sale. Because of that doctrine, it is said that the interests of the beneficiaries are from the inception of the trust in the proceeds of sale. Such a view is untenable as an explanation of overreaching. First, a disposition under a mere *power* of sale will overreach just as much as a disposition under a trust for sale, and this is so even though the doctrine of conversion is usually relevant to determine whether beneficial interests are in land or in personalty. Overreaching applies as much to trusts for sale of personalty as to trusts of realty. Thirdly, overreaching is concerned to transfer trusts from the original subject-matter of the trust to the *actual* proceeds *after* sale. The beneficial interests of those entitled under a trust for sale, by reason of the doctrine of conversion, are regarded for certain purposes as interests in the *notional* proceeds of sale *from the date of the creation of the trust*. There is no inevitability about the application of the doctrine of conversion to trusts for sale, and indeed the doctrine suffers from inherent logical flaws. The correct approach in every case is, it is suggested, to ask whether, as a matter of policy and for the particular purpose in issue, the interests of the beneficiaries should be regarded as interests in the subject matter of the trust or in the proceeds. It is not easy to predict whether the doctrine of conversion will ever again be used to explain overreaching. Lord Oliver, who in analysing the interests of tenants in common in *City of London Building Society* v *Flegg* [1988] 1 AC 54, favoured a strict application of the doctrine of conversion, certainly assumed that overreaching occurred on sale, but at the same time cited with approval the statement that '[t]he whole purpose of the trust for sale is to make sure, by shifting the equitable interests away from the land and into the proceeds of sale, that a purchaser of the land takes free from the equitable interests'.

The third misconception—apparently confined to trusts for sale of land—has it that overreaching will take place whenever the trustees for sale make *any* disposition, whether it is within their powers or not, provided the proceeds of the disposition are made to two trustees or to a trust corporation in accordance with the Law of Property Act 1925, s. 27(2). This view forms the foundation of the Law Commission's Working Paper No. 106, *Trusts of Land: Overreaching*, and seems to rest on the assumption that the provisions of the Law of Property Act 1925 a self-contained code for the operation of overreaching. It is said to derive support from the decision of the House of Lords in *City of London Building Society* v *Flegg*.

Leaving aside the statutory provisions of the Law of Property Act for the present, it would be very odd indeed if *ultra vires* dispositions could overreach. Dispositive powers are not inherently different from powers of appointment, and it would be reasonable to expect some parallel to the equitable doctrine of fraud on a power to be applicable to powers of disposition. If an *intra vires* appointment made in fraud of an equitable power is void, the same might be expected *a fortiori* of a transfer of property made in the absence or in excess of a power of disposition. An analysis of the authorities suggests that this is indeed the case.

16.2   Courts Settling Disputes Regarding Trusts of Land

LAW OF PROPERTY ACT 1925

30.   Powers of court where trustees for sale refuse to exercise powers

(1)   If the trustees for sale refuse to sell or to exercise any of the powers conferred by either of the last two sections, or any requisite consent cannot be obtained, any person interested may apply to the court for a vesting or other order for giving effect to the proposed transaction or for an order directing the trustees for sale to give effect thereto, and the court may make such order as it thinks fit.

(2)   The county court has jurisdiction under this section where the land which is to be dealt with in the court does not exceed the county court limit in capital value or net annual value for rating.

(Note: s. 30 is now repealed and replaced by ss. 13–15 of the Trusts of Land etc. Act 1996 — see below.)

TRUSTS OF LAND AND APPOINTMENT OF TRUSTEES ACT 1996

13. Exclusion and restriction of right to occupy

(1)   Where two or more beneficiaries are (or apart from this subsection would be) entitled under section 12 to occupy land, the trustees of land may exclude or restrict the entitlement of any one or more (but not all) of them.

(2)   Trustees may not under subsection (1)—

(a)   unreasonably exclude any beneficiary's entitlement to occupy land, or

(b)   restrict any such entitlement to an unreasonable extent.

(3)   The trustees of land may from time to time impose reasonable conditions on any beneficiary in relation to his occupation of land by reason of his entitlement under section 12.

(4)   The matters to which trustees are to have regard in exercising the powers conferred by this section include—

(a)   the intentions of the person or persons (if any) who created the trust,

(b)   the purposes for which the land is held, and

(c)   the circumstances and wishes of each of the beneficiaries who is (or apart from any previous exercise by the trustees of those powers would be) entitled to occupy the land under section 12.

(5)   The conditions which may be imposed on a beneficiary under subsection (3) include, in particular, conditions requiring him—

(a)   to pay any outgoings or expenses in respect of the land, or

(b)   to assume any other obligation in relation to the land or to any activity which is or is proposed to be conducted there.

(6)   Where the entitlement of any beneficiary to occupy land under section 12 has been excluded or restricted, the conditions which may be imposed on any other beneficiary under subsection (3) include, in particular, conditions requiring him to—

(a)   make payments by way of compensation to the beneficiary whose entitlement has been excluded or restricted, or

(b)   forgo any payment or other benefit to which he would otherwise be entitled under the trust so as to benefit that beneficiary.

(7)   The powers conferred on trustees by this section may not be exercised—

(a)   so as prevent any person who is in occupation of land (whether or not by reason of an entitlement under section 12) from continuing to occupy the land, or

(b)   in a manner likely to result in any such person ceasing to occupy the land, unless he consents or the court has given approval.

(8)   The matters to which the court is to have regard in determining whether to give approval under subsection (7) include the matters mentioned in subsection (4)(a) to (c).

Powers of court

14. Applications for order

(1)   Any person who is a trustee of land or has an interest in property subject to a trust of land may make an application to the court for an order under this section.

(2)   On an application for an order under this section the court may make any such order—

(a)   relating to the exercise by the trustees of any of their functions (including an order relieving them of any obligation to obtain the consent of, or to consult, any person in connection with the exercise of any of their functions), or

(b)   declaring the nature or extent of a person's interest in property subject to the trust,

as the court thinks fit.

(3)   The court may not under this section make any order as to the appointment or removal of trustees.

(4)   The powers conferred on the court by this section are exercisable on an application whether it is made before or after the commencement of this Act.

16.2.1 FACTORS TO BE CONSIDERED IN SETTLING DISPUTES

15. Matters relevant in determining applications

(1)   The matters to which the court is to have regard in determining an application for an order under section 14 include—

(a)   the intentions of the person or persons (if any) who created the trust,

(b)   the purposes for which the property subject to the trust is held,

(c)   the welfare of any minor who occupies or might reasonably be expected to occupy any land subject to the trust as his home, and

(d)   the interests of any secured creditor of any beneficiary.

(2)   In the case of an application relating to the exercise in relation to any land of the powers conferred on the trustees by section 13, the matters to which the court is to have regard also include the circumstances and wishes of each of the beneficiaries who is (or apart from any previous exercise by the trustees of those powers would be) entitled to occupy the land under section 12.

(3)   In the case of any other application, other than one relating to the exercise of the power mentioned in section 6(2), the matters to which the court is to have regard also include the circumstances and wishes of any beneficiaries of full age and entitled to an interest in possession in property subject to the trust or (in case of dispute) of the majority (according to the value of their combined interests).

. . .

16.2.2   SOLUTIONS THE COURT MAY ADOPT

(Note: s.30 of the Law of Property Act 1925 is now repealed and replaced by ss. 13–15 of the Trusts of Land etc. Act 1996.)

16.2.2.1   Refuse a sale

RE BUCHANAN-WOLLASTON'S CONVEYANCE [1939] 1 Ch 738, Court of Appeal

FACTS: A piece of open ground at Lowestoft in Suffolk separated four houses from the sea. That piece of land was up for sale, the owners of the four houses pooled their money together in order to buy the land as tenants in common. They were anxious to preserve their view of the sea. One of the four subsequently sold his house and moved away. He then applied to the court for an order that the piece of land should be sold and the proceeds divided. He argued that as the land was held on trust for sale it followed that if any of the four asked for a sale, a sale must take pace.
HELD: This argument was firmly rejected. Where land was bought for a specific purpose and that purpose could still be fulfilled, the courts would normally refuse to order a sale.

SIR WILFRID GREEN MR: . . . The statutory trust for sale is one which must be exercised and was intended by the Legislature to be exercised subject to the power of the Court to enforce it. That appears in s. 30. But the Legislature must be taken to have known the principles upon which the court of equity proceeds when asked by one of a body of trustees, or other persons who are not in agreement, to lend its assistance for the purpose of carrying out a trust; the Legislature must be taken to have known the principles upon which those powers are exercised, and the power of the Court to enforce the trust for sale must be exercised in regard to the statutory trust for sale according to well-known and ordinary principles. I am not going to enter into a discussion of the question whether or not the provisions of the Act in creating this trust for sale have the effect of overriding or nullifying any provisions in the instrument which in some way clog or fetter the trust for sale. That is a question which came into the discussion in the case of *In re Flint* [1927] 1 Ch 570, before Astbury J. If and when that particular question comes to be considered again, it will require perhaps some full examination, but what I am saying now is not affected by the decision in that case, because it seems to me that the court of equity, when asked to enforce the trust for sale, whether one created by a settlement or a will or one created by the statute, must look into all the circumstances of the case and consider whether or not, at the particular moment and in the particular circumstances when the application is made to it, it is right and proper that such an order shall be made. In considering a question of that kind, in circumstances such as these, the Court is bound to look at the contract into which the parties have entered and to ask itself the question whether or not the person applying for execution of the trust for sale is a person whose voice should be allowed to prevail. In the present case, Farwell J approached the matter from that angle and gave a perfectly definite and unhesitating answer to it, with which I entirely agree. He said in effect 'Here is a person who has contracted with others for a particular purpose, and the effect of the contract is to impose upon the power of the trustees to sell this land, certain restrictions.' Without going into the question which I mentioned a moment ago as to overriding or not overriding those things, he said: 'It is not right that the court of equity should in those circumstances, on the invitation of a person who has not acted in accordance with the contract, and is opposed by other persons interested, exercise the power of the Court and make an order for sale.' That, of course, does not mean that in other circumstances, at some future time, the Court will not lend its aid. Circumstances may change. If all the parties died and all their houses were sold, I apprehend, for example, that the Court, if asked to enforce a statutory trust for sale, would not be disposed to listen to arguments against such a sale adduced by people who had no real interest in keeping this land unsold. Questions of that kind can be decided if and when they arise. . . .

RE EVER'S TRUST [1980] 3 All ER 399, Court of Appeal

FACTS: A cohabiting couple bought a house as joint tenants, in order to house themselves and the three children for who they had responsibility. The relationship broke down, and the man left. The other four members of the family continued to live in the house. The man applied to court under s. 30 of the Law of Property Act 1925 for an order of sale.
HELD: The application for sale was refused. The greater part of the purpose of acquiring the house (housing the family of five) could still be fulfilled.

ORMROD LJ: . . . Under s. 30 the primary question is whether the court should come to the aid of the applicant at the particular moment, and in the particular circumstances when the application is made to it *Re Buchanan-Wollaston's Conveyance* [1939] 2 All ER 302 at 308, [1939] Ch 738 at 747). In the present case, at the present moment and in the existing circumstances, it would be wrong to order a sale. But circumstances may change unpredictably. It may not be appropriate to order a sale when the child reaches 16 years, a purely arbitrary date, or it may become appropriate to do so much sooner, for example on the mother's remarriage or on it becoming financially possible for her to buy the father out. In such circumstances it will probably be wiser simply to dismiss the application while indicating the sort of circumstances which would, *prima facie*, justify a further application. The ensuing uncertainty is unfortunate, but, under this section, the court has no power to adjust property rights or to redraft the terms of the trust. Ideally, the parties should now negotiate a settlement on the basis that neither of them is in a position to dictate terms. We would, therefore, dismiss the father's appeal, but would vary the order to dismiss the application on the mother's undertaking to discharge the liability under the mortgage, to pay the outgoings and maintain the property, and to indemnify the father so long as she is occupying the property.

16.2.2.2 Refuse a sale but charge a co-owner in possession rent

DENNIS v McDONALD [1981] 1 WLR 810, Family Division, Purchas J; [1982] 1 All ER 590, Court of Appeal, Arnold P

FACTS: A co-habiting couple bought a house as tenants in common in equal shares. They eventually had five children. The relationship broke up because of the man's violence. The woman left home, but only had care of the two youngest children. The three older children continued to live with their father in the house. He continued to make the mortgage repayments. The woman made an application under s. 30 of the Law of Property Act 1925 for an order for sale of the property.
HELD: The order for sale was refused. One of the primary purposes of the trust as originally envisaged was to provide a home for the family, and this purpose was still subsisting. However, the man would have to pay an 'occupation rent' to the woman throughout the duration of his residence in the property. This rent was fixed at half a 'fair rent' for the premises.

PURCHAS J: . . . The main argument has revolved around the right or otherwise of the plaintiff to receive an occupation rent as a co-tenant who is excluded from the property. Mr Coningsby has referred me to a judgment of Lord Denning MR in *Jones (AE)* v *Jones (FW)* [1977] 1 WLR 438, 441:

> First the claim for rent. It is quite plain that these two people were in equity tenants in common having a three-quarter and one-quarter share respectively. One was in occupation of the house. The other not. Now the common law said clearly that one tenant in common is not entitled to rent from another tenant in common, even though that other occupies the whole . . . As between tenants in common, they are both equally entitled to occupation and one cannot claim rent from the other. Of course, if there was an ouster, that would be another matter: or if there was a letting to a stranger for rent that would be different, but there can be no claim for rent by one tenant in common against the other whether at law or in equity.

In *Jones (AE)* v *Jones (FW)* the plaintiff failed not only on the ground that no occupation rent could be claimed by one tenant in common from another but also upon, the ground of equitable estoppel. . . .

In the instant case the plaintiff is clearly not a free agent. She was caused to leave the family home as a result of the violence or threatened violence of the defendant. In any event, whatever might have been the cause of the breakdown of the association, it would be quite unreasonable to expect the plaintiff to exercise her rights as a tenant in common to occupy the property as she had done before the breakdown of her association with the defendant. In my judgment she falls into exactly the kind of category of person excluded from the property in the way envisaged by Lord Cottenham LC in *M'Mahon* v *Burchell* 2 Ph 127. Therefore, the basic principle that a tenant in common is not liable to pay an occupation rent by virtue merely of his being in sole occupation of the property does not apply in the case where an association similar to a matrimonial association has broken down and one party is, for practical purposes, excluded from the family home. . . .

ARNOLD P: . . . [it is said] there is that one should look, not at the detriment to the plaintiff, but at the advantage to the defendant and that he should be regarded as illicitly enjoying, and therefore accountable for, one-half of what he would have to pay for the property if he entered the property market as a willing tenant and found a willing landlord ready to let it to him.

I am bound to say in the circumstances of this case that that is somewhat unrealistic. He occupies this property not because he has been able to negotiate in the market and obtain it but because he is a tenant in common. He occupies it in respect of, and by right of, his beneficial interest. He is not, therefore, subject to the vagaries of the market and starts off with a right of occupation. Something would have to be allowed in some way for that. Moreover, it is difficult to see what justification there is for charging a person in his position with such extra payment as a tenant would have to make by reason of the scarcity of relevant accommodation in the market. If one is setting out to achieve a fair solution in a situation in which plainly the defendant has to pay something, I can think of no better way of regulating that than by doing one's best to assess a fair rent for the property, with all its advantages and defects . . .

(Compare s. 13 of the Trusts of Land and Appointment of Trustees Act 1996 at **16.2** above.)

16.2.2.3   Order a sale

JONES v *CHALLENGER* [1961] 1 QB 176, Court of Appeal

FACTS: Husband and wife bought their matrimonial home as joint tenants. The marriage broke down and the wife went to live with another man. The husband was left alone in the house. The wife applied for an order of sale under the Law of Property Act 1925 s. 30.
HELD: With the end of the marriage the underlying purpose of the trust had come to an end. Consequently, the Court of Appeal ordered a sale.

DEVLIN LJ: . . . In the case we have to consider, the house was acquired as the matrimonial home. That was the purpose of the joint tenancy and, for so long as that purpose was still alive, I think that the right test to be applied would be that in *In re Buchanan-Wollaston's Conveyance* [1939] 1 Ch 738. But with the end of the marriage, that purpose was dissolved and the primacy of the duty to sell was restored. No doubt there is still a discretion. If the husband wanted time to obtain alternative accommodation, the sale could be postponed for that purpose, but he has not asked for that. If he was prepared to buy out the wife's interest, it might be proper to allow it, but he has not accepted a suggestion that terms of that sort should be made. In these circumstances, there is no way in which the discretion can properly be exercised except by an order to sell, because, since they cannot now both enjoy occupation of the property, that is the only way whereby the beneficiaries can derive equal benefit from their investment, which is the primary object of the trust. . . .

16.2.2.4 Order a sale but suspend the order for a short period

The possibility of making an order in this form was expressly recognised by the Court of Appeal in *Jones* v *Challenger*.

16.3 The Modern Position of Husband and Wife Co-owners on a Marriage Break-up

WILLIAMS v *WILLIAMS* [1977] 1 All ER 28, Court of Appeal

FACTS: A married couple purchased a house in joint names, the husband providing the majority of the purchase price. The marriage was later dissolved and the wife remained in the house with the four sons of the family. She paid the mortgage instalments thereafter. The youngest son having reached the age of 12, the husband applied under the Law of Property Act 1925, s. 30 for an order of sale. The judge at first instance granted the order of sale as requested. The wife appealed.
HELD: The appeal was allowed.

LORD DENNING MR: . . . It seems to me that in this case the judge was in error in applying the old approach. He did not give proper effect to the modern view, which is to have regard to the needs of the family as a whole before a sale is ordered. We have here the wife and the four sons still in the house. The youngest son is only 13 years of age and still at school. It would not be proper at this stage to order the sale of the house, unless it were shown that alternative accommodation could be provided at a cheaper rate, and some capital released. That has not been shown here.

The truth is that the approach to these cases has been transformed since the Matrimonial Proceedings and Property Act 1970 and the Matrimonial Causes Act 1973 which have given the power to the court after a divorce to order the transfer of property. In exercising any discretion under s. 30 of the Law of Property Act 1925, those Acts must be taken into account. The discretion should be exercised on the principles stated by this court in *Jackson* v *Jackson* [1971] 1 WLR 1539, 1543.

I would add this: An application about a matrimonial home should not be restricted to s. 30 of the Law of Property Act 1925. In view of the wide powers of transfer and adjustment which are available under the new matrimonial property legislation it seems to me that the applications should be made to the Family Division under the relevant provisions. If taken out in another division, they should be transferred to a judge of the Family Division. In this very case it seems to me that the right course (which the wife's advisers ought to have taken before) is that they should now, and at once, take out the appropriate application under s. 24 of the Matrimonial Causes Act 1973 for any necessary orders and so on to be made with regard to the house and the property. That application should be brought on together with an application under s. 30.

I would therefore be in favour of allowing the appeal, setting aside the order for sale made by Foster J and remitting the matter for further consideration by a judge of the Family Division when an application has been taken out under the matrimonial property legislation. I would allow the appeal accordingly. . . .

MESHER v MESHER AND HALL [1980] 1 All ER 126, Court of Appeal

FACTS: This case properly belongs in a book on family law. The matrimonial home was in the joint names of husband and wife. On an application for a property adjustment order under ss. 23–25 of the Matrimonial Causes Act 1973 the judge at first instance ordered that the property should be transferred into the wife's sole name. The husband appealed.
HELD: The judge's order was set aside and a new order made, in the terms set out at the end of the following extract.

DAVIES LJ: . . . matters are very evenly balanced; and in these circumstances counsel for the husband submits that it would be quite wrong to deprive the husband of the substantial asset which his half-interest in the house represents. Indeed he referred us to the very recent decision of this court in *Wachtel* v *Wachtel* [1973] 1 All ER 829 and suggested that as a result of the observations of Lord Denning MR in that case there would be something to be said for cutting down the wife's share to one-third. But he did not ask for such an order. He was content that this valuable asset should be divided equally.

Counsel for the wife, however, strongly supported the order. She pointed out that, after 14 years of marriage, it was the husband who broke it up, as the judge rightly said, and that, despite what this court said in *Wachtel* v *Wachtel*, under the express words of s. 5(1) of the Matrimonial Proceedings and Property Act 1970, conduct is a matter to put into the scales. She points out that owing to the forthcoming marriage between the wife and Mr Jones, the husband will be absolved from the liability to maintain the wife and that the order of £4 per week in respect of the daughter is on the low side.

So far as that last point is concerned, it is obviously open to the wife to apply for an increase if the circumstances justify it. But as far as the main problem is concerned, one has to take a broad approach to the whole case. What is wanted here is to see that the wife and daughter, together no doubt in the near future with Mr Jones, should have a home in which to live rather than that she should have a large sum of available capital. With that end in view, I have come to the conclusion that counsel's submission for the husband is right. It would, in my judgment, be wrong to strip the husband entirely of any interest in the house. I would set aside the judge's order so far as concerns the house and substitute instead an order that the house is held by the parties in equal shares on trust for sale but that it is not to be sold until the child of the marriage reaches a specified age or with the leave of the court. . . .

THOMPSON v THOMPSON [1985] 3 WLR 17, Court of Appeal

FACTS: The order of a court of the family division in divorce proceedings, made in 1981, directed that the ex-husband and ex-wife, who remained the trustees for sale, should postpone sale of the home 'until the youngest child of the family . . . reaches the age of 17 years or finishes further education, whichever is later, or further order'. The ex-wife continued to live in the home with the two children, the youngest of whom was (in 1985) aged 11. The ex-wife wanted to move from the home; ironically the ex-husband would not agree. She sought and obtained an order for sale under section 24A of the Matrimonial Causes Act 1973.
HELD: The order was granted. *Mesher* v *Mesher* [1980] 1 All ER 126 followed.

ALLEN v ALLEN [1974] 3 All ER 389, Court of Appeal

This case is included here as it provides an example of a form of property adjustment order that can be made under the Matrimonial Causes Act 1973, s. 24.

BUCKLEY LJ: . . . Taking all the circumstances into consideration I have come to the conclusion that the solution favoured by the learned judge was in fact a solution which would be the most satisfactory for these boys in particular and for the family as a whole. I think the learned judge, therefore, arrived at the right conclusion. But I think it would be better that his order should be varied in its terms (the precise drafting can be considered later) to provide that the former matrimonial home should be transferred to the husband and the wife, to be held on trust for sale, with a direction that the sale should not take place until the younger child had attained the age of 17 years, or had finished his full-time education, whichever date should be the earlier, without either the consent of both the parents or under an order of the court, and that during that limited period the property should be held in trust for the wife to the exclusion of the husband for the purpose of her providing a home there for the children of the family, and, in particular, the two boys, and that at the expiration of that limited period it should then be held on trust for the two spouses in equal shares.

Now it would follow from that that the husband would no longer have any right to reside in the home during the limited period which I have referred to, and I think it right that the order should be so framed as to give him a reasonable time to get out. The learned judge ordered him to leave within two months from the date of his order, and I think it would be right if the order is altered on the lines I suggest that he should still be given a reasonable time, whatever might now be a reasonable time, to find other accommodation and to make his move.

In substance, therefore, I for my part would dismiss this appeal, but I would vary the learned judge's order in the way I have indicated.

HARVEY v HARVEY [1982] 2 WLR 283, Court of Appeal

FACTS: The parties' marriage had broken down and the judge at first instance had made a 'Mesher' order (see above) in terms that the husband should leave the matrimonial home and that the property should be transferred into the joint names of the parties, to be held by them on trust for sale in equal shares; sale to be postponed until the youngest child attained the age of 16 or completed her full-time education, whichever was later. At the time of sale the wife would, under the 'Mesher' order be at liberty to purchase the husband's share at a fair valuation to be made at the time. The husband had left the home and obtained council accommodation. The wife appealed.

HELD: A new order was substituted for that of the judge, in terms appearing in the following extract from the judgment of Purchas J.

PURCHAS J: . . . The judge made an order in relation to the matrimonial home which provided that the husband, who at that time was in occupation, should vacate it with the purpose of the wife returning with the children. The order also provided that the property should be held in the joint names of the two parties to the marriage, on trust for sale in equal shares, that sale to be postponed until the youngest child of the family should attain the age of 16 years or complete her full time education, whichever was the later date and then further provided that the wife should be at liberty to purchase the husband's share at a valuation then to be made. Unless the circumstances of the family alter dramatically during the next few years, the latter part of that order would appear to be mainly academic in all the circumstances. . . .

I would vary the judge's order, first of all to say that the asset, the matrimonial home at 143 Wakeman Road, London, N.W.10, be transferred into the joint names of the wife and the husband on trust for sale in shares of two-thirds to the wife and one-third to the husband, and further that such sale shall be postponed during the lifetime of the wife her re-marriage, or voluntary removal from the premises, or her becoming dependent upon another man. I have in mind that if she begins to cohabit with another man in the premises, then obviously that man ought to take over the responsibility of providing accommodation for her. Until one or other of those events occur, she should be entitled to continue to reside at these premises, but after the mortgage has been paid off, or the youngest child has reached the age of 18, whichever is the latter, she should pay an occupation rent to be assessed by the registrar. To that extent I would allow this appeal and vary the order made by the judge.

16.4   The Rights of Co-owners in Equity — are they Interests in Land?

RE KEMPTHORNE [1930] 1 Ch 268, Chancery Division

FACTS: The testator owned a half-share in land as tenant in common. He died in 1927. His will was in terms which might be baldly summarised thus: 'I leave my real estate to X and my personal estate to Y'. The main question for resolution was whether the his 'undivided share' under the tenancy in common went to X or Y.

HELD: The testator's share as a tenant in common went to Y.

LAWRENCE LJ: . . . Maugham J in deciding this case, followed the decision of Clauson J, in *In re Price* [1928] Ch 579. In that case Clauson J, after carefully and exhaustively reviewing the provisions of the new Acts, came to the conclusion that the statutory imposition of a trust for sale operated to convert an undivided share of real estate into a corresponding share of the proceeds of sale of the entirety, and accordingly that as from the passing of the Act of 1925 the interest of the owner of the undivided share became personal estate and passed as such. I agree with Clauson J that this is the true effect of the recent legislation in the case of an unsettled undivided share of real estate. It follows, therefore, that on January 1, 1926, before the will in the present case became operative, the testator's undivided shares in question ceased to be 'freehold property,' and on his death they passed under the bequest of his personal estate.

Mr Grant contended that the decision in *In re Price* was wrong, and that the undivided shares in question remained 'freehold property,' In support of this contention he relied on the provisions of s. 28(1) of the Act of 1925. That section, however, so far from supporting his contention tends in the opposite direction. It recognizes the distinction between settled land and land held upon trust for sale, and, in the concluding words of the first paragraph, negatives the idea that the proceeds of sale under a trust for sale should devolve in the same manner as capital money arising from a sale of settled land. It enacts in terms that all capital money arising under the powers which the trustees might exercise under s. 28 should (unless paid or applied for any of the purposes authorized by the Settled Land Act, 1925) 'be applicable in the same manner as if the money represented proceeds of sale arising under the trust for sale'; and the sub-section goes on to provide that all land acquired under this sub-section (that is to say, by the exercise of any of the powers thereby conferred) should be conveyed to the trustees on trust for sale; thus drawing a sharp distinction between capital money arising from a sale of land under a trust for sale and capital money arising from a sale of settled land (whether consisting of an undivided share or of the entirety) under the provisions of the Settled Land Act, 1925. In the latter case, s. 75(5) of the Settled Land Act, 1925, provides that the proceeds of sale shall devolve in the same manner as the land from which such proceeds arise would have devolved, whereas in the case of a sale under the statutory trust for sale there is no provision to be found in either of the Acts which operates to re-convert the proceeds into land. . . .

16.4.1   THE MODERN POSITION — THE RIGHTS OF CO-OWNERS ARE INTERESTS IN LAND

BULL v *BULL* [1955] 1 QB 234, Queen's Bench Division

FACTS: Bull, 'the son', bought a house. His mother paid a substantial part of the purchase price. The mother thus acquired an equitable interest in the house. It followed that the son held the house on trust for sale for himself and his mother as tenants in common. The son later got married, and the mother fell out with her new daughter-in-law. The son sided with his wife, and told his mother to leave. When she refused he sued to evict her, contending that she was a trespasser. He argued that she had no interest in the land itself, but only an interest 'in money'.

HELD: Notwithstanding the imposition of a trust for sale by the 1925 legislation, the mother had a right to live in the home.

DENNING LJ: . . . My conclusion is . . . that the son, although he is the legal owner of the house, has no right to turn his mother out. She has an equitable interest which entitles her to remain in the house as tenant in common with him until the house is sold. If they fall out the house should be sold and the proceeds divided between them in the proper proportions; but he cannot at his will turn her out into the street. The house cannot be sold with vacant possession unless she consents to it. If she unreasonably refuses her consent, the son, by taking proper steps, can obtain an order for sale from the court and in aid of it the court can order the mother to go; but the court would only make such an order if it was satisfied that it was right and proper to do so and on such terms as to alternative accommodation as it thought right to impose. . . .

(Note: The Trusts of Land etc. Act 1996 vindicates the approach of Denning LJ in *Bull* v *Bull* [1955] 1 QB 234.)

16.5 Law of Property (Joint Tenants) Act 1964

LAW OF PROPERTY (JOINT TENANTS) ACT 1964
(as amended by the Law of Property (Miscellaneous Provisions) Act 1994)

1. Assumptions on sale of land by survivor of joint tenants

(1) For the purposes of section 36(2) of the Law of Property Act 1925, as amended by section 7 of and the Schedule to the Law of Property (Amendment) Act 1926, the survivor of two or more joint tenants shall in favour of a purchaser of the legal estate, be deemed to be solely and beneficially interested if [. . .] the conveyance includes a statement that he is so interested.

Provided that the foregoing provisions of this subsection shall not apply if, at any time before the date of the conveyance by the survivor—

(a) a memorandum of severance (that is to say a note or memorandum signed by the joint tenants or one of them and recording that the joint tenancy was severed in equity on a date therein specified) had been endorsed on or annexed to the conveyance by virtue of which the legal estate was vested in the joint tenants; or

(b) [a bankruptcy order] made against any of the joint tenants, or a petition for such an order, had been registered under the Land Charges Act 1925, being an order or petition of which the purchaser has notice, by virtue of the registration, on the date of the conveyance by the survivor.

(2) The foregoing provisions of this section shall apply with the necessary modifications in relation to a conveyance by the personal representatives of the survivor of joint tenants as they apply in relation to a conveyance by such a survivor.

. . .

3. Exclusion of registered land

This Act shall not apply to any land the title of which has been registered under the provisions of the Land Registration Acts 1925 and 1936.

16.6 Co-ownership of Registered Land

RE GORMAN (A BANKRUPT) [1990] 1 WLR 616, Chancery Division

FACTS: The land registry transfer to husband and wife co-proprietors did not specify whether they held as joint tenants in equity, or as tenants in common. However, the transfer did declare that the survivor of them could give a valid receipt for capital monies. Further, the registration did not include any restriction on transfer by the survivor of them. The couple divorced and the husband was later declared bankrupt. The present action was brought by the husband's trustee in bankruptcy for an order for the sale of the property. The judge held that the property belonged solely to the wife, on the basis, *inter alia*, that she had paid off all the mortgage instalments. The trustee appealed.

HELD: The appeal was allowed. The declaration that the survivor of the husband and wife could give a valid receipt of capital monies was consistent only with the existence of a joint tenancy in equity. Accordingly the land was now held by them as tenants in common in equal shares, the husband's bankruptcy having severed the joint tenancy, and so the trustee in bankruptcy would be entitled to recover the husband's share by sale.

VINELOTT J: . . . The position is shortly this. Section 58(3) of the Land Registration Act 1925 provides, so far as material, that in the case of joint proprietors, where the number of proprietors is reduced to below a certain level:

no disposition shall be registered except under an order of the court, or of the registrar after inquiry into title [the subsection then continues]— and, subject to general rules, such as entry under this subsection as may be prescribed shall be obligatory unless it is shown for their own benefit, or can give valid receipts for capital money, or that one of them is a trust corporation.

I observe in passing that the language of that subsection is in fact reflected in the declaration in this case. Rules have been made and, under s. 144(2) of the Act of 1925, the rules are to 'be of the same force as if enacted in this Act.' Rule 213(1) and (2) of the Land Registration Rules 1925 provides:

(1) An entry under section 58(3) shall be in form 62, and need only be made where, by law, the survivor of the joint proprietors will not have power to give a valid receipt for capital on a disposition of the land or charge, or where the registrar, for any special reason, considers that such an entry would be desirable. (2) Such an entry may at any time be made with the consent of joint proprietors entitled in their own right.

Form 62 reads:

When the number of joint proprietors has been reduced to one, unless such proprietor is a trust corporation, no registered disposition of the land . . . shall be made except under an order of the registrar, after an inquiry into title, or an order of the court.

The effect of subrules (1) and (2), together with s. 58(3), is that in the case of joint proprietors an entry in the terms of form 62 must be included, unless the registrar is satisfied that the survivor of joint proprietors will have power to give a valid receipt for the purchase price. The law is so stated in *Ruoff and Roper, Registered Conveyancing*, 5th edn. (1986), p. 398, where it is said:

Where two or more persons (not being charitable or Settled Land Act trustees) are jointly registered as proprietors, the Chief Land Registrar is under an obligation to enter a restriction to prevent a sole survivor of them from executing a disposition which involves capital money. The situation is precisely that with which the practitioner is familiar in unregistered conveyancing.

It is plain in the circumstances of this case, that the registrar must have been satisfied that the declaration represented an agreement between Mr and Mrs Gorman, and that he could only have been so satisfied if either the original transfer had been signed by both, or if he had been informed by the solicitors who acted for Mr and Mrs Gorman that it reflected an agreement between them. Both were represented by the same firm of solicitors. They were in fact Mrs Gorman's family solicitors.

Mr Hunter then submitted that the claim that the declaration on the transfer, even if unsigned, was evidence of an agreement, is a new point not raised before the judge and which this court, sitting as an appellate court, ought not to entertain. He submitted that Mrs Gorman might have been able to rebut this claim, if properly raised at the proper time. Then, he submitted, he might have been able to adduce evidence that the declaration was added without her knowledge or consent and was added by her solicitors as what he called 'a conveyancing device,' that is to facilitate a sale by the survivor without the need to appoint an additional trustee.

I do not think there is any substance in that argument. First, it cannot be said that it was a conveyancing device. If not in truth joint tenants, the effect of putting the transfer before the registrar as recording an agreement between them, was that the parties were deprived of the protection of an entry which would prevent a survivor from dealing with the property for his or her own benefit. In taking that course, the solicitors would have been guilty of grave dereliction of their duty to their clients.

As to the claim that the point is a new point, the position is this. Mr Parker, in opening his case, relied on the declaration as concluding the question as to the beneficial title of the property. During or shortly after the short adjournment it was drawn to his attention, either by Mr Hunter or the judge (I am not certain which) that the transfer had not been signed by the transferees; he nonetheless relied on the transfer as evidence of an agreement between the parties. No claim was made that the declaration had been added to the transfer without Mrs Gorman's knowledge and consent, and Mr Hunter did not apply for an adjournment to adduce evidence to this effect. The reason is not far to seek. Mrs Gorman was well aware that the trustee relied on the declaration in the transfer. At no time did she suggest, either before the application was made by the trustee, or in her evidence in opposition to it, that the declaration had been made without her authority. In her first affidavit in opposition she said:

> My late father did not trust my husband and at the time of giving me £2,000 he expressed the wish that the property be held by me alone. My former husband would not agree and persuaded me to arrange for the property to be transferred into our joint names. I was not aware at that time that it was possible to hold a property in joint names and for the beneficial interest to be expressed unequally.

That, as I see it, is a clear statement that she understood at the time of the transfer that the property would be conveyed into the joint names of herself and her husband and would not be held in trust for themselves as tenants in common in unequal shares.

16.7   End of Chapter Assessment Question

In 1988 four friends, Steven, Julia, Mark and Tracey, purchased a cottage called 'The Retreat' for the purpose of a holiday home. The conveyance to them contained no express declaration of a trust for sale. Title to The Retreat was unregistered. The purchase money was provided equally and at the time of the purchase Tracey was only 17 years of age.

In January 1997 Julia became short of cash and therefore obtained a bank loan which was secured on her interest in The Retreat.

Some months later, Steven also found himself in financial difficulties. However his solution to the problem was to create frequent arguments with the others in which he would demand that they 'buy him out'. These outbursts were ignored by the others and Steven eventually stopped using The Retreat.

In October 1997 Steven and Julia were killed in a car accident. By their wills Steven left all his property to his mother Violet, and Julia left all her property to her sister, Karen. Mark is keen to sell The Retreat and has just found a purchaser who wants an early completion. Tracey vehemently opposes the proposed sale as since the deaths of Steven and Julia she has been living at The Retreat permanently. Violet is in agreement with Mark, but Karen is uncertain.

Advise Mark as to:

(a)   exactly who owns The Retreat and in what proportions;

(b)   his prospects of forcing a sale.

16.8   End of Chapter Assessment Outline Answer

The Legal Ownership of the Retreat
As the friends were co-owners, a trust for sale was imposed on them in 1988. However, only Steven, Julia and Mark became trustees, as Tracey was under 18 and only adults can be appointed trustees. Tracey would NOT become a trustee on her attaining the age of 18.
   The only event after 1988 to affect the trusteeship of the legal title is the death of Steven and Julia. This event (as a result of the survivorship rule) leaves Mark as the only trustee, though not (as we shall see) the sole beneficiary.

Can Mark Sell Without a Court Order?
In theory, yes, in practical reality, no. Mark appears to be a sole surviving joint tenant, so he might try and take advantage of the Law of Property (Joint Tenants) Act 1964. Alternatively, to give added reassurance to the purchaser, he could appoint a friend as co-trustee, and the two of them convey The Retreat to the purchaser. Either way a sale would overreach the equitable interests of Tracey and any other beneficiary.
   The practical reality is, however, that no purchaser, even a very keen one, is going to buy with Tracey in permanent occupation. Undoubtedly Tracey has the right to occupy the property until it is sold (see *Bull* and *Boland*). On the sale taking place her rights will be overreached (*Flegg*) and she will become a trespasser vis-à-vis the purchaser. But the purchaser will 'acquire' the problem of taking proceedings to evict Tracey. No sane purchaser (particularly one keen to move in quickly) is going to buy in these circumstances.
   Thus Mark will be forced to take proceedings under s. 14, Trusts of Land and Appointment of Trustees Act 1996. (See below.)

The Equitable Owneship of The Retreat
The initial position
There appears to be nothing to rebut the initial presumption of joint tenancy. Note in particular that the four contributed equally to the cost. However, there might be a tenancy

in common (in equal shares) if the court found there was a business element to the arrangements, e.g. if they envisaged holiday lettings of The Retreat when none of them wanted to use it themselves.

Current Position if Parties Initially Tenants in Common
An equitable interest as tenants in common can be left by will. Therefore after the car crash Violet and Karen would become tenants in common in equity alongside Mark and Tracey.

Current Position if Parties Initially Equitable Joint Tenants

The Effect of Julia's Mortgage
This clearly severs her equitable interest, converting it into a one quarter share as tenant in common. On her death this equitable interest will pass by her will (subject to the mortgage) to Karen.

The Effect of Steven's Frequent Arguments
It is possible to sever by informal argreement, or by conduct which indicates that the parties are treating the joint tenancy as at an end (*Burgess* v *Rawnsley*). As the outbursts were ignored by the other three it seems that there has been no informal severance by conduct/agreement.

However, Lord Denning was of the view in *Burgess* that an oral unilateral statement would effect a severance. This rather impractical view is unsupported by authority, but if it were correct then presumably the outbursts would affect a severance. As a result Violet would inherit a quarter share.

If (as is probably the case) Steven has not severed, then Violet does not inherit any interest in The Retreat. The 'survivorship' rule operates between joint tenants; the law of succession has no application to a joint tenancy interest. The current equitable ownership would be Julia one quarter with the other three-quarters belonging to Mark and Tracey as joint tenants.

Mark's prospects of getting an order of sale
Violet's support is probably irrelevant, as she only has an interest if either the parties were initially tenants in common or if Steven has severed. If Violet has no interest and Karen comes out against a sale then a majority by value would be against sale.

But it is submitted that Mark has the trump card. The purpose for which the property was acquired has clearly failed, and that normally means that the court in its discretion will order a sale under s. 14, Trusts of Land etc. Act 1996. (See *Jones* v *Challenger,* contrast *Re Buchanan-Wollaston* and see, now, s. 15, Trusts of Land etc. Act 1996.)

A refusal of sale would be very unfair on Mark, as he would be left with his money locked up in an asset he no longer has any use for. In *Dennis* v *McDonald* the Court of Appeal adopted a compromise whereby a sale was refused but the co-owner in occupation had to pay a rent. However, that was a case of a broken-down cohabitation, very different from this one!

A much more sensible compromise, *and one which can be reached without the expense of litigation,* is for Tracey to buy out the interests of the other parties involved. Mark should propose this in '*Calderbank*' letters sent to Tracey and Karen. (A '*Calderbank*' letter is a letter sent 'without prejudice' to legal action that might be taken by the person sending the letter.)

CHAPTER SEVENTEEN

LEASES — THE BASIC REQUIREMENTS

17.1 Duration of Leases

17.1.1 FIXED-TERM LEASES

LACE v *CHANTLER* [1944] 1 KB 368, Court of Appeal

FACTS: The question in the Court of Appeal, was whether a lease 'for the duration of the war' was valid as a legal lease.

HELD: It was not possible to construe the lease as a long lease determinable on the cessation of the war. It was therefore a lease of indeterminate maximum duration and thus was not capable of being a legal lease.

LORD GREENE MR: Normally there could be no question that this was an ordinary weekly tenancy, duly determinable by a week's notice, but the parties in the rent-book agreed to a term which appears there expressed by the words 'furnished for duration,' which must mean the duration of the war. The question immediately arises whether a tenancy for the duration of the war creates a good leasehold interest. In my opinion, it does not. A term created by a leasehold tenancy agreement must be expressed either with certainty and specifically or by reference to something which can, at the time when the lease takes effect, be looked to as a certain ascertainment of what the term is meant to be. In the present case, when this tenancy agreement took effect, the term was completely uncertain. It was impossible to say how long the tenancy would last. Mr Sturge in his argument has maintained that such a lease would be valid, and that, even if the term is uncertain at its beginning when the lease takes effect, the fact that at some future time it will be rendered certain is sufficient to make it a good lease. In my opinion, that argument is not to be sustained. . . .

The question then arises whether it can take effect in any other way. It was suggested that the difficulty would be got over by construing the tenancy as a lease for a long period, e.g., ninety-nine years, determinable on the cessation of the war. In my opinion, it is impossible to construe this tenancy in that way. It is true that, in *Great Northern Railway Co.* v *Arnold* (1916) 33 TLR 114, Rowlatt J found it possible to treat a tenancy for the duration of the last war, the rent being payable weekly, as though a lease for nine hundred and ninety-nine years terminable on the cessation of the war had been created. He had some assistance in arriving at that conclusion in the fact that there was a definite undertaking by the landlords not to serve a notice to quit during the period. The actual words, as stated in the head-note, were: 'The landlords said that they did not intend that he should be subject to a week's notice.' That case can, in my opinion, only be supported because of the presence of that term of the agreement.

Is there any other possible construction? It is not contended that this tenancy agreement can be construed as though it were a grant of a freehold interest. The only way in which one could convert this into a freehold interest would be by construing it as an agreement for a life tenancy terminable at the end of the war. It is impossible to construe this agreement as anything of the kind.

Lastly, Mr Sturge argued that the agreement could be construed as an agreement to grant a licence. In my opinion, it is impossible to construe it in that sense. The intention was to create a tenancy and nothing else. The law says that it is bad as a tenancy. The court is not then justified in treating the contract as something different from what the parties intended, and regarding it merely as a contract for the granting of a licence. That would be setting up a new bargain which neither of the parties ever intended to enter into. The relationship between the parties must be ascertained on the footing that the tenant was in occupation and was paying a weekly rent. Accordingly, it must be the relationship of weekly tenant and landlord and nothing else.

PRUDENTIAL ASSURANCE CO. LTD v LONDON RESIDUARY BODY AND OTHERS
[1992] 2 AC 386, House of Lords

FACTS: This case involved a 'lease' granted by a council, and intended to 'continue until . . . the land is required by the council for the purposes of the widening of' a highway. The issue was whether the tenancy might be determined earlier.
HELD: As all leases need by definition to be of a certain duration, it followed that the lease granted by the council was void. However, the tenant's possession, and payment of a yearly rent, meant that the tenant had established an informal legal yearly tenancy. Such a tenancy could be determined on the giving of six months' notice.

LORD TEMPLEMAN: Now it is said that when in the present case the tenant entered pursuant to the agreement and paid a yearly rent he became a tenant from year to year on the terms of the agreement including clause 6 which prevents the landlord from giving notice to quit until the land is required for road widening. This submission would make a nonsense of the rule that a grant for an uncertain term does not create a lease and would make nonsense of the concept of a tenancy from year to year because it is of the essence of a tenancy from year to year that both the landlord and the tenant shall be entitled to give notice determining the tenancy. . . .

My Lords, I consider that the principle in *Lace* v *Chantler* [1944] KB 368 reaffirming 500 years of judicial acceptance of the requirement that a term must be certain applies to all leases and tenancy agreements. A tenancy from year to year is saved from being uncertain because each party has power by notice to determine at the end of any year. The term continues until determined as if both parties made a new agreement at the end of each year for a new term for the ensuing year. A power for nobody to determine or for one party only to be able to determine is inconsistent with the concept of a term from year to year: see *Doe d Warner* v *Browne*, 8 East 165 and *Cheshire Lines Committee* v *Lewis & Co.*, 50 LJQB 121. In *In re Midland Railway Co's Agreement* [1971] Ch 725 there was no 'clearly expressed bargain' that the term should continue until the crack of doom if the demised land was not required for the landlord's undertaking or if the undertaking ceased to exist. In the present case there was no 'clearly expressed bargain' that the tenant shall be entitled to enjoy his 'temporary structures' in perpetuity if Walworth Road is never widened. In any event principle and precedent dictate that it is beyond the power of the landlord and the tenant to create a term which is uncertain.

A lease can be made for five years subject to the tenant's right to determine if the war ends before the expiry of five years. A lease can be made from year to year subject to a fetter on the right of the landlord to determine the lease before the expiry of five years unless the war ends. Both leases are valid because they create a determinable certain term of five years. A lease might purport to be made for the duration of the war subject to the tenant's right to determine before the end of the war. A lease might be made from year to year subject to a fetter on the right of the landlord to determine the lease before the war ends. Both leases would be invalid because each purported to create an uncertain term. A term must either be certain or uncertain. It cannot be partly certain because the tenant can determine it at any time and partly uncertain because the landlord cannot determine it for an uncertain period. If the landlord does not grant and the tenant does not take a certain term the grant does not create a lease.

The decision of the Court of Appeal in *In re Midland Railway Co.'s Agreement* [1971] Ch 725 was taken a little further in *Ashburn Anstalt* v *Arnold* [1989] Ch 1. That case, if it was correct, would make it unnecessary for a lease to be of a certain duration. In an agreement for the sale of land the vendor reserved the right to remain at the property after completion as licensee and to trade therefrom without payment of rent.

> save that it can be required by Matlodge [the purchaser] to give possession on not less than one quarter's notice in writing upon Matlodge certifying that it is ready at the expiration of such notice forthwith to proceed with the development of the property and the neighbouring property involving, *inter alia*, the demolition of the property.

The Court of Appeal held that this reservation created a tenancy. The tenancy was not from year to year but for a term which would continue until Matlodge certified that it was ready to proceed with the development of the property. The Court of Appeal held that the term was not uncertain because the vendor could either give a quarter's notice or vacate the property without giving notice. But of course the same could be said of the situation in *Lace v Chantler* [1944] KB 368. The cumulative result of the two Court of Appeal authorities *In re Midland Railway Co.'s Agreement* [1971] Ch 725 and *Ashburn's* case [1989] Ch 1 would therefore destroy the need for any term to be certain.

In the present case the Court of Appeal were bound by the decisions in *In re Midland Railway Co.'s Agreement* and *Ashburn's* case. In my opinion both these cases were wrongly decided. A grant for an uncertain term does not create a lease. A grant for an uncertain term which takes the form of a yearly tenancy which cannot be determined by the landlord does not create a lease. I would allow the appeal. The trial judge, Millett J, reached the conclusion that the six months' notice served by the London Residuary Body was a good notice. He was of course bound by the Court of Appeal decisions but managed to construe the memorandum of agreement so as to render clause 6 ineffective in fettering the right of the landlord to serve a notice to quit after the landlord had ceased to be a road widening authority. In the circumstances this question of construction need not be considered. For the reasons which I have given the order made by Millett J must be restored. The plaintiffs must pay the costs of the second to fourth defendants before the House and in the courts below.

17.1.2   PERIODIC TENANCIES

LADIES' HOSIERY AND UNDERWEAR, LTD v *PARKER*
[1930] 1 Ch 304, Court of Appeal

FACTS: A fixed-term lease had come to an end and the tenant had remained in occupation. In other words, the tenant had 'held over' informally. In due course the landlord sold his reversion to the plaintiff company, but the plaintiff company received no rent from the tenant. The plaintiff brought the present action for an order of possession, asserting that the defendant was, at most, merely a weekly tenant.

HELD: Although it might, on other facts, be possible to infer that the defendant had continued in possession as a yearly tenant, such an inference was not possible here. The defendant was a weekly tenant. The 'period' of the tenancy should be determined by reference to the period according to which the rent had been calculated, not by reference to the time of rental payments. Thus a rent of £1,000 per annum, paid weekly, would give rise to a yearly tenancy. In the present case rent was set at £2.00 per week. Accordingly, this was a weekly periodic tenancy.

MAUGHAM J: . . . In the present case, the lease or agreement is one for three years at a rent of £2 a week. It is not a lease for three years at a rent of £104 per annum payable weekly: and it is observable that £2 a week is a rent which, as we all know, is not exactly divisible into the number of days either of an ordinary year or of a leap year. I cannot find, and counsel have been unable to find, any case exactly in point; but I have come to the conclusion that there is no reason for extending the views, which are binding on me, as to the terms which justify the inference that a tenancy is from year to year, and that in this case, narrow as the distinction is, the holding over of the premises after the expiration of the agreement of October 10 1914, would have resulted only, and did result only, in the tenant's being a tenant from week to week.

In coming to that conclusion I derive support from the judgment of Parke B in *Braythwayte* v *Hitchcock* (1842) 10 M & W 494. He says: 'Although the law is clearly settled, that where there has been an agreement for a lease and an occupation without payment of rent, the occupier is a mere tenant at will; yet it has been held that if he subsequently pays rent under that agreement, he thereby becomes tenant from year to year. Payment of rent, indeed, must be understood to mean a payment with reference to a yearly holding; for in *Richardson* v *Langridge* (1811) 4 Taunt 128, a party who had paid rent under an agreement of this description, but had not paid it with reference to a year, or any aliquot part of a year, was held nevertheless to be a tenant at will only'. My conclusion, therefore, is that when the defendant Henry Alfred Parker, after the expiration of that agreement, paid the sum of £2 a week to his landlord Jenkins, he was *prima facie* not paying it with reference to a year or an aliquot part of a year, but was paying it with reference to the week in respect of which he made the payment.

In the result the plaintiff company will have a judgment for possession of the premises at the back of No. 18, and the defendants must pay the costs of the action.

The Court of Appeal (Lord Hanworth MR, Lawrence and Romer LJJ) dismissed the appeal.

17.1.3 SPECIAL PROBLEMS CONNECTED WITH THE DURATION OF LEASES

17.1.3.1 Leases for lives

LAW OF PROPERTY ACT 1925

149. Abolition of interesse termini, and as to reversionary leases and leases for lives

. . .

(6)   Any lease or underlease, at a rent, or in consideration of a fine, for life or lives or for any term of years determinable with life or lives, or on the marriage of the lessee, or any contract therefor, made before or after the commencement of this Act, or created by virtue of Part V of the Law of Property Act 1922, shall take effect as a lease, underlease or contract therefor, for a term of ninety years determinable after the death or marriage (as the case may be) of the original lessee, or of the survivor of the original lessees, by at least one month's notice in writing given to determine the same on one of the quarter days applicable to the tenancy, either by the lessor or the persons deriving title under him, to the person entitled to the leasehold interest, or if no such person is in existence by affixing the same to the premises, or by the lessee or other persons in whom the leasehold interest is vested to the lessor or the persons deriving title under him:

Provided that—

(a)   this subsection shall not apply to any term taking effect in equity under a settlement or created out of an equitable interest under a settlement for mortgage, indemnity, or other like purposes;

(b)   the person in whom the leasehold interest is vested by virtue of Part V of the Law of Property Act 1922, shall, for the purposes of this subsection, be deemed an original lessee;

(c)   if the lease, underlease, or contract therefor is made determinable on the dropping of the lives of persons other than or besides the lessees, then the notice shall be capable of being served after the death of any person or of the survivor of any persons (whether or not including the lessees) on the cesser of whose life or lives the lease, underlease, or contract is made determinable, instead of after the death of the original lessee or of the survivor of the original lessees;

(d)   if there are no quarter days specially applicable to the tenancy, notice may be given to determine the tenancy on one of the usual quarter days.

17.1.3.2 Perpetually renewable leases

CAERPHILLY CONCRETE PRODUCTS LTD v *OWEN*
[1972] 1 WLR 372, Court of Appeal

FACTS: A lease granted a tenant the right to request, by writing, a renewal of the lease for a further five years 'at the same rent and containing the like covenants and provisos as are herein contained (including the option to renew such lease for a further term of five years at the expiration thereof)'. The question was whether this created a perpetually renewable lease convertible, under s. 145 and Schedule 15, para. 5 of the Law of Property Act 1922, into a lease for a term of 2,000 years.

HELD: The lease was perpetually renewable.

SACHS LJ: The question for determination in this appeal is whether the lease of May 6, 1963, is upon a proper construction of clause 4(3) a perpetually renewable lease. That clause, so far as relevant, reads:

> That the landlord will on the written request of the tenant made six months before the expiration of the term hereby created . . . at the expense of the tenant grant to him a lease of the said demised land for the further term of five years from the expiration of the said term hereby granted at the same rent and containing the like covenants and provisos as are herein contained (including an option to renew such lease for the further term of five years at the expiration thereof). . .

I, too, have underlined the words in brackets. It is trite to say that when construing a document such as a lease it is the prime purpose of the courts to seek to adopt a meaning that conforms to the intentions of the parties. Not even the most impeccable conveyancing logic, however neatly expressed, can convince me that in the instant case it was the mutual intention of the parties that the lease should be perpetually renewable. So far as the landlord is concerned it seems to me highly unlikely that he really intended that this particular lease could or should be 'for ever.' My doubts on this question of intention extend also to the tenant—for I would acquit him of any intent to lay a trap through the operation of the words enclosed in the brackets, which we know to have been added to the draft at the very last moment by his solicitors. It is difficult indeed, at any rate so far as I am concerned, to think that two business men would be talking in terms of five years if both—or indeed either— of them truly meant that a lease should be granted which went on *ad infinitum*.

Were I in a position to give effect to the views just expressed that would result in the landlord succeeding in this appeal: but it is necessary to consider whether the authorities which were so fully and so helpfully cited to us permit such a result. An examination of the relevant decisions discloses an area of law in which the courts have manoeuvred themselves into an unhappy position. On the one hand in judgment after judgment (for instance, *Baynham's* case (1796) 3 Ves 295, 298; *Moore* v *Foley* (1801) 6 Ves 232, 235–236 and *Swinburne* v *Milburn* (1884) 9 App Cas 844, 850) it has been proclaimed that the courts lean against holding that a lease is to that extent renewable. On the other hand, by strict adherence to precedent relating to the phrase 'including the present covenant' when following a covenant conferring a right to a renewal on the like covenants and provisos as are contained in the first lease, they appear to have bound themselves to hold that the use of a certain set of words (to which I will refer as 'the formula') causes the lease to be perpetually renewable, even when no layman—at least if he has some elementary knowledge of business—would dream of granting such a lease and, if aware of the technical meaning of the particular phraseology, would almost certainly be aghast at its devastating effect and refuse to sign. One reason for the courts so binding themselves is said to be that the formula is one the effect of which is well known to trained conveyancers, and that this is advantageous, however much of a trap it may constitute for others.

Wilkinson, H. W., Renewable Leases (1981) 131 NLJ 683

. . . Parties who do not want to make a perpetually renewable lease should say so. The *Encyclopaedia of Forms and Precedents* 4th edn, vol 11, form 2: 55, pp 340, 341 has a precedent which uses the vital words,

> subject in all other respects to the same stipulations as are herein contained except this clause for renewal.

If that type of phrase is not used, there can be danger. The judges in the *Caerphilly* case saw no remedy apart from statutory intervention. Indeed, Stamp LJ pointed out that statute so far has had the opposite effect from that intended,

One of the purposes of the Law of Property Act 1922 in converting a purported perpetually renewable lease into a long term of years, was, according to the learned editors of *Wolstenholme and Cherry's Conveyancing Statutes*, to discourage the creation of such leases; and to the extent that it has not done so this is a matter for the legislature.

Need such a reform await legislation? It is suggested that if an appropriate case got to the House of Lords their lordships could say that a perpetually renewable lease is only to be construed out of words which in clear terms provide for it.

17.1.3.3 Tenancy at will

MANFIELD v BOTCHIN [1970] 2 QB 612, Queen's Bench Division

FACTS: A written tenancy agreement prescribed that the tenancy should be a tenancy at will, and that an annual rent should be paid. The tenant claimed the protection of the Landlord and Tenant Act 1954, Part II, on the basis that the tenancy was a yearly tenancy according to the rental period.
HELD: The tenancy agreement had created a tenancy at will, not a yearly tenancy. The protection of the Act would not be available to the tenant.

COOKE J: Clause 1 of the agreement read as follows:

The company shall let and [the tenant] shall take the said premises on a tenancy at will commencing from December 5 1964, at a rental to be calculated at the rate of £1,560 per annum and paid on demand at such time or times as the company may think fit Provided always that if the company should demand the aforesaid rent at fixed periods such demand or acceptance of rent shall not be deemed to create any periodic tenancy. . . .

In my view, the fact that rent was reserved at an annual rate is not in the present case sufficient to override the expressed intention of the parties to create a tenancy at will. The agreement does not provide for the payment of rent at fixed times, but only on demand. It is questionable whether the terms of this provision would strictly empower the landlords to demand rent in advance. If, however, the provision does empower the landlords to demand rent in advance, it seems to me that any advance payment made on such a demand would of necessity be a provisional payment only; and if during the period for which an advance payment had been made either the landlords or the tenant were to exercise his right to determine the tenancy forthwith an appropriate adjustment would have to be made. . . .

Has, then, anything occurred since the date of the agreement which has altered the relationship of the parties? The tenant relies on the fact that the tenancy subsisted for nearly five years before the landlords purported to determine it. I cannot think that that is a circumstance which indicates that the parties have altered their relationship since the agreement was made. There is nothing in the actual duration of the tenancy which is inconsistent with the agreement which the parties made, for under the agreement the duration of the tenancy is wholly indeterminate.

Then the tenant relies on the fact that in the main rent was regularly demanded and paid on a monthly basis. I find nothing in this fact which indicates an alteration in the relationship between the parties. Regular demands for and payment of rent are not in themselves inconsistent with a tenancy at will, and indeed in this case they are actually contemplated by the agreement itself, just as they were contemplated in *Doe* d *Bastow* v *Cox* (1874) 11 QB 122. . . .

HESLOP v BURNS AND ANOTHER [1974] 3 All ER 406, Court of Appeal

FACTS: A fairly wealthy person allowed two friends to occupy a house he owned rent-free. After his death, the friends remained in possession. They claimed that they had a tenancy at will, which, by s. 9 of the Limitation Act 1939, was deemed to have determined a year after its commencement. Thereafter, they claimed they had occupied the freehold a 'squatters' (see the chapter on adverse possession) and now owned the freehold as of right.

HELD: Such a friendly arrangement (made without intent to create legal relations) regarding the occupation the house was to be treated as a licence, not as a tenancy at will. Accordingly, the 'friends' had no right to exclude the deceased (by his executors) from taking possession of the freehold.

STAMP LJ: . . . On the facts of this case it is, in my judgment, abundantly clear that the parties did not enter into any arrangement, far less any arrangement intended to create a legal relationship, as to the terms on which the defendants should occupy the property. There was no contract, no arrangement, no statement by the deceased. The defendants, as I see it, were allowed to move into the property and occupy it simply as a result of the bounty of the deceased and without any arrangements as to the terms on which they should do so. There was no evidence of any discussion whatsoever taking place as to the terms of the occupation. It was by the effect of the bounty of the deceased or, if you will, because of his feelings of affection for Mrs Burns, that the home was provided, and it was, I think, for those reasons that the defendants remained there.

The fact, which was relied on by counsel for the defendants, that the deceased had already said, in relation to each of the properties in Fowler Street and Love Walk, that he would leave it to the defendants, is no evidence that it was the intention of the deceased that the defendants should in the meantime be tenants at will rather than licensees. Counsel for the defendants submitted that, since the deceased intended to provide the defendants with a home, he must have intended to give them an interest in the property. But a tenancy at will was no more apt to achieve that purpose than a revocable personal licence to occupy the property; and if one asks the question what interest he intended them to have, it could only, consistently with counsel's submission, be an interest during the rest of the life of the deceased of such a nature as would exclude him from any right to turn them out. No such interest was created and I find it impossible to infer an intention on the part of the deceased to create such a situation. In my judgment the proper inference is that the defendants at the outset entered into occupation of the premises as licensees and not as tenants at will; not with a right to exclude the deceased from possession. . . .

17.2 The Distinction Between Leases and Licences

17.2.1 EXCLUSIVE POSSESSION AS THE FOUNDATION OF THE LEASE/LICENCE DISTINCTION

STREET v MOUNTFORD [1985] 1 AC 809, House of Lords

FACTS: Street granted to Mountford the right to occupy two rooms by a form of agreement described as being a 'licence'. The agreement was subject to a number of conditions. Mountford signed a declaration by which she acknowledged that the agreement did not give her a protected tenancy. Street sought an order of the county court declaring that the agreement was a licence, and did not constitute a tenancy.
HELD: The agreement was a tenancy, despite the use of the word 'licence'. The test to distinguish a lease from a licence was one of substance, not of form. The crucial question to ask was whether the agreement conferred 'exclusive possession'.

LORD TEMPLEMAN: . . . My Lords, there is no doubt that the traditional distinction between a tenancy and a licence of land lay in the grant of land for a term at a rent with exclusive possession. In some cases it was not clear at first sight whether exclusive possession was in fact granted. . . .

In the case of residential accommodation there is no difficulty in deciding whether the grant confers exclusive possession. An occupier of residential accommodation at a rent for a term is either a lodger or a tenant. The occupier is a lodger if the landlord provides attendance or services which require the landlord or his servants to exercise unrestricted access to and use of the premises. A lodger is entitled to live in the premises but cannot call the place his own. In Allan v Liverpool Overseers (1874) LR 9 QB 180, 191–192 Blackburn J said:

A lodger in a house, although he has the exclusive use of rooms in the house, in the sense that nobody else is to be there, and though his goods are stowed there, yet he is not in exclusive occupation in that sense, because the landlord is there for the purpose of being able, as landlords commonly do in the case of lodgings, to have his own servants to look after the house and the furniture, and has retained to himself the occupation, though he has agreed to give the exclusive enjoyment of the occupation to the lodger.

If on the other hand residential accommodation is granted for a term at a rent with exclusive possession, the landlord providing neither attendance nor services, the grant is a tenancy; any express reservation to the landlord of limited rights to enter and view the state of the premises and to repair and maintain the premises only serves to emphasise the fact that the grantee is entitled to exclusive possession and is a tenant. In the present case it is conceded that Mrs Mountford is entitled to exclusive possession and is not a lodger. Mr Street provided neither attendance nor services and only reserved the limited rights of inspection and maintenance and the like set forth in clause 3 of the agreement. On the traditional view of the matter, Mrs Mountford not being a lodger must be a tenant.

There can be no tenancy unless the occupier enjoys exclusive possession; but an occupier who enjoys exclusive possession is not necessarily a tenant. He may be owner in fee simple, a trespasser, a mortgagee in possession, an object of charity or a service occupier. To constitute a tenancy the occupier must be granted exclusive possession for a fixed or periodic term certain in consideration of a premium or periodical payments. The grant may be express, or may be inferred where the owner accepts weekly or other periodical payments from the occupier.

Occupation by service occupier may be eliminated. A service occupier is a servant who occupies his master's premises in order to perform his duties as a servant. In those circumstances the possession and occupation of the servant is treated as the possession and occupation of the master and the relationship of landlord and tenant is not created; . . .

In the present case, the agreement dated 7 March 1983 professed an intention by both parties to create a licence and their belief that they had in fact created a licence. It was submitted on behalf of Mr Street that the court cannot in these circumstances decide that the agreement created a tenancy without interfering with the freedom of contract enjoyed by both parties. My Lords, Mr Street enjoyed freedom to offer Mrs Mountford the right to occupy the rooms comprised in the agreement on such lawful terms as Mr Street pleased. Mrs Mountford enjoyed freedom to negotiate with Mr Street to obtain different terms. Both parties enjoyed freedom to contract or not to contract and both parties exercised that freedom by contracting on the terms set forth in the written agreement and on no other terms. But the consequences in law of the agreement, once concluded, can only be determined by consideration of the effect of the agreement. If the agreement satisfied all the requirements of a tenancy, then the agreement produced a tenancy and the parties cannot alter the effect of the agreement by insisting that they only created a licence. The manufacture of a five-pronged implement for manual digging results in a fork even if the manufacturer, unfamiliar with the English language, insists that he intended to make and has made a spade.

It was also submitted that in deciding whether the agreement created a tenancy or a licence, the court should ignore the Rent Acts. If Mr Street has succeeded, where owners have failed these past 70 years, in driving a coach and horses through the Rent Acts, he must be left to enjoy the benefit of his ingenuity unless and until Parliament intervenes. I accept that the Rent Acts are irrelevant to the problem of determining the legal effect of the rights granted by the agreement. Like the professed intention of the parties, the Rent Acts cannot alter the effect of the agreement. . . .

. . . in my opinion in order to ascertain the nature and quality of the occupancy and to see whether the occupier has or has not a stake in the room or only permission for himself personally to occupy, the court must decide whether upon its true construction the agreement confers on the occupier exclusive possession. If exclusive possession at a rent for a term does not constitute a tenancy then the distinction between a contractual tenancy and a contractual licence of land becomes wholly unidentifiable.

In *Somma* v *Hazelhurst* [1978] 1 WLR 1014, a young unmarried couple H and S occupied a double bedsitting room for which they paid a weekly rent. The landlord did not provide services or attendance and the couple were not lodgers but tenants enjoying exclusive possession. But the Court of Appeal did not ask themselves whether H and S were lodgers or tenants and did not draw the correct conclusion from the fact that H and S enjoyed exclusive possession. The Court of Appeal were diverted from the correct inquiries by the fact that the landlord obliged H and S to enter into separate agreements and reserved power to determine each agreement separately. The landlord also insisted that the room should not in form be let to either H or S or to both H and S but that each should sign an agreement to share the room in common with such other persons as the landlord might from time to time nominate, The sham nature of this obligation would have been only slightly more obvious if H and S had been married or if the room had been furnished with a double bed instead of two single beds. If the landlord had served notice on H to leave and had required S to share the room with a strange man, the notice would only have been a disguised notice to quit on both H and S. The room was let and taken as residential accommodation with exclusive possession in order that H and S might live together in undisturbed quasi-connubial bliss making weekly payments. The agreements signed by H and S constituted the grant to H and S jointly of exclusive possession at a rent for a term for the purposes for which the room was taken and the agreement therefore created a tenancy. Although the Rent Acts must not be allowed to alter or influence the construction of an agreement, the court should, in my opinion, be astute to detect and frustrate sham devices and artificial transactions whose only object is to disguise the grant of a tenancy and to evade the Rent Acts. I would disapprove of the decision in this case that H and S were only licensees and for the same reason would disapprove of the decision in *Aldrington Garages Ltd v Fielder* (1978) 37 P & CR 461 and *Sturolson & Co v Weniz* (1984) 272, EG 326.

In the present case the Court of Appeal, 49 P & CR 324 held that the agreement dated 7 March 1983 only created a licence. Slade LJ, at p. 329 accepted that the agreement and in particular clause 3 of the agreement 'shows that the right to occupy the premises conferred on the defendant was intended as an exclusive right of occupation, in that it was thought necessary to give a special and express power to the plaintiff to enter. . .' Before your Lordships it was conceded that the agreement conferred the right of exclusive possession on Mrs Mountford. Even without clause 3 the result would have been the same. By the agreement Mrs Mountford was granted the right to occupy residential accommodation. The landlord did not provide any services or attendance. It was plain that Mrs Mountford was not a lodger. Slade LJ proceeded to analyse all the provisions of the agreement, not for the purpose of deciding whether his finding of exclusive possession was correct, but for the purpose of assigning some of the provisions of the agreement to the category of terms which he thought are usually to be found in a tenancy agreement and of assigning other provisions to the category of terms which he thought are usually to be found in a licence. Slade LJ may or may not have been right that in a letting of a furnished room it was 'most unusual to find a provision in a tenancy agreement obliging the tenant to keep his rooms in a 'tidy condition' (p. 329). If Slade LJ was right about this and other provisions there is still no logical method of evaluating the results of his survey. Slade LJ reached the conclusion that 'the agreement bears all the hallmarks of a licence rather than a tenancy save for the one important feature of exclusive occupation': p. 329. But in addition to the hallmark of exclusive occupation of residential accommodation there were the hallmarks of weekly payments for a periodical term. Unless these three hallmarks are decisive, it really becomes impossible to distinguish a contractual tenancy from a contractual licence save by reference to the professed intention of the parties or by the judge awarding marks for drafting. Slade LJ was finally impressed by the statement at the foot of the agreement by Mrs Mountford 'I understand and accept that a licence in the above form does not and is not intended to give me a tenancy protected under the Rent Acts.' Slade LJ said, at p. 330:

> it seems to me that, if the defendant is to displace the express statement of intention embodied in the declaration, she must show that the declaration was either a deliberate sham or at least an inaccurate statement of what was the true substance of the real transaction agreed between the parties; . . .

My Lords, the only intention which is relevant is the intention demonstrated by the agreement to grant exclusive possession for a term at a rent. Sometimes it may be difficult to discover whether, on the true construction of an agreement, exclusive possession is conferred. Sometimes it may appear from the surrounding circumstances that there was no intention to create legal relationships. Sometimes it may appear from the surrounding circumstances that the right to exclusive possession is referable to a legal relationship other than a tenancy. Legal relationships to which the grant of exclusive possession might be referable and which would or might negative the grant of an estate or interest in the land include occupancy under a contract for the sale of the land, occupancy pursuant to a contract of employment or occupancy referable to the holding of an office. But where as in the present case the only circumstances are that residential accommodation is offered and accepted with exclusive possession for a term at a rent, the result is a tenancy.

The position was well summarised by Windeyer J sitting in the High Court of Australia in *Radaich v Smith* (1959) 101 CLR 209, 222, where he said:

> What then is the fundamental right which a tenant has that distinguishes his position from that of a licensee? It is an interest in land as distinct from a personal permission to enter the land and use it for some stipulated purpose or purposes. And how is it to be ascertained whether such an interest in land has been given? By seeing whether the grantee was given a legal right of exclusive possession of the land for a term or from year to year or for a life or lives. If he was, he is a tenant. And he cannot be other than a tenant, because a legal right of exclusive possession is a tenancy and the creation of such a right is a demise. To say that a man who has, by agreement with a landlord, a right of exclusive possession of land for a term is not a tenant is simply to contradict the first proposition by the second. A right of exclusive possession is secured by the right of a lessee to maintain ejectment and, after his entry, trespass. A reservation to the landlord, either by contract or statute, of a limited right of entry, as for example to view or repair, is, of course, not inconsistent with the grant of exclusive possession. Subject to such reservations, a tenant for a term or from year to year or for a life or lives can exclude his landlord as well as strangers from the demised premises. All this is long established law: see *Cole on Ejectment* (1857) pp. 72, 73, 287, 458.

My Lords, I gratefully adopt the logic and the language of Windeyer J. Henceforth the courts which deal with these problems will, save in exceptional circumstances, only be concerned to inquire whether as a result of an agreement relating to residential accommodation the occupier is a lodger or a tenant. In the present case I am satisfied that Mrs Mountford is a tenant, that the appeal should be allowed, that the order of the Court of Appeal should be set aside and that the respondent should be ordered to pay the costs of the appellant here and below.

Waite, A. J., 'Leases and Licences: The True Distinguishing Test' (1987) 50 MLR 226

. . . In *Crancour Ltd v Da Silvaesa* (1986) 52 P & CR 204 Ralph Gibson LJ said:

> It is not necessary in my opinion for this court to decide . . . whether the principles laid down in *Street v Mountford* [1985] 1 AC 809 mean that, as a matter of law, premises made available for a term at a rent for residential accommodation must imply a grant of exclusive possession, whatever the terms and circumstances of the agreement, unless the landlord provides attendance or services which require the landlord or his servants to exercise unrestricted access to and use of the premises. I incline to the view that *Street v Mountford* does lay down such a rule where the accommodation is intended for use as ordinary separate and private residential accommodation and in the absence of any exceptional circumstances. I understand the basis of the rule to be that possession of rooms for occupation as ordinary residential accommodation must, from its nature, be intended by both parties to be exclusive except where, as stated, the landlord requires unrestricted access for the provision of services or attendance.

It is suggested that this approach is open to criticism. It involves reading too much into a single passage in *Street v Mountford*. It is submitted that the touchstone of a tenancy remains exclusive possession. Lord Templeman's 'lodger' test is simply one of several ways in which a claim to exclusive possession can be negatived. . . . A fundamental question underlying the whole of the present discussion relates to the nature of the requisite exclusive possession. Must there be a right to exclusive possession or does the fact of it suffice? . . . The text of Lord Templeman's speech in *Street* v *Mountford* is somewhat ambiguous. However, if the above analysis of the sham is accepted then it is the right to (*i.e.* the grant of) exclusive possession which is decisive. This is clearly the view of the judges in *Crancour*. Ralph Gibson LJ in dealing with Lord Templeman's analysis of *Somma* v *Hazlehurst* [1978] 1 WLR 1014 said; 'the House of Lords is there saying, first, that the agreement in that case constituted the grant of exclusive possession; second, that the written obligation to share the room was not effective to alter the true nature of the grant . . .' In any case the 'right' as opposed to 'fact' analysis must be correct in principle since a lease is a derivative as opposed to original interest. It must therefore be based on a grant.

A final word is necessary about Lord Templeman's restricted 'lodger' test. It is clear that it is only where the landlord requires unrestricted access to the premises in order to provide attendance or services that the requisite exclusive possession is negated. Some useful guidance on the meaning of ' unrestricted ' has been provided by Ralph Gibson LJ in *Crancour*. The term means that the landlord can come and go at his own convenience irrespective of the presence of the occupier. The amount and frequency of the attendance and services are relevant but not overriding factors. Inevitably there is a grey area which is likely to provide the opportunity for litigation. No doubt equally inevitably the draughts-men will attempt to plug the gap. However, the shadow of the sham will always hover over this type of agreement, and will ensure that 'off the peg' agreements cannot be used to avoid Rent Act protection.

ADDISCOMBE GARDENS v *CRABBE* [1958] 1 QB 513, Court of Appeal

FACTS: The question was whether an agreement for the 'rental' of tennis courts in consideration of monthly payments of 'court fees' was a lease or a licence. The agreement required the grantee to keep the courts 'in good and tenantable repair and condition' and to surrender them at the end of the 'licence' in such condition. It also permitted the owner to enter 'at all reasonable times' to inspect the condition of the premises. In return, the owner, agreed to allow the grantees to 'quietly enjoy' the premises.
HELD: On the question of whether this agreement constituted a lease or a licence, it was held to constitute a lease. The answer was determined by law, and not by the label the parties put on the agreement.

JENKINS L: stated the facts and continued: It is vital to the plaintiffs' claim for possession of the premises that they should be able to establish that this document described as a licence is in truth a licence, as opposed to a tenancy agreement. If it is a mere licence, then the plaintiffs' claim to possession must follow, for the rights granted by it have some time since expired. If, on the other hand, although described as a licence, it has the effect of a tenancy agreement, then *prima facie* the plaintiffs must be faced, before they can get possession, with the task of compliance with the provisions of the Landlord and Tenant Act, 1954. . . .

. . . Taking all those considerations together, I am of opinion that the judge was perfectly right in holding, as he did, that this was a tenancy. He was particularly impressed by the express provision entitling the grantors to enter the premises 'to inspect the condition thereof and for all other reasonable purposes'; and he held that to be an indication that the right to occupy the premises granted to the grantees was intended to be an exclusive right of occupation, that circumstance, as I have said, being at lowest a strong circumstance in favour of the view that there is a tenancy as opposed to a licence.

FAMILY HOUSING ASSOCIATION v *JONES* [1990] 1 WLR 779, Court of Appeal

FACTS: The plaintiff housing association granted a homeless family the right to live in temporary accommodation. Under the agreement, described as a 'licence' and expressed to deny exclusive possession to the occupier, the occupiers were to pay a weekly 'accommodation charge'. The association retained a key, in order to execute emergency repairs and to provide certain counselling services to tenants. When offered alternative accommodation, the occupiers refused to vacate the premises. The judge at first instance held that the occupier was a licensee, and granted possession to the association. The occupiers appealed.

HELD: The appeal was allowed. According to the substantive test for 'a lease' the present arrangement could not properly be described as a licence. It was a weekly tenancy.

BALCOMBE LJ : *Licence or tenancy*

The decision of the House of Lords in *Street* v *Mountford* [1985] AC 809 represented a sea-change in the law on this subject. Although the difference between a licence and a tenancy had been long established, it was believed by many that a right of exclusive occupation could be granted to an occupier, and that right did not amount to exclusive possession, and hence create a tenancy, if that were the genuine intention of the parties. Lord Templeman, with whose speech all the other Law Lords agreed, disposed of that belief. . . .

Mr Neuberger, for the housing association before us, did not seek to support the judge's findings that there was no defined term or that occupation could be given up without notice. Clearly the payment of an 'accommodation charge' on a weekly basis is no different from the payment of a weekly rent, which without more creates a weekly tenancy, while payment of that charge in advance would appear to prevent the housing association from determining Mrs Jones's right to occupy at least before the end of the week in respect of which that charge had been paid; in any event even a licence cannot be determined except on reasonable notice: see *Minister of Health* v *Bellotti* [1944] KB 298. Furthermore, the 'genuine and express agreement that exclusive possession was not granted'—clause 5 of the agreement of 5 February 1985—is as much a label as is the reference to a 'licence' in the same clause and, to use Lord Templeman's spade/fork analogy (even though most garden forks have four tines or prongs), cannot prevent the agreement creating a tenancy if that is its true effect.

This was a self-contained flat, and it is clear that Mrs Jones and Nicolas were to be its only occupants. Mrs Jones paid a weekly charge for her right to occupy the flat. Thus the agreement fulfils all the requirements which Lords Templeman, Oliver of Aylmerton and Donaldson of Lymington MR in the several passages quoted above indicate as being appropriate for the creation of a tenancy; the only possible contra-indications are the retention of a key by the housing association and the purposes for which that key was retained. (I leave out of account the judge's reliance on the temporary nature of the accommodation granted: a weekly tenancy, provided it is not a secure tenancy and can be determined on a week's notice, is just as consistent with the provision of temporary accommodation as is a licence.) So I return to the question of the retention of the key and the purposes for which it was retained.

The retention of a key by itself cannot be decisive; a landlord under an undoubted tenancy may retain a key to enable him to exercise a right reserved to him by the tenancy to enter the demised premises to inspect the state of repair. As Lord Donaldson of Lymington MR said in *Aslan* v *Murphy* [1990] 1 WLR 776 there is a spectrum ranging from tenant at the one end to lodger at the other. Whilst the rights retained by the housing association in the present case may be slightly greater than those usually retained by a landlord under a lease, I entertain no doubt that they fall at the 'tenant' end of the spectrum, not the 'lodger' end.

In my judgment, the judge was incorrect in holding that the agreement of 5 February 1985 created a licence: it created a weekly tenancy.

17.2.2   THE MEANING OF EXCLUSIVE POSSESSION

MARCHANT v *CHARTERS* [1977] 1 WLR 1181, Court of Appeal

FACTS: The 'grantee' occupied an apartment in the grantor's premises. The grantor provided daily cleaning and regular changes of bed linen. The question was whether the grantee was a typical 'lodger', that is, a licensee, or whether they were a tenant.
HELD: The grantee was only a licensee.

LORD DENNING MR: . . . Gathering the cases together, what does it come to? What is the test to see whether the occupier of one room in a house is a tenant or a licensee? It does not depend on whether he or she has exclusive possession or not. It does not depend on whether the room is furnished or not. It does not depend on whether the occupation is permanent or temporary. It does not depend on the label which the parties put upon it. All these are factors which may influence the decision but none of them is conclusive. All the circumstances have to be worked out. Eventually the answer depends on the nature and quality of the occupancy. Was it intended that the occupier should have a stake in the room or did he have only permission for himself personally to occupy the room, whether under a contract or not? In which case he is a licensee.

Looking at the position in this case, in my opinion Mr Charters was not a tenant of this one room. He was only a licensee. A contractual licensee, no doubt, but still only a licensee. So he does not have security of tenure under the Rent Acts. He is not protected against eviction. On this point I differ from the judge. It is sufficient for the deciding of this case. Mr Charters has no right to stay. . . .

17.2.3   RETENTION OF KEYS BY THE GRANTOR

ASLAN v *MURPHY* [1990] 1 WLR 766, Court of Appeal

FACTS: The plaintiff owned a basement room occupied exclusively by the defendant. The agreement under which the occupant held the premises provided that he had a mere 'licence' to occupy the room in common with other licensees, the owner retained the keys to the room. The occupant was also required to vacate the room for 90 minutes each day. The judge at first instance held that the agreement created a 'licence'. The occupier appealed.
HELD: The occupier had been granted exclusive possession and was, accordingly, a tenant of the room. This fact could not be altered unilaterally by the threat of introducing another licensee into the premises.

LORD DONALDSON OF LYMINGTON MR: . . . *General principles*
The status of a tenant is essentially different from that of a lodger and owners of property are free to make accommodation available on either basis. Which basis applies in any particular case depends upon what was the true bargain between the parties. It is the ascertainment of that true bargain which lies at the heart of the problem.

Labelling
The labels which parties agree to attach to themselves or to their agreements are never conclusive and in this particular field, in which there is enormous pressure on the homeless to agree to any label which will facilitate the obtaining of accommodation, they give no guidance at all. As Lord Templeman said in *Street* v *Mountford* [1985] AC 809, 819:

> The manufacture of a five-pronged implement for manual digging results in a fork even if the manufacturer, unfamiliar with the English language, insists that he intended to make and has made a spade.

Exclusive or non-exclusive occupation
This is the touchstone by which the 'spade' of tenancy falls to be distinguished from the 'fork' of lodging. In this context it is necessary to consider the rights and duties of the person making the accommodation available ('the owner') and the rights of other occupiers. The occupier has in the end to be a tenant or a lodger. He cannot be both. But there is a spectrum of exclusivity ranging from the occupier of a detached property under a full repairing lease, who is without doubt a tenant, to the overnight occupier of a hotel bedroom who, however up-market the hotel, is without doubt a lodger. The dividing line—the sorting of the forks from the spades—will not necessarily or even usually depend upon a single factor, but upon a combination of factors.

Pretences
Quite apart from labelling, parties may succumb to the temptation to agree to pretend to have particular rights and duties which are not in fact any part of the true bargain. *Prima facie*, the parties must be taken to mean what they say, but given the pressures on both

parties to pretend, albeit for different reasons, the courts would be acting unrealistically if they did not keep a weather eye open for pretences, taking due account of how the parties have acted in performance of their apparent bargain. This identification and exposure of such pretences does not necessarily lead to the conclusion that their agreement is a sham, but only to the conclusion that the terms of the true bargain are not wholly the same as those of the bargain appearing on the face of the agreement. It is the true rather than the apparent bargain which determines the question 'tenant or lodger?'

The effect of the Rent Acts

If an occupier would otherwise be protected by the Rent Acts, he does not lose that protection by agreeing that he will surrender it either immediately or in the future and whether directly and in terms or indirectly, e.g. by agreeing to substitute a shared for an exclusive right of occupation should the owner so require; *Antoniades* v *Villiers* [1990] AC 417, 461. . . .

The judge was, of course, quite right to approach the matter on this basis that it is not a crime, nor is it contrary to public policy, for a property owner to license occupiers to occupy a property on terms which do not give rise to a tenancy. Where he went wrong was in considering whether the whole agreement was a sham and, having concluded that it was not, giving effect to its terms, i.e. taking it throughout at face value. What he should have done, and I am sure would have done if he had known of the House of Lords approach to the problem, was to consider whether the whole agreement was a sham and, if it was not, whether in the light of the factual situation the provisions for sharing the room and those depriving the defendant of the right to occupy it for 90 minutes out of each 24 hours were part of the true bargain between the parties or were pretences. Both provisions were wholly unrealistic and were clearly pretences.

In this court an attempt to uphold the judge's decision was made upon a different basis, namely, the landlord's right to retain the keys. The provisions relevant to this aspect of the agreement are:

1. . . . The licensor will retain the keys to the room and has absolute right of entry at all times for the purpose of exercising such control and (without prejudice to the generality of the foregoing) for the purpose of effecting any repairs or cleaning to the room or building or for the purpose of providing the attendance mentioned in clause 4 hereof or for the purpose of removing or substituting such articles of furniture from the room as the licensor might see fit. The said right of entry is exercisable by the licensor or his servants or agents with or without any other persons (including prospective future licensee of the room). . . . 4. The licensor will provide the following attendance for the licensee: (1) housekeeping (2) lighting of common parts (3) cleaning of common parts (4) window cleaning (5) intercom (6) telephone coin box (7) cleaning of room (8) collection of rubbish (9) provision and laundering of bed linen (10) hot water (11) provision of household supplies.

Provisions as to keys are often relied upon in support of the contention that an occupier is a lodger rather than a tenant. Thus in *Duke* v *Wynne* [1990] 1 WLR 766 . . . the agreement required the occupier 'not to interfere with or change the locks on any part of the premises, [or] give the key to any other than an authorised occupier of the premises.' Provisions as to keys, if not a pretence which they often are, do not have any magic in themselves. It is not a requirement of a tenancy that the occupier shall have exclusive possession of the keys to the property. What matters is what underlies the provisions as to keys. Why does the owner want a key, want to prevent keys being issued to the friends of the occupier or want to prevent the lock being changed?

A landlord may well need a key in order that he may be able to enter quickly in the event of emergency: fire, burst pipes or whatever. He may need a key to enable him or those authorised by him to read meters or to do repairs which are his responsibility. None of these underlying reasons would of themselves indicate that the true bargain between the parties was such that the occupier was in law a lodger. On the other hand, if the true bargain is that the owner will provide genuine services which can only be provided by having keys, such as frequent cleaning, daily bed-making, the provision of clean linen at regular intervals and the like, there are materials from which it is possible to infer that the occupier is a lodger rather than a tenant. But the inference arises not from the provisions as to keys, but from the reason why those provisions formed part of the bargain. On the facts of this case, the argument based upon the provisions as to keys must and does fail for the judge found that 'during the currency of the present agreement virtually 'no services' had been provided.' These provisions may or may not have been pretences, but they are without significance in the context of the question which we had to decide.

17.2.4   POSSESSORY LICENCES AFTER *STREET* v *MOUNTFORD*

17.2.4.1   Acts of generosity or friendship where there is no intent to create legal relations

RHODES v *DALBY* [1971] 2 All ER 1144, Chancery Division

FACTS: Two men were long-standing friends. One owned a bungalow, but was going abroad for two years. The two men signed a document described as 'a gentleman's agreement' not intended to create legal relations. Under that agreement the friend staying in this country took possession of the bungalow during the two year absence. He agreed to pay a quite high 'rent' for being able to live in the bungalow.
HELD: The arrangement was a licence.

GOFF J: . . . The plaintiff fastens on the word 'let', and on the payment of rent. But he cannot use it out of its context. What was admitted was that it was let on a gentleman's agreement. Counsel for the plaintiff very properly conceded that a gentleman's agreement normally means something which is not legally enforceable. I do not see how a letting on a gentleman's agreement, without further explanation, can be held sufficient evidence of a tenancy. . . .

Harris, J. W., Licences and Tenancies—The Generosity Factor (1969) 32 MLR 92

The commonest single factor which appears to have influenced the courts in finding a licence rather than a tenancy, is the element of charitable disposition on the part of the landowner. This may be called 'the generosity factor.' It appears typically in 'family,' 'friendly' or 'personal' arrangements.

A recent example of the generosity factor appeared in *Abbeyfield (Harpenden) Society Ltd* v *Woods* [1968] 1 WLR 374. A charitable society rented an unfurnished bed-sittingroom to Mr Woods at £9 per week, in a home for old people, on terms that the society would provide food, heating and light and the services of a resident house-keeper. The crucial letter from the Society's officer to Mr Woods contained these words:

I hope you will understand that in order to make the Abbeyfield House run properly, the Society must reserve the right to take possession of your room should it at its discretion think fit. You will, however, be given at least one month's notice of the Society's desire to take possession, and I do assure you that this right will only be exercised in the event of the Society considering it absolutely essential in the interests of yourself and of the other residents of this house.

It was held by the Court of Appeal that Mr Woods was not entitled to the protection of the Rent Acts, because the relationship was that of licensor and licensee. Lord Denning MR, said:

The modern cases show that a man may be a licensee even though he has exclusive possession, even though the word 'rent' is used, and even though the word 'tenancy' is used. The court must look at this agreement as a whole and see whether a tenancy really was intended. In this case there is, besides the one room, the provision of services, meals, a resident housekeeper, and such like. The whole arrangement was so personal in nature that the proper inference is, as the judge found, that he was a licensee on the terms stated in the letter, namely, that the Society would give him one month's notice and would only exercise that right in the event of the Society considering it absolutely essential in the interests of himself and the other residents of the house.

Lord Denning has often used the adjective 'personal' to describe the particular quality of the relationship between licensor and licensee. In *Cobb* v *Lane* [1952] 1 All ER 1199 and *Errington* v *Errington* [1952] 1 KB 290 he contrasted the 'personal privilege' created by a licence with the 'interest in land' created by any tenancy. The ordinary meaning of 'personal' in the context of Mr Woods' relationship with his landlords would seem to be 'intimate'; and yet there can certainly be tenancies in which the tenant has just as much an every-day relationship with his landlord as did Mr Woods with the plaintiff Society. Express tenancy agreements in respect of single rooms, where the landlord agrees to provide services, would, if the above words of Lord Denning were taken as a literal guide, all be in danger of being cut down to mere licences. 'Personal' is evidently equivalent to 'non-commercial' or 'charitable'—the generosity factor. Where one party is let into possession of another's land there is, below the level of the various relationships of estate created by grant, the relationship of licensor and licensee created by concession. This is a concept not susceptible of exact definition, and therefore it confers on the judge a discretion to preserve the deserving landlord from the effects of legislation designed to protect tenants.

17.2.4.2 Service occupancies

CRANE v MORRIS [1965] 3 All ER 77, Court of Appeal

FACTS: The defendant was employed as a farm worker and granted exclusive possession of a cottage on the farm upon condition that he remained in the employ of the plaintiff. The defendant did not pay rent. When the defendant left the plaintiff's employ and took up work in a factory, the plaintiff brought an action to regain possession of the premises.
HELD: The defendant was a mere licensee, not a service tenant.

LORD DENNING MR: . . . At one time it was said (as the judge said here) that, for there to be a service occupation and not a tenancy, the servant must be *required* to occupy the house in order to perform his duties, as distinct from being *permitted* to occupy it. It was also said that the difference between a licence and a tenancy was that, on a tenancy, the occupier had exclusive possession, but on a licence, he had not exclusive possession. We have got long past those days. It is now perfectly well settled that a man may be a licensee (and no tenant) even though he has exclusive possession; see *Errington* v *Errington* [1952] 1 KB 290. And a servant may be a licensee (and no tenant) even though he is not required to live in the house but only permitted to do so for the convenience of his work; see *Torbett* v *Faulkner* [1952] 2 TLR 659. In this particular case I have no doubt whatever that the defendant was not a tenant. He was a licensee in the house, with permission to stay there rent free, so long as he remained in the employment of the farmer. Once he ceased to be in that employment, he could be turned out, being given, of course, a reasonable time to go. It is not necessary to give a licensee notice to quit, any more than it is a tenant at will. A demand is sufficient: and a writ claiming possession is itself a sufficient demand. . . .

NORRIS v CHECKSFIELD [1991] 1 WLR 1241, Court of Appeal

FACTS: A coach mechanic had been granted a 'licence' to use a bungalow close to the depot where he worked. A condition of the grant was that he would apply for a passenger service vehicle licence and would drive coaches for his employer. Upon discovering that the mechanic was a disqualified driver, the employer terminated his employment and brought an action for possession of the premises. The judge granted the order and the employee appealed.
HELD: The appeal was dismissed. There was a sufficient connection between the employment and the licence to describe it as a 'service licence'. Such a licence came to an end summarily upon the termination of the employment to which it related.

WOOLF LJ: . . . In relation to the thorny issue as to when an employee is a licensee and not a tenant of premises belonging to his employer which he is allowed to occupy, Mr Seaward, who appeared on behalf of the employee, was prepared to accept Mr Zeidman's submission on behalf of the employer. Mr Zeidman submitted that an employee can be a licensee, although his occupation of the premises is not *necessary* for the purposes of the employment, if he is genuinely *required* to occupy the premises for the *better performance* of his duties. In my judgment this submission accurately reflects the law. We have been referred to a number of authorities which set out different tests. The most helpful decision is that of the House of Lords in *Glasgow Corporation* v *Johnstone* [1965] AC 609. In that case Lord Reid, with whose speech Lord Wilberforce agreed, said . . . that it would be sufficient if the employee's occupation was of 'material assistance' to his employment. It need not be '*necessary*' for his employment. The same view was taken by Lord Evershed and Lord Hodson. Lord Guest stated the position which must exist for there to be a licence in the following terms, at p. 629:

> The residence must be ancillary to the duties which the servant has to perform (*Smith* v *Seghill Overseers* (1875) LR 10 QB 422) or, put in another way, the requirement must be with a view to the more efficient performance of the servant's duties (*Fox* v *Dalby* (1874) LR 10 CP 285).

As Mr Seaward correctly submitted, it would not suffice if the occupation was a 'fringe benefit' or merely an inducement to encourage the employee to work better. . . .

17.2.5   FLAT-SHARING AGREEMENTS

ANTONIADES v *VILLIERS* [1990] 1 AC 417, House of Lords;
AG SECURITIES v *VAUGHAN* [1990] 1 AC 417, House of Lords

Antoniades v *Villiers*

FACTS: V1 and V2 (a co-habiting couple) each signed on the same day an agreement giving them the right to use a small flat. Clause 16 of each agreement provided: 'The licensor shall be entitled at any time to use the rooms together with the licensee and permit other persons to use all of the rooms together with the licensee'. The question was whether the agreements together constituted a lease of the premises, or whether they were individual licenses.
HELD: The practical reality was that the two documents, read together, granted exclusive possession to the appellants and therefore created a lease. Clause 16 should be ignored. It had been inserted by the grantor as a 'pretence', in an effort to show that V1 and V2 did not together have exclusive possession. The purported 'licences' were 'shams'.

AG Securities v *Vaughan*

FACTS: AGS owned a four-bedroomed flat. Each of the four occupiers had signed a non-exclusive licence. Each licence was signed on a different date, was for a different period, and was at a different rent. The question was whether this arrangement had created one lease or four licences.
HELD: There were four separate licences.

LORD TEMPLEMAN: . . . Parties to an agreement cannot contract out of the Rent Acts; if they were able to do so the Acts would be a dead letter because in a state of housing shortage a person seeking residential accommodation may agree to anything to obtain shelter. The Rent Acts protect a tenant but they do not protect a licensee. Since parties to an agreement cannot contract out of the Rent Acts, a document which expresses the intention, genuine or bogus, of both parties or of one party to create a licence will nevertheless create a tenancy if the rights and obligations enjoyed and imposed satisfy the legal requirements of a tenancy. A person seeking residential accommodation may concur in any expression of intention in order to obtain shelter. Since parties to an agreement cannot contract out of the Rent Acts, a document expressed in the language of a licence must nevertheless be examined and construed by the court in order to decide whether the rights and obligations enjoyed and imposed create a licence or a tenancy. A person seeking residential accommodation may sign a document couched in any language in order to obtain shelter. Since parties to an agreement cannot contract out of the Rent Acts, the grant of a tenancy to two persons jointly cannot be concealed, accidentally or by design, by the creation of two documents in the form of licences. Two persons seeking residential accommodation may sign any number of documents in order to obtain joint shelter. In considering one or more documents for the purpose of deciding whether a tenancy has been created, the court must consider the surrounding circumstances including any relationship between the prospective occupiers, the course of negotiations and the nature and extent of the accommodation and the intended and actual mode of occupation of the accommodation. If the owner of a one-bedroomed flat granted a licence to a husband to occupy the flat provided he shared the flat with his wife and nobody else and granted a similar licence to the wife provided she shared the flat with the husband and nobody else, the court would be bound to consider the effect of both documents together. If the licence to the husband required him to pay a licence fee of £50 per month and the licence to the wife required her to pay a further licence fee of £50 per month, the two documents read together in the light of the property to be occupied and the obvious intended mode of occupation would confer exclusive occupation on the husband and wife jointly and a tenancy at the rent of £100.

Landlords dislike the Rent Acts and wish to enjoy the benefits of letting property without the burden of the restrictions imposed by the Acts. Landlords believe that the Rent Acts unfairly interfere with freedom of contract and exacerbate the housing shortage. Tenants on the other hand believe that the Acts are a necessary protection against the exploitation of people who do not own the freehold or long leases of their homes. The court lacks the knowledge and the power to form any judgment on these arguments which fall to be considered and determined by Parliament. The duty of the court is to enforce the Acts and in so doing to observe on principle which is inherent in the Acts and has been long recognised, the principle that parties cannot contract out of the Acts. . . .

LORD OLIVER OF AYLMERTON: . . .

Antoniades v *Villiers and another*   The appellants in this appeal are a young couple who at all material times were living together as man and wife. In about November 1984 they learned from a letting agency that a flat was available in a house at 6, Whiteley Road, London SE19, owned by the respondent, Mr Antoniades. They inspected the flat together and were told that the rent would be £174 per month. They were given the choice of having the bedroom furnished with a double bed or two single beds and they chose a double bed. So, right from the inception, there was never any question but that the appellants were seeking to establish a joint home and they have, at all material times, been the sole occupants of the flat.

There is equally no question but that the premises are not suitable for occupation by more than one couple, save on a very temporary basis. The small living-room contains a sofa capable of being converted into a double bed and also a bed-table capable of being opened out to form a narrow single bed. The appellants did in fact have a friend to stay with them for a time in what the trial judge found to be cramped conditions, but the size of the accommodation and the facilities available clearly do not make the flat suitable for multiple occupation. When it came to drawing up the contractual arrangements under which the appellants were to be let into possession, each was asked to and did sign a separate licence agreement in the terms set out in the speech of my noble and learned friend, Lord Templeman, under which each assumed an individual, but not a joint, responsibility for payment of one half of the sum of £174 previously quoted as the rent.

There is an air of total unreality about these documents read as separate and individual licences in the light of the circumstance that the appellants were together seeking a flat as a quasi-matrimonial home. A separate licensee does not realistically assume responsibility for all repairs and all outgoings. Nor in the circumstances can any realistic significance be given to clauses 16 and 17 of the document. It cannot realistically have been contemplated that the respondent would either himself use or occupy any part of the flat or put some other person in to share accommodation specifically adapted for the occupation by a couple living together. These clauses cannot be considered as seriously intended to have any practical operation or to serve any purpose apart from the purely technical one of seeking to avoid the ordinary legal consequences attendant upon letting the appellants into possession at a monthly rent. The unreality is enhanced by the reservation of the right of eviction without court order, which cannot seriously have been thought to be effective, and by the accompanying agreement not to get married, which can only have been designed to prevent a situation arising in which it would be quite impossible to argue that the 'licensees' were enjoying separate rights of occupation.

The conclusion seems to me irresistible that these two so-called licences, executed contemporaneously and entered into in the circumstances already outlined, have to be read together as constituting in reality one single transaction under which the appellants became joint occupiers. That of course does not conclude the case because the question still remains, what is the effect?. . .

If the documents fall to be taken seriously at their face value and to be construed according to their terms, I see, for my part, no escape from the conclusion at which the Court of Appeal arrived. If it is once accepted that the respondent enjoyed the right—whether he exercised it or not—to share the accommodation with the appellants, either himself or by introducing one or more other persons to use the flat with them, it is, as it seems to me, incontestable that the appellants cannot claim to have had exclusive possession. . . .

If the real transaction was, as the judge found, one under which the appellants became joint tenants with exclusive possession, on the footing that the two agreements are to be construed together, then it would follow that they were together jointly and severally responsible for the whole rent. It would equally follow that they could effectively exclude the respondent and his nominees.

Although the facts are not precisely on all fours with *Somma* v *Hazelhurst* [1978] 1 WLR 1014, they are strikingly similar and the judge was, in my judgment, entitled to conclude that the appellants had exclusive possession of the premises. I read his finding that, 'the licences are artificial transactions designed to evade the Rent Acts' as a finding that they were sham documents designed to conceal the true nature of the transaction. There was, in my judgment, material on which he could properly reach this conclusion and I, too, would allow the appeal.

AG Securities v *Vaughan and others*

The facts in this appeal are startlingly different from those in the case of *Antoniades*. To begin with the appeal concerns a substantial flat in a mansion block consisting of four bedrooms, a lounge, a sitting-room and usual offices. The trial judge found, as a fact, that the premises could without difficulty provide residential accommodation for four persons. There is no question but that the agreements with which the appeal is concerned reflect the true bargain between the parties. It is the purpose and intention of both parties to each agreement that it should confer an individual right on the licensee named, that he should be liable only for the payment which he had undertaken, and that his agreement should be capable of termination without reference to the agreements with other persons occupying the flat. . . .

I pause to note that it has never been contended that any individual occupier has a tenancy of a particular room in the flat with a right to use the remainder of the flat in common with the tenants of other rooms. I can envisage that as a possibility in cases of arrangements of this kind if the facts support the marking out with the landlord's concurrence of a particular room as the exclusive domain of a particular individual. But to support that there would, I think, have to be proved the grant of an identifiable part of the flat and that simply does not fit with the system described in the evidence of the instant case.

The real question—and it is this upon which the respondents rely—is what is the position when the flat is occupied concurrently by all four licensees? What is said then is that since the licensor has now exhausted, for the time being, his right of nomination, the four occupants collectively have exclusive possession of the premises because they can collectively exclude the licensor himself. Because, it is argued, (1) they have thus exclusive possession and, (2) there is an ascertainable term during which all have the right to use and occupy, and (3) they are occupying in consideration of the payment of periodic sums of money, *Street* v *Mountford* [1985] AC 809 shows that they are collectively tenants of the premises. They are not lodgers. Therefore they must be tenants. And because each is not individually a tenant, they must together be joint tenants.

My Lords, there appear to me to be a number of fallacies here. In the first place, the assertion of an exclusive possession rests, as it seems to me, upon assuming what it is sought to prove. If, of course, each licence agreement creates a tenancy, each tenant will be sharing with other persons whose rights to be there rest upon their own estates which, once they have been granted, they enjoy in their own right independently of the landlord. Collectively they have the right to exclude everyone other than those who have concurrent estates. But if the licence agreement is what it purports to be, that is to say, merely an agreement for permissive enjoyment as the invitee of the landlord, then each shares the use of the premises with other invitees of the same landlord. The landlord is not excluded for he continues to enjoy the premises through his invitees, even though he may for the time being have precluded himself by contract with each from withdrawing the invitation. Secondly, the fact that under each agreement an individual has the privilege of user and occupation for a term which overlaps the term of user and occupation of other persons in the premises, does not create a single indivisible term of occupation for all four consisting of an amalgam of the individual overlapping periods. Thirdly, there is no single sum of money payable in respect of use and occupation. Each person is individually liable for the amount which he has agreed, which may differ in practice from the amounts paid by all or some of the others.

The respondents are compelled to support their claims by a strange and unnatural theory that, as each occupant terminates his agreement, there is an implied surrender by the other three and an implied grant of a new joint tenancy to them together with the new incumbent when he enters under his individual agreement. With great respect to the majority in the Court of Appeal, this appears to me to be entirely unreal. For my part, I agree with the dissenting judgment of Sir George Waller in finding no unity of interest, no unity of title, certainly no unity of time and, as I think, no unity of possession. I find it impossible to say that the agreements entered into with the respondents created either individually or collectively a single tenancy either of the entire flat or of any part of it. I agree that the appeal should be allowed.

Hill, J., 'Shared Accommodation and Exclusive Possession' (1989) 52 MLR 408

III Sham transactions

In the context of shared residential accommodation, the fact that each occupier entered a separate 'licence agreement' with the owner does not preclude the possibility that the occupiers are tenants. However, for this to be the case it must be established that the agreements are in some sense sham. While the fundamental characteristic of a sham transaction is that the form disguises the substance, it is important to be aware that not all shams are of the same type. In the present context three different types of sham should be distinguished (although it is quite possible for all three types of sham to arise in a single case). First, and least problematical, is the situation where the terminology employed in an agreement misrepresents the legal category into which the arrangement falls. Secondly, documents may include clauses by which neither party intends to be bound and which are obviously a smokescreen to cover the real intentions of both contracting parties, Thirdly, where there are a number of transactions creating a composite whole the court may look at the overall result of what is achieved rather than considering the individual transactions in isolation. For example, where a number of occupiers enter separate licence agreements the courts may treat the occupiers as joint tenants. In cases involving composite transactions the substance of the relationship between the occupiers and the owner may be determined either by reading the interdependent written agreements together (ignoring smokescreen clauses) or by reference to a parallel oral or implied agreement. . . .

IV Implications

A disappointing feature of the speeches in *AG Securities* v *Vaughan* and *Antoniades* v *Villiers* is the House of Lords' failure to address the problems which result from the fact that the exploitation of the lease/licence distinction is merely one of a number of devices employed by landlords to avoid the Rent Act 1977 (and now the Housing Act 1988). Any individual decision which appears to extend the ambit of statutory protection (such as *Antoniades* v *Villiers*) will have no more than a marginal impact in terms of its practical effects if landlords' legal advisers can continue to circumvent the legislation simply by redrafting their standard-form agreements or by employing alternative avoidance mechanisms. The absence of a broader perspective runs the risk of the rights of residential occupiers depending on arbitrary distinctions, and the courts 'awarding marks for drafting.'

Although in *Antoniades* v *Villiers* and *AG Securities* v *Vaughan* the House of Lords declined to address the issue of avoidance of statutory schemes of protection on a broader level, the principles which have been formulated in the context of the lease/licence distinction are applicable to analogous situations. It is suggested that the tripartite structure employed in the previous section offers an appropriate framework through which the courts can work out solutions to the various avoidance devices employed by private sector landlords.

In a number of cases the courts have considered the authenticity of holiday lettings (which are not within the scope of statutory schemes of protection). Although on occasion the courts have declined to question the label employed by the landlord more recently in *R* v *Rent Officer for London Borough of Camden, ex parte Plant* (1980) 257 EG 713 it was held that a purported 'holiday let' for six months was not genuine since the landlord knew that the occupiers were student nurses and therefore were not occupying the premises for the purpose of a holiday. This decision is consistent with the lease/licence cases in the sense that the court accepted that it was not bound by the label employed by the parties to the agreement. Similarly, although smokescreen clauses are used primarily with a view to exploiting the lease/licence distinction, the approach taken by the House of Lords in *Antoniades* v *Villiers* [see **17.2.5**] may be applicable in other contexts. For example, a contrived attempt to bring a tenancy agreement within the exception contained in section 7 of the Rent Act 1977 by providing 'board' might be regarded as a sham.

In relation to the lease/licence cases the third category of sham—interdependent transactions—presents the most problems. The same is true in the context of other avoidance devices, as can be seen from two cases decided by the Court of Appeal shortly before the House of Lords heard *Antoniades* v *Villiers* and *AG Securities* v *Vaughan* [see **17.2.5**]. In *Gisborne* v *Burton* [1988] 3 WLR 921 a landowner granted an agricultural tenancy to his wife, who immediately granted a sub-tenancy of the land to the defendant. The purpose of this arrangement was to prevent the defendant from acquiring the rights which are available to tenants under the Agricultural Holdings Act 1948. In the Court of Appeal Dillon LJ, having examined the principles employed by the courts in tax avoidance cases took the view that:

> a similar principle must be applicable wherever there is a pre-ordained series of transactions which is intended to avoid some mandatory statutory provision, even if not of a fiscal nature. You must look at the effect of the scheme as a whole, instead of concentrating on each pre-ordained step individually, and you do not, as it were, blow the whistle at half time.

Russell LJ, having noted that he had 'not derived a lot of assistance from the tax avoidance cases,' nevertheless decided that the series of transactions was a sham. Accordingly, notwithstanding the formal position the real substance of the two transactions was held to be the grant of a tenancy to the defendant.

Although one commentator expressed the view that '*Gisborne* may prove useful to residential tenants' advisers who try to argue that tenants have security of tenure, particularly in the case of 'artificial' company let agreements' in *Hilton* v *Plustitle Ltd* [1989] 1 WLR 149 the Court of Appeal held that a tenancy granted to an off-the-shelf company purchased by the sole occupier of residential premises was not a sham. As a result the occupier was denied the benefits of the Rent Act 1977.

The recent decisions of the House of Lords suggest that the approach taken by the Court of Appeal in *Gisborne* v *Burton* is the correct one. In *Antoniades* v *Villiers* it was held that the form of a predetermined series of transactions (two licence agreements) cannot be allowed to disguise the true substance of the arrangement (the grant of a joint tenancy). In a case such as *Hilton* v *Plustitle Ltd* which involves the purchase of an off-the-shelf company the artificial nature of the series of transactions is transparent. Accordingly, the true substance of the arrangement is the grant of tenancy to the occupier, rather than the company. On the other hand, where a tenancy of residential premises is granted to a company with an independent existence there is no sham since there is no pre-ordained or interdependent series of transactions.

Conclusion

Street v *Mountford* [1985] 1 AC 809 presented a very straightforward issue: there was a single agreement between Mrs Mountford and the landlord, and it was conceded by the landlord that Mrs Mountford had exclusive possession. From the foregoing discussion it has been seen that Lord Templeman's speech in *Street* v *Mountford* provides rather limited assistance when considering the questions posed by the use of licence agreements in the context of shared accommodation. The statement that 'exclusive possession for a term at a rent' results in a tenancy does not help in determining whether or not exclusive possession has been granted.

In 1987 the Law Commission said that *Street* v *Mountford* was 'not likely to have ended the battle; rather it settled a series of skirmishes and moved the front line.' This assessment is vindicated by the cases discussed in this note. Although in *Antoniades* v *Villiers* and *AG Securities* v *Vaughan* the House of Lords has gone some way towards clarifying the dividing line between leases and licences, some questions have not been given an unequivocal answer. More significantly, the House of Lords has still to consider expressly the viability of other avoidance devices (in particular the company let). The war is not over yet.

17.2.6 'PRETENCE' CLAUSES DESIGNED TO NEGATE EXCLUSIVE POSSESSION

ASLAN v *MURPHY* and *DUKE* v *WYNNE* [1990] 1 WLR 766

FACTS: In the first case, A granted to M the use of a tiny basement room. The licence included a term that A could introduce another occupant. It also included another provision that M had no right to use the room between 1030 and 1200 hours.
HELD: Both these clauses were found to be 'pretences', and M was held to be a tenant.

FACTS: In the second case D granted to Mr and Mrs W (who had two children living with them) a three-bedroom house for two years. D again reserved the right to introduce other occupiers to the property. This clause was found to be a 'pretence'. D had no genuine intention of introducing other person(s) to the house.
HELD: Mr and Mrs W were found to have a lease.

17.3 Formalities for Leases

17.3.1 LEGAL LEASES BY EXPRESS GRANT

LAW OF PROPERTY ACT 1925

54. Creation of interests in land by parol
(1) All interests in land created by parol and not put in writing and signed by the persons so creating the same, or by their agents thereunto lawfully authorised in writing, have, notwithstanding any consideration having been given for the same, the force and effect of interests at will only.
(2) Nothing in the foregoing provisions of this Part of this Act shall affect the creation by parol of leases taking effect in possession for a term not exceeding three years (whether or not the lessee is given power to extend the term) at the best rent which can be reasonably obtained without taking a fine.

17.3.2 LEGAL LEASES BY OPERATION OF LAW

JAVAD v *MOHAMMED AQIL* [1991] 1 WLR 1007, Court of Appeal

FACTS: The plaintiff landlord allowed the defendant to take possession of the premises upon payment of a lump sum equivalent to advance rent for the first quarter of the year. The arrangement was made in anticipation of the agreement of terms for a fixed-term lease. In the event, the parties could not agree the terms of the lease, but during the period of the negotiations the defendant remained in possession of the premises amd made two further payments in respect of quarterly rent. When the plaintiff ultimately brought proceedings for possession, the defendant claimed that he had a periodic tenancy and was therefore entitled to three months' notice before eviction.

HELD: In the circumstances the defendant was to be treated as a tenant at will. There were too many unresolved differences between the parties to infer a period tenancy.

NICHOLLS LJ: . . . A tenancy, or lease, is an interest in land. With exceptions immaterial for present purposes, a tenancy springs from a consensual arrangement between two parties: one person grants to another the right to possession of land for a lesser term than he, the grantor, has in the land. The extent of the right thus granted and accepted depends primarily upon the intention of the parties.

As with other consensually-based arrangements, parties frequently proceed with an arrangement whereby one person takes possession of another's land for payment without having agreed or directed their minds to one or more fundamental aspects of their transaction. In such cases the law, where appropriate, has to step in and fill the gaps in a way which is sensible and reasonable. The law will imply, from what was agreed and all the surrounding circumstances, the terms the parties are to be taken to have intended to apply. Thus if one party permits another to go into possession of his land on payment of a rent of so much per week or month, failing more the inference sensibly and reasonably to be drawn is that the parties intended that there should be a weekly or monthly tenancy. Likewise, if one party permits another to remain in possession after the expiration of his tenancy. But I emphasise the qualification 'failing more.' Frequently there will be more: Indeed, nowadays there normally will be other material surrounding circumstances. The simple situation is unlikely to arise often, not least because of the extent to which statute has intervened in landlord-tenant relationships. Where there is more than the simple situation, the inference sensibly and reasonably to be drawn will depend upon a fair consideration of all the circumstances, of which the payment of rent on a periodical basis is only one, albeit a very important one. This is so, however large or small may be the amount of the payment.

To this I add one observation, having in mind the facts of the present case. Where parties are negotiating the terms of a proposed lease, and the prospective tenant is let into possession or permitted to remain in possession in advance of, and in anticipation of, terms being agreed, the fact that the parties have not yet agreed terms will be a factor to be taken into account in ascertaining their intention. It will often be a weighty factor. Frequently in such cases a sum called 'rent' is paid at once in accordance with the terms of the proposed lease: for example, quarterly in advance. But, depending on all the circumstances, parties are not to be supposed thereby to have agreed that the prospective tenant shall be a quarterly tenant. They cannot sensibly be taken to have agreed that he shall have a periodic tenancy, with all the consequences flowing from that, at a time when they are still not agreed about the terms on which the prospective tenant shall have possession under the proposed lease, and when he has been permitted to go into possession or remain in possession merely as an interim measure in the expectation that all will be regulated and regularised in due course when terms are agreed and a formal lease granted.

Of course, when one party permits another to enter or remain upon his land on payment of a sum of money, and that other has no statutory entitlement to be there, almost inevitably there will be some consensual relationship between them. It may be no more than a licence determinable at any time, or a tenancy at will. But when and so long as such parties are in the throes of negotiating larger terms, caution must be exercised before inferring or imputing to the parties an intention to give to the occupant more than a very limited interest, be it licence or tenancy. Otherwise the court would be in danger of inferring or imputing from conduct, such as payment of rent and the carrying out of repairs, whose explanation lies in the parties' expectation that they will be able to reach agreement on the larger terms, an intention to grant a lesser interest, such as a periodic tenancy, which the parties never had in contemplation at all. . . .

I would dismiss this appeal. Entry into possession while negotiations proceed is one of the classic circumstances in which a tenancy at will may exist . . .

17.4 End of Chapter Assessment Question

Whether a transaction under which someone acquires the right to use another's property is a lease or a license depends largely, but not exclusively, on whether the transaction grants 'exclusive possession'.

Discuss.

17.5 End of Chapter Assessment Outline Answer

The Basic Test of Exclusive Possession

The first major case to discuss the *way* in which a lease should be distinguished from a licence was *Wells* v *Hull Corporation*. The facts of this 1875 case are very far removed from twentieth century cases, which usually involve residential properties.

Hull Corporation owned a dry dock which it 'let' for short periods (usually a week) to shipowners for the purposes of carrying out repairs. The court held that whether the transaction constituted a lease or a licence turned on whether the grantee shipowner had been given 'exclusive possession' of the dock. The grantee would have 'exclusive possession' if he had been granted the *overall general control* of the dock.

On the facts the shipowners were held only to have licences as they lacked the necessary control of the dock. Under the terms of the standard form used by the Corporation, the Corporation continued to operate the dock gates, the pumps, and also supervised the cleaning out of the dock at the end of each day's repair work. These clauses meant that the shipowners did not have exclusive possession.

Moving forward more than a hundred years it can be said that nowadays the most obvious type of licensee in modern conditions is the traditional lodger. His 'landlady' (in the colloquial sense) retains control of his room, cleaning out, tidying up and changing bed linen. In *Marchant* v *Charters* [see **17.2.2**], a case in 1977 which presumably survives *Street* v *Mountford*, the grantee was not a lodger in the time-honoured sense but the occupant of a service flat. The grantor provided daily cleaning and regular changes of bed linen; the grantee was held to have only a licence.

Service Occupancies

Reading *Wells* v *Hull Corporation* one might get the impression that there was a hard and fast rule, 'If a grant gives exclusive possession it must amount to a lease.' Even in the nineteenth century this was not the case, for the law has long recognised the concept of the 'Service Occupancy' under which an employee has a licence to occupy his employer's house/flat.

The employee usually has exclusive possession, but he in law will only have a licence if the house/flat is provided so that he can be 'ready on the job'. Normally the employee is required by his contract of employment to live in the accommodation, but in *Crane Morris* (1965) the employee was permitted but not obliged to live in a house which the employer had provided very close to the place of work. The employee was held to be a service occupier licencee.

An interesting recent case is *Norris* v *Checksfield* (1991). An employee, who was already working as a coach fitter, was granted by his employer exclusive possession of a bungalow very near the depot. It was envisaged by the employer that in the near future the employee would take a PSV driver's test and would then be 'on call' to cover for emergencies such as a regular driver going sick. The employee never took the test; it was held that he was only a service occupier licencee.

Possessory Licences from 1945 to 1985

After the second world war there were a number of cases which seemed to indicate that if a transaction (which was not a service occupancy) granted exclusive possession, a licence not a lease would arise if it could be proved that 'the intent of the parties' was that there should only be a licence.

This problematic line of cases possibly started with *Marcroft Wagons* v *Smith* in 1951. There the existing tenancy of a house had terminated, but the grantors allowed the daughter of the ex-tenants to continue to live there for six months while she sought alternative accommodation. They charged her the same rent as before, but refused to give her a rent book or any other documentation. The daughter was held to be only a licencee. The Court of Appeal held that a lease had not been 'intended'.

As a result of this and other cases grantors thought, 'If we draft our grants so that they are *called* possessory licences we are on to a winner. We will escape all the restrictions of the Rent Acts.

Things come to a head in Street v Mountford

In this case Street granted Mountford the exclusive possession of a flat. The document they both signed included the kind of provisions you would expect in a residential lease, but it also explicitly stated that the transaction was not a lease, only a licence. The Court of Appeal held that the subjective 'intent of the parties' was decisive, and that Mountford only had a licence.

Celebrations by grantors of residential properties were however very short-lived. When *Street* reached the House of Lords, the House overruled the Court of Appeal. In particular the House held that the test for whether a transaction was a lease or a licence was NOT the subjective 'intent of the parties'.

The House of Lords held (in effect reverting to the nineteenth century position) that it was the objective test of exclusive possession which determined whether a transaction was a lease or a licence. A transaction which granted exclusive possession created a lease unless it fell within certain exceptions.

The exceptions recognised by the Lords were four in number. Service occupancies and occupation by virtue of an office (e.g. a vicar in his vicarage) were two. The other two exceptions are where a purchaser of premises is allowed into possession ahead of completion and where somebody allows friend(s) to occupy his premises as an act of generosity.

The 1974 case of *Heslop* v *Burns* is a clear illustration of this last exception. There an impoverished couple lived rent free in the house of a wealthy benefactor. They were held only to be licensees. Whether *Marcroft* v *Smith* comes within this exception is more debatable. The grantors had some understandable sympathy for the daughter, but they did charge her rent!

Non-exclusive Licenses

Another trick adopted by residential grantors even prior to *Street* was examined by the House of Lords in *Antoniades* v *Villiers*. There the two partners to a cohabitation had each signed a separate 'non-exclusive' license over a very small flat. One of the clauses of each agreement read 'The licensor shall be entitled at any time to use the rooms together with the licensee and permit other persons to use all of the rooms together with the licensee.'

The House of Lords held that the documents had to be read together as creating one lease, and that the clause just quoted had to be rejected as a 'pretence'.

A case decided at the same time as *Antoniades*, *AG Securities* v *Vaughan* has however shown a way forward for grantors still determined to give only licences over their property. The grantors had granted four non-exclusive-licences over a four bedroom flat, each licence commencing on a different day, for a different duration and at a different rent. The House of Lords held that there were four licences, overruling a Court of Appeal decision that the four documents should be read as creating one lease.

Grantors retaining Rights over the Premises

It is quite clear that if a grantor retains keys to premises the use of which he has granted to other(s), that does not prevent the transaction from giving exclusive possession and therefore being a lease. But what if the grantor inserts into a grant a clause deliberately designed to negate exclusive possession? In *Aslan* v *Murphy* Aslan granted to Murphy the use of a tiny basement flat, but with a strange looking clause inserted that Murphy had no right to use the premises between 1030 and 1200 every day. The licensor also had 'the right' to introduce into the flat another occupant.

In practice these clauses were never enforced and the Court of Appeal in effect held that they were 'pretences' (cf. *Antoniades* v *Villiers*). Murphy was held to have a lease.

This robust approach of in effect deleting from transactions clauses inserted by grantors which *on paper but not in reality* negate the granting of exclusive possession calls into question the 1971 decision of the Court of Appeal in *Shell-Mex* v *Manchester Garages*.

Shell granted the use of a filling station to the defendants for one year. The grant included a strange clause under which Shell could alter the layout of the premises. The clause even entitled Shell to move the very extensive underground storage tanks. The Court of Appeal held that the defendants only had a licence.

It is submitted that if this case were to recur the courts would apply (in the commercial field) the same approach as has been applied to dwellings. The artificial clauses about layout would be ignored as 'pretences'; the garage would have exclusive possession and therefore a one year lease protected by the Landlord and Tenant Act 1954, Part II.

CHAPTER EIGHTEEN

OBLIGATIONS IN LEASES

18.1 Rent — Certain Basic Points

18.1.1 RENT REVIEWS

UNITED SCIENTIFIC HOLDINGS LTD v BURNLEY BOROUGH COUNCIL
[1977] 2 All ER 62, House of Lords

FACTS: A rent-review clause in a lease provided for the upwards-only variation of the rent at 10 year intervals. On the date for the first increase in rent the level of the reviewed rent had not been agreed between the parties. The tenant sought a declaration that, since time was of the essence, the landlord had lost its right to raise the rent for the second period of ten years.

HELD: Time was not of the essence. The new rent could still be determined in accordance with the formula set-out in the lease.

LORD DIPLOCK: My Lords, during the last two decades since inflation, particularly in the property market, has been rife, it has been usual to include in leases for a term of years, except when the term is very short, a clause providing for the annual rent to be reviewed at fixed intervals during the term and for the market rent current at reach review date if it be higher, to be substituted for the rent previously payable. The wording of such clauses varies; there are several different ones now included in the books of precedents; but a feature common to nearly all of them is that not only do they specify a procedure for the determination of the revised rent by agreement between the parties or, failing that, by an independent valuer or arbitrator, but they also set out a time-table for taking some or all of the steps in that procedure which, if followed, would enable the revised rent to be settled not later than the review date.

The question in both of these appeals, which have been heard together, is whether a failure to keep strictly to the time-table laid down in the review clause deprives the landlord of his right to have the rent reviewed and consequently of his right to receive an increased rent during the period that will elapse until the next review date. . . .

It is not disputed that the parties to a lease may provide expressly that time is or time is not of the essence of the contract in respect of all or any of the steps required to be taken by the landlord to obtain the determination of an increased rent, and that if they do so the court will give effect to their expressed intention. But many rent review cases that are now maturing do not contain express provision in these terms. . . .

The rent review clauses that have given rise to the two instant appeals, as well as nearly all those which have been considered in the reported cases, if they result in any alteration of the rent previously payable can only have the effect of providing for the payment of a higher rent than would be payable by the tenant if the review clause had not been brought into operation. So the only party who can benefit from a review of rent under these clauses is the landlord. It is accordingly unlikely that the tenant would take the initiative in obtaining a review of the rent, even where the clause contains provision for his doing so—as it does in the second of the instant appeals.

It was this concentration of initiative and benefit in the landlord that led the Court of Appeal in the second appeal to regard the rent review clause as conferring upon the landlord a unilateral right to bring into existence a new contractual relationship between the parties. This they regarded as sufficiently analogous to an option, to make time of the essence of the occurrence of each one of the events in the time-table laid down in a review clause for the determination of the new rent. For my part, I consider the analogy to be misleading. The determination of the new rent under the procedure stipulated in the rent review clause neither brings into existence a fresh contract between the landlord and the tenant nor does it put an end to one that had existed previously. It is an event upon the occurrence of which the tenant has in his existing contract already accepted an obligation to pay to the landlord the rent so determined for the period to which the rent review relates. The tenant's acceptance of that obligation was an inseverable part of the whole consideration of the landlord's grant of a term of years of the length agreed. Without it, in a period during which inflation was anticipated, the landlord would either have been unwilling to grant a lease for a longer period than up to the first review date or would have demanded a higher rent to be paid throughout the term than that payable before the first review date. By the time of each review of rent the tenant will have already received a substantial part of the whole benefit which it was intended that he should obtain in return for his acceptance of the obligation to pay the higher rent for the succeeding period.

My Lords, I see no relevant difference between the obligation undertaken by a tenant under a rent review clause in a lease and any other obligation in a synallagmatic contract that is expressed to arise upon the occurrence of a described event, where a postponement of that event beyond the time stipulated in the contract is not so prolonged as to deprive the obligor of substantially the whole benefit that it was intended he should obtain by accepting the obligation.

So upon the question of principle which these two appeals were brought to settle, I would hold that in the absence of any contra-indications in the express words of the lease or in the interrelation of the rent review clause itself and other clauses or in the surrounding circumstances the presumption is that the time-table specified in a rent review clause for completion of the various steps for determining the rent payable in respect of the period following the review date is not of the essence of the contract. . . .

AMHERST v *JAMES WALKER GOLDSMITH & SILVERSMITH LTD*
[1983] 1 Ch 305, Court of Appeal

FACTS: Amherst was the landlord of a shop and James Walker Ltd, the well-known 'high street chain', was the tenant. Amherst claimed a rent review four years late.
HELD: Amherst succeeded in his claim. The crucial point was that the rent on one shop was a relatively insignificant consideration for a big firm like James Walker.

OLIVER LJ: Essentially, as it seems to me, the question is one of construction not of remedies and what one has to ask is whether, as a matter of construction of the contract, compliance with the time stipulation is so essential to the contract that any failure to comply with it entitles the other party, without more, to treat the contract as repudiated. Of course, that does not mean either that the contract is to be treated for all purposes as if the time had never been mentioned or that, when it comes to exerting any remedies for breach of contract, the ordinary rules of specific performance are suspended or abrogated. Thus, albeit the contract is not to be construed as if time were essential, damages may still be obtained for failure to comply with the fixed date for completion if damage can be shown: see *Raineri* v *Miles* [1981] AC 1050.

Equally where, as a matter of construction, time is not of the essence, it does not follow that the party in default may not, by extensive delay or other conduct, disentitle himself from having it specifically performed: see, e.g., *Cornwall* v *Henson* [1900] 2 Ch 298 and *MEPC Ltd* v *Christian-Edwards* [1978] Ch 281.

But the question of how the contract should be construed and the question of whether a party in default may have deprived himself of a right to rely on the contract must now, in my judgment, be treated as logically distinct and separate questions, whatever may be the historical origin of the rule of construction.

Mr Rich's submission treats the service of a renewal notice after the time stipulated as a submission to the court of the issue whether or not the contract should be performed. But the landlord, in serving notice, is not invoking the aid of the court to perform the contract. He is exercising the right which the contract, as properly construed, confers upon him. If it is to be construed in the sense that time is of the essence, he has no right to serve the notice. If it is not, then the right subsists, unless the tenant can show either that the contract, or that part of the contract, has been abrogated or that the landlord has precluded himself from exercising it. He may do that by showing that the contract has been repudiated—for instance, where he has served a notice calling upon the landlord to exercise his right within a reasonable time or not at all and such notice is ignored—or that some event has happened which estops the landlord from relying on his right. But I know of no ground for saying that mere delay, however lengthy, destroys the contractual right. It may put the other party in a position where, by taking the proper steps, he may become entitled to treat himself as discharged from his obligation; but that does not occur automatically and from the mere passage of time. I know of no authority for the proposition that the effect of construing a time stipulation as not being of the essence is to substitute a fresh implied term that the contract shall be performed within a reasonable time and even if such a term is to be substituted the passage of a reasonable time would not automatically abrogate the contract. It is, I think, important to distinguish between that which entitles a party to treat the contract as at an end and that which entitles the party not in default to enforce it. No one contests that, once the stipulated date is passed, proceedings may be instituted to enforce the agreement (see, e.g. *Woods* v *Mackenzie Hill Ltd* [1975] 1 WLR 613), but that is quite a different question. . . .

In my judgment, therefore, the deputy judge was right in the conclusion at which he arrived, although I would in fact go further and suggest that, despite what Lord Salmon said in *United Scientific Holdings Ltd* v *Burnley Borough Council* [1978] AC 904, even delay plus hardship to the tenants would not disentitle the landlord to exercise the right which he has on the true construction of the contract unless the combination amounted to an estoppel. In my judgment, the contractual right continues to exist unless and until it is abrogated by mutual agreement or the contract is discharged by breach or, to adopt the example of Lord Diplock in the *United Scientific* case, by the obligor being substantially deprived of the whole benefit that it was intended that he should have (which I take to be a reference, in effect, to frustration or failure of consideration and which I cannot envisage as arising in this sort of case). Apart from these circumstances, the only way in which I can envisage the landlord as being precluded from relying upon the clause is by an estoppel . . .

Finally, I should add that I am not, for my part, persuaded that in fact the instant case is one where 'unreasonable' delay has occurred. The expression 'unreasonable delay' does, I think, require some definition. It must, I think, mean something more than 'prolonged delay' and it may, I suppose, be used to express the notion either of delay for which no acceptable reason can be advanced or delay which no reasonable man would incur acting in his own interest. But if this is its meaning then the absence of reason has no necessary relation to duration. If on the other hand, as I suspect, the phrase is used to describe such delay as it would not in the circumstances be reasonable to expect the other party to put up with, then it seems to me that it contains within it, by necessary implication, the notion of hardship or prejudice, for how otherwise is the other party harmed by it?

In the instant case certainly no prejudice is shown nor does it seem to me that there has been any substantial delay which is not perfectly rationally accounted for. The landlord's solicitors tried to rectify their omission within a month of the contract date and they can hardly be blamed, in the state of the law as it then stood, for not pursuing the matter further prior to 1978. If, thereafter, they had appreciated that their original letter did not, in fact, comply with the lease not only as to date but in point of form also, they could, no doubt, have issued a fresh notice before issuing the first originating summons, so that all matters could be dealt with in one set of proceedings. That they did not do so may be unfortunate, but it has been extremely beneficial to the tenants who got a further uncovenanted reprieve; but I cannot, speaking for myself, regard their failure to do so as 'unreasonable.'. . .

18.2   Repairs

18.2.1   LIABILITY TO REPAIR – GENERAL

BARRETT v *LOUNOVA (1982) LTD* [1990] 1 QB 348, Court of Appeal

FACTS: In a lease of a dwelling house the tenant had covenanted to carry out all the internal repairs on the premises. The question was, 'who should be responsible for carrying out the external repairs?'
HELD: In order to 'give business efficacy to the agreement', there was an implied obligation on the landlord to do the external repairs.

KERR LJ: . . . I turn to the issue whether or not there is to be implied a term to the effect that the landlord was bound to keep the outside in reasonable repair, as the recorder decided.
   In that regard it is common ground that he directed himself correctly when he said:

> Clearly on the authorities the law does not permit the court to imply terms merely on the basis that implication would seem to be reasonable or fair. In essence, what is required before such implication is made is either a situation where the parties to the agreement, if asked about the suggested implied term would have said words such as 'Oh yes, of course we both agree. Is there any need to mention it?;' or where it is not merely desirable but necessary to imply such a term to give business efficacy or in other words necessary to make the contract workable, which amounts to the same thing.

Those two ways of putting the test as to whether or not a term should be implied, sometimes referred to as 'the officious bystander test' and the 'business efficacy test,' are of course correct.
   But whether or not, on applying those tests, the implication falls to be made is not easy, and the authorities are of no direct assistance . . . on the basis that an obligation to keep the outside in a proper state of repair must be imposed on someone, three answers are possible.
   First, that the tenant is obliged to keep the outside in repair as well as the inside, at any rate to such extent as may be necessary to enable him to perform his covenant. I would reject that as being unbusinesslike and unrealistic. In the case of a tenancy of this nature, which was to become a monthly tenancy after one year, the rent being paid weekly, it is clearly unrealistic to conclude that this could have been the common intention. In that context it is to be noted that in *Warren* v *Keen* [1954] 1 QB 15, this court held that a weekly tenant was under no implied obligation to do any repairs to the structure of the premises due to wear and tear or lapse of time or otherwise, and that it was doubtful whether he was even obliged to ensure that the premises remained wind and watertight. Any construction which casts upon the tenant the obligation to keep the outside in proper repair must in my view be rejected for these reasons; and also because there is an express tenant's covenant relating to the inside, so that it would be wrong, as a matter of elementary construction, to imply a covenant relating to the outside as well.
   The second solution would be the implication of a joint obligation on both parties to keep the outside in good repair. I reject that as being obviously unworkable and I do not think that Mr Pryor really suggested the contrary.
   That leaves one with the third solution, an implied obligation on the landlord. In my view this is the only solution which makes business sense. The recorder reached the same conclusion by following much the same route, and I agree with him.
   Accordingly I would dismiss this appeal.

18.2.2   THE LANDLORD AND TENANT ACT 1985

LANDLORD AND TENANT ACT 1985

8.   Implied terms as to fitness for human habitation
   (1)   In a contract to which this section applies for the letting of a house for human habitation there is implied, notwithstanding any stipulation to the contrary—

(a)   a condition that the house is fit for human habitation at the commencement of the tenancy, and

(b)   an undertaking that the house will be kept by the landlord fit for human habitation during the tenancy.

(2)   The landlord or person authorised by him in writing, may at reasonable times of the day, on giving 24 hours' notice in writing to the tenant or occupier, enter premises to which this section applies for the purpose of viewing their state and condition.

(3)   This section applies to a contract if—

(a)   the rent does not exceed the figure applicable in accordance with subsection (4), and

(b)   the letting is not on such terms as to the tenant's responsibility as are mentioned in subsection (5).

(4)   . . .

(5)   This section does not apply where a house is let for a term of three years or more (the lease not being determinable at the option of either party before the expiration of three years) upon terms that the tenant puts the premises into a condition reasonably fit for human habitation.

(6)   In this section 'house' includes—

(a)   a part of a house, and

(b)   any yard, garden, outhouses and appurtenances belonging to the house or usually enjoyed with it.

10.   Fitness for human habitation

In determining for the purposes of this Act whether a house is unfit for human habitation, regard shall be had to its condition in respect of the following matters—

repair,

stability,

freedom from damp,

internal arrangement,

natural lighting,

ventilation,

drainage and sanitary conveniences,

facilities for preparation and cooking of food and for the disposal of waste water;

and the house shall be regarded as unfit for human habitation if, and only if, it is so far defective in one or more of those matters that it is not reasonably suitable for occupation in that condition.

11.   Repairing obligations in short leases

(1)   In a lease to which this section applies (as to which, see sections 13 and 14) there is implied a covenant by the lessor—

(a)   to keep in repair the structure and exterior of the dwelling-house (including drains, gutters and external pipes),

(b)   to keep in repair and proper working order the installations in the dwelling-house for the supply of water, gas and electricity and for sanitation (including basins, sinks, baths and sanitary conveniences, but not other fixtures, fittings and appliances for making use of the supply of water, gas or electricity), and

(c)   to keep in repair and proper working order the installations in the dwelling-house for space heating and heating water.

(1A)   If a lease to which this section applies is a lease of a dwelling-house which forms part only of a building, then, subject to subsection (1B), the covenant implied by subsection (1) shall have effect as if—

(a)   the reference in paragraph (a) of that subsection to the dwelling-house included a reference to any part of the building in which the lessor has an estate or interest; and

(b)   any reference in paragraphs (b) and (c) of that subsection to an installation in the dwelling-house included a reference to an installation which, directly or indirectly, serves the dwelling-house and which either—

(i)   forms part of any part of a building in which the lessor has an estate or interest; or

(ii)   is owned by the lessor or under his control.

(1B)   Nothing in subsection (1A) shall be construed as requiring the lessor to carry out any works or repairs unless the disrepair (or failure to maintain in working order) is such as to affect the lessee's enjoyment of the dwelling-house or of any common parts, as defined in section 60(1) of the Landlord and Tenant Act 1987, which the lessee, as such, is entitled to use.

(2)   The covenant implied by subsection (1) ('the lessor's repairing covenant') shall not be construed as requiring the lessor—

(a)   to carry out works or repairs for which the lessee is liable by virtue of his duty to use the premises in a tenant-like manner, or would be so liable but for an express covenant on his part,

(b)   to rebuild or reinstate the premises in the case of destruction or damage by fire, or by tempest, flood or other inevitable accident, or

(c)   to keep in repair or maintain anything which the lessee is entitled to remove from the dwelling-house.

(3)   In determining the standard of repair required by the lessor's repairing covenant, regard shall be had to the age, character and prospective life of the dwelling-house and the locality in which it is situated.

(3A)   In any case where—

(a)   the lessor's repairing covenant has effect as mentioned in subsection (1A), and

(b)   in order to comply with the covenant the lessor needs to carry out works or repairs otherwise than in, or to an installation in, the dwelling-house, and

(c)   the lessor does not have a sufficient right in the part of the building or the installation concerned to enable him to carry out the required works or repairs,

then, in any proceedings relating to a failure to comply with the lessor's repairing covenant, so far as it requires the lessor to carry out the works or repairs in question, it shall be a defence for the lessor to prove that he used all reasonable endeavours to obtain, but was unable to obtain, such rights as would be adequate to enable him to carry out the works or repairs.

(4)   A covenant by the lessee for the repair of the premises is of no effect so far as it relates to the matters mentioned in subsection (1)(a) to (c), except so far as it imposes on the lessee any of the requirements mentioned in subsection (2)(a) or (c).

(5)   The reference in subsection (4) to a covenant by the lessee for the repair of the premises includes a covenant—

(a)   to put in repair or deliver up in repair,

(b)   to paint, point or render,

(c)   to pay money in lieu of repairs by the lessee, or

(d)   to pay money on account of repairs by the lessor.

(6)   In a lease in which the lessor's repairing covenant is implied there is also implied a covenant by the lessee that the lessor, or any person authorised by him in writing, may at reasonable times of the day and on giving 24 hours' notice in writing to the occupier, enter the premises comprised in the lease for the purpose of viewing their condition and state of repair.

12.   Restriction on contracting out of s. 11

(1)   A covenant or agreement, whether contained in a lease to which section 11 applies or in an agreement collateral to such a lease, is void in so far as it purports—

(a)   to exclude or limit the obligations of the lessor or the immunities of the lessee under that section, or

(b)   to authorise any forfeiture or impose on the lessee any penalty, disability or obligation in the event of his enforcing or relying upon those obligations or immunities, unless the inclusion of the provision was authorised by the county court.

(2)   The county court may, by order made with the consent of the parties, authorise the inclusion in a lease, or in an agreement collateral to a lease, of provisions excluding or modifying in relation to the lease, the provisions of section 11 with respect to the repairing obligations of the parties if it appears to the court that it is reasonable to do so, having regard to all the circumstances of the case, including the other terms and conditions of the lease.

13.   Leases to which s. 11 applies: general rule

(1)   Section 11 (repairing obligations) applies to a lease of a dwelling-house granted on or after 24th October 1961 for a term of less than seven years.

(2)   In determining whether a lease is one to which section 11 applies—

(a)   any part of the term which falls before the grant shall be left out of account and the lease shall be treated as a lease for a term commencing with the grant,

(b)   a lease which is determinable at the option of the lessor before the expiration of seven years from the commencement of the term shall be treated as a lease for a term of less than seven years, and

(c)   a lease (other than a lease to which paragraph (b) applies) shall not be treated as a lease for a term of less than seven years if it confers on the lessee an option for renewal for a term which, together with the original term, amounts to seven years or more.

(3)   This section has effect subject to—

section 14 (leases to which section 11 applies: exceptions), and

section 32(2) (provisions not applying to tenancies within Part II of the Landlord and Tenant Act 1954).

14.   Leases to which s. 11 applies: exceptions

(1)   Section 11 (repairing obligations) does not apply to a new lease granted to an existing tenant, or to a former tenant still in possession, if the previous lease was not a lease to which section 11 applied (and, in the case of a lease granted before 24th October 1961, would not have been if it had been granted on or after that date).

(2)   In subsection (1)—

'existing tenant' means a person who is when, or immediately before, the new lease is granted, the lessee under another lease of the dwelling-house;

'former tenant still in possession' means a person who—

(a)   was the lessee under another lease of the dwelling-house which terminated at some time before the new lease was granted, and

(b)   between the termination of that other lease and the grant of the new lease was continuously in possession of the dwelling-house or of the rents and profits of the dwelling-house; and

'the previous lease' means the other lease referred to in the above definitions.

(3)   Section 11 does not apply to a lease of a dwelling-house which is a tenancy of an agricultural holding within the meaning of the Agricultural Holdings Act 1986.

(4)   Section 11 does not apply to a lease granted on or after 3rd October 1980 to—

a local authority,

a new town corporation,

an urban development corporation,

the Development Board for Rural Wales,

a registered housing association,

a co-operative housing association, or

an educational institution or other body specified, or of a class specified, by regulations under section 8 of the Rent Act 1977 (bodies making student lettings)

a housing action trust established under Part III of the Housing Act 1988.

(5)   Section 11 does not apply to a lease granted on or after 3rd October 1980 to—

(a)   Her Majesty in right of the Crown (unless the lease is under the management of the Crown Estate Commissioners), or

(b)   a government department or a person holding in trust for Her Majesty for the purposes of a government department.

QUICK v TAFF ELY BOROUGH COUNCIL [1986] 1 QB 809, Court of Appeal

FACTS: The plaintiff was tenant of a council house. Condensation, created by the type of windows in the house, caused woodwork, furniture and clothes to rot. The tenant brought proceedings for an order of specific performance of the landlord's obligation to repair the 'structure and exterior' of the premises.

HELD: The council was not liable. Evidence of lack of amenity was not evidence of a need for repair.

DILLON LJ: . . . In my judgment, the key factor in the present case is that disrepair is related to the physical condition of whatever has to be repaired, and not to questions of lack of amenity or inefficiency. I find helpful the observation of Atkin LJ in *Anstruther-Gough-*

Calthorpe v *McOscar* [1924] 1 KB 716, 734 that repair 'connotes the idea of making good damage so as to leave the subject so far as possible as though it had not been damaged.' Where decorative repair is in question one must look for damage to the decorations but where, as here, the obligation is merely to keep the structure and exterior of the house in repair, the covenant will only come into operation where there has been damage to the structure and exterior which requires to be made good.

If there is such damage caused by an unsuspected inherent defect, then it may be necessary to cure the defect, and thus to some extent improve without wholly renewing the property as the only practicable way of making good the damage to the subject matter of the repairing covenant. That, as I read the case, was the basis of the decision in *Ravenseft* v *Davstone Ltd* [1980] QB 12. There there was an inherent defect when the building, a relatively new one, was built in that no expansion joints had been included because it had not been realised that the different coefficients of expansion of the stone of the cladding and the concrete of the structure made it necessary to include such joints. There was, however, also physical damage to the subject matter of the covenant in that, because of the differing coefficients of expansion, the stones of the cladding had become bowed, detached from the structure, loose and in danger of falling. Forbes J in a very valuable judgment rejected the argument that no liability arose under a repairing covenant if it could be shown that the disrepair was due to an inherent defect in the building. He allowed in the damages under the repairing covenant the cost of putting in expansion joints, and in that respect improving the building, because, as he put it, at p. 22, on the evidence 'In no realistic sense . . . could it be said that there was any other possible way of reinstating this cladding than by providing the expansion joints which were, in fact, provided.'. . .

In the present case the liability of the council was to keep the structure and exterior of the house in repair—not the decorations. Though there is ample evidence of damage to the decorations and to bedding, clothing and other fabrics, evidence of damage to the subject matter of the covenant, the structure and exterior of the house, is far to seek. Though the condensation comes about from the effect of the warm atmosphere in the rooms on the cold surfaces of the walls and windows, there is no evidence at all of physical damage to the walls—as opposed to the decorations—or the windows. . . .

LAWTON LJ: It is with regret that I have decided that this appeal on the points taken in this court by the defendant council must be allowed. The case will have to be remitted to the county court for Judge Francis to reassess the damages, if they cannot be agreed, as I hope they will be.

When I read the papers in this case I was surprised to find that the plaintiff had not based his claim on an allegation that at all material times the house let to him by the council had not been fit for human habitation. The uncontradicted evidence, accepted by the trial judge, showed that furniture, furnishings and clothes had rotted because of damp and the sitting room could not be used because of the smell of damp.

18.2.3 THE CRUCIAL PRINCIPLE IN *O'BRIEN* v *ROBINSON*

O'BRIEN AND ANOTHER v *ROBINSON* [1973] AC 912, House of Lords

FACTS: A tenant and his wife were injured when the ceiling of their flat suddenly and unexpectedly caved in upon them. Some years ago the tenants of the flat above had caused violent vibrations of the ceiling by prolonged 'dancing' and 'banging on the floors'. The tenant sued the landlord for damages for personal injuries.
HELD: The landlord's liability to repair did not arise until latent defects had become apparent and their existence made known to him. On that basis the landlord in the present case was not liable.

LORD MORRIS OF BORTH-Y-GEST: . . . In the case of *Morgan* v *Liverpool Corporation* [1927] 2 KB 131 one basis of claim was that there had been a failure to perform the statutory undertaking that the house would be 'kept in all respects reasonably fit for human habitation.' As I have shown, there was at that date a statutory right in a landlord to enter for the purposes of inspection. The accident which gave rise to the claim was that when the upper portion of a window was being opened one of the cords of the window sash broke with the result that the top part of the window slipped down and caught and injured the plaintiff's hand. In the argument on behalf of the plaintiff in the Court of Appeal it was admitted that the defect was a latent one (of which the plaintiff did not know and about which accordingly he could not give any notice) but it was contended that there was a statutory obligation on the landlord which was different from that contained in an ordinary covenant and that in the Act (Housing Act 1925), there were no words requiring that any notice should be given to the landlord. Furthermore, reliance was placed on the statutory right of the landlord to enter and inspect. Apart from any such statutory right the facts of the case showed that there was a notice posted up in the house containing certain conditions which included a reservation by the landlord of the right of entering the house at any time without previous notice in order to view the state of repair. The Court of Appeal held that the landlord was not liable and that any liability was conditional upon his having been given notice of any defects even though they were latent ones and that this result was not affected by the fact that the landlord had a right to enter in order to inspect. There were divisions of opinion on certain points which arose: in particular on the point whether by reason of the breaking of the sash cord the particular dwelling (which was most limited in size) was rendered unfit for human habitation. But all three Lords Justices were of the opinion that the claim failed because the landlord did not have notice and because in such a case as that under consideration notice was required before the liability of the landlord to repair existed. Lord Hanworth MR said (at p. 141) that it had 'long been established law that where there is a covenant on the part of a landlord to keep the premises in repair, the tenant must give notice to the landlord of what is out of repair . . .' He held that notice was required whether or not the landlord had means of access: he said that the fact that the origin of a covenant was statutory did not give the covenant any higher authority than one inserted in a contract by the parties. Atkin LJ said that in ordinary circumstances the obligation of a landlord to do repairs does not come into existence until he has had notice of the defect which his contract to repair requires him to make good. He said, at p. 151:

> I think the power of access that is given, extensive though it may be, does not take the case away from the principle from which the courts have inferred the condition that the liability is not to arise except on notice. The position is quite a satisfactory one, because as soon as the tenant is aware of the defect he must then give notice, and if the landlord does not repair it, the landlord will be liable. If in fact the tenant is not able to ascertain the defect, there seems to be no reason why the landlord should be exposed to what remains still the same injustice of being required to repair a defect of which he does not know, which seems to me to be the real reason for the rule. This was a case in which notice was not given to the landlord. As I have said, it appears to me that, as soon as the defect became so known by the fall of the sash, the tenant was able to give notice to the landlord and did give notice. In my view the landlord then became under a liability to repair in the circumstances of this case, because if he did not, the house would be in a state not in all respects fit for human habitation; but as no notice was given, I think the landlord was not liable. . . .

LORD DIPLOCK: . . . this appeal must fail unless the tenant can show that before the ceiling fell the landlord had information about the existence of a defect in the ceiling such as would put him on inquiry as to whether works of repair to it were needed. . . .

BRITISH TELECOMMUNICATIONS PLC v SUN LIFE ASSURANCE SOCIETY PLC
[1995] 4 All ER 44, Court of Appeal

FACTS: The plaintiff company was the tenant of premises on the sixth and seventh floors of a building under a lease which required the defendant company, as landlord, to keep the building as a whole, and not merely the demised premises, in 'complete good and substantial repair and condition'. In the summer of 1986 a bulge appeared in the brick cladding forming part of the external walls and main structure of the building at fifth floor level. On 1 September 1986 the landlord was informed of the disrepair, which was caused by the fact that the external cladding had been badly fixed to the inner wall. The landlord immediately erected scaffolding and temporary protection and took steps preparatory to carrying out the necessary remedial work, which began in February 1988. In the meantime the tenant brought proceedings against the landlord, claiming damages for breach of its repairing covenant which, the tenant contended, occurred immediately the bulge in the cladding appeared. The judge ruled, on a preliminary issue of construction, that the landlord was in breach of its covenant to keep the other parts of the building in which the demised premises were situated in repair immediately they ceased to be in repair. The landlord appealed, contending that the breach, if any, occurred only on the expiration of a reasonable period for doing the repairs following the appearance of the defect.

HELD: A covenant in a lease to keep the demised premises in 'complete good and substantial repair and condition' which extended to the building as a whole obliged the landlord to keep the other parts of the building in which the demised premises were situated in repair at all times so that there was a breach of the repairing obligation immediately a defect occurred. The landlord was therefore in breach of covenant as soon as the property ceased to be in a state of repair and not at the later time when he had information about the existence of the defect and had failed to carry out the necessary works with reasonable expedition, since that exception to the general rule only applied where the defect occurred in the demised premises themselves and not where it occurred in a part of the premises not demised to the tenant.

NOURSE LJ: . . . It is now established by a line of authority culminating in the decision of the House of Lords in *O'Brien* v *Robinson* [1973] AC 912 that, where a defect occurs in the demised premises themselves, a landlord is in breach of his obligation to keep them in repair only when he has information about the existence of the defect such as would put a reasonable landlord on inquiry as to whether works of repair to it are needed and he has failed to carry out the necessary works with reasonable expedition thereafter (see [1973] AC 912 at 928, 930 per Lord Diplock). It has come as something of a surprise to me to learn that there is no decision of comparable authority governing the case where the defect occurs in premises not comprised in the demised premises themselves.

The basic submission of Mr Reynolds QC, for the defendant, is that to such a case the rule established by *O'Brien* v *Robinson* applies by analogy. He accepts that, since the premises affected by the defect are either in his possession or under his control, the landlord must be treated as having the necessary knowledge of it. But he submits that the landlord is in breach of his obligation to keep the premises in repair only when the defect occurs and he has failed to carry out the necessary repairs with reasonable expedition thereafter. In support of these submissions Mr Reynolds referred us at some length to the judgments in the Court of Appeal in Ireland in *Murphy* v *Hurly* [1921] 2 IR 335 and the speeches in the House of Lords (see [1922] 1 AC 369), but I did not find those references to be of any significant assistance.

For a reason which will appear in due course, I was for much of the argument inclined to the view that Mr Reynolds' submissions were, or at all events ought to be, correct. But a consideration of the authorities on which the rule established by *O'Brien* v *Robinson* is founded has satisfied me that it is in truth an exception from the general rule and, moreover, one which proves it. . . .

. . . The general rule is that a covenant to keep premises in repair obliges the covenantor to keep them in repair at all times, so that there is a breach of the obligation immediately a defect occurs. There is an exception where the obligation is the landlord's and the defect occurs in the demised premises themselves, in which case he is in breach of his obligation only when he has information about the existence of the defect such as would put a reasonable landlord on inquiry as to whether works of repair are needed and he has failed to carry out the necessary works with reasonable expedition thereafter.

I desire to make two further points. First, I express no concluded view as to the case where a defect is caused by an occurrence wholly outside the landlord's control. Suppose, for example, that the roof of the house in *Melles & Co.* v *Holme* [1918] 2 KB 100 had been damaged by a branch from a tree standing on neighbouring property not in the possession or control of the landlords and that the rainwater had found its way down into the plaintiff's rooms by that means. The stance adopted by Mr Gaunt QC, for the plaintiff, was that such a case would be covered by the general rule, and it was that which caused me to start by thinking that Mr Reynolds' submissions ought to be correct. On reflection and provisionally, I can see no reason why such a case should not, for reasons similar to those expressed in *Makin v Watkinson* (1870) LR 6 Exch 25, be made the subject of a further exception to the general rule. That point will have to be decided if and when it arises for decision.

Secondly, Mr Gaunt was disposed to accept that the position might be different in a case where the landlord's obligation was not to keep the premises in repair, but simply to repair them. Having confined myself to the former obligation, I say nothing about the latter, which is in any event, as I believe, a rarity in modern leases and tenancy agreements.

I would dismiss this appeal.

HEATH v DROWN [1973] AC 498, House of Lords

FACTS: It became necessary to execute extensive repairs to business premises occupied by a tenant. Accordingly, the landlord sought re-possession of the premises in order to carry out the repairs.

HELD: Temporary re-possession by the landlord was consistent with the continuing existence of the tenant's lease, but extensive repairs, necessitating long-term re-possession was not. Accordingly, although the tenant might ordinarily be entitled to a statutory renewal of the lease at the end of the term, such renewal would not be granted in the present case. The landlord was granted absolute possession.

LORD REID: In my view, the crucial findings are that the work would take at least four months, that during that time it would not be reasonably possible for the appellant to carry on her business—an employment agency—in the premises, that whatever terms might be put in the new lease there were likely to be disputes which would frustrate the respondent's operations and that therefore he needs exclusive possession. The clear meaning is, I think, that the only reasonable course is that the tenant shall have no right to enter the premises while the work is in progress: it is not enough that the respondent shall have access, he must also be enabled to exclude the appellant. . . .

I do not profess to be an expert in the English law of real property and this matter was not fully argued. But I understand that the granting of a new lease would necessarily imply that the tenant is given legal possession from its commencement and throughout its duration. But it is found as a fact that the landlord needs exclusive physical possession for a period of at least four months. So far as I know it would be a novelty to provide in a lease that during so long a period the tenant, although liable for the full rent, shall have no right even to enter the demised premises. I do not see in what sense the tenant could during that period be said to have legal possession. . . .

I would therefore dismiss this appeal.

18.2.4   MEANING OF EXPRESS COVENANTS TO REPAIR

ANSTRUTHER-GOUGH-CALTHORPE v McOSCAR AND ANOTHER
[1924] 1 KB 716, Court of Appeal

FACTS: A 95 year lease was granted in 1825 of three houses. They were built in 1825, in a very pleasant position on the then edge of the built-up area of London. By the time the lease expired in 1920 the area (in the vicinity of King's Cross station) had become very 'run down'. The landlord brought an action against the tenant for breaking the covenant to repair.

HELD: The tenant should have maintained the property to the 1825 standard.

SCRUTTON LJ: . . . The question in dispute seems to be whether, as the purposes for which such a subject matter is ordinarily used may vary from time to time, the standard of repair is to vary from time to time, or remains as it was when the subject matter was demised. For instance, where a fashionable mansion let for a long term of years has fallen to the position of a tenement house for the poorer classes, is the standard of repair to become less onerous than when the house is let? To take an illustration of Bankes LJ, if the sub-tenants of a tenement house do not want a front door, is the tenant to be excused from keeping a properly repaired front door on the premises?

In my view this question has been decided, as far as this Court is concerned, by the decision in *Morgan* v *Hardy* (1886) 17 QBD 770. In that case the referee had to decide between the claim that the premises must be properly repaired and the contention that, as the premises and the neighbourhood had deteriorated, and in consequence of such deterioration a great portion of the repairs required 'were not suited to the said premises and were unnecessary for their use and enjoyment', they need not be considered in awarding damages. This Court, affirming Denman J, said very summarily that it was a wholly untenable proposition to say that the depreciation of the neighbourhood ought to lower the amount of damages for breach of a covenant to repair. This can only mean that the fact that the class of persons who would use the house at the end of the term had deteriorated, so that their requirements in the way of repairs were less, was immaterial in ascertaining the repairs that the tenant was bound to execute. *Morgan* v *Hardy* was the case of a fifty years' lease.

In *Proudfoot* v *Hart* (1890) 25 QBD 42 the lease was for three years only, and the covenant was to keep in good tenantable repair. There was no suggestion of any change in character of the house or its probable tenants between the beginning and the end of the term. Lopes LJ framed a definition which Lord Esher adopted as follows: 'Such repair, as having regard to the age, character, and locality of the house, would make it reasonably fit for the occupation of a reasonably minded tenant of the class who would be likely to take it.' I do not think there was any intention of suggesting that a deterioration in the class of tenants would lower the standard of repairs; the point was not before the Court, and had been decided the other way by the Court four years previously. Therefore in my view we are bound to look to the character of the house and its ordinary uses at the time of the demise. It must then be put in repair and kept in repair. An improvement of its tenants or its neighbourhood will not increase the standard of repair, nor will their deterioration lower that standard. . . .

18.2.5   THE REPAIR/RECONSTRUCTION DISTINCTION

RAVENSEFT PROPERTIES LTD v *DAVSTONE (HOLDINGS) LTD*
[1979] 2 WLR 897, Queen's Bench Division

FACTS: Stone-cladding on a concrete block of flats began to bow away from the wall. In order to address the risk of stones falling, the landlord made full repairs. The tenant, a property development company, had covenanted to be liable for repairs and so the landlord company brought the present action to recover the cost of the works it had carried out.
HELD: It was a question of degree whether the works carried out by the landlord were properly to be described as 'repairs' or 'improvements'. On these facts the works were to be regarded as repairs, because at the end of the lease the tenant would return to the landlord substantially the same building that the landlord had originally leased out. Accordingly, the tenant would be liable to re-imburse the landlord's costs of repair.

FORBES J: . . . it is always a question of degree whether that which the tenant is being asked to do can properly be described as repair, or whether on the contrary it would involve giving back to the landlord a wholly different thing from that which he demised.

In deciding this question, the proportion which the cost of the disputed work bears to the value or cost of the whole premises, may sometimes be helpful as a guide. In this case the figures have not been finally worked out in complete detail. I have, however, the evidence of Mr Clark, the contracts manager for the Stone Firms Ltd, the contractors who actually carried out the work. He was not himself responsible for any of the work as he joined that company after the work was completed. He is, however, familiar with that company's methods of charging and so on, and he has studied the drawings and the analysed quotations produced by the company. From these he has been able to give me, not a detailed and accurate costing, but a reliable, broad, estimate of the cost of that part of the remedial work relating solely to the insertion of expansion joints. It is, as he said, an indication of the order of magnitude of the cost. Although cross-examined by Mr Colyer, no rebutting evidence was called and I accept Mr Clark's estimate that the cost would have been in the region of £5,000. The total cost of the remedial works was around £55,000, the balance of £50,000 being for re-fixing the stones and other ancillary works which was not, as I find, necessary to cure any defect of design, but to remedy what was originally defective workmanship. For comparison, the cost of building a structure of this kind in 1973 would have been in the region of £3 million, or rather more. I find myself wholly unable to accept that the cost of inserting these joints could possibly be regarded as a substantial part of the cost of the repairs, much less a substantial part of the value or cost of the building. Mr Colyer urges me not to consider cost and that may, perhaps, in some circumstances, be right. He argues that the result of carrying out this improvement is to give back to the landlord a safe building instead of a dangerous one and this means the premises now are of a wholly different character. Further, he argues that because they are of a wholly different character, the work on expansion joints, the work necessary to cure the inherent defect, is an improvement of a character which transforms the nature of the premises demised, and, therefore, cannot fall within the ambit of the covenant to repair. I cannot accept this. The expansion joints form but a trivial part of this whole building and looking at it as a question of degree, I do not consider that they amount to such a change in the character of the building as to take them out of the ambit of the covenant to repair.

I pass to Mr Colyer's second point, namely, that the tenant is not liable under the repair covenant for that part of any work of repair necessary to remedy an inherent defect. Again it seems to me that this must be a question of degree. . . .

LURCOTT v WAKELY & WHEELER [1911] 1 KB 905, Court of Appeal

FACTS: The tenant had covenanted to keep the premises in thorough repair and good condition. Shortly before the end of the term the local council condemned one wall of the house as dangerous and served notice on the landlord to demolish and replace it. Having done so, the landlord sought to recover the costs from the tenant.
HELD: The tenant was liable under the covenant to repair to reimburse the landlord.

COZENS-HARDY MR: . . . It was [in *Lister* v *Lane* [1893] 2 QB 212] held by the Court of Appeal, and I see no reason to quarrel with their decision, that the change of circumstances which had arisen could not have been in the contemplation of the parties and that it would not be reasonable to construe the covenant to repair as applicable to that change of circumstances. But then when I come to what I should have thought was everyday experience in cases of this kind, when I come to consider what is to happen when by reason of the elements acting on an old building, say, a chimney stack is blown down, is it possible for the tenant to say he is not liable to put that up because the collapse was due merely to age and the elements? I am astonished to hear that such a contention can be raised. So, if a tenant under a repairing lease finds that a floor has become so rotten that it cannot be patched up, that it is in such a condition that it cannot bear the weight of human beings or of furniture upon it, can it be said that the tenant is exempt from the liability of replacing that floor, and repairing it in the only way in which it can be repaired in order to make the house habitable, merely because the state of the floor is due to time and the elements? I am entirely unable to follow that argument. *Proudfoot* v *Hart* (1890) 25 QBD 42 seems to lay down a perfectly sound and intelligible proposition on this point, namely, that in such a case it is the duty of the tenant, if he cannot patch up the floor so as to make it a floor, to replace that which is no longer a floor by something which is a floor. . .

18.2.6   REMEDIES FOR BREACH OF LANDLORD'S EXPRESS COVENANTS TO REPAIR

18.2.6.1   No rent-strikes, *but . . .*

LEE-PARKER AND ANOTHER v IZZET AND OTHERS
[1971] 1 WLR 1688, Chancery Division

FACTS: Tenants, having executed certain repairs on their own account, sought to withhold rent to cover the cost they had incurred. The landlord should have carried out the repairs himself.

HELD: The tenants could withhold rent to cover the repairs. This was not by way of lien or set-off, but was an ancient common law right. The tenants would not have been able to withhold rent had they not executed the repairs themselves at their own cost.

GOFF J: . . . the third and fourth defendants further claim a lien for the cost of the repairs or alternatively for the value of any permanent improvement effected thereby, and they also claim a set off against rent in their capacity as tenants.

First, they say that in so far as the first defendant was, as landlord, liable to do the repairs by the express or implied terms of the tenancy agreement, including the covenants imported by section 32(1) of the Housing Act 1961, they, having done them themselves, are entitled to treat the expenditure as a payment of rent, for which reliance is placed on *Taylor v Beal* (1591) Cro Eliz 222. That is dicta only and the actual decision must have been the other way, because one of the majority in opinion thought the point was not open on the pleadings. However, *Woodfall's Landlord and Tenant* says the case—that is, the *dicta*—would still seem to be the law: see 27th edn. (1968), vol. 1, p. 655 para. 1490. The case is dealt with in *Foa's General Law of Landlord & Tenant*, 8th edn. (1957), on the question of distress only, at p. 559, citing also *Davies v Stacey* (1840) 12 Ad & El 506, where the point was left open. *Foa* states, at p. 559:

> Where the lessor covenants to repair and neglects to do so, and the repairs are thereupon executed by the lessee, a payment made by the lessee for the cost of such repairs is not (it is submitted) equivalent to payment of rent so as to reduce the amount for which the landlord may distrain.

. . . I do not think this is bound up with technical rules of set off. It is an ancient common law right. I therefore declare that so far as the repairs are within the express or implied covenants of the landlord, the third and fourth defendants are entitled to recoup themselves out of future rents and defend any action for payment thereof. It does not follow however that the full amount expended by the third and fourth defendants on such repairs can properly be treated as payment of rent. It is a question of fact in every case whether and to what extent the expenditure was proper. . . .

18.2.6.2 Specific performance for breach of a repairing obligation

JEUNE v QUEENS CROSS PROPERTIES LTD [1973] 3 All ER 97, Chancery Division

FACTS: The plaintiff tenants sought an order that the defendant landlord should reinstate a York Stone balcony which had partially collapsed at the front of their house in Westbourne Terrace, London, W2.
HELD: The Court made an order for specific performance of the landlord's repairing covenant because the landlord was plainly in breach of the covenant and there was no doubt as to what precisely was required to be done to remedy the breach.

PENNYCUICK V-C: . . . the principle that a landlord cannot obtain against his tenant an order for specific performance of a covenant to repair . . . does not . . . apply to a landlord's covenant to repair, although it is said there may be some other explanation for the words, 'The difficulty upon this doctrine of a Court of Equity is, that there is no mutuality in it.'

Counsel for the plaintiff has looked through various textbooks on the law of landlord and tenant and assures me that, although *Hill v Barclay* (1810) 16 Ves 402 is repeatedly cited, there is no other authority in point. It is worthwhile to refer to two passages in Halsbury's Laws of England. In the landlord and tenant volume it is stated:

> Unless the lease contains a proviso empowering the landlord to re-enter for forfeiture on breach of the covenant to repair, the landlord's remedy is an action for damages; for specific performance of such a covenant will not ordinarily be granted.

Reference is made there to *Hill v Barclay*. In the specific performance volume there is this passage: 'In particular, the court does not, as a rule, order the specific performance of a contract to build or repair.' It then goes on to refer to the circumstances in which specific performance of a contract to build will be granted.

There is nothing at all there inconsistent with a power in the court to make an order on a landlord to do specific work under a covenant to repair. I cannot myself see any reason in principle why, in an appropriate case, an order should not be made against a landlord to do some specific work pursuant to his covenant to repair. Obviously, it is a jurisdiction which should be carefully exercised. But in a case such as the present where there has been a plain breach of a covenant to repair and there is no doubt at all what is required to be done to remedy the breach, I cannot see why an order for specific performance should not be made. . . .

18.2.6.3   Appointing a receiver

SUPREME COURT ACT 1981

37.   Powers of High Court with respect to injunctions and receivers
(1)   The High Court may by order (whether interlocutory or final) grant an injunction or appoint a receiver in all cases in which it appears to the court to be just and convenient to do so.

(2)   Any such order may be made either unconditionally or on such terms and conditions as the court thinks just.

(3)   The power of the High Court under subsection (1) to grant an interlocutory injunction restraining a party to any proceedings from removing from the jurisdiction of the High Court, or otherwise dealing with, assets located within that jurisdiction shall be exercisable in cases where that party is, as well as in cases where he is not, domiciled resident or present within that jurisdiction.

(4)   The power of the High Court to appoint a receiver by way of equitable execution shall operate in relation to all legal estates and interests in land; and that power—
    (a)   may be exercised in relation to an estate or interest in land whether or not a charge has been imposed on that land under section 1 of the Charging Orders Act 1979 for the purpose of enforcing the judgment, order or award in question; and
    (b)   shall be in addition to, and not in derogation of, any power of any court to appoint a receiver in proceedings for enforcing such a charge.

(5)   Where an order under the said section 1 imposing a charge for the purpose of enforcing a judgment, order or award has been, or has effect as if, registered under section 6 of the Land Charges Act 1972, subsection (4) of the said section 6 (effect of non-registration of writs and orders registrable under that section) shall not apply to an order appointing a receiver made either—
    (a)   in proceedings for enforcing the charge; or
    (b)   by way of equitable execution of the judgment, order or award or, as the case may be, of so much of it as requires payment of moneys secured by the charge.

HART v EMELKIRK [1983] 1 WLR 1289, Chancery Division

FACTS: The landlord of two blocks of flats in London had failed to comply with a covenant to repair. The tenants therefore brought an action to force the landlord to carry out the repairs. Pending the hearing of that action, the tenants applied for the appointment of a receiver to 'stand in the landlord's shoes' and collect their rents and meet the landlord's obligations. HELD: The court appointed a receiver as requested.

GOULDING J: . . . The action is brought to obtain a mandatory injunction against the defendant company to comply with the landlord's covenants and also for damages, and counsel for the defendant company tells me that third party proceedings are likely. But what I am asked to do today by the plaintiffs in each of the two actions dealing with adjoining blocks of flats, is to appoint a named surveyor to receive the rents and profits of each property and all other moneys payable under any lease of any part thereof and to manage the property in accordance with the rights and obligations of the reversioner until trial or further order. I am asked to say that the person so appointed may give a good receipt for certain sums of money which one of the plaintiffs in each case has received as representing (or apparently representing) what remains of a reserve fund, intended under the leases to be built up by tenants' contributions, and that the receiver may have to resort to those funds in course of management.

Now, I know of no precedent for such relief but I also know of no authority that forbids it under the provisions of the Judicature Acts now represented by Supreme Court Act 1981. Section 37(1) provides:

> The High Court may by order (whether interlocutory or final) . . . appoint a receiver in all cases in which it appears to the court to be just and convenient to do so.

It clearly appears to me to be just to appoint a receiver in this case because it is done to support the enforcement by the court of covenants affecting property: compare *Riches* v *Owen* (1868) LR 3 Ch App 820. It is also convenient because, as I said, the properties are in a condition that demands urgent action. . .

EVANS v CLAYHOPE PROPERTIES LTD [1987] 1 WLR 225, Chancery Division

FACTS: Tenants of a block of flats brought an action against a landlord, seeking to enforce compliance with the landlord's covenant of repair. Pending the full hearing of the action, the court appointed a receiver to receive the rent and meet the landlord's continuing obligations in respect to the premises. Unfortunately the rents received by the receiver were not sufficient to meet his own remuneration, and the landlord's obligations. The receiver brought the present action to recover his expenses from the landlord.
HELD: The receiver's application was refused. The receiver was an officer appointed by the court and could only be indemnified out of assets under the control of the court. He could not be remunerated out of the landlord's general funds.

VINELOTT J: . . . The question raised in this application is whether, where a receiver has been appointed by the court in circumstances such as those which arose in *Hart* v *Emelkirk Ltd* [1983] 1 WLR 1289 and the receiver incurs expenditure or becomes entitled to remuneration in excess of moneys which he was appointed to receive the court has jurisdiction on an interlocutory application while the litigation is still proceeding to order that the balance of that expenditure or remuneration over the sums available to the receiver should be paid by one of the parties to the action.

. . . The use of the court's power to appoint a receiver to enforce a landlord's obligation to repair property, is a new development which poses many novel questions. They will have to be answered in time. I think that it is undesirable that I should attempt to do more than answer the precise question raised by the application now before me. Mr Heath also submitted that the court could and should extend the receiver's powers so as to authorise him to charge Dover Mansions to raise money for the purpose of meeting his remuneration. That application is made at a late stage. On the basis of the evidence before me, the prospect that moneys could be raised by way of charge is simply chimerical. The income derived from Dover Mansions is very small and as matters stand there is no real prospect that it could be enhanced by letting the unlet flats, whether at rack rents or at a premium, while the block remains in the present state of disrepair. There is, therefore, effectively no security which could be offered to a lender. Whether the court could authorise a receiver appointed in these circumstances to create a charge and meet his own remuneration, so indirectly throwing the burden on the landlord, is again a question which I do not think I should attempt to answer.

The position is a most unfortunate one. It may serve as a reminder of the limitations inherent in the power of the court to appoint a receiver. A receiver should not take office unless he is satisfied that the assets of which he is appointed a receiver will be adequate to meet his remuneration, or that he has an enforceable indemnity by a party to the litigation capable of meeting his remuneration. Moreover, although the appointment of a receiver in order, indirectly, to ensure that property is kept in repair in accordance with covenants to repair entered into by a landlord, is a valuable extension of the power of the court to appoint a receiver for the preservation of property in cases where urgent repairs are necessary, where the landlord is plainly in breach of a covenant to repair and where the income of the property will enable the receiver to remedy the want of repair (in particular where, as in *Hart* v *Emelkirk Ltd* [1983] 1 WLR 1289, a service charge capable of being recovered by the landlord, and capable of being vested in the receiver can be imposed in advance of the carrying out of works of repair to meet their eventual cost) the appointment of a receiver in a case where the income including any service charge, or any other property or money which can be put under the control of the receiver, is patently inadequate to meet the cost of repair, is likely to prove ineffective and may even frustrate the carrying out of repairs that the landlord is willing to carry out. . . .

18.2.6.4   Appointing a receiver manager

The tenants of a privately owned block of residential flats have a right to apply to court for the appointment of a receiver-manager.

LANDLORD AND TENANT ACT 1987

21.   Tenant's right to apply to court for appointment of manager

(1)   The tenant of a flat contained in any premises to which this Part applies may, subject to the following provisions of this Part, apply to *the court* for an order under section 24 appointing a manager to act in relation to those premises.

(2)   Subject to subsection (3), this Part applies to premises consisting of the whole or part of a building if the building or part contains two or more flats.

(3)   This Part does not apply to any such premises at a time when—

(a)   the interest of the landlord in the premises is held by an exempt landlord or a resident landlord, or

(b)   the premises are included within the functional land of any charity.

(4)   An application for an order under section 24 may be made—

(a)   jointly by tenants of two or more flats if they are each entitled to make such an application by virtue of this section, and

(b)   in respect of two or more premises to which this Part applies;
and, in relation to any such joint application as is mentioned in paragraph (a), references in this Part to a single tenant shall be construed accordingly.

(5)   Where the tenancy of a flat contained in any such premises is held by joint tenants, an application for an order under section 24 in respect of those premises may be made by any one or more of those tenants.

(6)   An application to the court for it to exercise in relation to any premises *any jurisdiction existing apart from this Act* to appoint a receiver or manager shall not be made by a tenant (in his capacity as such) in any circumstances in which an application could be made by him for an order under section 24 appointing a manager to act in relation to those premises.

(7)   References in this Part to a tenant do not include references to a tenant under a tenancy to which Part II of the Landlord and Tenant Act 1954 applies.

22.   Preliminary notice by tenant

(1)   Before an application for an order under section 24 is made in respect of any premises to which this Part applies by a tenant of a flat in those premises, a notice under this section must (subject to subsection (3)) be served on the landlord by the tenant.

(2)   A notice under this section must—

(a)   specify the tenant's name, the address of his flat and an address in England and Wales (which may be the address of his flat) at which the landlord may serve notices, including notices in proceedings, on him in connection with this Part;

(b)   state that the tenant intends to make an application for an order under section 24 to be made by *the court* in respect of such premises to which this Part applies as are specified in the notice, but (if paragraph (d) is applicable) that he will not do so if the landlord complies with the requirement specified in pursuance of that paragraph;

(c)   specify the grounds on which *the court* would be asked to make such an order and the matters that would be relied on by the tenant for the purpose of establishing those grounds;

(d)   where those matters are capable of being remedied by the landlord, require the landlord, within such reasonable period as is specified in the notice, to take such steps for the purpose of remedying them as are so specified; and

(e)   contain such information (if any) as the Secretary of State may by regulations prescribe.

(3)   *The court* may (whether on the hearing of an application for an order under section 24 or not) by order dispense with the requirement to serve a notice under this section in a

case where it is satisfied that it would not be reasonably practicable to serve such a notice on the landlord, but *the court* may, when doing so, direct that such other notices are served, or such other steps are taken, as it thinks fit.

(4)   In a case where—

(a)   a notice under this section has been served on the landlord, and

(b)   his interest in the premises specified in pursuance of subsection (2)(b) is subject to a mortgage,

the landlord shall, as soon as is reasonably practicable after receiving the notice, serve on the mortgagee a copy of the notice.

23.   Application to court for appointment of manager

(1)   No application for an order under section 24 shall be made to *the court* unless—

(a)   in a case where a notice has been served under section 22, either—

(i)   the period specified in pursuance of paragraph (d) of subsection (2) of that section has expired without the landlord having taken the steps that he was required to take in pursuance of that provision, or

(ii)   that paragraph was not applicable in the circumstances of the case; or

(b)   in a case where the requirement to serve such a notice has been dispensed with by an order under subsection (3) of that section, either—

(i)   any notices required to be served, and any other steps required to be taken, by virtue of the order have been served or (as the case may be) taken, or

(ii)   no direction was given by *the court* when making the order.

(2)   *Rules of court* shall make provision—

(a)   for requiring notice of an application for an order under section 24 in respect of any premises to be served on such descriptions of persons as may be specified in the *rules*; and

(b)   for enabling persons served with any such notice to be joined as parties to the proceedings.

24.   Appointment of manager by the court

(1)   The court may, on an application for an order under this section, by order (whether interlocutory or final) appoint a manager to carry out in relation to any premises to which this Part applies—

(a)   such functions in connection with the management of the premises, or

(b)   such functions of a receiver,

or both, as the court thinks fit.

(2)   The court may only make an order under this section in the following circumstances, namely—

(a)   where the court is satisfied—

(i)   that the landlord either is in breach of any obligation owed by him to the tenant under his tenancy and relating to the management of the premises in question or any part of them or (in the case of an obligation dependent on notice) would be in breach of any such obligation but for the fact that it has not been reasonably practicable for the tenant to give him the appropriate notice, and

(ii)   that the circumstances by virtue of which he is (or would be) in breach of any such obligation are likely to continue, and

(iii)   that it is just and convenient to make the order in all the circumstances of the case; or

(b)   where the court is satisfied that other circumstances exist which make it just and convenient for the order to be made.

. . .

(4)   An order under this section may make provision with respect to—

(a)   such matters relating to the exercise by the manager of his functions under the order, and

(b)   such incidental or ancillary matters,

as the court thinks fit; and, on any subsequent application made for the purpose by the manager, the court may give him directions with respect to any such matters.

(5)   Without prejudice to the generality of subsection (4), an order under this section may provide—

(a)   for rights and liabilities arising under contracts to which the manager is not a party to become rights and liabilities of the manager;

(b)   for the manager to be entitled to prosecute claims in respect of causes of action (whether contractual or tortious) accruing before or after the date of his appointment;

(c)   for remuneration to be paid to the manager by the landlord, or by the tenants of the premises in respect of which the order is made or by all or any of those persons;

(d)   for the manager's functions to be exercisable by him (subject to subsection (9)) either during a specified period or without limit of time.

(6)   Any such order may be granted subject to such conditions as the court thinks fit, and in particular its operation may be suspended on terms fixed by the court.

(7)   ...

(8)   The Land Charges Act 1972 and the Land Registration Act 1925 shall apply in relation to an order made under this section as they apply in relation to an order appointing a receiver or sequestrator of land. . . .

18.2.6.5   Local authorities taking action against private landlords

Where a house, flat, or block of flats is in disrepair, the local district council can serve a notice on the landlord requiring specified repairs. If the landlord fails to comply, the council can enter the property, carry out the repairs, and charge them to the landlord. (See the Housing Acts 1957–88.)

18.2.6.6   Measure of damages against landlords

CALABAR PROPERTIES LTD v STITCHER **[1984] 1 WLR 287, Court of Appeal**

FACTS: Defects in the external parts of certain rented premises had resulted in the interior becoming damp. Consequently, the tenants withheld payment of ground rent and were sued by the landlords. The tenants counter-claimed for damages for breach of the landlord's covenant to keep external parts in good repair. After some time the dampness, which had resulted in ill health, forced the tenants to vacate the premises. The judge at first instance found for the tenants and awarded damages for the cost of repairing the flat and for disappointment, discomfort, loss of enjoyment and ill health. However, the judge refused to award damages for loss of use and wasted rent etc. during the period for which the house was uninhabitable. The defendant appealed against the award of damages.

HELD: The appeal was dismissed. The judge had been correct to limit the award of damages to the difference in value between the flat as it was and the flat as it would have been had the repair obligations been met. No damages could be awarded in respect of the defendant's cost of renting alternative accommodation, no counterclaim had been made for those costs, and it was now too late to claim them.

GRIFFITHS LJ: . . . The object of awarding damages against a landlord for breach of his covenant to repair is not to punish the landlord but, so far as money can, to restore the tenant to the position he would have been in had there been no breach. This object will not be achieved by applying one set of rules to all cases regardless of the particular circumstances of the case. The facts of each case must be looked at carefully to see what damage the tenant has suffered and how he may be fairly compensated by a monetary award.

In this case on the findings of the judge the plaintiff landlords, after notice of the defect, neglected their obligation to repair for such a length of time that the flat eventually became uninhabitable. It was also clear that unless ordered to do so by an order of the court, the plaintiffs had no intention of carrying out the repairs. In these circumstances the defendant had two options that were reasonably open to her: either of selling the flat and moving elsewhere, or alternatively of moving into temporary accommodation and bringing an action against the plaintiffs to force them to carry out the repairs, and then returning to the flat after the repairs were done. If the defendant had chosen the first option then the measure of damages would indeed have been the difference in the price she received for the flat in its damaged condition and that which it would have fetched in the open market if the plaintiffs had observed their repairing covenant. If however the defendant did not wish to sell the flat but to continue to live in it after the plaintiffs had carried out the necessary structural repairs it was wholly artificial to award her damages on the basis of loss in market value, because once the plaintiffs had carried out the repairs and any consequential redecoration of the interior was completed there would be no loss in market value. The defendant should be awarded the cost to which she was put in taking alternative accommodation, the cost of redecorating, and some award for all the unpleasantness of living in the flat as it deteriorated until it became uninhabitable. These three heads of damage will, so far as money can, compensate the defendant for the plaintiffs' breach.

18.2.7 DAMAGES AGAINST A TENANT IN BREACH OF REPAIRING OBLIGATIONS

LEASEHOLD PROPERTY (REPAIRS) ACT 1938

1. Restriction on enforcement of repairing covenants in long leases of small houses

(1) Where a lessor serves on a lessee under subsection (1) of section one hundred and forty-six of the Law of Property Act 1925, a notice that relates to a breach of a covenant or agreement to keep or put in repair during the currency of the lease [all or any of the property comprised in the lease], and at the date of the service of the notice [three] years or more of the term of the lease remain unexpired, the lessee may within twenty-eight days from that date serve on the lessor a counter-notice to the effect that he claims the benefit of this Act.

(2) A right to damages for a breach of such a covenant as aforesaid shall not be enforceable by action commenced at any time at which [three] years or more of the term of the lease remain unexpired unless the lessor has served on the lessee not less than one month before the commencement of the action such a notice as is specified in subsection (1) of section one hundred and forty-six of the Law of Property Act 1925, and where a notice is served under this subsection, the lessee may, within twenty-eight days from the date of the service thereof, serve on the lessor a counter-notice to the effect that he claims the benefit of this Act.

(3) Where a counter-notice is served by a lessee under this section, then, notwithstanding anything in any enactment or rule of law, no proceedings, by action or otherwise, shall be taken by the lessor for the enforcement of any right of re-entry or forfeiture under any proviso or stipulation in the lease for breach of the covenant or agreement in question, or for damages for breach thereof, otherwise than with the leave of the court.

(4) A notice served under subsection (1) of section one hundred and forty-six of the Law of Property Act 1925, in the circumstances specified in subsection (1) of this section, and a notice served under subsection (2) of this section shall not be valid unless it contains a statement, in characters not less conspicuous than those used in any other part of the notice, to the effect that the lessee is entitled under this Act to serve on the lessor a counter-notice claiming the benefit of this Act, and a statement in the like characters specifying the time within which, and the manner in which, under this Act a counter-notice may be served and specifying the name and address for service of the lessor.

(5) Leave for the purposes of this section shall not be given unless the lessor proves—

(a) that the immediate remedying of the breach in question is requisite for preventing substantial diminution in the value of his reversion, or that the value thereof has been substantially diminished by the breach;

(b) that the immediate remedying of the breach is required for giving effect in relation to the [premises] to the purposes of any enactment, or of any byelaw or other provision having effect under an enactment, [or for giving effect to any order of a court or requirement of any authority under any enactment or any such byelaw or other provision as aforesaid];

(c) in a case in which the lessee is not in occupation of the whole of the [premises as respects which the covenant or agreement is proposed to be enforced], that the immediate remedying of the breach is required in the interests of the occupier of [those premises] or of part thereof;

(d) that the breach can be immediately remedied at an expense that is relatively small in comparison with the much greater expense that would probably be occasioned by postponement of the necessary work; or

(e) special circumstances which in the opinion of the court, render it just and equitable that leave should be given.

(6) The court may, in granting or in refusing leave for the purposes of this section, impose such terms and conditions on the lessor or on the lessee as it may think fit.

2. Restriction on right to recover expenses of survey, etc

A lessor on whom a counter-notice is served under the preceding section shall not be entitled to the benefit of subsection (3) of section one hundred and forty-six of the Law of Property Act 1925, (which relates to costs and expenses incurred by a lessor in reference to breaches of covenant), so far as regards any costs or expenses incurred in reference to the breach in question, unless he makes an application for leave for the purposes of the preceding section, and on such an application the court shall have power to direct whether and to what extent the lessor is to be entitled to the benefit thereof.

18.3 Covenants Against Assigning, Sub-letting and Parting with Possession

18.3.1 QUALIFIED COVENANTS

LANDLORD AND TENANT ACT 1927

19. Provisions as to covenants not to assign, etc, without licence or consent

(1) In all leases whether made before or after the commencement of this Act containing a covenant condition or agreement against assigning, underletting, charging or parting with the possession of demised premises or any part thereof without licence or consent, such covenant condition or agreement shall, notwithstanding any express provision to the contrary, be deemed to be subject—

(a) to a proviso to the effect that such licence or consent is not to be unreasonably withheld, but this proviso does not preclude the right of the landlord to require payment of a reasonable sum in respect of any legal or other expenses incurred in connection with such licence or consent; . . .

LANDLORD AND TENANT ACT 1988

1. Qualified duty to consent to assigning, underletting etc of premises

(1) This section applies in any case where—

(a) a tenancy includes a covenant on the part of the tenant not to enter into one or more of the following transactions, that is—

(i) assigning,

(ii) underletting

(iii) charging, or

(iv) parting with the possession of,

the premises comprised in the tenancy or any part of the premises without the consent of the landlord or some other person, but

(b) the covenant is subject to the qualification that the consent is not to be unreasonably withheld (whether or not it is also subject to any other qualification).

(2) In this section and section 2 of this Act—

(a) references to a proposed transaction are to any assignment, underletting, charging or parting with possession to which the covenant relates, and

(b) references to the person who may consent to such a transaction are to the person who under the covenant may consent to the tenant entering into the proposed transaction.

(3) Where there is served on the person who may consent to a proposed transaction a written application by the tenant for consent to the transaction, he owes a duty to the tenant within a reasonable time—

(a) to give consent, except in a case where it is reasonable not to give consent,

(b) to serve on the tenant written notice of his decision whether or not to give consent specifying in addition—

(i)   if the consent is given subject to conditions, the conditions,

(ii)   if the consent is withheld, the reasons for withholding it.

(4)   Giving consent subject to any condition that is not a reasonable condition does not satisfy the duty under subsection (3)(a) above.

(5)   For the purposes of this Act it is reasonable for a person not to give consent to a proposed transaction only in a case where, if he withheld consent and the tenant completed the transaction, the tenant would be in breach of a covenant.

(6)   It is for the person who owed any duty under subsection (3) above—

(a)   if he gave consent and the question arises whether he gave it within a reasonable time, to show that he did,

(b)   if he gave consent subject to any condition and the question arises whether the condition was a reasonable condition, to show that it was,

(c)   if he did not give consent and the question arises whether it was reasonable for him not to do so, to show that it was reasonable,

and, if the question arises whether he served notice under that subsection within a reasonable time, to show that he did.

LANDLORD AND TENANT (COVENANTS) ACT 1995

22.   Imposition of conditions regulating giving of landlord's consent to assignments

After subsection (1) of section 19 of the Landlord and Tenant Act 1927 (provisions as to covenants not to assign etc. without licence or consent) there shall be inserted—

(1A)   Where the landlord and the tenant under a qualifying lease have entered into an agreement specifying for the purposes of this subsection—

(a)   any circumstances in which the landlord may withhold his licence or consent to an assignment of the demised premises or any part of them, or

(b)   any conditions subject to which any such licence or consent may be granted, then the landlord—

(i)   shall not be regarded as unreasonably withholding his licence or consent to any such assignment if he withholds it on the ground (and it is the case) that any such circumstances exist, and

(ii)   if he gives any such licence or consent subject to any such conditions, shall not be regarded as giving it subject to unreasonable conditions;

and section 1 of the Landlord and Tenant Act 1988 (qualified duty to consent to assignment etc.) shall have effect subject to the provisions of this subsection. . . .

LAW OF PROPERTY ACT 1925

144.   No fine to be exacted for licence to assign

In all leases containing a covenant, condition, or agreement against assigning, underletting, or parting with the possession, or disposing of the land or property leased without licence or consent, such covenant, condition, or agreement shall, unless the lease contains an express provision to the contrary, be deemed to be subject to a proviso to the effect that no fine or sum of money in the nature of a fine shall be payable for or in respect of such licence or consent; but this proviso does not preclude the right to require the payment of a reasonable sum in respect of any legal or other expense incurred in relation to such licence or consent.

18.3.2   WHEN IS A CONSENT UNREASONABLY WITHELD?

INTERNATIONAL DRILLING FLUIDS LTD v LOUISVILLE INVESTMENTS (UXBRIDGE) LTD [1986] 1 Ch 513, Court of Appeal

FACTS: A lease was granted for thirty years and provided that the demised premises should not be used 'for any purpose other than as offices'. The lease could not be assigned without the landlord's permission (known, somewhat confusingly, as the landlord's 'licence'), but such licence was not to be unreasonably witheld. The tenant requested the landlord's consent to an assignment. The landlord refused, on the ground, *inter alia*, that

the proposed use of the premises as offices would reduce the value of the landlord's reversion and create parking problems. The judge held that the landlord's refusal to give consent to the assignment had been unreasonable. The landlord appealed.
HELD: The appeal was dismissed.

BALCOMBE LJ: From the authorities I deduce the following propositions of law.
(1) The purpose of a covenant against assignment without the consent of the landlord, such consent not to be unreasonably withheld, is to protect the lessor from having his premises used or occupied in an undesirable way, or by an undesirable tenant or assignee: *per* A L Smith LJ in *Bates v Donaldson* [1896] 2 QB 241, 247, approved by all the members of the Court of Appeal in *Houlder Brothers & Co. Ltd v Gibbs* [1925] Ch 575.
(2) As a corollary to the first proposition, a landlord is not entitled to refuse his consent to an assignment on grounds which have nothing whatever to do with the relationship of landlord and tenant in regard to the subject matter of the lease: see *Houlder Brothers & Co. Ltd v Gibbs*, a decision which (despite some criticism) is binding on this court: *Bickel v Duke of Westminster* [1977] QB 517. A recent example of a case where the landlord's consent was unreasonably withheld because the refusal was designed to achieve a collateral purpose unconnected with the terms of the lease is *Bromley Park Garden Estates Ltd v Moss* [1982] 1 WLR 1019.
(3) The onus of proving that consent has been unreasonably withheld is on the tenant: see *Shanly v Ward* (1913) 29 TLR 714 and *Pimms Ltd v Tallow Chandlers Company* [1964] 2 QB 547, 564. [Now see Landlord and Tenant Act 1988.]
(4) It is not necessary for the landlord to prove that the conclusions which led him to refuse consent were justified, if they were conclusions which might be reached by a reasonable man in the circumstances: *Pimms Ltd v Tallow Chandlers Company* [1964] 2 QB 547, 564.
(5) It may be reasonable for the landlord to refuse his consent to an assignment on the ground of the purpose for which the proposed assignee intends to use the premises, even though that purpose is not forbidden by the lease: see *Bates v Donaldson* [1896] 2 QB 241, 244.
(6) There is a divergence of authority on the question, in considering whether the landlord's refusal of consent is reasonable, whether it is permissible to have regard to the consequences to the tenant if consent to the proposed assignment is withheld. In an early case at first instance, *Sheppard v Hong Kong and Shanghae Banking Corporation* (1872) 20 WR 459, 460, Malins V-C said that by withholding their consent the lessors threw a very heavy burden on the lessees and they therefore ought to show good grounds for refusing it. In *Houlder Brothers & Co Ltd v Gibbs* [1925] Ch 575, 584, Warrington LJ said:

> An act must be regarded as reasonable or unreasonable in reference to the circumstances under which it is committed, and when the question arises on the construction of a contract the outstanding circumstances to be considered are the nature of the contract to be construed, and the relations between the parties resulting from it.

In a recent decision of this court, *Leeward Securities Ltd v Lilyheath Properties Ltd* (1983) 271 EG 279 concerning a sub-letting which would attract the protection of the Rent Act, both Oliver LJ and O'Connor LJ made it clear in their judgments that they could envisage circumstances in which it might be unreasonable to refuse consent to an underletting, if the result would be that there was no way in which the tenant (the sub-landlord) could reasonably exploit the premises except by creating a tenancy to which the Rent Act protection would apply, and which inevitably would affect the value of the landlord's reversion. O'Connor LJ said, at p. 283:

> It must not be thought that, because the introduction of a Rent Act tenant inevitably has an adverse effect upon the value of the reversion, that that is a sufficient ground for the landlords to say that they can withhold consent and that the court will hold that that is reasonable.

To the opposite effect are the *dicta, obiter* but nevertheless weighty, of Viscount Dunedin and Lord Phillimore in *Viscount Tredegar v Harwood* [1929] AC 72, 78, 82. There are numerous other dicta to the effect that a landlord need consider only his own interest: see, e.g., *West Layton Ltd* v *Ford* [1979] QB 593, 605, and *Bromley Park Garden Estates Ltd* v *Moss* [1982] 1 WLR 1019, 1027. Those *dicta* must be qualified, since a landlord's interests, collateral to the purposes of the lease, are in any event ineligible for consideration: see proposition (2) above. But in my judgment a proper reconciliation of those two streams of authority can be achieved by saying that while a landlord need usually only consider his own relevant interests, there may be cases where there is such a disproportion between the benefit to the landlord and the detriment to the tenant if the landlord withholds his consent to an assignment that it is unreasonable for the landlord to refuse consent.

(7) Subject to the propositions set out above, it is in each case a question of fact, depending upon all the circumstances, whether the landlord's consent to an assignment is being unreasonably withheld: see *Bickel* v *Duke of Westminster* [1977] QB 517, 524, and *West Layton Ltd* v *Ford* [1979] QB 593, 604, 606–607.

In the present case, the judge, having made the findings of specific fact set out above, carefully considered the relevant authorities. He then reached the conclusion that the views of the landlords' expert witnesses about the effect of the proposed assignment on the value of the reversion, although views which could be held by reasonable professional men, did not in the circumstances of this case, where there was no prospect of the landlords wishing to realise the reversion, constitute a ground for reasonable apprehension of damage to their interests. That was a decision on the facts to which the judge was entitled to come. He made no error of law in reaching his decision; he took into account nothing which he ought not to have considered, and he omitted nothing which he ought to have considered. In my judgment, this court ought not to interfere.

But in any event, in my judgment, the judge reached the right decision. Although he did not expressly mention the disproportionate harm to the tenants if the landlords were entitled to refuse consent to the assignment, compared with the minimum disadvantage which he clearly considered the landlords would suffer by a diminution in the paper value of the reversion—'paper value' because he was satisfied there was no prospect of the landlords wishing to realise the reversion—he clearly recognised the curious results to which the landlords' arguments, based solely upon a consideration of their own interests, could lead. As he said in his judgment:

It seems to me that, if Mr Lewison is right, the more substantial the lessee, the more easily the landlord would be able to justify a refusal of consent to an assignment, since unless the proposed assignee's covenant was as strong as the assignor's, a reasonable man might form the view that the market would consider the reversion less attractive if the lease were vested in the assignor. To take the matter to extremes, if a lease was made in favour of a government department it would be unassignable except to another government department; for as Mr Matthews [one of the expert witnesses] accepted in cross-examination, the market would prefer to have the government as the lessee, whether the premises were being used as serviced offices or not, even if they were standing empty, rather than a company, however strong its covenant.

In my judgment, the gross unfairness to the tenants of the example postulated by the judge strengthens the arguments in favour, in an appropriate case of which the instant case is one, of it being unreasonable for the landlord not to consider the detriment to the tenant if consent is refused, where the detriment is extreme and disproportionate to the benefit to the landlord.

NORFOLK CAPITAL GROUP LTD v *KITWAY LTD* [1976] 3 All ER 787, Court of Appeal

FACTS: A long lease of a house was vested in a limited company. It was proposed to assign the lease to a human tenant who would be able to take advantage of certain sections of protective legislation not available to 'artificial persons' (as companies are often referred to). This fact would have the effect of reducing the value of the landlord's reversion.
HELD: The landlords were reasonable in vetoing the assignments.

MEGAW LJ: . . . In so far as there is any authority which can be said to bear on this question, Mr Barnes has rightly called our attention to a decision at first instance of Lawson J in *Welch* v *Birrane*, in 1974, reported only in (1974) 29 P & CR 102. In that case Lawson J had to deal with the question of a refusal by a landlord to give consent to an assignment the effect of which would have been to enable the proposed assignee, in course of time, had the proposed assignee so desired, to claim the advantages of the Leasehold Reform Act 1967. There were further complications in that case which ultimately led to the decision in favour of the tenant. The judge held that the landlord in that case had waived his right to challenge the assignment that had been made without his consent. But the judge did decide, as the first question, whether the landlord in those circumstances could be said unreasonably to have refused his consent; and the judge decided that question before going on to the other question, whether there had been a waiver. Lawson J as I understand his judgment, decided that issue on two separate grounds, each of which stood apart from the other. The first of those grounds, as I understand it, was that the very fact that there is this potential disadvantage to a landlord under the Leasehold Reform Act 1967 if the proposed assignment were to go through is in itself sufficient to prevent that refusal from being unreasonable. . . .

In my judgment, the case ends where it began. Looking at it as a matter of ordinary common sense and the ordinary use of words, from which I do not think that the law ought to be regarded as departing unless there is clear authority that requires one so to hold, the refusal of the landlord, in the circumstances of this case, to give his consent to an assignment which has the potential effect that this assignment would have is something that cannot be fairly described as being 'unreasonable.' Accordingly, I would dismiss the appeal. . . .

PREMIER CONFECTIONARY (LONDON) COMPANY LTD v LONDON COMMERCIAL SALE ROOMS LTD [1933] Ch 904, Chancery Division

FACTS: A tenant of two tobacconist shops sought the landlord's written consent to an assignment of one of the shops to a respectable tenant. The landlord reposed to give consent in the belief that occupation of the shops by separate tenants would be detrimental to the property.
HELD: The landlord's consent had not been unreasonably withheld.

BENNETT J: If the defendants have in law the right to consider the possible effect upon their property of the shop and the kiosk being in the occupation of different tenants, I have no doubt that in withholding their consent to the assignment of the kiosk to Mrs Kramer they did not act unreasonably. They acted as a reasonable man might have acted in the circumstances. The real question is whether as a matter of law the defendants, for the purpose of determining whether or not they would give their consent to the assignment, had the right to consider the effect upon their property, and in particular upon the shop which is a part of it, of the kiosk being occupied separately from the shop, and by a tenant bound to carry on there a trade which will compete with the trade for which the shop is best suited. In my judgment, they have.

In *Houlder Brothers & Co.* v *Gibbs* [1925] Ch 575 the Master of the Rolls, Warrington and Sargant LJJ all accepted and acted upon the reasoning of A. L. Smith LJ in *Bates* v *Donaldson* [1896] 2 QB 241. Sargant LJ in particular proceeded upon the footing that the statement of A. L. Smith LJ that the covenant in question in that case was inserted 'in order to protect the lessor from having his premises used or occupied in an undesirable way, or by an undesirable tenant or assignee,' was a statement which shows the limits which are to be put upon such a clause as the clause in question. If a reasonable man might think that the proposed user of the premises, or the proposed occupation of the premises will be undesirable, then, in my judgment, it is within the right of the landlord to withhold his consent to an assignment which will result in that undesirable use or occupation. The defendants in this case have withheld their consent because they in good faith think that in all the circumstances the occupation of the kiosk by Mrs Kramer is undesirable.

Mr Morton for the plaintiffs contended that the defendants are really seeking to consolidate the two agreements, and that if they had intended that the shop and the kiosk should always be in the occupation of one tenant they should have inserted a stipulation to that effect in the agreement of September 14, 1928. The argument (if I followed it rightly) was that it was not reasonable for a landlord to withhold his consent to a proposed assignment if the subject-matter with regard to which the proposed assignment was objected to might have been made the subject-matter of an express stipulation at the time the tenancy was created. In my judgment, this is not the law. It is, in my opinion, clear from the judgments delivered by the members of the Court of Appeal in *Bates v Donaldson* [1896] 2 QB 241 and in *Houlder Brothers & Co. v Gibbs* [1925] Ch 575 that a landlord may withhold his consent to an assignment because he objects to the use the proposed assignee intends to make of the premises proposed to be assigned, although that use is not forbidden by the terms of the tenancy or by any rule of law.

I decide this case in favour of the defendants for the following reasons: (a) Because the proposed assignment will result in the kiosk being occupied separately from the shop; (b) Because that is a matter which the defendants are entitled to consider in determining whether or not they will give their consent; (c) Because the defendants believe that the separation of the kiosk from the shop may injuriously affect their property; and (d) Because that opinion is one which may be entertained by reasonable persons and is not wholly unreasonable.

18.4   Surrender Clauses

BOCARDO SA v S & M HOTELS LTD AND ANOTHER [1980] 1 WLR 17, Court of Appeal

FACTS: A clause of a long commercial lease required the tenant to offer to surrender its lease to the landlord before asking for consent to assign. The tenant pleaded that such an arrangement fell foul of section 19(1) of the Landlord and Tenant Act 1927, and was void. HELD: The provision as to surrender was valid.

MEGAW LJ: . . . if one is to assume, as for the reasons which I have given it seems to me right for us to assume, that section 19(1) does not prevent or limit freedom of contract to ban assignments altogether by agreement in the lease, why should the subsection be treated as having the effect of preventing or limiting freedom of contract to ban assignments during a part of the lease? Counsel for the landlords, I think rightly, submitted that the courts could not treat section 19(1) as invalidating a contractual proviso that no assignment should be made—that no question of assignment by consent should arise—during, say, the first, or the last, seven years of a 14-year lease. Why, then, as a matter of policy or practical sense or logic should the courts hold that section 19(1) invalidates a proviso that, before the tenant's right of assignment with consent shall arise, a condition precedent shall be fulfilled: namely, the tenant's obligation first to offer a surrender? If by agreement an assignment by consent can be precluded altogether, what logical reason or policy can be invoked to preclude a limited right of the tenant to assign with consent; the limitation being that the landlord, if he wishes, can insist on a surrender?. . .

GREENE v *CHURCH COMMISSIONERS FOR ENGLAND*
[1974] 1 Ch 467, Court of Appeal

FACTS: The plaintiff had taken a lease by assignment. The original tenant had agreed to offer to surrender his lease before making any request to assign the premises. The plaintiff claimed not to be bound by the agreement to surrender. He argued that the landlord's right to require a surrender was an estate contract, registrable as a class C(iv) Land Charge, and as it had not been registered it would be void against a purchaser from the original tenant. HELD: The plaintiff's argument succeeded.

LORD DENNING MR: This case raises a point of widespread application. It concerns a clause, now common in leases, by which the landlord can insist on a surrender. The question is whether it ought to be registered as a land charge. . . .

The question is, therefore: Was this proviso a 'contract' to surrender?

. . . help is to be found by the word 'including' in Class C(iv). That word is very appropriate to show the wide meaning which the legislature attributes to 'contract' in the opening words. It uses the word 'contract' in a sense which *includes* a valid option to purchase or a right of pre-emption. So it does *include* contracts which are binding on one side only. The word 'including' is used so as to remove any doubt as to the width of the word 'contract' in the opening words. It makes it clear that it is used in the wide sense, which includes an offer binding on one side, which the other can accept or reject as he pleases. . . .

In my opinion, therefore, the word 'contract' in the opening words of Class C(iv) includes a contract which is binding on one side only. It includes a contract by which one party binds himself, in a particular event, to convey or create a legal estate, even though the other is not bound to accept it: and only becomes bound by some further act of acceptance. Such is the case where the owner of a legal estate gives another an option to purchase, or gives him a right of pre-emption, or where a lessee gives to a tenant an option to renew a lease (as in *Beesly* v *Hallwood Estates Ltd* [1961] Ch 105 itself), or where a lessee gives to a lessor a right to accept or reject a surrender (as in this case). . . .

CHAPTER NINETEEN

THE RUNNING OF COVENANTS IN A LEASE

19.1 Which Covenants Touch and Concern the Land?

KUMAR v DUNNING [1987] 2 All ER 801, Court of Appeal

FACTS: The landlord gave consent to an assignment of the lease, but made his consent conditional upon the provision by a third party of a guarantee that the new tenant would pay the rent. Such a third party is called a 'surety'. If the assignee fails to make rental payments, the surely will be required to make them instead. The question in the present case was whether a puchaser of the leasehold reversion would be entitled to enforce the guarantee. HELD: The guarantee was enforceable by the new landlord because it 'touched and concerned' the land. The guarantee was of benefit to nobody but the present owner of the freehold, it would therefore be artificial to treat the benefit of the guarantee as something personal to the original freeholder only.

SIR NICOLAS BROWNE-WILKINSON V-C: The test whether a covenant touches and concerns land is that formulated by Bayley J in *Mayor of Congleton* v *Pattison* (1808) 10 East 130 at 138, 103 ER 725 at 728 and adopted by Farwell J in *Rogers* v *Hosegood* [1900] 2 Ch 388 at 395: '. . . the covenant must either affect the land as regards mode of occupation, or it must be such as per se, and not merely from collateral circumstances, affects the value of the land'. But although the test is certain, its exact meaning when applied to different sets of circumstances is very obscure. In *Grant* v *Edmondson* [1931] 1 Ch 1 at 28, [1930] All ER Rep 48 at 59 Romer LJ said:

> In connection with the subject of covenants running with the land, it is impossible to reason by analogy. The established rules concerning it are purely arbitrary, and the distinctions, for the most part, quite illogical.

Before seeking to analyse the authorities, I will first state how the matter strikes me as a matter of impression. The surety convenant is given as a support or buttress to covenants given by a tenant to a landlord. The covenants by the tenant relate not only to the payment of rent, but also to repair, insurance and user of the premises. All such covenants by a tenant in favour of the landlord touch and concern the land, i.e. the reversion of the landlord. The performance of some covenants by tenants relate to things done on the land itself (e.g. repair and user covenants). Other tenants' covenants (e.g. payment of rent and insurance) require nothing to be done on the land itself. They are mere covenants for the payment of money. The covenant to pay rent is the major cause of the landlord's reversion having any value during the continuance of the term. Where there is privity of estate, the tenants' covenant to pay rent touches and concerns the land: see *Parker* v *Webb* (1693) 3 Salk 5, 91 ER 656. As it seems to me, in principle a covenant by a third party guaranteeing the performance by the tenant of his obligations should touch and concern the reversion as much as do the tenants' covenants themselves.

This view accords with what, to my mind, is the commercial common sense and justice of the case. When, as in the present case, the lease has been assigned on the terms that the sureties will guarantee performance by the assignee of the lease, justice and common sense ought to require the sureties, not the original tenant, to be primarily liable in the event of default by the assignee. So long as the reversion is not assigned, that will be the position. Why should the position between the original tenant and the sureties be rendered completely different just because the reversion has been assigned, a transaction wholly outside the control of the original tenant and the sureties?

Yet in all save one of the cases decided at first instance, the court has held that the surety covenant does not touch and concern the land. The exception is *Pinemain Ltd* v *Tuck* (4 March 1986, unreported) where the question was left open. In *Pinemain Ltd* v *Welbeck International Ltd* (1984) 272 EG 1166 Edward Nugee QC sitting as a deputy High Court judge held that the surety covenant to run at law (as opposed to a negative covenant running with the land in equity) it was necessary that the covenant should require something to be done which afffected the land itself, not merely its value. I find this view difficult to reconcile with those cases which establish that a tenant's covenant to pay rent and to insure touch and concern the land. Moreover, Mr Nugee's view is, to my mind, inconsistent with the decision in *Dyson* v *Forster* [1909] AC 98, [1908–10] All ER Rep 212 which I will mention later. . . .

Reverting to the test laid down in the *Congleton* case, it is clear that the surety covenant in the present case does not 'affect the land as to the mode of occupation'. The question is whether it affects the value of the reversion 'per se and not merely from collateral circumstances'. The meaning of those latter words has been expounded in a number of cases which have not often been cited subsequently. In *Vernon* v *Smith* (1821) 5 B & Ald 1, [1814–23] All ER Rep 677 the question was whether a covenant by the tenant to insure the demised premises was enforceable by the assignee of the reversion. Although the case was one of privity of estate, the enforceability of the covenant depended on whether the covenant touched and concerned the land. It was argued that the covenant was merely to pay money to a third party. The majority of the court decided that the covenant was enforceable on the narrow point that the assignee of the reversion would have an interest in the insurance moneys.

. . . The benefit of the covenant to repay could not touch and concern the land because someone other than the owner for the time being of the term could take the benefit of it.

19.2   Liability of Original Parties after Assignment

LAW OF PROPERTY ACT 1925

141.   Rent and benefit of lessee's covenants to run with the reversion

(1)   Rent reserved by a lease, and the benefit of every covenant or provision therein contained, having reference to the subject-matter thereof, and on the lessee's part to be observed or performed, and every condition of re-entry and other condition therein contained, shall be annexed and incident to and shall go with the reversionary estate in the land, or in any part thereof, immediately expectant on the term granted by the lease, notwithstanding severance of that reversionary estates, and without prejudice to any liability affecting a covenantor or his estate.

(2)   Any such rent, covenant or provision shall be capable of being recovered, received, enforced, and taken advantage of, by the person from time to time entitled, subject to the term, to the income of the whole or any part, as the case may require, of the land leased.

ARLESFORD TRADING CO. LTD v *SERVANSINGH* **[1971] 3 All ER 113, Court of Appeal**

FACTS: The original tenant covenanted on behalf of himself and his succesors in title, for the benefit of the landlord and its successors in title, to pay, half yearly, a ground rent and cetain service charges. The tenant assigned the remainder of the term of the 99 year lease to a new tenant. The new tenant failed to make the payments of ground rent and service charges. Later, the reversion also changed hands. It was assigned by the original landlord to the plaintiff. The plaintiff brought the present action against the original tenant for recovery of the sums due.

HELD: The new landlord was successful. An original tenant generally remained liable, throughout the full term of the lease, for any breaches of covenants touching and concerning the land. This was in accordance with s. 141 of the Law of Property Act 1925.

RUSSELL LJ: . . . Now it has been established in this court that an assignee of the reversion can claim, against the lessee, arrears of rent accrued prior to the assignment, and to re-enter on the ground of the failure to have paid such arrears; this is by force of s. 141 of the Law of Property Act 1925: see *London and County (A & D) Ltd* v *Wilfred Sportsman Ltd (Greenwoods (Hosiers and Outfitters) Ltd, third party)* [1917] Ch 764. In that case, however, the claim to re-enter and forfeit the lease was against the original lessee (and his chargee). It is pointed out that in the present case the defendant assigned his lease before the reversion was asigned to the plaintiffs and that there has never been privity of estate between the plaintiffs and the defendant, contrary to what appears from the note of the judgment to have been the judge's view. But it is argued for the plaintiffs that an original lessee remains at all times liable under the lessee's covenants throughout the lease, and that assignment of the reversion does not automatically release him from that liability. This agreement is in our judgment correct; so that if there is no special feature in this case the plaintiffs undoubtedly have a right as assignee of the reversion, and with it of the benefit of the lessee's covenants for rent etc to sue for arrears of rent.

Was there a special feature which denies the plaintiffs the right to sue the defendant? It is plain that Drayville Properties Ltd could not have asserted against the assignee of the lease (or his mortgagee) that there was any subsisting breach of the covenant for rent. This is because of the production of the receipt for the June 1969 instalment. It was manifestly the intention that the lease should be assigned 'clean', so to speak, of any liability for those three unpaid instalments. Equally, the plaintiffs could not have asserted against the assignee of the term (or his mortgagee) the failure in the payment of those three instalments. But does it follow from that that the postponed obligation of the defendant to pay those three instalments no longer had sufficiently the quality of an obligation to pay rent etc under the lease to enable the assignee of the reversion to assert against the defendant that the benefit of that obligation was assigned together with the reversion? In our judgment the answer is in the negative. The obligation on the defendant remained on him in his capacity as lessee under the lease, and the ability to enforce against him passed with the reversion to the plaintiffs.

In our judgment accordingly the appeal fails.

19.2.1 INDEMNITIES BETWEEN ASSIGNEES OF A LEASE

LAW OF PROPERTY (MISCELLANEOUS PROVISIONS) ACT 1994

1. Covenants to be implied on a disposition of property

(1) In an instrument effecting or purporting to effect a disposition of property there shall be implied on the part of the person making the disposition, whether or not the disposition is for valuable consideration, such of the covenants specified in sections 2 to 5 as are applicable to the disposition.

(2) Of those sections—

(a) sections 2, 3(1) and (2), 4 and 5 apply where dispositions are expressed to be made with full title guarantee; and

(b) sections 2, 3(3), 4 and 5 apply where dispositions are expressed to be made with limited title guarantee.

(3) Sections 2 to 4 have effect subject to section 6 (no liability under covenants in certain cases); and sections 2 to 5 have effect subject to section 8(1) (limitation or extension of covenants by instrument effecting the disposition).

(4) In this Part—

'disposition' includes the creation of a term of years; and

'instrument' includes an instrument which is not a deed; and

'property' includes a thing in action, and any interest in real or personal property.

2. Right to dispose and further assurance

(1)   If the disposition is expressed to be made with full title guarantee or with limited title guarantee there shall be implied the following covenants—

(a)   that the person making the disposition has the right (with the concurrence of any other person conveying the property) to dispose of the property as he purports to, and

(b)   that that person will at his own cost do all that he reasonably can to give the person to whom he disposes of the property the title he purports to give.

(2)   The latter obligation includes—

(a)   in relation to a disposition of an interest in land the title to which is registered, doing all that he reasonably can to ensure that the person to whom the disposition is made is entitled to be registered as proprietor with at least the class of title registered immediately before the disposition; and

(b)   in relation to a disposition of an interest in land the title to which is required to be registered by virtue of the disposition, giving all reasonable assistance fully to establish to the satisfaction of the Chief Land Registrar the right of the person to whom the disposition is made to registration as proprietor.

(3)   In the case of a disposition of an existing legal interest in land, the following presumptions apply, subject to the terms of the instrument, in ascertaining for the purposes of the covenants implied by this section what the person making the disposition purports to dispose of—

(a)   where the title to the interest is registered, it shall be presumed that the disposition is of the whole of that interest;

(b)   where the title to the interest is not registered, then—

(i)   if it appears from the instrument that the interest is a leasehold interest, it shall be presumed that the disposition is of the property for the unexpired portion of the term of years created by the lease; and

(ii)   in any other case, it shall be presumed that what is disposed of is the fee simple.

LAW OF PROPERTY ACT 1925

77. Implied covenants in conveyance subject to rents

(1)   In addition to the covenants implied under Part I of the Law of Property (Miscellaneous Provisions) Act 1994, there shall in the several cases in this section mentioned, be deemed to be included and implied, a covenant to the effect in this section stated, by and with such persons as are hereinafter mentioned, that is to say:—

. . .

(C)   In a conveyance for valuable consideration, other than a mortgage, of the entirety of the land comprised in a lease, for the residue of the term or interest created by the lease, a covenant by the assignee or joint and several covenants by the assignees (if more than one) with the conveying parties and with each of them (if more than one) in the terms set out in Part IX of the Second Schedule to this Act. . . .

SECOND SCHEDULE

PART IX   COVENANT IN A CONVEYANCE FOR VALUABLE CONSIDERATION, OTHER THAN A MORTGAGE, OF THE ENTIRETY OF THE LAND COMPRISED IN A LEASE FOR THE RESIDUE OF THE TERM OR INTEREST CREATED BY THE LEASE

That the assignees, or the persons deriving title under them, will at all times, from the date of the conveyance or other date therein stated, duly pay all rent becoming due under the lease creating the term or interest for which the land is conveyed, and observe and perform all the covenants, agreements and conditions therein contained and thenceforth on the part of the lessees to be observed and performed:

And also will at all times, from the date aforesaid, save harmless and keep indemnified the conveying parties and their estates and effects, from and against all proceedings, costs, claims and expenses on account of any omission to pay the said rent or any breach of any of the said covenants, agreements and conditions.

19.3   Position of Covenants Which Do Not Touch and Concern

19.3.1   POSITION OF OPTIONS TO RENEW THE LEASE

REGENT OIL CO. LTD v *J A GREGORY (HATCH END) LTD*
[1965] 3 All ER 673, Court of Appeal

FACTS: C Ltd, the tenant of a petrol filling station, borrowed £4,000 from the plaintiff and undertook to repay the sum, without interest, over ten years. Simultaneous with the mortgage, the tenant also covenated to purchase all its petrol, oil etc. from the plaintiff company, and from none other. Later, C Ltd, assigned the lease to a new tenant. The question was whether the covenants as to the purchase of petrol, oil etc touched and concerned the land, so as to run with the assignment and bind the new tenant.
HELD: The covenant touched and concerned the land and was not merely personal. The new tenant was bound.

19.4   Position of Equitable Leases

PURCHASE v *LICHFIELD BREWERY COMPANY*
[1915] 1 KB 184, King's Bench Division

FACTS: The tenant of an equitable lease agreed to assign a lease to new tenants, but the deed to that effect was never executed by the proposed assignees, nor did they take up possession of the demised land. The plaintiff landlord brought this action to recover rent from the proposed assignees. They refused to pay rent, on grounds that they had never taken up possession.
HELD: There could not be privity of estate between the landlord and the new tenants, because the original tenant had never possessed a legal estate capable of being assigned. Accordingly, the proposed assignees were not liable to pay rent on the premises.

HORRIDGE J: . . . Assuming that Lunnis was in a position to have enforced specific performance against the plaintiff and had the right to treat himself as being a lessee under the lease which would have been granted under a decree for specific performance, still it does not follow that his assignee is in the same position. The only case cited to establish such a right in an assignee is *Dowell* v *Dew* 12 LJ (Ch) 158; but in that case the assignee of the agreement had entered and paid rent and had been recognized as tenant by the owner of the property. Knight Bruce V-C said that the agreement was assignable 'and especially with the assent of the landlord for the time being.' In that case there was privity of contract. Even then the landlord was entitled if he thought fit to insist on the personal liability of his lessee on the covenants in the lease as if it had been granted to him. Such a case as the present one seems remote from the case which Jessel MR was considering when he said, in *Walsh* v *Lonsdale* 21 ChD 9, 'There is an agreement for a lease under which possession has been given. Now since the Judicature Act the possession is held under the agreement . . . The tenant holds under an agreement for a lease. He holds, therefore, under the same terms in equity as if a lease had been granted, it being a case in which both parties admit that relief is capable of being given by specific performance.' In my opinion as assignee of a mere agreement for a lease who never took possession and never attorned tenant could not before the Judicature Acts and cannot now in his own right enforce specific performance against the landlord. He could not establish such a direct relation between himself and the landlord as would induce a Court of Equity, regarding that as done which ought to be done, to treat him as a person in whom a lease had been vested. I do not think that the case of *Williams* v *Bosanquet* 1 Brod & B 238 applies because in that case the lease was under seal and it was validly assigned by deed to the mortgagees.

LUSH J: . . . I do not think it is necessary to say how the case might have stood if the defendants had ever taken possession. They are liable, if at all, on the principle of *Walsh* v *Lonsdale* 21 ChD 9. In that case the tenant was in possession under the agreement. In the present case the defendants never did take possession. The agreement contained a provision against assigning. The defendants were only mortgagees. It does not follow from *Walsh* v *Lonsdale* that a Court of Equity would decree specific performance against mere mortgagees who only took an assignment by way of security. In my opinion it would leave the parties to their position at law. Accordingly the matter stands thus: A tenant under an agreement, whose only title to call himself a lessee depends on his right to specific performance of the agreement, assigns his right to assignees. The assignees never had a term vested in them because no term was ever created; therefore there was never privity of estate. They never went into possession or were recognized by the landlord; therefore there was never privity of contract. It is impossible that specific performance of a contract can be decreed against a person with whom there is neither privity of contract nor privity of estate. Therefore these assignees are not liable to perform the terms of the agreement and this appeal must be allowed.

BOYER v WARBEY [1953] 1 QB 234, Court of Appeal

DENNING LJ: . . . I know that before the Judicature Act 1873, it was said that the doctrine of covenants running with the land only applied to covenants under seal and not to agreements under hand: see *Elliott* v *Johnson* (1868) LR 2 QB 120. But since the fusion of law and equity, the position is different. The distinction between agreements under hand and covenants under seal has been largely obliterated. There is no valid reason nowadays why the doctrine of covenants running with the land—or with the reversion—should not apply equally to agreements under hand as to covenants under seal, and I think we should so hold, not only in the case of agreements for more than three years which need the intervention of equity to perfect them, but also in the case of agreements for three years or less which do not. . . .

19.5 Position of Sub-Tenants and Head Landlords

19.5.1 RESTRICTIVE COVENANTS IN THE HEAD LEASE

A head landlord can enforce restrictive covenants in the lease against a sub-tenant, despite the absence of privity of estate, where:
(a) the lease is unregistered title and the sub-tenant has notice of the restrictive covenants (usually the sub-tenant will have notice of the restrictive covenants in the head lease as the head tenant will, for his own protection, at least tell the sub-tenant about them); or
(b) the lease is registered title. Restrictive covenants in registered leases are automatically binding on sub-tenants by virtue of the Land Registration Act 1925, s. 23(1)(a) and (2).

LAND REGISTRATION ACT 1925

23. Effect of registration of dispositions of leaseholds
(1) In the case of a leasehold estate registered with an absolute title, a disposition (including a subdemise thereof) for valuable consideration shall, when registered, be deemed to vest in the transferee or underlessee the estate transferred or created to the extent of the registered estate, or for the term created by the subdemise, as the case may require, with all implied or expressed rights, privileges, and appurtenances attached to the estate transferred or created, including (subject to any entry to the contrary on the register) the appropriate rights and interests which would under the Law of Property Act 1925, have been transferred if the land had not been registered, but subject as follows:—
(a) To all implied and express covenants, obligations, and liabilities incident to the estate transferred or created; and
(b) To the incumbrances and other entries (if any) appearing in the register [and any charge for [inheritance tax] subject to which the disposition takes effect under section 73 of this Act]; and

(c)   Unless the contrary is expressed on the register, to the overriding interests, if any, effecting the estate transferred or created,
but free from all other estates and interests whatsoever, including estates and interests of His Majesty; and the transfer or subdemise shall operate in like manner as if the registered transferor or sublessor were (subject to any entry to the contrary on the register) absolutely entitled to the registered lease for his own benefit.

(2)   In the case of a leasehold estate registered with a good leasehold title, a disposition (including a subdemise thereof) for valuable consideration shall, when registered, have the same effect as it would have had if the land had been registered with an absolute title, save that it shall not effect or prejudice the enforcement of any right or interest affecting or in derogation of the title of the lessor to grant the lease.

19.6   The Landlord and Tenant (Covenants) Act 1995

1.   Tenancies to which the Act applies
(1)   Sections 3 to 16 and 21 apply only to new tenancies.
(2)   Sections 17 to 20 apply to both new and other tenancies.
(3)   For the purposes of this section a tenancy is a new tenancy if it is granted on or after the date on which this Act comes into force otherwise than in pursuance of—
    (a)   an agreement entered into before that date, or
    (b)   an order of a court made before that date.
(4)   Subsection (3) has effect subject to section 20(1) in the case of overriding leases granted under section 19.
(5)   Without prejudice to the generality of subsection (3), that subsection applies to the grant of a tenancy where by virtue of any variation of a tenancy there is a deemed surrender and regrant as it applies to any other grant of a tenancy.
(6)   Where a tenancy granted on or after the date on which this Act comes into force is so granted in pursuance of an option granted before that date, the tenancy shall be regarded for the purposes of subsection (3) as granted in pursuance of an agreement entered into before that date (and accordingly is not a new tenancy), whether or not the option was exercised before that date.
(7)   In subsection (6) 'option' includes right of first refusal.

2.   Covenants to which the Act applies
(1)   This Act applies to a landlord covenant or a tenant covenant of a tenancy—
    (a)   whether or not the covenant has reference to the subject matter of the tenancy, and
    (b)   whether the covenant is express, implied or imposed by law,
but does not apply to a covenant falling within subsection (2).
(2)   Nothing in this Act affects any covenant imposed in pursuance of—
    (a)   section 35 or 155 of the Housing Act 1985 (covenants for repayment of discount on early disposals);
    (b)   paragraph 1 of Schedule 6A to that Act (covenants requiring redemption of landlord's share); or
    (c)   paragraph 1 or 3 of Schedule 2 to the Housing Associations Act 1985 (covenants for repayment of discount on early disposals or for restricting disposals).

3.   Transmission of benefit and burden of covenants
(1)   The benefit and burden of all landlord and tenant covenants of a tenancy—
    (a)   shall be annexed and incident to the whole, and to each and every part, of the premises demised by the tenancy and of the reversion in them, and
    (b)   shall in accordance with this section pass on an assignment of the whole or any part of those premises or of the reversion in them.
(2)   Where the assignment is by the tenant under the tenancy, then as from the assignment the assignee—
    (a)   becomes bound by the tenant covenants of the tenancy except to the extent that—
        (i)   immediately before the assignment they did not bind the assignor, or

(ii)   they fall to be complied with in relation to any demised premises not comprised in the assignment; and

(b)   becomes entitled to the benefit of the landlord covenants of the tenancy except to the extent that they fall to be complied with in relation to any such premises.

(3)   Where the assignment is by the landlord under the tenancy, then as from the assignment the assignee—

(a)   becomes bound by the landlord covenants of the tenancy except to the extent that—

(i)   immediately before the assignment they did not bind the assignor, or

(ii)   they fall to be complied with in relation to any demised premises not comprised in the assignment; and

(b)   becomes entitled to the benefit of the tenant covenants of the tenancy except to the extent that they fall to be complied with in relation to any such premises.

(4)   In determining for the purposes of subsection (2) or (3) whether any covenant bound the assignor immediately before the assignment, any waiver or release of the covenant which (in whatever terms) is expressed to be personal to the assignor shall be disregarded.

(5)   Any landlord or tenant covenant of a tenancy which is restrictive of the user of land shall, as well as being capable of enforcement against an assignee, be capable of being enforced against any other person who is the owner or occupier of any demised premises to which the covenant relates, even though there is no express provision in the tenancy to that effect.

(6)   Nothing in this section shall operate—

(a)   in the case of a covenant which (in whatever terms) is expressed to be personal to any person, to make the covenant enforceable by or (as the case may be) against any other person; or

(b)   to make a covenant enforceable against any person if, apart from this section, it would not be enforceable against him by reason of its not having been registered under the Land Registration Act 1925 or the Land Charges Act 1972.

(7)   To the extent that there remains in force any rule of law by virtue of which the burden of a covenant whose subject matter is not in existence at the time when it is made does not run with the land affected unless the covenantor covenants on behalf of himself and his assigns, that rule of law is hereby abolished in relation to tenancies.

4.   Transmission of rights of re-entry

The benefit of a landlord's right of re-entry under a tenancy—

(a)   shall be annexed and incident to the whole, and to each and every part, of the reversion in the premises demised by the tenancy, and

(b)   shall pass on an assignment of the whole or any part of the reversion in those premises.

5.   Tenant released from covenants on assignment of tenancy

(1)   This section applies where a tenant assigns premises demised to him under a tenancy.

(2)   If the tenant assigns the whole of the premises demised to him, he—

(a)   is released from the tenant covenants of the tenancy, and

(b)   ceases to be entitled to the benefit of the landlord covenants of the tenancy,

as from the assignment.

(3)   If the tenant assigns part only of the premises demised to him, then as from the assignment he—

(a)   is released from the tenant covenants of the tenancy, and

(b)   ceases to be entitled to the benefit of the landlord covenants of the tenancy,

only to the extent that those covenants fall to be complied with in relation to that part of the demised premises.

(4)   This section applies as mentioned in subsection (1) whether or not the tenant is tenant of the whole of the premises comprised in the tenancy.

6.   Landlord may be released from covenants on assignment of reversion

(1)   This section applies where a landlord assigns the reversion in premises of which he is the landlord under a tenancy.

(2)   If the landlord assigns the reversion in the whole of the premises of which he is the landlord—

(a)   he may apply to be released from the landlord covenants of the tenancy in accordance with section 8; and

(b)   if he is so released from all of those covenants, he ceases to be entitled to the benefit of the tenant covenants of the tenancy as from the assignment.

(3)   If the landlord assigns the reversion in part only of the premises of which he is the landlord—

(a)   he may apply to be so released from the landlord covenants of the tenancy to the extent that they fall to be complied with in relation to that part of those premises; and

(b)   if he is, to that extent, so released from all of those covenants, then as from the assignment he ceases to be entitled to the benefit of the tenant covenants only to the extent that they fall to be complied with in relation to that part of those premises.

(4)   This section applies as mentioned in subsection (1) whether or not the landlord is landlord of the whole of the premises comprised in the tenancy.

7.   Former landlord may be released from covenants on assignment of reversion

(1)   This section applies where—

(a)   a landlord assigns the reversion in premises of which he is the landlord under a tenancy, and

(b)   immediately before the assignment a former landlord of the premises remains bound by a landlord covenant of the tenancy ('the relevant covenant').

(2)   If immediately before the assignment the former landlord does not remain the landlord of any other premises demised by the tenancy, he may apply to be released from the relevant covenant in accordance with section 8.

(3)   In any other case the former landlord may apply to be so released from the relevant covenant to the extent that it falls to be complied with in relation to any premises comprised in the assignment.

(4)   If the former landlord is so released from every landlord covenant by which he remained bound immediately before the assignment, he ceases to be entitled to the benefit of the tenant covenants of the tenancy.

(5)   If the former landlord is so released from every such landlord covenant to the extent that it falls to be complied with in relation to any premises comprised in the assignment, he ceases to be entitled to the benefit of the tenant covenants of the tenancy to the extent that they fall to be so complied with.

(6)   This section applies as mentioned in subsection (1)—

(a)   whether or not the landlord making the assignment is landlord of the whole of the premises comprised in the tenancy; and

(b)   whether or not the former landlord has previously applied (whether under section 6 or this section) to be released from the relevant covenant.

8.   Procedure for seeking release from a covenant under section 6 or 7

(1)   For the purposes of section 6 or 7 an application for the release of a covenant to any extent is made by serving on the tenant, either before or within the period of four weeks beginning with the date of the assignment in question, a notice informing him of—

(a)   the proposed assignment or (as the case may be) the fact that the assignment has taken place, and

(b)   the request for the covenant to be released to that extent.

(2)   Where an application for the release of a covenant is made in accordance with subsection (1), the covenant is released to the extent mentioned in the notice if—

(a)   the tenant does not, within the period of four weeks beginning with the day on which the notice is served, serve on the landlord or former landlord a notice in writing objecting to the release, or

(b)   the tenant does so serve such a notice but the court, on the application of the landlord or former landlord, makes a declaration that it is reasonable for the covenant to be so released, or

(c)   the tenant serves on the landlord or former landlord a notice in writing consenting to the release and, if he has previously served a notice objecting to it, stating that that notice is withdrawn.

(3)   Any release from a covenant in accordance with this section shall be regarded as occurring at the time when the assignment in question takes place.

(4)   In this section—

(a)   'the tenant' means the tenant of the premises comprised in the assignment in question (or, if different parts of those premises are held under the tenancy by different tenants, each of those tenants);

(b)   any reference to the landlord or the former landlord is a reference to the landlord referred to in section 6 or the former landlord referred to in section 7, as the case may be; and

(c)   'the court' means a county court.

15.   Enforcement of covenants

(1)   Where any tenant covenant of a tenancy, or any right of re-entry contained in a tenancy, is enforceable by the reversioner in respect of any premises demised by the tenancy, it shall also be so enforceable by—

(a)   any person (other than the reversioner) who, as the holder of the immediate reversion in those premises, is for the time being entitled to the rents and profits under the tenancy in respect of those premises, or

(b)   any mortgagee in possession of the reversion in those premises who is so entitled.

(2)   Where any landlord covenant of a tenancy is enforceable against the reversioner in respect of any premises demised by the tenancy, it shall also be so enforceable against any person falling within subsection (1)(a) or (b).

(3)   Where any landlord covenant of a tenancy is enforceable by the tenant in respect of any premises demised by the tenancy, it shall also be so enforceable by any mortgagee in possession of those premises under a mortgage granted by the tenant.

(4)   Where any tenant covenant of a tenancy, or any right of re-entry contained in a tenancy, is enforceable against the tenant in respect of any premises demised by the tenancy, it shall also be so enforceable against any such mortgagee.

(5)   Nothing in this section shall operate

(a)   in the case of a covenant which (in whatever terms) is expressed to be personal to any person, to make the covenant enforceable by or (as the case may be) against any other person; or

(b)   to make a covenant enforceable against any person if, apart from this section, it would not be enforceable against him by reason of its not having been registered under the Land Registration Act 1925 or the Land Charges Act 1972.

(6)   In this section—

'mortgagee' and 'mortgage' include 'chargee' and 'charge' respectively;

'the reversioner', in relation to a tenancy, means the holder for the time being of the interest of the landlord under the tenancy.

16.   Tenant guaranteeing performance of covenant by assignee

(1)   Where on an assignment a tenant is to any extent released from a tenant covenant of a tenancy by virtue of this Act ('the relevant covenant'), nothing in this Act (and in particular section 25) shall preclude him from entering into an authorised guarantee agreement with respect to the performance of that covenant by the assignee.

(2)   For the purposes of this section an agreement is an authorised guarantee agreement if—

(a)   under it the tenant guarantees the performance of the relevant covenant to any extent by the assignee; and

(b)   it is entered into in the circumstances set out in subsection (3); and

(c)   its provisions conform with subsections (4) and (5).

(3)   Those circumstances are as follows—

(a)   by virtue of a covenant against assignment (whether absolute or qualified) the assignment cannot be effected without the consent of the landlord under the tenancy or some other person;

(b)   any such consent is given subject to a condition (lawfully imposed) that the tenant is to enter into an agreement guaranteeing the performance of the covenant by the assignee; and

(c)   the agreement is entered into by the tenant in pursuance of that condition.

(4)   An agreement is not an authorised guarantee agreement to the extent that it purports—

(a) to impose on the tenant any requirement to guarantee in any way the performance of the relevant covenant by any person other than the assignee; or

(b) to impose on the tenant any liability, restriction or other requirement (of whatever nature) in relation to any time after the assignee is released from that covenant by virtue of this Act.

(5) Subject to subsection (4), an authorised guarantee agreement may—

(a) impose on the tenant any liability as sole or principal debtor in respect of any obligation owed by the assignee under the relevant covenant;

(b) impose on the tenant liabilities as guarantor in respect of the assignee's performance of that covenant which are no more onerous than those to which he would be subject in the event of his being liable as sole or principal debtor in respect of any obligation owed by the assignee under that covenant;

(c) require the tenant, in the event of the tenancy assigned by him being disclaimed, to enter into a new tenancy of the premises comprised in the assignment—

(i) whose term expires not later than the term of the tenancy assigned by the tenant, and

(ii) whose tenant covenants are no more onerous than those of that tenancy;

(d) make provision incidental or supplementary to any provision made by virtue of any of paragraphs (a) to (c).

(6) Where a person ('the former tenant') is to any extent released from a covenant of a tenancy by virtue of section 11(2) as from an assignment and the assignor under the assignment enters into an authorised guarantee agreement with the landlord with respect to the performance of that covenant by the assignee under the assignment—

(a) the landlord may require the former tenant to enter into an agreement under which he guarantees, on terms corresponding to those of that authorised guarantee agreement, the performance of that covenant by the assignee under the assignment; and

(b) if its provisions conform with subsections (4) and (5), any such agreement shall be an authorised guarantee agreement for the purposes of this section; and

(c) in the application of this section in relation to any such agreement—

(i) subsections (2)(b) and (c) and (3) shall be omitted, and

(ii) any reference to the tenant or to the assignee shall be read as a reference to the former tenant or to the assignee under the assignment.

(7) For the purposes of subsection (1) it is immaterial that—

(a) the tenant has already made an authorised guarantee agreement in respect of a previous assignment by him of the tenancy referred to in that subsection, it having been subsequently revested in him following a disclaimer on behalf of the previous assignee, or

(b) the tenancy referred to in that subsection is a new tenancy entered into by the tenant in pursuance of an authorised guarantee agreement;
and in any such case subsections (2) to (5) shall apply accordingly.

(8) It is hereby declared that the rules of law relating to guarantees (and in particular those relating to the release of sureties) are, subject to its terms, applicable in relation to any authorised guarantee agreement as in relation to any other guarantee agreement.

17. Restriction on liability of former tenant or his guarantor for rent or service charge etc

(1) This section applies where a person ('the former tenant') is as a result of an assignment no longer a tenant under a tenancy but—

(a) (in the case of a tenancy which is a new tenancy) he has under an authorised guarantee agreement guaranteed the performance by his assignee of a tenant covenant of the tenancy under which any fixed charge is payable; or

(b) (in the case of any tenancy) he remains bound by such a covenant.

(2) The former tenant shall not be liable under that agreement or (as the case may be) the covenant to pay any amount in respect of any fixed charge payable under the covenant unless, within the period of six months beginning with the date when the charge becomes due, the landlord serves on the former tenant a notice informing him—

(a) that the charge is now due; and

(b) that in respect of the charge the landlord intends to recover from the former tenant such amount as is specified in the notice and (where payable) interest calculated on such basis as is so specified.

(3)   Where a person ('the guarantor') has agreed to guarantee the performance by the former tenant of such a covenant as is mentioned in subsection (1), the guarantor shall not be liable under the agreement to pay any amount in respect of any fixed charge payable under the covenant unless, within the period of six months beginning with the date when the charge becomes due, the landlord serves on the guarantor a notice informing him—

(a)   that the charge is now due; and

(b)   that in respect of the charge the landlord intends to recover from the guarantor such amount as is specified in the notice and (where payable) interest calculated on such basis as is so specified.

(4)   Where the landlord has duly served a notice under subsection (2) or (3), the amount (exclusive of interest) which the former tenant or (as the case may be) the guarantor is liable to pay in respect of the fixed charge in question shall not exceed the amount specified in the notice unless—

(a)   his liability in respect of the charge is subsequently determined to be for a greater amount,

(b)   the notice informed him of the possibility that that liability would be so determined, and

(c)   within the period of three months beginning with the date of the determination, the landlord serves on him a further notice informing him that the landlord intends to recover that greater amount from him (plus interest, where payable).

(5)   For the purposes of subsection (2) or (3) any fixed charge which has become due before the date on which this Act comes into force shall be treated as becoming due on that date; but neither of those subsections applies to any such charge if before that date proceedings have been instituted by the landlord for the recovery from the former tenant of any amount in respect of it.

(6)   In this section—

'fixed charge', in relation to tenancy, means—

(a)   rent,

(b)   any service charge as defined by section 18 of the Landlord and Tenant Act 1985 (the words 'of a dwelling' being disregarded for this purpose), and

(c)   any amount payable under a tenant covenant of the tenancy providing for the payment of a liquidated sum in the event of a failure to comply with any such covenant;

'landlord', in relation to a fixed charge, includes any person who has a right to enforce payment of the charge.

19.7 End of Chapter Assessment Question

In 1980 Lisa leased (by deed) a house to Tommy for 40 years. The lease includes the following covenants:

(a) the tenant should pay £2,000 per year rent;

(b) the tenant should not use the house for any purpose other than as a private dwelling;

(c) the tenant should not assign, sub-let or part with possession except with the landlord's consent.

The lease does not contain a forfeiture clause.

Lisa believes that Tommy intends to assign or sub-let to Percy. She is alarmed at that prospect, as Percy uses a number of houses in the area as branches of his very extensive accountacy practice.

Advise Lisa:

(i) as to the possible legal consequences if she withheld her consent to an assignment or sub-letting to Percy;

(ii) as to her position if she gave her consent to an assignment or sub-letting, but subsequently wishes to enforce covenants (a) or (b).

19.8 End of Chapter Assessment Outline Answer

The lease omits a forfeiture clause, thus limiting the remedies Lisa can seek for breach of covenant. She can sue for damages, and also an injunction to restrain non-residential user, but she will be unable to reclaim possession, even if the breach is extremely serious.

A second preliminary point is that if Tommy assigned or sublet to Percy without even asking for Lisa's consent, that would be a breach of covenant. Lisa could claim damages, but the transaction would be valid (*Peabody* v *Higgins*). If Percy was a man of excellent character to whom no reasonable objection could have been taken the damages might be nominal.

Assuming that Tommy asks (in writing) for consent to assign or sub-let to Percy, then the Landlord and Tenant Acts 1927 and 1988 apply to covenant (iii), a 'qualified covenant' against assignment etc. The 1927 Act (section 19) implies into covenant (iii) a proviso that Lisa must not unreasonably withhold her consent.

The 1988 Act is even more significant, placing on Landlords (like Lisa) a series of duties if they receive from a tenant with respect to a qualified covenant a written request for consent to an assignment or sub-letting. Firstly, Lisa must give an answer within a 'reasonable time'. Secondly she must give consent, unless there are reasonable grounds for refusing. Thirdly, if she says 'no' then she must give written reasons. Moreover, if she breaches any of these duties, Tommy can sue for damages.

The 1988 Act also establishes that in any dispute over a landlord's actions where there is a qualified covenant, the onus of proof will be on the landlord to show that (s)he is being reasonable.

Thus Lisa is advised to say 'yes' to any written request from Tommy, unless she has good grounds for objecting which she can prove to the satisfaction of the court. Caselaw (particularly the *Louisville Investments* case) indicates that purely personal objections (e.g. 'I cannot stand accountants') will not suffice. The landlord's objections must relate to the character of the assignee/sub-tenant or his proposed use for the premises. If Percy were of proven bad character, e.g. a convicted criminal or male prostitute, that would be good grounds for objection.

More importantly, if Lisa could prove that Percy intended to use the premises for inappropriate purposes, e.g. that he was definitely going to use the house as an office, that would be good grounds for saying 'no'.

It follows from this discussion that the answer to part (a) largely depends on whether Lisa is confident that she has reasonable grounds of objection provable in court. If this is so, then she will win any litigation commenced by Tommy. She might even consider herself seeking an injunction to restrain the proposed sub-letting/assignment.

If, in response to Tommy, she advances inadequate reasons, she may be lucky. Tommy may not want to risk litigation, and abandon his proposed transaction. Lisa will have bluffed her way out. But Tommy may well call Lisa's bluff, and when told 'no' go ahead and assign or sub-let without consent. Proceedings then commenced by Lisa would fail.

Tommy might alternatively claim a declaration that Lisa witholding her consent unreasonably and/or a claim damages under the 1988 Act. Tommy would win. Moreover, if because of delay caused by litigation Percy lost interest in the premises, the damages could be substantial.

With respect to part (b) of the question, if Lisa wishes to enforce covenants (i) or (ii) against Tommy, then the position is the same, whether Tommy has sub-let or assigned. Tommy, being the original tenant, is liable for the duration of the lease. He contracted for forty years, so he (or his personal representatives after his death) remain liable for that period. This will be so, whether the breach about which Lisa is complaining is actually committed by Tommy, Percy or an assignee from Percy.

With respect to enforcement against Percy, it matters whether the transaction is an assignment or sub-lease. If an assignment, then Lisa and Percy will come into a relationship known as 'Privity of Estate'. Such privity exists where two parties are in a direct landlord and tenant relationship. Where parties are in Privity of Estate, then covenants which 'touch and concern the land' are enforceable between them.

Covenants to pay rent and relating to user of the premises touch and concern the land. Thus if rent arrears build up, Lisa will have the choice of suing Tommy (contract) or Percy (privity of estate). She can only recover one lot of damages. She should sue whoever has the most money.

If the house is used for other than a private dwelling, she can again sue either Tommy or Percy, though if she wants an injunction preventing the user she should sue Percy.

If the transaction is a subletting, then there is no Privity of Estate between Lisa and Percy, a there is no direct relationship of landlord and tenant. (Tommy, as it were, stands between them.) Thus the covenant to pay rent would only be enforceable against Tommy.

Covenant (iii) is special. It is a restrictive covenant, which can be enforced by a landlord (Lisa) against a subtenant (Percy), not by invoking landlord and tenant law, but by invoking restrictive covenants law. If the lease is registered title, then the covenant automatically binds a sub-tenant. (Land Registration Act section 23). If the lease is unregistered, then Percy is only bound if he has notice of the covenant. Lisa can ensure this by consenting to the sub-letting on condition that Tommy tells Percy about the covenant. (Case law and the 1988 Act allow consent on conditions, providing they are reasonable. Clearly this condition is reasonable.)

CHAPTER TWENTY

TERMINATION OF LEASES

20.1 Ways in Which Leases May Terminate

20.1.1 NATURAL EXPIRY

This occurs where the term of a fixed-term lease runs out. Also known as termination by 'Effluxion of Time'.

20.1.2 GIVING OF NOTICE

See **17.1**.

20.1.3 MERGER

This occurs where the tenant buys the landlord's reversion.

20.1.4 SURRENDER

A lease is surrendered where it is terminated by mutual agreement between landlord and tenant.

20.1.5 FRUSTRATION

NATIONAL CARRIERS LTD v PANALPINA (NORTHERN) LTD
[1981] 1 All ER 161, House of Lords

FACTS: In January 1974 the defendants took a ten-year lease of a warehouse. In May 1979 the local authority closed the only access road to the warehouse. The closure was likely to last 20 months. The tenants refused to pay any further rent, arguing that the lease was frustrated by the lack of any road access.

HELD: The doctrine of frustration did apply to leases, but a twenty months interruption in the enjoyment of a ten year lease was not such a drastic change in the rights of the parties as to amount to a frustration terminating the lease.

LORD HAILSHAM OF ST MARYLEBONE LC: . . . Is there anything in principle which ought to prevent a lease from ever being frustrated? I think there is not. In favour of the opposite opinion, the difference in principle between real and chattel property was strongly urged. But I find it difficult to accept this, once it has been decided, as has long been the case, that time and demise charters even of the largest ships and of considerable duration can in principle be frustrated. . . . I accept of course that systems of developed land draw a vital distinction between land, which is relatively permanent, and other types of property, which are relatively perishable. But one can overdo the contrast. Coastal erosion as well as the 'vast convulsion of nature' postulated by Viscount Simon LC in the *Cricklewood case* [1945] 1 All ER 252 at 255–256, [1945] AC 221 at 229 can, even in this island, cause houses, gardens, even villages and their churches to fall into the North Sea . . .

20.1.6   FORFEITURE

See below.

20.2   Forfeiture of Leases

20.2.1   MODES OF FORFEITURE

CRIMINAL LAW ACT 1977

6.   Violence for securing entry

(1)   Subject to the following provisions of this section, any person who, without lawful authority, uses or threatens violence for the purpose of securing entry into any premises for himself or for any other person is guilty of an offence, provided that—

(a)   there is someone present on those premises at the time who is opposed to the entry which the violence is intended to secure; and

(b)   the person using or threatening the violence knows that that is the case.

(2)   The fact that a person has any interest in or right to possession or occupation of any premises shall not for the purposes of subsection (1) above constitute lawful authority for the use or threat of violence by him or anyone else for the purpose of securing his entry into those premises.

(3)   In any proceedings for an offence under this section it shall be a defence for the accused to prove—

(a)   that at the time of the alleged offence he or any other person on whose behalf he was acting was a displaced residential occupier of the premises in question; or

(b)   that part of the premises in question constitutes premises of which he or any other person on whose behalf he was acting was a displaced residential occupier and that the part of the premises to which he was seeking to secure entry constitutes an access of which he or, as the case may be, that other person is also a displaced residential occupier.

(4)   It is immaterial for the purposes of this section—

(a)   whether the violence in question is directed against the person or against property; and

(b)   whether the entry which the violence is intended to secure is for the purpose of acquiring possession of the premises in question or for any other purpose.

(5)   A person guilty of an offence under this section shall be liable on summary conviction to imprisonment for a term not exceeding six months or to a fine not exceeding [level 5 on the standard scale] or to both.

(6)   A constable in uniform may arrest without warrant anyone who is, or whom he, with reasonable cause, suspects to be, guilty of an offence under this section.

(7)   . . .

BILLSON v RESIDENTIAL APARTMENTS LTD **[1992] 2 WLR 15, House of Lords**

FACTS: A tenant undertook major reconstruction works without their landlord's consent and in express breach of covenant. The landlord served a Law of Property Act 1925, s. 146 (1) notice forfeiting the lease. Having failed to remedy the breach the landlords peaceably re-entered the vacant premises and changed the locks. Only later did the tenant apply for relief from forfeiture.

HELD: The tenants were too late to apply for relief.

LORD TEMPLEMAN: . . . When a tenant receives a s. 146 notice he will not know whether the landlord can be persuaded that there is no breach or persuaded to accept in due course that any breach has been remedied and that he has been offered adequate and satisfactory compensation or whether the landlord will seek to determine the lease by issuing and serving a writ or will seek to determine the lease by re-entering the premises. The tenant will not wish to institute proceedings seeking relief from forfeiture if those proceedings will be aggressive and hostile and may be premature and unnecessary. Parliament cannot have intended that if the landlord employs the civilised method of determining the lease by issuing and serving a writ, then the tenant will be entitled to apply for relief, but if the landlord employs the dubious and dangerous method of determining the lease by re-entering the premises, then the tenant will be debarred from applying for relief. . . .

My Lords, I accept the conclusion that a landlord who serves a notice under s. 146(1) can be said, for the purposes of s. 146(2) to be proceeding to enforce his rights under the lease. A tenant authorised by s. 146(2) to apply to the court for relief against forfeiture if he fails to comply with a s. 146 notice may make that application after service of the notice for the purpose of elucidating the issues raised by the notice, ascertaining the intentions of the landlord, and setting in train the machinery by which the dispute between the landlord and the tenant can be determined by negotiation or by the court. But the fact that the tenant may apply to the court for relief after service of the s. 146 notice does not mean that if he does not do so he loses the right conferred on him by s. 146(2) to apply for relief if and when the landlord proceeds, not by action but 'otherwise' by exercising a right of re-entry. No absurdity follows from a construction which allows the tenant to apply for relief before and after a landlord re-enters without first obtaining a court order. . . .

The results of s. 146 and the authorities are as follows. A tenant may apply for appropriate declarations and for relief from forfeiture under s. 146(2) after the issue of a s. 146 notice but he is not prejudiced if he does not do so. A tenant cannot apply for relief after a landlord has forfeited a lease by issuing and serving a writ, has recovered judgment and has entered into possession pursuant to that judgment. If the judgment is set aside or successfully appealed the tenant will be able to apply for relief in the landlord's action but the court in deciding whether to grant relief will take into account any consequences of the original order and repossession and the delay of the tenant. A tenant may apply for relief after a landlord has forfeited by re-entry without first obtaining a court order for that purpose but the court in deciding whether to grant relief will take into account all the circumstances, including delay, on the part of the tenant. Any past judicial observations which might suggest that a tenant is debarred from applying for relief after the landlord has re-entered without first obtaining a court order for that purpose are not to be so construed.

I would therefore allow the appeal and set aside the orders of the trial judge and the Court of Appeal.

20.2.2 FORFEITURE OF A LEASE OF A DWELLING HOUSE

PROTECTION FROM EVICTION ACT 1977

1. Unlawful eviction and harassment of occupier

(1) In this section 'residential occupier', in relation to any premises, means a person occupying the premises as a residence, whether under a contract or by virtue of any enactment or rule of law giving him the right to remain in occupation or restricting the right of any other person to recover possession of the premises.

(2) If any person unlawfully deprives the residential occupier of any premises of his occupation of the premises or any part thereof, or attempts to do so, he shall be guilty of an offence unless he proves that he believed, and had reasonable cause to believe, that the residential occupier had ceased to reside in the premises.

(3) If any person with intent to cause the residential occupier of any premises—

(a) to give up the occupation of the premises or any part thereof; or

(b) to refrain from exercising any right or pursuing any remedy in respect of the premises or part thereof;

does acts [likely] to interfere with the peace or comfort of the residential occupier or members of his household, or persistently withdraws or withholds services reasonably required for the occupation of the premises as a residence, he shall be guilty of an offence.

(3A)   Subject to subsection (3B) below, the landlord of a residential occupier or an agent of the landlord shall be guilty of an offence if—

(a)   he does acts likely to interfere with the peace or comfort of the residential occupier or members of his household, or

(b)   he persistently withdraws or withholds services reasonably required for the occupation of the premises in question as a residence,

and (in either case) he knows, or has reasonable cause to believe, that that conduct is likely to cause the residential occupier to give up the occupation of the whole or part of the premises or to refrain from exercising any right or pursuing any remedy in respect of the whole or part of the premises.

(3B)   A person shall not be guilty of an offence under subsection (3A) above if he proves that he had reasonable grounds for doing the acts or withdrawing or withholding the services in question. . . .

2.   Restriction on re-entry without due process of law

Where any premises are let as a dwelling on a lease which is subject to a right of re-entry or forfeiture it shall not be lawful to enforce that right otherwise than by proceedings in the court while any person is lawfully residing in the premises or part of them.

HOUSING ACT 1988

27.   Damages for unlawful eviction

(1)   This section applies if, at any time after 9th June 1988, a landlord (in this section referred to as 'the landlord in default') or any person acting on behalf of the landlord in default unlawfully deprives the residential occupier of any premises of his occupation of the whole or part of the premises.

(2)   This section also applies if, at any time after 9th June 1988, a landlord (in this section referred to as 'the landlord in default') or any person acting on behalf of the landlord in default—

(a)   attempts unlawfully to deprive the residential occupier of any premises of his occupation of the whole or part of the premises, or

(b)   knowing or having reasonable cause to believe that the conduct is likely to cause the residential occupier of any premises—

(i)   to give up his occupation of the premises or any part thereof, or

(ii)   to refrain from exercising any right or pursuing any remedy in respect of the premises or any part thereof,

does acts likely to interfere with the peace or comfort of the residential occupier or members of his household, or persistently withdraws or withholds services reasonably required for the occupation of the premises as a residence, and, as a result, the residential occupier gives up his occupation of the premises as a residence.

(3)   Subject to the following provisions of this section, where this section applies, the landlord in default shall, by virtue of this section, be liable to pay to the former residential occupier, in respect of his loss of the right to occupy the premises in question as his residence, damages . . .

20.3   Waiver of Forfeiture

CENTRAL ESTATES (BELGRAVIA) LTD v WOOLGAR (No. 2)
[1972] 3 All ER 610, Court of Appeal

FACTS: Woolgar, an OAP and a First World War veteran, was tenant of a long lease (due to expire in 1993) of a sizeable house in central London. He had a fall from grace, and was convicted of using the premises as a (homosexual) brothel. In view of his past exemplary record he was granted a conditional discharge by the magistrates. The landlords, however, decided to forfeit the lease for breach of the covenant in the lease prohibiting illegal user, and served on Woolgar the warning notice required by section 146 of the Law of Property Act 1925. The landlords were anxious to forfeit the lease as the property would be much more valuable to them with 'vacant possession'. A minor official of the landlords then made a crucial mistake. He sent to Woolgar a rent demand for a future instalment of rent. HELD: The rent demand waived the breach, even though it had been sent out in error and Woolgar had not been in any way misled by the demand (even after the demand was sent he still personally believed that he was going to be evicted from the premises). The test of an 'unequivocal act' of waiver was what the 'reasonable onlooker' would think.

LORD DENNING MR: . . . The material question is whether the demand and acceptance of rent in September 1970 was a waiver of the forfeiture. If it was, the landlords were not entitled to issue this plaint for possession as they did in December 1970. The judge held there was not a waiver because, as he found, the tenant when he paid the rent knew full well that the landlords' intention to forfeit the lease remained unchanged.

The cases on waiver are collected in the notes to *Dumpor's Case* (1603) 4 Co Rep 119b in Smith's Leading Cases. Those notes show that the demand and acceptance of rent has a very different effect according to how the question arises. If it is sought to say there is *a new tenancy* by acceptance of rent; for instance, after a notice to quit has expired, the question always is, as Lord Mansfield said, *'quo animo* the rent was received, and what the real intention of both parties was': see *Doe d Cheny* v *Batten* (1775) 1 Cowp 243 and *Clarke* v *Grant* [1949] 1 All ER 768. But, if it is sought to say that an existing lease *continues in existence* by waiver of forfeiture, then the intention of the parties does not matter. It is sufficient if there is an unequivocal act done by the landlord which recognises the existence of the lease after having knowledge of the ground of forfeiture. The law was well stated by Parker J in *Matthews* v *Smallwood* [1910] 1 Ch 777, which was accepted by this court in *Oak Property Co. Ltd* v *Chapman* [1947] 2 All ER 1:

> It is also, I think, reasonably clear upon the cases that whether the act, coupled with the knowledge, constitutes a waiver is a question which the law decides, and therefore, it is not open to a lessor who has knowledge of the breach to say 'I will treat the tenancy as existing, and I will receive the rent, or I will take advantage of my power as landlord to distrain; but I tell you that all I shall do will be without prejudice to my right to re-enter, which I intend to reserve'. That is a position which he is not entitled to take up. If, knowing of the breach, he does distrain, or does receive the rent, then by law he waives the breach, and nothing which he can say by way of protest against the law will avail him anything.

. . . So we have simply to ask: was this rent demanded and accepted by the landlords' agents with knowledge of the breach? It does not matter that they did not intend to waive. The very fact that they accepted the rent with the knowledge constitutes the waiver. The position here is quite plain. The agents, who had full authority to manage these properties on behalf of the landlords, did demand and accept the rent with full knowledge. It may be that the instructions did not get down the chain of command from the partner to the subordinate clerk who issued the demands and gave the receipts for rent. That cannot affect, to my mind, the legal position. It comes within the general rule that the knowledge of the agent—and of his clerks—is the knowledge of the principal. A principal cannot escape the doctrine of waiver by saying that one clerk had the knowledge and the other received the rent. They must be regarded as one for this purpose. The landlords' agents knew the position and they accepted the rent with knowledge. That is a waiver. . . .

BLACKSTONES LTD v *BURNETTS* [1973] 3 All ER 782, Queen's Bench Division

FACTS: Burnetts had a lease from Blackstones of premises in central London. There was a qualified covenant against sub-letting. Burnetts got Blackstones' consent to sub-let to two people, A and D, trading in partnership. However, Burnetts actually sub-let to a different person, Flat Finders Ltd. (A and D were the directors of that company). The landlord's solicitors got to hear of what had happened. The solicitors seem to have been ignorant of the very basic principle of company law that a company is a separate person from its shareholders and directors. They sought counsel's opinion as to whether there had been a breach of the qualified covenant against sub-letting (clearly there had been such a breach). While this 'opinion' was awaited a clerk in the landlord's office sent out a rent demand for the next quarter's rent.

HELD: The rent demand had waived the breach of the qualified covenant against sub-letting.

SWANWICK J: . . . in forfeiture cases the consequences of an action relied on as a waiver are a matter of law and not of actual intention and that it is irrelevant *quo animo* such an act was done. It is also clear from the last mentioned case that a principal is affected by the knowledge of his agent and that he cannot escape the consequences of an act done by one agent by saying that it was not that agent but another that had the actual knowledge. . . .

The basic questions on this issue therefore are: (a) is a demand for future rent, if made with knowledge of a breach which entitles the landlord to forfeit, sufficient by itself to constitute an election to continue the lease and therefore a waiver? (b) If so, what knowledge is necessary and did Mr Fraser have it at the relevant time?

. . . My view, both on principle and on such persuasive authority as has been cited to me, is that an unambiguous demand for future rent in advance—such as was made here—does in law amount to an election and does constitute a waiver if, at the time it is made, the landlord has sufficient knowledge of the facts to put him to his election. To my perhaps simple mind there is a fundamental inconsistency between contending that a lease has been determined and demanding rent on the basis of its future continuance. . . .

In my judgment, again without the guidance of any direct authority, the knowledge required to put a landlord to his election is knowledge of the basic facts that in law constitute a breach of covenant entitling him to forfeit the lease. Once he or his agent knows these facts, an appropriate act by himself or any agent will in law effect a waiver or a forfeiture. His knowledge or ignorance of the law is, in my judgment, irrelevant. If it were not so, a vast gap would be opened in the administration of the law of landlord and tenant, and a facile escape route for landlords would be provided. Indeed, if this were the position, unscrupulous landlords could hardly have failed in the past to take advantage of it long before now. . . .

20.4   Relief from Forfeiture

LAW OF PROPERTY ACT 1925

146.   Restrictions on and relief against forfeiture of leases and underleases

(1)   A right of re-entry or forfeiture under any proviso or stipulation in a lease for a breach of any covenant or condition in the lease shall not be enforceable, by action or otherwise, unless and until the lessor serves on the lessee a notice—

(a)   specifying the particular breach complained of; and

(b)   if the breach is capable of remedy, requiring the lessee to remedy the breach; and

(c)   in any case, requiring the lessee to make compensation in money for the breach; and the lesee fails, within a reasonable time thereafter, to remedy the breach, if it is capable of remedy, and to make reasonable compensation in money, to the satisfaction of the lessor, for the breach.

(2)   Where a lessor is proceeding, by action or otherwise, to enforce such a right of re-entry or forfeiture, the lessee may, in the lessor's action, if any, or in any action brought by himself, apply to the court for relief; and the court may grant or refuse relief, as the court, having regard to the proceedings and conduct of the parties under the foregoing provisions of this section, and to all the other circumstances, thinks fit; and in case of relief may grant it on such terms; if any, as to costs, expenses, damages, compensation, penalty, or otherwise, including the granting of an injunction to restrain any like breach in the future, as the court, in the circumstances of each case, thinks fit.

(3)   A lessor shall be entitled to recover as a debt due to him from a lessee, and in addition to damages (if any), all reasonable costs and expenses properly incurred by the lessor in the employment of a solicitor and surveyor or valuer, or otherwise, in reference to any breach giving rise to a right of re-entry or forfeiture which, at the request of the lessee, is waived by the lessor, or from which the lessee is relieved, under the provisions of this Act.

(4)   Where a lessor is proceeding by action or otherwise to enforce a right of re-entry or forfeiture under any covenant, proviso, or stipulation in a lease, or for non-payment of

rent, the court may, on application by any person claiming as under-lessee any estate or interest in the property comprised in the lease or any part thereof, either in the lessor's action (if any) or in any action brought by such person for that purpose, make an order vesting, for the whole term of the lease or any less term, the property comprised in the lease or any part thereof in any person entitled as under-lessee to any estate or interest in such property upon such conditions as to execution of any deed or other document, payment of rent, costs, expenses, damages, compensation, giving security, or otherwise, as the court in the circumstances of each case may think fit, but in no case shall any such under-lessee be entitled to require a lease to be granted to him for any longer term than he had under his original sub-lease.

20.4.1   RELIEF FROM FORFEITURE FOR NON-PAYMENT OF RENT

BELGRAVIA INSURANCE CO. LTD v MEAH [1964] 1 QB 436, Court of Appeal

FACTS: The tenant in this case had fallen into arrears with rental payments, and did not resist an order forfeiting the lease and granting possession to the landlord. However, a mortgagee who had a mortgage of the tenant's interest applied to the court for relief from forfeiture of the lease. The mortgagee undertook to carry out outstanding repairs, and to pay arrears of rent.
HELD: Relief was granted.

LORD DENNING MR: . . . During the nineteenth century it was held (following Lord Eldon LC's views in *Hill* v *Barclay* (1810) 16 Ves 402), that the Court of Chancery had no jurisdiction to grant a lessee relief from forfeiture for any breaches except non-payment of rent. This was remedied in 1881 by s. 14 of the Conveyancing Act 1881 (which did not apply to non-payment of rent). But that section did not apply to under-lessees. So Parliament enacted s. 4 of the Conveyancing Act 1892, so as to include them. But this section was held to apply, not only to other breaches, but also to non-payment of rent: see *Gray* v *Bonsall* [1904] 1 KB 601. In 1925 the whole law, as so evolved, was consolidated in section 146 of the Law of Property Act 1925. Section 146(4) enabled the court to grant relief to an under-lessee, not only in case of other breaches but also non-payment of rent, on such conditions 'as the court in the circumstances of each case may think fit.' It seems to me that, in exercising this discretion, the court will, in the ordinary way, grant relief to an under-lessee on the terms of paying the rent in arrear, performing the covenants, and paying all the costs: see *Gray* v *Bonsall, per* Romer LJ. In short, on the same terms as the old Court of Chancery would have done. The only difference is that it is not necessary to make the lessee a party.

. . . In any case, whether under the old Chancery jurisdiction or under s. 146(4) of the Law of Property Act 1925, it is clear that the court may always refuse relief, if the conduct of the applicant is such as to make it inequitable that relief should be given to him: see *Bowser* v *Colby* [1956] 2 QB 1, *per* Wigram V.-C., and *Gill* v *Lewis* (1841) 1 Hare 109, *per* Hodson LJ.

The master and the judge seem to have thought that this was such a case. The judge said that the applicant had a history which disentitled him to relief. I cannot share this view. The episode of the drains and of the proposed assignment was over four years ago and should no longer be held against him. The recent difficulties with the defendant, and the proposal about Noor, do not reflect adversely on the applicant, or at any rate not so adversely as to disentitle him to relief. It seems to me that if he is prepared to pay all the rent in arrear and all proper costs and to put the premises in repair to the satisfaction of a surveyor, he should be granted relief. . . .

SUPREME COURT ACT 1981

38.   Relief against forfeiture for non-payment of rent

(1)   In any action in the High Court for the forfeiture of a lease for non-payment of rent, the court shall have power to grant relief against forfeiture in a summary manner, and may do so subject to the same terms and conditions as to the payment of rent, costs or otherwise as could have been imposed by it in such an action immediately before the commencement of this Act.

(2)   Where the lessee or a person deriving title under him is granted relief under this section, he shall hold the demised premises in accordance with the terms of the lease without the necessity for a new lease.

20.4.2   FORFEITURE FOR BREACH OF COVENANT OTHER THAN RENT

20.4.2.1   Remediable or irremediable breaches?

EXPERT CLOTHING SERVICE AND SALES LTD v *HILLGATE HOUSE LTD AND ANOTHER* **[1985] 2 All ER 998, Court of Appeal**

FACTS: The tenant had breached a covenant to reconstruct the premises by an agreed date. The landlords served a notice under s. 146 Law of Property Act 1925 that the lease was forfeit due to an irremediable breach of covenant. The tenants claimed relief from forfeiture on the basis that the notice had been defective. They claimed that the breach was capable of remedy, and the notice had not given them an opportunity to effect that remedy.
HELD: The tenant was granted relief. The breach was 'remediable' by the tenant belatedly carrying out the works of reconstruction.

SLADE LJ: I would, for my part, accept the submission of counsel for the defendants that the breach of a positive covenant (whether it be a continuing breach or a once and for all breach) will ordinarily be capable of remedy. As Bristow J pointed out in the course of argument, the concept of capability of remedy for the purpose of s. 146 must surely be directed to the question whether the harm that has been done to the landlord by the relevant breach is for practical purposes capable of being retrieved. In the ordinary case, the breach of a promise to do something by a certain time can for practical purposes be remedied by the thing being done, even out of time. For these reasons I reject the plaintiffs' argument that the breach of the covenant to reconstruct by 28 September 1982 was not capable of remedy *merely* because it was not a continuing breach.

I would add this point. If this breach was, on these grounds alone, not capable of remedy, the very same grounds would appear to render the breach of the lessees' covenant to give notice of the charge in favour of Lloyds Bank likewise incapable of remedy. But counsel for the plaintiffs has not attempted to maintain the latter proposition, which would have been very difficult to sustain having regard to what one may suppose was the intention of the legislature in enacting s. 146(1).

As his second main line of argument in this context, he submitted that the breach of the covenant to reconstruct was not capable of remedy because of the operation of the new rent review provisions incorporated in the lease by the schedule to the order of 29 June 1981. He pointed out that under these provisions the landlords, on a rent review, would have an option which they would clearly wish to exercise, to review the rent on the basis of the premises as reconstructed. He submitted that there was no ready way in which the plaintiffs could be effectively restored to the same position under the rent review clause as that in which they would have found themselves if the premises had been reconstructed by the due date.

Respectfully differing from the judge on this point, I do not think that this submission is well founded. When the rent review clause comes to be applied, the defendants cannot rely on their own wrong (consisting of the failure to reconstruct) to reduce the rent which would otherwise have been payable as from the review date. The proper approach must be to asume for the purpose of the assessment that the required reconstruction has taken place. As counsel for the defendants pointed out, surveyors are quite accustomed to this kind of artificial assumption in rent review valuations. With the appropriate expert advice there would be little difficulty in ascertaining the rent to which the plaintiffs would have been entitled on the first rent review, and indeed on any subsequent rent review, if the defendants had complied with their building obligations in due time. While counsel for the plaintiffs pointed out that, if this had been done, the premises might have been sublet by the rent review date and this would itself have facilitated the ascertainment of a fair rack market annual rental value, there is no certainty whatever that any such subletting would have taken place. In the context of the rent review clause, any damage resulting from the relevant breach of covenant was, in my opinion, capable of being remedied simply by the payment by the defendants of an appropriate sum of money.

SCALA HOUSE AND DISTRICT PROPERTY CO. LTD v FORBES
[1973] 3 All ER 308, Court of Appeal

FACTS: A tenant broke a covenant against sub-letting and the landlord gave notice forfeiting the lease. The tenant applied for relief from forfeiture.
HELD: The breach was a once-and-for-all breach, it was incapable of remedy. Relief was refused.

RUSSELL LJ: . . . So the first question is whether a breach of covenant such as is involved in the present case is capable of remedy. If it is capable of remedy, and is remedied in reasonable time, the lessor is unable to prove that a condition precedent to his ability to seek to forfeit by action or otherwise has been fulfilled. Here at once is a problem. An unlawful subletting is a breach once and for all. The subterm has been created.

. . . breach by an unlawful subletting is not capable of remedy at all. In my judgment the introduction of such breaches into the relevant section for the first time by s. 146 of the 1925 Act operates only to confer a statutory ability to relieve the lessee from forfeiture on that ground. The subterm has been effectively created subject only to risks of forfeiture; it is a complete breach once for all; it is not in any sense a continuing breach. If the law were otherwise a lessee, when a subtenancy is current at the time of the s. 146 notice, would have a chance of remedying the situation without having to apply for relief. But if the unlawful subletting had determined before the notice, the lessee could only seek relief from forfeiture. The only escape from that wholly unsatisfactory difference would be to hold that in the second example by some analogy the lessor was disabled from issuing a writ for possession. But I can find nothing in the section to justify that limitation on the common law right of re-entry, bearing especially in mind that a lessor might discover a whole series of past expired unlawful subletting which might well justify a refusal to grant relief in forfeiture proceedings.

I stress again that where there has been an unlawful subletting which has determined (and which has not been waived) there has been a breach which at common law entitles the lessor to re-enter; nothing can be done to remedy that breach; the expiry of the subterm has not annulled or remedied the breach; in such case the lessor plainly need not, in his s. 146 notice, call on the lessee to remedy the breach which is not capable of remedy, and is free to issue his writ for possession, the possibility of relief remaining. . . .

GLASS v KENCAKES LTD AND OTHERS [1964] 3 All ER 807, Queen's Bench Division

FACTS: The tenant of a lease containing a covenant against illegal/immoral user sub-let to a sub-tenant who used the premises for the purpose of prostitution. The original tenant was not aware of the breach. When the landlord became aware of the immoral user he served a notice under s. 146 of the Law of Property Act alleging that the lease was forfeit because of an irremediable breach of covenant. The tenant, in turn, served a notice to the same effect on the sub-tenant.
HELD: The tenant was granted relief from forfeiture, but the sub-lease was declared forfeit. The judge held that the tenant had remedied his (arguably technical) breach of the head lease by evicting the sub-tenant before the property became tainted with a stigma.

PAULL J: As I see it, the result of the agreement between counsel is that cl. (2) must be taken to read:

> The above-mentioned covenants have been broken and the particular breach complain-ed of is that the first and third floors of the said premises have been used [as] other than residential flats in that they have been used for a business purpose, that is for the purpose of prostitution, an immoral business.

It is this breach which is said to be incapable of remedy. On the strict wording of the notice clearly the plaintiff fails. That is agreed by counsel for the plaintiff. What follows in this judgment therefore must be read as based on a notice stating the words which I have set out. . . .

The question before me therefore resolves itself into a question which can be simply stated, but which I have found very difficult to decide. I would state it in these words: Where the covenant, the breach of which is complained of, is a covenant that premises shall only be used in a certain manner and that covenant is broken by a sub-tenant of the lessee, is it capable of remedy by the lessee where the user which constitutes the breach is in fact an immoral user but where the lessee does not know that there is any such or any breach and the circumstances are such that the lessee has no reason to suppose that any, and in particular any such, breach has been or is being committed by the sub-tenant? If the position is that in some circumstances such a breach is capable of remedy and in some circumstances not, is the breach in this case capable of remedy?

. . . I think that the following propositions may be stated: (i) The mere fact that the breach complained of is a breach of user by a sub-tenant contrary to a covenant in the lease does not render the breach incapable of remedy. If one of the tenants of these flats in Queensway had, unknown to the defendants, carried on a small business of dressmaking in the flats, I would hold without hesitation that the breach was capable of remedy so far as the defendants are concerned, but it may be that the remedy would have to consist not only of stopping the tenants from carrying on that business but of bringing an action for forfeiture—it being then left to the court to decide whether the particular tenants should be granted relief. (ii) The fact that the business user involves immorality does not in itself render the breach incapable of remedy provided that the lessees neither knew nor had any reason to know of the fact that the flat was being so used. The remedy in such a case, however, must involve not only that immediate steps are taken to stop such a user so soon as the user is known, but that an action for a claim for forfeiture of the sub-tenant's lease must be started within a reasonable time. If therefore the lessee has known of such a breach for a reasonable time before the notice is served, the breach is incapable of remedy unless such steps have been taken. (iii) It does not follow that such a breach is always capable of remedy. All the circumstances must be taken into consideration. For example, if the notice is not the first notice which has had to be served, or if there are particularly revolting circumstances attaching to the user, or great publicity, then it might well be that the slate could not be wiped clean, or, to use another phrase, the damage to the property might be so great as to render the breach incapable of remedy.

At first sight propositions (ii) and (iii) would seem to put the landlord in great difficulties as to the form of his notice, since a mistake would be fatal. However, Harman J, in *Hoffman's case* [*Hoffman* v *Fineberg* [1948] 1 All ER 592] said that a form calling on the tenants to remedy the breach and adding the words 'if it is capable of remedy' probably is a good notice, and I would go further and say that I can see no reason why it should not be a good notice. If such a notice is served then the landlord, having allowed a reasonable time to elapse, can bring his action claiming (a) that the breach is incapable of remedy, or (b) if it is capable of remedy that it has not been remedied, and (c) in any event asking that the court should not permit the lease to continue.

After some hesitation, in my judgment the breach in this case is capable of remedy, and indeed was remedied within a reasonable time. . . .

SAVVA AND SAVVA v *HOUSSEIN* (1997) 73 P & CR 150, Court of Appeal

FACTS: The landlords claimed possession against the tenant for breaching covenants not to put up signs or make alterations to the property without consent, on the ground that the breaches were incapable of remedy.

HELD: A tenant's breach of a negative covenant was capable of remedy for the purposes of s. 146(1) of the Law of Property Act 1925 if the harm caused by the breach could effectively be remedied.

STAUGHTON LJ: . . . In this case the question is whether the breaches, if there were breaches, were capable of remedy. They amount to doing things without the consent of the landlord. That is what the covenant did not allow. In the case of *Billson* v *Residential Apartments Limited* (1990) 60 P & CR 392 Mummery J touched on the question whether such a breach could ever be capable of remedy. He said:

I reject the defendant's arguments on the ground that the breach of covenant committed by making the alterations in the property without the plaintiffs' consent 'first had and obtained' was not capable of remedy by the defendants. It was a breach of the covenant for the defendants to embark on alterations to the property without first applying for and seeking to obtain the plaintiffs' consent. Now that the alterations have been made without consent it is impossible for the defendants to comply with the covenant which required them first to apply for consent so that they could either obtain it or, if they did not obtain it, be in a position to contend that they were entitled to make improvements because the plaintiffs had unreasonably withheld consent.

In those circumstances I hold that the breach was not capable of remedy.

When that case reached the Court of Appeal, the Vice Chancellor said:

The judge held, first, that since the alterations had been started without **prior** consent of the plaintiffs the breach was irremediable. Second, he held that even if he was wrong on the first point, remedying the breach would consist, not in doing the works of reinstatement, but in stopping the works, submitting the necessary plans and specifications and then awaiting the giving or unreasonable withholding of consent.

I prefer to express no view on the judge's first ground of decision, beyond expressing some doubt as to whether he was right in holding that the breach was irremediable.

It is established law in this court that the breach of a covenant not to assign without consent cannot be remedied. That was decided in *Scala House & District Property Co. Ltd* v *Forbes* [1974] QB 575. Even then relief from forfeiture was granted, so that may not be of any great consequence.

In my judgment, except in a case of breach of a covenant not to assign without consent, the question is: whether the remedy referred to is the process of restoring the situation to what it would have been if the covenant had never been broken, or whether it is sufficient that the mischief resulting from a breach of the covenant can be removed. When something has been done without consent, it is not possible to restore the matter wholly to the situation which it was in before the breach. The moving finger writes and cannot be recalled. That is not to my mind what is meant by a remedy, it is a remedy if the mischief caused by the breach can be removed. In the case of a covenant not to make alterations without consent or not to display signs without consent, if there is a breach of that, the mischief can be removed by removing the signs or restoring the property to the state it was in before the alterations.

I would hold that all the breaches complained of in this case were capable of remedy. It follows that the notice under s. 146 should have required them to be remedied. As it did not, . . . the notice was not a valid one. In those circumstances there is no question of forfeiture here. There is, I suppose, still a claim for damages for breach of covenant, or there may be. But if there were breaches here they were not such as to give rise to any damages, at any rate for the time being. There was, as I have mentioned, a provision about restoring the property at the end of the term. . . .

ALDOUS LJ: I agree with the judgment of Staughton LJ. In particular, I believe that the breaches of the covenant relied on by the plaintiff in this court were capable of being remedied. It follows that the s. 146 notice was inappropriate. It also follows that the statement of law of Mummery J referred to by my Lord in *Billson* v *Residential Apartments Limited*, cannot be supported.

In one sense a breach can never be remedied because there must have been non-compliance with the covenant for there to be a breach. That cannot be the solution. Thus, the fact there has been a breach does not determine whether it can be remedied in the way contemplated by the Law of Property Act 1925, s. 146. That was decided in *Expert Clothing Service & Sales Ltd* v *Hillgate House Ltd* [1986] 1 Ch 340:

Breach of a positive covenant to do something, could ordinarily for practical purposes, be remedied by the thing being actually done.

I can see no reason why similar reasoning should not apply to some negative covenants. An important purpose of s. 146 is to give tenants, who have not complied with their obligations, one last chance to do so before the landlord re-enters. Slade LJ in *Expert Clothing*, proposed this test:

> If the section 146 notice had required the lessee to remedy the breach and the lessors had then allowed a reasonable time to elapse to enable the lessee fully to comply with the relevant covenant, would such compliance coupled with the payment of any appropriate monetary compensation have effectively remedied the harm which the lessors had suffered or were likely to suffer from the breach?

It is only if the answer to that question is 'no' can it be said that the breach is not capable of being remedied.

What was proposed as the question to ask by Slade LJ, albeit in relation to a case of dispute about a positive covenant, is relevant to consideration as to whether a negative covenant can be remedied. There is in my view nothing in the statute, nor in logic, which requires different considerations between a positive and negative covenant, although it may be right to differentiate between particular covenants. The test is one of effect. If a breach has been remedied then it must have been capable of being remedied.

For the reasons given by my Lord I agree with the order proposed.

20.4.3   RELIEF TO SUB-TENANTS

CHATHAM EMPIRE THEATRE (1955) LTD v *ULTRANS LTD AND OTHERS*
[1961] 2 All ER 381, Queen's Bench Division

FACTS: A head lease had been granted by the plaintiff to the first defendant's predecessor in title. The premises subject to the head lease included a theatre, a cinema, a car park and a restaurant. The first defendant sub-let the cinema, car park and restaurant to other parties but retained possession of the theatre. The defendant company failed to pay the rent due under the head-lease and ultimately went insolvent. The plaintiff served a forfeiture notice on the first defendant company. The sub-tenants of the cinema applied for relief from forfeiture. Against the sub-tenant's application the plaintiff argued that relief should not be granted unless the sub-tenants were prepared to pay the full arrears of rent due under the head-lease.
HELD: The sub-tenants were entitled to relief from forfeiture.

SALMON J: . . . It seems to me quite plain that s. 146(4) LPA 1925 confers on the court the widest discretion as to the terms on which relief should be granted. Counsel for the defendants contends that the defendants should be required to pay only £195 per quarter for the three relevant quarters, that is to say, £585. The defendants had, of course, paid this sum to Ultrans, Ltd., who have not paid it to the plaintiffs. Counsel says that the defendants ought only to pay that part of the arrears attributable to their property, the property which was sub-let to them. Counsel for the plaintiffs says that the whole of the arrears in respect of the whole property in the head lease ought to be paid by the defendants. That really is the chief issue between the parties.

In my judgment it is clearly equitable that the landlord should be put in the same position as he was in before the forfeiture *qua* that part of the property, namely, the cinema, let to the defendants. In my judgment the defendants ought to be required as a condition of obtaining relief, to pay £585 plus an element for the premium and not the whole of the £2,730. One can envisage a case in which a block of property comprising a large number of shops and other premises is let to one corporation for £30,000 a year. The corporation then sub-lets the separate shops to various small shopkeepers at perhaps £300 a year each. After some time the corporation goes into liquidation owing perhaps half a year's rent. It is quite plain that the legislature gives the right to the small shopkeeper to come and ask for relief. If counsel for the plaintiffs' contention is correct, the apparently wide discretion conferred by s. 146(4) is so limited that the court could not give relief to the small shopkeeper unless he paid the £15,000 rent in arrear in respect of the whole block. It is suggested that that would not work any hardship because he could recoup himself from the corporation. That does not really commend itself to me as a practical argument because, in the first place, he will not be able to find the £15,000, and in any event the insolvent corporation could not pay. I cannot believe that in circumstances such as those the court's discretion is fettered as contended on behalf of the plaintiffs. I should have thought that if the shopkeeper paid his proportion of the arrears, namely, £150, and it was otherwise just and equitable that there should be relief, he should obtain relief on that basis. I can certainly conceive of cases where it would be quite wrong to give a sub-lessee relief on this basis; great hardship could be caused to the head lessor if granting relief to one or two of many sub-tenants would make it impossible for him to deal with the premises as a whole. Every case must be considered on its own facts. . . .

20.5   Leasehold Property (Repairs) Act 1938

LEASEHOLD PROPERTY (REPAIRS) ACT 1938

1.   Restriction on enforcement of repairing covenants in long leases of small houses

(1)   Where a lessor serves on a lessee under subsection (1) of section one hundred and forty-six of the Law of Property Act 1925, a notice that relates to a breach of a covenant or agreement to keep or put in repair during the currency of the lease all or any of the property comprised in the lease, and at the date of the service of the notice three years or more of the term of the lease remain unexpired, the lessee may within twenty-eight days from that date serve on the lessor a counter-notice to the effect that he claims the benefit of this Act.

(2)   A right to damages for a breach of such a covenant as aforesaid shall not be enforceable by action commenced at any time at which three years or more of the term of the lease remain unexpired unless the lessor has served on the lessee not less than one month before the commencement of the action such a notice as is specified in subsection (1) of section one hundred and forty-six of the Law of Property Act 1925, and where a notice is served under this subsection, the lessee may, within twenty-eight days from the date of the service thereof, serve on the lessor a counter-notice to the effect that he claims the benefit of this Act.

(3)   Where a counter-notice is served by a lessee under this section, then, notwithstanding anything in any enactment or rule of law, no proceedings, by action or otherwise, shall be taken by the lessor for the enforcement of any right of re-entry or forfeiture under any proviso or stipulation in the lease for breach of the covenant or agreement in question, or for damages for breach thereof, otherwise than with the leave of the court.

(4)   A notice served under subsection (1) of section one hundred and forty-six of the Law of Property Act 1925, in the circumstances specified in subsection (1) of this section, and a notice served under subsection (2) of this section shall not be valid unless it contains a statement, in characters not less conspicuous than those used in any other part of the notice, to the effect that the lessee is entitled under this Act to serve on the lessor a counter-notice claiming the benefit of this Act, and a statement in the like characters specifying the time within which, and the manner in which, under this Act a counter-notice may be served and specifying the name and address for service of the lessor.

(5)   Leave for the purposes of this section shall not be given unless the lessor proves—

(a)   that the immediate remedying of the breach in question is requisite for preventing substantial diminution in the value of his reversion, or that the value thereof has been substantially diminished by the breach;

(b).   that the immediate remedying of the breach is required for giving effect in relation to the premises to the purposes of any enactment, or of any byelaw or other provision having effect under an enactment, or for giving effect to any order of a court or requirement of any authority under any enactment or any such byelaw or other provision as aforesaid;

(c)   in a case in which the lessee is not in occupation of the whole of the premises as respects which the covenant or agreement is proposed to be enforced, that the immediate remedying of the breach is required in the interests of the occupier of those premises or of part thereof;

(d)   that the breach can be immediately remedied at an expense that is relatively small in comparison with the much greater expense that would probably be occasioned by postponement of the necessary work; or

(e) special circumstances which in the opinion of the court, render it just and equitable that leave should be given.

(6) The court may, in granting or in refusing leave for the purposes of this section, impose such terms and conditions on the lessor or on the lessee as it may think fit.

ASSOCIATED BRITISH PORTS v *CH BAILEY PLC* [1990] 1 All ER 929, House of Lords

FACTS: Landlords of a dry-dock which had fallen into disuse served a forfeiture notice (under s. 146 of the Law of Property Act 1925) on the tenant, alleging breaches of their repairing covenant which would cost £600,000 to remedy. The tenants served a counter notice under the Leasehold Property (Repairs) Act 1938). The landlords brought proceedings for forfeiture, claiming that the continued disrepair of the premises would cause a substantial diminution of the value of the reversion. A master, a judge and then the Court of Appeal all confirmed that the landlord should succeed. The tenant appealed to the House of Lords.

HELD: The tenant's appeal was allowed. The landlord had to prove on the balance of probabilities that forfeiture was necessary to prevent a diminution of the value of the reversion. The landlord in this case had merely shown an arguable case.

LORD TEMPLEMAN: . . . save in special circumstances, the landlord must prove that the immediate remedying of a breach of the repairing covenant is required in order to save the landlord of the LP(R)A 1938 from substantial loss or damage which the landlord would otherwise sustain. By s. 1(6) the court can specify action to be taken by the tenant or impose other conditions in granting or withholding leave for the landlord to sue for forfeiture or damages.

In *National Real Estate and Finance Co. Ltd* v *Hassan* [1939] 2 KB 61 at 78, cf [1939] 2 All ER 154 at 161 Goddard LJ said that the mischief that the 1938 Act was designed to remedy—

> was speculators buying up small property in an indifferent state of repair, and then serving a schedule of dilapidations upon the tenants, which the tenants cannot comply with . . . this is the general mischief, that the speculator buys at a very low price, turns out the tenants, and gets the reversion which he has never paid for, which is a great hardship to the tenants.

Parliament must have concluded that similar mischief was caused to tenants of all properties because, by s. 51(3) of the Landlord and Tenant Act 1954, leases of all properties, except agricultural property, become subject to the 1938 Act. In the present case the landlords are not speculators or purchasers but have served a notice of dilapidation which can only be complied with by expenditure exceeding £600,000 which, according to the tenants, will be useless expenditure to the tenants and of minimal value to the landlords. If the landlords are allowed to pursue their remedies, the landlords may be able to recover the demised premises in the year 1990 instead of the year 2049.

Section 1 of the 1938 Act prevents the landlord from bringing proceedings for forfeiture and damages 'otherwise than with the leave of the court'. The immunity from suit thus conferred on the tenants is absolute unless the landlords prove that at least one of the requirements imposed by paras (a) to (e) of s. 1(5) is satisfied. The landlords have only established a prima facie or arguable case. The landlords have not proved in accordance with the balance of probabilities in the light of the evidence adduced by both the landlords and the tenants that the immediate remedying of the tenants' breach of their repairing covenant is requisite for preventing substantial diminution in the value of the landlords' reversion or that the breach has substantially diminished that value. The landlords submit that they need only establish a prima facie or arguable case and must then, on the true construction of the 1938 Act, be granted leave to institute proceedings for forfeiture and damages. In the course of those proceedings the tenants may seek to satisfy the court that they should be granted relief from forfeiture for their admitted breaches of covenant on the ground that the immediate remedying of the tenants' breaches of covenant is not required for the protection of the landlords. It is said, on behalf of the landlords, that the authorities and the practice of the courts support the view that in an application under s. 1 of the 1938 Act, the landlords are entitled to leave to pursue their remedies if they adduce evidence which consists of material on which, if it were accepted as accurate, an arguable case can be put forward. The justification for this course is said to be the avoidance of duplication and the saving of time and expense. If the landlords and the tenants produce their best evidence and the landlords prove the need for immediate remedying of breaches of covenant as required by the 1938 Act, the same or better evidence must be rehearsed in the ensuing action for forfeiture if the tenants resist forfeiture or seek relief from forfeiture. . .

SEDAC INVESTMENTS LTD v *TANNER AND OTHERS* [1982] 3 All ER 646, Chancery Division

FACTS: A local Conservative Club had convenanted to carry out repairs of the premises of which they were tenant, but had allowed the building to fall into a dangerous state of disrepair. The landlords (under pressure from the local authority) carried out the repairs themselves. The landlords then served a forfeiture notice under s. 146 of the Law of Property Act 1925 on the tenant. The tenant argued that the notice had been invalid for the purposes of s. 1 of the Leasehold Property (Repairs) Act 1938.
HELD: The tenant was granted relief from forfeiture. The s. 146 notice had not been validly served. It should have been served before the repairs were remedied.

MICHAEL WHEELER QC: . . . I am forced to the conclusion that in a case such as the present, where the lessor remedied the breach before attempting to serve a notice under s. 146(1), he has thereby put it out of his power to serve a valid s. 146 notice at all, with the result that he has deprived the lessee of his right to serve a counter-notice, and the consequence of this seems inevitably to be that the court has no jurisdiction to give the lessor leave to commence proceedings for damages because that jurisdiction arises, as I have already indicated, only where (and because) the lessee has served a valid counter-notice.

It is also true, as was pointed out in argument, that in the present case the lessors might have protected their position in other ways. For example, (1) they might have invoked cl. 2(4) of the lease and called on the lessees to remedy the breach; and they could have reinforced this by seeking, or threatening to seek, a mandatory injunction on the lessees to undertake the necessary remedial work; alternatively, (2) they might have served a notice under s. 146(1) (however general and imprecise the terms of that notice might, in the circumstances, have had to be) and might have also stated that in view of the urgency they regarded it as essential (and, ex hypothesi, as reasonable) that the lessees should at least commence to remedy the breach within, say, 48 hours.

As to these alternatives, they must, if they are valid, apply to any similar situation whether more or less urgent than in the present case. Suffice it to say that I do not consider either of them to be of any practical value in a case of real emergency.

In the present case, the basic trouble has arisen partly from the urgency of the repairs which were undoubtedly required (Mr Laker's evidence on this score is uncontroverted and is accepted as correct by counsel for the lessees) and partly from the fact that at the time when the damage to the wall was first noticed neither side (and I state this as a fact rather than as a criticism) was apparently aware of their respective legal rights and obligations. The lessees were unaware of the nature and extent of their liabilities under the repairing covenant in the lease; and the lessors were unaware of their rights under cl. 2(4) of the lease.

So it was that when the emergency arose (an emergency which the lessees themselves first brought to the attention of the lessors) it was the latter who (rightly as the factual position was to prove) took immediate emergency action. True it is that they did so really on their own initiative and without, as their counsel accepted, first giving the lessees the opportunity to take remedial action themselves. But the fact remains that the emergency basically arose as a result of the lessees' failure to comply with their obligations under the repairing covenant in the lease.

Nevertheless, for the reasons which I have given, I feel bound to conclude that in the present case the lessees are correct in arguing that the purported s. 146 notice given by the lessors did not (and on the facts could not) comply with the requirements of s. 1(2) of the 1938 Act and accordingly that I have no jurisdiction to give leave to the lessors as contemplated by that section to take proceedings to enforce their claim for damages for breach of the repairing covenant. But, in case this matter should go further, I wish to make it clear that, if I felt that as a matter of law I had such jurisdiction, I would, on the facts of this case, unhesitatingly exercise my judicial discretion in favour of the plaintiff lessors. . . .

JERVIS v *HARRIS* **[1996] 1 All ER 303, Court of Appeal**

FACTS: A tenant failed to comply with a repairing covenant in a lease which expressly conferred on a landlord the right to enter on the demised premises, carry out the repairs himself and recover the cost from the tenant.

HELD: An action by the landlord to recover the cost of the repairs is a claim in debt for reimbursement of sums spent in carrying out the repairs himself rather than a claim for damages for breach of the covenant to repair within s. 1 of the Leasehold Property (Repairs) Act 1938, and accordingly the landlord does not require leave under s. 1(3) to bring the action against the tenant.

MILLETT LJ: . . .

The 1938 Act issue

Clause 2(10) of the underlease authorises the landlord or the superior landlords to enter upon the demised premises from time to time during the term granted to view the state of repair and to give notice in writing to the tenant of any defects or want of repair. The tenant is required within three months to make good all such defects or want of repair of which he has been given notice and in default the landlord or the superior landlords may do the work themselves and recover the costs and expenses of the work from the tenant on demand.

. . . a clause such as cl. 2(10) . . . enables the landlord to take remedial action himself to avoid any loss consequent on the tenant's failure to repair. Once the landlord has carried out the repairs himself, the value of his interest in the property is restored. The work of repair enures to the benefit of the tenant as well as the landlord. The landlord is out of pocket, but that is because he has carried out repairs, not because the property is in disrepair.

Counsel for the defendant emphasises that the landlord's right under cl. 2(10) to enter the property and effect the necessary repairs at the tenant's expense cannot arise unless there has first been a breach by the tenant of his repairing obligations, not only under cl. 2(7) to keep the property in repair, but also under cl. 2(10) itself to effect repairs on notice. He accepts that s. 1 of the 1938 Act can have no application in the absence of any repairing covenant on the part of the tenant; but where the landlord's right to reimbursement depends on an anterior breach of his repairing obligations by the tenant, he submits, the section applies.

I do not accept this. Leaving aside for the moment the landlord's claim to reimbursement, his contractual right to enter the property and effect the repairs himself if the tenant does not do so is plainly outside the section. Nothing in the section requires him to obtain the leave of the court either before entry or before service of notice of disrepair. Should he then decide to bring proceedings for forfeiture or damages for breach of covenant, whether to repair or to repair on notice, he must first obtain the leave of the court under the section. But if he chooses instead to effect the repairs himself, there is nothing in the section which requires him to obtain the leave of the court before doing so. . . .

The landlord's claim to reimbursement is not triggered by the tenant's breach of covenant but by his own expenditure in carrying out repairs. The fact that the property is in disrepair is not enough. The landlord must have carried out work to remedy the want of repair; and his right to do so does not depend upon the existence of any covenant on the part of the tenant, but simply upon there being a want of repair which the tenant has failed to remedy within the stated period after notice. The fact that the tenant is thereby also in breach of covenant is neither here nor there. It merely means that the landlord has an alternative remedy of claiming damages for breach of covenant. But the presence of an alternative remedy which the landlord does not choose to enforce cannot affect the proper characterisation of the remedy which he does. . . .

20.6   Reform of Forfeiture of Leases

Clarke, A., Property Law (1992) 45 *Current Legal Problems* 81 at 104

. . . Forfeiture displays the best and worst features of a self-help remedy. When exercised extra-judicially it is fast and effective remedy for breach, and it is sufficiently drastic in effect to deter breaches. In fact it has been so successful in this jurisdiction that it has developed at the expense of doctrines of repudiatory breach and frustration. On the other hand, its bad features are, first, that it affects the interests of third parties, who may have had no knowledge of the breach and no means of preventing it, and secondly that its effect between the parties bears no relation to the effect of the breach: it can inflict loss on the tenant quite disproportionate to the blameworthiness of the breach, and it can produce a windfall profit for the landlord. *Cardigan Properties Ltd* v *Consolidated Property Investments Ltd* [1991] 7 EG 132 provides a good illustration. The freeholder had granted a 999-year lease of a residential block at a peppercorn rent for a premium of £770,000. Twelve years later the lease was assigned to the present tenant for £6,829,000, who bought it with the aid of a loan secured by a mortgage of the lease. In circumstances which were only marginally the fault of the tenant and created no real risk to the freeholder, the freeholder sought to forfeit by actual re-entry on the grounds of breach of the tenant's covenant to insure. In fact the court found that the re-entry was premature (insufficient time had been given for the remedy of the breach): had the court not done so it would, in the present state of the law, have been powerless to prevent the freeholder obtaining a windfall worth over £6,000,000 at the expense of the tenant and its wholly blameless mortgagee.

Unsurprisingly, given its potential for producing such dramatic results, both equity and statute have from an early stage intervened to regulate the exercise of the right to forfeit. Equity intervened as part of its general jurisdiction to grant relief against penalties, forfeiture of property, and unconscionable insistence on legal rights. The first statutory intervention was in fact made to regulate the equitable jurisdiction to grant relief against forfeiture for non-payment of rent: the Landlord and Tenant Act 1730, passed to relieve landlords who had been adversely affected by the courts of equity granting relief from forfeiture for non-payment of rent long after the lease had been forfeited at law, effectively barred a tenant from relief unless application was made within six months after the landlord obtained judgment. Later statutes introduced more positive but piecemeal regulation of forfeiture, which developed parallel to, or more accurately, entwined with, developments in the equitable jurisdiction.

The present interplay between equity and the complicated network of statute in this area is difficult to follow, and a matter of current controversy. In particular, there are two complicating factors. The first is that forfeiture for non-payment of rent has developed separately from forfeiture for breach of other covenants. The second is that most of the statutory provisions deal with forfeiture and relief as procedural rather than substantive matters: as a consequence, some (whether deliberately or accidentally) deal only with court proceedings for forfeiture, making no provision for forfeiture by actual re-entry, and others deal only with county court, or only with High Court, proceedings.

For present purposes, the essential problem is this. Both equity and statute—sometimes pulling together and at other times working against each other—have sought to ensure that forfeiture is used only as security for the performance of the obligations under the lease, by allowing the tenant, and any subtenant or mortgagee of the tenant's interest, relief against the forfeiture in all appropriate cases. But given the piecemeal development of the equitable and statutory jurisdictions, it is not surprising that there are gaps in the protection. The gap currently being exploited by landlords is that in the case of a breach of covenant other than to pay rent, the court appears to have no jurisdiction to grant relief against forfeiture to a tenant, subtenant, or mortgagee once the forfeiture is completed: since forfeiture by actual re-entry is completed as soon as the landlord enters, and no notice of re-entry is required, the opportunity to apply for relief can be removed by stealth. . . .

The Law Commission (Law Com. No. 142) Codification of the Law of Landlord and Tenant: Forfeiture of Tenancies, London: HMSO, 21 March 1985

SUMMARY OF RECOMMENDATIONS

(1) The law of forfeiture has become unnecessarily complicated, is no longer coherent and gives rise to injustices. The report recommends its replacement by a new system. In cases where the fault is that of the landlord, the tenant now has no means of terminating the tenancy. The report recommends that he should have a right to do so which is broadly analogous to that of the landlord under the new system. . . .

THE DETAILS OF THE TERMINATION ORDER SCHEMES PROPOSED

(6)   The scheme is based upon a system under which there would be no distinction between termination for non-payment of rent and termination for other reasons and under which the tenancy would continue in full force until the court made an order—a *'termination order'*—determining the date on which it should end. . . .

GROUNDS FOR A TERMINATION ORDER: 'TERMINATION ORDER EVENTS'

(10)   Grounds on which the landlord may base an application for a termination order may conveniently be called *'termination order events'*. They should be of three kinds. . . .

(a)   **Breaches of covenant**

(11)   All breaches of covenant by the tenant should be termination order events. We use the word 'covenant' in the wide sense, to include all the obligations owed by tenant to landlord, whether they are expressly undertaken or implied at common law or by statute. . . .

(12)   Although under the present law breaches of covenant are grounds for forfeiture only if they are expressly made so by the inclusion in the tenancy of a 'forfeiture clause', no such special provision should be necessary to make them termination order events. But:

(a)   This should not apply to tenancies granted before the date on which the implementing legislation comes into force: in such tenancies a breach of covenant should be a termination order event only if covered by a forfeiture clause.

(b)   If a tenancy, though granted after that date, is granted in pursuance of a binding obligation in existence before that date, and the obligation was such that a forfeiture clause was not to be included (or was not to be included in relation to some of the tenant's covenants) then the obligation should be interpreted as requiring the inclusion of an express term excluding the termination order scheme in relation to the tenant's covenants (or some of them as the case may be). . . .

(13)   Where an obligation entered into before the date on which the implementing legislation comes into force was such that a forfeiture clause *was* to be included in a tenancy granted after that date, that requirement should be treated as fulfilled if the tenancy maintains silence on the point, so allowing breaches of covenant to be termination order events. . . .

(b)   **Disguised breaches of covenant**

(14)   Termination order events should also include all events on the happening of which the tenancy (whether through the inclusion of a condition or limitation or for any other reason) is to cease (whether immediately or after a period) or the landlord is to have the right (whether or not on notice) to apply for a termination order, to forfeit the tenancy or to bring it to an end in any other way or to require its surrender or its assignment to a person nominated or to be nominated by him—being events against which a landlord would be expected to protect himself (if he protected himself at all) through the imposition of a covenant upon the tenant. . . .

(c)   **Insolvency events**

(15)   Termination order events should also include all events on the happening of which the tenancy (whether through the inclusion of a condition, limitation or for any other reason) is to cease (whether immediately or after a period) or the landlord is to have the right (whether or not on notice) to apply for a termination order, to forfeit the tenancy or bring it to an end in any other way, or to require its surrender or its assignment to a person nominated or to be nominated by him—being events having to do with the actual or threatened bankruptcy or insolvency of the tenant or any surety and including (but without prejudice to the generality of the foregoing words):

bankruptcy of, or the commission of any act of bankruptcy by, or the making of a receiving order against, a tenant or surety who is an individual;

entering into liquidation, compulsory or voluntary, by any tenant or surety which is a company, or having a receiver appointed in respect of any of its assets;

a tenant or surety entering into any arrangement or composition for the benefit of creditors; or

a tenant suffering the tenancy to be taken in execution; or a tenant or surety suffering any distress or execution to be levied on goods. . . .

PART VI   WAIVER

(21)   The law which now governs the circumstances in which a landlord is debarred by waiver from forfeiting a tenancy on a particular ground is unsatisfactory. A termination order event should be regarded as waived if, and only if, the landlord's conduct, after he has knowledge of the event, is such that it would lead a reasonable tenant to believe, and does in fact lead the actual tenant to believe, that he will not seek a termination order on the ground of that event. . . .

(22)   And if the event is a continuing breach of covenant, it should be a question of fact whether and how far the landlord has led the tenant reasonably to believe that he has waived it for the future as well as for the past. . . .

(23)   It should be possible, according to analogous rules, for the landlord to grant a waiver which is conditional upon some action on the part of the tenant. . . .

(24)   A termination order event should generally remain available as a ground for a termination order despite the fact that its consequences may have been remedied. . . .

Wilkinson, H. W., The Rush to Simplification [1994] Conv 177

Termination of Tenancies Bill
The Law Commission seems to have taken an objection to all that beautiful and involved learning which has for so long been a delight to the industrious student. Once more it has produced proposals for 'simplifying' the law, heedless of the wise maxim derived from our transatlantic cousins, 'if it ain't real broke, don't fix it.'. . .

Outline of the Scheme
The Law Commission outlines its proposed new scheme as follows. A landlord will no longer be able to forfeit a lease for breach of covenant or insolvency, or for failure to fulfill a condition. He will instead have the right to bring termination order proceedings to end the lease. A proviso for re-entry or other such provision would not be needed in the lease, but the right to bring termination proceedings could be excluded (or presumably restricted) by an express term. The tenancy will continue until a court orders that it should end. The court order could be of two types, the first that it will end on a stated day, the other that it will end if the tenant has not taken specified remedial action within a stated period. Any derivative interests will come to an end unless the landlord or the owner of the derivative interest makes an appropriate application to the court and an order in his favour is made. A Termination of Tenancies Bill is included in the report.

The Bill and Notes
By clause 1 and 2, the landlord's power to determine a tenancy by re-entry or forfeiture is abolished and the only way in which termination may be procured is by a termination order event taking place and a court then making a termination order. Exceptions would be where the landlord believes and has reasonable cause to believe that the tenant has abandoned the whole of the property and one or more termination order events has taken place. The landlord must serve a notice on the tenant and if no counter-notice is received the tenancy will end six months later. In the meantime the landlord will be able to enter and 'take such steps as are immediately necessary for securing the property and preserving it from damage.' The explanatory note says that entering the property to secure it would not terminate the tenancy but would absolve the landlord from any liability for trespass. By clause 40(2) guidance is given as to the meaning of 'abandonment'; it has both a physical and a mental element ('is not occupying it' and 'has no intention of occupying it'). Conviction for knowingly using premises as a brothel, under the Sexual Offences Act 1956, is a ground for the landlord to require assignment of the lease to someone else, or termination in a case of non-compliance.

By clause 5, a breach of any of the tenant's obligations (meaning by clause 47(1) created by covenant and owed by the tenant to the landlord in his capacity as landlord) is a termination order event, whether an act or an omission, repudiatory or not. Now, here is the earth-shaking change. By clause 5(3) a breach of the tenant's obligation to pay rent becomes a termination order event 'without a formal demand having been made,' but there is to be a period of 21 days' grace (or such other period as is stipulated) after the date the rent is overdue for payment to be made. Some leases are so framed that they may be terminated by the landlord where an event occurs which does not arise from the act or omission of the tenant 'neutral events.' Examples are given of the grant of planning permission or the bankruptcy of a surety. By clause 39, in such cases, the landlord may determine the tenancy by giving not less than one month's notice from the date of the notice. He must give the notice not later than six months after the event came to his knowledge and he must not have waived compliance.

By clause 4 the court could make a termination order or a remedial order. Under the latter, by clauses 8 and 9 it could order a payment to the landlord, the discontinuance of a breach and the obtaining of a surety.

The Law Commission considered that the present law on waiver of breaches was too technical and that waiver was too easy to make inadvertently, such as by demanding rent through an employee of an estate agent when instructions had been given not to do so. By clause 11(1) the rule is proposed to be that a landlord may choose to waive but is only to be held to do so against his will if,

(a)   his conduct, after it came to the knowledge of the tenant, would have led a reasonable tenant to believe and in fact led the tenant to believe, that the landlord would not seek to rely on it, or;

(b)   in the case of non-compliance with a condition, that the landlord's conduct, after it came to the tenant's knowledge, would have led a reasonable tenant to believe, and did in fact lead the tenant to believe, that the landlord would not seek to rely on the breach if the condition were fulfilled and the condition was in fact fulfilled. Thus this particular breach of obligation would not remain a ground for termination after it had been remedied.

By clause 13 and 14 there are three cases in which the court will have a duty to make an absolute termination order. The first is where it is satisfied that a termination event of a serious character has occurred whilst the tenant has held the tenancy or that terminating events have been frequent during that time (even if not acted on by the landlord) and in addition it appears to the court that the tenant is therefore such an unsatisfactory tenant that he ought not to remain tenant. The purpose of this is to deal with the 'stigma' cases but to decide each on its merits. The second case is where the tenancy has been assigned to forestall the risk of an absolute order under the first provision and where in addition it appears to the court that there is a substantial risk of the continuance of the termination events (this is to prevent profitable continued misuse of the property). The third case is where there has been an assignment in breach of the tenant's obligations or an insolvency event (defined in clause 47(2)) has occurred and the court is satisfied that a remedial order will not provide an adequate remedy. . . .

The new proposals affect all types of lease, residential, agricultural and business but they do not override any special protection given by statute to various classes of tenant, such as under the Landlord and Tenant Act 1954 for business tenants.

Ah well, those who think that the law of forfeiture produces 'needless complication' may yet have their way. Next they will wish to simplify the rules of chess.

20.7 End of Chapter Assessment Question

In 1983 Letitia leased (by deed) a shop to Tamsin for 40 years. The lease includes a covenant under which the tenant undertakes to ensure that the shop is not used for illegal purposes. Rent is payable quarterly and in advance to Letitia's agent Rocky. The lease also includes a forfeiture clause which can be invoked if the tenant breaks any of the covenants.

In 1995 Tamsin lawfully assigned the lease to Ann. In early 1996 Dandy, one of Ann's shop assistants, took advantage of the fact that Ann did not normally arrive at the shop until 9.30 a.m. He started an early morning 'side-line' selling Cocaine. After only a month Ann found out about the illegal trade. She immediately dismissed Dandy and reported his activities to the police. Last week Dandy was convicted of drug-trafficking.

Letitia has just read of Dandy's conviction in the local newspaper. She has decided to endeavour to forfeit the lease. She tells you, 'The rent under the existing lease is ridiculously low; if I can get Ann out a new tenant would be willing to pay three times as much'.

Advise Letitia.

20.8 End of Chapter Assessment Outline Answer

There is one point of which Letitia should be warned almost the moment she has sat down in the office. As she wishes to forfeit the lease she should be careful not to do anything which might be construed by a court as 'Waiver'. In particular she should inform Rocky that he should neither demand nor accept any further instalments of rent.

Demanding/accepting rent is always a waiver of forfeiture even if done by an agent of the landlord who is ignorant of the landlord's intent to forfeit. (See *Belgravia* v *Woolgar*.) Letitia should immediately insist that Rocky marks his file relating to the shop 'No rent to be collected'. If Rocky uses a computer system to send out rent demands/reminders, the computer must be reprogrammed immediately.

The forfeiture process instituted by Letitia should proceed in two stages.

(1) Serve a notice under section 146 of the LPA and then (after waiting a reasonable time).
(2) Issue a writ claiming forfeiture of the lease and possession of the property.

(It is still theoretically possible to forfeit a lease without court proceedings, using 'peaceable re-entry'. Letitia might be tempted to do what the landlords did in *Billson* v *Residential Apartments*; sneak in very early one morning when no-one is at the shop.

However the House of Lords decision in *Billson* makes peaceable re-entry an undesirable course. Under the Lords' decision a tenant can claim relief from forfeiture after the landlord has peaceably re-entered, perhaps quite a long time after. Thus after the peaceable re-entry no new tenant would be keen to take a lease of the property for fear that Ann would reappear claiming relief.)

The section 146 notice should be served on Ann (the current tenant, see *Old Grovebury*). Extreme care should be taken in drafting the notice. If the notice is not correctly drafted, any court proceedings for forfeiture commenced after the notice will be abortive, and Letitia will have to start all over again.

The notice should give full details of the breach of covenant, and if Letitia wants monetary compensation the notice should contain a demand for such compensation.

If Ann's breach is 'capable of remedy' the notice should include a demand that the breach be remedied. This 'capable of remedy' point is notoriously tricky.

Normally a breach by a tenant of a covenant against illegal user is irremediable. The damage has been done; the property has been besmirched; everyone knows that the house is a brothel or the shop a drug den. . . . However Letitia's case looks slightly like the problematic case of *Glass* v *Kencakes* where Paull J (not a specialist land lawyer) held that illegal user by a sub-tenant in breach of the head lease had been remedied by evicting the sub-tenant before the property became tainted.

Letitia is therefore advised to play safe. She should include in the section 146 notice a clause, 'Remedy this breach if capable of remedy'. Moreover she should wait at least three months between serving the notice and issuing her writ. (A fortnight wait would be sufficient if the breach were irremediable.)

Having got to court (and getting there is clearly going to take at minimum a few months) Letitia should be warned that Ann will probably apply (by way of counterclaim) for relief from forfeiture. Although relief from forfeiture is in the discretion of the court, Ann's case for relief is strong. (The breach may be technically incapable of remedy, but the Court of Appeal in *Woolgar* and now the Lords in *Billson* have made it clear that relief can be granted with respect to an irremediable breach.)

Ann has a strong case for relief as the breach was not committed by her personally but by her employee. She sacked Dandy the moment she found out. To grant forfeiture would be to deprive Ann of a very valuable asset—a lease with 26 years to run at (seemingly) a cheap rent. When Ann acquired the lease in 1995 she presumably had to pay quite a substantial price to Tamsin.

Probably Letitia's only hope is to come to court in a state of righteous indignation, fuming, 'I will not have my shop used as an emporium for HARD drugs such as Cocaine. Ann should have been careful whom she employed, and should have been at the shop every day when it opened.'

It would be fatal to her chances of forfeiture for Letitia to let on that she only wanted Ann out in order to get in a tenant who was willing to pay a much higher rent (*cf. Woolgar*). Moreover, if Ann proves that Letitia already has a new tenant lined up, that would destroy any claim that the property had been tainted.

It would thus appear that Letitia is likely to spend a lot of money, time and energy pursuing forfeiture proceedings which will probably end with relief from forfeiture being granted. It is probably not worth all the effort, particularly when it is remembered that Letitia will not be able to collect any rent while the forfeiture proceedings are pending.

Letitia may feel confident that she can relet the property at a much higher rent. In the current economic climate her confidence may be misplaced. We see a lot of empty shops, even in the (relatively) prosperous South-East. If the shop was left unlet for any length of time Letitia might even have a problem with 'shop squatters'.

Letitia might, as an alternative to forfeiture, consider suing for damages. She has the choice of suing Tamsin (privity of contract) or Ann (privity of estate). However, as Letitia's reversion is not due to come into possession until 2023, it is difficult to see her recovering anything more than nominal damages.

CHAPTER TWENTY-ONE

ADVERSE POSSESSION AND THE LIMITATION ACTS

21.1 Introduction

**Lawson, F. H., and Rudden, B., The Law of Property, 2nd edn,
Oxford: Clarendon Press, 1982, p. 51**

LIMITATION OF ACTIONS AND RIGHTS

. . . Persons acquiring movables seldom trouble themselves with questions of title. But with land the barring of title by twelve years' adverse possession is important.

It operates as follows. Let us suppose that A has the best title to a piece of land which we shall call Blackacre—that is to say, a title which has no known title superior to it—and whilst he is away B takes possession of it. B now, by the very fact that he possesses Blackacre, has title to it, but one that can be defeated by A. If, however, A does not take steps to recover possession for twelve years, by ousting B or bringing an action against him, he loses his title, and B's title, which was formerly the best but one, becomes the best. But his title does not then become a new one; it is still the same one that he obtained by dispossessing A; and this may have important consequences which are too technical to detain us here.

It might be thought that a purchaser of land would feel safe in limiting his researches into his vendor's title to a period of twelve years in the past. This is unfortunately not the case. For there may be persons who have rights in the land which will entitle them to possession at some future date. Until that time they will have no right to recover possession from an intruder, and the Limitation Act gives them some years from that time and not from the original intrusion in which to recover possession. No limit can be set to the period during which the purchaser should push back his investigations in order to be absolutely safe. However, as a practical matter some period must be fixed and the law has chosen to say that, unless a special agreement has been made to the contrary, a purchaser is entitled to trace back the vendor's title only to some good root of title at least fifteen years old. A good root of title is some document, such as a conveyance on sale, which transferred the interest which the purchaser seeks to acquire, which dealt completely with the title to it in law and equity, and contained nothing to cast doubts upon the title of the vendor. . . .

BUCKINGHAMSHIRE COUNTY COUNCIL v MORAN
[1989] 2 All ER 225, Court of Appeal

FACTS: In 1955, the plaintiff council had acquired a plot of land near some houses, intending at some future date to use the land for a road diversion. Before then the land was to be left vacant. In fact, the resident of a house adjoining the plot decided to maintain the plot of land and treated it as part of their own garden. The only access to the plot was through their garden. In 1971 the defendant bought the house and continued to treat the plot as if it were part of his garden, even though he was fully aware that the council owned it. Indeed, in a letter to the council he had asserted his belief that he was entitled to use the plot until the proposed road diversion was built. The council, in reply, refuted his claimed entitlement to use the land, but they took no measures to regain possession of the land at that time. Only in 1985 did they eventually issue a writ claiming possession of the plot. The defendant raised s. 15(1) of the Limitation Act 1980 in his defence, claiming that the council were time-barred from bringing an action to recover possession, on account of 12 years adverse possession.

HELD: The council's claim for possession was barred by the Limitation Act 1980. The defendant had established the necessary adverse possession.

SLADE LJ: On this appeal counsel for the council has accepted that if the plot was in adverse possession of the defendant more that 12 years before action was bought (i.e. on 28 October 1973) it has not ceased to be in adverse possession since that time. Ultimately, therefore, the crucial question will be: was the defendant in adverse possession of the plot on 28 October 1973?

Possession is never 'adverse' within the meaning of the 1980 Act if it is enjoyed under a lawful title. If, therefore a person occupies or uses land by licence of the owner with the paper title and his licence has not been duly determined, he cannot be treated as having been in 'adverse possession' as against the owner with the paper title.

Before the passing of the 1980 Act certain decisions of this court, in particular *Wallis's Cayton Bay Holiday Camp* v *Shell-Mex and BP Ltd* [1974] 3 All ER 575, [1975] QB 94 and *Gray* v *Wykeham-Martin* [1977] CA Transcript 10A, were thought to have established a general doctrine that in one special type of case there would be implied in favour of the would-be adverse possessor, *without any specific factual basis for such implication*, a licence permitting him to commit the acts of possession on which he sought to rely; the effect of implying such a licence would, of course, be to prevent the squatter's possession from being 'adverse'. That special type of case was broadly one where the acts of an intruder, however continuous and far-reaching, did not substantially interfere with any plans which the owners might have for the future use of undeveloped land.

... The doctrine of the implied licence has now been abrogated by para. 8(4) of Sch. 1 to the 1980 Act, which provides:

> For the purpose of determining whether a person occupying any land is in adverse possession of the land it shall not be assumed by implication of law that his occupation is by permission of the person entitled to the land merely by virtue of the fact that his occupation is not inconsistent with the latter's present or future enjoyment of the land. This provision shall not be taken as prejudicing a finding to the effect that a person's occupation of any land is by implied permission of the person entitled to the land in any case where such a finding is justified on the actual facts of the case.

In the light of this provision, it would at first sight appear that there is now no reason why the words 'possess' and 'dispossess' or similar expressions should not be given their ordinary legal meaning in the context of the 1980 Act. However, counsel for the council, while accepting that the implied licence doctrine is now abrogated, nevertheless submits that para. 8(4) (I quote from his skeleton argument)—

> leaves intact the special rule formulated by Bramwell LJ in *Leigh* v *Jack* ((1879) 5 Ex D 264) and Sir John Pennycuick in *Treloar* v *Nute* ([1977] 1 All ER 230, [1976] 1 WLR 1295) that where land is acquired or retained by the owner for a specific future purpose then acts of trespass which are not inconsistent with such purpose do not amount to dispossession. ...

... it must, in my judgment, be too broad a proposition to suggest that an owner who retains a piece of land with a view to its utilisation for a specific purpose in the future can never be treated as dispossessed, however firm and obvious the intention to dispossess, and however drastic the acts of dispossession of the person seeking to dispossess him may be. ...

I turn then to consider the first of the two requisite elements of possession. First, as at 28 October 1973 did the defendant have factual possession of the plot? I venture to repeat what I said in *Powell* v *McFarlane* (1977) 38 P & CR 452 at 470–471:

Factual possession signifies an appropriate degree of physical control. It must be a single and [exclusive] possession . . . Thus an owner of land and a person intruding on that land without his consent cannot both be in possession of the land at the same time. The question what acts constitute a sufficient degree of exclusive physical control must depend on the circumstances, in particular the nature of the land and the manner in which land of that nature is commonly used or enjoyed.

On evidence it would appear clear that by 28 October 1973 the defendant had acquired complete and exclusive physical control of the plot. He had secured a complete enclosure of the plot and its annexation to Dolphin Place. Any intruder could have gained access to the plot only by way of Dolphin Place, unless he was prepared to climb the locked gate fronting the highway or to scramble through one or other of the hedges bordering the plot. The defendant had put a new lock and chain on the gate and had fastened it. He and his mother had been dealing with the plot as any occupying owners might have been expected to deal with it. They had incorporated it into the garden of Dolphin Place. They had planted bulbs and daffodils in the grass. They had maintained it as part of that garden and had trimmed the hedges. I cannot accept counsel's submission for the council that the defendant's acts of possession were trivial. It is hard to see what more he could have done to acquire complete physical control of the plot by October 1973. In my judgment, he had plainly acquired factual possession of the plot by that time.

However as the judge said, the more difficult question is whether the defendant had the necessary *animus possidendi*. As to this, counsel for the council accepted the correctness of the following statement (so far as it went) which I made in *Powell* v *McFarlane* (at 471–472):

. . . the *animus possidendi* involves the intention, in one's own name and on one's own behalf, to exclude the world at large, including the owner with the paper title if he be not himself the possessor, so far as is reasonably practicable and so far as the processes of the law will allow.

At least at first sight the following observations of Lord Halsbury in *Marshall* v *Taylor* [1895] 1 Ch 641 at 645 (which were referred to by Hoffmann J in his judgment) are very pertinent to the present case:

The true nature of this particular strip of land is that it is inclosed. It cannot be denied that the person who says he owns it could not get to it in any ordinary way. I do not deny that he could have crept through the hedge, or, if it had been a brick wall, that he could have climbed over the wall; but that was not the ordinary and usual mode of access. That is the exclusion—the dispossession—which seems to me to be so important in this case.

As a number of authorities indicate, inclosure by itself *prima facie* indicates the requisite *animus possidendi*. As Cockburn CJ said in *Seddon* v *Smith* (1987) 36 LT 168 at 169: 'Enclosure is the strongest possible evidence of adverse possession . . .' Russell LJ in *George Wimpey & Co. Ltd* v *Sohn* [1966] 1 All ER 232 at 240, [1967] Ch 487 at 511 similarly observed: 'Ordinarily, of course, enclosure is the most cogent evidence of adverse possession and of dispossession of the true owner.' While counsel for the council pointed out that the plot was always accessible from the north where no boundary demarcation existed, it was only accessible from the defendant's own property, Dolphin Place. In my judgment, therefore, he must be treated as having inclosed it.

Counsel for the council, however, submitted that, even if inclosure had occurred, the defendant's intention must be assessed in the light of the particular circumstances of this case. The defendant knew that the council had acquired and retained the plot with the specific intention of building a road across it at some future time. The council had no use for the land in the interim. It was for all practical purposes waste land. None of the defendant's acts, he submitted, were inconsistent with the council's known future intentions. . . .

If the defendant had stopped short of placing a new lock and chain on the gate, I might perhaps have felt able to accept these submissions. Counsel for the council submitted that this act did not unequivocally show an intention to exclude the council as well as other people. It is well established that it is no use for an alleged adverse possessor to rely on acts which are merely equivocal as regards the intention to exclude the true owner: see for example *Tecbild Ltd* v *Chamberlain* (1969) 20 P & CR 633 at 642 per Sachs LJ. In my judgment, however, the placing of the new lock and chain and gate did amount to a final unequivocal demonstration of the defendant's intention to possess the land. . . .

The other main point which counsel for the council has argued in support of this appeal has caused me slightly more difficulty. In his submission there can be no sufficient *animus possidendi* to constitute adverse possession for the purpose of the 1980 Act unless there exists the intention to exclude the owner with the paper title in *all* future circumstances. The defendant's oral statements to Mr Harris in the conversation of 10 November 1975, as recorded in the attendance note, do appear to have constituted an implicit acknowledgment by the defendant that he would be obliged to leave the plot if in the future the council required it for the purpose of constructing the proposed new road. The letter of 18 December 1975, which I have concluded should be admitted in evidence, contains an express acknowledgment of this nature. If the intention to exclude the owner with the paper title in *all* future circumstances is a necessary constituent of the *animus possidendi*, the attendance notice and the letter of 18 December 1975 show that this constituent was absent in the present case.

There are some dicta in the authorities which might be read as suggesting that an intention to *own* the land is required. Lindley MR, for example, in *Littledale* v *Liverpool College* [1900] 1 Ch 19 at 23, referred to the 'acts of ownership' relied on by the plaintiffs. Russell LJ in *George Wimpey & Co. Ltd* v *Sohn* [1966] 1 All ER 232 at 240, [1967] Ch 487 at 510 said:

> . . . I am not satisfied that the actions of the *predecessors* in bricking up the doorway and maintaining a lock on the gate to the roadway were necessarily referable to an intention to occupy the [land] as their own absolute property. (Russell LJ's emphasis.)

At one point in my judgment in *Powell* v *McFarlane* (1977) 38 P & CR 452 at 478 I suggested that:

> . . . any objective informed observer might probably have inferred that the plaintiff was using the land simply for the benefit of his family's cow or cows, during such periods as the absent owner took no steps to stop him, without any intention to appropriate the land as his own.

Nevertheless, I agree with the judge that 'What is required for this purpose is not an intention to own or even an intention to acquire ownership but an intention to possess', that is to say an intention *for the time being* to possess the land to the exclusion of all other persons, including the owner with the paper title. No authorities cited to us establish the contrary proposition. The conversation with Mr Harris, as recorded in the attendance note and the letter of 18 December 1975, to my mind demonstrate the intention of the defendant for the time being to continue in possession of the plot to the exclusion of the council unless and until the proposed bypass is built. The form of the conveyance to the defendant and of the contemporaneous statutory declaration which he obtained from Mr and Mrs Wall are, of course, entirely consistent with the existence of an intention on his part to take and keep adverse possession of the plot, at least unless and until that event occurred.

In the light of the line of authorities to which we have been referred, beginning with *Leigh* v *Jack*, I have already accepted that the court should be slow to make a finding of adverse possession in a case such as the present. However, as the judge pointed out, in none of those earlier cases, where the owner with the paper title successfully defended his title, was there present the significant feature of complete inclosure of the land in question by the trespasser. On the evidence in the present case he was, in my judgment, right in concluding that the defendant had acquired adverse possession of the plot by 28 October 1973 and had remained in adverse possession of it ever since. There is no evidence that any representative of the council has even set foot on the plot since that date.

This appeal, which has been well argued on both sides, should in my judgment be dismissed.

21.2 The Limitation Act 1980

THE LIMITATION ACT 1980

15. Time limit for actions to recover land

(1) No action shall be brought by any person to recover any land after the expiration of twelve years from the date on which the right of action accrued to him or, if it first accrued to some person through whom he claims, to that person.

(2) Subject to the following provisions of this section, where—

(a) the estate or interest claimed was an estate or interest in revision or remainder or any other future estate or interest and the right of action to recover the land accrued on the date on which the estate or interest fell into possession by the determination of the preceding estate or interest; and

(b) the person entitled to the preceding estate or interest (not being a term of years absolute) was not in possession of the land on that date;

no action shall be brought by the person entitled to the succeeding estate or interest after the expiration of twelve years from the date on which the right of action accrued to the person entitled to the preceding estate or interest or six years from the date on which the right of action accrued to the person entitled to the succeeding estate or interest, whichever period last expires.

(3) Subsection (2) above shall not apply to any estate or interest which falls into possession on the determination of an entailed interest and which might have been barred by the person entitled to the entailed interest.

(4) No person shall bring an action to recover any estate or interest in land under an assurance taking effect after the right of action to recover the land had accrued to the person by whom the assurance was made or some person through whom he claimed or some person entitled to a preceding estate or interest, unless the action is brought within the period during which the person by whom the assurance was made could have brought such an action.

(5) Where any person is entitled to any estate or interest in land in possession and, while so entitled, is also entitled to any future estate or interest in that land, and his right to recover the estate or interest in possession is barred under this Act, no action shall be brought by that person, or by any person claiming through him, in respect of the future estate or interest, unless in the meantime possession of the land has been recovered by a person entitled to an intermediate estate or interest.

(6) Part I of Schedule 1 to this Act contains provisions for determining the date of accrual of rights of action to recover land in the cases there mentioned.

(7) Part II of that Schedule contains provisions modifying the provisions of this section in their application to actions brought by, or by a person claiming through, the Crown or any spiritual or eleemosynary corporation sole.

SCHEDULE I

Right of action not to accrue or continue unless there is adverse possession

8.—(1) No right of action to recover land shall be treated as accruing unless the land is in the possession of some person in whose favour the period of limitation can run (referred to below in this paragraph as 'adverse possession'); and where under the preceding provisions of this Schedule any such right of action is treated as accruing on a certain date and no person is in adverse possession on that date, the right of action shall not be treated as accruing unless and until adverse possession is taken of the land.

(2) Where a right of action to recover land has accrued and after its accrual, before the right is barred, the land ceases to be in adverse possession, the right of action shall no longer be treated as having accrued and no fresh right of action shall be treated as accruing unless and until the land is again taken into adverse possession.

(3) For the purpose of this paragraph—

(a) possession of any land subject to a rentcharge by a person (other that the person entitled to the rentcharge) who does not pay the rent shall be treated as adverse possession of the rentcharge; and

(b)   receipt of rent under a lease by a person wrongfully claiming to be entitled to the land in reversion immediately expectant on the determination of the lease shall be treated as adverse possession of the land.

(4)   For the purpose of determining whether a person occupying any land is in adverse possession of the land it shall not be assumed by implication of law that his occupation is by permission of the person entitled to the land merely by virtue of the fact that his occupation is not inconsistent with the latter's present or future enjoyment of the land.

This provision shall not be taken as prejudicing a finding to the effect that a person's occupation of any land is by implied permission of the person entitled to the land in any case where such a finding is justified on the actual facts of the case.

21.2.1   COMMENCEMENT OF ADVERSE POSSESSION

TRELOAR v NUTE [1977] 1 All ER 230, Court of Appeal

FACTS: The plaintiff and the defendant were adjoining farmers. The plaintiff (an elderly lady) had about one-seventh of an acre of waste ground which she totally forgot about. The defendant and his father in effect took over the ground. They levelled it off. (There had been a gully.) They then used it for various purposes such as an informal motor-bike trials course and a rubbish dump. Eventually the defendant started to build a bungalow on the ground. At this point Mrs Treloar issued a writ claiming to re-possess the land.
HELD: The defendant and his father were able to prove that they had been using the ground for more than twelve years and that the possession was adverse to Mrs Treloar's title. Her title was therefore extinguished and Nute (junior) was declared to hold a new title to the land.

SIR JOHN PENNYCUICK: . . . It is not in any doubt that under the 1939 Act as under the previous law, the person claiming by possession must show either (1) discontinuance by the paper owner followed by possession or (2) dispossession or, as it is sometimes called, 'ouster' of the paper owner. Clearly, possession concurrent with the paper owner is insufficient. On the other hand, where the person claiming by possession establishes possession in the full sense of exclusive possession, that by itself connotes absence of possession on the part of the paper owner and I doubt if there is any real difference in the concept of taking possession and the concept of dispossession except in the special type of case where the owner, although not technically in possession, has some purpose to which he intends to put the land in the future. . . .

The judge found, as we read his judgment, that the defendant's father took possession of the disputed land outside the limitation period but that this possession was not adverse by reason that it caused no inconvenience to the plaintiff. In our judgment the second part of this finding is contrary to the plain terms of [the Act], which in effect defines adverse possession as possession of some person in whose favour the period of limitation can run. It is not permissible to import into this definition a requirement that the owner must be inconvenienced or otherwise affected by that possession. Apart from the cases relating to special purpose no authority has been cited to us which would support the requirement of inconvenience to the owner and we are not ourselves aware of any such authority. On the contrary, so far as our own experience goes the typical instance in which a possessory title is treated as having been acquired is that in which a squatter establishes himself on a piece of land for which the owner has no use. Indeed, if inconvenience to the owner had to be established it would be difficult ever to acquire a possessory title since the owner if inconvenienced would be likely to take proceedings. . . .

21.2.2   THE 'ADVERSE' IN ADVERSE POSSESSION

HYDE v PEARCE [1982] 1 All ER 1029, Court of Appeal

FACTS: In 1958, the plaintiff agreed, at an auction, to purchase a plot of land. He went into possession without telling the vendors and the auctioneers agreed to lend him the keys on the understanding that he would return them on demand. Shortly after the plaintiff had moved into the premises, there arose a boundary dispute with a neighbour. The vendors sided with the neighbour and demanded that the plaintiff return the keys to the premises. He refused to do so. The vendors took no further action to remove the plaintiff. However, in 1972, the vendors sold the land to the defendant. That sale overreached any estate contract the plaintiff might have had, because he had never protected it by registering a land charge. The plaintiff was imprisoned about this time and when he emerged from prison he discovered that the defendant had demolished, reconstructed and taken possession of the house. He brought an action claiming that the vendor's title had been extinguished by his adverse possession, and that, therefore, the defendant had no title in the house.

HELD: The existence of the plaintiff's estate contract, which he had owned up until the sale to the defendant, was inconsistent with his claim to have acquired title by adverse possession. The defendant was declared the true owner of the property.

TEMPLEMAN LJ: . . . We were also referred to certain cases in which it was held that time did not begin to run under the Limitation Act because of the peculiar nature of the position of the person claiming a title under that Act. For example, in *Thomas v Thomas* (1855) 2 K & J 79, 69 ER 701, a father, who entered on property, was held not to have a possessory title as against his own children because, as I understand it, he clothed himself with the capacity of a trustee and a trustee cannot assert a possessory title against beneficiaries. . . .

. . . in the peculiar circumstances of this case, it seems to me that it is not sufficient to show that a right of action had accrued. The plaintiff must show some further quality, namely adverse possession. The plaintiff was allowed in possession as a purchaser pending completion; and he was allowed to stay there because he was a purchaser. If he had been a mere trespasser no doubt the vendors would have brought proceedings. But the vendors, in all the circumstances of the case, seem to have decided by accident or design to allow matters to drift on without taking steps to evict him from the premises, relying on the fact that it would all turn out right in the end when the purchase price was ascertained and completion took place. . . .

In my judgment, the plaintiff, having in effect been able to go in and stay under the contract, cannot now repudiate the contract with hindsight. As I have said, if, at any time, he made it clear that he was no longer bound by the contract, then different considerations would apply. Equally, no doubt, if he had made that clear, then the vendors would have taken action against him. It is only the fact that he was there as a purchaser pending completion which has enabled time to run in his favour, as he says, and which enables him to claim a title by adverse possession. Accordingly, in my judgment, although the full period by the 1939 Act has elapsed, the plaintiff has not shown that he was in adverse possession. . . .

21.2.3   THE 'APPARENTLY ABANDONED PLOT' PROBLEM

(Note that the following case must now be read subject to the case of *Bucks C.C.* v *Moran* and sch. 1, para. 8(4) of the Limitation Act 1980, above.)

WALLIS'S CAYTON BAY HOLIDAY CAMP LTD v *SHELL-MEX AND BP LTD*
[1974] 3 All ER 575, Court of Appeal

FACTS: The defendants acquired one-and-a-third acres in the middle of a field for the purposes of a new filling station. This one-and-a-third acres adjoined the site of a proposed new road, but neither the road nor the one-and-a-third acres were marked off by boundary markers. All a passer-by would see was an arable field no different from its neighbours. The field belonged to Wallis's, which it farmed, together with adjoining fields, through a subsidiary company. For eleven-and-a-half years Wallis's farming activities extended to the one-and-a-third acres. Then the local authority abandoned the scheme for the new road. Shell promptly wrote to Wallis's offering to sell the one-and-a-third acres. Wallis's did not reply. Instead they carried on their farming for eight more months and then claimed that they had acquired title through adverse possession.

HELD: Wallis's failed to establish title by adverse possession. The period of adverse possession had not commenced until after Shell had abandoned its plans for the land. There had therefore only been a few months of adverse possession, not the necessary twelve years.

LORD DENNING MR: . . . When the true owner of land intends to use it for a particular purpose in the future, but meanwhile has no immediate use for it, and so leaves it unoccupied, he does not lose his title to it simply because some other person enters on it and uses it for some temporary purpose, like stacking materials; or for some seasonal purpose, like growing vegetables. Not even if this temporary or seasonal purpose continues year after year for 12 years, or more: see *Leigh* v *Jack* (1879) 5 ExD 264, *Williams Brothers Direct Supply Stores Ltd* v *Raftery* [1957] 3 All ER 593, *Tecbild Ltd* v *Chamberlain* (1969) 20 P & CR 633. The reason is not because the user does not amount to actual possession. The line between acts of user and acts of possession is too fine for words. The reason behind the decisions is because it does not lie in that other person's mouth to assert that he used the land of his own wrong as a trespasser. Rather his user is to be ascribed to the licence or permission of the true owner. By using the land, knowing that it does not belong to him, he impliedly assumes that the owner will permit it; and the owner, by not turning him off, impliedly gives permission. And it has been held many times in this court that acts done under licence or permitted by the owner do not give a licensee a title under the Limitation Act 1939. They do not amount to adverse possession: see *Cobb* v *Lane* [1952] 1 All ER 1199 . . . in this court. . . .

21.3   Adverse Possession and Tenants

21.3.1   WHAT IF AN ADVERSE POSSESSOR DISPLACES A TENANT?

See **21.6.**

21.3.2   THE PROBLEM OF A TENANT ENCROACHING ON ADJOINING LAND

SMIRK v *LYNDALE DEVELOPMENTS LTD* [1975] 1 Ch 317, Court of Appeal

FACTS: The plaintiff, a British Railways employee, had a weekly service tenancy of a house owned by his employer. During the period of his occupation he took it upon himself to cultivate adjoining land ('the blue plot') which was also owned by his employer. His employer eventually sold the title to the house and 'the blue plot' to the defendant. The plaintiff claimed to have acquired title to 'the blue plot' by adverse possession.
HELD: Where a lessee encroaches upon other land, the encroachment is presumed to be an extension of the 'locus' of the lease (the tenant is presumed to be merely expanding the area granted to him). The plaintiff failed, therefore, to show that he had acquired title to 'the blue plot' by adverse possession.

LAWTON LJ: [Approved the following *dictum* of Pennycuik V-C in the court below] . . .

> Whatever accrued or accruing right the plaintiff may have had to include the blue plot in his tenancy from British Railways, this right must have determined with his tenancy under British Railways, and obviously no new right can have accrued against [the defendant] during the short time in which [the defendant has] been his landlord. There can be no ground for treating a period of two different tenancies as continuous for the present purposes. Contrast the position where a possessory title is acquired by successive squatters or against successive freeholders. The tenant, so long as the presumption applies, can do no more than acquire an addition to the subject-matter of the tenancy and his interest in that additional subject-matter must necessarily determine together with his interest in the original subject-matter.

21.4 Time Starts Running Afresh by Acknowledgment of Title

EDGINGTON v CLARK AND ANOTHER [1963] 3 All ER 468, Court of Appeal

FACTS: A person in adverse possession of certain freehold property wrote a letter to an agent of the owner making an offer to purchase the land. The offer was accepted and a deposit paid, but the purchase was never completed.

HELD: The letter showed that the adverse possessor acknowledged the title of the original owner. The period of adverse possession would begin afresh from the date of that acknowledgment.

UPJOHN LJ: . . . If a man makes an offer to purchase freehold property, even though it be subject to contract, he is quite clearly saying that as between himself and the person to whom he makes the offer, he realises that the offeree has a better title to the freehold land than himself, and that would seem to be the plainest possible form of acknowledgment.

Counsel for the plaintiff, however, has ingeniously argued that when an intending purchaser makes an offer to purchase, he does not thereby acknowledge that the vendor can prove or establish the title which the purchaser is entitled to have on a sale and purchase of land, and he says that the letters properly understood merely mean: 'If you can prove your title which I am bound to accept, then I will buy', and accordingly, so the argument proceeds, there is no acknowledgment of the vendor's title. We are quite unable to accept that argument. Of course an intending purchaser does not acknowledge that the vendor has a marketable title when he makes an offer to purchase. That is a matter for inspection of title and requisitions at a later stage; but what he does acknowledge is that as between the intending purchaser and the vendor, the vendor has the better title to the land and that seems to us all that is required.

. . . The question whether a particular writing amounts to an acknowledgment must depend on the true construction of the document in all the surrounding circumstances, and it is quite plain that in that case there was no acknowledgment by the writing, for it challenges the ownership of the true owner, but offers by way of compromise to accept a tenancy. Had a bargain been concluded, then no doubt that would have been an acknowledgment because by agreeing to become a tenant, the writer could not deny his landlord's title, and that, we think, is the explanation of the concluding words at the end of the judgment. Accordingly that case does not help the plaintiff. . . .

21.4.1 ACKNOWLEDGMENT OF TITLE MADE BY PERSON IN WHOSE FAVOUR TIME HAS ALREADY RUN IS OF NO EFFECT

COLCHESTER BOROUGH COUNCIL v SMITH AND OTHERS [1992] 2 All ER 561, Court of Appeal

FACTS: The fourth defendant, Maurice Tillson, had been (apparently) in adverse possession of the plaintiff's land for well over twelve years. Despite that fact, the plaintiff began proceedings for possession against him. These proceedings were compromised on the terms:

(a) that Tillson accepted the plaintiff still owned the land;
(b) that the plaintiff granted Tillson a lease of the land.

In later proceedings for possession brought on the expiry of the lease, Tillson claimed that he had a freehold title by virtue of adverse possession.

HELD: Tillson was bound by the earlier compromise and therefore estopped from disputing the plaintiff's title to the freehold.

BUTLER-SLOSS LJ: . . . Where parties to a dispute reach a compromise which brings that dispute to an end and avoids the need for litigation or further litigation, such a compromise is a valuable part of the resolution of disputes within the machinery of the administration of justice. The compromise has to be genuine, entered into freely by all parties to it without concealment of essential information or undue advantage taken by one party of another party, and preferably with the assistance of lawyers. Consequently, an agreement to compromise an action or a dispute which may lead to litigation is binding and is enforceable against the party seeking subsequently to repudiate it. As Roskill LJ said in *Binder* v *Alachouzos* [1972] 2 All ER 189 at 194, [1972] 2 QB 151 at 160, 'any other course would cause very great difficulty in the administration of justice'.

In my view the courts have an interest in upholding agreements to compromise disputes. The terms of the agreement to compromise under review are therefore in a wholly different position from the situations caught within the scope of the Limitation Acts, such as payment of rent or acknowledgment of title. The agreement to compromise at 3 November 1983 is therefore binding upon the appellant, and I also would dismiss this appeal.

21.5 Nature of Title acquired under Limitation Acts where Title Adversely Possessed against is Unregistered

RE NISBET AND POTTS' CONTRACT [1906] 1 Ch 386, Court of Appeal

FACTS: A 'squatter' had extinguished the unregistered title of the original freeholder by adverse possession. The question was whether this had the effect of releasing the adverse possessor's new title from a restrictive covenant to which the original freehold had been subject.
HELD: The 'squatter' was bound by the restriction. The covenantee had not, as yet, had any cause to enforce the restriction, so it would be a nonsense to hold that the enforcement of the covenant in the future had been time-barred by the squatter's adverse possession. Nor could the squatter claim to be a 'purchaser' for value of the legal estate without notice of the restrictive covenant.

COLLINS MR: . . . the Statute of Limitations, as one would expect, does not purport to annul by lapse of time any rights other than those which persons might have, and ought to have, exercised during the period limited. The statute does not begin to run in any case against a person until that person has been put to what is generally called his 'right of entry.' Unless the circumstances have been such as to put the person who is to be barred by the lapse of time upon the assertion of his right, the time does not begin to run against him. All that the statute does is this. By s. 34 it says: 'At the determination of the period limited by this Act to any person for making an entry or distress, or bringing any writ of quare impedit or other action or suit, the right and title of such person to the land, rent, or advowson, for the recovery whereof such entry, distress, action, or suit respectively might have been made or brought within such period, shall be extinguished.' That is the whole right the squatter acquires, namely, the extinguishment of a title adverse to his own. But how does that affect the question here? What machinery is there in the Statute of Limitations affecting the right of a covenantee who has the benefit of a restrictive covenant? Nothing in the Act has been pointed out to us which touches that right at all. In fact, unless and until the right of the covenantee has been in some way infringed, so that it becomes necessary for him to enforce that right, there is no reason, either in principle or in fairness, why his right should be in any way affected. . . .

21.6 Adverse Possession Where the Title Possessed Against is Registered Land

LAND REGISTRATION ACT 1925

75. Acquisition of title by possession
(1)   The Limitation Acts shall apply to registered land in the same manner and to the same extent as those Acts apply to land not registered, except that where, if the land were

not registered, the estate of the person registered as proprietor would be extinguished, such estate shall not be extinguished but shall be deemed to be held by the proprietor for the time being in trust for the person who, by virtue of the said Acts, has acquired title against any proprietor, but without prejudice to the estates and interests of any other person interested in the land whose estate or interest is not extinguished by those Acts.

(2)   Any person claiming to have acquired a title under the Limitation Acts to a registered estate in the land may apply to be registered as proprietor thereof.

(3)   The registrar shall, on being satisfied as to the applicant's title, enter the applicant as proprietor either with absolute, good leasehold, qualified, or possessory title, as the case may require, but without prejudice to any estate or interest protected by any entry on the register which may not have been extinguished under the Limitation Acts, and such registration shall, subject as aforesaid, have the same effect as the registration of a first proprietor; but the proprietor or the applicant or any other person interested may apply to the court for the determination of any question arising under this section.

(4)   . . .

(5)   Rules may be made for applying (subject to any necessary modifications) the provisions of this section to cases where an easement, right or privilege has been acquired by prescription.

21.7   Adverse Possession Against the Registered Proprietor of a Lease

21.7.1   TWELVE YEARS' ADVERSE POSSESSION BUT NO RECTIFICATION OF THE REGISTER

FAIRWEATHER v ST MARYLEBONE PROPERTY CO. LTD
[1962] 2 All ER 288, House of Lords

FACTS: A squatter had established title by adverse possession against a tenant holding land under a 99 year lease of registered title. The tenant then surrendered its lease to the landlord.

HELD: (Lord Morris of Borth y Gest dissenting) the surrender was effective to extinguish the 'squatters' right to possess the land.

LORD DENNING: My Lords, I have come to the clear conclusion that a surrender operates as a determination of the term. It is not an assignment of it. I am aware that no less an authority than Lindley LJ, once said that: 'The surrender of the term only operated as an assignment of the surrenderor's interest in it', see *David* v *Sabin* [1893] 1 Ch 533. But if that be true, it is not by any rule of the common law, only by force of statute: and then only in the case of underleases, not in the case of trespasser or squatter. . . .

The question may be asked: why did the common law on a surrender protect the underlessee from eviction? The answer is to be found in Coke on Littleton II, p. 338b, where it is said that

> having regard to the parties to the surrender, the estate is absolutely drowned . . . But having regard to strangers, who were not parties or privies thereunto, lest by a voluntary surrender they may receive prejudice touching any right or interest they had before the surrender, the estate surrendered hath in consideration of law a continuance.

This passage applies in favour of an underlessee so as to protect him from eviction during the term of his underlease: but it does not apply in favour of a trespasser. The reason for the difference is because the underlessee comes in under a grant from the lessee; and the lessee cannot, by a surrender, derogate from his own grant, see *Davenport's Case* (1610) 8 Co. Rep 144b, *Mellor* v *Watkins* (1874) LR 9 QB 405 by Blackburn J. But a trespasser comes in by wrong and not by grant of the lessee. If the lessee surrenders his term, the freeholder is at once entitled to evict the trespasser for the simple reason that, on the surrender, the lease is determined, and there is no bar whatever to the freeholder recovering possession, see *Ecclesiastical Comrs of England and Wales v Rowe* (1880) 5 App Cas 736. And I see no reason why the same reasoning should not apply even though, at the date of the surrender, the trespasser is a squatter who has been there more than twelve years for, as against the freeholder he is still a trespasser. The freeholder's right to possession does not arise until the lease is determined by the surrender. It then comes into being and time begins to run against him under s. 6(1) of the Limitation Act 1939.

The only reason, it seems to me, which can be urged against this conclusion is that it means that a squatter's title can be destroyed by the leaseholder and freeholder putting their heads together. It is said that they can by a surrender—or by a surrender and regrant—destroy the squatter's title completely and get rid of him. So be it. There is no way of preventing it. But I would point out that, if we were to deny the two of them this right, they could achieve the same result in another way. They could easily do it by the leaseholder submitting to a forfeiture. If the leaseholder chooses not to pay the rent, the freeholder can determine the lease under the proviso for re-entry. The squatter cannot stop him. He cannot pay the rent without the authority of the leaseholder. He cannot apply for relief against forfeiture. The squatter's title can thus be defeated by a forfeiture—or by a forfeiture and regrant—just as it can by a surrender—or by a surrender and regrant. So there is nothing in the point.

My Lords, so far as these questions under the Limitation Acts are concerned, I must say that I see no difference between a surrender or merger or a forfeiture. On each of those events the lease is determined and the freeholder is entitled to evict the squatter, even though the squatter has been on the land during the lease for more than twelve years: and on the determination of the lease, time then begins to run against the freeholder. . . .

One word about s. 75(1) of the Land Registration Act, 1925. That point was not raised in the county court and its availability depends on facts which were not proved. I do not think that it is open to the appellant here. But in any case I doubt if that puts registered land on a very different footing from unregistered land. It is machinery so as to apply the Limitation Acts to registered land but it does not alter the substantive position very materially. The registered leaseholder clearly remains liable on the covenants and subject to the conditions of the lease, including the proviso for re-entry: and I do not see why, on a surrender, the freeholder should not recover possession from a squatter, just as he can on a forfeiture. The freeholder has no notice of the trust in favour of the squatter and his interests are not to be prejudiced by the fact that the leasehold is registered. I say no more because the point is not available here. Suffice it to say that for the reasons I have given, I would dismiss this appeal.

21.7.2   TWELVE YEARS' ADVERSE POSSESSION AND THERE IS RECTIFICATION OF THE REGISTER

SPECTRUM INVESTMENT CO. AND ANOTHER v HOLMES
[1981] 1 All ER 6, Chancery Division

FACTS: The facts are best understood chronologically. The freehold of the premises was registered in 1901 and a 99 year lease was granted to a lessee from Christmas Day, 1902. This lease was registered early in 1903. In 1939 the lessee granted an oral weekly tenancy to Mrs Holmes. The lessee then assigned the lease to Mrs David, who was duly registered as proprietor thereof. Mrs Holmes stopped paying rent in 1944. She died in 1951 and her daughter, Miss Holmes, took up possession as her successor. Miss Holmes was registered with possessory title to the lease in 1968 and Mrs David's registered proprietorship was removed by the rectification of the register in 1968. In April 1975 the freehold reversion was transferred to the plaintiff, Spectrum Investment Co. In May 1975 Mrs David surrendered her lease to the plaintiff. The plaintiff then brought proceedings for possession against Miss Holmes.

HELD: The purported surrender by Mrs David had no effect. She ceased to have any interest capable of being surrendered from the moment that the register was rectified.

BROWNE-WILKINSON J: . . . I can now shortly state the contentions of Spectrum. Spectrum submits that the Land Registration Act 1925 introduces mere machinery for proving title to and transferring land and does not affect the substantive rights which parties enjoy under the general law. Accordingly it is said that the rights of Spectrum (as established by *Fairweather* v *St Marylebone Property Co. Ltd* [1962] 2 All ER 288, [1963] AC 510) must be reflected in the provisions of the Land Registration Act 1925 and are preserved by the words in s. 11 which expressly provide that registration with possessory title 'shall not affect or prejudice the enforcement of any estate, right, or interest (whether in respect of the lessor's title or otherwise) adverse to or in derogation of' the proprietor with possessory title. So, it is said, having obtained a surrender of the lease from Mrs David, Spectrum's right to possession as against Miss Holmes is preserved.

There is in my judgment a short answer to the claim by Spectrum. Accepting for the moment the broad proposition that the Land Registration Act 1925 was not intended to alter substantive rights, it undoubtedly was intended to alter the manner in which such rights were to be established and transferred. The surrender by Mrs David to Spectrum is the linchpin of Spectrum's claim. But in my judgment that surrender has not been affected by the only means authorised by the 1925 Act for the disposal of a registered leasehold interest by act of the parties.

. . . It is clear from the references in s. 75(3) that s. 75 apples to leasehold interest. Under s. 75(3) the registrar is under a mandatory duty to register the squatter on the application made by the squatter under sub-s. (2) if the registrar is satisfied as to the squatter's title. For what does the squatter make application? I will read s. 75(2) again: 'Any person claiming to have acquired a title under the Limitation Acts to a registered estate in the land may apply to be registered as proprietor thereof.' To my mind the words are clear and unequivocal: the squatter claims to have acquired a title to 'a registered estate in the land' (i.e. the leasehold interest) and applies to be registered as a proprietor '*thereof*' (my emphasis). Therefore, under s. 75(2), references to the squatter having acquired title to a registered estate must include the rights which under the Limitation Act 1939 the squatter acquires in relation to leasehold interests. Subsection (2) then refers to the squatter applying to be registered as proprietor 'thereof'. This word can, in my judgment, only refer back to the registered estate in the land against which the squatter has acquired title under the 1939 Act, i.e. the leasehold interest. The clear words of the Act therefore seem to require that, once the 12 years have run, the squatter is entitled to be registered as proprietor of the lease itself, and is bound to be so registered if he applies for registration. It follows that in my judgment Miss Holmes (as the squatter) is correctly registered as proprietor of the lease itself in accordance with the clear requirements of s. 75 of the 1925 Act. If that is right, Mrs David cannot be entitled to rectification of the register as against Miss Holmes, and she can therefore never get into a position in which she is competent to surrender the lease to Spectrum.

I am conscious that in so deciding I am reaching a conclusion which produces at least a limited divergence between squatter's rights over registered and unregistered land. Once the squatter is rightly registered as proprietor under s. 75(3) the documentary lessee and the freeholder can no longer defeat the squatter's rights by a surrender. But I am not deciding anything as to the position during the period between the date when the squatter obtains his title by adverse possession and the date on which he obtains registration of it. This is the period covered by sub-s. (1) of s. 75 which is the subsection on which Lord Radcliffe ([1962] 2 All ER 288 at 296, [1963] AC 510 at 542) and Sir John Pennycuick ([1976] 3 All ER 521 at 530, [1978] QB 264 at 275) were commenting. It may well be, as their *dicta* suggest, that during the period preceding any registration of the squatter's rights, the documentary lessee (as registered proprietor of the lease) and the freeholder can deal with the legal estate with reference to a person whose rights are not recorded on the register. But once the Act provides for registration of the squatter's title, it must in my judgment follow that the squatter's rights (once registered) cannot be overridden. The difference between registered and unregistered land in this respect is an inevitable consequence of the fact that the Land Registration Act 1925 provides for registration of the squatter as proprietor and that registered proprietors have rights. . . .

Smith, P. F., 'Limitation and the Land Registration Act 1925' (1981) 131 NLJ 718

The interrelation of the Limitation Act 1939 and the Land Registration Act 1925 raises two problems of some difficulty which it is the object of this article to examine. The first question concerns the nature of a squatter's title acquired against registered land; the second matter is whether in any sense it is true to say that a squatter is given by the combined effects of the Limitation Act 1939 and the Land Registration Act 1925, a 'parliamentary conveyance'.

Construction of LRA, s. 75

Neither the authorities nor the leading texts offer very much guidance as to the nature of the title conferred on the squatter (one registered) by s. 75 of the 1925 Act, but two points do emerge. The first of these is that, contrary to the position with unregistered land, the squatter with a registered title has no new estate. Secondly, despite this, the general view appears to be that s. 75(1) is in effect mere machinery and does not affect the substance of the matter. Thus, not untypically, it is said in *Williams on Title* (4th edn, p. 844) when dealing with the provision:

> It is arguable that s. 75 achieves a parliamentary conveyance to the squatter, a proposition which is diametrically opposed to the accepted construction of the Limitation Acts. It is thought, however, that this conclusion will be resisted by the courts. . . .

Not surprisingly, as was suggested above, the latest authority on the point, *Spectrum Investment Ltd* v *Holmes* [1981] 1 All ER 6, was non-committal on the point, the reason for this being partly the decision that the purported surrender was invalid as an unauthorised disposition, and partly, no doubt, caution.

It is thought, with respect, that the proper construction of s. 75(1) leads to the tentative conclusion that the broad denial of its effecting a parliamentary conveyance is as misleading as its complete and unqualified acceptance would be. After all, it has already been seen that the estate of the squatter, once registered under the 1925 Act, is capable of resisting disfeasance by a subsequent 'surrender' by the documentary lessee. This is not so in the case of unregistered land where the effect of the squat is purely extinctive.

Secondly, and this is of more difficulty, if the squatter's registered leasehold title is incapable of disfeasance by subsequent surrender, it is possible that the squatter steps into the position of the lessee for the residue of the term, so that in general, the freeholder's right to possession will not vest until the term date.

Thirdly, it is fairly clear that, as is the case with unregistered land, the squatter's registration will not of itself defeat prior interests and titles, and this appears to be recognised in s. 75(1) of the Land Registration Act, in these words:

> . . . without prejudice to the estates and interests of any other person interested in the land whose estate or interest is not extinguished by those Acts. . . .

Nugee, E.G., 'Limitation and the Land Registration Act 1925' (1981) 131 NLJ 774

Dear Madam,

Your contributor Mr P. F. Smith (*NLJ* July 9, p. 718) finds difficulties in the interrelation of the Limitation Act 1939 and the Land Registration Act 1925 some of which do not really exist. The key is that, to quote Jessel MR in *Rosenberg* v *Cook* 8 QBD 162, 165, 'The title of the disseisor is in this country a freehold title'. When a squatter takes possession of land adversely to the owner, he obtains a legal estate in fee simple from the moment he does so. True it is defeasible by the owner, but it is good against the rest of the world. The best exposition is in Megarry & Wade's *Law of Real Property* 4th edn, pp. 1002–10, especially at 1007.

The fact that the owner's title is registered is neither here nor there. If S, the squatter, acquires a legal estate in fee simple from the moment he goes into adverse possession when R's title is unregistered, he does so equally clearly if R's title is registered—R's title is quite distinct, and there is nothing in the Land Registration Act 1925 to prevent S from acquiring an independent legal estate in fee simple. His estate does not require registration in order that its legal nature be recognised, for S does not acquire it by disposition from R, and it is not within the categories of estate the registration of which is compulsory under s. 123. The law has always recognised that two legal estates in fee simple can co-exist in the same land, one being defeasible by the other; and the Land Registration Act 1925 contains nothing to alter the general law in this respect.

When 12 years have elapsed, S still has his original legal estate, but it has ceased to be defeasible by R. R, however, remains on the register as the proprietor of *his* legal estate. Since the register is intended to mirror the true legal position, the Act provides that the estate which is registered in R's name is not simply extinguished as it would have been had it been unregistered; but R ceases to have any beneficial interest in it, and becomes a bare trustee of it for S. S then has two interests in the land—his own legal estate acquired by adverse possession, and the equitable title to the estate of which R is still the registered proprietor. In practice what happens is that when S applies to be registered, the Land Registry close R's title and open a new one for S, thereby recognising that the reality of the position is that R's title has been extinguished and S's has become indefeasible.

Mr Smith's statement that 'contrary to the position with unregistered land, the squatter with a registered title' (by which he presumably means the squatter on land the title to which is registered in the name of someone else) 'has no new estate' is, with respect, wrong. The Land Registry will in fact register a squatter with possessory title before he has been in adverse possession for 12 years, at any rate if no one else has a registered title (see 27 Conv 372), and in such a case they must be accepting that there are two legal estates in fee simple co-existing, since the title of the original owner cannot have been extinguished. . . .

Yours faithfully,

E. G. Nugee QC

Lincoln's Inn

London WC2

21.8   End of Chapter Assessment Question

Edwina holds an 80 year lease (granted in 1968) over Greenacre and a freehold title to Redacre. The two plots adjoin and Edwina uses most of the land for her business as a scrap merchant. However she has left vacant part of the land ('Grey Land'). Grey Land is partly within Greenacre and partly within Redacre.

In 1985 Freda, the owner of nearby Great House, started to cultivate Grey Land as an ornamental garden. Freda admits that, 'I have known all along that Grey Land belongs to Edwina'. Indeed in 1998 Freda wrote to Edwina offering to buy Grey Land. (Edwina did not reply to this letter.)

Edwina's business is now expanding, and she wishes to regain possession of Grey Land.

Advise Edwina.

21.9   End of Chapter Assessment Outline Answer

It would appear that Freda (if she is properly advised) will claim title to Grey Land by virtue of adverse possession.

In the 1989 case of *Bucks CC* v *Moran*, Moran extended his large garden on to land which he well knew was owned by the Council and was intended to be used for a projected by-pass. Moran nevertheless took control of the Council's land, and clearly had *animus possidendi*, i.e. an intent to exclude everyone else from the relevant land. As Moran's control continued for more than twelve years the Court of Appeal held that he had destroyed the Council's title by his adverse possession and acquired a new title for himself based on his own long possession.

Similarly Freda can argue that her cultivation of Grey Land for the last fourteen years was adverse possession. (One imagines that she intended to keep everyone from trampling over her beautiful garden!) Following *Moran* it will not matter that Freda knew 'all along that Grey Land belonged to Edwina'.

Edwina may well say to us something like, 'I always intended to make use of Grey Land but I just never got round to doing so.' In the past that might well have helped Edwina, as a line of cases (one as recent as 1974, *Wallis* v *Shell*) had held that if the owner of a paper title to some disused land retained plans for that land, there could be no adverse possession against that land until those plans were either abandoned or rendered impossible.

However in 1979 Parliament passed what is now Schedule 1, para. 8(4) of the Limitation Act 1980. The wording is obscure, but in *Moran* the Court of Appeal held that para. 8(4) overrules the line of cases culminating in *Wallis*.

The *Wallis'* line of cases had produced the unfortunate result that ownership of land could depend on obscure plans locked up in the minds of paper title owners, rather than on the easily observed physical fact of long possession. It is submitted that if the interpretation of para. 8(4) in Moran was challenged in the House of Lords, the House (currently very concerned to produce a sensible and workable Land Law) would rule that *Moran* was entirely correct.

The letter which Freda wrote in 1998 has come too late for our client. If it had been written in (say) 1994 it would have constituted an acknowledgement of title which would have stopped time running in Freda's favour. But by 1997 time had already run in Freda's favour; the rights of a paper title holder (Edward) once they have been 'time barred' cannot be revived by a subsequent acknowledgment.

It follows from the above that Edwina has no chance of regaining possession of that part of the Grey Land which falls within Redacre, ('Redgrey'). If Redgrey is unregistered title, her legal freehold title was destroyed in 1997. If Redgrey is registered title, Edwina still holds the legal title. But she will hold it on bare trust for Freda (s. 75, LRA). Moreover, Freda could at any time claim rectification of the register; on rectification, Edwina would not be entitled to any compensation.

With respect to the part of Grey Land falling within Greenacre ('Greengrey') Edwina is in a better position. If the lease is unregistered title then the current position is as follows. Although Edwina's lease is time-barred *vis-à-vis* Freda, it still has a notional existence *vis-à-vis* the landlord. Time will not start running against the landlord until this notional lease expires. Edwina could thus follow the procedure used successfully in *Fairweather* v *St Marylebone*. She should come to an arrangement with the landlord with respect to Greengrey under which:

(a)   Edwina and the landlord terminate by surrender the notional lease with respect to Greengrey;
(b)   The landlord sues Freda for possession; the landlord is bound to win;
(c)   The landlord then grants Edwina a fresh lease of Greengrey.

If the lease of Greengrey is registered title, then according to the House of Lords in *St Marylebone* the procedure just outlined will still be effective, notwithstanding the trust imposed by s. 75, LRA. However Edwina should act very quickly. Freda might well apply for rectification of the register so as to become proprietor of the lease over Greengrey. Once Freda has obtained rectification of the register not even a notional lease exists between the landlord and Edwina. It would then be too late for Edwina to exploit the procedure of surrender-action for possession-new lease. (See *Spectrum Investments* v *Holmes*.)

CHAPTER TWENTY-TWO

RECTIFICATION OF THE REGISTER OF TITLE

22.1 The Statutory Framework

LAND REGISTRATION ACT 1925

82. Rectification of the register

(1) The register may be rectified pursuant to an order of the court or by the registrar, subject to an appeal to the court, in any of the following cases, but subject to the provisions of this section:—

(a) Subject to any express provisions of this Act to the contrary, where a court of competent jurisdiction has decided that any person is entitled to any estate right or interest in or to any registered land or charge, and as a consequence of such decision such court is of opinion that a rectification of the register is required, and makes an order to that effect;

(b) Subject to any express provision of this Act to the contrary, where the court, on the application in the prescribed manner of any person who is aggrieved by any entry made in, or by the omission of any entry from, the register, or by any default being made, or unnecessary delay taking place, in the making of any entry in the register, makes an order for the rectification of the register;

(c) In any case and at any time with the consent of all persons interested;

(d) Where the court or the registrar is satisfied that any entry in the register has been obtained by fraud;

(e) Where two or more persons are, by mistake, registered as proprietors of the same registered estate or of the same charge;

(f) Where a mortgagee has been registered as proprietor of the land instead of as proprietor of a charge and a right of redemption is subsisting;

(g) Where a legal estate has been registered in the name of a person who if the land had not been registered would not have been the estate owner; and

(h) In any other case where, by reason of any error or omission in the register, or by reason of any entry made under a mistake, it may be deemed just to rectify the register.

(2) The register may be rectified under this section, notwithstanding that the rectification may affect any estates, rights, charges, or interests acquired or protected by registration, or by any entry on the register, or otherwise.

(3) The register shall not be rectified, except for the purpose of giving effect to an overriding interest [or an order of the court], so as to affect the title of the proprietor who is in possession—

(a) unless the proprietor has caused or substantially contributed to the error or omission by fraud or lack of proper care; or

(b) . . .

(c) unless for any other reason, in any particular case, it is considered that it would be unjust not to rectify the register against him.

(4) Where a person is in possession of registered land in right of a minor interest, he shall, for the purposes of this section, be deemed to be in possession as agent for the proprietor.

(5) The registrar shall obey the order of any competent court in relation to any registered land on being served with the order or an official copy thereof.

(6) On every rectification of the register the land certificate and any charge certificate which may be affected shall be produced to the registrar unless an order to the contrary is made by him.

NORWICH AND PETERBOROUGH BUILDING SOCIETY v STEED
[1993] Ch 116, Court of Appeal

FACTS: The defendant had emigrated to the United States, leaving his home in the occupation of his mother, his sister and his brother in law. He executed a power of attorney in favour of his mother, in terms which permitted her, *inter alia*, to sell the property. The sister produced a transfer showing that the mother had sold the land to her and the brother in law, her husband. The mother denied ever having consented to such a sale. In any event, the sister and brother in law were duly registered as proprietors of the property. Unfortunately, they fell behind with repayments of mortgage instalments and the building society brought proceedings for possession. The defendant resisted the building society's claim to possess the premises, and counterclaimed for rectification of the register on the basis that the transfer had been forged and was, therefore, not his deed (this plea is known as '*non est factum*'). He withdrew the allegation of forgery when expert evidence was adduced to show that the mother (who had since died) probably had executed the transfer. HELD: As the defendant no longer alleged fraud, and as his claim of *non est factum* had failed, there were no grounds for rectification. Section 82(1) of the Land Registration Act 1925 did not confer on the court a general jurisdiction to achieve a just and equitable solution.

SCOTT LJ: . . . As a matter of principle, if, as I think, the defendant's case for rectification as against the building society cannot be brought under any of the paragraphs of s. 82(1), I would conclude that that must be an end to the rectification claim.

22.1.1 RECTIFICATION AGAINST A REGISTERED PROPRIETOR IN POSSESSION

22.1.1.1 Registered proprietor 'to blame' for the wrong registration

RE 139 HIGH STREET, DEPTFORD [1951] 1 ChD 950, Chancery Division

FACTS: Prior to 1948 number 139 was unregistered title. In 1948 V sold to P number 139. The conveyance, which had no plan attached, described the land as 'all that shop and dwelling-house situate and known as 139, High Street, Deptford in the County of London'. P applied for first registration. Apparently V, P, their respective legal advisers, and the Land Registry all thought that number 139 included a small piece of disused land at the rear of No 139, next to a railway line. P was registered as proprietor of the dwelling house/shop and the land at the rear. In fact, this land actually 'belonged to' British Railways. The registration thus deprived the railway of that piece of land. When British Railways found out, it sought rectification of the register.
HELD: Rectification was granted. The judge held that P was caught by section 82(3)(a), because P had 'contributed' to the error at the Registry.

WYNN-PARRY J: . . . The respondent, by his solicitor, merely put forward an application in the usual form, describing the property as '139 Deptford High Street,' and accompanying the application with the conveyance containing the description to which I have already referred:

> all that shop and dwelling-house situate at and known as 139 High Street, Deptford, in the county of London.

Counsel for the respondent, on the one hand, contends that, in doing that and nothing more, the respondent did something which cannot in any sense be said to have contributed to the mistake, the mistake being that of the Land Registry in including the disputed land in the registration. It is submitted by the applicants, on the other hand, that the respondent must be said to have contributed to the mistake. The question must be one of construction as to what is included in the language of the parcels. To resolve that, reference must be made to the surrounding circumstances so far as, in accordance with the well-established rules, they can be taken into consideration. When one looks at the surrounding circumstances, one finds that at the date of the contract and the conveyance the only access to the disputed land was through the immediately adjoining premises, which, quite clearly, were known as '139 High Street, Deptford,' and that, therefore, as a matter of construction, this conveyance intended to include, and did include, the disputed land in the description '139 High Street, Deptford.' On that view it is contended by counsel for the applicants that, by putting that description forward, the respondent contributed to the mistake, because the necessary consequence of putting forward the application must have been that the Land Registry officials would make the usual inquiries and, if necessary, a survey of the premises, and they would, therefore, be led to fall into the same mistake as had been made by the respondent and his vendors. It is not an easy point to resolve, but it appears to me that the determining factor is the circumstance that, so far as the physical aspect of the matter is concerned, the disputed land must have appeared to anyone looking at the properties in question to form part of 139 High Street, Deptford. It was, apparently, so obvious that the vendors to the respondent fell into the mistake, the respondent himself fell into the mistake, and the Land Registry fell into the mistake. On that view of the matter, it appears to me, notwithstanding the arguments both practical and theoretical of counsel for the respondent, to follow, necessarily, that the respondent must be held to have contributed to the mistake, within the meaning of s. 82(3)(a) of the Act of 1925. . . .

22.1.1.2   Unjust not to rectify the register

EPPS v *ESSO PETROLEUM CO. LTD* [1973] 2 All ER 465, Chancery Division

FACTS: C owned a site in Gillingham on which he built a house and a garage, leaving a strip of land between them. In 1955 C's personal representatives conveyed the house and the strip to Edna Jones. She covenanted to erect a wall between the strip and the garage, but failed to do so. The existing fence between strip and house remained *in situ*. The strip therefore appeared to 'belong' to the garage. In 1957 Gillingham became an area of compulsory registration. In 1959 C's personal representatives conveyed the garage and strip to Ball. Ball applied for first registration, and was registered as proprietor of both garage and strip. There was thus a 'double conveyancing' situation, but Ball had legal title to the strip due to his registration. Since 1959 the strip had been used as part of the garage. In 1964 Ball sold the garage including the strip to Esso; Esso became registered proprietor. In 1968 Edna Jones' personal representatives sold the house and purported to sell the strip to Epps, but the Land Registry refused to register him as proprietor of the strip. He applied for rectification, and relied particularly on section 82(3)(c).
HELD: Rectification was refused.

TEMPLEMAN J: . . . if an order for rectification is made the defendants will be entitled to indemnity on 1973 values, and if the claim for rectification is refused then they will keep the land, but the plaintiffs will not get compensation.

   The question I have to determine is whether that is sufficient to upset the justice of the defendants' claim that there should not be rectification in the present instance. Is it sufficient—and this is the test—to make it unjust not to rectify the register against the defendants? Counsel for the plaintiffs pointed out that as far as the defendants are concerned the disputed strip formed, he calculated, four per cent of the garage premises. He said it could not make a lot of difference to the defendants' garage; on the other hand, it was of importance to 4 Darland Avenue, because it provided a private garage, an asset which is important in commuter territory.

   In my judgment, however, this cannot be solved merely on the question of money. The defendants bought the land; they bought it to exploit for their commercial purposes; they did not buy it in order to sell a strip for a 1973 value, which in real terms will not, in my judgment, adequately indemnify them. Although the strip is at the back of the garage, in the same way as it could be used as a private garage for 4 Darland Avenue, so it could be used by the defendants for commercial purposes, and in fact they say now they intend to use it in connection with a car wash; if they are deprived of it they will be in considerable difficulty, and will not have all the facilities which a modern garage requires. I think that may be putting it a bit high, but the fact of the matter is that this strip is worth more to the defendants than the pounds, shillings and pence which they will receive by indemnity, even on a 1973 basis.

Accordingly, in my judgment, that argument is not sufficient to overturn all the other arguments in favour of the defendants, and I decline to order rectification of the register.

22.2 Indemnity

LAND REGISTRATION ACT 1925
as amended by s. 2 of the Land Registration Act 1997

83. Indemnity for errors or omissions in the register

(1)   Where the register is rectified under this Act, then, subject to the provisions of this Act—

(a)   any person suffering loss by reason of the rectification shall be entitled to be indemnified; and

(b)   if, notwithstanding the rectification, the person in whose favour the register is rectified suffers loss by reason of an error or omission in the register in respect of which it is so rectified, he also shall be entitled to be indemnified.

(2)   Where an error or omission has occurred in the register, but the register is not rectified, any person suffering loss by reason of the error or omission shall, subject to the provisions of this Act, be entitled to be indemnified.

(3)   Where any person suffers loss by reason of the loss or destruction of any document lodged at the registry for inspection or safe custody or by reason of an error in any official search, he shall be entitled to be indemnified under this Act.

(4)   Subject to the following provisions of this section, a proprietor of any registered land or charge claiming in good faith under a forged disposition shall, where the register is rectified, be deemed to have suffered loss by reason of such rectification and shall be entitled to be indemnified under this Act.

(5)   No indemnity shall be payable under this Act—

(a)   on account of any loss suffered by a claimant wholly or partly as a result of his own fraud or wholly as a result of his own lack of proper care;

(b)   on account of any mines or minerals, or the existence of any right to work or get mines or minerals, unless it is noted on the register that the mines or minerals are included in the title; or

(c)   on account of any costs or expenses (of whatever nature) incurred without the consent of the registrar, unless—

(i)   by reason of urgency it was not practicable to apply for the registrar's consent before they were incurred, and

(ii)   the registrar subsequently approves them for the purposes of this paragraph.

(6)   Where any loss suffered by a claimant is suffered partly as a result of his own lack of proper care, any indemnity payable to him shall be reduced to such extent as is just and equitable having regard to his share in the responsibility for the loss.

(7)   For the purposes of subsections (5)(a) and (6) above, any fraud or lack of proper care on the part of a person from whom the claimant derives title (otherwise than under a disposition for valuable consideration which is registered or protected on the register) shall be treated as if it were fraud or lack of proper care on the part of the claimant (and the reference in subsection (6) to the claimant's share in the responsibility for the loss shall be construed accordingly).

(8)   Where an indemnity is paid in respect of the loss of an estate or interest in or charge on land, the amount so paid shall not exceed—

(a)   where the register is not rectified, the value of the estate, interest or charge at the time when the error or omission which caused the loss was made;

(b)   where the register is rectified, the value (if there had been no rectification) of the estate, interest or charge, immediately before the time of rectification.

(9)   Subject to subsection (5)(c) above, as restricted by section 2(2) of the Land Registration and Land Charges Act 1971—

(a)   an indemnity under any provision of this Act shall include such amount, if any, as may be reasonable in respect of any costs or expenses properly incurred by the claimant in relation to the matter; and

(b)   a claimant for an indemnity under any such provision shall be entitled to an indemnity thereunder of such amount, if any, as may be reasonable in respect of any such costs or expenses, notwithstanding that no other indemnity money is payable thereunder.

(10)   Where indemnity is paid to a claimant in respect of any loss, the registrar, on behalf of the Crown, shall be entitled—

(a)   to recover the amount paid from any person who caused or substantially contributed to the loss by his fraud; or

(b)   for the purpose of recovering the amount paid, to enforce—

(i)   any right of action (of whatever nature and however arising) which the claimant would have been entitled to enforce had the indemnity not been paid, and

(ii)   where the register has been rectified, any right of action (of whatever nature and however arising) which the person in whose favour the register has been rectified would have been entitled to enforce had it not been rectified.

(11)   Subsection (10) above does not prejudice any other rights of recovery which by virtue of any enactment are exercisable by the registrar where he has made a payment of indemnity.

(12)   A liability to pay indemnity under this Act shall be deemed to be a simple contract debt; and for the purposes of the Limitation Act 1980, the cause of action shall be deemed to arise at the time when the claimant knows, or but for his own default might have known, of the existence of his claim.

(13)   This section applies to the Crown in like manner as it applies to a private person.

22.2.1   INDEMNITY FOR A REGISTERED PROPRIETOR WHERE RECTIFICATION IS GRANTED

RE CHOWOOD'S REGISTERED LAND [1933] 1 Ch 574, Chancery Division

FACTS: An adverse possessor had gained title to part of a piece of land of which Chowood Ltd was registered proprietor. The adverse possessor sought rectification of the register.
HELD: Rectification was granted. Chowood Ltd was held not to be entitled to any indemnity. The adverse possessor had an overriding interest under section 70(1)(f) of the Land Registration Act 1925, and Chowood lost nothing as a result of the rectification.

CLAUSON J: . . . Immediately before the rectification of the register the position, as I have indicated above, was that Chowood's estate was 'subject to rights acquired or in course of being acquired under the Limitation Acts.' On the facts as they appeared in the case of Chowood, Ltd v Lyall [1930] 2 Ch 156 (and the findings of fact in that case are by agreement to be treated as binding between the present parties), Lyall was in possession of the strip when Chowood's title was registered, and, of course, also when the Land Registration Act 1925, came into force, and also immediately before and at the date of the rectification of the register. Further, that possession was, at each of those dates, protected against any claim by Chowood to enter upon it, the protection flowing from the fact, established by Lyall in the former litigation, that Lyall and her predecessors had had possession for such length of time as would be an answer under the Limitation Acts to any such claim by Chowood. It appears to me to follow that Lyall's rights were accordingly rights acquired under the Limitation Acts. It was suggested that the words 'subject to the provisions of this Act' affect the matter. I cannot see why. The reference seems to be to s. 75, which contains very special provisions which prevent rights acquired under the Limitation Acts from operating under certain cirumstances to extinguish the estate of the registered proprietor. This does not seem to have any operation upon the position in the case with which I am now dealing. It was further suggested that Lyall's title depended to some extent on what was called a paper title, and not solely on the Limitation Acts. I do not say what the position might have been if Lyall's paper title had disclosed, for example, a grant to her by Ralli's predecessor in title which could be used to defeat Chowood's claim to the strip without recourse to the Statute of Limitations. Such a case can be dealt with when it arises. In the present case Lyall's paper title was of value simply as some evidence of length of possession, and had no other operation; the paper title, save in so far as it supported a plea of possession for the statutory period, would not have helped to defeat Chowood's claim. It results from this that Chowood's title was all along subject to the rights which Lyall has succeeded in establishing; and the loss, if it may properly be so called, which Chowood has suffered is that they have not got, and since the Act of 1925 came into force (whatever may have been the position before) have never had title to the strip, except subject to an overriding right in Lyall. That loss was occasioned by Chowood failing to ascertain that, when they bought, Lyall was in possession, and in possession under such circumstances that Ralli could not make a title to the strip. The loss was occasioned by paying Ralli for a strip to which Ralli could not make title. The rectification of the register merely recognised the existing position, and put Chowood in no worse a position than they were in before.

In these circumstances I must hold that Chowood have suffered no loss by reason of the rectification of the register. . . .

22.3   End of Chapter Assessment Question

The Aberconwy District (Llandudno, Conwy, Llanrwst etc.) became an area of compulsory registration of title on the 1 December 1988.

In early 1988 Geoffrey purchased a small piece of land 'Lomasacre' situated in Aberconwy. Lomasacre formed a small part of the vast 'Brooke Estate' owned by John. Geoffrey did his own conveyancing; as a result no indorsement referring to the sale off of Lomasacre was placed on the deeds to the Brooke Estate.

Geoffrey has only visited Lomasacre on one occasion since he purchased it; on that occasion he dumped some rusting railings on part of the land.

Last week John sold the whole of the Brooke Estate to Malcolm; Malcolm believes that Lomasacre is part of the land he has purchased. He has successfully applied for registration as proprietor of the whole of the Brooke Estate.

Discuss.

22.4   End of Chapter Assessment Outline Answer

The problem scenario describes a 'double conveyancing' situation. John sold Lomasacre to Geoffrey in early 1988, before it became compulsory to register Lomasacre with a separate title. In these circumstances Geoffrey should have ensured that the sale of Lomasacre had been endorsed on the deeds of the Brook Estate. He failed to do so. Recently John sold the whole of the Brooke Estate to Malcolm, with the result that Lomasacre has been conveyed twice. On these facts it is clear that Geoffrey has the best title to Lomasacre. However, to the scenario must be added the fact that Malcolm has been registered successfully as proprietor of the whole of the Brook Estate, including Lomasacre. Now Geoffrey's only hope of asserting his title to Lomasacre is to obtain rectification of the register.

   In the case of *Norwich and Peterborough Building Society* v *Steed* (1993) [see **22.1**], the Court of Appeal emphasised that the court's powers to order rectification of the register are strictly confined to the grounds set out in s. 82 of the Land Registration Act 1925. The basic grounds for rectifying the register are set out in s. 82(1) of the Land Registration Act 1925. If, however, as in the present case, rectification of the register is sought against a 'registered proprietor in possession', the conditions in s. 82(3) will also have to be satisfied.

   Section 82(1)(b) provides that the register may be rectified 'on the application . . . of any person who is aggrieved by any entry made in, or by the ommission of an entry from, the register'. This section covers Geoffrey's claim. Section 82(1) further provides that rectification may take place if all the parties consent (not likely here); if the court is satisfied that an entry has been obtained by fraud (there is no suggestion that Malcolm has acted fraudulently); where a legal estate has been registered in the name of a person who if the land had not been registered would not have been the estate owner (this paragraph, s. 82(1)(g), is clearly the most appropriate to Geoffrey's claim); and in any other case where by reason of any error or omission in the register, or by reason of an entry made under a mistake, it may be deemed just to rectify the register.

   It is clear that Geoffrey will seek rectification under s. 82(1)(g). However, he will have to satisfy the requirements of s. 82(3) which are designed to protect registered proprietors in possession, such as Malcolm in our case. Before 1977, s. 82(3)(a) provided for rectification against a registered proprietor in possession where the proprietor had caused or substantially contributed, by his act, neglect or default, to the fraud, mistake or omission. This provision was applied in *Re 139 Deptford High Street* (1951) [see **22.1.2.1**]. In that case a purchaser applied for first registration of title, just as Malcolm has done in our case. The purchaser was registered as proprietor of a large piece of land, but he was mistakenly registered as proprietor also of a small piece of land that did not belong to him (as in our case). The true owner of the small plot applied for rectification of the register and was successful. The court held that the purchaser had 'contributed' to the error at the registry by presenting documents for registration which were inaccurate. It did not matter that the purchaser had been neither fraudulent nor negligent (in that case the vendor had mistakenly believed that the disputed piece of land had been properly sold to the purchaser, and so the purchaser had not been negligent) in putting forward the innacurate documents. Accordingly, it is likely that Geoffrey would have succeeded on the facts of the present case if he had been claiming rectification before 1977.

However, in 1977 s. 82(3)(a) was amended to give even more protection to the registered proprietor in possession. Under the new provision rectification can be granted only where '. . . the proprietor has caused or substantially contributed to the error or omission by fraud or lack of proper care'. Accordingly, Geoffrey will only obtain rectification today if he can show that Malcolm knew that the documents he had presented for registration had been inaccurate (a case of fraud) or that he ought to have known that the documents were inaccurate (a case of 'lack of proper care'). There is no evidence that Malcolm had actual knowledge of Geoffrey's right. And it is doubtful that he ought to have known. The presence of 'rusty' railings on a part of the Brook Estate, suggests, if anything, that the land has not been used for some time. Malcolm may, perhaps, have asked John how the rusty railings came to be there, and if John's answer led Malcolm to suspect the presence of a third party, it may be that Malcolm 'ought to have concluded' that a third party had rights over the land. However, this is a most unlikely set of circumstances.

The most likely conclusion is that Geoffrey will be refused rectification under s. 82(3)(a). Consequently, Geoffrey will fail to obtain rectification unless he can show that 'for any other reason . . . it would be unjust not to rectify the register' (s. 82(3)(c)). It is clear from the wording of that paragraph (particularly the use of a double negative [see **22.1**]) that this provision should only be used in a case where it is absolutely clear that justice demands that the register should be rectified. One question the courts will ask is whether, if Geoffrey is refused rectification, cash compensation at the market value of his lost land will be adequate compensation (*Epps* v *Esso* (1973) [see **22.1.2.2**]). Considering the infrequent and uneconomic use to which Geoffrey has put his land the conclusion seems inevitable that justice will not demand a rectification, and that rectification will be refused.

The question of compensation remains. According to s. 83(2) of the Land Registration Act 1925 [see **22.2**] 'where an error or omission has occurred in the register, but the register is not rectified, any person suffering loss by reason of such error or omisssion, shall, subject to the provisions of this Act, be entitled to be indemnified'. The land 'lost' is valued at the date that the error occurred (today) which is probably bad news for Malcolm because the land will have been devalued due to the presence of the rusty railings.

CHAPTER TWENTY-THREE

THE ESSENTIAL CHARACTERISTICS OF EASEMENTS

23.1   Preliminary Considerations

MILLER v *EMCER PRODUCTS LTD* [1956] 1 All ER 237, Court of Appeal

FACTS: A tenant claimed the right to use a lavatory on another floor of the building in which he lived. The tenants of that floor objected to his use of it. One question was whether the right to use the toilet would be capable of being an easement.
HELD: It was.

ROMER LJ: . . . The question remains, however, as to the nature of the right which the landlords purported to include in the demise, and, in particular whether it was a licence or an easement? In my judgment, the right had all the requisite characteristics of an easement. There is no doubt what were intended to be the dominant and servient tenements respectively, and the right was appurtenant to the former and calculated to enhance its beneficial use and enjoyment. It is true that during the times when the dominant owner exercised the right, the owner of the servient tenement would be excluded, but this in greater or less degree is a common feature of many easements (e.g., rights of way) and does not amount to such an ouster of the servient owner's rights as was held by Upjohn J, to be incompatible with a legal easement in *Copeland* v *Greenhalf* [1952] 1 All ER 809. No case precisely in point on this issue was brought to our attention, but the right to use a lavatory is not dissimilar, I think, to the right to use a neighbour's kitchen for washing, the validity of which as an easement was assumed without question in *Heywood* v *Mallalieu* (1883) 25 ChD 357. No objection can fairly be made based on uncertainty, and it follows, in my judgment, that the right may properly be regarded as an easement which the landlords were professing to grant for a term of years; and such an easement would rank as an interest in or over land capable of being created at law by virtue of the Law of Property Act 1925, s. 1(2)(a).

. . . the easement which the landlords purported to grant to the tenant in relation to the lavatories is within the covenant for quiet enjoyment.

RE ELLENBOROUGH PARK [1955] 3 All ER 667, Court of Appeal

FACTS: The owners of houses situated around a 'private square' in Weston-super-Mare claimed the right to use a private garden in the middle of the square for the purpose of exercise and relaxation.
HELD: The neighbouring owners had easements over the garden.

SIR RAYMOND EVERSHED MR: For the purposes of the argument before us counsel were content to adopt, as correct, the four characteristics formulated in Dr. Cheshire's Modern Real Property (7th edn.), p. 456 et seq. They are (i) There must be a dominant and a servient tenement: (ii) an easement must accommodate the dominant tenement: (iii) dominant and servient owners must be different persons: and (iv) a right over land cannot amount to an easement unless it is capable of forming the subject-matter of a grant.

The four characteristics stated by Dr. Cheshire correspond with the qualities discussed by Gale in his second chapter, sections 2, 5, 3, and 6 and 8 respectively. Two of the four may be disregarded for present purposes, *viz*, the first and the third. If the garden or park is, as it is alleged to be, the servient tenement in the present case, then it is undoubtedly distinct from the alleged dominant tenements, *viz*, the freeholds of the several houses whose owners claim to exercise the rights. It is equally clear that if these lands respectively constitute the servient and dominant tenements, then they are owned by different persons. The argument in the case is found accordingly to turn on the meaning and application to the circumstances of the present case of the second and fourth conditions; i.e., first, whether the alleged easement can be said in truth to 'accommodate' the dominant tenement, in other words, whether there exists the required 'connection' between the one and the other; and, second, whether the right alleged is 'capable of forming the subject-matter of a grant'. The exact significance of this fourth and last condition is, at first sight perhaps, not entirely clear. As between the original parties to the 'grant' it is not in doubt that rights of this kind would be capable of taking effect by way of contract or licence. But for the purposes of the present case, as the arguments made clear, the cognate questions involved under this condition are: whether the rights purported to be given are expressed in terms of too wide and vague a character; whether, if and so far as effective, such rights would amount to rights of joint occupation or would substantially deprive the owners of the park of proprietorship or legal possession; whether, if and so far as effective, such rights constitute mere rights of recreation, possessing no quality of utility or benefit; and on such grounds cannot qualify as easements. . . .

Can it be said, then, of the right of full enjoyment of the park in question, which was granted by the conveyance of December 23, 1864, and which, for reasons already given, was, in our view, intended to be annexed to the property conveyed to Mr Porter, that it accommodated and served that property? It is clear that the right did, in some degree enhance the value of the property and this consideration cannot be dismissed as wholly irrelevant. It is, of course, a point to be noted; but we agree with the submission of counsel for the owners of the park that it is in no way decisive of the problem; it is not sufficient to show that the right increased the value of the property conveyed unless it is also shown that it was connected with the normal enjoyment of that property. It appears to us that the question whether or not this connection exists, is primarily one of fact, and depends largely on the nature of the alleged dominant tenement and the nature of the right granted.

. . . The park became a communal garden for the benefit and enjoyment of those whose houses adjoined it or were in its close proximity. Its flower beds, lawns and walks were calculated to afford all the amenities which it is the purpose of the garden of a house to provide; and apart from the fact that these amenities extended to a number of householders instead of being confined to one (which on this aspect of the case is immaterial) we can see no difference in principle between Ellenborough Park and a garden in the ordinary signification of that word. It is the collective garden of the neighbouring houses to whose use it was dedicated by the owners of the estate and as such amply satisfied, in our judgment, the requirement of connection with the dominant tenements to which it is appurtenant. The result is not affected by the circumstance that the right to the park is in this case enjoyed by some few houses which are not immediately fronting on the park. The test for present purposes, no doubt, is that the park should constitute in a real and intelligible sense the garden (albeit the communal garden) of the houses to which the enjoyment is annexed. But we think that the test is satisfied as regards these few neighbouring, though not adjacent, houses. We think that the extension of the right of enjoyment to these few houses does not negative the presence of the necessary 'nexus' between the subject-matter enjoyed and the premises to which the enjoyment is expressed to belong. . . .

We turn next to Dr. Cheshire's fourth condition for an easement—that the right must be capable of forming the subject-matter of a grant. As we have earlier stated, satisfaction of the condition in the present case depends on a consideration of the questions, whether the right conferred is too wide and vague, whether it is inconsistent with the proprietorship or possession of the alleged servient owners, and whether it is a mere right of recreation without utility or benefit.

To the first of these questions the interpretation which we have given to the typical deed provides, in our judgment, the answer; for we have construed the right conferred as being both well defined and commonly understood. In these essential respects the right may be said to be distinct from the indefinite and unregulated privilege which, we think, would ordinarily be understood by the Latin term *'jus spatiandi'*, a privilege of wandering at will over all and every part of another's field or park, and which, though easily intelligible as the subject-matter of a personal licence, is something substantially different from the subject-matter of the grant in question, *viz*, the provision for a limited number of houses in a uniform crescent of one single large but private garden. Our interpretation of the deed also provides, we think, the answer to the second question; for the right conferred no more amounts to a joint occupation of the park with its owners, no more excludes the proprietorship or possession of the latter, than a right of way granted through a passage or than the use by the public of the gardens of Lincoln's Inn Fields (to take one of our former examples) amount to joint occupation of that garden with the London County Council, or involve an inconsistency with the possession or proprietorship of the council as lessees. It is conceded that in any event the owners of the park are entitled to cut the timber growing on the park and to retain its proceeds. We have said that in our judgment, under the deed, the flowers and shrubs grown in the garden are equally the property of the owners of the park. We see nothing repugnant to a man's proprietorship or possession of a piece of land that he should decide to make of it and maintain it as an ornamental garden, and should grant rights to a limited number of other persons to come into it for the enjoyment of its amenities.

. . . If the proposition be well-founded, we do not think that the right to use a garden of the character with which we are concerned in this case can be called one of mere recreation and amusement. . . .

The third of the questions embraced in Dr. Cheshire's fourth condition rests primarily on a proposition stated in Theobald's The Law of Land (1929), at p. 263, where it is said that an easement 'must be a right of utility and benefit and not one of mere recreation and amusement.'

PHIPPS v PEAR [1964] 2 All ER 35, Court of Appeal

FACTS: A house was demolished, leaving a wall of a neighbouring house exposed which had not been built to withstand the weather. When frost began to cause cracks to appear in the wall the owner of the exposed house brought an action against his neighbour, claiming an easement of protection from the weather.
HELD: There was no such right known to the law, and none should be recognised.

LORD DENNING MR: . . . There are two kinds of easement known to the law: positive easements, such as a right of way, which give the owner of land *a right himself to do something* on or to his neighbour's land: and negative easements, such as a right of light, which gives him *a right to stop his neighbour doing something* on his (the neighbour's) own land. The right of support does not fall neatly into either category. It seems in some way to partake of the nature of a positive easement rather than a negative easement. The one building, by its weight, exerts a thrust, not only downwards, but also sideways on to the adjoining building or the adjoining land, and is thus doing something to the neighbour's land, exerting a thrust on it; see *Dalton v Angus* (1881) 6 App Cas 740 per Lord Selborne, LC. But a right to protection from the weather (if it exists) is entirely negative. It is a right to stop your neighbour pulling down his own house. Seeing that it is a negative easement, it must be looked at with caution, because the law has been very chary of creating any new negative easements. . . .

23.2 There Must be a Dominant and a Servient Tenement

An easement can exist only if it is attached to ('appurtenant to') a piece of dominant land. Suppose Gillian owns Wideviews Farm, situated in rural Derbyshire. She executes a deed in favour of Wendy (a keen walker) granting Wendy the right to use a path which crosses the farm. Wendy owns no land whatsoever. Though the right granted by the deed will give Wendy a lot of pleasure, it is certainly not an easement.

23.3 The Easement Must Accommodate the Dominant Tenement

PUGH v SAVAGE [1970] 2 All ER 353, Court of Appeal

FACTS: The question which arose in this case was whether a 'right of way' existing over one field to get to another field, where a third field lay between the dominant and servient tenements, could exist as a valid easement.
HELD: The right of way was a valid easement.

CROSS LJ: . . . *Todrick v Western National Omnibus Co. Ltd* [1934] Ch 561 shows that a right of way may exist for the benefit of a dominant tenement although between the dominant tenement and the servient tenement there is some intervening land. In the *Todrick* case itself, that intervening land was in fact owned by the owner of the dominant tenement, but all three members of the court expressed the view that, providing that the dominant owner was able to get across the intervening land, though only by the consent of a third party, the way claimed might still be a good right of way if it was sufficiently close to the dominant land to be sensibly described as appurtenant to and for the benefit of the dominant land. . . .

HILL v TUPPER (1863) 159 English Reports 51, Court of Exchequer

FACTS: The Basingstoke Canal Company owned the canal and some land on the banks of the canal. They leased the land on the banks of the canal to Hill for the purposes of a boatyard. The lease included a clause granting Hill the exclusive right to put pleasure boats on the canal. Tupper nevertheless started placing his pleasure boats on the canal. Hill sued Tupper, claiming that his 'pleasure boat monopoly' (as I like to call it) was an easement. If the court had accepted that claim, it would have meant that the pleasure boat monopoly was a property right which could be protected by suing anybody who interfered with it.
HELD: The pleasure boat monopoly was not an easement. The monopoly did not 'accommodate' the land leased to Hill. Rather it was for the benefit of Hill's business. Therefore, Hill's only remedy was to sue the canal company for breach of contract.

MARTIN B: . . . This grant is no doubt a valid grant between the canal company and their tenant, the plaintiff in this action; but in order to enable the plaintiff to maintain his action against the defendant he must establish that, by the grant, an estate vested in him so as to enable him to maintain an action on the case against a stranger for an infringement of his alleged rights, which he has failed to do. No case has been cited to show that such a right as this can be created, or that an owner can carve out his property into an indefinite number of hitherto unknown estates. To admit the right here claimed would be to open a door to the creation of such a variety of pieces and parcels of interests in land, and to such an indefinite increase of possible estates, that we ought not to do it. The plaintiff is entitled to the benefit of his covenant as against his lessors, the canal company; but if strangers infringe or molest him in the enjoyment of his rights, he must use the company's name to bring an action against such wrongdoers, and in this there is no hardship. . . .

23.4 'An Easement Must be Capable of Forming the Subject Matter of a Grant'

23.4.1 AN EASEMENT MUST BE CAPABLE OF REASONABLY EXACT DEFINITION

HARRIS v DE PINNA (1886) 33 ChD 238, Court of Appeal

FACTS: The owner of a timber-drying shed claimed the right to have an uninterrupted flow of air to his shed. He sought to enforce this right against a neighbour who had built two warehouses on nearby land.

HELD: There could be no easement for a general flow of air.

COTTON LJ: . . . Then, coming to what is said also to be a very important matter—air—have the plaintiffs made out any right in respect of air? It must be claimed either under the common law, or by a presumed grant, or under the statute.

. . . As regards light that is an entirely different matter from air. Light, the principal light which we enjoy, comes to us in a direct line, in direct pencils, and the light which is thrown over a neighbour's land goes over a very short space indeed. But here it is not a claim to air as coming in a defined channel over a neighbour's land, but it is a claim which is made in respect of a building not in any way closed up but made with openings,—merely a skeleton of a building if I may say so—with timbers supporting the floor and roof, and cross-beams to keep them in their position and make them steady; to prevent the plaintiffs' neighbour from doing anything which will prevent the current of air over his open yard from coming to the whole face of the plaintiffs' buildings as freely as it originally came when he did not choose, and it was not necessary for him, to apply the land for the purpose for which he is now intending to apply it. That, in my opinion, would be a most serious interference with the right which every one has to use his property, so long as he does not interfere with those rights of his neighbour in respect of which the law gives such neighbour a right of complaint if they should be interfered with. In my opinion, therefore, there is no case made out here for holding that the plaintiffs are entitled to that right of air which they claim as against the defendant. . . .

COLLS v HOME AND COLONIAL STORES LTD [1904] AC 179, House of Lords

FACTS: Home and Colonial Stores Ltd held premises from which they carried on their trade. They sought an injunction to restrain Colls from building on the opposite side of the road. They based their claim on the need to protect their right to light.
HELD: The injunction was refused. It was not sufficient to show that the erection of buildings would result in there being less light than before. A substantial deprivation must be shown.

EARL OF HALSBURY LC: . . . Light, like air, is the common property of all, or, to speak more accurately, it is the common right of all to enjoy it, but it is the exclusive property of none. If the same proposition against which I am protesting could be maintained in respect of air the progressive building of any town would be impossible. The access of air is undoubtedly interfered with by the buildings which are being built every day round London. The difference between the town and country is very appreciable to the dweller in cities when he goes to the open country, or to the top of a mountain, or even a small hill in the country; but would the possessor for twenty years of a house on the edge of a town be at liberty to restrain his neighbour from building near him because he had enjoyed the free access of air without buildings near him for twenty years? No doubt this is an extreme case, but it is one of the extreme cases which tries the principle.

23.4.2 AN EASEMENT MUST NOT BE SO EXTENSIVE AS TO AMOUNT TO A CLAIM TO JOINT POSSESSION OF THE SERVIENT LAND

COPELAND v GREENHALF [1952] 1 All ER 809, Chancery Division

FACTS: The case involved a claim for an easement. The alleged servient land was a strip of land about 150 feet long and 20 feet wide. The servient owners used the strip to gain access to their orchard. The alleged dominant owners were 'wheelwrights' (i.e. vehicle repairers). For many years they parked vehicles awaiting repair on the strip. These vehicles often occupied a large part of the strip, but the 'wheelwrights' were always careful to leave a gap through which the 'servient owners' could pass to get to their orchard. The wheelrights eventually claimed that they had a prescriptive easement to park their vehicles on the strip.
HELD: The wheelwrights were, in effect, claiming joint possession of the land. Such a claim was too extensive to qualify as an easement.

UPJOHN J: . . . in my judgment the right claimed here goes wholly outside any normal idea of an easement, that is, a right of the occupier of a dominant tenement over a servient tenement. This claim really amounts to a claim to a joint user of the land by the defendant. Practically he is claiming the whole beneficial user of the strip of land on the south-east side of the track so that he can leave there as many or as few lorries as he likes for any time that he likes and enter on it by himself, his servants and agents, to do repair work. In my judgment, that is not a claim which can be established as an easement. It is virtually a claim to possession, if necessary to the exclusion of the owner, or, at any rate, to a joint user, and no authority has been cited to me which would justify me in coming to the conclusion that a right of this wide and undefined nature can be the proper subject-matter of an easement. It seems to me that for this claim to succeed it must really amount to a right of possession by long adverse possession. I say nothing, of course, as to the creation of such rights by grant or by covenant. I am dealing solely with the question of a claim arising by prescription. . . .

LONDON AND BLENHEIM ESTATES LTD v LADBROKE RETAIL PARKS LTD
[1993] 1 All ER 307, Chancery Division

This case is referred to because it contains an interesting *obiter dictum* on whether a right to park cars on land is capable of being an easement. It was held that the right is capable of being an easement.

JUDGE PAUL BAKER QC: . . . *Wright v Macadam* [see **22.2.4.1**] was not cited in *Copeland* v *Greenhalf* [1952] 1 All ER 809, [1952] Ch 488, which directly concerned the parking of vehicles. The alleged servient tenement was a strip of land about 150 feet long running from the road with a width varying between 15 feet and 35 feet. It was wholly occupied with vehicles and agricultural implements save for a gangway allowing access from the road to the land beyond. The defendant was a wheelwright whose premises were on the other side of the road. The vehicles were his or his customers awaiting repair or collection. The plaintiff owned the strip and the land beyond. Upjohn J said ([1952] 1 All ER 809 at 812, [1952] Ch 488 at 498):

> . . . in my judgment the right claimed here goes wholly outside any normal idea of an easement, that is, a right of the occupier of a dominant tenement over a servient tenement. This claim really amounts to a claim to a joint user of the land by the defendant. Practically he is claiming the whole beneficial user of the strip of land on the south-east side of the track so that he can leave there as many or as few lorries as he likes for any time that he likes and enter on it by himself, his servants and agents, to do repair work. In my judgment, that is not a claim which can be established as an easement.

It is unfortunate that *Wright v Macadam* was not cited, but it probably would not have made any difference. The matter must be one of degree. A small coal shed in a large property is one thing. The exclusive use of a large part of the alleged servient tenement is another. Hence I do not accept the submission that *Copeland v Greenhalf* was wrongly decided.

. . . the grantee of a right of way cannot complain of obstructions in some part of the way so long as his right is not substantially interfered with. In the present case the right on its true construction is dependent upon the continued existence of car parking facilities for other persons. That leaves the main point under this head, whether the right to park cars can exist at all as an easement. I would not regard it as a valid objection that charges are made, whether for the parking itself or the general upkeep of the park. The essential question is one of degree. If the right granted in relation to the area over which it is to be exercisable is such that it would leave the servient owner without any reasonable use of his land whether for parking or anything else, it could not be an easement, though it might be some larger or different grant. The rights sought in the present case do not appear to approach anywhere near that degree of invasion of the servient land. If that is so—and I emphasise that I have not gone into the facts—I would regard the right claimed as a valid easement.

23.5   Access to Neighbouring Land Act 1992

ACCESS TO NEIGHBOURING LAND ACT 1992

1. Access orders

(1)   A person—

(a)   who, for the purpose of carrying out works to any land (the 'dominant land'), desires to enter upon any adjoining or adjacent land (the 'servient land'), and

(b)   who needs, but does not have, the consent of some other person to that entry, may make an application to the court for an order under this section ('an access order') against that other person.

(2)   On an application under this section, the court shall make an access order if, and only if, it is satisfied—

(a)   that the works are reasonably necessary for the preservation of the whole or any part of the dominant land; and

(b)   that they cannot be carried out, or would be substantially more difficult to carry out, without entry upon the servient land;

but this subsection is subject to subsection (3) below.

(3)   The court shall not make an access order in any case where it is satisfied that, were it to make such an order—

(a)   the respondent or any other person would suffer interference with, or disturbance of, his use or enjoyment of the servient land, or

(b)   the respondent, or any other person (whether of full age or capacity or not) in occupation of the whole or any part of the servient land, would suffer hardship,

to such a degree by reason of the entry (notwithstanding any requirement of this Act or any term or condition that may be imposed under it) that it would be unreasonable to make the order.

(4)   Where the court is satisfied on an application under this section that it is reasonably necessary to carry out any basic preservation works to the dominant land, those works shall be taken for the purposes of this Act to be reasonably necessary for the preservation of the land; and in this subsection 'basic preservation works' means any of the following, that is to say—

(a)   the maintenance, repair or renewal of any part of a building or other structure comprised in, or situate on, the dominant land;

(b)   the clearance, repair or renewal of any drain, sewer, pipe or cable so comprised or situate;

(c)   the treatment, cutting back, felling, removal or replacement of any hedge, tree, shrub or other growing thing which is so comprised and which is, or is in danger of becoming, damaged, diseased, dangerous, insecurely rooted or dead;

(d)   the filling in, or clearance, of any ditch so comprised;

but this subsection is without prejudice to the generality of the works which may, apart from it, be regarded by the court as reasonably necessary for the preservation of any land.

. . .

3. Effect of access order

(1)   An access order requires the respondent, so far as he has power to do so, to permit the applicant or any of his associates to do anything which the applicant or associate is authorised or required to do under or by virtue of the order of this section.

(2)   Except as otherwise provided by or under this Act, an access order authorises the applicant or any of his associates, without the consent of the respondent,—

(a)   to enter upon the servient land for the purpose of carrying out the specified works;

(b)   to bring on to that land, leave there during the period permitted by the order and, before the end of that period, remove, such materials, plant and equipment as are reasonably necessary for the carrying out of those works; and

(c)   to bring on to that land any waste arising from the carrying out of those works, if it is reasonably necessary to do so in the course of removing it from the dominant land;

but nothing in this Act or in any access order shall authorise the applicant or any of his associates to leave anything in, on or over the servient land (otherwise than in discharge of their duty to make good that land) after their entry for the purpose of carrying out works to the dominant land ceases to be authorised under or by virtue of the order. . . .

CHAPTER TWENTY-FOUR

EXPRESS AND IMPLIED GRANT OF EASEMENTS

24.1 Express Grant and Reservation of Easements (and Profits)

ST EDMUNDSBURY AND IPSWICH DIOCESAN BOARD OF FINANCE AND ANOTHER v CLARK (No. 2) [1975] 1 All ER 722, Court of Appeal

FACTS: The Church of England originally owned a chuchyard and the adjoining rectory grounds. In 1945 the Church of England sold the rectory and its grounds to Clark. The only access to the church building was across the rectory grounds. So the conveyance to Clark included an express reservation of an easement of way along an existing track across the rectory grounds to and from the church. Unfortunately this reservation did not make it clear whether this right of way was 'on foot only' or whether vehicles could use the track. Clark, to the inconvenience of weddings, funerals etc, insisted that the right of way was 'on foot only'. Evidence had been adduced to show that in 1945 there had been at the churchyard end of the track two solid gateposts only about four feet apart.
HELD: The physical circumstances of the pieces of land at the time of the grant/reservation had to be taken into account; if, but only if, the doubts were not resolved by looking at the physical circumstances, the court should give the benefit of the doubt to the dominant owner and construe the grant in his favour. In the present case the finding of fact as to the size of the gap between the gateposts proved fatal to the Church's claim. The Court concluded that the narrow gap through the gateposts meant that in 1945 the right of way must have been 'on foot only'. In view of that finding of fact there was no room for doubt such as would warrant an exercise of discretion in favour of the dominant owner.

SIR JOHN PENNYCUICK: . . . Counsel for the parochial church council relied, above all, on the undoubted facts that the disputed strip is wide enough—nine feet from tree root to tree root—for cars, including lorries, to drive along it without difficulty and that its surface in 1945 was sufficiently firm and even for them to do so. This is an important factor, but far from conclusive. One may well have a strip of land capable of being used by cars but not adapted or appropriate for the passage of cars.

   Counsel for the parochial church council relied on another factor which seemed to us of importance, namely, that from time to time building materials would have to be taken to the church and there was no other route available. One would certainly expect the parties to have had this consideration in mind in 1945, when the church was in rather a dilapidated condition. They could not, of course, have foreseen the 1968 fire.

   We mention at this point, in order to avoid misunderstanding, that if there is no right of way for vehicles over the disputed strip, the Church authorities may have a vehicular right of way of necessity to the church for the purpose of taking up building materials and the like. This possibility does not arise on the pleadings; but if there be such, it is open to Mr Clark to select any reasonably convenient line, and he has in fact offered a longer vehicular way round to the north of the church for the repairs.

There was some evidence as to the use of a small part of the disputed strip by hearses. But this did not, we think, turn out to be a factor of much importance. No serious difficulty arises in carrying a coffin over this short stretch and it would in any event be met at the entrance to the churchyard and carried into the church. Nor did any point arise as to weddings. In a parish of this size, neither weddings nor funerals are of frequent occurrence. The ordinary churchgoer, arrived by car or on foot, would be negligibly inconvenienced by a few yards extra walk.

Counsel for the parochial church council sought to discount the gate at the churchyard end by pointing out its poor condition in 1945. This is a valid point so far as it goes. Obviously a broken-down wooden gate is of less significance than, for instance, a solid iron barrier. But the gate remains, to our mind, a factor of the first importance. . . .

24.2   Implied Grant of Easements (and Profits)

24.2.1   WAYS OF NECESSITY

CORPORATION OF LONDON v *RIGGS* (1880) 13 ChD 798, Master of the Rolls

FACTS: Riggs acquired a 'land-locked' piece of farm-land in the middle of Epping Forest. Epping Forest was (and still is) the property of the City of London. Riggs started building 'tea rooms' on his land. It was not disputed that Riggs had a 'way of necessity' to and from his land, but the Corporation of London objected to his building activities.
HELD: The way of necessity could only be used for those purposes for which the dominant and was being used at the time the necessity arose (i.e. at the time the land became isolated). In the present case the land had been used for farming purposes at that time, therefore neither contractors building the tea-rooms, nor his future clientele, could use the way.

JESSEL MR: . . . What does the necessity of the case require? The object of implying the re-grant, as stated by the older Judges, was that if you did not give the owner of the reserved close some right of way or other, he could neither use nor occupy the reserved close, nor derive any benefit from it. But what is the extent of the benefit he is to have? Is he entitled to say, I have reserved to myself more than that which enables me to enjoy it as it is at the time of the grant? And if that is the true rule, that he is not to have more than necessity requires, as distinguished from what convenience may require, it appears to me that the right of way must be limited to that which is necessary at the time of the grant; that is, he is supposed to take a re-grant to himself of such a right of way as will enable him to enjoy the reserved thing as it is.

That appears to me to be the meaning of a right of way of necessity. If you imply more, you reserve to him not only that which enables him to enjoy the thing he has reserved as it is, but that which enables him to enjoy it in the same way and to the same extent as if he reserved a general right of way for all purposes: that is—as in the case I have before me—a man who reserves two acres of arable land in the middle of a large piece of land is to be entitled to cover the reserved land with houses, and call on his grantee to allow him to make a wide metalled road up to it. I do not think that is a fair meaning of a way of necessity: I think it must be limited by the necessity at the time of the grant; and that the man who does not take the pains to secure an actual grant of a right of way for all purposes is not entitled to be put in a better position than to be able to enjoy that which he had at the time the grant was made. . . .

24.2.2   INTENDED EASEMENTS

CORY v *DAVIES* [1923] 2 Ch 95, Chancery Division

FACTS: A property developer had built three houses serviced by a private road which had openings at each end where it joined the public highway. The tenant of one of the houses locked the gates of the private road nearest to his house, so as to prevent traffic using that route. The tenants of the other houses sought an injunction preventing the defendant from locking the gate in the future. They also sought a declaration that they were entitled to use the right of way.

HELD: The circumstances showed that it had been the common intention of the tenants that the private drive should be open for their mutual benefit. Accordingly the grant of an easement to that effect would be implied into the lease of each plot.

PO LAWRENCE J: . . . the circumstances in the present case are such that, in order to give effect to the common intention of the parties, the law will imply the appropriate grants and reservations in the three contemporaneous leases of May 8 1857. This common intention would be given complete effect to, if there were implied in the lease of each plot a grant to the lessee of the right, during the term, to use the drive and entrance gates and a reservation to the lessor and to his lessees, as owner and occupiers of the houses erected on the other two plots, of the right to use the drive and entrance gates, so far as such drive and gates were constructed on the demised plot. The present case, in my opinion, falls within the second of the two classes of cases in which, according to Lord Parker's speech in *Pwllbach Colliery Co.* v *Woodman* [1915] AC 634 easements may impliedly be created. Lord Parker there states that this class of cases does not depend upon the terms of the grant itself, but upon the circumstances under which the grant was made, and that the Court will readily imply the grant or reservation of such easements as may be necessary to give effect to the common intention of the parties to the grant with reference to the manner or purpose in and for which the land granted or some land retained by the grantor is to be used, pointing out, however, that it is an essential condition of the implied creation of such easements that the parties should intend that the subject of the grant or the land retained by the grantor should be used in some definite and particular manner and that it is not enough that the user intended by the parties might or might not involve that definite and particular use. The defendants, however, contend that the Court ought not to act on this principle, because in the circumstances of this case its application would involve the implication of a reservation in favour of the lessor, and that such an implication is contrary to the principle laid down in *Wheeldon* v *Burrows* [see **24.2.3**]. That case, no doubt, lays down the general rule that, if a grantor intends to reserve any right over the tenement granted, it is his duty to reserve it expressly in the grant, and I think that there is great force in the argument that this general rule applies a fortiori where the grant, as in the present case, contains certain express reservations in favour of the grantor. It is evident, however, from the judgment in *Wheeldon* v *Burrows*, that there are exceptions to this general rule, and I am of opinion that the present case forms one of these exceptions. The three leases of May 8 1857, were really parts of one transaction, by which the lessor was at the same moment disposing of the sites of all the three plots, that is to say, of the whole of the land over which the easements were to extend, and the easements were only required for the beneficial enjoyment by the lessees of the three plots. In fact the lessor in granting the three leases containing covenants to lay out the three plots in the form of a terrace was only giving effect to the arrangement made between the three lessees, and, therefore, this is not a case where the lessor or anybody deriving title under him by virtue of a subsequent grant is claiming the benefit of an implied reservation in favour of the lessor for his own benefit. In these circumstances the Court ought not, in my opinion, to let the general rule stand in the way of holding that the appropriate grants and reservations, in order to carry out the common intention of the parties, ought to be implied. . . .

WONG v *BEAUMONT PROPERTY TRUST LTD* [1964] 2 All ER 119, Court of Appeal

FACTS: A landlord had granted a lease of the basement of premises to Blackaby. He covenanted—

   (a)   to run the premises as a 'popular restaurant';
   (b)   to comply with Public Health Regulations;
   (c)   to eliminate 'all noxious smells'.

Blackaby's attempt to run the premises as an English Restaurant were a miserable failure. He assigned the lease to Wong, who converted the restaurant to Chinese food, with resounding success. However, the tenant upstairs complained about the dreadful 'noxious smells' coming from the basement. Public Health Officers were called in. They told Wong that unless a ventilation shaft was run from the basement up the back of the above-ground floors of the building, Wong would have to close down. The landlords refused to let Wong put up the ventilating shaft, so Wong commenced proceedings claiming that he had an easement entitling him to put up the shaft. The county court judge found as a fact that, at the time the lease was granted to Blackaby, a ventilating shaft was necessary for the restaurant to function successfully and eliminate smells.

HELD: The fact that neither of the original parties realised that a ventilation shaft was necessary was not fatal to establishing an easement on the basis of an implied grant based on the intentions of the parties. The inference of an easement had been necessary to accord with their general intentions.

LORD DENNING MR: The whole question in the case now is: Is the tenant entitled to put up this duct outside the building without the landlords' consent? The Midland Bank readily consent because they dislike very much the odours and smells which come up. The public health inspector says it is absolutely essential, if the business is to be carried on at all, that this ventilation duct should be put in. But the landlords object. It is difficult to see any good reason for the landlords' refusal. The judge has found that the duct would hardly make any appreciable difference to the landlords at all. Of course, it would be unsightly for a big duct to be put up on the back wall; but the back of these premises is unsightly anyway. It faces a back street and is hardly seen by anyone.

. . . The question is: Has the tenant a right to put up this duct without the landlords' consent? If he is to have any right at all, it must be by way of easement and not merely by way of implied contract. He is not the original lessee, nor are the defendants the original lessors. Each is a successor in title. As between them, a right of this kind, if it exists at all, must be by way of an easement. In particular, an easement of necessity. The law on the matter was stated by Lord Parker of Waddington in *Pwllbach Colliery Co. Ltd* v *Woodman* [1915] AC 634, where he said, omitting immaterial words:

> The law will readily imply the grant or reservation of such easements as may be necessary to give effect to the common intention of the parties to a grant of real property, with reference to the manner or purposes in and for which the land granted . . . is to be used . . . But it is essential for this purpose that the parties should intend that the subject of the grant . . . should be used in some definite and particular manner. It is not enough that the subject of the grant . . . should be intended to be used in a manner which may or may not involve this definite and particular use.

That is the principle which underlies all easements of necessity. . . .

. . . Here was the grant of a lease to the lessee for the very purpose of carrying on a restaurant business. It was to be a popular restaurant, and it was to be developed and extended. There was a covenant not to cause any nuisance; and to control and eliminate all smells; and to comply with the food hygiene regulations. That was 'a definite and particular manner' in which the business had to be conducted. It could not be carried on in that manner at all unless a ventilation system was installed by a duct of this kind. In these circumstances it seems to me that, if the business is to be carried on at all—if, in the words of Rolle's Abridgment, the lessee is to 'have any benefit by the grant' at all—he must of necessity be able to put a ventilation duct up the wall. It may be that in Mr Blackaby's time it would not have needed such a large duct as is now needed in the tenant's time; but nevertheless a duct of some kind would have had to be put up the wall. The tenant may need a bigger one. That does not matter. A man who has a right to an easement can use it in any proper way, so long as he does not substantially increase the burden on the servient tenement. In this case a bigger duct will not substantially increase the burden.

There is one point in which this case goes further than the earlier cases which have been cited. It is this. It was not realised by the parties, at the time of the lease, that this duct would be necessary. But it was in fact necessary from the very beginning. That seems to me sufficient to bring the principle into play. In order to use this place as a restaurant, there must be implied an easement, by the necessity of the case, to carry a duct up this wall. . . .

24.2.3 THE RULE IN *WHEELDON* v *BURROWS*

WHEELDON v *BURROWS* (1879) 12 ChD 31, Court of Appeal

FACTS: A workshop and an adjacent piece of land belonging to the same owner were put up for sale by auction. The piece of land was sold first, and the workshop was sold later. Both properties were sold to different purchasers. The workshop had the benefit of light coming in from the area of the piece of land.

HELD: There was no implied reservation in the sale of the workshop of the right to receive light coming from the area of the piece of land.

THESIGER LJ: . . . on the grant by the owner of a tenement or part of that tenement as it is then used and enjoyed, there will pass to the grantee all those continuous and apparent easements (by which, of course, I mean *quasi* easements), or, in other words, all those easements which are necessary to the reasonable enjoyment of the property granted, and which have been and are at the time of the grant used by the owners of the entirety for the benefit of the part granted. . . .

. . . in the case of a grant you may imply a grant of such continuous and apparent easements or such easements as are necessary to the reasonable enjoyment of the property conveyed, and have in fact been enjoyed during the unity of ownership, but that, with the exception which I have referred to of easements of necessity, you cannot imply a similar reservation in favour of the grantor of land. . . .

24.2.3.1 The almost magical conversion of 'nebulous rights' into easements

BORMAN v *GRIFFITH* [1930] 1 Ch 49, Chancery Division

FACTS: James owned a sizeable country estate. The estate included a mansion leased to Griffith for the purposes of a school. Running across the estate from the mansion to the main road was a properly made up private driveway. On that private driveway was a smaller house known as 'The Gardens'.

In 1923, James agreed to lease 'The Gardens' to Borman, a poultry farmer. This agreement said nothing about access to 'The Gardens'. However, at the time of the agreement James was constructing an alternative access route to 'The Gardens'. In wet weather this alternative route proved impassable for the lorries which served Borman's business. The lorries therefore used the main driveway, despite opposition from Griffith.

HELD: (Applying *Wheeldon* v *Burrows*, see above) An easement to use the driveway was to be implied into the 1923 agreement. The three elements of the rule were satisfied.

MAUGHAM J: . . . The plaintiff relies on s. 62, sub-ss. 1 and 2, of the Law of Property Act, 1925, under which certain general words are deemed to be included in a conveyance . . . 'conveyance' is defined in s. 205, sub-s. 1 (ii), to include 'a lease . . . and every other assurance of property or of an interest therein by any instrument, except a will.'

If the contract of October 10, 1923 is an 'assurance of property or of an interest therein,' a very curious result follows, for the definition of 'conveyance' in the Conveyancing Act, 1881, is limited to documents made by deed, and the contract in the present case is not by deed. . . .

On the whole, I think that it is not a 'conveyance,' because it is not an 'assurance of property or of an interest therein.'. . . In my view, the principles laid down in . . . *Wheeldon* v *Burrows* (1879) 12 ChD 31 . . . are applicable. Without going through all those cases in detail, I may state the principle as follows—namely, that where, as in the present case, two properties belonging to a single owner and about to be granted are separated by a common road, or where a plainly visible road exists over the one for the apparent use of the other, and that road is necessary for the reasonable enjoyment of the property, a right to use the road will pass with the quasi-dominant tenement, unless by the terms of the contract that right is excluded: and in my opinion, if the present position were that the plaintiff was claiming against the lessor specific performance of the agreement of October 10 1923, he would be entitled to be given a right of way for all reasonable purposes along the drive, including the part that passes the farm on the way to the orchard.

It is true that the easement, or, rather, quasi-easement, is not continuous. But the authorities are sufficient to show that a grantor of property, in circumstances where an obvious, i.e., visible and made road is necessary for the reasonable enjoyment of the property by the grantee, must be taken *prima facie* to have intended to grant a right to use it. . . .

24.2.4   SECTION 62 OF THE LAW OF PROPERTY ACT 1925

LAW OF PROPERTY ACT 1925

62.   General words implied in conveyances

(1)   A conveyance of land shall be deemed to include and shall by virtue of this Act operate to convey, with the land, all buildings, erections, fixtures, commons, hedges, ditches, fences, ways, waters, watercourses, liberties, privileges, easements, rights, and advantages whatsoever, appertaining or reputed to appertain to the land, or any part thereof, or, at the time of conveyance, demised, occupied, or enjoyed with or reputed or known as part or parcel of or appurtenant to the land or any part thereof. . . .

(4)   This section applies only if and as far as a contrary intention is not expressed in the conveyance, and has effect subject to the terms of the conveyance and to the provisions therein contained.

(5)   This section shall not be construed as giving to any person a better title to any property, right, or thing in this section mentioned than the title which the conveyance gives to him to the land or manor expressed to be conveyed, or as conveying to him any property, right, or thing in this section mentioned, further or otherwise than as the same could have been conveyed to him by the conveying parties. . . .

65.   Reservation of legal estates

(1)   A reservation of a legal estate shall operate at law without any execution of the conveyance by the grantee of the legal estate out of which the reservation is made, or any regrant by him, so as to create the legal estate reserved, and so as to vest the same in possession in the person (whether being the grantor or not) for whose benefit the reservation is made.

(2)   A conveyance of a legal estate expressed to be made subject to another legal estate not in existence immediately before the date of the conveyance, shall operate as a reservation unless a contrary intention appears.

(3)   This section applies only to reservations made after the commencement of this Act.

24.2.4.1   The breadth of the s. 62 principle

WRIGHT v *MACADAM* [1949] 2 All ER 565, Court of Appeal

FACTS: The defendant leased a top-floor flat to Mrs Wright. While this first lease was still running Macadam gave Mrs Wright permission to store her coal in a coal-shed situated in the garden to the small block of flats. When Wright's first lease ran out, it was renewed for a further period. At the time of renewal nothing was said about the coal shed. Later, during the running of the second lease, Macadam demanded that Wright pay one shilling and sixpence (seven-and-a-half new pence) per week for the use of the coal-shed. She refused. HELD: On the renewal of the lease to Wright, there was implied into the renewed lease an easement to store coal in the coal-shed. The crucial point was the existence of the privilege at the time the lease was renewed. The statutory 'magic' of the Law of Property Act 1925, s. 62 therefore converted Wright's privilege into a full easement.

JENKINS LJ: . . . The question in the present case, therefore, is whether the right to use the coal shed at the date of the letting of August 28 1943, was a liberty, privilege, easement, right or advantage appertaining, or reputed to appertain, to the land, or any part thereof, or, at the time of the conveyance, demised, occupied or enjoyed with the land—i.e., the flat—or any part thereof. It is enough for the tenants' purposes if they can bring the right claimed within the widest part of s. 62(1), i.e., if they can show that the right was at the time of the material letting demised, occupied or enjoyed with the flat or any part thereof. The predecessor of s. 62 of the Act of 1925, in the shape of s. 6 of the Act of 1881, has been the subject of a good deal of judicial discussion, and I think the effect of the cases can be thus summarised. First, the section is not confined to rights which, as a matter of law, were so annexed or appurtenant to the property conveyed at the time of the conveyance as to make them actual legally enforceable rights. Thus, on the severance of a piece of land in common ownership, the *quasi* easements *de facto* enjoyed in respect of it by one part of the land over another will pass although, of course, as a matter of law, no man can have a right appendant or appurtenant to one part of his property exercisable by him over the other part of his property. Secondly, the right, in order to pass, need not be one to which the owner or occupier for the time being of the land has had what may be described as a permanent title. A right enjoyed merely by permission is enough.

. . . I am of opinion that the learned judge came to a wrong conclusion when he held that s. 62 of the Law of Property Act 1925, had no application. He said that the right to use the coal-shed was merely a temporary right. That, as I have said, is no sufficient ground for excluding the operation of s. 62, having regard to the principle laid down in the *International Tea Stores case* [1903] 2 Ch 165. Further, he said that this was never a right or advantage appurtenant to the flat, but it is not only rights or advantages that are appurtenant to given premises that pass under s. 62. It is enough, as I have already said, that the right or advantage should, in fact, be enjoyed with the premises. Accordingly, it seems to me that the learned judge was wrong in excluding the operation of s. 62. . . .

GOLDBERG v *EDWARDS* [1950] 1 Ch 247, Court of Appeal

FACTS: Edwards owned a main building, together with an annex at the back of the main building. He leased the annex to Goldberg. That lease included an express grant of an easement of way permitting all visitors to the annex to gain access using an open yard at the side of the building. While this first lease was still in force Edwards gave permission for visitors to the annex to pass through the hallway of the main building. (That way they did not get wet!)

The first lease expired, but Goldberg was granted a new lease, with the same express clause regarding use of the open yard at the side. The new lease made no express mention of the hallway, but Goldberg claimed that the new lease impliedly granted him an easement to use the hallway.

HELD: Goldberg's claim under *Wheeldon* v *Burrows* failed, because a right to use the hallway, while it had its advantages, was not 'necessary for the reasonable or convenient enjoyment' of the annex. Despite losing on the *Wheeldon* v *Burrows* issue, Goldberg won the case; he was held to have acquired (on the renewal of his lease) an implied easement to use the hallway under the Law of Property Act 1925, s. 62.

EVERSHED MR : . . . in my judgment it does not follow that a way through the front door of another's premises and through the ground floor and passages is even *prima facie* necessary for the reasonable or convenient enjoyment of premises behind. It would take strong evidence to show that it was so, for the right to pass through another's premises, particularly when they are business premises, is, I think, a considerable burden upon the quasi-servient tenement in any case. But the evidence is that these premises at the back before the plaintiff's tenancy were wholly or partly in the occupation of another person who carried on another type of business there, and who apparently enjoyed them both reasonably and conveniently without any necessity for passing through the front part of the premises. I therefore reject the argument based on implied grant, and turn to s. 62.

. . . the privilege granted here was not temporary, like, for instance, a temporary right of light when it is obvious that buildings shortly to be erected will obscure it. The present privilege is in some ways indeed not dissimilar to that which in *Wright* v *Macadam* [1949] 2 KB 744 was held to be covered by s. 62, namely, a privilege for the tenant to use a shed for storing her coal. I therefore think that, if the right which I have defined was one which was being enjoyed at the time of the conveyance, it is covered by s. 62.

That therefore leaves the final point: what is the 'time of conveyance' within the meaning of s. 62, sub-ss. 1 and 2? The arrangement about this use of the passage appears to have been made at various dates, the last of which was January 13 1947. The plaintiffs went into occupation of the annexe on January 18 1947. The fitting of the bell and signboard took place after that. Several months passed (why, I know not, and it is quite immaterial) before the lease was executed on July 10 1947, though the term was expressed to run from January 18. It is plain that before July 10 there was no written instrument whatever. Possession may no doubt have been attributable to an oral agreement of which, having regard to the position, specific performance might have been granted; but I fail to find any instrument in writing within the meaning of s. 62 before the lease of July 10. It seems to me, therefore, that the phrase 'at the time of conveyance' must mean in this case July 10. I am unable to accept the view that one should construe that as meaning at the time when the term granted by the lease is stated to have begun. On July 10 1947, under the privilege granted, this right of ingress and egress was being enjoyed in fact. As I have held, though it is limited to the lessees themselves and does not extend to other persons, it would be capable of formulation and incorporation as a term of the lease, and it is, in my judgment, covered by s. 62. To that extent, therefore, but to that limited extent only, the plaintiffs are entitled to succeed. . . .

24.2.4.2 The limits on s. 62

SOVMOTS INVESTMENTS LTD v SECRETARY OF STATE FOR THE ENVIRONMENT AND OTHERS [1977] 2 All ER 385, House of Lords

FACTS: A London Borough Council made a compulsory purchase order of a number of maisonettes. The council argued that certain additional rights must be taken to have passed with the maisonettes, for without those rights the maisonettes could not be used for residential purposes. The rights claimed included such things as ways for water, electricity and sewage.

HELD: (Lord Russell of Killowen dissenting) The additional rights did not automatically pass with the maisonettes. Accordingly, the maisonettes could not be used for their intended residential purposes. Consequently, the Borough Council had been acting *ultra vires* in making the compulsory purchase order with a view to providing housing.

LORD WILBERFORCE: The main argument before the inspector and in the courts below was that in this case and under the compulsory purchase order as made no specific power to require the creation of ancillary rights was necessary because these would pass to the acquiring authority under either, or both, of the first rule in *Wheeldon v Burrows* (1879) 12 ChD 31 ('the rule') or of s. 62 of the Law of Property Act 1925. . . . Under s. 62 a conveyance of land operates to convey with the land all ways, watercourses, liberties, privileges, easements, rights and advantages whatsoever, appertaining or reputed to appertain to the land, or any part thereof, or, at the time of conveyance, demised, occupied or enjoyed with, or reputed or known as part or parcel or appurtenant to the land or any part thereof.

My Lords, there are very comprehensive expressions here, but it does not take much analysis to see that they have no relevance to the situation under consideration.

The rule is a rule of intention, based on the proposition that a man may not derogate from his grant. He cannot grant or agree to grant land and at the same time deny to his grantee what is at the time of the grant obviously necessary for its reasonable enjoyment. To apply this to a case where a public authority is taking from an owner his land without his will is to stand the rule on its head: it means substituting for the intention of a reasonable voluntary grantor the unilateral, opposed, intentions of the acquirer.

Moreover, and this point is relevant to a later argument, the words I have emphasised show that for the rule to apply there must be actual, and apparent, use and enjoyment at the time of the grant. But no such use or enjoyment had, at Centre Point, taken place at all.

Equally, s. 62 does not fit this case. The reason is that when land is under one ownership one cannot speak in any intelligible sense of rights, or privileges, or easements being exercised over one part for the benefit of another. Whatever the owner does, he does as owner and, until a separation occurs, of ownership or at least of occupation, the condition for the existence of rights, etc, does not exist: see *Bolton v Bolton* (1879) 11 ChD 968, per Fry J, and *Long v Gowlett* [1923] 2 Ch 177, in my opinion a correct decision.

A separation of ownership, in a case like the present, will arise on conveyance of one of the parts (e.g. the maisonettes), but this separation cannot be projected back to the stage of the compulsory purchase order so as, by anticipation, to bring into existence rights not existing in fact. . . .

24.2.4.3 *Graham v Philcox*

GRAHAM v PHILCOX [1984] 2 All ER 643, Court of Appeal

FACTS: L owned a large garden with a house at one end of that garden. In 1960 L leased the house to T. This lease included an express grant to T of an easement of way over the garden for the duration of the lease. In 1975 (while T's lease was still running) L sold the fee simple reversion in the house to G. The 1975 conveyance made no mention of a right of way. HELD: Section 62 implied into the 1975 conveyance the grant to G of a fee simple easement of way over the garden.

PURCHAS LJ: . . . With great respect to the judge, I think that he was wrong in deciding that the easement and right created in the first instance in the lease was coterminous with it or even with any further occupation by the grantee under statutory protection. The right of way having been created by direct grant and its use continuing even though under statutory protection at the time of the conveyance, the use and enjoyment of that easement fell within the terms of s. 62 of the 1925 Act and the judge was in error in holding that it did not. Nor, for the reasons I have already given, can I accept the submissions made by counsel for the defendants that by enlarging the physical dimensions or indeed altering the nature of the dominant tenement from two individual flats to one dwelling house has the easement, right or advantage been destroyed. The occupier of the dominant tenement, however, will be and will remain subject to the rules requiring that the character and extent of the burden imposed on the servient tenement must not be enlarged. For want of a better definition, this burden must be said to be commensurate with the reasonable user of the means of access by the occupier, his servants, agents, invitees or licensees occupying a single dwelling unit. If by any change in the nature of his enjoyment of the dominant tenement the occupier thereof increases the burden on the servient tenement beyond this, then he will be liable to the consequences of excessive user which may be imposed on any person enjoying an easement, right or benefit of this kind. . .

24.3 Implied Reservation of Easements

RE WEBB'S LEASE [1951] Ch 808, Court of Appeal

FACTS: The landlord, the head-lessee of business premises where he carried on his business of a butcher and merchant, leased the floors above his shop to Webb. The tenancy covered the outer walls of the upper floors where the landlord had for some time prior to the tenancy displayed an advertisement in respect of his trade. The landlord had neglected to reserve the right to continue to display the advertisement and claimed that the reservation of an easement to that end ought to be implied into the grant of the tenancy. HELD: The landlord's claim to an easement by reservation failed.

JENKINS LJ: . . . The landlord did not include in the provisions of the lease, as executed, any reservation of advertising rights over any part of the outer walls. At the date of the lease the advertisements now in dispute were in their present positions on the walls and plainly to be seen. Moreover, they had existed in their present positions continuously since before the commencement of the tenant's original tenancy in 1939, and the tenant never objected to their presence at any time during his original tenancy or at the time of the granting of the lease of August 11 1949, or thereafter until January 1950. There is no evidence that either party ever even mentioned the subject of the advertisements to the other during the whole of this period of more than ten years. This being in substance the whole of the available facts, the question is whether on those bare facts, without more, the court can and ought as a matter of law to imply in favour of the landlord a reservation during the term of twenty-one years granted by the lease of August 11 1949, of advertising rights over the outer walls demised, at all events, to the extent required to enable him to maintain the existing advertisements and to retain for his own benefit any periodical payments receivable from the Borough Billposting Co. in respect of the site of the Brymay poster. . . .

In *Wheeldon* v *Burrows* (12 ChD 49), Thesiger LJ, states two propositions as 'the general rules governing cases of this kind.' The first concerns easements passing to the grantee and is not relevant here. The second he states (*ibid*) as being

> . . . that, if the grantor intends to reserve any right over the tenement granted, it is his duty to reserve it expressly in the grant. Those are the general rules governing cases of this kind, but the second of those rules is subject to certain exceptions. One of those exceptions is the well-known exception which attaches to cases of what are called ways of necessity; and I do not dispute for a moment that there may be, and probably are, certain other exceptions, to which I shall refer before I close my observations upon this case. Both of the general rules which I have mentioned are founded upon a maxim which is as well established by authority as it is consonant to reason and common sense, *viz*, that a grantor shall not derogate from his grant.

The learned lord justice deals further with the question of exceptions (*ibid*, 59), but, apart from the case of easements of necessity, he does not appear to have been disposed to admit any further exceptions other than cases of mutual easements and cases in which the same vendor sells by auction different lots to different persons at the same time, where the purchaser of one lot may be entitled to an easement over another lot even though the latter was in fact actually conveyed before the former: see *Swansborough* v *Coventry* (1832) 9 Bing 305. . . . (i) If the landlord intended to reserve any such rights over the demised premises it was his duty to reserve them expressly in the lease of August 11 1949: *Wheeldon* v *Burrows*. (ii) The landlord having failed in this duty, the onus was on him to establish the facts to prove, and prove clearly, that his case was an exception to the rule: *Aldridge* v *Wright* [1929] 2 KB 117. (iii) The mere fact that the tenant knew at the date of the lease of August 11 1949, that the landlord was using the outer walls of the demised premises for the display of the advertisements in question did not suffice to absolve the landlord from his duty of expressly reserving any rights in respect of them he intended to claim, or to take the case out of the general rule: see *Suffield* v *Brown* 4 De GJ & Sm 199, *Crossley & Sons Ltd* v *Lightowler* LR 2 Ch 478. . . .

CHAPTER TWENTY-FIVE

PRESCRIPTION FOR EASEMENTS (AND PROFITS)

25.1 The Complexities of Prescription Law

Unfortunately there are no less than three forms of prescription for easements and profits:

(a) common law prescription;

(b) lost modern grant;

(c) the Prescription Act 1832.

25.2 Rules Common to All Three Forms of Prescription

User, to be prescriptive, must be 'as of right'. User is only 'as of right' if it is *nec vi, nec clam, nec precario*, i.e., 'without force, without secrecy and without permission'.

25.2.1 WITHOUT FORCE

In this context, 'force' has been given a very wide meaning, and the courts have ruled that user, to be prescriptive, must not be contentious in any way. Thus, fisticuffs man-to-man, the breaking down of barriers and the climbing over of fences are all 'forcible' user and therefore not prescriptive.

The courts have also held that user in face of express oral or written protests from the alleged servient owner should be deemed to be 'forcible', even though there is no actual violence.

25.2.2 WITHOUT SECRECY

LLOYDS BANK LIMITED AND ANOTHER v DALTON
[1942] 1 Ch 466, Chancery Division

FACTS: Dalton owned the servient building, which was a large dye-works. The dominant building was a small outhouse which claimed a prescriptive easement of support against the dye-works. The outhouse had for well over twenty years leant against the wall of the dye-works. That wall was a blank wall without any windows. The outhouse could therefore not be seen from the works, nor could it be seen from the public road.

HELD: The court rejected Dalton's contention that there was a 'secret' user, not capable of giving rise to an easement by prescription. A reasonable owner would surely go around his premises from time to time. A reasonable owner would therefore at some stage have discovered the outhouse.

BENNETT J: . . . It was not suggested that the plaintiffs' predecessors in title, in executing their works, had acted secretly. The defendant rested his case exclusively on the fact proved that in March 1939, the yard and the outbuilding were not visible from the dye-works or from a highway or other public place.

It is clear law, I think, that an easement of support cannot be acquired unless the owner of the servient tenement has knowledge that his land or his building is in fact supporting the dominant tenement. . . .

. . . in *Union Lighterage Co.* v *London Graving Dock Co.* [1902] 2 Ch 557 Romer LJ stated the principle in these terms: '. . . on principle, it appears to me that a prescriptive right to an easement over a man's land should only be acquired when the enjoyment has been open—that is to say, of such a character that an ordinary owner of the land, diligent in the protection of his interests, would have, or must be taken to have, a reasonable opportunity of becoming aware of that enjoyment.'

In the present case the dominant tenement had in fact been supported by the servient tenement for more than forty years before March 1939. The two tenements were on the slope of this hill. They were contiguous, and the defendant's tenement was below the plaintiffs' tenement. The buildings on the slope were close to one another. There was an open passage leading from Castle Terrace on to the plaintiffs' yard. Once in the plaintiffs' yard, it must have been obvious that the north-east end of that yard and of the outbuilding were supported by the dye-works, and the south-west wall of the dye-works. Lastly, the defendant was not called to give evidence at the trial. It is notorious that the owners of land and buildings are interested in their boundaries, and, in my judgment, the facts proved at the trial of this case lead irresistibly to the conclusion that the successive owners of the dye-works, assuming them to have been reasonable persons, diligent in the protection of their interests, either must have known or must be taken to have had reasonable opportunity of becoming aware of the fact that the dye-works were supporting the north-east part of the plaintiffs' yard and of the outbuilding standing thereon. For these reasons, the plea of claim, in my judgment, fails. . . .

LIVERPOOL CORPORATION v H COGHILL & SON [1918] 1 Ch 307, Chancery Division

FACTS: Coghill ran a chemical factory which operated 24 hours a day. For many years Coghill poured borax effluent into the corporation's sewers. Coghill always did so very early in the morning. This was not out of any deliberate attempt to conceal what he was doing. Discharging effluent at night suited its 'production cycle'.
HELD: Coghill could not claim a prescriptive right. Its user was in law 'secret', even though there had been no deliberate attempt at concealment.

EVE J: . . . how can this intermittent use, or rather misuse, of surface and rain water gullies and drains wholly upon and within the limits of the defendants' premises be made the foundation of a legal right to pour a poisonous waste liquor (for such *ex hypothesi* it must be, or no necessity for asserting the easement would exist) into the plaintiffs' sewers, unless notice is brought home to the plaintiffs of what the defendants were doing? There has been no assertion by conduct or otherwise on the part of the defendants that they claimed to do these things as of right, nor have they produced any evidence to prove any notice of their acts to the corporation or their predecessors, or established the existence of any state of things from which such notice could legitimately be inferred. On the contrary, I am quite satisfied on the evidence of Mr Everett, who covers the period between 1879 and 1895, fortified by the resolution of July 30 1873, that the plaintiffs' predecessors had no knowledge of the facts. No attempt has been made to fix the corporation with notice since 1895, and when the matter of injury to the farm was taken up by their responsible officials in 1908 their whole course of conduct was quite inconsistent with their having any notice of what was going on inside the defendants' works. If, then, the methods adopted by the defendants could in any circumstances have been made the foundation of a prescriptive right, a point upon which I express no opinion, I am satisfied that in the circumstances here disclosed the enjoyment has not been of such a character as to establish any such right. It has throughout been secret, not surreptitious or actively concealed from, but unknown to and unsuspected by the plaintiffs and their predecessors, and incapable, therefore, of being relied upon as the foundation of rights to their prejudice. As Thesiger LJ says in the course of the judgment of the Court of Appeal in *Sturges* v *Bridgman* (1879) 11 ChD 852, 'Consent or acquiescence of the owner of the servient tenement lies at the root of prescription, and of the fiction of a lost grant, and hence the acts or user, which go to the proof of either the one or the other, must be in the language of the civil law, nec vi, nec clam, nec precario; for a man cannot, as a general rule, be said to consent or acquiesce in the acquisition by his neighbour of an easement through an enjoyment of which he has no knowledge, actual or constructive.'...

25.2.3   WITHOUT PERMISSION

MILLS v *SILVER* [1991] 1 All ER 449, Court of Appeal

FACTS: In 1986 the defendant purchased a derelict farm set some distance from a public road. The defendant relied upon an old statutory declaration which indicated that the previous owner of the farm had for many years regularly and openly used a particular track to gain access to the farm. The defendant proceeded to use the track for passage on foot and by motor vehicle. The plaintiff objected to the use of vehicles, particularly when the defendant laid down 700 tons of stone along the track, to make a solid road. They sought an injunction and damages for trespass against the defendant.
HELD: The previous owner of the 'servient' land had not given permission for the previous owner of the 'dominant' land to use the track, nor had he objected to the use of it. He had merely 'tolerated' or acquiesced in the use of the track. Nevertheless, this did not defeat the defendant's claim that an easement had been acquired by prescriptive user 'as of right'. The defendants would be able to pass and repass, with or without vehicles, over the track. However, the laying of 700 tons of stone was an excessive exercise of the right to a right of way. Damages were awarded for the trespass.

DILLON LJ: . . . I turn now to the judge's point of tolerance. The question is whether the judge has correctly directed himself in law. To put it another way, did the tolerance of the successive servient owners, James Price until 1970 and in his case tolerance out of good neighbourliness and because the use was too insignificant to matter to him or cause him any inconvenience, of such vehicular use of the disputed track as there was in Joe Phillips's time preclude a prescriptive right being acquired, even though no express permission was ever granted to Joe Phillips and no reservations as to his use of the disputed track with vehicles were ever communicated to him by anyone?

The topic of tolerance has bulked fairly large in recent decisions of this court dealing with claims to prescriptive rights, since the decision in *Alfred F Beckett Ltd* v *Lyons* [1967] 1 All ER 833, [1967] Ch 449. If passages in successive judgments are taken on their own out of context and added together, it would be easy to say, as, with all respect, it seems to me that the judge did in the present case, that there is an established principle of law that no prescriptive right can be acquired if the user by the dominant owner of the servient tenement in the particular manner for the appropriate number of years has been tolerated without objection by the servient owner.

But there cannot be any such principle of law because it is, with rights of way, fundamentally inconsistent with the whole notion of acquisition of rights by prescription. It is difficult to see how, if there is such a principle, there could ever be a prescriptive right of way. It follows that the various passages in the judgments in question cannot be taken on their own out of context. If each case is looked at on its own and regarded as a whole, none lays down any such far-reaching principle. In my judgment, the judge in the present case has misapplied the authorities, by taking passages out of context, and misdirected himself in arriving at the supposed principle of law which he has sought to apply. . . .

25.2.4   USER MUST BE CONTINUOUS

HOLLINS v *VERNEY* (1884) 13 QB 304, Court of Appeal

FACTS: The case concerned a claim to an easement of way. The alleged dominant owner had only used the right of way three times in the last twenty years.

HELD: The claim for a prescriptive easement failed. User must be regular enough for it to be reasonable to expect that the servient owner would be aware that some right was being asserted.

LINDLEY LJ: . . . as the enjoyment which is pointed out by the Prescription Act 1832 is an enjoyment which is open as well as of right, it seems to follow that no actual user can be sufficient to satisfy the statute, unless during the whole of the statutory term (whether acts of user be proved in each year or not) the user is enough at any rate to carry to the mind of a reasonable person who is in possession of the servient tenement, the fact that a continuous right to enjoyment is being asserted, and ought to be resisted if such right is not recognised, and if resistance to it is intended. Can a user which is confined to the rare occasions on which the alleged right is supposed in this instance to have been exercised, satisfy even this test? It seems to us that it cannot: that it is not, and could not reasonably be treated as the assertion of a continuous right to enjoy; and when there is no assertion by conduct of a continuous right to enjoy, it appears to us that there cannot be an actual enjoyment within the meaning of the statute. Without therefore professing to be able to draw the line sharply between long and short periods of non-user, without holding that non-user for a year or even more is necessarily fatal in all cases, without attempting to define that which the statute has left indefinite, we are of opinion that no jury can properly find that the right claimed by the defendant in this case has been established by evidence of such limited user as was mainly relied upon, and as was contended by the defendant to be sufficient in the present case.

25.2.5   USER MUST BE BY OR ON BEHALF OF A FEE SIMPLE AGAINST A FEE SIMPLE

SIMMONS v DOBSON [1991] 4 All ER 25, Court of Appeal

FACTS: The plaintiff was the tenant of one property and the defendant was tenant of an adjoining property. Freehold title to both properties was held by the same freeholder. The plaintiff sought to show that, according to the doctrine of lost modern grant, they had the right to use a passageway over the defendant's premises.
HELD: A tenant could not claim an easement by the doctrine of lost modern grant. The doctrine gave rise to a form of common law prescription, it could therefore only apply between freeholders.

FOX LJ: . . . Now, in relation to common law prescription generally, user had to be by or on behalf of a fee simple owner against a fee simple owner. An easement can be granted expressly by a tenant for life or tenant for years so as to bind their respective limited interests, but such rights cannot be acquired by prescription. . . .

While, therefore, there appears to be no case which directly decides that there can be no lost modern grant by or to a person who owns a lesser estate than the fee, the *dicta* are to the contrary and are very strong and of long standing. I take them to represent settled law. I should mention for completeness that the law in Ireland has gone the other way: see *Flynn v Harte* [1913] 2 IR 322 and *Tallon v Ennis* [1937] IR 549.

As to any departure from that state of the law, there are, I think, difficulties of principle. It is clear that common law prescription and prescription under the 1832 Act are, as a matter of decision, not available by or to owners of less estates than the fee. Lost modern grant is merely a form of common law prescription. It is based upon a fiction which was designed to meet, and did meet, a particular problem. It would, I think, be anomalous to extend the fiction further by departure, in relation to lost modern grant, from the fundamental principle of common law prescription referred to by Lindley LJ.

I would allow the appeal.

PALK v SHINNER (1852) 118 English Reports 215

FACTS: Palk leased his land to various tenants. From 1820 onwards the tenants crossed Shinner's land 'as of right' to get to the land leased to them. From 1821 onwards Shinner's land was leased to X. User as of right by the tenants continued until the dispute broke out in about 1850.

HELD: Judgment was given for Palk. His tenants were to be regarded as acting on his behalf. Palk thus acquired a fee simple easement.

LORD CAMPBELL CJ: I am of opinion that the plaintiff is entitled to our judgment. I think that there was evidence from which the jury might find that he was entitled to claim a right of way under s. 2 of stat. 2 & 3 W. 4, c. 71. I do not say that the evidence was conclusive; but it was sufficient to justify their finding; and that finding ought not to be disturbed unless the plaintiff's claim is defeated by s. 8. I am of opinion that it is not. The period during which the land over which the right of way is claimed has been leased for a term exceeding three years is not, under that section, to be excluded from the computation of a twenty years' enjoyment, though it is, no doubt, to be excluded from the computation of an enjoyment for forty years. Sect. 7 excludes certain times, including that of a tenancy for life, but not that of a tenancy for years, from the computation of the 'periods' thereinbefore 'mentioned'; and a twenty years' enjoyment is one of those periods. But s. 8 provides for the exclusion of certain other times, among which is a tenancy of more than three years, not from the periods thereinbefore mentioned, but from one particular period only, expressly mentioned, namely, that of an enjoyment for forty years. It is clear, therefore, that it was not intended to exclude from the computation of an enjoyment for twenty years. Great reliance was placed upon *Bright* v *Walker* (1 CM & R 211, 4 Tyr 502); but, on examination into that case, it appears that there was no necessity for the Court to give any opinion as to the effect of s. 8; for the right of way there claimed was clearly destroyed, under s. 7, by reason of a tenancy for life. But, even supposing s. 8 to apply to a twenty years' enjoyment as well as to an enjoyment for forty years, the right by enjoyment in the present case is not destroyed, inasmuch as the condition, that the claim shall be resisted by the reversioner within three years after the determination of the tenancy for years, has not been complied with.

25.3   Prescription at Common Law

(For a general discussion see the dictum of Fox LJ in *Simmons* v *Dobson* (**25.2.5**, above).)

A claim for an easement or a profit by 'prescription at common law' is very rarely successful. The theory of this form of prescription is that once upon a time a deed was executed by the then servient owner in favour of the then dominant owner granting the relevant easement or profit. However, this deed was granted so long ago that its execution is 'outside the scope of legal memory'.

Unfortunately legal memory is elephantine, and stretches back to 1189 (the year of the accession of Richard I). In effect, if you claim a prescriptive easement (or profit) at common law, you have bodly to assert that you and your predecessors have been exercising the right ever since 1189.

Fortunately you do not have to produce evidence of user covering the whole of the last 800 or so years. If 20 years' user is proved, user right back to 1189 will be presumed. But the presumption can be rebutted by showing any of the following facts:

(a)   at some time since 1189 the right was not exercised; or
(b)   at some time since 1189 the right could not have been exercised; or
(c)   at some time since 1189 dominant and servient plots were in common ownership.

25.4   Prescription by Lost Modern Grant

(See the dictum of Fox LJ in *Simmons* v *Dobson* (**25.2.5** above).)

CHARLES DALTON v HENRY ANGUS & Co. (1881) 6 App Cas 740, House of Lords

This case is included here because it contains an important statement in the House of Lords affirming the validity of the doctrine of lost modern grant.

THE LORD CHANCELLOR (LORD SELBORNE): . . . 'My Brother Hayes said, presumed grants of windows and of support were idle fictions which ought never to have been invented; perhaps so, but the fact that they were shews that the inventors and everybody else supposed that *real grants of such a nature would be* good.' The rule as to prescription is thus stated in Sir Francis North's argument in *Potter v North* 1 Vent 387: 'The law allows prescriptions but in supply of the loss of a grant. Ancient grants happen to be lost many times, and it would be hard that no title could be made to things that lie in grant but by shewing of a grant; therefore, upon usage *temps dont*, &c., the law presumes a grant and a lawful beginning, and allows such usage for a good title; but still it is but in supply of the loss of a grant; and, therefore, for such things *as can have no lawful beginning*, nor be created at this day *by any manner of grant, or reservation, or deed that can be supposed*, no prescription is good.' Ashhurst J, in *Lord Pelham v Pickersgill* 1 TR 667, laid it down as the general rule, that 'every prescription is good, if by any possibility it can be supposed to have had a legal commencement.'. . .

TEHIDY MINERALS LTD AND ANOTHER v NORMAN AND OTHERS
[1971] 2 All ER 475, Court of Appeal

FACTS: In January 1920 a group of farmers started grazing their sheep on the servient land. They continued to do so 'as of right' until October 1941, when the land was requisitioned by the war office for military training. The farmers continued to graze their sheep on the land, but it was conceded that the post 1941 grazing was by permission. (Permission came first from the war office and then, after the land had been derequisitioned, the servient owners.) The farmers claimed a prescriptive profit of pasture.

HELD: The farmers succeeded under the doctrine of 'lost modern grant'. The 'presumption' of lost modern grant arose because the claimant had produced strong evidence of twenty years user 'as of right'. It would not rebut the 'presumption' for the servient owner to show that the grant never in fact took place. The servient owner could only rebut the 'presumption' by showing that during the relevant period (in this case January 1920 to October 1921) the grant was impossible at law.

BUCKLEY LJ: No defendant has sought to prove any actual grant of common rights; at the trial the defendants relied on common law prescription, on the Prescription Act 1832, and on the doctrine of lost modern grant.

. . . The co-existence of three separate methods of prescribing is, in our view, anomalous and undesirable, for it results in much unnecessary complication and confusion. We hope that it may be possible for the legislature to effect a long overdue simplification in this branch of the law.

. . . In our judgment *Angus & Co.* v *Dalton* (1877) 3 QBD 85 decides that, where there has been upwards of 20 years' uninterrupted enjoyment of an easement, such enjoyment having the necessary qualities to fulfil the requirements of prescription, then unless, for some reason such as incapacity on the part of the person or persons who might at some time before the commencement of the 20-year period have made a grant, the existence of such a grant is impossible, the law will adopt a legal fiction that such a grant was made, in spite of any direct evidence that no such grant was in fact made. If this legal fiction is not to be displaced by direct evidence that no grant was made, it would be strange if it could be displaced by circumstantial evidence leading to the same conclusion, and in our judgment it must follow that circumstantial evidence tending to negative the existence of a grant (other than evidence establishing impossibility) should not be permitted to displace the fiction. Precisely the same reasoning must, we think, apply to a presumed lost grant of a profit à prendre as to an easement.

In the present case, if we are to presume lost grants, we must do so in respect of each of the four farms, Higher and Lower Hill, Cabilla and Pinsla Park. Each of the presumed grants must be supposed to have been made between 20 January 1920 and 28 November 1921, and to have been since lost in circumstances of which no one now has any recollection. This combination of circumstances seems to us to be exceedingly improbable, and we feel sympathy for the view expressed by Farwell J in *A-G v Simpson*, where that learned judge said:

It cannot be the duty of a judge to presume a grant of the non-existence of which he is convinced, nor can he be constrained to hold that such a grant is reasonably possible within the meaning of the authorities.

In view, however, of the decision in *Angus & Co.* v *Dalton* we consider that it is not open to us in the present case to follow this line. . . .

For these reasons we think that grants of common rights of grazing over Tawna Down must be presumed to have been made since 19 January 1920 and before 6 October 1921, in respect of each of the four farms at present under consideration. We are therefore of opinion that prescriptive rights to grazing on the down must be regarded as having been in force at the date of the requisition in respect of all seven farms under discussion. What ensued thereafter can only have had the effect of suspending these rights unless it can be said that any of the claimants or any predecessor in title of his has abandoned his grazing rights. For the plaintiffs it is contended that the arrangements of October 1960 amounted to abandonment by the commoners of their rights over Tawna Down. We do not agree. For reasons which we have already indicated we think that that arrangement was of a temporary and terminable character. Abandonment of an easement or of a profit à prendre can only, we think, be treated as having taken place where the person entitled to it has demonstrated a fixed intention never at any time thereafter to assert the right himself or to attempt to transmit it to anyone else. The fact that the commoners are content for the time being to subject the management of the grazing on the down to the control of the association is not, in our view, a circumstance which gives rise to any such conclusion. The commoners may well find it more advantageous for the time being to subject themselves to the control of the association in order to obtain the benefits of the fencing and maintenance by the association of the grazing on the down than to exercise their common rights. It does not at all follow from this that if at some time in the future the arrangement should come to an end, the commoners might not wish to reassert their common rights. We do not think that any abandonment has been shown to have taken place. . . .

OAKLEY v BOSTON [1975] 3 All ER 405, Court of Appeal

FACTS: Land surrounding a Church of England rectory was 'glebe land' vested in the rector of the parish in his capacity as a 'corporation sole'. The owner of adjoining land had continually used, 'as of right', a pathway of the rectory land from 1914 to 1962. In 1962 the adjoining land was sold to a new owner who used the pathway only occasionally. In 1965 the rectory was sold to the plaintiffs. They sought an injunction to restrain the adjoining owner from 'trespassing' on their land.

HELD: There could be no presumption of a lost modern grant made sometime between 1914 and 1942 (the relevant period in order to establish user as of right for twenty years up to 1962). This was because a vicar who owns land in his official capacity as an 'ecclesiastical corporation sole' has no power to grant easements. The claim for prescription by lost modern grant failed because the grant was a legal impossibility.

25.5 Prescription Under the Prescription Act 1832

PRESCRIPTION ACT 1832

1. Claims to right of common and other profits à prendre, not to be defeated after thirty years enjoyment by merely showing the commencement; after sixty years enjoyment the right to be absolute, unless had by consent or agreement

. . . No claim which may be lawfully made at the common law, by custom, prescription, or grant, to any right of common or other profit or benefit to be taken and enjoyed from or upon any land of our sovereign lord the King . . . or any land being parcel of the duchy of Lancaster or the duchy of Cornwall, or of any ecclesiastical or lay person, or body corporate, except such matters and things as are herein specially provided for, and except tithes, rent, and services, shall, where such right, profit, or benefit have been actually taken and enjoyed by any person claiming right thereto without interruption for the full period of thirty years, be defeated or destroyed by showing only that such right, profit, or benefit was first taken or enjoyed at any time prior to such period of thirty years, but nevertheless such claim may be defeated in any other way by which the same is now liable to be defeated; and when such right, profit, or benefit shall have been so taken and enjoyed as aforesaid for the full period of sixty years, the right thereto shall be deemed absolute and indefeasible, unless it shall appear that the same was taken and enjoyed by some consent or agreement expressly made or given for that purpose by deed or writing.

2.   In claims of rights of way or other easement the periods to be twenty years and forty years

. . . No claim which may be lawfully made at the common law, by custom, prescription, or grant, to any way or other easement, or to any watercourse, or the use of any water, to be enjoyed or derived upon, over, or from any land or water of our said lord the King . . . or being parcel of the duchy of Lancaster or of the duchy of Cornwall, or being the property of any ecclesiastical or lay person, or body corporate, when such way or other matter as herein last before mentioned shall have been actually enjoyed by any person claiming right thereto without interruption for the full period of twenty years, shall be defeated or destroyed by showing only that such way or other matter was first enjoyed at any time prior to such period of twenty years, but nevertheless such claim may be defeated in any other way by which the same is now liable to be defeated; and where such way or other matter as herein last before mentioned shall have been so enjoyed as aforesaid for the full period of forty years, the right thereto shall be deemed absolute and indefeasible, unless it shall appear that the same was enjoyed by some consent or agreement expressly given or made for that purpose by deed or writing.

3.   Right to the use of light enjoyed for twenty years indefeasible, unless shewn to have been by consent

. . . When the access and use of light to and for any dwelling house, workshop, or other building shall have been actually enjoyed therewith for the full period of twenty years without interruption, the right thereto shall be deemed absolute and indefeasible, any local usage or custom to the contrary notwithstanding, unless it shall appear that the same was enjoyed by some consent or agreement expressly made or given for that purpose by deed or writing.

5.   In actions on the case the claimant may allege his right generally, as at present. In pleas to trespass and other pleadings, etc, the period mentioned in this Act may be alleged; and exceptions, etc, to be replied to specially

. . . In all actions upon the case and other pleadings, wherein the party claiming may now by law allege his right generally, without averring the existence of such right from time immemorial, such general allegation shall still be deemed sufficient, and if the same shall be denied, all and every the matters in this Act mentioned and provided, which shall be applicable to the case, shall be admissible in evidence to sustain or rebut such allegation; and . . . in all pleadings to actions of trespass, and in all other pleadings wherein before the passing of this Act it would have been necessary to allege the right to have existed from time immemorial, it shall be sufficient to allege the enjoyment thereof as of right by the occupiers of the tenement in respect whereof the same is claimed for and during such of the periods mentioned in this Act as may be applicable to the case, and without claiming in the name or right of the owner of the fee, as is now usually done; and if the other party shall intend to rely on any proviso, exception, incapacity, disability, contract, agreement, or other matter herein-before mentioned, or on any cause or matter of fact or of law not consistent with the simple fact of enjoyment, the same shall be specially alleged and set forth in answer to the allegation of the party claiming, and shall not be received in evidence on any general traverse or denial of such allegation.

6.   Restricting the presumption to be allowed in support of claims herein provided for

. . . In the several cases mentioned in and provided for by this Act, no presumption shall be allowed or made in favour or support of any claim, upon proof of the exercise or enjoyment of the right or matter claimed for any less period of time or number of years than for such period or number mentioned in this Act as may be applicable to the case and to the nature of the claim.

25.5.1 THE 'NEXT BEFORE ACTION' AND 'WITHOUT INTERRUPTION' RULES

PRESCRIPTION ACT 1832

4. Before mentioned periods to be deemed those next before suits for claiming to which such periods relate—What shall constitute an interruption

. . . Each of the respective periods of years herein-before mentioned shall be deemed and taken to be the period next before some suit or action wherein the claim or matter to which such period may relate shall have been or shall be brought into question; and . . . no act or other matter shall be deemed to be an interruption, within the meaning of this statute, unless the same shall have been or shall be submitted to or acquiesced in for one year after the party interrupted shall have had or shall have notice thereof, and of the person making or authorising the same to be made.

25.5.1.1 Interruption of user as of right in the twentieth year

FLIGHT v *THOMAS* (1841) 8 English Reports 91, House of Lords

FACTS: The dominant owner had enjoyed an easement of way as of right for 19 years and eleven months. He was then interrupted by an obstruction. He waited a few months before issuing the writ, thus twenty months had elapsed from the commencement of his user as of right.

HELD: The dominant owner was held to have a prescriptive easement.

THE LORD CHANCELLOR: . . . The argument at the bar rested principally on this, that there had not been 20 years' enjoyment. That there had not been one year's interruption acquiesced in is clear from the facts stated in the bill of exceptions; but the ground of the objection to the direction of the learned Judge was, that there had not been 20 years' enjoyment of the window. Now, in point of fact, there is no doubt that there had not been 20 years' enjoyment, according to the ordinary meaning and usage of that term; but the question is not whether there had been 20 years' enjoyment in the ordinary sense, but whether there had or had not been 20 years' enjoyment within the meaning of the Act . . .

. . . The words of the fourth section of the Act are positive that no interruption for less than one year shall be deemed an interruption within the meaning of this Act—the meaning and purpose of the Act being to give 20 years' enjoyment the effect of absolute right—that no interruption of the enjoyment of that right for less than one year shall have effect for the purposes of the Act.

25.5.2 DIFFERENCES BETWEEN LONGER AND SHORTER PERIODS UNDER THE PRESCRIPTION ACT 1832

GARDNER v *HODGSON'S KINGSTON BREWERY COMPANY LTD* [1903] AC 229, House of Lords

FACTS: The owner of a house used a track from his stables through the yard of an adjoining inn in order to access a public road. Evidence showed that he paid fifteen shillings a year to the owners of the yard. There was no agreement in writing and no evidence to show conclusively that the payment of the fifteen shillings was in consideration of the use of the track.

HELD: The payment of fifteen shillings was presumed to have been made in consideration of the right to use the track. Therefore the use of the track had been 'by permission', not 'as of right'. Accordingly, there could be no prescription under the Prescription Act 1832.

EARL OF HALSBURY LC: In a certain sense a man has a right to enjoy what he has paid for, and, therefore, if the appellant here at any time during the year when she had paid for the right to use this way had been hindered, she would have had a right to complain that what I will call her contract had been broken, and that during the year she had a right to use the way. I do not think that this would have established a right in the proper sense, because, being but a parol licence, it might be withdrawn, and her action would be for damages, but she would have no *right* to the way. And in no sense could the right be the right contemplated by the Act. That right means a right to exercise the right claimed against the will of the person over whose property it is sought to be exercised. It does not and cannot mean a user enjoyed from time to time at the will and pleasure of the owner of the property over which the user is sought. At any time after the first year the owner of the Red Lion might refuse to renew the permission to use this way. I think, therefore, that there is no evidence whatever of a user 'as of right'.

25.5.3   PRESCRIPTION FOR EASEMENTS OF LIGHT

25.5.3.1   Rights of Light Act 1959

RIGHTS OF LIGHT ACT 1959

2.   Registration of notice in lieu of obstruction of access of light
(1)   For the purpose of preventing the access and use of light from being taken to be enjoyed without interruption, any person who is an owner of land (in this and the next following section referred to as the 'servient land') over which light passes to a dwelling-house, workshop or other building (in this and the next following section referred to as 'the dominant building') may apply to the local authority in whose area the dominant building is situated for the registration of a notice under this section. . . .

3.   Effect of registered notice and proceedings relating thereto
(1)   Where, in pursuance of an application made in accordance with the last preceding section, a notice is registered thereunder, then, for the purpose of determining whether any person is entitled (by virtue of the Prescription Act 1832, or otherwise) to a right to the access of light to the dominant building across the servient land, the access of light to that building across that land shall be treated as obstructed to the same extent, and with the like consequences, as if an opaque structure, of the dimensions specified in the application,—
(a)   had, on the date of registration of the notice, been erected in the position on the servient land specified in the application, and had been so erected by the person who made the application, and
(b)   had remained in that position during the period for which the notice has effect and had been removed at the end of that period.
(2)   For the purposes of this section a notice registered under the last preceding section shall be taken to have effect until either—
(a)   the registration is cancelled, or
(b)   the period of one year beginning with the date of registration of the notice expires, or
(c)   in the case of a notice registered in pursuance of an application accompanied by a certificate issued under paragraph (b) of subsection (3) of the last preceding section, the period specified in the certificate expires without such a further certificate as is mentioned in paragraph (c) of subsection (5) of that section having before the end of that period been lodged with the local authority,
and shall cease to have effect on the occurrence of any one of those events.
(3)   Subject to the following provisions of this section, any person who, if such a structure as is mentioned in subsection (1) of this section had been erected as therein mentioned, would have had a right of action in any court in respect of that structure, on the grounds that he was entitled to a right to the access of light to the dominant building across the servient land, and that the said right was infringed by that structure, shall have the like right of action in that court in respect of the registration of a notice under the last preceding section:
Provided that an action shall not be begun by virtue of this subsection after the notice in question has ceased to have effect.
(4)   Where, at any time during the period for which a notice registered under the last preceding section has effect, the circumstances are such that, if the access of light to the dominant building had been enjoyed continuously from a date one year earlier than the

date on which the enjoyment thereof in fact began, a person would have had a right of action in any court by virtue of the last preceding subsection in respect of the registration of the notice, that person shall have the like right of action in that court by virtue of this subsection in respect of the registration of the notice.

(5)   The remedies available to the plaintiff in an action brought by virtue of subsection (3) or subsection (4) of this section (apart from any order as to costs) shall be such declaration as the court may consider appropriate in the circumstances, and an order directing the registration of the notice to be cancelled or varied, as the court may determine.

(6)   For the purposes of section four of the Prescription Act 1832 (under which a period of enjoyment of any of the rights to which that Act applies is not to be treated as interrupted except by a matter submitted to or acquiesced in for one year after notice thereof)—

(a)   as from the date of registration of a notice under the last preceding section, all persons interested in the dominant building or any part thereof shall be deemed to have notice of the registration thereof and of the person on whose application it was registered;

(b)   until such time as an action is brought by virtue of subsection (3) or subsection (4) of this section in respect of the registration of a notice under the last preceding section, all persons interested in the dominant building or any part thereof shall be deemed to acquiesce in the obstruction which, in accordance with subsection (1) of this section, is to be treated as resulting from the registration of the notice;

(c)   as from the date on which such an action is brought, no person shall be treated as submitting to or acquiescing in that obstruction:

Provided that, if in any such action, the court decides against the claim of the plaintiff, the court may direct that the preceding provisions of this subsection shall apply in relation to the notice as if that action had not been brought.

25.6   End of Chapter Assessment Questions

1.   Last month Finnegan, owner of Blackacre and Whiteacre, two neighbouring farms, sold and conveyed Blackacre to Milligan. The conveyance contained no provision relating to easements and profits.

Advise Milligan regarding the following:

(a)   The only direct access to Blackacre is a narrow footpath insufficiently wide to accommodate motor traffic. Milligan wishes to make use of the private driveway which runs from Blackacre through Whiteacre and leads into the adjoining public highway.

(b)   Some drains run from Blackacre under Whiteacre. Milligan wishes to make use of those drains.

(c)   Cyrus, the owner of Redacre, an adjoining farm, claims that he can continue to graze his sheep on a hill-side forming part of Blackacre where sheep from Redacre have been grazed 'as long as anyone can remember'.

2.   In 1976 Louise acquired the freehold to Grand House. Grand House adjoins West Field, the freehold to which was then owned by Nellie. Over the years Nellie has leased West Field to Olive for short periods.

On acquiring Grand House, Louise immediately leased it to Terry for 70 years. Soon after taking the lease, Terry started to pasture the five sheep he owned in West Field, and to take a short cut across West Field to get to the nearest station. He continued both of these activities until September 1998, without any objection from Nellie or Olive.

In September 1998 Gurinder acquired the freehold to West Field from Nellie, and immediately ordered Terry not to make any further use of West Field. Initially Terry complied with this demand, but now both he and Louise are threatening legal action.

It is now January 1999. Advise Gurinder.

25.7   End of Chapter Assessment Outline Answers

QUESTION 1

Regarding (a) and (b) Milligan will have to try and rely on the (rather complex) rules for implied grant of easements. There are no less than four separate rules in which an easement can arise by implied grant.

The first rule is 'way of necessity'. This rule is relevant only to (a). It only applies if land is sold which is completely 'land-locked', i.e. there is absolutely no way in and out except over the vendor's land. This does not appear to be the case with Blackacre, as there is the 'narrow footpath'. This path may not be adequate for farming purposes, but its existence is sufficient to prevent there being a way of necessity.

The second rule is the rule of 'intended easements'. If land is granted by a vendor or lessor to be used for a particular purpose *known to the vendor/lessor*, then there is implied into the conveyance/lease any easement over land retained by the vendor/lessor which is ABSOLUTELY ESSENTIAL in order to carry out that 'particular purpose'. (See the ventilation shaft case of *Wong* v *Beaumont*.)

With respect to (a) Milligan must argue:

(i)   that Finnegan knew that Milligan intended to use Blackacre as a farm; AND

(ii)   that a right to use the private driveway was absolutely essential to carry on a farm business.

Milligan should have no difficulty proving point (i), but point (ii) is very problematic. Finnegan would probably sucsessfully contend that there were possible alternatives (e.g. widening and surfacing the narrow footpath to take motor traffic) and that therefore using the driveway was not *absolutely essential*.

With respect to (b) Milligan will have to argue that it is absolutely essential that he use the existing drains under Whiteacre. But Finnegan is likely to respond that alternative drains could be always laid not passing under Whiteacre. If that is the case, then Milligan has no chance under the intended easements rule.

Milligan's best chance would appear to be with the third rule of implied grant, the rule in *Wheeldon* v *Burrows*. Under this rule pre-existing nebulous rights known as 'privileges' and 'quasi-easements' can be magically converted into easements on the conveyance of the dominant land.

A 'privilege' would arise if the owner of two plots had leased one of them and then later granted the tenant some licence over the land he retained. There appears no evidence of Finnegan having done this. A quasi-easement would exist where the owner of two plots makes use of one plot for the benefit of the other in circumstances where had the plots been in separate ownership the 'use' could have been granted as an easement. It seems very likely that prior to the sale of Blackacre Finnegan made use of quasi-easements over the driveway and the drains.

If the following three conditions were satisfied one or both of these quasi-easements would be converted into full easements in favour of Blackacre the moment Blackacre was conveyed to Milligan.

(1)   The quasi-easement was 'continuous and apparent', i.e. regularly used, and detectable by inspection of the plots of land.

(2)   The quasi-easement was used for the benefit of the dominant land immediately prior to its being conveyed.

(3)   The quasi-easement was necessary for the reasonable or convenient enjoyment of the dominant land.

Element (2) is presumably satisfied with respect to both (a) and (b). (1) is clearly satisfied with respect to the driveway, but whether the drains are 'apparent' will depend upon whether there was evidence *on the surface* (man-hole covers, gratings, etc) of their existence.

It is submitted that element (3) is satisfied with respect to both (a) and (b). While the driveway and drains are probably not 'absolutely essential', they probably do satisfy the lesser test of necessity laid down for *Wheeldon* v *Burrows*.

The fourth rule for implied grant, section 62, can apply only to 'privileges'; and is therefore seemingly of no help to Milligan's claims.

With respect to (c) Cyrus is going to claim a profit of pasture by prescription. The basic idea underlying prescription for easements and profits is that if the dominant owner has been exercising his claim *'as of right'* for the past twenty years he thereby acquires an easement/profit to exercise his claim permanently.

For user to be 'as of right' it must be open ('without secrecy'), without force and without permission. Cyrus' user has clearly been open, but if his user depended upon a permission (even an oral one) granted by Finnegan or one of his predecessors, there could be no prescription. (Exceptionally, if there was a purely oral permission given more than sixty years ago and never repeated a claim under section one of the Prescription Act 1832 would apparently succeed.)

If Cyrus' user was in the face of active opposition from Finnegan (protests or more obstructive behaviour), then user would be forceable and not prescriptive. Assuming Cyrus' user was as of right he would not *ipso facto* acquire a prescriptive profit. He must also satisfy one of the three alternative prescription periods, common law, or the Prescription Act 1832 or lost modern grant.

Cyrus probably will not succeed under the common law rule, as he has to assert that he and his predecessors have been grazing sheep on the hillside since 1189. But the

Prescription Act section one will almost certainly be available, which requires thirty (not twenty) years user as of right 'next before action'.

If Cyrus can only show between twenty and thirty years user as of right he will probably be able to rely on the presumption of lost modern grant. This presumption could only be rebutted by showing that throughout the relevant period the grant of a profit was a legal impossibility.

QUESTION 2

For reasons which will emerge, there is no need to treat the claims of Louise and Terry separately. Louise will claim that a prescriptive easement of way and a prescriptive profit of pasture have been acquired over West Field, and that those rights are 'appurtenant' to the freehold in Grand House. Terry will claim that, as current Tenant of Grand House, he is automatically entitled to the benefit of those rights appurtenant to Grand House.

There are two stages to the establishing of a claim for a prescriptive easement or profit. Firstly, the dominant owner must show that certain general rules common to all three forms of Prescription are satisfied. Secondly, he/she must show that the 'User as of Right' satisfies the rules specific to one of the three forms of prescription.

The General Rules

Louise and Terry will firstly have to show that there has been continuous user as of right, i.e. open user without permission from the servient owner and without force or dispute in any form.

For user to be 'open' it must be such as would indicate to a reasonable servient owner that a right was being exercised (*Lloyds Bank* v *Dalton*). The grazing was obviously 'open', as presumably was the crossing the field to get to the station, unless Terry only used the short cut at night-time, which is highly unlikely.

We are told that user was 'without any objection', so there is no question of 'forcible user'. Gurinder's only hope under the 'user as of right' heading would be to prove that Nellie gave express permission to Terry for his activities. An oral permission would be sufficient, but it must be stressed that mere acquiescence in the prescriber's activities, which seems to be the case here, does not equal permission.

Louise and Terry must also satisfy the general rule that user be 'by or on behalf of a fee simple against a fee simple'. A prescriptive easement is always in fee simple, and is (theoretically) a grant from the servient freeholder to the dominant freeholder.

The application of this rule has two aspects. Firstly any prescriptive user by a lessee such as Terry is deemed to be as agent for his landlord. Thus Terry could not have prescribed against land owned by Louise, but any prescriptive right which he establishes against a third party such as Nellie is appurtenant to her freehold, though he gets the benefit for the seventy years of his lease.

Secondly, user as of right to be prescriptive must commence against a freeholder in physical possession. Thus if the commencement of the grazing and the 'short cutting' was during one of the 'short periods' when Nellie had let the field to Olive, Gurinder will be able to defeat the claims for prescriptive rights.

The Forms of Prescription

Assuming that Gurinder is unable to defeat the prescriptive rights under the general rules just discussed, Terry and Louise will invoke the Prescription Act 1832 for the (alleged) right of way, and lost modern grant for the profit of grazing. (Any claim under the third form of prescription, common law, is bound to fail as user clearly commenced in about 1974, long after 1189.)

Under the Prescription Act 1832 Louise and Terry will have to show user as of right for twenty years 'next before action'. Their claim will succeed (they can show user 1974–95) despite the fact that for about seven months Terry complied with the demand not to exercise his 'rights'. Provided Louise and Terry issue their writ before the break in user has lasted one year, they should win.

Section four of the 1832 Act requires the user to be 'next before action', i.e. (normally) immediately preceding the issue of the writ in the case in which the easement is disputed. But it then provides that an 'interruption' of user for less than twelve months shall not count as an interruption to defeat the claim.

Louise and Terry will not be able to rely on the 1832 Act for their claim to a prescriptive profit. This is simply because section one of the Act lays down a minimum period of 30 years user for profits. Louise and Terry (like the farmers in *Tehidy Minerals* v *Norman*) will thus have to fall back on the 'last resort' form of prescription, 'lost modern grant'.

To succeed under this heading they will have to show strong evidence of at least twenty years user as of right. If they can do so (and it seems they can) the court will, by way of legal fiction, presume that a deed was executed 'in modern times' but that deed has been mislaid. . . .

In lost modern grant cases nobody really believes that a deed existed. Yet recent cases rule that the presumption of lost grant cannot be rebutted by factual proof (however convincing) that there was no deed. The presumption can only be rebutted by showing that the grant was throughout 'the relevant time' impossible as a matter of law.

The 'relevant time' begins when user as of right commenced, and ends twenty years before user as of right ceased. In our case the relevant time would be (circa) 1974 to September 1975. If throughout those months the granting of a valid profit would have been legally impossible because (say) the land was requisitioned or because Nellie was under some special legal disability like the vicar in *Oakley* v *Boston*, then Gurinder would defeat the claim to a Profit. But it should be stressed that cases where the alleged servient owner can show legal impossibility are rare.

CHAPTER TWENTY-SIX

RESTRICTIVE COVENANTS — THE BASIC PRINCIPLES

26.1 Restrictive and Positive Covenants Distinguished

AUSTERBERRY v *CORPORATION OF OLDHAM* (1885) 24 ChD 750, Court of Appeal

FACTS: Mr Elliot conveyed freehold land to trustees of a joint stock company which company wished to use the land to build a road. The trustees covenanted in the deed, for themselves, their heirs and assigns, that they would make the road and keep it in repair. The trustees duly made the road, creating an access to Mr Elliot's land. Later Mr Elliot sold his land to Austerberry and the trustees sold their land to the defendant. The main question in the case was whether Austerberry could enforce the repairing covenant against the defendant.
HELD: The covenant was unenforceable. This was because the covenant was a 'positive covenant', that is, one which imposed a positive burden on the owner of the servient land.

COTTON LJ: . . . where there is a restrictive covenant, the burden and benefit of which do not run at law, Courts of Equity restrain anyone who takes the property with notice of that covenant from using it in a way inconsistent with the covenant. But here the covenant which is attempted to be insisted upon on this appeal is a covenant to lay out money in doing certain work upon this land; and, that being so, in my opinion—and the Court of Appeal has already expressed a similar opinion in a case which was before it—that is not a covenant which a Court of Equity will enforce: it will not enforce a covenant not running at law when it is sought to enforce that covenant in such a way as to require the successors in title of the covenantor, to spend money, and in that way to undertake a burden upon themselves. The covenantor must not use the property for a purpose inconsistent with the use for which it was originally granted: but in my opinion a Court of Equity does not and ought not to enforce a covenant binding only in equity in such a way as to require the successors of the covenantor himself, they having entered into no covenant, to expend sums of money in accordance with what the original covenantor bound himself to do.

RHONE v *STEPHENS* [1994] 2 All ER 65, House of Lords

FACTS: The owners of a house and cottage under the same roof sold the cottage and covenanted in the conveyance that they would maintain the roof above the cottage. Since then both properties had been sold on to new owners. Later, the roof of the cottage began to leak. The plaintiffs, the new owners of the cottage, sought to enforce the repairing covenant against the new owners of the house.
HELD: The positive covenant was not enforceable at common law. To permit it to be so enforced would destroy the notion of privity of contract between the original parties. Nor could the burden of the covenant run in equity to bind the new owner of the house.

LORD TEMPLEMAN: . . . Equity can . . . prevent or punish the breach of a negative covenant which restricts the user of land or the exercise of other rights in connection with land. Restrictive covenants deprive an owner of a right which he could otherwise exercise.

Equity cannot compel an owner to comply with a positive covenant entered into by his predecessors in title without flatly contradicting the common law rule that a person cannot be made liable upon a contract unless he was a party to it. Enforcement of a positive covenant lies in contract; a positive covenant compels an owner to exercise his rights. Enforcement of a negative covenant lies in property; a negative covenant deprives the owner of a right over property. As Lord Cottenham LC said in *Tulk v Moxhay* 2 Ph 774 at 778, [1843–60] All ER Rep 9 at 11:

> . . . if an equity is attached to the property by the owner, no one purchasing with notice of that equity can stand in a different situation from the party from whom he purchased. . . .

For over 100 years it has been clear and accepted law that equity will enforce negative covenants against freehold land but has no power to enforce positive covenants against successors in title of the land. To enforce a positive covenant would be to enforce a personal obligation against a person who has not covenanted. To enforce negative covenants is only to treat the land as subject to a restriction.

Mr Munby, who argued the appeal persuasively on behalf of the plaintiffs, referred to an article by Professor Sir William Wade, 'Covenants—"a broad and reasonable view" (1972) 31 CLJ 157, and other articles in which the present state of the law is subjected to severe criticism. In 1965 the *Report of the Committee on Positive Covenants Affecting Land* (Cmnd 2719), which was a report by a committee appointed by the Lord Chancellor and under the chairmanship of Lord Wilberforce, referred to difficulties caused by the decision in the *Austerberry* case and recommended legislation to provide that positive covenants which relate to the use of land and are intended to benefit specified other land should run with the land. In *Transfer of Land: Appurtenant Rights* (Law Commission working paper no 36, published on 5 July 1971) the present law on positive rights was described as being illogical, uncertain, incomplete and inflexible. The Law Commission Report *Transfer of Land: The Law of Positive and Restrictive Covenants* (Law Com No 127) laid before Parliament in 1984 made recommendations for the reform of the law relating to positive and restrictive obligations and submitted a draft Bill for that purpose. Nothing has been done.

In these circumstances your Lordships were invited to overrule the decision of the Court of Appeal in the *Austerberry* case [(1885) 24 ChD 750]. To do so would destroy the distinction between law and equity and to convert the rule of equity into a rule of notice. It is plain from the articles, reports and papers to which we were referred that judicial legislation to overrule the *Austerberry* case would create a number of difficulties, anomalies and uncertainties and affect the rights and liabilities of people who have for over 100 years bought and sold land in the knowledge, imparted at an elementary stage to every student of the law of real property, that positive covenants affecting freehold land are not directly enforceable except against the original covenantor. Parliamentary legislation to deal with the decision in the *Austerberry* case would require careful consideration of the consequences. . . .

Snape, J., The Burden of Positive Covenants (1994) 58 Conv 477

In *Rhone v Stephens (Executrix)* [1994] 2 All ER 65, the House of Lords has definitively ruled that, in freehold land, the burden of a *positive* covenant (e.g. to repair) will not *in equity* run with the land. In other words, the burden of a positive covenant cannot in equity be enforced against successors in title of the original covenantor by the original covenantee/ successors in title of the original covenantee. This is unsurprising although, until *Rhone v Stephens*, the rule had not been tested in a higher court for over a century. At common law, irrespective of whether a covenant is positive or restrictive, the burden does not generally run. The crucial difference between the equitable and common law positions, reinforced in *Rhone v Stephens*, is that the burden of a restrictive covenant *may* be enforced against successors in title of the original covenantor under the rule in *Tulk v Moxhay* [see **26.2.1**].

There are a number of ways of circumventing these rules so as to make, in effect, the *burden* of a positive covenant 'run.' Property lawyers have known about them for years. Perhaps three stand out from the others. One makes use of the rule that the original covenantor remains liable on his covenant. On selling the relevant property, the covenantor (i.e. the vendor) takes an indemnity from the purchaser in the conveyance, to cover his continuing liability for breaches of covenant by the purchaser/successors in title of the purchaser. This obviously creates a strong incentive for the purchaser to observe the covenant. Another involves the reservation of a rentcharge on the sale of the relevant property, to which is annexed a right of entry allowing the rentcharge owner (the covenantor/vendor) to enter, make good the breach and charge the cost to the purchaser in possession. A third possibility is, with extreme care, to make use of the so-called 'conditional benefit principle'. Whilst ensuring that the condition is relevant to the exercise of the right, it is necessary to make taking a benefit under the deed conditional on the assumption of the burden of the positive covenant. However, it is apparent from *Rhone* v *Stephens* itself that there are certain cases where this third possibility cannot be applied, because the person intended to be subject to the burden is not free to choose whether to take the benefit and may have no continuing interest in claiming it. . . .

26.2 Passing the Burden of a Restrictive Covenant

26.2.1 THE COVENANT MUST BE NEGATIVE IN SUBSTANCE

TULK v *MOXHAY* (1848) [1843–60] All ER Rep 9, Lord Chancellor's Court

FACTS: The fee simple owner of land in Leicester Square, London sold the land to Mr Elms. Elms covenanted in the conveyance, for himself, his heirs and assigns, that he would 'keep and maintain the said piece of ground . . . uncovered with any buildings, in neat and ornamental order'. The land was later sold by Elms to the defendant. That conveyance did not recite the covenant, but the defendant admitted that he had actual notice of it in any event. The defendant intended to build on the land.
HELD: An injunction was granted against the defendant to restrain a breach of the covenant.

LORD COTTENHAM LC: That this court has jurisdiction to enforce a contract between the owner of land and his neighbour purchasing a part of it that the purchaser shall either use or abstain from using the land purchased in a particular way is what I never knew disputed. Here there is no question about the contract. The owner of certain houses in the square sells the land adjoining, with a covenant from the purchaser not to use it for any other purpose than as a square garden. It is now contended, not that the vendee could violate that contract, but that he might sell the piece of land, and that the purchaser from him may violate it without this court having any power to interfere. If that were so, it would be impossible for an owner of land to sell part of it without incurring the risk of rendering what he retains worthless. It is said that, the covenant being one which does not run with the land, this court cannot enforce it, but the question is not whether the covenant runs with the land, but whether a party shall be permitted to use the land in a manner inconsistent with the contract entered into by his vendor, with notice of which he purchased. Of course, the price would be affected by the covenant, and nothing could be more inequitable than that the original purchaser should be able to sell the property the next day for a greater price, in consideration of the assignee being allowed to escape from the liability which he had himself undertaken. . . .

(Note that in *Haywood* v *Brunswick Permanent Benefit Building Society* (1881) 8 QBD 403 Cotton LJ suggested a simple test for determining whether a covenant is restrictive (i.e. negative in substance). He held that a covenant will not be restrictive if the covenantor is required 'to put his hand into his pocket' in order to fulfil his covenant.)

26.2.2 THE COVENANT MUST BE MADE WITH AN INTENT TO BURDEN THE SERVIENT LAND

LAW OF PROPERTY ACT 1925

79. Burden of covenants relating to land

(1) A covenant relating to any land of a covenantor or capable of being bound by him, shall, unless a contrary intention is expressed, be deemed to be made by the covenantor on

behalf of himself his successors in title and the persons deriving title under him or them, and, subject as aforesaid, shall have effect as if such successors and other persons were expressed.

This subsection extends to a covenant to do some act relating to the land, notwithstanding that the subject-matter may not be in existence when the covenant is made.

(2) For the purposes of this section in connexion with covenants restrictive of the user of land 'successors in title' shall be deemed to include the owners and occupiers for the time being of such land.

(3) This section applies only to covenants made after the commencement of this Act.

26.2.3 THE COVENANT MUST BE MADE TO PROTECT DOMINANT LAND RETAINED BY THE COVENANTEE

LONDON COUNTY COUNCIL v *ALLEN* [1914] 3 KB 642, Court of Appeal

FACTS: The LCC sold a large amount of land to Mr Allen, a builder. With respect to one small part of the land, Mr Allen covenanted not to build upon it. This small parcel was intended as an open space for the local residents. The LCC retained no other land in the vicinity. Mr Allen sold the small parcel to his wife, who commenced building work. The LCC sought an injunction.
HELD: The injunction was refused. The LCC had no dominant land, so it could not claim the benefit of the restrictive covenant.

BUCKLEY LJ: . . . The reasoning of Lord Cottenham's judgment in *Tulk* v *Moxhay* [1843–60] All ER Rep 9 is that if an owner of land sells part of it reserving the rest, and takes from his purchaser a covenant that the purchaser shall use or abstain from using the land purchased in a particular way, that covenant (being one for the protection of the land reserved) is enforceable against a sub-purchaser with notice. The reason given is that, if that were not so, it would be impossible for an owner of land to sell part of it without incurring the risk of rendering what he retains worthless. If the vendor has retained no land which can be protected by the restrictive covenant, the basis of the reasoning of the judgment is swept away. In *Haywood* v *Brunswick Permanent Benefit Building Society* (1881) 8 QBD 403 the Court of Appeal declined to extend the doctrine of *Tulk* v *Moxhay* [1843–60] All ER Rep 9 to covenants other than restrictive covenants. They rejected the doctrine that, inasmuch as the defendants took the land with notice of the covenants, they were bound in equity to perform them. That therefore is not the principle upon which the equitable doctrine rests. In the present case we are asked to extend the doctrine of *Tulk* v *Moxhay* so as to affirm that a restrictive covenant can be enforced against a derivative owner taking with notice by a person who never has had or who does not retain any land to be protected by the restrictive covenant in question. In my opinion the doctrine does not extend to that case. The doctrine is that a covenant not running with the land, but being a negative covenant entered into by an owner of land with an adjoining owner, binds the land in equity and is enforceable against a derivative owner taking with notice. The doctrine ceases to be applicable when the person seeking to enforce the covenant against the derivative owner has no land to be protected by the negative covenant. The fact of notice is in that case irrelevant. . . .

NEWTON ABBOT CO-OP v *WILLIAMS AND TREADGOLD* [1952] 1 All ER 279, Chancery Division

FACTS: Mrs Mardon owned two shops in the small central Devon town of Bovey Tracey. The shops were about fifty yards apart on opposite sides of the street. In 1923 Mrs Mardon sold one of the shops. In the conveyance of that shop there was imposed a restrictive covenant which said that no ironmongery was to be sold from the shop. The restrictive covenant did not identify the dominant land. However, the shop across the road retained by Mrs Mardon was an ironmongers.
HELD: There was a valid restrictive covenant which bound a subsequent purchaser of the shop sold by Mrs Mardon in 1923. Although the dominant land was not expressly identified in the conveyance which contained the restrictive covenant, it could be identified by examining the geography of the locality. That, in the view of the judge, was sufficient.

UPJOHN J: . . . the sole issue before me is whether the plaintiffs are entitled to the benefit of the restrictive covenant, and, if so, whether they are entitled to enforce it against the defendants. I will deal with the first point first. Counsel for the plaintiffs submitted, first, that the benefit of the restrictive covenant was annexed to Devonia so as to pass with the assignment of Devonia in equity without any express mention in such subsequent assignment—in other words, that the covenant runs with the land. Alternatively, he said that the plaintiffs are the express assigns of the benefit of the covenant, and as such are entitled to enforce it. In this difficult branch of the law one thing, in my judgment, is clear, viz, that in order to annex the benefit of a restrictive covenant to land so that it runs with the land without express assignment on a subsequent assignment of the land, the land for the benefit of which it is taken must be clearly identified in the conveyance containing the covenant. That has been established in a number of cases of high authority.

. . . Looking at the 1923 conveyance, I can find nothing whatever which identifies the land for the benefit of which the covenant is alleged to be taken. Counsel for the plaintiffs relies on the fact that Mrs Mardon is described as of Devonia, Fore Street, but that, in my judgment, is quite insufficient to annex the benefit of the covenant to those premises. There is no other mention whatever of Devonia in the conveyance. In my judgment, therefore, the plaintiffs fail on this point.

I turn, then, to his second submission, viz, that the plaintiffs are express assigns of the benefit of the restrictive covenant. Counsel for the defendants contends that, even if his submissions (with which I shall deal later) are wrong and the covenant was taken by Mrs Mardon for the benefit of Devonia to enable her to dispose of it to better advantage, yet there is here no complete chain of assignments vesting the benefit in the plaintiffs. He says that there was never any assignment of the benefit of the covenant by the executors of Mrs Mardon to Leonard Soper Mardon, and, therefore, he was not in a position to assign the benefit of the covenant to the plaintiffs' predecessors in title. He relied on *Ives* v *Brown* [1919] 2 Ch 314 and *Lord Northbourne* v *Johnston & Son* [1922] 2 Ch 309. In my judgment, those authorities do not support his contention. The position as I see it was this. On the footing that the restrictive covenant was not annexed to the land so as to run with it, the benefit of the covenant is capable of passing by operation of law as well as by express assignment and formed part of Mrs Mardon's personal estate on her death: see *Ives* v *Brown*. It follows, therefore, that when her estate was duly wound up and administered—and this case has been argued before me on the footing that that happened many years ago—the benefit of the covenant was held by the executors as bare trustees for the residuary legatee, Leonard Soper Mardon, who was himself one of the executors. He, therefore, became entitled to the benefit of this restrictive covenant in equity, and, in my judgment, he was entitled to assign the benefit in equity on an assignment of Devonia. No doubt, had the covenant been assigned to him by the executors, he could also have assigned it at law.

. . . Counsel's second point was that in order that the benefit of the covenant may be assignable the land for which the benefit of the covenant is taken must in some way be referred to in the conveyance creating the covenant. . . .

In my judgment, therefore, the problem which I have to consider is, first, when Mrs Mardon took the covenant in 1923, did she retain other land capable of being benefited by the covenant? If not, *cadit quaestio*. Secondly, was such land 'ascertainable' or 'certain' in this sense, that the existence and situation of the land must be indicated in the conveyance or otherwise shown with reasonable certainty. Apart from the fact that Mrs Mardon is described as of Devonia, there is nothing in the 1923 conveyance to define the land for the benefit of which the restrictive covenant was taken, and I do not think that carries one very far, but, for the reasons I have given, I am, in my judgment, entitled to look at the surrounding circumstances to see if the land to be benefited is shown 'otherwise' with reasonable certainty. That is a question of fact, and, on the admitted facts, bearing in mind the close juxtaposition of Devonia and the defendants' premises, in my judgment, the only reasonable inference to draw from the circumstances at the time of the 1923 conveyance was that Mrs Mardon took the covenant restrictive of the user of the defendants' premises for the benefit of her own business of ironmonger and of her property Devonia where at all material times she was carrying on that business, which last-mentioned fact must have been apparent to the purchasers in 1923. I should, perhaps, mention that at the date of her death, Mrs Mardon owned other property in Fore Street, but counsel on neither side founded any argument on that circumstance. It follows, therefore, in my judgment, that Mrs Mardon could on any subsequent sale of her land Devonia, if she so chose, as part of the transaction of sale, assign the benefit of the covenant so as to enable the purchaser from her and his assignees of the land and covenant to enforce it against an owner of the defendants' premises taking with notice and her legatee, Leonard Soper Mardon, was in no worse position. I do not regard the fact that he assigned the covenant in the deed containing the assignment of the business as affecting the matter. I say nothing as to the position when the plaintiffs' lease expires so that their estate in Devonia comes to an end, nor whether Leonard Soper Mardon, having apparently assigned away the entire benefit of the covenant, will then be in any position further to enforce it. . . .

26.3   Remedies to Enforce a Restrictive Covenant

WROTHAM PARK ESTATE COMPANY v *PARKSIDE HOMES LTD AND OTHERS*
[1974] 2 All ER 321, Chancery Division

FACTS: In 1935, the Wrotham Park Estate, then owned by the Earl of Strafford, extended to about 4,000 acres. In that year the Earl sold 47 acres out of the Estate. This land was subject to a restrictive covenant 'not to develop the . . . land for building purposes except in strict accordance with plans [approved by the owners of Wrotham Park Estate].' The covenant was expressed to be for the benefit of 'Wrotham Park Estate'. The plaintiff company later acquired Wrotham Park Estate. The defendant, Parkside Homes Ltd, acquired a small part of the servient land. The defendant obtained planning permission from the local authority to build 13 'middle class' houses on the land. It did not, however, submit its plans to the plaintiff for approval. It believed that the plaintiff was not entitled to enforce the covenant. In January 1972, the defendant started to lay the foundations. On 14 February the plaintiff issued a writ claiming an injunction to restrain building. The plaintiff failed, however, to seek an 'interlocutory' (temporary) injunction to restrain development pending the full trial of the dispute. Parkside, accordingly, completed the building operations and the first residents moved into their new homes.
HELD: The judge refused to order that the houses should be demolished. Instead, he awarded the plaintiff damages equivalent to the 'price' it could reasonably have asked for releasing the covenant.

BRIGHTMAN J: . . . I must now consider the relief to which the plaintiffs are entitled, that is to say a mandatory injunction or damages (both are not sought): if damages, whether substantial or nominal; or a declaration of the plaintiffs' rights as the sole relief. The plaintiffs made it abundantly clear at the outset of the case that the relief they primarily sought was a mandatory injunction. This did not spring from outraged feelings or from indifference to the welfare of those who have made the offending houses their homes. It sprang from the belief, sincerely held, that there was no other effective way of preserving the integrity of the planning restrictions imposed by the terms of the Blake conveyance. Quite apart from the benefit to the Wrotham Park estate, the plaintiffs, as I have already said, take the view that they have a moral obligation towards the residents of the building estates to enforce the restrictive covenants so far as they are lawfully entitled to do so. I agree. The plaintiffs do not seek to bulldoze the occupiers out of their homes but are content that they shall have a period of two years in which to acquire other homes with the help of the £20,000 or so that will come to each of them under the indemnity assurance that has been arranged. . . .

Counsel for the plaintiffs submitted, and I accept, that it is no answer to a claim for a mandatory injunction that the plaintiffs, having issued proceedings, deliberately held their hand and did not seek the assistance of the court for the purpose of preserving the status quo. On the other hand, it is, in my view, equally true that a plaintiff is not entitled 'as of course' to have everything pulled down that was built after the issue of the writ. The erection of the houses, whether one likes it or not, is a fait accompli and the houses are now the homes of people. I accept that this particular fait accompli is reversible and could be undone. But I cannot close my eyes to the fact that the houses now exist. It would, in my opinion, be an unpardonable waste of much needed houses to direct that they now be pulled down and I have never had a moment's doubt during the hearing of this case that such an order ought to be refused. No damage of a financial nature has been done to the plaintiffs by the breach of the layout stipulation. The plaintiffs' use of the Wrotham Park estate has not been and will not be impeded. It is totally unnecessary to demolish the houses in order to preserve the integrity of the restrictive covenants imposed on the rest of area 14. Without hesitation I decline to grant a mandatory injunction. But the fact that these houses will remain does not spell out a charter entitling others to despoil adjacent areas of land in breach of valid restrictions imposed by the conveyances. A developer who tries that course may be in for a rude awakening.

. . . In my judgment a just substitute for a mandatory injunction would be such a sum of money as might reasonably have been demanded by the plaintiffs from Parkside as a quid pro quo for relaxing the covenant. The plaintiffs submitted that that sum should be a substantial proportion of the development value of the land. This is currently put at no less than £10,000 per plot, i.e. £140,000 on the assumption that the plots are undeveloped. Mr Parker gave evidence that a half or a third of the development value was commonly demanded by a landowner whose property stood in the way of a development. I do not agree with that approach to damages in this type of case. I bear in mind the following factors: (1) The layout covenant is not an asset which the estate owner ever contemplated he would have either the opportunity or the desire to turn to account. It has no commercial or even nuisance value. For it cannot be turned to account except to the detriment of the existing residents who are people the estate owner professes to protect. (2) The breach of covenant which has actually taken place is over a very small area and the impact of this particular breach on the Wrotham Park estate is insignificant. The validity of the covenant over the rest of area 14 is unaffected.

. . . I think that damages must be assessed in such a case on a basis which is fair and, in all the circumstances, in my judgment a sum equal to 5 per cent of Parkside's anticipated profit is the most that is fair. I accordingly award the sum of £2,500 in substitution for mandatory injunctions. . . .

CHAPTER TWENTY-SEVEN

THE PASSING OF THE BENEFIT OF RESTRICTIVE COVENANTS

27.1 Introduction

LAW OF PROPERTY ACT 1925

78. Benefit of covenants relating to land

(1) A covenant relating to any land of the covenantee shall be deemed to be made with the covenantee and his successors in title and the persons deriving title under him or them, and shall have effect as if such successors and other persons were expressed.

For the purposes of this subsection in connexion with covenants restrictive of the user of land 'successors in title' shall be deemed to include the owners and occupiers for the time being of the land of the covenantee intended to be benefited.

(2) This section applies to covenants made after the commencement of this Act, but the repeal of section fifty-eight of the Conveyancing Act 1881 does not affect the operation of covenants to which that section applied.

FEDERATED HOMES LTD v *MILL LODGE PROPERTIES LTD* [1980] 1 All ER 371, Court of Appeal

FACTS: A firm called Mackenzie Hill Ltd owned a large amount of development land in Newport Pagnell (just north of Milton Keynes). It had outline planning permission to develop the land with 1,250 houses. It sold part of that land to Mill Lodge. The conveyance included a restrictive covenant:—

In carrying out the development of the . . . land the purchaser shall not build at a greater density than a total of 300 dwellings so as not to reduce the number of units which the vendor might eventually erect on the retained land under the existing planning consent.

Mackenzie Hill later sold the land they retained in the area to Federated Homes. The Court of Appeal had (*inter alia*) to decide whether the above clause effected an annexation so that on the sale of the 'retained land' the right to enforce the covenant passed automatically to Federated Homes.

HELD: The clause effected a valid annexation of the benefit of the covenant to the land owned by Federated Homes Ltd.

BRIGHTMAN LJ: In my judgment the benefit of this covenant was annexed to the retained land, and I think that this is a consequence of s. 78 of the Law of Property Act 1925, which reads:

(1) A covenant relating to any land of the covenantee shall be deemed to be made with the covenantee and his successors in title and the persons deriving title under him or them, and shall have effect as if such successors and other persons were expressed. For the purposes of this subsection in connexion with covenants restrictive of the user of

land 'successors in title' shall be deemed to include the owners and occupiers for the time being of the land of the covenantee intended to be benefited.

(2)   This section applies to covenants made after the commencement of this Act, but the repeal of section fifty-eight of the Conveyancing Act 1881, does not affect the operation of covenants to which that section applied.

Counsel for the defendants submitted that there were three possible views about s. 78. One view, which he described as 'the orthodox view' hitherto held, is that it is merely a statutory shorthand for reducing the length of legal documents. A second view, which was the one that counsel for the defendants was inclined to place in the forefront of his argument, is that the section only applies, or at any rate only achieves annexation, when the land intended to be benefited is signified in the document by express words or necessary implication as the intended beneficiary of the covenant. A third view is that the section applies if the covenant in fact touches and concerns the land of the covenantee, whether that be gleaned from the document itself or from evidence outside the document.

For myself, I reject the narrowest interpretation of s. 78, the supposed orthodox view, which seems to me to fly in the face of the wording of the section. Before I express my reasons I will say that I do not find it necessary to choose between the second and third views because, in my opinion, this covenant relates to land of the covenantee on either interpretation of s. 78. Clause 5(iv) shows quite clearly that the covenant is for the protection of the retained land and that land is described in cl. 2 as 'any adjoining or adjacent property retained by the Vendor'. This formulation is sufficient for annexation purposes: see *Rogers* v *Hosegood* [1900] 2 Ch 388.

There is in my judgment no doubt that this covenant 'related to the land of the covenantee', or, to use the old-fashioned expression, that it touched and concerned the land, even if counsel for the defendants is correct in his submission that the document must show an intention to benefit identified land. The result of such application is that one must read cl. 5(iv) as if it were written: 'The purchaser hereby covenants with the vendor and its successors in title and the persons deriving title under it or them, including the owners and occupiers for the time being of the retained land, that in carrying out the development of the blue land the purchaser shall not build at a greater density than a total of 300 dwellings so as not to reduce the number of units which the vendor might eventually erect on the retained land under the existing planning consent.' I leave out of consideration s. 79 as unnecessary to be considered in this context, since Mill Lodge is the original covenantor.

The first point to notice about s. 78(1) is that the wording is significantly different from the wording of its predecessor, s. 58(1) of the Conveyancing and Law of Property Act 1881. The distinction is underlined by sub-s. (2) of s. 78, which applies sub-s. (1) only to covenants made after the commencement of the Act. Section 58(1) of the earlier Act did not include the covenantee's successors in title or persons deriving title under him or them, nor the owners or occupiers for the time being of the land of the covenantee intended to be benefited. The section was confined, in relation to realty, to the covenantee, his heirs and assigns, words which suggest a more limited scope of operation than is found in s. 78.

If, as the language of s. 78 implies, a covenant relating to land which is restrictive of the user thereof is enforceable at the suit of (1) a successor in title of the covenantee, (2) a person deriving title under the covenantee or under his successors in title, and (3) the owner or occupier of the land intended to be benefited by the covenant, it must, in my view, follow that the covenant runs with the land, because ex hypothesi every successor in title to the land, every derivative proprietor of the land and every other owner and occupier has a right by statute to the covenant. In other words, if the condition precedent of s. 78 is satisfied, that is to say, there exists a covenant which touches and concerns the land of the covenantee, that covenant runs with the land for the benefit of his successors in title, persons deriving title under him or them and other owners and occupiers.

This approach to s. 78 has been advocated by distinguished textbook writers: see Dr Radcliffe in the Law Quarterly Review, Professor Wade in the Cambridge Law Journal under the apt cross-heading 'What is wrong with section 78?', and Megarry and Wade on the Law of Real Property. Counsel pointed out to us that the fourth edition of Megarry and Wade's textbook indicates a change of mind on this topic since the third edition was published in 1966.

Although the section does not seem to have been extensively used in the course of argument in this type of case, the construction of s. 78 which appeals to me appears to be consistent with at least two cases decided in this court. The first is *Smith* v *River Douglas Catchment Board* [1949] 2 All ER 179. In that case an agreement was made in April 1938 between certain landowners and the catchment board under which the catchment board undertook to make good the banks of a certain brook and to maintain the same, and the landowners undertook to contribute towards the cost. In 1940 the first plaintiff took a conveyance from one of the landowners of a part of the land together with an express assignment of the benefit of the agreement. In 1944 the second plaintiff took a tenancy of that land without any express assignment of the benefit of the agreement. In 1946 the brook burst its banks and the land owned by the first plaintiff and tenanted by the second plaintiff was inundated. The two important points are that the agreement was not expressed to be for the benefit of the landowner's successors in title; and there was no assignment of the benefit of the agreement in favour of the second plaintiff, the tenant. In reliance, as I understand the case, on s. 78 of the Law of Property Act 1925, it was held that the second plaintiff was entitled to sue the catchment board for damages for breach of the agreement. It seems to me that that conclusion can only have been reached on the basis that s. 78 had the effect of causing the benefit of the agreement to run with the land so as to be capable of being sued on by the tenant. . . .

I find the idea of the annexation of a covenant to the whole of the land but not to a part of it a difficult conception fully to grasp. I can understand that a covenantee may expressly or by necessary implication retain the benefit of a covenant wholly under his own control, so that the benefit will not pass unless the covenantee chooses to assign; but I would have thought, if the benefit of a covenant is, on a proper construction of a document, annexed to the land, *prima facie* it is annexed to every part thereof, unless the contrary clearly appears. . . .

In the end, I come to the conclusion that s. 78 of the Law of Property Act 1925 caused the benefit of the restrictive covenant in question to run with the red land and therefore to be annexed to it, with the result that the plaintiff company is able to enforce the covenant against Mill Lodge, not only in its capacity as owner of the green land, but also in its capacity as owner of the red land. . . .

27.2   Annexation

Todd, P. N., 'Annexation After Federated Homes' (1985) 49 Conv 177

. . . the view of the operation of section 78 taken by Brightman LJ in *Federated Homes* is very radical. It seems to be that at least for any post-1926 covenant, once the covenant 'relates to' the benefited land, annexation is a matter of law:

> If the condition precedent of section 78 is satisfied—that is to say, there exists a covenant which touches and concerns the land of the covenantee—that covenant runs with the land for the benefit of his successors in title, persons deriving title under them and other owners and occupiers.

On the widest interpretation of this statement, restrictive covenants run with land automatically. The question does not seem to depend on words expressing or implying annexation, or on surrounding circumstances, and may even be independent of the intention of the parties. Thus, Mr Newsom, commenting on the above statement of Brightman LJ states:

> This can only mean that the benefit of the covenant is automatically annexed to 'the land of the covenantee' which it 'touches and concerns.' This is a new doctrine and it is at least a little surprising that Parliament should have forced annexation upon the parties even if they clearly did *not* intend it; but that is what the Lord Justice implied.

Indeed, the case is ostensibly even more radical than this, as the automatic annexation doctrine applies not merely for the benefit of the land as a whole, but for the benefit of each and every part of the land.

Given that this interpretation of the case is widely held, it is perhaps not surprising that *Federated Homes* has attracted such extensive comment and criticism. If the decision is correct, the wide view of it suggests that the law on the passing of benefit of all restrictive covenants has been revolutionised, and is much simpler than had previously been thought. . . .

Though it is no doubt possible to argue this very wide interpretation of *Federated Homes*, however, I would suggest that a much narrower view is probably more appropriate. The case may not be an authority for automatic annexation at all, and may not, I suggest, apply to all post-1926 covenants.

A NARROWER VIEW

. . . There are other reasons also for inferring that Brightman LJ did not intend annexation to be independent of intention. He relies heavily on the academic authority of Professor H W R Wade, as expressed in an article in the *Cambridge Law Journal* in 1972, where he asked 'What is wrong with Section 78.' In this article, Professor Wade argued that the rules for the transmission of restrictive covenants both should be and have been recently relaxed. He believed that there had been a relaxation of the law by the Chancery judges in the 20 years prior to 1972, such that the precise words of the conveyance became less important, and evidence of intention to annex gleaned from the surrounding circumstances more important. One result of this, he suggested, was that the words implied into a conveyance by section 78 should be sufficient to annex any covenant to land, if they can be taken along with surrounding circumstances indicating intention to so annex. It is important to note that he does not seem to assume that the words of the section are sufficient to automatically annex any covenant to land:

> If the covenant in fact relates to any land of the covenantee, his successors in title, widely defined for the purposes of restrictive covenants, are presumed to be intended to benefit,

but

> Whether, if so capable [of 'touching and concerning' or 'relating to' land], it [a covenant] actually does so relate to any given land is a matter of intention, to be collected from the deed and the surrounding circumstances; there are no rules of formality.

This suggests that far from arguing for automatic annexation, Professor Wade would gather intention from surrounding circumstances, both as to whether the covenant actually relates to the land, and also if it does, (possibly) as to whether the presumption of intention to benefit is rebutted. In relation to section 78 in particular, therefore, what seems to be argued is that if from the surrounding circumstances an intention to annex is apparent, no further words of annexation are required apart from those implied anyway by section 78. . . .

My conclusion, therefore, is that *Federated Homes* does not, in fact, stand for such an automatic annexation theory, but that Brightman LJ's views are similar to Professor Wade's, namely that the wording of section 78 is sufficient without more to annex a covenant to land so long as enough evidence can be found from surrounding circumstances that it is intended to 'relate to' the land in question. . . .

27.2.1 THE TRADITIONAL VIEWPOINT ON ANNEXATION

JAMAICA MUTUAL LIFE ASSURANCE SOCIETY v HILLSBOROUGH AND OTHERS
[1989] 1 WLR 1101, Privy Council

FACTS: The owners of land sold plots to various parties, subject to a covenant against sub-division of the plots and prohibiting the use of the plots for the carrying on of any trade or business. The instruments of transfer of the plots did not expressly identify the land which the covenants were intended to benefit. One of the owners of the plots applied to the Supreme Court of Jamaica for a declaration as to the extent to which they were bound by the restrictive covenants contained in the instrument of transfer.

HELD: In the absence of express assignment of the benefit of the covenant to the vendors' successors in title, and in the absence of any possible inference that the vendors intended to annex the benefit of the covenants to the land retained by them, the benefit of the covenant had not passed and could not be enforced against the owner of the plot.

LORD JAUNCEY of Tullichettle: . . . There were in the instrument of transfer to Maurice William Facey no words stating that the restrictions therein were intended for the benefit of any land retained by Dunn and others. . . . .

In *Renals* v *Cowlishaw* (1878) 9 ChD 125, 130, Hall V-C said:

> that in order to enable a purchaser as an assign (such purchaser not being an assign of all that the vendor retained when he executed the conveyance containing the covenants, and that conveyance not shewing that the benefit of the covenant was intended to enure for the time being of each portion of the estate so retained or of the portion of the estate of which the plaintiff is assign) to claim the benefit of a restrictive covenant, this, at least, must appear, that the assign acquired his property with the benefit of the covenant, that is, it must appear that the benefit of the covenant was part of the subject-matter of the purchase.

In *Rogers* v *Hosegood* [1900] 2 Ch 388, 407–408, Collins LJ said:

> When, as in *Renals* v *Cowlishaw*, there is no indication in the original conveyance, or in the circumstances attending it, that the burden of the restrictive covenant is imposed for the benefit of the land reserved, or any particular part of it, then it becomes necessary to examine the circumstances under which any part of the land reserved is sold, in order to see whether a benefit, not originally annexed to it, has become annexed to it on the sale, so that the purchaser is deemed to have bought it with the land . . .

Both *Renals* v *Cowlishaw* and *Rogers* v *Hosegood* were referred to with approval in *Reid* v *Bickerstaff* [1909] 2 Ch 305 where Cozens-Hardy MR in the context of a submission that the benefit of a covenant was annexed to adjoining lands of the vendors said, at p. 321:

> As to the second proposition the plaintiffs have a more plausible case, but I think they fail in establishing it. It is plain that they are not assignees of the covenant, of the existence of which they were not aware. It is equally plain that there is nothing in the deed of 1840, or in any document prior or subsequent thereto, to indicate that the covenant was entered into for the benefit of the particular parcels of which the plaintiffs are now owners. I cannot hold that the mere fact that the plaintiffs' land is adjacent and would be more valuable if the covenant were annexed to the land suffices to justify the court in holding that it was so annexed as to pass without mention by a simple conveyance of the adjacent land.

Applying the principles to be derived from these three cases to the matters to which their Lordships have just referred their Lordships consider that Carey JA was mistaken in concluding that the covenant in the applicant's title was annexed to any land. . . .

27.2.1.1 Annexation to the whole or each and every part?

On the traditional view of the law, a restrictive covenant which is annexed to 'Blackacre' is presumptively annexed only to the whole of Blackacre. This presumption can be rebutted if the conveyance includes some phrase such as 'this covenant is annexed to Blackacre and each and every part thereof'.

When drafting a restrictive covenant for the benefit of a large piece of land, the solicitor acting for the dominant owner needs to decide whether:

(a) to annex the covenant only to the whole of the dominant land; or
(b) to annex the covenant to 'each and every part of the dominant land'.

Each alternative has its advantages and disadvantages.

27.2.1.2 The disadvantages of annexation only to the whole of the dominant land— the 'small plot–big plot' situation

RE BALLARD'S CONVEYANCE [1937] 2 All ER 691, Chancery Division

FACTS: The owners of the 'Childwickbury Estate' sold sixteen acres on the edge of their 1,700 acre estate, subject to a restrictive covenant that the land sold should be used for agricultural purposes only. The covenant was expressed to be for the benefit of 'the whole of the Childwickbury Estate'.

HELD: There was no valid annexation. For a valid annexation the current owners of Childwickbury would have to have proved that all 1,700 acres were benefited by the 'agriculture only' covenant. In the judge's view, those parts of the estate close to the sixteen acres were capable of benefiting from the covenant, but those further away were not. The covenant was therefore unenforceable.

CLAUSON J: I . . . hold that the land for the benefit of which the covenant was taken was the land (about 1,700 acres) now vested in Childwickbury Stud, Ltd, by conveyance from Mr Joel, and that the fact that it claims by virtue of a purchase from Mrs Ballard would not affect its title to sue.

That brings me to the remaining question, namely: Is the covenant one which, in the circumstances of the case, comes within the category of a covenant the benefit of which is capable of running with the land for the benefit of which it was taken? A necessary qualification, in order that the covenant may come within that category, is that it concerns or touches the land with which it is to run : see *per* Farwell J, in *Rogers* v *Hosegood* [1900] 2 Ch 388, at p. 395. That land is an area of some 1,700 acres. It appears to me quite obvious that, while a breach of the stipulations might possibly affect a portion of that area in the vicinity of Mr Wright's land, far the largest part of this area of 1,700 acres could not possibly be affected by any breach of any of the stipulations.

Counsel for the respondent company asked for an adjournment in order to consider whether it would call evidence (as I was prepared to allow it to do) to prove that a breach of the stipulations, or of some of them, might affect the whole of this large area. However, ultimately no such evidence was called.

The result seems to me to be that I am bound to hold that, while the covenant may concern or touch some comparatively small portion of the land to which it has been sought to annex it, it fails to concern or touch far the largest part of the land. I asked in vain for any authority which would justify me in severing the covenant, and treating it as annexed to or running with such part of the land as is touched by or concerned with it, though, as regards the remainder of the land, namely, such part as is not touched by or concerned with the covenant, the covenant is not, and cannot be, annexed to it, and accordingly does not, and cannot, run with it. . . .

27.2.1.3 The modern trend in 'small plot' 'big plot' cases

MARTEN v FLIGHT REFUELLING LTD [1961] 2 All ER 696, Chancery Division

FACTS: Mrs Marten had a beneficial interest under a strict settlement in the 7,500 acre Crichel Estate, Dorset. When she was still an infant, the trustees of the settlement sold a farm comprising part of the estate (562 acres, in fact) to Mr Harding. He covenanted that he would use the land for agricultural purposes only. In course of time the defendant company came to own the 'farm', and began to use the land for industrial purposes. When Mrs Marten attained majority, the trustees executed an assent vesting the estate in her, but the assent made no express mention of the covenant. Mrs Marten brought the present action for an injunction restraining the defendant's industrial use of the 'farm' land.

HELD: She was entitled to the benefit of the restrictive covenant. Accordingly, the injunction was granted.

WILBERFORCE J: . . . an intention to benefit may be found from surrounding or attending circumstances. . .

. . . it was said that a mere examination of the figures showed that the covenant could not benefit the estate: the Crichel Estate extends to some seven thousand five hundred acres, and it was asked how such covenant could benefit the estate as a whole. In my view, there is no such manifest impossibility about this. I have already referred to the character of the estate, and I can well imagine that for the owner of it, whether he wished to retain it in his family or to sell it as a whole, it might be of very real benefit to be able to preserve a former outlying portion from development. This seems to me to be a question of fact to be determined on the evidence: and I note that, when a similar argument was placed before the court in *Re Ballard's Conveyance* [see **27.2.1.2**], Clauson J, while accepting it in the absence of evidence, showed it to be his opinion that evidence could have been called. . . .

27.2.1.4   Annexation destroyed on sub-division of the dominant land

RUSSEL v *ARCHDALE* [1962] 3 All ER 305, Chancery Division

FACTS: A company owned certain land which it conveyed to the defendant, the company retaining other land in the neighbourhood. The defendant purchaser entered into various restrictive covenants 'so as to . . . benefit and protect the vendor's adjoining and neighbouring land'. Some years later the plaintiffs bought *part* of the company's retained land. The conveyance was expressed to include the benefit of the covenants entered into by the defendants. On the question whether the plaintiffs could enforce the restrictive covenants:
HELD: The annexation of the covenants to 'the vendor's adjoining and neighbouring land' was an annexation to the *whole* of the vendor's adjoining and neighbouring land and not to *each and every part* of it. Accordingly, as the plaintiffs had acquired a part only of the land, they could not enforce the benefit of the covenant.

BUCKLEY J: No doubt every case of this kind, being one of construction, must be determined on the facts and the actual language used, but . . . I cannot see that the mere fact that the land intended to be benefited is described by such an expression as 'the land retained by the vendor', is sufficient to enable the court to come to the conclusion that the covenant is intended to benefit each and every part of that land. . . . That being so, it must follow that the plaintiffs cannot enforce the covenant merely by reason of its annexation to the 'adjoining and neighbouring land' of the vendors under the conveyance of July 6 1938, since they (the plaintiffs) have acquired part only of that land.

27.2.1.5   The disadvantage of annexation to each and every part

When the dominant land is sub-divided, the number of owners entitled to enforce the covenant is bound to increase; with a large dominant area the number of dominant owners could initially be one, but later be enormous.

27.2.2   THE POTENTIAL EFFECTS OF THE *FEDERATED HOMES* CASE— A HIGHLY QUESTIONABLE NEW FORM OF ANNEXATION

27.2.2.1   Drafting of restrictive covenants in the light of *Federated Homes*

ROAKE v *CHADHA AND ANOTHER* [1983] 3 All ER 503, Chancery Division

FACTS: A clause in a 1934 conveyance expressly stated that the benefit of a number of restrictive convenants was not to pass by annexation.
HELD: The judge rejected an argument that the benefit of the covenants had nevertheless been annexed by virtue of s. 78 of the Law of Property Act 1925. Careful drafting had excluded the effect of s. 78.

HIS HONOUR JUDGE PAUL BAKER QC: . . . Counsel for the plaintiffs' method of applying it is simplicity itself. The *Federated Homes* case shows that s. 78 brings about annexation, and that the operation of the section cannot be excluded by a contrary intention. As I have indicated, he supports this last point by reference to s. 79, which is expressed to operate 'unless a contrary intention is expressed', a qualification which, as we have already noticed, is absent from s. 78. Counsel for the plaintiffs could not suggest any reason of policy why s. 78 should be mandatory, unlike, for example, s. 146 of the 1925 Act, which deals with restrictions on the right to forfeiture of leases and which, by an express provision, 'has effect notwithstanding any stipulation to the contrary'.

I am thus far from satisfied that s. 78 has the mandatory operation which counsel for the plaintiffs claimed for it. But, even if one accepts that it is not subject to a contrary intention, I do not consider that it has the effect of annexing the benefit of the covenant in each and every case irrespective of the other express terms of the covenant. I notice that Brightman LJ did not go so far as that, for he said in the *Federated Homes* case [1980] 1 All ER 371 at 381, [1980] 1 WLR 594 at 606:

> I find the idea of the annexation of a covenant to the whole of the land but not to a part of it a difficult conception fully to grasp. I can understand that a covenantee may expressly or by necessary implication retain the benefit of a covenant wholly under his own control, so that the benefit will not pass unless the covenantee chooses to assign; but I would have thought, if the benefit of a covenant is, on a proper construction of a document, annexed to the land, *prima facie* it is annexed to every part thereof, unless the contrary clearly appears.

So at least in some circumstances Brightman LJ is considering that despite s. 78 the benefit may be retained and not pass or be annexed to and run with land. In this connection, I was also referred by counsel for the defendants to Sir Lancelot Elphinstone's *Covenants Affecting Land* (1946) p. 17, where the author says, with reference to this point (and I quote from a footnote on that page):

> . . . but it is thought that, as a covenant must be construed as a whole, the court would give due effect to words excluding or modifying the operation of the section.

The true position as I see it is that, even where a covenant is deemed to be made with successors in title as s. 78 requires, one still has to construe the covenant as a whole to see whether the benefit of the covenant is annexed. Where one finds, as in the *Federated Homes* case, the covenant is not qualified in any way, annexation may be readily inferred; but, where, as in the present case, it is expressly provided that 'this covenant shall not enure for the benefit of any owner or subsequent purchaser of any part of the Vendor's Sudbury Court Estate at Wembley unless the benefit of this covenant shall be expressly assigned', one cannot just ignore these words. . . .

27.3   Assignment of the Benefit of Restrictive Covenants

27.3.1   THE RULES FOR A VALID ASSIGNMENT

MILES v *EASTER* [1933] Ch 611, Court of Appeal

FACTS: A 1908 conveyance contained a covenant made by the purchasers that they would not do anything which might cause a nuisance to the vendor's land. The conveyance showed that the vendors retained land in the vicinity, referring as it did to a 'foreshore belonging to the vendors', but the deed did not go further in defining the land.
HELD: Due to uncertainty as to the land intended to benefit, the plaintiff had failed to show that the benefit of the restrictive covenant made in the 1908 deed had vested in them.

ROMER LJ: . . . It is plain, however, from these and other cases, and notably that of *Renals* v *Cowlishaw* (1878) 9 ChD 125, that if the restrictive covenant be taken not merely for some personal purpose or object of the vendor, but for the benefit of some other land of his in the sense that it would enable him to dispose of that land to greater advantage, the covenant, though not annexed to such land so as to run with any part of it, may be enforced against an assignee of the covenantor taking with notice, both by the covenantee and by persons to whom the benefit of such covenant has been assigned, subject however to certain conditions. In the first place, the 'other land' must be land that is capable of being benefited by the covenant—otherwise it would be impossible to infer that the object of the covenant was to enable the vendor to dispose of his land to greater advantage. In the next place, this land must be 'ascertainable' or 'certain,' to use the words of Romer and Scrutton LJJ respectively. For, although the Court will readily infer the intention to benefit the other land of the vendor where the existence and situation of such land are indicated in the conveyance or have been otherwise shown with reasonable certainty, it is impossible to do so from vague references in the conveyance or in other documents laid before the Court as to the existence of other lands of the vendor, the extent and situation of which are undefined. In the third place, the covenant cannot be enforced by the covenantee against an assign of the purchaser after the covenantee has parted with the whole of his land.

. . . it is impossible to ascertain with any certainty what lands retained by the covenantees when the conveyance of October 23 1908, was executed were intended to be protected by the covenant so that the covenantees might thereafter dispose of them to greater advantage. That conveyance shows that the vendors were possessed of other land in the vicinity, reference being made in the deed to 'foreshore belonging to the vendors west of the harbour entrance,' without further defining it, and to land coloured yellow on the plan attached to the deed in terms that clearly indicate their ownership of such land. But our attention is also called to certain transactions between the covenantees and a company called The Service Land Company Ltd, in the month of January 1912, that show that in October 1908, the covenantees were possessed of still other lands at Lancing and Shoreham of considerable, though, so far as the Court is concerned, of undefined extent. Referring to these other lands, Bennett J said: 'There was no evidence before me as to where such other lands were situate or as to the area thereof. There was no evidence before me as to the purposes for which the Shoreham Company acquired these lands, whether for the purpose of resale or for development as a building estate. . . . I am really left to guess at the reasons, if any, which led to the introduction in the conveyance of October 23 1908, of the purchaser's covenant.' In these circumstances, the learned judge declined to draw the conclusion that the covenant was inserted in the conveyance for the protection of all the other lands of the Shoreham Company so as to enable them to dispose of such lands to the best advantage. And he was justified in so doing. It is impossible to ascertain whether all or some, and if so which, part of such lands were capable of being protected by the reservation of the covenant. When, therefore, by indentures of October 19 1920, and October 15 1921, the Shoreham Company and the Seaside Company (to whom the Shoreham Company had previously sold the whole of their still unsold lands) purported to assign to the defendant Easter the benefit of the restrictive covenant, there can be no sure ground for thinking that any of such still unsold lands were lands for the protection of which the covenant had been obtained. It is plain that at that time all the lands coloured green had been disposed of. The defendants have accordingly failed to show that there is now vested in them, or either of them, the right to enforce the restrictive covenant contained in the deed of October 23, 1908. . . .

27.4 Building Schemes or Schemes of Development

27.4.1 THE CONDITIONS REQUIRED FOR A VALID BUILDING SCHEME

ELLISTON v *REACHER* [1908] 2 Ch 374, Chancery Division

FACTS: A building scheme was created in 1861. The plots were sold from an office in Ipswich, but the scheme itself was on 10 acres of land at Felixstowe. Anybody entering the office at Ipswich would have seen on the wall a large plan of the scheme, with the restrictive covenants endorsed prominently on the plan. Potential purchasers could buy a copy of this plan for 1s 6d. The covenants were of a kind to preserve the 'exclusive' nature of the area.

HELD: It was a natural inference from the advertising that the creator of the scheme intended the covenants to be mutually enforceable.

PARKER J: I pass, therefore, to the consideration of the question whether the plaintiffs can enforce these restrictive covenants. In my judgment, in order to bring the principles of *Renals* v *Cowlishaw* (1878) 9 ChD 125 and *Spicer* v *Martin* (1888) 14 App Cas 12 into operation it must be proved that both the plaintiffs and defendants derive title under a common vendor; that previously to selling the lands to which the plaintiffs and defendants are respectively entitled the vendor laid out his estate, or a defined portion thereof (including the lands purchased by the plaintiffs and defendants respectively), for sale in lots subject to restrictions intended to be imposed on all the lots, and which, though varying in details as to particular lots, are consistent and consistent only with some general scheme of development; that these restrictions were intended by the common vendor to be and were for the benefit of all the lots intended to be sold, whether or not they were also intended to be and were for the benefit of other land retained by the vendor; and that both the plaintiffs and the defendants, or their predecessors in title, purchased their lots from the common vendor upon the footing that the restrictions subject to which the purchases were made were to enure for the benefit of the other lots included in the general scheme whether or not they were also to enure for the benefit of other lands retained by the vendors. If these four points be established, I think that the plaintiffs would in equity be entitled to enforce the restrictive covenants entered into by the defendants or their predecessors with the common vendor irrespective of the dates of the respective purchases. I may observe, with reference to the third point, that the vendor's object in imposing the restrictions must in general be gathered from all the circumstances of the case, including in particular the nature of the restrictions. If a general observance of the restrictions is in fact calculated to enhance the values of the several lots offered for sale, it is an easy inference that the vendor intended the restrictions to be for the benefit of all the lots, even though he might retain other land the value of which might be similarly enhanced, for a vendor may naturally be expected to aim at obtaining the highest possible price for his land. Further, if the first three points be established, the fourth point may readily be inferred, provided the purchasers have notice of the facts involved in the three first points; but if the purchaser purchases in ignorance of any material part of those facts, it would be difficult, if not impossible, to establish the fourth point. It is also observable that the equity arising out of the establishment of the four points I have mentioned has been sometimes explained by the implication of mutual contracts between the various purchasers, and sometimes by the implication of a contract between each purchaser and the common vendor, that each purchaser is to have the benefit of all the covenants by the other purchasers, so that each purchase is in equity an assign of the benefit of these covenants. In my opinion the implication of mutual contract is not always a perfectly satisfactory explanation. It may be satisfactory where all the lots are sold by auction at the same time, but when, as in cases such as *Spicer* v *Martin*, there is no sale by auction, but all the various sales are by private treaty and at various intervals of time, the circumstances may, at the date of one or more of the sales, be such as to preclude the possibility of any actual contract. For example, a prior purchaser may be dead or incapable of contracting at the time of a subsequent purchase, and in any event it is unlikely that the prior and subsequent purchasers are ever brought into personal relationship, and yet the equity may exist between them. It is, I think, enough to say, using Lord Macnaghten's words in *Spicer* v *Martin*, that where the four points I have mentioned are established, the community of interest imports in equity the reciprocity of obligation which is in fact contemplated by each at the time of his own purchase. . . .

Proceeding with the facts as we know them, it appears that, though the lots were according to the sale plan to be offered to the members of the society in August 1860, the society did not complete its title to the property until early in January 1861. The unexecuted engrossment bears date a few days after such completion. It appears also that the society prepared and procured to be printed a form of conveyance for use on the sale of every lot, and that such printed form was in fact used on the sales of the lots purchased by the predecessors in title of the plaintiffs and defendants respectively. Further, a copy of the sale plan was pasted on canvas and hung up in the offices of the society, and as and when plots were sold such plots were marked off on the plan in Indian ink. Most if not all of the plots were so marked off as sold before the end of the year 1865. . . .

Under all the circumstances of the case it is in my opinion sufficiently established not only that the predecessors of the plaintiffs and the defendants respectively had notice of the intention of their common vendors that the restrictions in question should enure for the benefit of all the lots offered for sale, but that they made their respective purchases on that footing. . . .

27.4.2 PROVING THAT THE CREATOR OF THE SCHEME INTENDED MUTUAL ENFORCEABILITY

BAXTER v FOUR OAKS PROPERTIES LTD [1965] 1 All ER 906, Chancery Division

FACTS: The 288 acre 'Four Oaks Estate' was sold in plots of various sizes over a period of ten years, each purchaser entering a mutual deed of covenants for the benefit of the owners of the other plots.
HELD: Where there was a mutual deed of covenant, the fact that the vendor had not laid out his land in plots before sale did not preclude a finding that a building scheme was in existence.

CROSS J: . . . In 1891 Lord Clanrikarde owned an estate of some 288 acres at Sutton Coldfield known as the 'Four Oaks Estate', the eastern boundary of which was formed by a public road called at the south end the Lichfield Road, and further north the Four Oaks Road. By various conveyances executed over a period of some ten years he sold the whole of the estate for building development in plots of various sizes. It was his intention that the whole estate should be residential but that the cost of the houses to be erected should not be uniform throughout. To effect the purpose which he had in mind, the whole estate was divided into several parts, the part with which this action is concerned being that abutting on the Lichfield and Four Oaks Road.

The first purchaser of a plot on this part was one Samuel Hope. On April 27 1891, an indenture (which I will call the 'Lichfield Road deed of covenant') was expressed to be made between Lord Clanrikarde of the one part and Samuel Hope and all other persons whose names are or might thereafter be entered in the second column of Sch. 2 thereto, being purchasers of lands forming parts of the Four Oaks Estate as delineated on the plan thereto annexed of the other part. The recital and operative part of this Indenture were as follows:

WHEREAS by an Indenture of Conveyance bearing even date with these presents and made between the said Marquess of Clanrikarde of the one part and the said Samuel Hope of the other part for the consideration therein mentioned the said Marquess of Clanrikarde hath conveyed to the said Samuel Hope his heirs and assigns a certain piece or parcel of land being part of the Four Oaks Estate and fronting on a road shown on the said plan and leading from Sutton Coldfield to Lichfield and Little Aston being the piece or parcel of land coloured blue on the said plan and identified by the name 'Hope' written upon it TO HOLD the same unto and to the use of the said Samuel Hope his heirs and assigns AND in the said Indenture of Conveyance is contained a covenant by the said Samuel Hope with the said Marquess of Clanrikarde that he the said Samuel Hope his heirs and assigns and all persons claiming under him will at all times hereafter perform and observe certain covenants and conditions as to building on the said piece or parcel of land and as to the user of the said piece or parcel of land therein specified AND WHEREAS it is intended that all other persons who may be or become purchasers of any lands forming part of the said Four Oaks Estate and fronting on the said road shall enter into covenants as to building on such lands as to the user thereof similar to the covenant in that behalf contained in the hereinbefore recited Indenture of Conveyance to the said Samuel Hope NOW THIS INDENTURE WITNESSETH that for giving effect to such covenants respectively IT IS HEREBY AGREED AND DECLARED that the said Samuel Hope and every other person who shall be or become a purchaser of any land forming part of the said Four Oaks Estate and fronting on the said road and their respective heirs and assigns and all persons claiming under them respectively shall whether they shall or shall not have respectively executed these presents perform and observe the covenants and conditions contained in Sch. 1 hereunder written so far as such covenants and conditions respectively may relate to the lands purchased by them respectively AND IT IS HEREBY FURTHER AGREED AND DECLARED that in the event of any breach by the said Samuel Hope or any such other person as aforesaid or by their respective heirs or assigns or by any person or persons claiming under them respectively of the said covenants and conditions respectively or any of them it shall be lawful for any other person for the time being entitled to any land being part of the said Four Oaks Estate and fronting on the said road or having any estate or interest in such land without any further consent or concurrence of the said Marquess of Clanrikarde his heirs or assigns to bring such action or take such steps as may be necessary or proper or restrain such breach PROVIDED ALWAYS that the covenant and conditions contained in Sch. 1 hereunder written shall not apply to or affect any lands forming part of the Four Oaks Estate other than such lands as front on the said road.

The covenants and conditions in Sch. 1 were as follows:

1. No dwellinghouse or other building (other than the existing cottage adjoining Doe Bank House or other than a building used for the purposes of and as appurtenant to a dwellinghouse) of a less cost for materials and labour of construction than £750 or in the case of a pair of semi-detached houses than £1,200 shall be erected or built or suffered to remain upon any part of the lands above mentioned between Hartopp Road and Bracebridge Road or of a less cost than £1,000 in the case of a single house or £1,500 in the case of a pair of semi-detached houses upon any part of the lands above mentioned between Bracebridge Road and Blackroot Road. 2. No dwellinghouse or other building other than a porch or oriel or bow window or balcony shall be erected or built or suffered to remain upon any part of the lands above mentioned so as to project beyond the building line shown on the plan hereto annexed. 3. No dwellinghouse or other building on any part of the lands above mentioned shall be used for the sale or supply of wine beers or spirits or for the sale or supply of victuals or as an hotel or inn or for any trade or business whatever or otherwise than as a private residence or for any purpose which may be or grow to the annoyance damage or disturbance of any person who may be or become the owner or occupier of any other part of the lands above mentioned. . . .

It is, of course, clear that a vendor who sells a piece of land to 'A' and subsequently sells another piece of land to 'B' cannot, as part of the later transaction, annex to 'A's' land the benefit of a restrictive covenant entered into by 'B' if it was not part of his bargain with 'A' at the time of the sale to him that 'A' should have the benefit of it. On the other hand, for well over one hundred years past where the owner of land deals with it on the footing of imposing restrictive obligations on the use of various parts of it as and when he sells them off for the common benefit of himself (in so far as he retains any land) and of the various purchasers *inter se* a court of equity has been prepared to give effect to this common intention notwithstanding any technical difficulties involved. In the early days it was not unusual for the common vendor to have prepared a deed of mutual covenant to be executed by each purchaser. If the various sales all took place at the same time—as they would, for instance, if all the land in question was put up for sale by auction in lots—then the various purchasers would, no doubt, be brought into direct contractual relations with one another on signing the deed; but if the common vendor sold off different lots of land at intervals, it might well happen that by the time a later purchaser executed the deed, one of the earlier purchasers was dead. In such a case it would be difficult to found the right of the successors in title of the deceased earlier purchaser to enforce the covenants against the later purchaser or his successors in title on any contract between the two original purchasers, even though each signed the deed.

The view taken by the courts has been rather that the common vendor imposed a common law on a defined area of land and that whenever he sold a piece of it to a purchaser who knew of the common law, that piece of land automatically became entitled to the benefit of, and subject to the burden of, the common law. With the passage in time it became apparent that there was no particular virtue in the execution of a deed of mutual covenant—save as evidence of the intention of the parties—and what came to be called 'building schemes' were enforced by the courts if satisfied that it was the intention of the parties that the various purchasers should have rights *inter se*, even though no attempt was made to bring them into direct contractual relations. . . .

LAW OF PROPERTY ACT 1925

56.   Persons taking who are not parties and as to indentures

(1)   A person may take an immediate or other interest in land or other property, or the benefit of any condition, right of entry, covenant or agreement over or respecting land or other property, although he may not be named as a party to the conveyance or other instrument.

(2)   A deed between parties, to effect its objects, has the effect of an indenture though not intended or expressed to be an indenture.

27.4.3   MODERN CASES EXPANDING THE BUILDING SCHEME PRINCIPLES

BAXTER v FOUR OAKS [1965] 1 All ER 906

FACTS: There was a Victorian building scheme with one special feature. The common vendor had fixed the area of his scheme but had not divided his land into plots before commencing selling. Rather, he had sold each purchaser as much land as he (the purchaser) desired.

HELD: Cross J found that the special feature of the case did not prevent there being a building scheme. In *Baxter* there was an organised scheme of covenants for a defined area, and those covenants had been incorporated into a mutual deed of covenant.

RE DOLPHIN'S CONVEYANCE [1970] 2 All ER 664

FACTS: In 1871, two sisters were tenants in common of the 30-acre 'Selly Hill Estate' on the (then) south-west edge of Birmingham. They started selling off sizeable parts of this estate. They then gave the remaining parts of Selly Hill to their nephew. He sold off further chunks of Selly Hill, until it had all gone by 1891.

As each chunk of Selly Hill was sold, restrictive covenants were imposed on the land. The purchasers (usually builders) promised to build only high class housing; each house was to have a minimum of a quarter of an acre of grounds.

On each sale the vendors (the sisters or the nephew) covenanted that if they sold further parts of Selly Hill, the same restrictive covenants would be imposed. The judge inferred from this promise by the vendors an intention that the covenants restricting the area to high-class housing were to be mutually enforceable.

HELD: The judge went on to hold that although:

(a)   there had been no scheme of restrictive covenants for the whole area decided upon before sale commenced; and

(b)   the selling of the estate had been spread over 20 years;

there was nevertheless in his view a situation within the building scheme principle. Thus current owners of large houses on Selly Hill could enforce the covenants against Birmingham Corporation, who had bought other parts of Selly Hill for high-density council housing.

27.5   The Chaotic State of the Law on the Running of Benefits of Covenants

The Law Commission (Law Com. No. 127) Transfer of Land: The Law of Positive and Restrictive Covenants, London: HMSO, 26 January 1984

4.10   A traveller in this area of the law, old though it is, walks on ground which is still shifting. Particularly striking examples come from the same two topics: the *Federated Homes* case has made radical and controversial changes in what was thought to be the law about annexation, and successive court decisions in recent years have altered the conditions thought to be essential for the establishment of a binding scheme.

4.11   Shifts in the law as interpreted by the courts may be wholly beneficial so far as future covenants are concerned, but they must of course apply equally to existing covenants and here their effects are much more mixed. If a land-owner sought legal advice periodically about the enforceability of a particular covenant, he would have to be told different things at different times; and his lot would not be a happy one if he had acted in good faith on advice given one year only to find it invalidated the next. . . .

[The Law Commission proposed that a new 'land obligation' should be created to replace existing and future restrictive covenants.]

4.22 . . . the new interest will, like an easement, normally subsist as a legal interest in land, and be enforceable by legal remedies, including an action for common law damages. The highly technical rules determining whether the benefit and the burden of restrictive covenants may pass to new owners of the land affected will also disappear; and any doubt which might otherwise arise as to whether an obligation was intended to run with the land or operate only between the parties will be removed by requiring parties who intend to create an obligation running with the land to label it by express words as a 'land obligation'. . . . It will not be enforceable between the original parties after they have parted with the land.

CHAPTER TWENTY-EIGHT

ESCAPING FROM RESTRICTIVE COVENANTS

28.1 Carry on Regardless

Some developers may boldly say, 'Let's ignore those restrictive covenants,' and start work hoping that no 'dominant owner' will come along and object. In some types of situation there is little risk in doing this.

28.2 'Doing a Parkside Homes'

In the Wrotham Park case—see **26.3** the defendants, Parkside Homes, commenced their building work, but took out an insurance policy to protect themselves (and the purchasers of their houses) should anyone succeed in a claim that the covenant could still be enforced. As we know, a claim to enforce the covenant did (unexpectedly) succeed. The £2,500 damages awarded by Brightman J was paid (as his Lordship well knew) by the insurers.

28.3 Attempt to Buy Out the Dominant Owners

You must first realise that if there are (say) 10 dominant owners, then all 10 must be persuaded to give up their rights to enforce the covenant. You must also appreciate that as a result of the chaos caused by modern cases such as *Federated Homes* and *Wrotham Park* (see **27.1** and **26.3**), it is often impossible to be certain that you have 'persuaded' every dominant owner.

28.4 Take Proceedings Under the Law of Property Act 1925, Section 84(2)

LAW OF PROPERTY ACT 1925

84. Power to discharge or modify restrictive covenants affecting land

(1)   [the Lands Tribunal] shall (without prejudice to any concurrent jurisdiction of the court) have power from time to time, on the application of any person interested in any freehold land affected by any restriction arising under covenant or otherwise as to the user thereof or the building thereon, by order wholly or partially to discharge or modify any such restriction . . . on being satisfied—

(a)   that by reason of changes in the character of the property or the neighbourhood or other circumstances of the case which [the Lands Tribunal] may deem material, the restriction ought to be deemed obsolete, or

(aa)   that in a case falling within subsection (1A) below the continued existence thereof would impede some reasonable user of the land for public or private purposes . . . or, as the case may be, would unless modified so impede such user; or

(b)   that the persons of full age and capacity for the time being or from time to time entitled to the benefit of the restriction, whether in respect of estates in fee simple or any lesser estates or interests in the property to which the benefit of the restriction is annexed, have agreed, either expressly or by implication, by their acts or omissions, to the same being discharged or modified; or

(c)   that the proposed discharge or modification will not injure the persons entitled to the benefit of the restriction:

and an order discharging or modifying a restriction under this subsection may direct the applicant to pay to any person entitled to the benefit of the restriction such sum by way of consideration as the Tribunal may think it just to award under one, but not both, of the following heads, that is to say, either—

(i)   a sum to make up for any loss or disadvantage suffered by that person in consequence of the discharge or modification; or

(ii)   a sum to make up for any effect which the restriction had, at the time when it was imposed, in reducing the consideration then received for the land affected by it.

(1A)   Subsection (1)(aa) above authorises the discharge or modification of a restriction by reference to its impeding some reasonable user of land in any case in which the Lands Tribunal is satisfied that the restriction, in impeding that user, either—

(a)   does not secure to persons entitled to the benefit of it any practical benefits of substantial value or advantage to them; or

(b)   is contrary to the public interest;

and that money will be an adequate compensation for the loss or disadvantage (if any) which any such person will suffer from the discharge or modification.

(1B)   In determining whether a case is one falling within subsection (1A) above, and in determining whether (in any such case or otherwise) a restriction ought to be discharged or modified, the Lands Tribunal shall take into account the development plan and any declared or ascertainable pattern for the grant or refusal of planning permissions in the relevant areas, as well as the period at which and context in which the restriction was created or imposed and any other material circumstances.

(1C)   It is hereby declared that the power conferred by this section to modify a restriction includes power to add such further provisions restricting the user of or the building on the land affected as appear to the Lands Tribunal to be reasonable in view of the relaxation of the existing provisions, and as may be accepted by the applicant; and the Lands Tribunal may accordingly refuse to modify a restriction without some such addition.

(2)   The court shall have power on the application of any person interested—

(a)   To declare whether or not in any particular case any freehold land is or would in any given event be affected by a restriction imposed by any instrument; or

(b)   To declare what, upon the true construction of any instrument purporting to impose a restriction, is the nature and extent of the restriction thereby imposed and whether the same is [or would in any given event be] enforceable and if so by whom. Neither subsections (7) and (11) of this section nor, unless the contrary is expressed, any later enactment providing for this section not to apply to any restrictions shall affect the operation of this subsection or the operation for purposes of this subsection of any other provisions of this section.

(3)   The Lands Tribunal shall, before making any order under this section, direct such enquiries, if any, to be made of any government department or local authority, and such notices, if any, whether by way of advertisement or otherwise, to be given to such of the persons who appear to be entitled to the benefit of the restriction intended to be discharged, modified, or dealt with as, having regard to any enquiries notices or other proceedings previously made, given or taken, the Lands Tribunal may think fit.

(3A)   On an application to the Lands Tribunal under this section the Lands Tribunal shall give any necessary directions as to the persons who are or are not to be admitted (as appearing to be entitled to the benefit of the restriction) to oppose the application, and no appeal shall lie against any such direction; but rules under the Lands Tribunal Act 1949 shall make provision whereby, in cases in which there arises on such an application (whether or not in connection with the admission of persons to oppose) any such question as is referred to in subsection (2)(a) or (b) of this section, the proceedings on the application can and, if the rules so provide, shall be suspended to enable the decision of the court to be obtained on that question by an application under that subsection, or by means of a case stated by the Lands Tribunal, or otherwise, as may be provided by those rules or by rules of court.

(4) . . .

(5) Any order made under this section shall be binding on all persons, whether ascertained or of full age or capacity or not, then entitled or thereafter capable of becoming entitled to the benefit of any restriction, which is thereby discharged, modified, or dealt with, and whether such persons are parties to the proceedings or have been served with notice or not. . . .

(6) An order may be made under this section notwithstanding that any instrument which is alleged to impose the restriction intended to be discharged, modified, or dealt with, may not have been produced to the court or the Lands Tribunal, and the court or [the Lands Tribunal] may act on such evidence of that instrument as it may think sufficient.

(7) . . .

(8) This section applies whether the land affected by the restrictions is registered or not, but, in the case of registered land, the Land Registrar shall give effect on the register to any order under this section in accordance with the Land Registration Act 1925.

(9) . . .

(10) . . .

(11) . . .

(12) Where a term of more than forty years is created in land (whether before or after the commencement of this Act) this section shall, after the expiration of twenty-five years of the term, apply to restrictions affecting such leasehold land in like manner as it would have applied had the land been freehold:

Providing that this subsection shall not apply to mining leases.

RE 6, 8, 10 AND 12 ELM AVENUE, NEW MILTON, EX PARTE NEW FOREST DISTRICT COUNCIL [1984] 3 All ER 632, Chancery Division

In this case the judge gave a clear exposition of the special procedure to be adopted when seeking, under s. 84(2) of the Law of Property Act 1925, a High Court declaration of a complete list of dominant owners entitled to claim the benefit of a restrictive covenant.

SCOTT J: . . . [This] brings me to consider the approach which ought to be adopted on an application for a declaration under s. 84(2) of the Law of Property Act 1925, as amended. The subsection provides a means by which the owners of land, which may appear to be subject to restrictive covenants, can come to the court and ask for a declaration that it is not so subject. If the court makes that declaration it has an *in rem* effect and the property is not then so subject. The negative is established by the declaration sought. The position seems to me to be not in the least comparable to the situation which pertains where there is a lis between somebody claiming to be entitled to the benefit of restrictions on the one hand and the owner of the property said to be subject to the restrictions and denying the entitlement of the plaintiff on the other hand. In such a case it is plain that the onus of establishing, on a balance of probabilities, that there is a scheme, and that the property for the benefit of which it is claimed is so entitled, lies on the person asserting those matters. But when an owner of land comes to the court for a declaration under s. 84(2) it does not seem to me that he can claim to be entitled to the declaration simply on the basis that if there had been an opponent who had been arguing for the benefit of the restrictions that opponent would, on the evidence before the court, have failed on a balance of probabilities. That seems to me to be an erroneous approach. If there had been such a person, what inquiries and what case would have been made by such person is not able to be identified. It is the practice that as a preliminary to bringing before the court a claim for a declaration under s. 84(2) notice should be given to all persons in the area who might conceivably be interested in claiming the benefit of the restrictions. That has been done in this case. But it has been done in this case in the context of the wish of the local authority to construct its car park and it is entirely possible that the overwhelming consents to the construction of the car park that have been received from persons living in the neighbourhood may be simply a reflection of the need for a car park in the area. I think I would be wrong in assuming that by giving those consents the persons giving them were acknowledging that they were not entitled to the benefit of the restrictions.

However that may be, in my judgment if a declaration is to be made under s. 84(2), the court ought to be clear that the property is not burdened by the relevant restrictions. On the evidence before me I am not so clear. It seems to me likely that there was a building scheme created by Mr Merefield in the 1920s. It seems to be at least possible that, subject to the local authority's position as having acquired for statutory purposes, that building scheme may still be enforceable. In those circumstances I do not feel prepared to make a declaration the effect of which would be not simply that the local authority can proceed to construct the car park without fear of interference by way of claims for injunction, but would also have the effect of precluding anyone from coming and claiming compensation for injurious affection. Any person so claiming must of course establish, and would have the onus of proving on the balance of probabilities, that he is entitled to the benefit of the restrictions. It may very well be that nobody can do that but I do not think it would be right for me to make a declaration which would prevent any person who desired to do that from attempting to do so. . . .

28.5   Commence Proceedings in the Lands Tribunal Under Section 84(1)

RE BASS LTD'S APPLICATION (1973) 26 P & CR 156, Lands Tribunal

FACTS: The applicants had bought some land in 'inner-city' Birmingham which was 'zoned' for industrial use. They obtained planning permission to establish a large depot for long distance beer-transporting lorries. It was estimated that some 250 lorries a day would come in and out of the depot. The land was, however, subject to a 'residential purposes only' restrictive covenant. Local residents, claiming to be the dominant owners of the covenant resisted Bass's application to have the restriction removed.
HELD: Bass's application failed, despite the finding that Bass performed 'so useful and agreeable a function.'

J STUART DANIEL QC: . . . The issue, which I think is a difficult one, is then whether the application should succeed under section 84(1)(aa). I accept Mr Eyre's distillation of the questions which therefore arise and I proceed to them. *Question 1. Is the proposed user a reasonable user of the land for private purposes?* In order to answer this question it is right, I think, to consider the question on the assumption that the covenants do not exist, otherwise the question is begged. The planning permissions are very persuasive in this connexion . . . I would not like it to be thought that the first question arising, that of reasonable user, could always be concluded in the affirmative by the production of a planning permission, but on balance and after some doubt, and assuming that the covenants were not there, I have decided that in the present case the proposal does in all the difficulties of the situation constitute a reasonable user of the land for private purposes.
Question 2.   Do the covenants impede the proposed user?
   There is no question but that the covenants do impede the proposed user.
Question 5.   Is impeding the proposed user contrary to the public interest?
   I am following Mr Eyre in taking his question 5 before giving my answers to his Questions 3 and 4. In doing so I recognise that it is right and sensible to juxtapose question 5 with question 2 because this enables the question of reasonable user and of public interest to be considered consecutively. But that does not of course mean that the questions are the same, they are simply related and sometimes overlapping; the proposition that a user is reasonable may be assisted by a planning permission; the proposition that impeding that user is contrary to public interest may also be assisted by a planning permission but in rather a different way. As I have just said a planning permission is immediately persuasive on the general question whether a user is reasonable. Mr Eyre submitted that prima facie a planning permission also meant that the proposal was in the public interest. But that is not the question. The question is whether impeding the proposal is contrary to the public interest. There is here more than a narrow nuance of difference; a planning permission only says, in effect, that a proposal will be allowed; it implies perhaps that such a proposal will

not be a bad thing but it does not necessarily imply that it will be positively a good thing and in the public interest, and that failure of the proposal to materialise would be positively bad. Many planning permissions have got through by the skin of their teeth, and I think that the assistance derived from a planning permission at this stage of things is little more than the negative assistance of enabling it to be said that at any rate there was not a refusal. Thus the proving that impeding the present proposal is contrary to public interest raises a different onus from the onus of proving the user to be a reasonable one. This is really obvious from the drafting of the section but I have spelled it out in the present case because I think it is necessary. I am by no means satisfied that to stop this proposal would be contrary to public interest. There is private interest, of course, and to serve the private interest of so large a concern as Bass Limited which performs so useful and agreeable a function does to some extent serve the public interest, but that is really as far as it goes and I do not think it goes far enough. . . . I do not think the planning documents prove anything on this issue. . . . I am not satisfied that impeding this proposal is contrary to the public interest, and that conclusion is made after having full regard to what I am now about to say on Question 3, to which I now turn.

Question 3.   Does impeding the proposed user secure to the objectors practical benefits?

This opens up the general merits on the amenity front and in particular the question of noise.

The Tribunal then considered the evidence in some further detail and concluded: The residents of City Road are already subjected to noise which is not only undesirable but is beyond the limit of what is acceptable. And this application proposes to increase it.

In that situation I feel quite unable to be satisfied that impeding this proposal does not secure to the objectors benefits of substantial value or advantage. The objectors' evidence made it very clear how they feared and disliked this proposal. It does not seem to me that any authority is needed for the proposition that prevention of such a proposal and therefore the assuaging of the fear and dislike it engenders is indeed a benefit of substantial advantage.

It is not only the noise. That perhaps is the factor most amenable to measurement, difficult though that is. Fumes, vibration, dirt, the appearance of things and the risk of accidents all add to the aggregate of debts and cumulatively strengthen my opinion that in impeding this proposal the objectors do secure practical benefits of substantial value and advantage. . . .

Questions 6 and 7 do not arise, because I have given an affirmative answer to Question 4 and a negative answer to Question 5. . . .

[Question 6 was—'If the answer to Question 4 is negative, would money be an adequate compensation?

Question 7 was—'If the answer to Question 5 is affirmative, would money be an adequate compensation?']

GILBERT v SPOOR [1982] 2 All ER 576, Court of Appeal

FACTS: This case involved an application to the Lands Tribunal for an order under s. 84(1) for the discharge or modification of a restrictive covenant against building. The applicant had obtained planning permission to build houses on the servient land.

HELD: The restrictive covenant would not be modified or discharged. The grant of planning permission was not a conclusive consideration.

EVELEIGH LJ: . . . We are only concerned with one restriction and the ground for the application based on s. 84(1)(aa) although the original application covered a wider field.

The resriction is contained in the first schedule to a conveyance dated 3 November 1954. So far as is material it reads:

Not to erect on the piece of land hereby conveyed any building whatsoever other than one private dwellinghouse with proper offices and outbuildings (including at the Purchaser's option a private garage). . .

The application was for an order that the restriction be discharged wholly or modified by—

Permitting the erection and maintenance on the said land of three dwelling houses with proper offices, outbuildings and garages, of design and specification approved by the Castle Morpeth Borough Council by and or pursuant to the said Council's grant of planning permission to the Applicant dated the 11th day of October one thousand nine hundred and seventy six. . .

It is clear from the introductory sentence of sub-s. (1) of s. 84 of the 1925 Act that its provisions apply as between the original parties and to restrictions of any kind: see the observations in *Ridley* v *Taylor* [1965] 2 All ER 51, [1965] 1 WLR 611. I therefore do not think that it is permissible to construe sub-s. (1A) only in the context of restrictive covenants which run with the land. The first task is to construe the section in isolation and then to relate it to the facts of the present case.

The words of the subsection, in my opinion, are used quite generally. The phrase 'any practical benefits of substantial value or advantage to them' is wide. The subsection does not speak of a restriction for the benefit or protection of land, which is a reasonably common phrase, but rather to a restriction which secures any practical benefits. The expression 'any practical benefits' is so wide that I would require very compelling considerations before I felt able to limit them in the manner contended for. When one remembers that Parliament is authorising the Lands Tribunal to take away from a person a vested right either in law or in equity, it is not surprising that the tribunal is required to consider the adverse effects on a broad basis.

Had this application been one where all the original parties were concerned, I do not understand counsel for the applicant to argue that the preservation of the view could not be said to be a practical benefit secured by the restriction. If this is correct, and I think that it is, I see no reason to give the words a different meaning because successors in title are involved. The successor in title may well have to establish certain conditions before the covenant is enforceable by him, but that fact will not alter the nature of the benefits or advantage in fact secured to him by the existence of the restriction.

In my judgment the tribunal was entitled to hold that the view was a benefit whether or not that benefit could be said to touch and concern the land. However, I am also of the view that the land of the objectors is, in each case, touched and concerned by the covenant. The covenant is intended to preserve the amenity or standard of the neighbourhood generally. The covenant is specifically aimed at density of housing. Extensive building can effect the amenity of a district in many ways. An estate can easily lose its character when buildings obstruct the views. It seems to me to be perfectly reasonable to say that the loss of a view 'at a point just a short distance from the land' may have an adverse effect on the land itself for the loss of the view could prove detrimental to the estate as a whole. In my opinion therefore the tribunal was entitled to find as it did. . . .

28.6   End of Chapter Assessment Question

In 1870 Mark bought the fee simple in Broadacre. Broadacre was then 10 acres of poor quality farm land, so Mark decided to sell the land for high class housing.

From 1871 to 1875 he sold off the whole of Broadacre in 40 plots of approximately a quarter of an acre each. In each conveyance he imposed restrictive covenants which (inter alia) prohibited the building of more than one house on each plot.

Luke has just purchased 'Redgables', a house built in 1873 on one of the plots sold by Mark. He has obtained planning permission to build a second house in the garden of 'Redgables'.

Luke's plans have caused alarm amongst some of his neighbours, and they are threatening proceedings for an injunction, claiming that they are entitled to enforce the 'one house per plot' restrictive covenant.

Other neighbours have indicated to Luke that they support him, and that they are also considering applying for planning permission to build a second house in their gardens.

Advise Luke.

28.7   End of Chapter Assessment Outline Answer

Prima facie there would appear to be a building scheme here, in which the restrictive covenants are mutually enforceable between the current owners of the plots. Compare, for instance, *Re Dolphin's Conveyance* (1970) [see **27.4.3**]. In that case the judge held that there was a valid building scheme of restrictive covenants for the whole estate, notwithstanding the fact that (as in the present case) the estate had not been divided into separate plots prior to the first plots being sold.

Assuming that each plot on Broadacre is subject to the scheme of restrictive covenants the question arises whether Luke can escape from the covenant restricting him to building one house on his plot.

A number of possible avenues of escape may be available to him.

First, he might carry on regardless and build a second house on his plot. Although, with neighbours threatening to seek an injunction against further building on his land this would appear to be inadvisable. Normally it will not be difficult for Luke's neighbours to obtain an interlocutory injunction, all they need to show is an 'arguable case' against Luke's plans. However, an injunction is an equitable remedy granted in the discretion of the court and it will not be awarded if the applicant has 'unclean hands'. Thus, if the neighbours who oppose Luke can be shown to have breached (substantially) any of the scheme covenants, they will be unlikely to obtain an injunction against him.

Secondly, he might carry on regardless, but take out insurance against the possibility that he might be subjected to an injunction. However, in the light of the threats he has received it is likely that insurance cover will be prohibitively expensive, or even refused altogether.

Thirdly, Luke might seek to identify all the 'dominant' owners (neighbours who are able to enforce the restrictive covenant) and attempt to persuade them to support him, perhaps by 'buying them out', although he is unlikely to be able to buy them all out without the financial support of those neighbours who support his plans. But how will Luke know that he has pursuaded all the dominant owners? The answer is that under s. 84(2) of the Law of Property Act 1925 the High Court can declare a definitive list of the dominant owners. Once such a declaration has been made Luke need not fear the claims of any dominant owner not appearing on the list. The High Court will only make a declaration under s. 84(2) if Luke has first circularised all his neighbours informing them that proceedings are pending, that they can be joined as parties and that they will be bound by the result (*Re Sunnyfield* [1932] 1 Ch 79).

If Luke is unable to pursuade all the dominant owners to release him from the restrictive covenant he may commence proceedings in the Lands Tribunal under s. 84(1) of the Law of Property Act 1925. The Lands Tribunal has the power, on such an application, to modify or discharge out of date restrictive covenants.

Under s. 84(1) there are a number of grounds on which a restrictive covenant may be discharged or modified [see **28.4**]. Luke is most likely to succeed under ground s. 84(1)(aa), which was introduced in 1969. The ground is that: 'the continued existence [of the restrictive covenant undischarged/modified] would impede some reasonable user of the land for public or private purposes'.

Section 84(1A) provides that two elements must be satisfied in order to succeed under s. 84(1)(aa). First, the restrictive covenant must (a) 'not secure to [the dominant owner(s)] any practical benefits of substantial value or advantage ...' **or** (b) must be 'contrary to the public interest'. Secondly, money must be 'an adequate compensation for the loss or disadvantage (if any) which any [dominant owner] will suffer from the discharge or modification'. In determining these issues '. . . the Lands Tribunal shall take into account the development plan and any declared or ascertainable pattern for the grant or refusal of planning permissions in the relevant area . . .' (s. 84(1B)). Thus Luke will rely on the development plan for his area if it suggests that there is a shortage of local housing. But it will not satisfy s. 84(1B) for Luke to point, merely, to the individual planning permission that has been granted to him.

In *Re Bass' Application* (1973) the tribunal analysed a ground (aa) application in terms of a series of questions [see **28.5**]. Applying those questions to the present case it is fairly clear that, (1) Luke's proposed user is reasonable (the grant of planning permission is usually conclusive evidence of this); (2) the covenants clearly impede that reasonable user; (3) impeding the user secures a practical benefit to the objectors (it preserves the appearance of his plot in keeping with the rest of Broadacre, and may prevent the obstruction of light from neighbouring premises); (4) the practical benefit (in 3) is substantial (but see below); (5) it is not against the public interest to impede the development (a grant of planning permission shows only that the development is not against the public interest); and consequently the tribunal is unlikely to discharge or modify the restrictive covenant.

If, on the other hand, the geography of Broadacre is such that Luke could build a second house without depriving his neighbours of a 'substantial' practical benefit (perhaps his plot is on the edge of the estate and obscured by trees) he might succeed under ground (aa) (*Re Banks' Application* (1976) P & CR 138). If such is the case the restrictive covenant will be modified or discharged, but only if money would be an adequate compensation to the dominant owners for the loss of the restriction. If compensation is awarded it will be calculated as 'a sum to make up for any loss' or, alternatively, 'as a sum to make up for the effect which the restriction had, at the time it was imposed, in reducing the consideration then received for the land affected by it'. One problem with the latter measure of compensation is that it is not inflation proof, another problem is that historic valuations are difficult to carry out. Accordingly, the first, less complicated, measure is the one normally used.

CHAPTER TWENTY-NINE

THE CREATION OF MORTGAGES

29.1 Introduction

Lawson, F. H. and Rudden, B., The Law of Property, 2nd edn,
Oxford: Clarendon Press, 1982, p. 198

. . .

The function of land mortgages
Since the days when the law of land mortgages was worked out two important changes have taken place. Firstly, ordinary people and not just the wealthy or the business community enter into mortgages to acquire their homes. Secondly, in this field, the private lender has almost disappeared along with the form of the mortgage that expected periodic payment only of *interest* with the capital advanced being repaid in a lump sum.

Nowadays the great mortgagees are the Building Societies who lend money to enable citizens to acquire a home and stipulate for repayment of both capital and income by instalments, so that after twenty or so years the debt and the mortgage are both extinguished. Their business is to earn money in the form of interest on loans made to purchasers of houses and mortgages are merely security for those loans. But they are *trustees* of their funds for their depositors. In one sense, therefore, the great lenders are merely conduit pipes. Ordinary people hand over their savings to them and receive interest on the money; and the funds thus amassed are lent to other ordinary people at interest.

Thus a mortgage looks two ways. The lender benefits the borrower by financing him, usually in the purchase of something like a home; the borrower benefits the lender by offering him a sound and safe investment. Any problems that might arise over a lender who suddenly needs his money back are solved by the interposition of Building Societies so that both lender and borrower are relieved from the anxieties of a one-to-one transaction.

29.2 Legal Mortgages of Fees Simple after 1925

29.2.1 MORTGAGE BY LONG LEASE ('MORTGAGE BY DEMISE')

The mortgagor grants to the mortgagee a lease for a very long period (usually 3,000 years) subject to a proviso for cesser on redemption, i.e. a provision that on the debt being repaid on a named date the lease should automatically terminate. This named date is the legal redemption date and is still usually fixed at a nominal six months from the date of the creation of the mortgage. The equitable right to redeem remains all important.

Any attempt after 1925 to create a mortgage by conveyance of the fee simple is converted by the Law of Property Act 1925, s. 85(2) to a mortgage by demise for 3,000 years, with a proviso for cesser on redemption.

Any legal mortgage existing on 1 January 1926 which had been created by conveyance of the fee simple was automatically converted into a mortgage by demise for 3,000 years. The fee simple was automatically revested in the mortgagor.

29.2.2   CHARGE BY WAY OF LEGAL MORTGAGE

LAW OF PROPERTY ACT 1925

Section 117   FOURTH SCHEDULE

FORMS RELATING TO STATUTORY CHARGES OR MORTGAGES OF FREEHOLD OR
LEASEHOLD LAND

FORM NO 1

STATUTORY CHARGE BY WAY OF LEGAL MORTGAGE

This Legal Charge made by way of Statutory Mortgage the .... day of ....
19 .. , between *A.* of [etc.] of the one part and *M.* of [etc.] of the other part Witnesseth that
in consideration of the sum of £............. now paid to *A.* by *M.* of which sum *A.* hereby
acknowledges the receipt *A.* As Mortgagor and As Beneficial Owner hereby charges by
way of legal mortgage All That [etc.] with the payment to *M.* on the .... day of ....
19 .. , of the principal sum of £............. as the mortgage money with interest thereon at the
rate of .... per centum per annum.
   In witness etc.

29.3   Equitable Mortgages of Legal Estates

29.3.1   EQUITABLE MORTGAGES AFTER 26 SEPTEMBER 1989

UNITED BANK OF KUWAIT PLC v *SAHIB AND OTHERS* **[1996] 3 All ER 215,**
Court of Appeal

FACTS: The plaintiff obtained judgment against the first defendant. The first defendant
then confirmed in writing to another bank, the second defendant, that the land certificate
to his land (he held the freehold jointly with his wife) was being held for the defendant
bank as security for a loan made by the defendant bank to him. The plaintiff claimed to be
entitled to an equitable charge on the freehold by deposit of the land certificate.
HELD: Section 2 of the Law of Property (Miscellaneous Provisions) Act 1989 precluded the
valid creation of an equitable mortgage in favour of the defendant bank. There was no
document in writing signed by both parties which amounted to a specifically enforceable
contract.

PETER GIBSON LJ: Since 1783 a deposit of title deeds relating to a property by way of
security has been taken to create an equitable mortgage of that property without any
writing, notwithstanding s. 4 of the Statute of Frauds (1677) and its successor, s. 40 of the
Law of Property Act 1925. The main question that arises on this appeal is whether this
much-criticised but well-established rule has survived the coming into force of s. 2 of the
Law of Property (Miscellaneous Provisions) Act 1989. . . .

The s. 2 point
Section 2 of the 1989 Act was enacted to give effect to the substance of that part of the Law
Commission's Report, *Transfer of Land: Formalities for Contracts for Sale etc of Land* (1987)
(Law Com No. 164), which recommended the repeal of s. 40 of the Law of Property Act
1925 and the abolition of the doctrine of part performance and proposed new requirements
for the making of a contract for the sale or other disposition of an interest in land. The
material parts of s. 2 are [see **5.2.2.1**].
   . . . 'Disposition' in s. 205(1)(ii) of the 1925 Act includes a conveyance, and 'conveyance'
includes a mortgage or charge. Section 40, which replaced s. 4 of the Statute of Frauds
(1677), contained provisions less stringent than the 1989 Act governing formalities relating
to contracts for the sale or other disposition of land or any interest in land, and by sub-s (2)
had preserved the law relating to part performance.

The effect of s. 2 is, therefore, that a contract for a mortgage of or charge on any interest in land or in the proceeds of sale of land can only be made in writing and only if the written document incorporates all the terms which the parties have expressly agreed and is signed by or on behalf of each party. In the present case it is not suggested that there is any such written document. . . .

Mr Pymont made seven submissions as to why s. 2 did not apply to a deposit of title deeds.

(1)   He submitted that there is nothing in the 1989 Act which expressly or by necessary implication repeals the provisions of the 1925 Act and later legislation recognising and extending the scope of a security by deposit of title deeds. He relied on four statutory provisions to the following effect: (a) s. 13 of the 1925 Act, which provides that that Act is not to affect prejudicially the right or interest of any person arising out of or consequent on the possession by him of any document relating to a legal estate in land; (b) s. 97 of that Act relating to unregistered land, which excepts from the operation of the section (governing the priority of legal and equitable mortgages) a mortgage protected by the deposit of documents relating to the legal estate affected; (c) s. 66 of the Land Registration Act 1925, which allows the proprietor of any registered land to create a lien on the registered land by deposit of the land certificate, such lien to be equivalent to a lien created in the case of unregistered land by the deposit by a legal and beneficial owner of the registered estate of the documents of title; and (d) s. 2(4) of the Land Charges Act 1972, which excepts from general equitable charges requiring registration under class C(iii) any equitable charge secured by a deposit of documents relating to the legal estate affected.

Mr Pymont submitted that it was significant that none of those provisions was referred to in the 1989 Act as having been repealed or otherwise affected by s. 2. He drew attention to the fact that some commentators have concluded from this that s. 2 was not intended to repeal the rule relating to the creation of security by deposit of title deeds: see *Snell's Equity* (29th edn, 1990) pp. 444–445, *Cheshire and Burn's Modern Law of Real Property* (15th edn, 1994) p. 670 and Bently and Coughlan 'Informal dealings with land after section 2' (1990) 10 LS 325 at 341.

I differ with reluctance from such distinguished property lawyers, but I am not persuaded that their views on this point are correct. The presence of s. 13 in the 1925 Act, as Mr Munby for UBK submitted, would appear to indicate that, without it, the Act, with its requirements of formalities for dispositions of interests in land, might have affected prejudicially the right or interest of a person with whom title deeds had been deposited. Significantly the 1989 Act, with its new and stricter requirements, contains no corresponding provision. Section 97 relates not to the requirements governing the validity of a mortgage but to priorities between mortgagees. Section 66 of the Land Registration Act 1925 begs the question what lien is created by the deposit by a legal and beneficial owner of the documents of title to unregistered land. Section 2(4) of the 1972 Act relates not to the validity of a charge, but to the way in which the deposit of the title deeds operates as a substitute for registration. In the scheme of the legislation, all mortgages must be registered unless protected by deposit of title deeds.

In any event, earlier legislative references to rights or interests created by the deposit of title deeds must now be read in the light of the 1989 Act. The new formalities required by s. 2 govern the validity of all dispositions of interests in land. I cannot see that the references relied on by Mr Pymont in the earlier legislation can displace what otherwise is the plain meaning and effect of s. 2 on contracts in whatever form to mortgage land.

(2)   Mr Pymont pointed to the fact that there is nothing in the Law Commission's report which initiated the reforms effected by the 1989 Act to suggest that security by deposit of title deeds was intended to be affected or was even considered.

I accept that there is nothing in the report that expressly refers to the deposit of title deeds by way of security, or suggests that it created a problem that needed attention. But the intention of the Law Commission to include in its proposals contracts to grant mortgages was made plain (see para. 4.3), and as a deposit of title deeds by way of security takes effect in an agreement to mortgage, in logic there is no reason why the creation of security by deposit of title deeds should have been excepted from the proposals. This is all the more likely when one considers the part played by the doctrine of part performance in the recognition by equity judges of the *Russel* v *Russel* doctrine (see further (5) below). In any event, if the wording of s. 2 is clear, as I think it is, the absence from the Law Commission's report of a reference to security by deposit of title deeds cannot alter the section's effect.

(3)   Mr Pymont then reverted to s. 2(4) of the 1972 Act excepting equitable charges not secured by a deposit of documents from the requirement of registration. He said that if a deposit of title deeds prima facie takes effect as a contract to create a mortgage, such a security would be registrable as a class C(iv) land charge, notwithstanding the exception from the requirement of registration as a class C(iii) land charge, and that cannot be right.

The wording of s. 2(4) is to my mind a clear indication that, for the purposes of that Act, a deposit of title deeds gave rise to a general equitable charge which would have been registrable as a class C(iii) land charge, but for being excepted. I accept that it was plainly not envisaged in that Act that it might also come within class C(iv). As I have already said, it was part of the scheme of the legislation that all mortgages should be registered unless protected by deposit. It would be inconsistent with that scheme that a deposit of title deeds by way of security should be an estate contract registrable as a Class C(iv) land charge. It may be that, as Mr Munby submitted, the contract to grant a mortgage inherent in the deposit of title deeds by way of security was not considered to be a mere estate contract. But whether or not that is right, I do not see that this statutory provision can affect the meaning of s. 2 of the 1989 Act.

(4)   Mr Pymont then said that the rule that a deposit of title deeds by way of security creates a mortgage is not dependent on any actual contract between the parties, though, if there is one, that contract will govern the parties' rights; if there is an actual contract, it must comply with s. 2; but that does not affect the legal presumptions or inferences which arise when there is a mere deposit.

I accept that there need not be an express contract between the depositor of the title deeds and the person with whom they are deposited for an equitable mortgage to arise (subject to s. 2). But I have already stated why it is clear from the authorities that the deposit is treated as rebuttable evidence of a contract to mortgage. Oral evidence is admissible to establish whether or not a deposit was intended to create a mortgage security, whether or not the original deposit was intended at the outset to be security for further advances, whether or not it was agreed subsequently that that deposit should be security for further advances and whether or not any memorandum of agreement accurately stated the terms of the contract or was complete. To allow inquiries of this sort after the 1989 Act in order to determine whether an equitable mortgage has been created and on what terms seems to me to be wholly inconsistent with the philosophy of s. 2, requiring as it does that the contract be made by a single document containing all the terms of the agreement if it is to be valid.

(5)   Mr Pymont then submitted that it is well established that an act of part performance could only be relied upon if it were an act done by the person seeking to enforce the contract. He said that that requirement is not fulfilled if a plaintiff, with whom the title deeds are deposited, seeks to rely on the defendant's act of depositing the title deeds.

It is clear that the rule relating to the creation of an equitable mortgage by deposit proceeded on the footing that the act of deposit constituted a sufficient act of part performance of the presumed agreement to mortgage. I accept that that is contrary to the normal rule that an act of part performance can only be relied upon if done by the plaintiff and not the defendant. But in *Maddison* v *Alderson* (1878) 8 App Cas 467 at 480 Lord Selborne LC said that the law of equitable mortgage by deposit of title deeds depended upon the same principles as the cases of part performance to which he had been referring, and in each of which a valid contract was an essential feature. In *Re Beetham, ex parte Broderick* (1886) 18 QBD 380 the Divisonal Court considered whether certain facts were sufficient to establish an equitable mortgage by deposit of title deeds. Cave J (with whom Wills J agreed) said (at 382–383):

> The law on the subject . . . forms a branch of the equitable doctrine of the specific performance of oral contracts relating to land based on part performance. It has been held that there is an inference from the mere deposit of title deeds that it was intended to give an interest in the land, and in that way there is something more than a mere oral contract, something in the nature of part performance, so as to take the case out of the Statute of Frauds.

. . . To the extent that part performance is an essential part of the rationale of the creation of an equitable mortgage by the deposit of title deeds, that too is inconsistent with the new philosophy of the 1989 Act. As the Law Commission said in its report (para. 4.13):

Inherent in the recommendation that contracts should be made in writing is the consequence that part performance would no longer have a role to play in contracts concerning land.

(6)   Mr Pymont then submitted that in other situations equity treats void dispositions (eg void leases and void mortgages) as agreements to dispose of what the disponor can dispose. He said that there was nothing in the Law Commission's report or in the problems there addressed to suggest that s. 2 was intended to affect such agreements.

I have already referred to the express reference in the Law Commission's report to the intention to include in its proposals contracts to grant mortgages. In the same paragraph (para. 4.3) it was made clear that contracts to grant leases were also to be included. In my judgment, for the like reasons to those given in (2) above, the absence from the report of express mention of the effect of void dispositions as agreements to dispose cannot alter the effect of s. 2.

(7)   Mr Pymont submitted that although equity will presume to infer an agreement from the deposit of title deeds, it does not follow that for all purposes the parties' rights are to be treated as if they lie in contract.

He sought to derive support for this proposition from the remarks of Hoffman J in *Spiro v Glencrown Properties Ltd* [1991] 1 All ER 600 at 606. There that judge was considering how, for the purposes of the 1989 Act, an option to buy land should be characterised. He pointed out that an option was neither an offer nor a conditional contract, not having all the incidents of the standard form of either of those concepts, and said that each analogy is in the proper context a valid way of characterising the situation created by an option. He continued:

The question in this case is not whether one analogy is true and the other false, but which is appropriate to be used in the construction of s. 2 of the Law of Property (Miscellaneous Provisions) Act 1989.

He concluded, not that the option fell outside the scope of s. 2, but that it came within it. In the present case, for the reasons given, it seems to me clear that the deposit of title deeds takes effect as a contract to mortgage and as such falls within s. 2. . . .

I therefore conclude that by reason of s. 2, the mere deposit of title deeds by way of security cannot any longer create a mortgage or charge. . . .

29.4   Equitable Mortgages of Equitable Interests

LAW OF PROPERTY ACT 1925

53.   Instruments required to be in writing

(1)   Subject to the provisions hereinafter contained with respect to the creation of interests in land by parol—

(a)   no interest in land can be created or disposed of except by writing signed by the person creating or conveying the same, or by his agent thereunto lawfully authorised in writing, or by will, or by operation of law;

(b)   a declaration of trust respecting any land or any interest therein must be manifested and proved by some writing signed by some person who is able to declare such trust or by his will;

(c)   a disposition of an equitable interest or trust subsisting at the time of the disposition, must be in writing signed by the person disposing of the same, or by his agent thereunto lawfully authorised in writing or by will.

(2)   This section does not affect the creation or operation of resulting, implied or constructive trusts.

CHAPTER THIRTY

THE REMEDIES OF MORTGAGEES

30.1 Introduction

Radcliffe, G. R. Y. and Cross, G., The English Legal System, 3rd edn, London: Butterworth & Co., 1954, p. 137

. . . A mortgage in the seventeenth century took the form of a conveyance of the property intended as security by the borrower to the lender, with a stipulation that if the money lent was repaid with interest on a given day the lender would reconvey the property to the borrower. If the money was not repaid the property would, according to the tenor of the bond, become the lender's. Cases, however, might arise in which it would be inequitable to hold that the property was forfeited for non-payment on the fixed day. For instance, the lender might intentionally evade payment by hiding or some unexpected accident might prevent the borrower from having the money ready. In such cases, since the common law adhered to the letter of the bond, equity gave relief, provided the money with interest and any costs which the lender had incurred were paid within a reasonable time. Gradually it came to be felt that the true object of the conveyance at law was to give the lender security for repayment of his loan and not to give him the chance of making a profit by forfeiting the estate, and that the lender ought not to be able in any case to claim to retain the security if his money was forthcoming from the borrower within a reasonable time of his demanding it. Thus there grew up the doctrine that although the time fixed at law for redemption was passed the borrower still had in equity a right to redeem which could only be extinguished by the lender's applying to the Chancery to destroy it. The Chancery would then calculate what was due, give the borrower six months to pay, and on his default declare the estate forfeited in equity as well as law to the lender.

The right to redeem a mortgaged estate by application to the Chancery was known as an 'equity of redemption' and was viewed by the seventeenth-century Chancellors as an equitable estate in the property remaining in the borrower. This estate could be dealt with by its owner with the same freedom with which a beneficiary could deal with an equitable interest in land held on trust for him by a trustee. Since a very large proportion of the land in the country was either held by trustees or incumbered with mortgages a great amount of the litigation regarding real property found its way into the Court of Chancery. This foothold which the Chancery gained in the sphere of the land law in the eighteenth century by reason of its jurisdiction in cases of equitable interests under settlements and over mortgages enabled the court in the nineteenth century, after the Court of Chancery Procedure Act 1852, gave it power to decide for itself the true construction of legal as opposed to equitable limitations of land without having to submit these questions to the common law courts, gradually to draw nearly the whole land law into its orbit. Thus to-day the branch of the law which was once the special province of the common lawyers in the Temple is now the recognised sphere of the equity lawyer in Lincoln's Inn. . . .

30.2 Foreclosure

30.2.1 FORECLOSURE AND DWELLING HOUSES

(See s. 8(3) of the Administration of Justice Act 1973 at **30.4.1.2.**)

30.3 The Mortgagee's Statutory Power of Sale

LAW OF PROPERTY ACT 1925
as amended by the Trusts of Land etc. Act 1996

101. **Powers incident to estate or interest of mortgage**

(1) A mortgagee, where the mortgage is made by deed, shall, by virtue of this Act, have the following powers, to the like extent as if they had been in terms conferred by the mortgage deed, but not further (namely):—

(i) A power, when the mortgage money has become due, to sell, or to concur with any other person in selling, the mortgaged property, or any part thereof, either subject to prior charges or not, and either together or in lots, by public auction or by private contract, subject to such conditions respecting title, or evidence of title, or other matter, as the mortgagee thinks fit, with power to vary any contract for sale, and to buy in at an auction, or to rescind any contract for sale, and to re-sell, without being answerable for any loss occasioned thereby; and

(ii) A power, at any time after the date of the mortgage deed, to insure and keep insured against loss or damage by fire any building, or any effects or property of an insurable nature, whether affixed to the freehold or not, being or forming part of the property which or an estate or interest wherein is mortgaged, and the premiums paid for any such insurance shall be a charge on the mortgaged property or estate or interest, in addition to the mortgage money, and with the same priority, and with interest at the same rate, as the mortgage money; and

(iii) A power, when the mortgage money has become due, to appoint a receiver of the income of the mortgaged property, or any part thereof; or, if the mortgaged property consists of an interest in income, or of a rentcharge or an annual or other periodical sum, a receiver of that property or any part thereof; and

(iv) A power, while the mortgagee is in possession, to cut and sell timber and other trees ripe for cutting, and not planted or left standing for shelter or ornament, or to contract for any such cutting and sale, to be completed within any time not exceeding twelve months from the making of the contract.

(2) Where the mortgage deed is executed after the thirty-first day of December, nineteen hundred and eleven, the power of sale aforesaid includes the following powers as incident thereto (namely):—

(i) A power to impose or reserve or make binding, as far as the law permits, by covenant, condition, or otherwise, on the unsold part of the mortgaged property or any part thereof, or on the purchaser and any property sold, any restriction or reservation with respect to building on or other user of land, or with respect to mines and minerals, or for the purpose of the more beneficial working thereof, or with respect to any other thing:

(ii) A power to sell the mortgaged property, or any part thereof, or all or any mines and minerals apart from the surface:—

(a) With or without a grant or reservation of rights of way, rights of water, easements, rights, and privileges for or connected with building or other purposes in relation to the property remaining in mortgage or any part thereof, or to any property sold: and

(b) With or without an exception or reservation of all or any of the mines and minerals in or under the mortgaged property, and with or without a grant or reservation of powers of working, wayleaves, or rights of way, rights of water and drainage and other powers, easements, rights, and privileges for or connected with mining purposes in relation to the property remaining unsold or any part thereof, or to any property sold: and

(c)   With or without covenants by the purchaser to expend money on the land sold.

(3)   The provisions of this Act relating to the foregoing powers, comprised either in this section, or in any other section regulating the exercise of those powers, may be varied or extended by the mortgage deed, and, as so varied or extended, shall, as far as may be, operate in the like manner and with all the like incidents, effects, and consequences, as if such variations or extensions were contained in this Act.

(4)   This section applies only if and as far as a contrary intention is not expressed in the mortgage deed, and has effect subject to the terms of the mortgage deed and to the provisions therein contained. . . .

102.   Provision as to mortgages of undivided shares in land

(1)   A person who was before the commencement of this Act a mortgagee of an undivided share in land shall have the same power to sell his [interest under the trust to which the land is subject], as, independently of this Act, he would have had in regard to the share in the land; and shall also have a right to require the [trustees] in whom the land is vested to account to him for the income attributable to that share or to appoint a receiver to receive the same from such trustees corresponding to the right which, independently of this Act, he would have had to take possession or to appoint a receiver of the rents and profits attributable to the same share.

(2)   The powers conferred by this section are exercisable by the persons deriving title under such mortgagee.

103.   Regulation of exercise of power of sale

A mortgagee shall not exercise the power of sale conferred by this Act unless and until—

(i)   Notice requiring payment of the mortgage money has been served on the mortgagor or one of two or more mortgagors, and default has been made in payment of the mortgage money, or of part thereof, for three months after such service; or

(ii)   Some interest under the mortgage is in arrear and unpaid for two months after becoming due; or

(iii)   There has been a breach of some provision contained in the mortgage deed or in this Act, or in an enactment replaced by this Act, and on the part of the mortgagor, or of some person concurring in making the mortgage, to be observed or performed, other than and besides a covenant for payment of the mortgage money or interest thereon.

30.3.1   MORTGAGEE'S DUTIES ON SELLING THE PROPERTY

CUCKMERE BRICK CO. LTD v MUTUAL FINANCE LTD [1971] 2 All ER 633,
Court of Appeal

FACTS: A property company owned a sizeable vacant site on the edge of Maidstone. The company had planning permission to develop the site for houses or flats. The mortgagees exercised their power of sale. They sold by auction. The adverts for the auction mentioned that there was planning permission for houses, but not the permission for flats. Because of this omission the site did not fetch as high a price as it should have.
HELD: The mortgagee had to account for the difference in price between what should have been obtained and what was actually obtained.

SALMON LJ: . . . It is well settled that a mortgagee is not a trustee of the power of sale for the mortgagor. Once the power has accrued, the mortgagee is entitled to exercise it for his own purposes whenever he chooses to do so. It matters not that the moment may be unpropitious and that by waiting a higher price could be obtained. He has the right to realise his security by turning it into money when he likes. Nor, in my view, is there anything to prevent a mortgagee from accepting the best bid he can get at an auction, even though the auction is badly attended and the bidding exceptionally low. Providing none of those adverse factors is due to any fault of the mortgagee, he can do as he likes. If the mortgagee's interests, as he sees them, conflict with those of the mortgagor, the mortgagee can give preference to his own interests, which of course he could not do were he a trustee of the power of sale for the mortgagor.

Counsel for the defendants contends that the mortgagee's sole obligation to the mortgagor in relation to a sale is to act in good faith; there is no duty of care, and accordingly no question of negligence by the mortgagee in the conduct of the sale can arise. If this contention is correct it follows that, even on the facts found by the learned judge, the defendants should have succeeded. It is impossible to pretend that the state of the authorities on this branch of the law is entirely satisfactory. There are some dicta which suggest that unless a mortgagee acts in bad faith he is safe. His only obligation to the mortgagor is not to cheat him. There are other *dicta* which suggest that, in addition to the duty of acting in good faith, the mortgagee is under a duty to take reasonable care to obtain whatever is the true market value of the mortgaged property at the moment he chooses to sell it: compare, for example, *Kennedy* v *de Trafford* [1896] 1 Ch 762 with *Tomlin* v *Luce* (1889) 43 ChD 191. The proposition that the mortgagee owes both duties, in my judgment, represents the true view of the law. Approaching the matter first of all on principle, it is to be observed that if the sale yields a surplus over the amount owed under the mortgage, the mortgagee holds this surplus in trust for the mortgagor. If the sale shows a deficiency, the mortgagor has to make it good out of his own pocket. The mortgagor is vitally affected by the result of the sale but its preparation and conduct is left entirely in the hands of the mortgagee. The proximity between them could scarcely be closer. Surely they are 'neighbours'. Given that the power of sale is for the benefit of the mortgagee and that he is entitled to choose the moment to sell which suits him, it would be strange indeed if he were under no legal obligation to take reasonable care to obtain what I call the true market value at the date of the sale. Some of the textbooks refer to the 'proper price', others to the 'best price'. Vaisey J in *Reliance Permanent Building Society* v *Harwood-Stamper* [1944] 2 All ER 75, seems to have attached great importance to the difference between these two descriptions of 'price'. My difficulty is that I cannot see any real difference between them. 'Proper price' is perhaps a little nebulous, and 'the best price' may suggest an exceptionally high price. That is why I prefer to call it 'the true market value'.

. . . I accordingly conclude, both on principle and authority, that a mortgagee in exercising his power of sale does owe a duty to take reasonable precaution to obtain the true market value of the mortgaged property at the date on which he decides to sell it. No doubt in deciding whether he has fallen short of that duty, the facts must be looked at broadly and he will not be adjudged to be in default unless he is plainly on the wrong side of the line.

CHINA AND SOUTH SEA BANK LTD v *TAN* [1989] 3 All ER 839, Privy Council

FACTS: A surety had guaranteed the repayment of a loan which the plaintiff bank had made to a company. The company defaulted on the loan at a time when the shares in the company were adequate security for the loan. However, the bank did not enforce its security (by selling the shares) until the shares were virtually worthless. The bank sought repayment of the loan under the guarantee given by the surety. The surety, in his defence, argued that the bank owed him a duty to have sold the shares at the time when the proceeds would have been sufficient to pay off the loan.
HELD: The surety was obliged to pay-off the company's debt to the bank.

LORD TEMPLEMAN: . . . If the creditor does nothing and the debtor declines into bankruptcy the mortgaged securities become valueless and if the surety decamps abroad the creditor loses his money. If disaster strikes the debtor and the mortgaged securities but the surety remains capable of repaying the debt then the creditor loses nothing. The surety contracts to pay if the debtor does not pay and the surety is bound by his contract. If the surety, perhaps less indolent or less well protected than the creditor, is worried that the mortgaged securities may decline in value then the surety may request the creditor to sell and if the creditor remains idle then the surety may bustle about, pay off the debt, take over the benefit of the securities and sell them. No creditor could carry on the business of lending if he could become liable to a mortgagee and to a surety or to either of them for a decline in value of mortgaged property, unless the creditor was personally responsible for the decline. Applying the rule as specified by Pollock CB in *Watts* v *Shuttleworth* (1860) 5 H & N 235 at 247–248, 157 ER 1171 at 1176, it appears to their Lordships that in the present case the creditor did no act injurious to the surety, did no act inconsistent with the rights of the surety and the creditor did not omit any act which his duty enjoyed him to do. The creditor was not under a duty to exercise his power of sale over the mortgaged securities at any particular time or at all. . . .

PARKER-TWEEDALE v DUNBAR BANK PLC AND OTHERS (No. 1) [1990] 2 All ER 577, Court of Appeal

FACTS: A matrimonial home was held by the wife on trust for sale for herself and her husband. Having defaulted in repaying a loan to the defendant bank, which it had secured by way of mortgage on the matrimonial home, the bank took possession and sold the house. The house was sold to a development company for £575,000 and one week later it was sold on to another company for £700,000. The husband brought this present action against the bank, claiming that the bank had owed him a duty of care to obtain a proper price upon sale of the property.

HELD: The duty of care owed by the bank to the mortgagor (the wife) did not extend to the husband, whose only interest in the house was a beneficial interest under a trust for sale.

NOURSE LJ: . . . It was settled by the decision of this court in *Cuckmere Brick Co. Ltd* v *Mutual Finance Ltd* [1972] 2 All ER 633, [1971] Ch 949 that a mortgagee, although he may exercise his power of sale at any time of his own choice, owes the mortgagor a duty to take reasonable care to obtain a proper price for the mortgaged property at that time. But there is no support, either in the authorities or on principle, for the proposition that where the mortgagor is a trustee, even a bare trustee, of the mortgaged property a like duty is owed to a beneficiary under the trust of whose interest the mortgagee has notice.

In seeking to support that proposition the plaintiff relied on the decision of this court in *Jarrett* v *Barclays Bank Ltd* [1946] 2 All ER 266, [1947] Ch 187. For reasons which were stated by Peter Gibson J and need not be repeated here, that case does not assist him. He also relied on the following passage in the judgment of Salmon LJ in *Cuckmere Brick Co. Ltd* v *Mutual Finance Ltd* [1971] 2 All ER 633 at 643–644, [1971] Ch 949 at 966:

> Approaching the matter first of all on principle, it is to be observed that if the sale yields a surplus over the amount owed under the mortgage, the mortgagee holds this surplus in trust for the mortgagor. If the sale shows a deficiency, the mortgagor has to make it good out of his own pocket. The mortgagor is vitally affected by the result of the sale but its preparation and conduct is left entirely in the hands of the mortgagee. The proximity between them could scarcely be closer. Surely they are 'neighbours'. Given that the power of sale is for the benefit of the mortgagee and that he is entitled to choose the moment to sell which suits him, it would be strange indeed if he were under no legal obligation to take reasonable care to obtain what I call the true market value at the date of the sale.

This reference to 'neighbours' has enabled the plaintiff to argue that the duty is owed to all those who are within the neighbourhood principle, i.e. to adapt the words of Lord Atkin in *Donoghue (or M'Alister)* v *Stevenson* [1932] AC 562 at 580–581, [1932] All ER Rep 1 at 11–12, to all persons who are so closely and directly affected by the sale that the mortgagee ought reasonably to have them in contemplation as being so affected when he is directing his mind to the sale. Further support for the application of the neighbourhood principle in this context can be gained from the judgment of Lord Denning MR in *Standard Chartered Bank Ltd* v *Walker* [1982] 3 All ER 938 at 942, [1982] 1 WLR 1410 at 1415, where it was held that the duty to take reasonable care to obtain a proper price was owed to a surety for the mortgage debt as well as to the mortgagor himself.

In my respectful opinion it is both unnecessary and confusing for the duties owed by a mortgagee to the mortgagor and the surety, if there is one, to be expressed in terms of the tort of negligence. The authorities which were considered in the careful judgments of this court in *Cuckmere Brick Co. Ltd* v *Mutual Finance Ltd* demonstrate that the duty owed by the mortgagee to the mortgagor was recognised by equity as arising out of the particular relationship between them. Thus Salmon LJ himself said ([1971] 2 All ER 633 at 644, [1971] Ch 949 at 967):

It would seem, therefore, that many years before the modern development of the law of negligence, the courts of equity had laid down a doctrine in relation to mortgages which is entirely consonant with the general principles later evolved by the common law.

The duty owed to the surety arises in the same way. In *China and South Sea Bank Ltd* v *Tan* [1989] 3 All ER 839 at 841, [1990] 2 WLR 56 at 58 Lord Templeman, in delivering the judgment of the Privy Council, having pointed out that the surety in that case admitted that the moneys secured by the guarantee were due, continued:

But the surety claims that the creditor owed the surety a duty to exercise the power of sale conferred by the mortgage and in that case the liability of the surety under the guarantee would either have been eliminated or very much reduced. The Court of Appeal [in Hong Kong] sought to find such a duty in the tort of negligence but the tort of negligence has not yet subsumed all torts and does not supplant the principles of equity or contradict contractual promises . . . Equity intervenes to protect a surety.

Once it is recognised that the duty owed by the mortgagee to the mortgagor arises out of the particular relationship between them, it is readily apparent that there is no warrant for extending its scope so as to include a beneficiary or beneficiaries under a trust of which the mortgagor is the trustee. The correctness of that view was fully established in the clear and compelling argument of counsel for Dunbar, who drew particular attention to the rights and duties of the trustee to protect the trust property against dissipation or depreciation in value and the impracticabilities and potential rights of double recovery inherent in giving the beneficiary an additional right to sue the mortgagee, a right which is in any event unnecessary.

The only exception for which counsel for Dunbar allowed was the special case where the trustee has unreasonably refused to sue on behalf of the trust or has committed some other breach of its duties to the beneficiaries, e.g. by consenting to an improvident sale, which disables or disqualifies him from acting on behalf of the trust. In such a case the beneficiary is permitted to sue on behalf of the trust. This exception is established by a series of authorities, some of which were recently considered by the Privy Council in *Hayim* v *Citibank NA* [1987] AC 730. In delivering the judgment of their Lordships, Lord Templeman said (at 748):

These authorities demonstrate that a beneficiary has no cause of action against a third party save in special circumstances which embrace a failure, excusable or inexcusable, by the trustees in the performance of the duty owed by the trustees to the beneficiary to protect the trust estate or to protect the interests of the beneficiary in the trust estate.

It is important to emphasise that when a beneficiary sues under the exception he does so in right of the trust and in the room of the trustee. . . .

30.4 Mortgagees Taking Possession

ASHLEY GUARANTEE PLC v *ZACARIA AND ANOTHER* [1993] 1 All ER 254,
Court of Appeal

FACTS: The plaintiff mortgagee lent money to a company which was secured by mortgage on the defendant's family home. The company defaulted in re-payment of the loan and the plaintiff brought an action to recover the sum of £151,000, or in default possession of the family home. The defendants contended that the company had counter-claims for unliquidated damages against the plaintiff, which if successful would yield funds sufficient to re-pay the loan. Accordingly, the defendants resisted the plaintiff's action for possession. HELD: The mortgagee was entitled to enter into possession at any time, subject only to the usual limitations on the re-possession of residential property. The existence of counter-claims was no ground for postponing possession and sale of the family home. The fact that the defendants were guarantors of the loan and not the principal debtors was no ground for allowing them to resist the order for possession.

NOURSE LJ: . . . Contract and statute apart, a legal mortgagee's right to possession of the mortgaged property cannot be defeated by a cross-claim on the part of the mortgagor, even if it is both liquidated and admitted and even if it exceeds the amount of the mortgage arrears.

. . . In my judgment that question must be answered in the negative. I can see no distinction in principle between a case where the mortgagor is the principal debtor of the mortgagee and one where he is only a guarantor. In each case the mortgagee has, as an incident of his estate in the land, a right to possession of the mortgaged property. In each case the cross-claims cannot be unilaterally appropriated in discharge of the mortgage debt. The fact that in the latter case the mortgagor is not primarily liable for payment of the debt is immaterial. When he comes to be made liable his position vis-à-vis the appropriation of the cross-claims is at best no different from, and certainly cannot be better than, that of a mortgagor who is the primary debtor. . . .

30.4.1   MORTGAGEE TAKING POSSESSION OF A DWELLING-HOUSE

CHELTENHAM AND GLOUCESTER PLC v KRAUSZ AND ANOTHER
[1997] 1 All ER 21, Court of Appeal

FACTS: The defendants defaulted on a loan of £58,300 from the plaintiff building society which was secured by a mortgage on their home. Following the issue of a warrant for possession which fell due for execution on 12 June 1995, the defendants negotiated a sale of the property for £65,000. However, by that time the mortgage debt amounted to some £83,000 and the plaintiff refused to agree to the sale on the ground that a higher price could be obtained. The defendants thereafter applied to the county court for an order suspending possession on the ground that they had found a purchaser and gave notice of their intention to apply to the High Court for an order for sale pursuant to s. 91 of the Law of Property Act 1925. The district judge dismissed their application. The county court judge allowed the defendants' appeal and ordered a stay of the warrant for possession pending determination of the application under s. 91. The plaintiff appealed.

HELD: The court had no power under s. 36 of the Administration of Justice Act 1970 (as amended by s. 8 of the Administration of Justice Act 1973) to suspend a warrant for possession of mortgaged property in order to enable the mortgagor to make an application for sale under s. 91 of the Law of Property Act 1925 where the proceeds of sale would not discharge the mortgage debt fully, unless other funds were available to the mortgagor to make up the shortfall.

PHILLIPS LJ: . . . This appeal requires consideration of the inter-relationship of two areas of the law relating to the mortgage of a dwelling house: (1) the circumstances in which the mortgagor is entitled to an order for the sale of the mortgaged property; and (2) the circumstances in which the court has jurisdiction to suspend entry into possession of the dwelling house by the mortgagee.

Mortgagor's right of sale
Section 91 of the 1925 Act provides as follows:

(1)   Any person entitled to redeem mortgaged property may have a judgment or order for sale instead of for redemption in an action brought by him either for redemption alone, or for sale alone, or for sale or redemption in the alternative.

(2)   In any action, whether for foreclosure, or for redemption, or for sale, or for the raising and payment in any manner of mortgage money, the court, on the request of the mortgagee, or of any person interested either in the mortgage money or in the right of redemption, and, notwithstanding that—(a) any other person dissents; or (b) the mortgagee or any person so interested does not appear in the action; and without allowing any time for redemption or for payment of any mortgage money, may direct a sale of the mortgaged property, on such terms as it thinks fit, including the deposit in court of a reasonable sum fixed by the court to meet the expenses of sale and to secure performance of the terms . . .

The origin and history of these provisions are described by Nicholls V-C in *Palk* v *Mortgage Services Funding plc* [1993] 2 All ER 481 at 484. Nicholls V-C also cited the statement of Jessel MR in *Union Bank of London* v *Ingram* (1882) 20 Ch D 463 at 464 about the essentially identical provisions of s. 25(2) of the Conveyancing and Law of Property Act 1881:

> The Act is a remedial Act, one effect of it being to allow a mortgagor whose property is worth more than the mortgage-money, but who cannot raise it, to obtain a sale and get the benefit of the surplus.

Until *Palk's* case it was the practice of the Chancery court only to entertain an application for sale by the mortgagor if the proceeds of sale were expected to be sufficient to discharge the entirety of the mortgage debt. In such circumstances the mortgagor might initiate proceedings by bringing an action for sale under s. 91(1), or, if the mortgagee sought to foreclose, the mortgagor could apply for an order for sale in place of foreclosure. The practice thus reflected the heading to s. 91: Sale of mortgaged property in action for redemption or foreclosure.

Palk's case established, for the first time, that the court has power under s. 91(2) to make an order for sale on the application of a mortgagor, notwithstanding that the proceeds of sale will be insufficient to discharge the mortgage debt. . . .

Barrett v *Halifax Building Society* (1995) 28 HLR 634 marks the next development in this area of the law, and one which demonstrates the importance of the present appeal. In that case the plaintiffs had mortgaged their home and then defaulted on their repayment obligations. The situation was one of negative equity—the mortgage debt substantially exceeded the value of their home. On 6 August 1992 the mortgagees obtained a possession order, with a view to exercising their power of sale. There were numerous suspensions of this order to give the plaintiffs a chance to discharge the instalment arrears. What then occurred was explained by the judge as follows (at 636):

> On 6 March 1995 there was a further suspension of the order for the purpose of leaving [the] mortgagors in possession of the property themselves to find a buyer notwithstanding that there was a deficit over the sum secured so that the property would be on the market, lived in and without it becoming known to the market that it was subject to a forced sale, thereby increasing the realisations available to discharge at least part of the amount due.

The plaintiffs then applied to the Chancery court for an order for sale pursuant to s. 91 of the 1925 Act. By the time that their action came on for hearing they had negotiated a sale of the property, subject to contract. They sought an order that they be permitted to proceed with that sale and to remain in possession until completion. The judge summarised the evidence on which they relied as follows (at 637):

> The evidence of the plaintiffs, including the expert evidence of a valuer, is that it is a recognised feature of today's property market that where a mortgagee obtains possession of property and sells in the exercise of its power of sale it is able to obtain a price which is usually not as good as the price which might have been obtained by the mortgagor had the mortgagor remained in possession and the fact of the forced sale not become apparent. It is also the plaintiffs' evidence that if the mortgagee building society were to take over the sale or were now to obtain possession and proceed to sell itself there would be likely to be a delay of some months at least before a fresh purchaser could be found and a sale completed.

The mortgagees resisted the order sought. They did not contend that they would be able to obtain a better price, but urged that if the sale went ahead it would break their established policy not to permit borrowers with negative equity themselves to conduct the sale of their property without also at the same time making proposals for the repayment of any resulting deficit. The judge held that this was not a material circumstance which he ought to take into account when exercising his discretion. He held (at 640):

I am left, therefore, with a case [in] which, on the evidence before me, there is no discernible advantage to the building society in refusing to allow this sale to complete, whereas there is an obvious advantage to the mortgagors to complete their proposed sale at what is accepted as the best price that is likely to be obtainable in the current market.

He proceeded to grant the plaintiffs the order that they sought.

Just as in *Palk's* case the report does not suggest that in *Barrett's* case any challenge was made by the mortgagees to the order suspending possession pending the plaintiffs' application to the Chancery court.

The consequences of the procedure followed in *Barrett's* case appear to me to be far reaching. In any case in which there is negative equity, it will be open to the mortgagor to resist an order for possession on the ground that he wishes to obtain a better price by remaining in possession and selling the property himself. In not every case will the primary motive for such an application be the wish to obtain a better price than that which the mortgagee is likely to obtain on a forced sale. Often the mortgagor will be anxious to postpone for as long as possible the evil day when he has to leave his home. This court has ample experience of hopeless applications for leave to appeal against possession orders designed to achieve just that end. There will be a danger, if the mortgagee does not obtain possession, that the mortgagor will delay the realisation of the property by seeking too high a price, or deliberately procrastinating on completion. At present there is a simple procedure for seeking possession in the county court and the issue tends to be whether there are arrears and whether the mortgagor is likely to be able to discharge these in a reasonable time. If possession is to be suspended whenever this appears reasonable in order to give mortgagors the opportunity to sell the property themselves, the courts are going to have to enter into an area of difficult factual inquiry in order to decide in the individual case whether or not this course will be to the common benefit of mortgagor and mortgagee. Furthermore, there will be obvious practical difficulties for mortgagees in monitoring the negotiations of mortgagors who are permitted time to market their properties.

For these reasons, it seems to me that the procedure followed and the decision reached in *Barrett's* case tend fundamentally to undermine the value of the mortgagee's entitlement to possession.

Having touched on the implications of the issue raised in this case I turn to consider whether, in law, the county court has jurisdiction to suspend possession in such circumstances. . . .

The effect of s. 36, as amended, on the power to suspend possession is as follows: (1) the power can be exercised to enable the mortgagor to pay off instalment arrears due under the mortgage agreement from sources other than the sale of the mortgaged property, but (2) if the mortgagor intends to sell the mortgaged property to provide the source of payment, the court must be satisfied that the proceeds will be sufficient to discharge the entirety of the mortgage debt (see *Royal Trust Co. of Canada* v *Markham* [1975] 3 All ER 433 and *National and Provincial Building Society* v *Lloyd* [1996] 1 All ER 630).

Before the decision in *Palk* it seemed that s. 36 of the 1970 Act and s. 91 of the 1925 Act were complementary. An application under s. 91 would only be contemplated where the proceeds of sale were expected to exceed the mortgage debt. In these circumstances s. 36 gave the court the power to suspend possession in order to enable an application for sale under s. 91 to be made. It is, however, quite clear that s. 36 does not empower the court to suspend possession in order to permit the mortgagor to sell the mortgaged premises where the proceeds of sale will not suffice to discharge the mortgage debt, unless of course other funds will be available to the mortgagor to make up the shortfall.

A mortgagor seeking relief in the circumstances of *Palk's* case is thus unable to invoke any statutory power to suspend the mortgagee's right to enter into possession.

For the mortgagors, Mr Smith argued that the provisions of s. 36 did not define exclusively the jurisdiction of the court to suspend possession. The section was accurately headed 'Additional powers of court in action by mortgagee for possession of dwelling-house'. The court enjoyed in addition a power to suspend possession as part of its inherent jurisdiction. He referred us to the general statement or principle, albeit in a criminal context, of Lord Morris of Borth-y-Gest in *Connelly* v *DPP* [1964] 2 All ER 401 at 409:

There can be no doubt that a court which is endowed with a particular jurisdiction has powers which are necessary to enable it to act effectively within such jurisdiction. I would regard them as powers which are inherent in its jurisdiction. A court must enjoy such powers in order to enforce its rules of practice and to suppress any abuses of its process and to defeat any attempted thwarting of its process.

Mr Smith elaborated his argument as follows:

On an application by a mortgagor for sale under s. 91 of the 1925 Act the court has power to order that the mortgagor be entrusted with the sale and that he remain in possession while effecting the sale (see *Barrett*). Should the mortgagee attempt to frustrate such an order by entering into possession, the court seized of the s. 91 application must have an inherent power to restrain him from doing so. In these circumstances, the county court must also have an inherent power to suspend an order or warrant for possession, at least for such short period as is necessary to enable the mortgagor to make a s. 91 application.

In my judgment this argument breaks down at a number of stages.

In *Royal Trust Co. of Canada* v *Markham* Sir John Pennycuick, when delivering the leading judgment of this court, cited with approval the passage from the judgment of Russell J in *Caunt's* case which I have myself cited above. He then said ([1975] 3 All ER 433 at 436–437):

A characteristic instance in which that sole exception is applicable is where the mortgagor has entered or is about to enter into a contract for the sale of the property at a price which will enable the mortgage to be paid off in full . . . So, as the law stood before 1970, the mortgagee had a right, subject only to that one exception mentioned by Russell J, to possession, and it was not in the power of the court to refuse him possession.

Megaw LJ added ([1975] 3 All ER 433 at 440):

There was, as I think is clear, no power, before the enactment of s. 36 of the Administration of Justice Act 1970, for a court to grant a stay or suspension of execution of an order for possession in a mortgagees' action, such as the present one, based on default in payment or breach of other obligations. Therefore, if there be such power to suspend or stay the execution of the order for possession, it can come only from the provisions of s. 36 of the 1970 Act as amended by s. 8 of the Administration of Justice Act 1973.

In my judgment, the very specific delimitation of the power given by s. 36 makes it clear that the legislature did not intend that the court should have any wider jurisdiction to curtail the mortgagee's right to possession. That right enables the mortgagee to exercise his power of sale in the manner he chooses and in the confidence that he can offer a purchaser vacant possession. Section 36 circumscribes that right where the proceeds of sale are likely to discharge the mortgage debt. It does not do so where the mortgage debt will not be fully discharged, and it is in those circumstances that the mortgagee's rights are of particular importance.

I recognise the principle of the inherent jurisdiction of the court, as explained by Lord Morris in *Connelly* v *DPP*, but I question whether that principle can justify the court in exercising its power to order a sale of mortgaged property under s. 91 in circumstances where the mortgagee is seeking to enter into possession in order to sell property in which there is negative equity and where the sole object with which the mortgagor seeks that order is to prevent the mortgagee exercising his right to possession so that the mortgagor can negotiate his own sale while in possession.

Even if one assumes that the Chancery court has power to order sale of mortgaged property on terms that displace the mortgagee's right to possession, I do not consider that it follows from this that the county court, as part of its inherent jurisdiction, can properly suspend an order or warrant for possession in order to enable a mortgagor to apply to the High Court for an order under s. 91. It seems to me incumbent on the mortgagor to seek from the High Court any relief which that court is empowered to give before the possession warrant takes effect.

In the present case the judge purported in 1995 to suspend a warrant for possession that was properly issued pursuant to an order for possession made in 1991. For the reasons I have given, I consider that he had no jurisdiction to make such an order and this appeal should be allowed.

30.4.1.1   The 1970 'reform'

ADMINISTRATION OF JUSTICE ACT 1970

36. Additional powers of court in action by mortgagee for possession of dwelling-house

(1)   Where the mortgagee under a mortgage of land which consists of or includes a dwelling-house brings an action in which he claims possession of the mortgaged property, not being an action for foreclosure in which a claim for possession of the mortgaged property is also made, the court may exercise any of the powers conferred on it by subsection (2) below if it appears to the court that in the event of its exercising the power the mortgagor is likely to be able within a reasonable period to pay any sums due under the mortgage or to remedy a default consisting of a breach of any other obligation arising under or by virtue of the mortgage.

(2)   The court—

   (a)   may adjourn the proceedings, or

   (b)   on giving judgment, or making an order, for delivery of possession of the mortgaged property, or at any time before the execution of such judgment or order, may—

      (i)   stay or suspend execution of the judgment or order, or

      (ii)   postpone the date for delivery of possession,

for such period or periods as the court thinks reasonable.

(3)   Any such adjournment, stay, suspension or postponement as is referred to in subsection (2) above may be made subject to such conditions with regard to payment by the mortgagor of any sum secured by the mortgage or the remedying of any default as the court thinks fit.

(4)   The court may from time to time vary or revoke any condition imposed by virtue of this section. . . .

30.4.1.2   A further 'reform' in 1973

ADMINISTRATION OF JUSTICE ACT 1973

8. Extension of powers of court in action by mortgagee of dwelling-house

(1)   Where by a mortgage of land which consists of or includes a dwelling-house, or by any agreement between the mortgagee under such a mortgage and the mortgagor, the mortgagor is entitled or is to be permitted to pay the principal sum secured by instalments or otherwise to defer payment of it in whole or in part, but provision is also made for earlier payment in the event of any default by the mortgagor or of a demand by the mortgagee or otherwise, then for purposes of section 36 of the Administration of Justice Act 1970 (under which a court has power to delay giving a mortgagee possession of the mortgaged property so as to allow the mortgagor a reasonable time to pay any sums due under the mortgage) a court may treat as due under the mortgage on account of the principal sum secured and of interest on it only such amounts as the mortgagor would have expected to be required to pay if there had been no such provision for earlier payment.

(2)   A court shall not exercise by virtue of subsection (1) above the powers conferred by section 36 of the Administration of Justice Act 1970 unless it appears to the court not only that the mortgagor is likely to be able within a reasonable period to pay any amounts regarded (in accordance with subsection (1) above) as due on account of the principal sum secured, together with the interest on those amounts, but also that he is likely to be able by the end of that period to pay any further amounts that he would have expected to be required to pay by then on account of that sum and of interest on it if there had been no such provision as is referred to in subsection (1) above for earlier payment.

(3)   Where subsection (1) above would apply to an action in which a mortgagee only claimed possession of the mortgaged property, and the mortgagee brings an action for

foreclosure (with or without also claiming possession of the property), then section 36 of the Administration of Justice Act 1970 together with subsections (1) and (2) above shall apply as they would apply if it were an action in which the mortgagee only claimed possession of the mortgaged property, except that—

    (a)   section 36(2)(b) shall apply only in relation to any claim for possession; and

    (b)   section 36(5) shall not apply. . . .

CHELTENHAM AND GLOUCESTER BUILDING SOCIETY v NORGAN
[1996] 1 All ER 449, Court of Appeal

FACTS: Mrs Norgan had lived with her husband and five sons in a period farmhouse in Wiltshire with eight acres of land, total value £225,000. They had borrowed £90,000 from the building society in 1986, on an instalment mortgage. The Cheltenham society was a member of the Council of Mortgage Lenders whose statement of current practice provided means of helping some borrowers in difficulty. Those included lengthening the term of a repayment loan, deferring interest payments for a period and capitalising interest.

HELD: The logic and spirit of the legislation required, especially where the lender was acting within the statement of current practice, that the court should take as its starting point the full term of the mortgage and pose at the outset the question: would it be possible for the borrower to maintain payment-off of the arrears by instalments over that period?

WAITE LJ: . . .

The legal background

The position at common law was that the court had only a very limited jurisdiction to grant relief to a mortgagor in default under the payment terms in the mortgage against the mortgagee's consequent claim to possession. It could do no more than to adjourn the application 'for a short time to afford to the mortgagor a chance of paying off the mortgagee in full or otherwise satisfying him; but this should not be done if there is no reasonable prospect of this occurring' (see *Birmingham Citizens Permanent Building Society* v *Caunt* [1962] 1 All ER 163 at 182 per Russell J). The rigour of this restriction was first mitigated by s. 36 of the Administration of Justice Act 1970, which provides [see **30.4.1.1** above] . . .

The reference in sub-s (1) to 'any sums due under the mortgage' was restrictively interpreted in case law as referring to the entire mortgage debt (see *Halifax Building Society* v *Clark* [1973] 2 All ER 33 at 38 per Pennycuick V-C). The effect was to restrict s. 36 relief in practice to a very limited range of cases—'for, if the mortgagor was already in difficulties with his instalments, the chances of his being able to pay off the whole principal as well in a reasonable time must be considered fairly slim' (see *Habib Bank Ltd* v *Tailor* [1982] 3 All ER 561 at 564 per Oliver LJ). That led to the enactment of s. 8 of the Administration of Justice Act 1973, which provides [see **30.4.1.2** above] . . .

The *Supreme Court Practice 1995* vol. 1, para. 88/5/9 succinctly summarises the effect of those two sections, in the common situation (also applicable in this case) where the whole mortgage debt becomes repayable on default, in this way:

> In such a case a Court may, in exercising its discretion under s. 36, treat the sum due under the mortgage as being only the arrears of instalments or interest. It may exercise its jurisdiction under the section if it appears that the borrower is likely to be able within a reasonable period to bring his payments up-to-date by paying off all arrears at the date of the order and the payments falling due after the date of the order . . .

The editors later comment in the same passage that the question as to what exactly is a 'reasonable period' for bringing the payments up to date is one on which there is little guidance. It is the question which lies at the heart of this appeal.

Dicta in two authorities have been particularly relevant to the debate. They are as follows.

    (1)   *First Middlesbrough Trading and Mortgage Co. Ltd* v *Cunningham* (1974) 28 P & CR 69. This was a case of default under an instalment mortgage. The original mortgage principal was £850 repayable by instalments of capital and interest at the rate of £3 per week. By the date of the hearing before the judge the amount of the instalments in arrear was £142 and

the total balance then owing on the mortgage was £514. The judge had made an order for possession in favour of the mortgagee, but suspended it for so long as the instalments due under the mortgage plus a further specific amount off the arrears were paid weekly. Although s. 8 had by then been enacted, the case had to be decided, because of the date of the hearing at first instance, under s. 36 as interpreted under the previous law, without reference to s. 8. Scarman LJ made it plain that he did not share the interpretation put upon s. 36 in *Halifax* v *Clark* but proceeded on the basis that it was right—ie that the 'sums due' were the whole of the mortgage debt. In determining what would be a reasonable period for repayment of 'any sums due under the mortgage' for the purposes of s. 36(2), he asked that question independently under the separate heads of repayment of the oustanding principal and future interest on the one hand and the repayment of arrears on the other.

As to the former, he said (at 75):

Since the object of the instalment mortgage was, with the consent of the mortgagee, to give the mortgagor the period of the mortgage to repay the capial sum and interest, one begins with a powerful presumption of fact in favour of the period of the mortgage being the 'reasonable period.'

As to the latter he said:

Arrears had, however, arisen. The judge, considering all the circumstances, took the view that the mortgagor would be able to maintain her agreed instalments and to pay a specified sum per week off the arrears on the basis (and I need not go into the detail of it) of the order he in fact made. Those arrears will be paid, under the judge's order, if it be complied with, well within the stipulated period for the repayment of the mortgage by the agreed instalments.

(2)   *Western Bank Ltd* v *Schindler* [1976] 2 All ER 393. That was an instance of a more unusual case, where the mortgagee was seeking possession as of right—that is to say in the absence of any default in payment by the mortgagor—in simple reliance on the legal estate conferred on it under a charge carrying a right to possession as soon (in the vivid phrase) as the ink was dry on it. The Court of Appeal held by a majority (Buckley and Scarman LJJ) that a distinction must be drawn between cases where the mortgagor is in default and those where he is not. In the former (default) case a reasonable period for the purposes of s. 36(2) must be measured 'by what is reasonable for the purposes indicated in the conditional clause in sub-s (1)' (see [1976] 2 All ER 393 at 400, per Buckley LJ); in other words it must be a reasonable period for the mortgagor to 'find the necessary money or remedy the default (see [1976] 2 All ER 393 at 404 per Scarman LJ). In the latter (no default) case Buckley LJ said 'In a suitable case the specified period might even be the whole remaining prospective life of the mortgage' (see [1976] 2 All ER 393 at 400).

Goff LJ dissented from the majority on the issue as to whether s. 36 had any application at all to cases where the mortgagor was not in default, but on the issue (as to which he was in agreement with the other members of the court) as to the application of that section to default cases he said that it was—

clear that the purpose of the section is to enable the court in any of the ways specified in sub-s (2) to grant a limited time, which may of course in a proper case be extended by a further exercise of the statutory powers, within which the mortgagor may put the matter right. (See [1976] 2 All ER 393 at 408.)

The factual background

The appellant, Christina Norgan, has lived with her husband and their family (now consisting of five sons aged from 6 to 18) since 1974 in a period farmhouse in Wiltshire with some eight acres of land, said now to be worth about £225,000. In November 1986 her husband required business finance and he accordingly arranged to realise his half share of the property by selling it to his wife and thus constituting her the sole owner. On 28 November 1986 he conveyed the property into her sole name in consideration of a payment of £90,000 which was financed by means of a mortgage with the Guardian Building Society (Guardian) executed on the same date by the wife, under which the property was charged with repayment to Guardian of a sum of £90,000. The terms of that charge (the mortgage) were that the principal sum should be repaid at the expiration of a term of 22 years with interest at 11.25% payable in monthly instalments. The mortgage was pension-linked and guaranteed by the husband. It was subject to Guardian's standard mortgage conditions, which included a power to vary interest by charging Guardian's standard rate currently in force, and also a provision that if at any time any monthly instalment should be in arrear and unpaid for one month after becoming due, Guardian would be entitled to take possession of the property.

Mr Norgan suffered misfortune in his business activities, as a result of which the appellant, his wife, ran into difficulty in keeping up the interest payments under the mortgage, which began to fall into arrears. In April 1990 Guardian was taken over by the plaintiffs, who were formerly the Cheltenham and Gloucester Building Society and are now Cheltenham and Gloucester plc. I will refer to them simply as 'Cheltenham'. By the date of the Cheltenham take-over the arrears of interest due under the mortgage were in the region of £7,000.

Cheltenham is a member of the Council of Mortgage Lenders, which publishes a statement (the CML statement) of current practice of mortgage lenders when dealing with mortgage arrears and possession cases. The current (February 1995) CML statement contains the following in a section headed 'Alleviating Arrears Problems':

7. Lenders have the following measures which they can use to help some borrowers in arrears difficulties—(a) In the case of a repayment loan the term of the loan can be lengthened, although in most cases this does not make a significant difference to the monthly repayments. (b) An endowment mortgage can be changed to a repayment, or interest only, mortgage with a subsequent reduction in monthly outgoings . . . (c) Part of the interest can be deferred for a period. This is particularly appropriate where there is a temporary shortfall of income (for example, because of an industrial dispute or a temporary illness), or where there has been a rapid increase in interest rates. Lenders would generally be willing to accept, for a reasonable period of time the most the borrower could reasonably afford . . . However, this is not a solution where, because of a permanent reduction in income, a borrower is unable to afford anywhere near the full mortgage repayments and there is no early prospect of a change in the situation [in the future]. (d) Linked to (c) is the possibility of capitalising interest. This is appropriate where arrears have been built up and when full monthly repayments can be resumed. The arrears can be added to the capital sum and repaid over the life of the loan . . .

8. In addition, lenders try to ensure that the borrower is aware of any income support or other social security benefits that may be available, and, in appropriate cases, many advise the borrower to consider letting the property or taking in a lodger . . .

On 14 May 1990 Cheltenham applied to the county court for a possession order. The claimed arrears of interest instalments then stood at £7,216. By the date of the hearing on 12 November of that year this figure had increased to £14,744. The then current rate for the interest instalments was £1,251 per month. The district judge, being told that Mrs Norgan was proposing to refinance the mortgage, made a possession order, but suspended it in the first instance for 28 days, directing that if the arrears were not cleared the mortgagor would be at liberty to apply for a further suspension on terms as to payment of current instalments and a proportion off the arrears. The mortgage was not refinanced, and Mrs Norgan applied for such a suspension, which was granted by the district judge on 17 December 1990, when she varied the suspension terms to provide for payment by Mrs Norgan of the current instalments of interest plus £445 per month off the arrears. Had those conditions been fully complied with, the claimed arrears (amounting by then to £16,023) would have been paid off within about three years.

No payments of the arrears were made, however, and Cheltenham obtained a warrant for possession. On 22 April 1991 the district judge suspended the warrant on the ground that a sum of £11,000 would be paid very shortly, and such a sum was indeed paid by Mrs Norgan in May 1991. There were no further payments, however, during the summer and Cheltenham again applied to issue the warrant. Mrs Norgan obtained a further suspension on terms as to payment of the current instalments of interest and £551 per month off the arrears. There was then a period of substantial improvement in the payment record, but only a slight inroad was made on the claimed arrears. By the autumn of 1992 they stood at £15,000. Nearly a year later (after an interval occupied by exploration of Mrs Norgan's eligibility for payment of housing benefit) the Benefits Agency on 9 September 1993 began payments (backdated to June of that year) to the credit of Mrs Norgan's mortgage account with Cheltenham. The claimed arrears remained substantial, and Cheltenham applied once again to issue the warrant.

That application, together with the mortgagor's cross-application for a further suspension, was heard by the district judge on 28 September 1993. He refused any further suspension and gave leave to issue the warrant, but granted a stay pending the mortgagor's appeal to the judge.

The hearing of that appeal before Judge O'Malley occupied three days, fragmented between dates in November 1993 and February and May 1994. Mrs Norgan appeared in person, with her husband acting as spokesman. Cheltenham was represented by counsel. The judge (as appears from the careful and detailed judgment which he later handed down) was taken through the authorities. He was confronted with the difficulty that the figures could not be agreed. . . .

. . . he followed the course of taking a figure which took some account of the disputed items, by reducing the claimed arrears as at the date of the hearing before him from £23,000 to £20,000, and proceeding on that as an approximate basis for the exercise of his discretion.

He then proceeded to announce his conclusion on the case in the following terms:

What, then, is a reasonable time within which to require the repayment of this sum? There is scant assistance to be derived from the decided cases. The experience of this court in appeals of this kind suggests that a period of two to four years is the maximum that will ordinarily be allowed. It is noteworthy too that District Judge Parmiter, whose article 'Wrongly dispossessed?' (1992) 16 LS Gaz 17 is written to assist mortgagors, refers to a Judicial Studies Board 'recommendation' of two years, with many judges apparently thinking 'in much longer terms'. He makes no reference to the dictum of Scarman LJ, although it is relatively well known to judges exercising this jurisdiction. I am persuaded by Mr Nesbitt that Scarman LJ's starting point, in *First Middlesbrough Trading and Mortgage Co. Ltd* v *Cunningham* (1974) 28 P & CR 69, of the whole of the rest of the term must be viewed in the context which existed before the passing of the 1973 Act. In the result, I consider that a reasonable time for the defendant to get up to date with the mortgage payments should be a far shorter period than that contended for by Mr Norgan. I would specify a period of the order of four years. In reaching this conclusion I take account of the fact that there is at present and there will for a considerable time be ample security for the plaintiff's loan. The statement of practice of the Council of Mortgage Lenders does not bind the plaintiffs to a particular course of action. It could be a factor in determining the length of the period regarded as reasonable for payment of arrears. However, the difficulty for the defendant in the present case is the magnitude of the arrears, and I am not persuaded that the plaintiffs in any way contributed to the size of those arrears. The defendant's case for the suspension of the warrant depends very largely on the whole of the rest of the term being held to be the reasonable period for payment of the arrears. My rejection of this submission and my finding that only a far shorter period would be reasonable, makes it impossible for the court's power under s. 36 to be exercised in the defendant's favour. There is a prospect that, given time, the finances of the Norgan family may improve sufficiently to discharge the liabilities under the mortgage. Mr Norgan is an able and resourceful man, but I am not satisfied that on the balance of probabilities the family finances *will* so improve. Whether the family is allowed the chance must be left to the plaintiffs to decide. They have established their claim to possession in law and have obtained an order for possession. They are entitled to enforcement of that order unless the defendant can establish the contrary. In this, as I find with much regret, she has failed. The appeal is dismissed. (Judge O'Malley's emphasis.)

The opposing arguments which Mr Croally and Mr Waters have developed in their helpful written and oral submissions are as follows. Mr Croally contends that there is a primary assumption that a reasonable period is the term of the mortgage, and for that he relies on the dicta already cited from *Cunningham* and *Schindler*. That assumption is reinforced, he says, in the present case by the fact that there is sufficient equity to protect the mortgagee's eventual entitlement to repayment of the principal debt in full in 2008, that the mortgagor has deposed on affidavit to budgeting proposals under which (with the help she now receives from the Department of Social Security) there is a reasonable prospect of her being able to pay off the arrears in full by the expiry of the mortgage term, and that such a proposal would accord with the policy declared on the face of the CML statement. Mr Waters contends that such an approach takes too narrow a view of the court's discretion. The delaying powers under s. 36 represent a substantial interference with the contractual right which the parties have themselves freely negotiated, namely the right of the mortgagee to repayment in full of the whole mortgage debt as soon as a default occurs. In the exercise of its discretion, therefore, the court is bound to be even-handed in its approach to the claims of each side, matching a concern on the one hand that the mortgagor should be allowed a proper opportunity of making good his default, with a concern that a mortgagee who has contracted for a steady flow of interest punctually paid by instalments as they fall due should not be compelled to wait for payment through an enforced capitalisation of interest. Given the number of these cases which comes before the courts every day, it would lead, so Mr Waters submits, to unnecessary cost and delay if in every case the court was required to undertake the sort of detailed inquiry which would be necessary if one is to weigh to a nicety the effect on the one hand upon the lender of having to submit to a phasing of repayment of arrears over the whole remaining term of the mortgage, and the ability on the other hand of the mortgagor to maintain such payments. It would be sufficient for the purposes of a just and fair exercise of the discretion if the courts were to be encouraged to adopt, as the judge did in this case and as many other judges (with encouragement from *The Supreme Court Practice*) regularly do, a period of years (be it two, four or six: Mr Waters leaves us to say which should be chosen) that can, without being applied blindly or rigidly, be adapted by the courts to the demands of each case.

Conclusion

There is no doubt that Mr Waters' argument has strong pragmatic advantages. In the present plight of the housing market possession cases play a major part in the caseload for the county courts. That is particularly true of the district judges, who deal with those cases in such numbers that they develop a 'feel' for them and have achieved an excellent disposal record. It is not surprising that they have found it convenient to adopt a relatively short period of years as the rough rule of thumb which aids a just determination of the 'reasonable period' for the purposes of ss. 36 and 8. Nevertheless, although I would not go quite so far with Mr Croally as to say it should be an 'assumption', it does seem to me that the logic and spirit of the legislation require, especially in cases where the parties are proceeding under arrangements such as those reflected in the CML statement, that the court should take as its starting point the full term of the mortgage and pose at the outset the question: would it be possible for the mortgagor to maintain payment-off of the arrears by instalments over that period? . . .

. . . There is likely to be a greater need to require of mortgagors that they should furnish the court with a detailed 'budget', of the kind that has been supplied by the mortgagor in her affidavit in the present case. But analysis of such budgets is part of the expertise in which the district judges have already become adept in their family jurisdiction and I would not expect that to present too great a difficulty. There will be instances, too, in which preliminary adjudication will be necessary to determine, when calculating the amount of arrears and assessing the future instalments for their payment-off, which items are to be attributed to the mortgagor's current payment obligations and which to his ultimate liability on capital account. The present case has shown—through the disparity introduced by the disputed items—how problematic that may sometimes prove to be. They are nevertheless disputes that it will be essential to resolve—in this case and others where they arise—before the court can undertake an accurate estimate of the amount which the mortgagor would be required to meet if the arrears were to be made repayable over the full remainder of the mortgage term. There may also be cases, as Mr Waters points out, in which it is less obvious than in this case that the mortgagee is adequately secured, and detailed evidence, if necessary by experts, may be required to see if and when the lender's security will become liable to be put at risk as a result of imposing postponement of payments in arrear. Problems such as these—which I suspect will arise only rarely in practice although they will undeniably be daunting when they do arise—should not however be allowed, in my judgment, to stand in the way of giving effect to the clearly intended scheme of the legislation.

There is another factor which, to my mind, weighs strongly in favour of adopting the full term of the mortgage as the starting point for calculating a 'reasonable period' for payment of arrears. It is prompted by experience in this very case. The parties have been before the court with depressing frequency over the years on applications to enforce, or further to suspend, the warrant of possession, while Mrs Norgan and her husband have struggled, sometimes with success and sometimes without, to meet whatever commitment was currently approved by the court. Cheltenham has (in the exercise of its power to do so under the terms of the mortgage) added to its security the costs it has incurred in connection with all these attendances. One of the disputed items turns upon the question whether such costs fall to be allocated to capital or to interest account. What is not in dispute, however, is that one day, be it sooner or later, those costs will have to be borne by the mortgagor, and if the day comes when she decides, or is compelled by circumstances, to move to more readily affordable accommodation, her resources for rehousing will be correspondingly reduced. It is an experience which brings home the disadvantages which both lender and borrower are liable to suffer if frequent attendance before the court becomes necessary as a result of multiple applications under s. 36, to say nothing of the heavy inroads made upon court hearing time. One advantage of taking the period most favourable to the mortgagor at the outset is that if his or her hopes of repayment prove to be ill-founded and the new instalments initially ordered as a condition of suspension are not maintained but themselves fall into arrear, the mortgagee can be heard with justice to say that the mortgagor has had his chance, and that the s. 36 powers (although of course capable in theory of being exercised again and again) should not be employed repeatedly to compel a lending institution which has already suffered interruption of the regular flow of interest to which it was entitled under the express terms of the mortgage, to accept assurances of future payment from a borrower in whom it has lost confidence.

It follows, for all these reasons, that in adopting for this case a period of repayment (four years) unrelated to the remaining term of the mortgage (thirteen years) the judge in my view fell into error. The fault was not his. He applied to a case which he examined with outstanding care and clarity a practice of convenience which has been developed to deal with a widely-framed statutory discretion, in respect of which guidance from authority has been limited.

In view of the long history of this litigation, and the anxiety it has involved, in particular for Mrs Norgan and her family, it would have been the wish of this court to determine all outstanding issues for ourselves, so that each side might have left this court knowing exactly where they stood. But, as Evans LJ made clear to the parties at the hearing, there are too many matters unresolved, on evidence which is still not wholly complete, to enable us to do so. I would therefore allow the appeal and remit the case to the county court for the following.

(1)   A determination of the disputed items and a finding as to what precisely is now, or (as the case may be) will at the expiry of the mortgage term be, due from the mortgagor on the capital and interest instalment account respectively, including in the latter account a precise figure for the current interest in arrear.

(2)   A calculation of: (a) the instalments which the mortgagor would be required to pay if the arrears so found were to be made payable by instalments over the whole of the remaining period of the mortgage term, and (b) the instalments of interest currently due under the mortgage.

(3)   A determination of the question whether, in the light of the court's findings as to the current and prospective ability of the mortgagor to discharge the instalments under (2)(a) and (b), there are any unusual circumstances justifying a departure from the remaining term of the mortgage as the period that is prima facie 'reasonable' for the purposes of ss. 36 and 8.

(4)   A determination of the question whether, in the light of its conclusions under (1), (2) and (3), this would be a suitable case in which to exercise the court's discretion to suspend the warrant of possession for any, and if so what period.

EVANS LJ: ... The statement issued by the Council of Mortgage Lenders said that members sought to take possession only as a last resort.

Given its stated policy, his Lordship did not see how the building society could properly say that it was not appropriate to take account of the whole of the remaining part of the original term when assessing a reasonable period for the payment of arrears.

Considerations which were likely to be relevant in establishing a reasonable period were:

(a) How much could the borrower reasonably afford to pay, both now and in the future?

(b) If the borrower had a temporary difficulty in meeting his obligations, how long was the difficulty likely to last?

(c) What was the reason for the arrears which had accumulated?

(d) How much remained of the original term?

(e) What were the relevant contractual terms and what type of mortgage was it, that is, when was the principal due to be repaid?

(f) Was it a case where the court should exercise its power to disregard accelerated payment provisions (section 8 of the 1973 Act)?

(g) Was it reasonable to expect the lender, in the circumstances of the particular case, to recoup the arrears of interest (i) over the whole of the original term, or (ii) within a shorter period, or even (iii) within a longer period, that is, by extending the repayment period? Was it reasonable to expect the lender to capitalise the interest or not?

(h) Were there any reasons affecting the security which should influence the length of the period for payment?

In the light of the answers to those questions, the court could proceed to exercise its overall discretion, taking account also of any further factors which might arise in the particular case. . . .

Madge, N., 'Mortgage possession proceedings' (1997) 147 NLJ 459

Although some mortgages are regulated by the Consumer Credit Act 1974, most mortgage possession proceedings are governed by the provisions of the Administration of Justice Acts 1970 and 1973. These Acts, although considered daily in the county courts, received very little attention from the Court of Appeal for the first twenty years of their existence. The last couple of years have, however, seen a significant increase in appeals and this has resulted in a dozen or so newly reported decisions. This body of case law has had a marked effect upon practice in the county courts.

Administration of Justice Act 1970, s. 36(1) provides:

Where the mortgagee under a mortgage of land which consists of or includes a dwelling-house brings an action in which he claims possession . . . (not being an action for foreclosure in which a claim for possession . . . is also made) the court may exercise any of [its] powers . . . if it appears to the court that in the event of its exercising the power the mortgagor is likely to be able within a *reasonable period* to pay any sums due under the mortgage or to remedy a default consisting of a breach of any other obligation arising under or by virtue of the mortgage.

Section 36(2) provides that the court:

(a) may adjourn the proceedings, or

(b) on giving judgment, or making an order, for delivery of possession . . . or at any time before execution of such judgment or order may:

(i) stay or suspend execution of the judgment or order, or

(ii) postpone the date for delivery of possession

for such period or periods as the court thinks reasonable.

The court's powers under s. 36 apply equally to repayment mortgages and endowment mortgages (*Bank of Scotland* v *Grimes* [1985] 2 All ER 254, CA). However, borrowers cannot rely upon s. 36 where a charge securing a bank overdraft provides that the sum owed shall only become payable on demand, (an 'all moneys charge') since, in those circumstances, there is no agreement to defer payment (see AJA 1973, s. 8 and *Habib Bank* v *Tailor* [1982] 3 All ER 561, CA). In those circumstances 'the court has no jurisdiction to decline the order or to adjourn the hearing, whether on terms of keeping up payments or paying arrears, if the mortgagee cannot be persuaded to agree to this course' (*Birmingham Citizens Permanent Building Society* v *Caunt* [1962] Ch 883, Ch D). In *Caunt* Russell J stated that the sole exception to this rule is that possession proceedings 'may be adjourned for a short time to afford the mortgagor a chance of paying off the mortgagee in full or otherwise satisfying him; but this should not be done if there is no reasonable prospect of this occurring. When I say the sole exception, I do not, of course, intend to exclude adjournments which in the ordinary course of procedure may be desirable in circumstances such as temporary inability of a party to attend, and so forth'. (p. 912)

The court's power under s. 36 to adjourn mortgage possession proceedings, stay or suspend execution or postpone the date for delivery of possession ceases after a warrant has been executed. (*Cheltenham and Gloucester Building Society* v *Obi* (1996) 28 HLR 22, CA.)

Criteria and evidence

The borrower must, on the balance of probabilities satisfy the court that it is *likely* that the arrears will be cleared within a *reasonable period*. The court cannot suspend an order for possession under s. 36, however hard the circumstances, if there is no prospect of the borrower reducing the arrears (*Abbey National Mortgages* v *Bernard* (1995) 71 P & CR 57, CA).

The defendant need not always produce evidence in the normal formal sense (for example, by affidavit or on oath). In *Cheltenham and Gloucester Building Society* v *Grant* (1994) 26 HLR 703, CA, where the building society unsuccessfully challenged the common practice of district judges exercising their discretion under AJA 1970 without hearing sworn evidence from borrowers, Nourse LJ stated that:

> It must be possible for [judges] to act without evidence, especially where, as here, the mortgagor was present in court and available to be questioned and no objection to the reception of informal material is made by the mortgagee. Clearly, it will sometimes be prudent for the mortgagor to put in an affidavit before the hearing. (p. 707)

The Court of Appeal declined to lay down rigid rules as to how 'busy district judges' should satisfy themselves as to the requirements in s. 36 and upheld the original order made by the district judge that a possession order should not be enforced without leave of the court while regular payments were made.

Reasonable period

One crucial question which has to be answered in every case is 'What is a reasonable period?' The phrase is not defined by the Administration of Justice Act.

In *Centrax Trustees* v *Ross* [1979] 2 All ER 952, Ch D, Goulding J stated that in assessing how long a reasonable period might be, the court must 'bear in mind the rights and obligations of both parties, including [the lender's] right to recover their money by selling the property if necessary, and the full past history of the security.'

In *First Middlesbrough Trading and Mortgage Co. Ltd* v *Cunningham* (1974) 28 P & CR 69, CA, Scarman LJ, when considering what is a 'reasonable period' within s. 36, stated:

> since the object of the instalment mortgage was, with the consent of the mortgagee, to give the mortgagor the period of the mortgage to repay the capital sum and interest, one begins with a powerful presumption of fact in favour of the period of the mortgage being the 'reasonable period'. (p. 75)

In *Western Bank* v *Schindler* [1977] Ch 1, CA Buckley LJ stated:

> What must be reasonable must depend on the circumstances of the case . . . In a suitable case the specified period might even be the whole remaining prospective life of the mortgage. ([1976] 2 All ER at p. 400)

These passages were *obiter* but were followed by the Court of Appeal in *Cheltenham and Gloucester Building Society* v *Norgan* [1996] 1 All ER 449, CA.

Waite LJ stated that in determining 'a reasonable period':

> the court should take as its starting point the full term of the mortgage and pose at the outset the question: would it be possible for the mortgagor to maintain payment off of the arrears by instalments over that period? (p. 458)

In *Norgan* there had been a history of arrears. In May 1990, when arrears stood at £7,216, the building society obtained a possession order suspended for 28 days. In December 1990, the terms of the suspension were varied, but not complied with, and the building society obtained a warrant. The warrant was twice suspended on terms, but when the borrower failed to comply, the building society applied to reissue the warrant and the borrower cross-applied for a further suspension. The district judge gave leave to reissue the warrant and refused any further suspension. By the time the appeal came on before the circuit judge the arrears were in the region of £20,000. He dismissed the borrower's appeal and she appealed to the Court of Appeal. The Court of Appeal allowed her appeal.

Evans LJ set out a number of considerations which are likely to be relevant when establishing what is a reasonable period. They include:

> (a) How much can the borrower reasonably afford to pay, both now and in the future? (b) If the borrower has a temporary difficulty in meeting his obligations, how long is the difficulty likely to last? (c) What was the reason for the arrears which have accumulated? (d) How much remains of the original term? (e) What are the relevant contractual terms, and what type of mortgage is it, i.e. when is the principal due to be repaid?

Other matters which may be relevant include family circumstance and the income of other members of the family. If arrears have accrued as a result of matrimonial breakdown, are any proceedings for ancillary relief likely to result in an order which will enable arrears to be paid off? Is the Benefit Agency (or should it be) paying anything towards the interest due on the mortgage?

Security at risk

Norgan was a case where the lender's security was not at risk. Courts are likely to be far more cautious about exercising s. 36 powers where there is already negative equity or where there is a risk of negative equity. In *Norgan*, Waite LJ recognised that there would be cases where evidence might 'be required to see if and when the lender's security will become liable to be put at risk as a result of imposing postponement of payments in arrear'. (p. 459)

Evans LJ indicated that courts should ask 'Are there any reasons affecting the security which should influence the period for payment?' (p. 463) Similarly in *First Middlesbrough Trading and Mortgage Co. Ltd* v *Cunningham* the Court of Appeal stated that when exercising its AJA discretion, one of the 'relevant surrounding circumstances' which the court is entitled to take into account is the fact that the debt might be inadequately secured. Sometimes, borrowers produce letters from estate agents in order to satisfy the court about the value of the property in comparison with the amount of the loan outstanding, but in *Bristol and West BS* v *Ellis* (1996) *The Times*, 2 May 1996, the Court of Appeal stated that judges should approach such estimates with 'reserve'. If a borrower's valuation is disputed, it may be necessary for there to be an adjournment for an independent valuation so that the court can determine whether the lender's security is at risk.

Sale of the property

In most cases borrowers try to satisfy the court that it is likely that the arrears will be cleared within a reasonable period by giving evidence about their income and expenditure. However, where borrowers' income is not sufficient to repay arrears, they may seek time in which to sell the property so that the outstanding balance (including arrears) can be paid from the proceeds of sale.

In *National and Provincial Building Society* v *Lloyd* [1996] 1 All ER 630, the Court of Appeal considered an appeal against a decision to suspend a possession order to give the borrower time to sell premises and so clear mortgage arrears. The building society argued that any such suspension should only be for a short period. Neill LJ rejected this submission. If there is clear evidence that completion of the sale of a property 'could take place in six or nine months or even a year', there was no reason why the court could not come to the conclusion that it was likely that the arrears would be repaid within a reasonable period. What is 'a reasonable period' is a question for the court in each individual case. However, in *Lloyd* there was insufficient evidence before the judge to show that the arrears would be paid within a reasonable period. Much of it was 'a mere expression of hope' and accordingly the building society's appeal against the suspension was allowed.

In *Bristol and West BS* v *Ellis, The Times*, 2 May 1996, the Court of Appeal confirmed that what is a reasonable period for sale depends on the individual circumstances of each case, particularly the extent to which the mortgage and arrears are secured by the value of the property. In *Ellis* the Court of Appeal allowed a lender's appeal against an order which would have allowed the borrower three to five years (when her children would have finished university education) to sell because there was insufficient evidence that Mrs Ellis could or would sell the property within that period or that the proceeds of sale would be sufficient to discharge the mortgage debt and arrears. The Court stated that the comments by Neill LJ in *National and Provincial BS* v *Lloyd* [1996] 1 All ER 630 that sale 'could take place in six or nine months or even a year' did not establish a year as the maximum period 'as a rule of law or as a matter of great guidance'. (See too *Cheltenham and Gloucester BS* v *Johnson* (1996) 28 HLR 885, CA where *Lloyd* was followed.)

In most cases where the security is not at risk, the court will adjourn or make a suspended order to allow the borrowers to arrange a sale. It is generally accepted that borrowers occupying premises achieve a better price on sale than lenders through 'forced sales'. For example in *Target None Loans Clothier* [1994] 1 All ER 439, CA borrowers paid no mortgage instalments for over 15 months and when possession proceedings came to court there were arrears of £46,000. The lenders sought an immediate possession order, but the district judge adjourned for 56 days under s. 36. When the Court of Appeal heard the appeal, there was a letter from estate agents indicating that an offer of £450,000 for the house had been received. Nolan LJ, after asking whether there was a prospect of an early sale, stated:

If so, is it better in the interests of all concerned for that to be effected by [the borrower] and his wife or by the mortgage company? If the view is the prospects of an early sale for the mortgagees as well as for [the borrower] are best served by deferring an order for possession, then it seems to me that that is a solid reason for making such an order . . . [1994] 1 All ER at p. 447)

The Court of Appeal made a possession order to take effect in three months.

Even if the power to suspend execution under Administration of Justice Act 1970, s. 36 cannot be exercised because it is unlikely that the borrower can repay arrears within a reasonable period, the county court still has a residual inherent jurisdiction to defer the giving up of possession in order to enable the lender to sell the property (*Cheltenham and Gloucester plc* v *Booker, The Times*, 20 November 1996, CA). In such circumstances the 1970 s. 36 cannot be exercised because it is unlikely that the borrower can repay arrears within a reasonable period, the county court still has a residual inherent jurisdiction to defer the giving up of possession in order to enable the lender to sell the property (*Cheltenham and Gloucester plc* v *Booker*). In such circumstances the court may give conduct of the sale of premises to the lender while postponing execution of a warrant for possession until completion of the sale, thus allowing the borrower to remain in occupation.

There is no reason in principle for the court to accede to a lender's insistence upon immediate possession if:

(a) possession will only be required on completion;
(b) the presence of the borrowers pending completion will enhance, or at least not depress, the sale price;
(c) the borrowers will co-operate in the sale; and
(d) they will give possession to the purchasers on completion.

However, in *Booker*, Millett LJ stated these conditions are seldom likely to be satisfied and the circumstances in which such a course would be appropriate are hard to imagine. Such an order would 'certainly be a rarity'.

If a lender does not agree to a borrower selling premises, the borrower may apply for an order for sale under Law of Property Act 1925, s. 91(2). Such an application may be made in a county court if 'the amount owing in respect of the mortgage or charge at the commencement of the proceedings does not exceed £30,000'. (The High Court and County Courts Jurisdiction Order 1991, para. 2(4).) If the amount owing is more than £30,000 a s. 91 application has to be made in the High Court. In *Cheltenham and Gloucester BS v Krausz* [1997] 1 All ER 21, the Court of Appeal held that a district judge in the county court has no jurisdiction to suspend a warrant in these circumstances.

Phillips LJ did not consider 'that the county court, as part of its inherent jurisdiction, can properly suspend an order or warrant for possession in order to enable a mortgagor to apply to the High Court for an order under s. 91. It [is] incumbent on the mortgagor to seek from the High Court any relief which the court is empowered to give before the warrant takes effect.' He noted that s. 36 makes it clear that Parliament did not intend that the court should have power to curtail mortgagees' rights to possession unless the proceeds of sales were likely to discharge the mortgage debt.

30.4.2 DUTY OF MORTGAGEE IN POSSESSION TO ACCOUNT STRICTLY

WHITE v CITY OF LONDON BREWERY COMPANY (1889) 42 ChD 237, Court of Appeal

FACTS: A pub, originally a 'free house', was mortgaged to a brewery, the mortgage (surprisingly) not containing a tie clause. The brewery took possession and leased the pub as a 'tied house'. The fact that the pub was tied to one brewery meant, in those days, that the pub attracted a lower rent than it would have, had it been a 'free house'.
HELD: In determining the amount owed by White to the brewery, under the mortgage, the brewery had to account on the basis of the higher rent which a 'free house' would have commanded.

COTTON LJ: . . . A mortgagee in possession must account for the rents which, but for his wilful default, he would have received. The plaintiff says that if he fails as to the brewers' profits yet he ought to have a larger sum in respect of the rents which the mortgagees would, but for their wilful default, have received. I think the learned Judge was a little indulgent to the plaintiff, but in these days if there is a question to be decided on the evidence before the Court, we are not inclined to restrict the suitor very closely to the pleadings. The learned Judge has allowed an addition of £20 a year from 19 August, 1874, down to the date of the sale, in addition to the rent obtained by the mortgagees. Before 1873, there had been a period during which the brewers were in occupation by their servant, then a period during which they let nominally at £30, but really at £15 a year, since half the £30 was paid by the tenant for the furniture and fixtures which belonged to the brewers; and then a period of letting at £60 a year. I was rather struck at first at there being no occupation rent charged against the brewers while they were in possession by their servant; it does not appear to have been asked for, but if it had been, is any case made for giving it? I think the evidence is the other way. At the time the brewers took possession, the trade in the neighbourhood was in a bad state. We know that when trade is in a bad state workmen have not money to spend in beer, so the custom would fall off, and when a public-house has got into a low state there is a difficulty in re-establishing its business. This house at the time when the brewers took possession could not be let, because nobody could carry it on without a loss, as the brewers found by experience. As soon after as they could let it at all, they let it to Moulton, who found a rent of £40 too high, and was allowed to remain at a rent of £30. On the evidence before us, there is nothing which satisfies my mind that they could by any possibility have obtained a larger rent than that, during the tenancy of Mr Moulton. Then I think the learned Judge was right in saying, when there was a change in the tenancy, that there was no ground for charging the brewers with more than the £60 rent which they received from Hake during the first year of his occupation; but after that time, when he had established himself, the learned Judge thought that something more ought to be allowed. The evidence on that question is of a somewhat doubtful character, but I think the Plaintiff has not established that more should be given him than what the learned Judge has allowed, viz. £20 a year, which comes altogether, as the Master of the Rolls has said, to £100. . . .

30.5   Power to Appoint a Receiver

DOWNSVIEW NOMINEES LTD AND ANOTHER v FIRST CITY CORP LTD AND ANOTHER [1993] 3 All ER 626, Privy Council

FACTS: A mortgagor brought this action against a mortgagee and a receiver appointed by it, claiming that the receiver had acted fraudulently, recklessly and in breach of his duties. HELD: A mortgagee must exercise its power to appoint receivers in good faith and for the sole purpose of enforcing its security, however the mortgagee owes the mortgagor no duty to be careful in selecting the receiver appointed.

LORD TEMPLEMAN: . . . The nature of the duties owed by a receiver and manager appointed by a debenture holder were authoritatively defined by Jenkins LJ in a characteristically learned and comprehensive judgment in *Re B Johnson & Co. (Builders) Ltd* [1955] 2 All ER 775 at 790–791, [1955] Ch 634 at 661–663:

> . . . the phrase 'manager of the company', *prima facie*, according to the ordinary meaning of the words, connotes a person holding, whether *de jure* or *de facto*, a post in or with the company of a nature charging him with the duty of managing the affairs of the company for the company's benefit; whereas a receiver and manager for debenture-holders is a person appointed by the debenture-holders to whom the company has given powers of management pursuant to the contract of loan constituted by the debenture and as a condition of obtaining the loan, to enable him to preserve and realise the assets comprised in the security for the benefit of the debenture-holders. The company gets the loan on terms that the lenders shall be entitled, for the purpose of making their security effective, to appoint a receiver with powers of sale and of management pending sale, and with full discretion as to the exercise and mode of exercising those powers. The primary duty of the receiver is to the debenture-holders and not to the company. He is receiver and manager of the property of the company for the debenture-holders, not manager of the company. The company is entitled to any surplus of assets remaining after the debenture debt has been discharged, and is entitled to proper accounts. The whole purpose of the receiver and manager's appointment would obviously be stultified if the company could claim that a receiver and manager owes it any duty comparable to the duty owed to a company by its own directors or managers. In determining whether a receiver and manager for the debenture-holders of a company has broken any duty owed by him to the company, regard must be had to the fact that he is a receiver and manager—i.e., a receiver, with ancillary powers of management—for the debenture-holders, and not simply a person appointed to manage the company's affairs for the benefit of the company . . . The duties of a receiver and manager for debenture-holders are widely different from those of a manager of the company. He is under no obligation to carry on the company's business at the expense of the debenture-holders. Therefore he commits no breach of duty to the company by refusing to do so, even though his discontinuance of the business may be detrimental from the company's point of view. Again, his power of sale is, in effect, that of a mortgagee, and he therefore commits no breach of duty to the company by a *bona fide* sale, even though he might have obtained a higher price and even though, from the point of view of the company, as distinct from the debenture-holders, the terms might be regarded as disadvantageous. In a word, in the absence of fraud or mala fides . . . the company cannot complain of any act or omission of the receiver and manager, provided that he does nothing that he is not empowered to do, and omits nothing that he is enjoined to do by the terms of his appointment. If the company conceives that it has any claim against the receiver and manager for breach of some duty owed by him to the company, the issue is not whether

the receiver and manager has done or omitted to do anything which it would be wrongful in a manager of a company to do or omit, but whether he has exceeded or abused or wrongfully omitted to use the special powers and discretions vested in him pursuant to the contract of loan constituted by the debenture for the special purpose of enabling the assets comprised in the debenture-holders' security to be preserved and realised.

The duties owed by a receiver and manager do not compel him to adopt any particular course of action, by selling the whole or part of the mortgaged property or by carrying on the business of the company or by exercising any other powers and discretions vested in him. But since a mortgage is only security for a debt, a receiver and manager commits a breach of his duty if he abuses his powers by exercising them otherwise than 'for the special purpose of enabling the assets comprised in the debenture holders' security to be preserved and realised' for the benefit of the debenture holder. . . .

. . . The general duty of care said to be owed by a mortgagee to subsequent incumbrancers and the mortgagor in negligence is inconsistent with the right of the mortgagee and the duties which the courts applying equitable principles have imposed on the mortgagee. If a mortgagee enters into possession he is liable to account for rent on the basis of wilful default; he must keep mortgage premises in repair; he is liable for waste. Those duties were imposed to ensure that a mortgagee is diligent in discharging his mortgage and returning the property to the mortgagor. If a mortgagee exercises his power of sale in good faith for the purpose of protecting his security, he is not liable to the mortgagor even though he might have obtained a higher price and even though the terms might be regarded as disadvantageous to the mortgagor. *Cuckmere Brick Co. Ltd v Mutual Finance Ltd* [1971] 2 All ER 633, [1971] Ch 949 is Court of Appeal authority for the proposition that, if the mortgagee decides to sell, he must take reasonable care to obtain a proper price but is no authority for any wider proposition. A receiver exercising his power of sale also owes the same specific duties as the mortgagee. But that apart, the general duty of a receiver and manager appointed by a debenture holder, as defined by Jenkins LJ in *Re B Johnson & Co. (Builders) Ltd* [1955] 2 All ER 775 at 790–791, [1955] Ch 634 at 661–663, leaves no room for the imposition of a general duty to use reasonable care in dealing with the assets of the company. The duties imposed by equity on a mortgagee and on a receiver and manager would be quite unnecessary if there existed a general duty in negligence to take reasonable care in the exercise of powers and to take reasonable care in dealing with the assets of the mortgagor company. . . .

Similar considerations apply to Downsview. A mortgagee owes a general duty to subsequent incumbrancers and to the mortgagor to use his powers for the sole purpose of securing repayment of the moneys owing under his mortgage and a duty to act in good faith. He also owes the specific duties which equity has imposed on him in the exercise of his powers to go into possession and his powers of sale. It may well be that a mortgagee who appoints a receiver and manager, knowing that the receiver and manager intends to exercise his powers for the purpose of frustrating the activities of the second mortgagee or for some other improper purpose or who fails to revoke the appointment of a receiver and manager when the mortgagee knows that the receiver and manager is abusing his powers, may himself be guilty of bad faith but in the present case this possibility need not be explored.

The liability of Mr Russell in the present case is firmly based not on negligence but on the breach of duty. . . .

30.6   A Possible Lifeline to Mortgagors with Negative Equity?

PALK AND ANOTHER v *MORTGAGE SERVICES FUNDING PLC* [1993] 2 All ER 481, Court of Appeal

FACTS: The Palks owned a house encumbered with a debt amounting to £358,000. They had found a prospective purchaser willing to pay just £283,000, and they wanted to sell the property and make up the difference out of their personal resources. The mortgagee refused to agree to this, and took proceedings for possession. It was the mortgagee's intention not to sell the house until 'the market improved', and in the meantime to let the house to a tenant. It was clear that the rent obtainable would be substantially less than the interest continuing to accrue. Thus the amount owed by the Palks would steadily increase, as would the amount of the 'negative equity'. The Palks therefore applied for an order of sale under section 91(2) of the Law of Property Act 1925, a provision granting the court a discretion to order a sale of mortgaged property.

HELD: The order for sale was granted. The mortgagee must not exercise its various powers in a manner wholly unfair to the mortgagor.

SIR DONALD NICHOLLS V-C: Anthony Palk is a victim of the recession.

In January 1990 he obtained an advance of £300,000 from Mortgage Services Funding plc (Mortgage Services). The loan was secured by a mortgage over the house owned by him and his wife Margaret: The Thatch, Warren Lane, Cross-in-Hand, Heathfield, East Sussex. . . .

Mr Palk is now bankrupt. His wife has appealed against the judge's decision. The amount, including interest, now owing under the mortgage is approximately £409,000.

The statute

The jurisdiction being invoked by Mrs Palk is statutory. Section 91(2) of the Law of Property Act 1925 provides:

> In any action, whether for foreclosure, or for redemption, or for sale, or for the raising and payment in any manner of mortgage money, the court, on the request of the mortgagee, or of any person interested either in the mortgage money or in the right of redemption, and, notwithstanding that—(a) any other person dissents; or (b) the mortgagee or any person so interested does not appear in the action; and without allowing any time for redemption or for payment of any mortgage money, may direct a sale of the mortgaged property, on such terms as it thinks fit, including the deposit in court of a reasonable sum fixed by the court to meet the expenses of sale and to secure performance of the terms.

. . . a mortgagee can sit back and do nothing. He is not obliged to take steps to realise his security. But if he does take steps to exercise his rights over his security, common law and equity alike have set bounds to the extent to which he can look after himself and ignore the mortgagor's interests. In the exercise of his rights over his security the mortgagee must act fairly towards the mortgagor. His interest in the property has priority over the interest of the mortgagor, and he is entitled to proceed on that footing. He can protect his own interest, but he is not entitled to conduct himself in a way which unfairly prejudices the mortgagor. If he takes possession he might prefer to do nothing and bide his time, waiting indefinitely for an improvement in the market, with the property empty meanwhile. That he cannot do. He is accountable for his actual receipts from the property. He is also accountable to the mortgagor for what he would have received but for his default. So he must take reasonable care to maximise his return from the property. He must also take reasonable care of the property. Similarly, if he sells the property: he cannot sell hastily at a knock-down price sufficient to pay off his debt. The mortgagor also has an interest in the property and is under a personal liability for the shortfall. The mortgagee must keep that in mind. He must exercise reasonable care to sell only at the proper market value. . . .

I have given two examples where the law imposes a duty on a mortgagee when he is exercising his powers: if he lets the property he must obtain a proper market rent, and if he sells he must obtain a proper price. . . .

However, and this is my second observation on the mortgagee's argument, whether in these circumstances Mortgage Services is in breach of any duty it owes to Mrs Palk is not a crucial question on this appeal, for this reason: an exercise by the court of its statutory power to direct a sale even against the wishes of Mortgage Services is not dependent on there first having been a breach of duty by the company. The discretion given to the court by s. 91(2) of the 1925 Act is not hedged about with preconditions. The question on this appeal is how ought the court to exercise its discretion under the statute in the particular circumstances and against the background that a mortgagee owes at least some duties in law to a mortgagor when exercising his rights over the mortgaged property. That

Mortgage Services is not, or may not be, in breach of any duty it owes Mrs Palk is only one of the circumstances to be taken into account. . . .

In my view this is a case in which a sale should be directed even though there will be a deficiency. It is just and equitable to order a sale because otherwise unfairness and injustice will follow. I can summarise the four factors which combine to produce this result. First, there is a substantial income shortfall: the rental under the proposed letting would fall significantly short of the interest Mrs Palk would save if the house were sold. Second, the only prospect of recoupment of the shortfall lies in the hope that there will be a substantial rise in house prices generally. This is not a case where a sale is being postponed for a reason specific to this property: for example, pending the outcome of an application for planning permission for development. Following on from this, third, on the scanty evidence before the court the likelihood of Mrs Palk suffering increased loss if the company's plan proceeds is so high as to make the plan oppressive to her. Her liability is open-ended and will increase indefinitely. This risk of increased loss to her under her repayment obligation far outweighs the prospect of any gain the company may make from its proposed realisation scheme for the house. The one is unacceptably disproportionate to the other. Fourth, directing a sale will not preclude the mortgagee from having the opportunity to wait and see what happens to house prices. The mortgagee can buy the property. A mortgagee cannot buy property from itself, but here the sale is directed by the court; it is not a sale by a mortgagee in exercise of its own power of sale. . . .

30.7   Reform

The Law Commission (Law Com. No. 204) Transfer of Land—Land Mortgages, London: HMSO, 13 November 1991

7.27   Foreclosure is not . . . an inevitable feature of a mortgage system . . . we recommend that foreclosure be abolished, and that a mortgagee under a formal land mortgage should be entitled to sell to himself in exercise of the statutory power of sale, subject to the following:

(a)   the mortgagee must first obtain leave of the court; and

(b)   the court should not grant leave unless satisfied by the mortgagee that this is the most advantageous method of realising the security, from the point of view of the mortgagor, any guarantors of the mortgagor, and any subsequent encumbrancers.

Standard Terms

5.5   The question of standardising the *content* of mortgages by producing standard terms or conditions raises rather different issues. In this context, statutory mortgage conditions can fulfil three different functions. The first is that, by setting out the *prima facie* rights and duties of the parties, they define the nature of the relationship created by the new mortgage. To the extent that standard terms are fulfilling this function they should be largely overriding (that is, not variable by the parties), to ensure that the essential nature of the transaction is preserved. While the parties would not be able to vary overriding provisions, either in the mortgage document or by any other oral or written agreement at that time or later, it will be seen that they are not all inflexible. For example, the mortgagee's duty to repair the property while in possession would be the equivalent of whatever obligation was imposed on the mortgagor during his period of possession of the property, and the mortgagor's statutory repairing duty would be capable of variation or total exclusion in accordance with the parties' wishes. Again, the freedom which the mortgagor would have to grant leases while he was in possession would be modified by the fact that no lease would bind the mortgagee or a receiver unless the mortgagee had given his written consent to it; the mortgagee would therefore have a complete discretion in deciding whether to be bound by leases created by the mortgagor.

5.6   The second function of standard terms is to provide minimum rights and protection for protected mortgagors. To the extent that standard terms have this mortgagor protection function, they should be overriding in protected mortgages but largely variable in non-protected mortgages. The third function is to produce simple, uniform, and modern formulations of provisions commonly found in all mortgages. The objective in drafting such conditions is to produce a formulation acceptable to most mortgagors and mortgagees in most circumstances, so that the parties would not usually choose to vary the standard conditions (whilst they remain free to do so). Some conditions may of course fulfil more than one of these functions. . . .

Redemption

6.42   Although we recommend below the abolition of the equitable jurisdiction to set aside any provision of a mortgage which constitutes a clog or fetter on the equity of redemption, we do not intend to interfere with the equitable right to redeem. In other words, under a formal or informal land mortgage (as in any other mortgage or charge over any other kind of property) the mortgagor will remain entitled to redeem the property freed from the mortgage by paying and discharging all obligations under it, even after the contractual date for payment and discharge has passed, up until the time when the mortgagor's interest is destroyed by a sale by the mortgagee. In the case of protected mortgages, we consider that further steps should be taken to ensure that redemption and discharge are not discouraged or penalised. In our view this is particularly important because of the lack of control protected mortgagors have over the identity of the mortgagee and over the rate of interest from time to time charged. . . . Nevertheless, mortgagees must inevitably retain a significant degree of discretion in both areas, and ultimately the only recourse of mortgagors dissatisfied with their mortgagees, or with the rate of interest charged, is to redeem the mortgage and borrow elsewhere. Whilst a shortage of mortgage funds may often make the right to redeem illusory in practice, we take the view that, in the case of protected mortgages, no restriction on the right to redeem at any any time ought to be permitted. Although most lenders would prefer to retain the flexibility of being able to impose whatever terms they consider appropriate in relation to redemption, they made no very strong objections to the provisions which we proposed in the Working Paper and recommend here, and which were strongly supported by consumers' organisations. Also, it should be noted that mortgagors whose mortgages secure regulated agreements under the Consumer Credit Act 1974 are already entitled to discharge the mortgage at any time.

6.43   Accordingly we recommend that in the case of protected mortgages:

(a)   any term of the mortgage which postpones the mortgagor's right to redeem should be void, unless the property includes non-residential premises (in which case the postponement of the right to redeem should be dealt with in the same way as in non-protected mortgages, that is subject to challenge under the court's general jurisdiction: see Part VIII below);

(b)   any term of the mortgage which requires the mortgagor to give notice of intention to redeem, or requires payment of interest in lieu of notice, should be void: such provisions, which were once very common in residential mortgage deeds although now not in regular use by institutional lenders, impose a financial penalty on mortgagors who want to repay early;

(c)   mortgagors whose repayments are calculated on the basis of the loan remaining outstanding for a specified period should be entitled to the appropriate rebate on earlier repayment; this should be dealt with by regulations similar to those currently achieving the same objective in relation to mortgages securing a regulated agreement under the Consumer Credit Act 1974.

30.8   End of Chapter Assessment Question

In 1993 Bertha borrowed £40,000 from the Doorway Building Society. The loan is secured by a first legal mortgage of Bertha's freehold house 'Arkwrite Towers'.

In 1995 Bertha borrowed a further £20,000 from Princewest Finance Ltd secured by a second legal mortage on Arkwrite Towers. The interest on this loan is 23%, and Bertha has fallen into arrears with her repayments to Princewest.

(a)   Explain whether it will be possible for Princewest to take possession of and sell Arkwrite Towers, and how such a sale would affect the position of the Doorway Building Society.

(b)   If Princewest sells Arkwrite Towers at less than its open market value, consider whether Bertha would have any remedy against either:

    (i)   Princewest, or

    (ii)   the purchaser from Princewest.

(c)   How must Princewest apply the proceeds of any sale of Arkwrite Towers?

30.9   End of Chapter Assessment Outline Answer

(a)   In order to take possession under the Criminal Law Act 1967, a mortgagee seeking possession in practice always seeks a court possession order. In the case of residential property repossession is always illegal unless it takes place by order of the court. Thus, assuming that 'Arkwrite Towers' is a dwelling house, Princewest will need to apply to court for a possession order under s. 36 of the Administration of Justice Act 1970.

Section 36 gives the court a wide discretion to adjourn possession proceedings, or to make a possession order but suspend its operation. The intention is to give the mortgagor time to find the money to pay off the mortgage. Possession will only be suspended or adjourned if it appears that the mortgagor will be able to repay the loan within a 'reasonable period'. Further protection is given to mortgagors of instalment mortgages by s. 8 of the Administration of Justice Act 1973 (most mortgages of dwelling houses are paid off by instalments). Section 8 authorises the court to suspend or adjourn possession in cases where it appears likely that the mortgagor will, within a reasonable period, be able to pay off instalments that are in arrears and catch-up with current instalment payments. A reasonable period will normally be around two years (depending upon the economic climate) although in the recent case of *Cheltenham and Gloucester Building Society* v *Norgan* [1996] 1 All ER 449, the Court of Appeal held that the court should take the full term of the mortgage (usually 25 years) as its starting point in determining the 'reasonable period' for repayment. Waite LJ stated that courts should ask at the outset the question: would it be possible for the borrower to maintain payment-off of the arrears by instalments over that period? It remains to be seen whether this radical decision will survive an appeal to the House of Lords.

Assuming that the building society has gained possession of the house it will now be able to sell, provided that the power of sale has arisen and has become exercisable. It will **arise** if the mortgage is by deed and if the legal redemption date has passed (the mortgage is four years old, and so the power of sale will almost certainly have arisen). The power to sell is **exercisable** if interest repayments are at least two months in arrears, as appears to be the case in the present scenario. Accordingly, it appears from the facts that sale will be possible if possession is secured.

The effect of a sale on the first mortgagee, Doorway, depends upon whether Doorway had allowed the sale to take place from its rights. If it did, Doorway will be entitled only to recover its share of the sale proceeds. If Doorway refused to allow the sale to continue free from its rights, the sale could still go ahead, but the house would yield greatly reduced sale proceeds, as any purchaser would be bound by the first mortgage.

(b)(i)   The Court of Appeal in *Cuckmere Brick Co.* v *Mutual Finance Co.* [1971] 2 All ER 633 held that in deciding **when** to sell the mortgagee is entitled to consult its own interests to the total exclusion of the mortgagor's interests. However, having decided to sell at a particular time, in conducting the sale a mortgagee owes a duty of care to the mortgagor to obtain the best price reasonably obtainable at that time. If the mortgagee fails to obtain the best price he will have to account for the difference. The onus of proving that the mortgagee is in breach of this duty is on the mortgagor, unless the purchaser from the mortgagee has a personal connection with the mortgagee, in which case the onus is on the mortgagee to show that reasonable efforts were made to obtain the best price (*Tse Kwong Lam* v *Wong Chit Sen* [1983] 1 WLR 1349).

(ii)   If a mortgagee attempts to convey the property before the power of sale has arisen, any conveyance will be completely invalid. Once the power of sale has arisen, a mortgagee can convey a good title to a purchaser free of the mortgagor's rights, whether or not the power of sale has become exercisable. A purchaser in good faith from a mortgagee need satisfy himself only that the power of sale has arisen; he is under no duty to enquire whether the power has become exercisable.

A purchaser from the mortgagee is under no duty to pay the best price. Provided he acts in good faith he will get a good title, even if the mortgagee should have obtained a higher price by taking greater care. It would be acting in bad faith if the purchaser conspired with the mortgagee to purchase at an undervalue.

(c)   Princewest is treated as 'trustee of the proceeds of sale'. Proceeds from the sale must be applied in the following order: First, in paying off the total debt owed to the prior mortgagee, Doorway Building Society, if Doorway had permitted the sale to proceed free from its mortgage. Secondly, in discharging any costs of sale and any attempted sale. Thirdly, in discharging the total debt (capital and interest) owed to Princewest. Finally, the balance (if any) must be paid to Bertha. If Princewest departs from this strict order it may be liable for breach of its trust.

CHAPTER THIRTY-ONE

SPECIAL LEGAL RULES GOVERNING MORTGAGES

31.1   Fire Insurance of the Mortgaged Property

See Law of Property Act 1925, s. 101(1)(ii) at **30.3**.

31.2   Leasing of the Mortgaged Property

CHATSWORTH PROPERTIES LTD v *EFFIOM* **[1971] 1 All ER 604, Court of Appeal**

FACTS: A mortgagee who had appointed a receiver of rented property gave the tenants the impression that the mortgagee was the new landlord of the premises. It had written to the tenants saying, 'Do not pay your rent to your former landlord, but to the receiver we have appointed'.

HELD: The mortgagee was held to have created a tenancy by estoppel in favour of the tenants.

SALMON LJ: . . . The vital letter in this case is a letter of 23 December 1968, written to the defendant by the plaintiffs' solicitors acting on their behalf. The letter is in these terms:

> We act for [the plaintiffs], who have to-day appointed a Receiver of the income, rents and profits of the above property. The Receiver is Mr R C Richardson of Messrs. C H & J W Willmott, 65 Goldhawk Road, W12. Please take notice that henceforth you should not pay any sums to your former landlords, Mr and Mrs Lamptey, but to Mr Richardson or to whom he shall direct. Further take notice that no credit will be given for monies paid from now on to Mr and Mrs Lamptey. Yours faithfully.

Then it is signed by the solicitors. Now what does this letter mean? Counsel for the plaintiffs says, quite rightly, that the test (sometimes described as 'objective') is not, what did the defendant understand by it? but, what would this letter mean to the ordinary reasonable man? Counsel for the plaintiffs says that a receiver appointed under a mortgage deed is the agent of the mortgagor and not of the mortgagee. I entirely agree. He says that the true view of this letter is that it is giving notice to the defendant that the plaintiffs have appointed a receiver under a mortgage into which Mr and Mrs Lamptey had entered, that it gave the defendant notice that Mr Richardson was Mr and Mrs Lamptey's agent to receive the rents, and that in future the rent should be paid to Mr Richardson as agent for Mr and Mrs Lamptey and not to them.

I am afraid that, persuasively as counsel for the plaintiffs has put the argument, I am quite unable to accept it. I do not think that the letter means anything of the kind. To begin with, it is to be noticed that it does not say a word about any 'mortgage deed' or 'legal charge'. There is not a spark of evidence that the defendant had any idea that the Lampteys had mortgaged their leasehold interest in the premises. The natural meaning to the ordinary person would be that Mr Richardson was appointed as the agent of the plaintiffs, on behalf of whom the letter was written, to receive the rent due to them in respect of the premises. It is said: well, that cannot be right; surely the fact that the word 'Receiver' is used in the letter—particularly with a large 'R'—ought to put the ordinary man on some sort of enquiry, even if he is not a lawyer. But even if one were to accede to that argument, and I am afraid I do not, the rest of the letter seems to me to make it abundantly plain that the one thing that would not be communicated to the mind of the ordinary man by this letter is that the plaintiffs had appointed Mr Richardson a receiver to collect rents on behalf of Mr and Mrs Lamptey as landlords. The passage to which I draw particular attention is the passage in which the letter says 'henceforth you should not pay any sums to your *former* landlords, Mr and Mrs Lamptey'. I think that that can only mean, to the ordinary person, that Mr and Mrs Lamptey were no longer his landlords: the rent must be paid to Mr Richardson, presumably as agents for the landlord. If any reasonable man received a letter such as that written on behalf of the plaintiffs, I think that he would come to the conclusion, a very sensible conclusion, that the letter was telling him not only that Mr and Mrs Lamptey had ceased to be his landlords but that the plaintiffs, on behalf of whom the letter was written, were his landlords and that they had appointed Mr Richardson to collect the rents from him on their behalf. Thereafter, without more ado, Mr Richardson collected the rent from the defendant in accordance with the terms of that letter. A new rent book was issued to the defendant describing the landlord as 'R C Richardson Receiver'. This in the circumstances would convey to the defendant only that Mr Richardson was the landlord's agent. In my view a fresh tenancy had indeed been created between the plaintiffs and the defendant; at any rate the plaintiffs are precluded from denying that they did become the defendant's landlords. . . .

31.3 The Rules of Equity Protecting the Equitable Right to Redeem

31.3.1 NO IRREDEEMABLE MORTGAGES

One consequence of this is that it is impossible to include, as a term of the mortgage, a provision giving the mortgage an option to purchase the mortgaged property. But if, after the land has been mortgaged, the mortgagor as a completely separate transaction grants an option to the mortgagee, the option is valid.

31.3.2 POSTPONEMENT OF REDEMPTION

FAIRCLOUGH v *SWAN BREWERY COMPANY LIMITED* [1912] AC 565, Privy Council

FACTS: A lease of a hotel with seventeen-and-a-half years to run was mortgaged to a brewery, redemption being postponed until there were just six weeks to run on the lease. HELD: The postponement of redemption was invalid.

LORD MACNAGHTEN: . . . It will be observed that the lease is made to expire on June 12 1925, and that the instrument of mortgage provides that without the consent in writing of the company the mortgage debt of £500 is not to be wholly paid off until May 1 1925, that is just six weeks before the actual expiration of the lease.

In December 1909, the company were prevented by accidental circumstances from supplying the appellant with beer in accordance with a covenant on their part contained in the mortgage deed. The appellant thereupon assumed to treat the tie as at an end, and obtained beer from other quarters. The company brought an action for damages and for an injunction. The appellant, who apparently had already offered to redeem, counterclaimed for redemption. McMillan J gave judgment for the company in the action, and assessed the damages at £8. On the counter-claim he gave judgment for the appellant, holding that by law he was entitled to redeem. On appeal to the Full Court an order was made in the action in favour of the company with a reference as to damages. The counter-claim was dismissed with costs. Hence the present appeal.

The arguments of counsel ranged over a very wide field. But the real point is a narrow one. It depends upon a doctrine of equity, which is not open to question.

'There is,' as Kindersley V-C said in *Gossip* v *Wright* (1863) 32 LJ Ch 648, 'no doubt that the broad rule is this: that the Court will not allow the right of redemption in any way to be hampered or crippled in that which the parties intended to be a security either by any contemporaneous instrument with the deed in question, or by anything which this Court would regard as a simultaneous arrangement or part of the same transaction.' The rule in comparatively recent times was unsettled by certain decisions in the Court of Chancery in England which seem to have misled the learned judges in the Full Court. But it is now firmly established by the House of Lords that the old rule still prevails and that equity will not permit any device or contrivance being part of the mortgage transaction or contemporaneous with it to prevent or impede redemption. The learned counsel on behalf of the respondents admitted, as he was bound to admit, that a mortgage cannot be made irredeemable. That is plainly forbidden. Is there any difference between forbidding redemption and permitting it, if the permission be a mere pretence? Here the provision for redemption is nugatory. The incumbrance on the lease the subject of the mortgage according to the letter of the bargain falls to be discharged before the lease terminates, but at a time when it is on the very point of expiring, when redemption can be of no advantage to the mortgagor even if he should be so fortunate as to get his deeds back before the actual termination of the lease. For all practical purposes this mortgage is irredeemable. It was obviously meant to be irredeemable. It was made irredeemable in and by the mortgage itself.

Their Lordships are therefore of opinion that the order of the Full Court should be discharged with costs, and the decision of McMillan J restored. Their Lordships will humbly advise His Majesty accordingly. . . .

ESSO PETROLEUM CO. LTD v *HARPER'S GARAGE (STOURPORT) LTD*
[1966] 1 All ER 725, Court of Appeal

FACTS: A mortgage of a petrol filling station included a term postponing redemption for 21 years, and another term requiring the mortgagor to buy the mortgagee's petrol.
HELD: The postponement was invalid. The mortgagor was able to repay the mortgage and thereby free themselves from the 'tie' to Esso.

LORD DENNING MR: . . . In my opinion if a covenant in a mortgage is bad as being in unreasonable restraint of trade, then a court of equity should refuse to enforce it just as much as a court of law. Equity should follow the law. It is true of course that in applying the doctrine of restraint of trade to a mortgage, it is very relevant that the mortgagee has lent money. In many cases it may be quite reasonable for the mortgagee to stipulate for a tie so long as the loan is outstanding. But in that case he must not preclude the mortgagor from paying off the loan. At any rate he must not insert a clause making the loan irredeemable for an unduly long period. If he does so, then the tie is bad as being in unreasonable restraint of trade and the proviso forbidding redemption is bad as being unconscionable or oppressive. It is the coupling of the two together—the tie for the long period and the proviso forbidding redemption for the same period—which makes both bad if the period is so long as to be in unreasonable restraint of trade.

I find nothing in the cases contrary to this view. The cases on mortgages to brewers do not help because the doctrine of restraint of trade was not considered in them. The actual decisions are quite consistent with what I have said. In *Biggs* v *Hoddinott* [1895–99] All ER Rep 625, the restraint was *reasonable* and a proviso forbidding redemption for five years was held valid. In *Morgan* v *Jeffreys* [1910] Ch 620, the restraint was unreasonable and a proviso against redemption for twenty-eight years was held invalid.

I hold, therefore, that the doctrine of restraint of trade does apply to mortgages. Applied to this case I think that the tie for twenty-one years—coupled with a proviso forbidding redemption for twenty-one years—was unreasonable and invalid. It might have been reasonable, when they were making a loan of £7,000, to provide for a tie for five years and no right to redeem for that period. But twenty-one years is far too long.

I would, therefore, dismiss Esso's claim for an injunction; because the tie clause was in unreasonable restraint of trade. I would allow Harpers' counter-claim for redemption; because the proviso prohibiting redemption for twenty-one years (seeing that it was coupled with the tie) was unconscionable or oppressive. I would allow the appeal accordingly.

KNIGHTSBRIDGE ESTATES TRUST LTD v *BYRNE* [1938] 4 All ER 618, Court of Appeal

FACTS: A London property company mortgaged land to an insurance company. The mortgage contained a term postponing redemption for forty years.
HELD: The postponement was valid.

SIR WILFRID GREENE MR: . . . The first argument was that the postponement of the contractual right to redeem for 40 years was void in itself. In other words, the making of such an agreement between mortgagor and mortgagee was prohibited by a rule of equity. It was not contended that a provision in a mortgage deed making the mortgage irredeemable for a period of years is necessarily void. The argument was that such a period must be a 'reasonable' one, and it was said that the period in the present case was an unreasonable one, by reason merely of its length. This argument was not the one accepted by the judge.

An argument such as this requires the closest scrutiny, for, if it is correct, it means that an agreement made between two competent parties, acting under expert advice and presumably knowing their own business best, is one which the law forbids them to make upon the ground that it is not 'reasonable'. If we were satisfied that the rule of equity was what it is said to be, we should be bound to give effect to it. However, in the absence of compelling authority, we are not prepared to say that such an agreement cannot lawfully be made. A decision to that effect would, in our view, involve an unjustified interference with the freedom of business men to enter into agreements best suited to their interests, and would impose upon them a test of 'reasonableness' laid down by the courts without reference to the business realities of the case. It is important to remember what those realities were. The appellants are a private company, and do not enjoy the facilities for raising money by a public issue possessed by public companies. They were the owners of a large and valuable block of property, and, so far as we know, they had no other assets. The property was subject to a mortgage at a high rate of interest, and this mortgage was liable to be called in at any time. In these circumstances, the respondents were, when the negotiations began, desirous of obtaining for themselves two advantages, (i) a reduction in the rate of interest, and (ii) the right to repay the mortgage moneys by instalments spread over a long period of years. The desirability of obtaining these terms from a business point of view is manifest, and it is not to be assumed that these respondents were actuated by anything but pure considerations of business in seeking to obtain them. The sum involved was a very large one, and the length of the period over which the instalments were spread is to be considered with reference to this fact. In the circumstances, it was the most natural thing in the world that the respondents should address themselves to a body desirous of obtaining a long-term investment for its money. The resulting agreement was a commercial agreement between two important corporations experienced in such matters, and has none of the features of an oppressive bargain where the borrower is at the mercy of an unscrupulous lender. In transactions of this kind, it is notorious that there is competition among the large insurance companies and other bodies having large funds to invest, and we are not prepared to view the agreement made as anything but a proper business transaction. It is said, however, not only that the period of postponement must be a reasonable one, but also that, in judging the 'reasonableness' of the period, the considerations which we have mentioned cannot be regarded, and that the court is bound to judge 'reasonableness' by a consideration of the terms of the mortgage deed itself, without regard to extraneous matters. In the absence of clear authority, we emphatically decline to consider a question of 'reasonableness' from a standpoint so unreal. To hold that the law is to tell business men what is reasonable in such circumstances, and to refuse to take into account the business considerations involved, would bring the law into disrepute. Fortunately, we do not find ourselves forced to come to any such conclusion. . . .

31.4 Collateral Advantages

31.4.1 VALIDITY WHILE THE MORTGAGE SUBSISTS

MULTISERVICE BOOKBINDING LTD v *MARDEN* [1978] 2 All ER 489, Chancery Division

FACTS: A clause in a mortgage deed provided for the capital repayments to increase proportionate to the decrease in value of the pound sterling against the Swiss franc ('the Swiss franc uplift'). The question was whether such a clause was an invalid collateral advantage.
HELD: The clause was valid as being neither oppressive or unconscionable.

BROWNE-WILKINSON J: I turn then to the question whether the mortgage is unconscionable or unreasonable. The plaintiffs' starting point on this aspect of the case is a submission that a lender on mortgage is only entitled to repayment of principal, interest and costs. If the lender additionally stipulates for a premium or other collateral advantage the court will not enforce such additional stipulation unless it is reasonable. Then it is submitted that cl 6 (providing for the payment of the Swiss franc uplift in addition to the nominal amount of capital and interest) is a premium which in all the circumstances is unreasonable. Alternatively it is said that the terms of the mortgage taken together are unreasonable. In my judgment the argument so advanced is based on a false premise. Since the repeal of the usury laws there has been no general principle that collateral advantages in mortgages have to be 'reasonable'. . . .

I therefore approach the second point on the basis that, in order to be freed from the necessity to comply with all the terms of the mortgage, the plaintiffs must show that the bargain, or some of its terms, was unfair and unconscionable; it is not enough to show that, in the eyes of the court, it was unreasonable.

In my judgment a bargain cannot be unfair and unconscionable unless one of the parties to it has imposed the objectionable terms in a morally reprehensible manner, that is to say, in a way which affects his conscience.

The classic example of an unconscionable bargain is where advantage has been taken of a young, inexperienced or ignorant person to introduce a term which no sensible well-advised person or party would have accepted. But I do not think the categories of unconscionable bargains are limited; the court can and should intervene where a bargain has been procured by unfair means.

. . . The defendant made a hard bargain. But the test is not reasonableness. The parties made a bargain which the plaintiffs, who are businessmen, went into with their eyes open, with the benefit of independent advice, without any compelling necessity to accept a loan on these terms and without any sharp practice by the defendant. I cannot see that there was anything unfair or oppressive or morally reprehensible in such a bargain entered into in such circumstances. . . .

CONSUMER CREDIT ACT 1974

137. Extortionate credit bargains
  (1) If the court finds a credit bargain extortionate it may reopen the credit agreement so as to do justice between the parties.
  (2) In this section and sections 138 to 140—
    (a) 'credit agreement' means any agreement between an individual (the 'debtor') and any other person (the 'creditor') by which the creditor provides the debtor with credit of any amount, and
    (b) 'credit bargain'—
      (i) where no transaction other than the credit agreement is to be taken into account in computing the total charge for credit, means the credit agreement, or
      (ii) where one or more other transactions are to be so taken into account, means the credit agreement and those other transactions, taken together.

138. When bargains are extortionate

(1) A credit bargain is extortionate if it—

(a) requires the debtor or a relative of his to make payments (whether unconditionally, or on certain contingencies) which are grossly exorbitant, or

(b) otherwise grossly contravenes ordinary principles of fair dealing.

(2) In determining whether a credit bargain is extortionate, regard shall be had to such evidence as is adduced concerning—

(a) interest rates prevailing at the time it was made,

(b) the factors mentioned in subsections (3) to (5), and

(c) any other relevant considerations.

(3) Factors applicable under subsection (2) in relation to the debtor include—

(a) his age, experience, business capacity and state of health; and

(b) the degree to which, at the time of making the credit bargain, he was under financial pressure, and the nature of that pressure.

(4) Factors applicable under subsection (2) in relation to the creditor include—

(a) the degree of risk accepted by him, having regard to the value of any security provided;

(b) his relationship to the debtor; and

(c) whether or not a colourable cash price was quoted for any goods or services included in the credit bargain.

(5) Factors applicable under subsection (2) in relation to a linked transaction include the question how far the transaction was reasonably required for the protection of debtor or creditor, or was in the interest of the debtor.

DAVIES v *DIRECTLOANS LTD* [1986] 2 All ER 783, Chancery Division

FACTS: The terms of a loan granted to a co-habiting couple to enable them to buy a house included an interest rate of 21.6% at a time when the market rate was approximately 17%. The couple's income was uncertain (they were professional artists) and they were unable to borrow from institutional lenders. When the mortgagors fell behind with repayments the mortgagee brought proceedings for possession. Before those proceedings were heard the plaintiffs managed to sell their property to an estate agent. The present action was brought to re-open the charge on the basis that it had been an 'extortionate credit bargain' within the terms of the Consumer Credit Act 1974, s. 138.

HELD: In view of the uncertain security against which the mortgagee had risked the loan, and in view of the fact that the loan had been made with the independent advice of a solicitor, the high rate of interest could not be described as 'extortionate' under s. 138 of the Consumer Credit Act 1974.

EDWARD NUGEE QC: On these facts the question posed by s. 138(1)(a) of the 1974 Act is whether the defendant has proved that the legal charge required the plaintiffs to make payments which were not grossly exorbitant. These words are not defined by the Act and must be given their ordinary meaning. 'Exorbitant' is defined by the *Shorter Oxford English Dictionary* as 'Exceeding ordinary or proper bounds; excessive; outrageously large'; 'grossly' is defined as 'excessively; flagrantly'. . . .

However that may be, whether the word 'grossly' adds any additional weight or not, I am more than satisfied that the payments which the defendant required the plaintiffs to make in the present case fall far short of rendering the credit bargain constituted by the legal charge extortionate within the meaning of s. 138 of the 1974 Act. I take into account that the rate of interest was fixed throughout the term of the mortgage (although the plaintiffs could, of course, redeem at any time if they could obtain finance more cheaply elsewhere or they wished to sell). But this is an inevitable feature of an agreement under which a loan is repayable by equal fixed instalments over a period of years, and one that may operate in favour of either party. Rates of interest in general rose substantially between the date of the contract and the date of the legal charge, but the defendant did not increase the rate of interest which it required the plaintiffs to pay, although by the date of the legal charge it was under no legal obligation to abide by the original terms of the brokerage agreement. Rates fell again during the period between the date of the legal charge and its redemption, but the building society rate never fell as low as it was at the date of the contract.

Counsel for the plaintiffs asked that, if the bargain was reopened, it should be on the basis that the proper rate of interest to charge was 18%. Although I accept his submission that the court should be astute to protect borrowers, and indeed this is clearly the policy underlying the 1974 Act, I cannot regard the difference between the 18% which he submitted was proper and the 21.6% which the defendant actually charged as anywhere near large enough to render the latter grossly exorbitant. Similarly there is in my judgment nothing in the terms of the legal charge or in any other of the facts in this case which comes anywhere near satisfying the terms of s. 138(1)(b) and rendering the credit bargain one which grossly contravenes ordinary principles of fair dealing.

Sir John Donaldson MR said in *Wills* v *Wood* [1983] CCLR 7 at 15:

It is, of course, clear that the Consumer Credit Act 1974 gives and is intended to give the court the widest possible control over credit bargains which, for a variety of reasons, might be considered 'extortionate'. But the word is 'extortionate', not 'unwise'. The jurisdiction seems to me to contemplate at least a substantial imbalance in bargaining power of which one party has taken advantage.

If the plaintiffs appear in retrospect to have been unwise, their lack of wisdom lay in contracting to buy the house at a time when their finances were not established on a sufficiently firm foundation. Given that initial decision, which was taken with the full benefit of advice from their own solicitor, I do not consider that it was unwise of them to have entered into the legal charge so as to enable them to complete the contract; and I am wholly satisfied that the defendant did not, either then or at the earlier contract stage, take advantage of such imbalance in bargaining power as existed, and that there was nothing extortionate about the terms of the legal charge. Accordingly the plaintiffs' claim fails and I dismiss this action.

31.4.2 COLLATERAL ADVANTAGES AFTER REDEMPTION

JAMES BRADLEY AND WILLIAM M BRADLEY v *CARRITT* [1902] AC 253,
House of Lords

FACTS: The mortgagor was the controlling shareholder of a tea company. The mortgagor was not the tea company itself, which of course is in law a separate person. The property mortgaged was the shares themselves. The mortgagee was a tea-broker. The mortgage included a collateral advantage under which the mortgagor promised that the mortgagee should always remain broker to the company.
HELD: The mortgagor, having paid off the mortgage, was released from the promise of permanent employment for the mortgagee.

LORD DAVEY: . . . In the present case the agreement is that the appellant W M Bradley will, 'as a shareholder,' use his best endeavours to secure the sale of the company's teas to the respondent or his firm, and in the event of the teas being sold through another broker will pay to the respondent the amount of the commission which he or his firm might have earned. In other words, he agrees to use the voting power attached to his shares in a particular way for the respondent's benefit. Now, what is a share? It is but a bundle of rights, of which the right of voting at meetings of the company is not the least valuable. My Lords, can it be said that the mortgagee does not retain a hold upon the shares which form the mortgaged property, or that the mortgagor has full redemption of it, when the latter is not free to exercise an important right in such manner as he may think most conducive to his own interests? He may think it advantageous to the company to employ another broker, or that the change would produce a better return on his shares, but if he gives effect to his opinion he incurs what is in effect a heavy penalty. Again, the appellant could not part with or otherwise deal with his shares without losing the influence in the company's counsels which might enable him to secure the performance of the first part of the agreement, or running a serious risk of liability under the second part. . . .

Prima facie a clause in a mortgage contract is limited to the duration of the mortgage relation between the contracting parties. In this clause we have the words 'always hereafter'; but I observe that in two other clauses (the third and the fifth) a similar phrase, 'at any time hereafter,' is used and is limited by the context to the duration of the mortgage. I am disposed to say that the words 'always hereafter,' having regard to the nature and purport of the agreement, in like manner mean at any time hereafter during the currency of the loan. But in the view which I take of the case it is not necessary for me to express a decided opinion on this question.

With regard to the appellant, James Bradley's, agreement, I think it was part of the same transaction and ancillary to the principal agreement, and by way of further security to the respondent and increased remuneration to him for the use of his money. And I am of opinion that it must be construed in the same way, and stand or fall with the principal agreement. . . .

31.4.3   A COLLATERAL ADVANTAGE AS AN INDEPENDENT AGREEMENT

KREGLINGER v *NEW PATAGONIA MEAT AND COLD STORAGE COMPANY LIMITED* [1914] AC 25, Privy Council

FACTS: The meat company were mortgagors, while the mortgagees were a firm of woolbrokers. The mortgage contained a provision that for the next five years the company should not sell any sheepskins to any other person without first offering them to the woolbrokers at the best price obtainable elsewhere. The woolbrokers accepted a slightly reduced rate of interest in return for this guarantee. The mortgagor repaid the debt after only two years.
HELD: The 'sheepskins clause' remained valid for the full five years, even though the mortgagors had redeemed the mortgage. The sheepskins agreement was not a collateral advantage of the mortgage, but was an 'independent' collateral contract, entered into as a condition of obtaining the loan.

VISCOUNT HALDANE LC: . . . My Lords, the question in the present case is whether the right to redeem has been interfered with. And this must, for the reasons to which I have adverted in considering the history of the doctrine of equity, depend on the answer to a question which is primarily one of fact. What was the true character of the transaction? Did the appellants make a bargain such that the right to redeem was cut down, or did they simply stipulate for a collateral undertaking, outside and clear of the mortgage, which would give them an exclusive option of purchase of the sheepskins of the respondents? The question is in my opinion not whether the two contracts were made at the same moment and evidenced by the same instrument, but whether they were in substance a single and undivided contract or two distinct contracts. Putting aside for the moment considerations turning on the character of the floating charge, such an option no doubt affects the freedom of the respondents in carrying on their business even after the mortgage has been paid off. But so might other arrangements which would be plainly collateral, an agreement, for example, to take permanently into the firm a new partner as a condition of obtaining fresh capital in the form of a loan. The question is one not of form but of substance, and it can be answered in each case only by looking at all the circumstances, and not by mere reliance on some abstract principle, or upon the *dicta* which have fallen *obiter* from judges in other and different cases. Some, at least, of the authorities on the subject disclose an embarrassment which has, in my opinion, arisen from neglect to bear this in mind. In applying a principle the ambit and validity of which depend on confining it steadily to the end for which it was established, the analogies of previous instances where it has been applied are apt to be misleading. For each case forms a real precedent only in so far as it affirms a principle, the relevancy of which in other cases turns on the true character of the particular transaction, and to that extent on circumstances.

My Lords, if in the case before the House your Lordships arrive at the conclusion that the agreement for an option to purchase the respondents' sheepskins was not in substance a fetter on the exercise of their right to redeem, but was in the nature of a collateral bargain the entering into which was a preliminary and separate condition of the loan, the decided cases cease to present any great difficulty. . . .

There is a further remark which I wish to make about *Bradley* v *Carritt* [1902] AC 253. It is impossible to read the report without seeing that there was a marked divergence of opinion among those members of your Lordships' House who took part in the decision as to the test by which the validity of contracts collateral to a mortgage is to be determined. Lord Davey observes that he cannot understand how, consistently with the doctrine of equity, a mortgagee can insist on retaining the benefit of a covenant in the mortgage contract materially affecting the enjoyment of the mortgaged property after redemption. Lord Lindley, on the other hand, doubts whether the covenant in question, a covenant that the mortgagor would use his influence as a shareholder to secure for the mortgagee in permanence the brokerage business of the company, ought to be looked on as really forming part of the terms of the security. He points out that when the usury laws were in force, and when every device for evading them had to be defeated by equity, the proposition that everything that was part of the mortgage transaction must cease with it, if it was not to infringe the doctrine that once a mortgage always a mortgage, was a convenient statement and as free from objection as most concise statements are, but that when the usury laws were abolished the language was too wide to be accurate.

My Lords, the views expressed by Lord Davey and Lord Lindley are not, so far as mere words go, contradictory. But I cannot shut my eyes to the fact that they represent divergent tendencies. Lord Davey seems to suggest that the doctrine about which, when expressed in general terms, there is little controversy had become finally crystallised in the particular expressions used in certain of the earlier authorities, and that, having become thus rigid, it is to-day fatal to the freedom of mortgagor and mortgagee to make their own bargains, even in cases where the reason for applying the doctrine has ceased to exist. The tendency of Lord Lindley's language is, on the other hand, to treat the application of such a rule as a question in which the Courts must not lose sight of the dominating principle underlying the reasons which originally influenced the terms of the rule, reasons which have, in certain cases, become modified as public policy has changed. Speaking for myself, and notwithsanding the high authority of Lord Davey, I think that the tendency of Lord Lindley's conclusion is the one which is most consonant with principle, and I see no valid reason why this House should not act in accordance with it in the case now under consideration. . . .

31.5 Redemption of Mortgages

31.5.1 MACHINERY OF REDEMPTION

LAW OF PROPERTY ACT 1925

115. Reconveyances of mortgages by endorsed receipts

(1)   A receipt endorsed on, written at the foot of, or annexed to, a mortgage for all money thereby secured, which states the name of the person who pays the money and is executed by the chargee by way of legal mortgage or the person in whom the mortgaged property is vested and who is legally entitled to give a receipt for the mortgage money shall operate, without any reconveyance, surrender, or release—

(a)   Where a mortgage takes effect by demise or subdemise, as a surrender of the term, so as to determine the term or merge the same in the reversion immediately expectant thereon;

(b)   Where the mortgage does not take effect by demise or subdemise, as a reconveyance thereof to the extent of the interest which is the subject matter of the mortgage, to the person who immediately before the execution of the receipt was entitled to the equity of redemption;

and in either case, as a discharge of the mortgaged property from all principal money and interest secured by, and from all claims under the mortgage, but without prejudice to any term or other interest which is paramount to the estate or interest of the mortgagee or other person in whom the mortgaged property was vested.

(2)   Provided that, where by the receipt the money appears to have been paid by a person who is not entitled to the immediate equity of redemption, the receipt shall operate as if the benefit of the mortgage had by deed been transferred to him; unless—

(a)   it is otherwise expressly provided; or

(b)   the mortgage is paid off out of capital money, or other money in the hands of a personal representative or trustee properly applicable for the discharge of the mortgage, and it is not expressly provided that the receipt is to operate as a transfer. . . .

31.6   Consolidation of Mortgages

Consolidation of mortgages occurs where a mortgagee has two mortgages created by the same mortgagor, and insists that if one mortgage is redeemed the other mortgage is redeemed as well. This right of consolidation is of practical value where the mortgagor proposes to repay a well-secured loan, but to leave a poorly-secured loan outstanding. The following conditions must be satisfied for consolidation to be effected:

(a)   At least one of the two mortgages must confer a right of consolidation. (Modern mortgages always include a clause entitling the mortgagee to consolidate.)

(b)   The legal redemption date on each mortgage must be past.

(c)   Both mortgages must have been made by the same mortgagor.

(d)   At some point of time (however long or short) both mortgages were in common ownership, and both equities of redemption were in common ownership.

CHAPTER THIRTY-TWO

PRIORITY OF MORTGAGES OF UNREGISTERED TITLES

32.1 Priority of Mortgages Where an Unregistered Legal Estate is Mortgaged

32.1.1 MORTGAGES REGISTRABLE AS LAND CHARGES

LAND CHARGES ACT 1972

4. Effect of land charges and protection of purchasers

(5) A land charge of Class B and a land charge of Class C (other than an estate contract) created or arising on or after 1st January 1926 shall be void as against a purchaser of the land charged with it, or of any interest in such land, unless the land charge is registered in the appropriate register before the completion of the purchase.

32.1.2 SECTION 97 OF THE LAW OF PROPERTY ACT 1925

LAW OF PROPERTY ACT 1925

97. Priorities as between puisne mortgages

Every mortgage affecting a legal estate in land made after the commencement of this Act, whether legal or equitable (not being a mortgage protected by the deposit of documents relating to the legal estate affected) shall rank according to its date of registration as a land charge pursuant to the Land Charges Act 1925.

This section does not apply [to mortgages or charges to which the Land Charges Act 1972 does not apply by virtue of section 14(3) of that Act (which excludes certain land charges created by instruments necessitating registration under the Land Registration Act 1925), or] to mortgages or charges of registered land. . . .

32.2 Tacking of Further Advances

32.2.1 WHEN CAN A FURTHER ADVANCE BE TACKED?

LAW OF PROPERTY ACT 1925

94. Tacking and further advances

(1) After the commencement of this Act, a prior mortgagee shall have a right to make further advances to rank in priority to subsequent mortgages (whether legal or equitable)—

    (a) if an arrangement has been made to that effect with the subsequent mortgagees; or

(b)   if he had no notice of such subsequent mortgages at the time when the further advance was made by him; or

(c)   whether or not he had such notice as aforesaid, where the mortgage imposes an obligation on him to make such further advances.

This subsection applies whether or not the prior mortgage was made expressly for securing further advances.

(2)   In relation to the making of further advances after the commencement of this Act a mortgagee shall not be deemed to have notice of a mortgage merely by reason that it was registered as a land charge if it was not so registered at the time when the original mortgage was created or when the last search (if any) by or on behalf of the mortgagee was made, whichever last happened.

This subsection only applies where the prior mortgage was made expressly for securing a current account or other further advances.

(3)   Save in regard to the making of further advances as aforesaid, the right to tack is hereby abolished:

Provided that nothing in this Act shall affect any priority acquired before the commencement of this Act by tacking, or in respect of further advances made without notice of a subsequent incumbrance or by arrangement with the subsequent incumbrancer.

(4)   This section applies to mortgages of land made before or after the commencement of this Act, but not to charges registered under the Land Registration Act 1925, or any enactment replaced by that Act.

CHAPTER THIRTY-THREE

MORTGAGES OF REGISTERED LAND

33.1 Introduction

MORTGAGE CORP LTD v NATIONWIDE CREDIT CORP LTD **[1993] 4 All ER 623,**
Court of Appeal

FACTS: X mortgaged a registered property to A by executing a charge. A did not register
the charge or protect its rights in any other way. X then executed a charge in favour of B
who (somewhat unusually) protected its interest by entering an ordinary notice on the
register. The question was whether A or B had priority.
HELD: If B had actually substantively registered its charge, B would undoubtedly have
gained priority. But entering an ordinary notice, while guaranteeing that the mortgage
binds later purchasers/mortgagees, does not give the mortgage priority over an earlier
created right, even though the earlier created right has not been protected by entry on the
register. A had priority, applying the general principle of 'first in time first in right'.

DILLON LJ: One of the oddities in the present case is that it is not clear whether the
plaintiffs' charge was in fact registered as a registered charge before the sale of the property
to the purchasers took place. On the other hand, there is a letter from the Land Registry of
19 March 1991, which says that the plaintiffs' charge had been substantively registered
under s. 26 of the 1925 Act and this is apparently echoed in a further letter from another
representative of the Land Registery. On the other hand, in the only affidavit sworn in the
proceedings, it is said by the plaintiffs' solicitor in relation to the plaintiffs' charge that it
was lodged in the registry for registration against the title in June 1990 but the registration
was still pending at the date of the affidavit, 10 June 1991, which was after completion of
the sale to the purchaser. In these circumstances, we must, I apprehend, conclude that it is
not shown, on the balance of probabilities, that the plaintiffs' charge was substantially
registered as a registered charge. Consequently the defendants do not bring the case within
s. 27(3) of the 1925 Act.
   It is anyhow necessary, however, to turn to s. 52 of the 1925 [Land Registration] Act,
which is concerned with the effect of notice under s. 49 of the Act. Section 52 provides as
follows:

   (1)   A disposition by the proprietor shall take effect subject to all estates, rights, and
   claims which are protected by way of notice on the register at the date of the registration
   or entry of notice of the disposition, but only if and so far as such estates, rights, and
   claims may be valid and are not (independently of this Act) overridden by the
   disposition.
   (2)   Where notice of a claim is entered on the register, such entry shall operate by way
   of notice only, and shall not operate to render the claim valid whether made adversely
   to or for the benefit of the registered land or charge.

The judge construed s. 52(1) as applying only where the document which gave rise to the estate, right or claim protected by the notice on the register had been entered into at a date which was earlier than the date on which the disposition whose registration was in question had been made, that is as he put it, the effect of a notice is limited to giving priority to a person who has registered the notice only in relation to interests granted subsequently to his interest.

As I read s. 52(1), the opening part applies generally irrespective of the date of the execution of the document which gave rise to the estate, right or claim protected by the notice on the register or the date of the making of the rival disposition which is to be registered or to be the subject of the entry of a later notice. So far as the opening part is concerned, the only relevant date is the date of registration or entry of notice. But the general effect of the opening part is then cut down by the final proviso, *viz*:

> . . . but only if and so far as such estates, rights, and claims may be valid and are not (independently of this Act) overridden by the disposition.

In the present case there is no difficulty over the first half of that proviso 'so far as such estates, rights, and claims may be valid', since the defendants' charge is unquestionably valid.

It is therefore necessary to consider the second half of the proviso: 'and are not (independently of this Act) overridden by the disposition.' As I see it, independently of the 1925 Act, the defendants' charge is necessarily overridden by the plaintiffs' charge. If, by virtue of s. 106, neither charge having been registered, both are regarded as taking effect only in equity, then the equitable rule as to the priorities that *qui prior est tempore potior est jure* applies; if they are considered independently even of s. 106 of the 1925 Act, then they are both charges by way of legal mortgage, and the later, in time, the defendants' charge can only take effect as a charge on the equity of redemption in the property subject to the plaintiffs' charge. I therefore agree with the judge's conclusion, though I am not sure that I have followed quite the same course of reasoning as he did.

In my judgment, s. 52 is enacted to prescribe the effect of a notice entered on the register. That may not necessarily be the same as the effect of a caution since the effect of a caution is prescribed by ss. 54 and 55. The effect of a notice, as determined under s. 52, will cut down any apparently wider effect that the general wording in other sections such as ss. 20 and 27(3) would otherwise have had. The particular qualifications imposed by the proviso to s. 52(1) are, first of all, that the interest protected by the notice must be valid apart from the notice and secondly that the interest protected by the notice would not independently of the 1925 Act be overridden by the rival disposition. Notice is indeed notice, but it does not give validity, if validity is not otherwise there, and it does not give priority which would not, apart from the 1925 Act, have been there. Therefore the plaintiffs' charge has priority to the defendants' charge. . . .

33.2 End of Chapter Assessment Question

'The rules governing the priority of mortgages of an unregistered title are both complex and uncertain. The rules governing the priority of mortgages of a registered title are by comparison straightforward, though the recent case of *Mortgage Corporation* v *Nationwide Credit Corporation* does create a problem for lenders who take a deposit of the land certificate.')

Discuss.

33.3 End of Chapter Assessment Outline Answer

Mortgages of Unregistered Titles

Where the mortgagee takes possession of the title deeds at the time the mortgage is created (usual in the case of a first mortgage)

A mortgage of this nature will not be registrable as a land charge. If the mortgage is legal the mortgagee can lose priority to a later mortgagee in limited circumstances only. Namely, (a) by deliberately (or in gross negligence) permitting the mortgagor to retake possession of the title deeds, thus allowing the mortgagor fraudulently to represent to a new lender that the property is not mortgaged; or (b) by prematurely endorsing a receipt on the mortgagee, thereby giving later mortgagees the impression that the first mortgage has been fully paid off. If the mortgage is equitable the same principles ((a) and (b)) apply. In addition, an equitable mortgage where the mortgagee has taken the title deeds is an example of an equitable interest not registrable as a land charge but still subject to the doctrine of notice. Therefore, such an equitable mortgagee could theoretically lose priority to a later legal mortgagee who took without notice of the earlier equitable mortgage. The risk is purely theoretical, however, because the absence of title deeds in such a case would give any later mortgagee notice of the first mortgage.

Where the mortgagee does not take possession of the title deeds at the time the mortgage is created

In such a case the mortgage will be registrable as a land charge. If it is a legal mortgage it will be a 'puisne' mortgage registrable as a class C(i) land charge. If it is an equitable mortgage it will be a general equitable charge registrable as a class C(iii) land charge. If a registrable mortgage is in fact promptly registered as a land charge then it is bound to have priority over subsequently created mortgages. The real 'complexity and uncertainty' in this area of law arises if a registrable mortgage is not registered, or is registered late (after the creation of a second mortgage of the land). In such a case s. 4(5) of the Land Charges Act 1972 and s. 97 of the Law of Property Act 1925 will apply.

Section 4(5) provides that if a registrable mortgage is not in fact registered it 'shall be void as against a purchaser of the land charged therewith, or any interest in that land'. Accordingly, in the normal course of events, if X grants a registrable mortgage to A which A omits to register, and then X grants a mortgage to B, it is B's mortgage which will have priority.

The picture becomes more confused if we now imagine that B's mortgage is also registrable, but has not been registered. According to s. 4(5) of the Land Charges Act 1972 nothing turns on whether B's mortgage has been registered, but s. 97 of the Law of Property Act 1925 could change the situation entirely. Section 97 provides that 'every mortgage affecting a legal estate in land . . . shall rank according to its date of registration as a land charge pursuant to the Land Charges Act'. If s. 97 is read literally, A, in the example given above, could regain priority over B by registering his mortgage after B has obtained her mortgage, but before B has registered her mortgage as a land charge. In short, there is a conflict in the results which flow from a literal application of ss. 4(5) and 97.

Which section should be followed? The conflict has existed for about 70 years and has not yet been resolved by any decided case, so the question is clearly not an easy one to answer. A literal reading of s. 4(5) suggests that an unregistered mortgage is rendered 'void' against the holder of a subsequent mortgage, and the usual rule is that once an interest in land is void against a purchaser (or mortgagee) subsequent registration cannot make it valid again. In further support of s. 4(5) it could be argued that a literal reading of s. 97 makes it clear that s. 97 is 'pursuant to the Land Charges Act' [see **32.1.1**] and that, accordingly, s. 4(5) of the 1972 Act should be followed.

Nevertheless, another literal reading of s. 97 leads to the clear conclusion that priority between registrable mortgages is to be determined, and to be determined only, according to the date of registration. Perhaps s. 97 will ultimately be favoured, but it would make mortgages distinct from other land charges (which would not be ideal), but it would at least be simple to apply. It would also make the rule for unregistered title similar to that for registered title.

Mortgages of Registered Titles

In contrast to the above, the rule for determining priority of mortgages of a registered title is very straightforward. If there is a series of registered charges, they rank in priority in the order they are entered on the register, not in the order of their creation. The rule is not dissimilar to the rule in s. 97 as applied to land charges in unregistered land, and lends further support to a literal application of s. 97.

Having stated that the rule is relatively straightforward it is true that the recent case of *Mortgage Corporation Ltd* v *Nationwide Credit Corporation Ltd* (1993) [see **33.1** for the facts] does create a problem for lenders who take a deposit of the land certificate instead of substantively registering their mortgage as a 'registered charge' (it is cheaper simply to take a deposit of the land certificate!). In the *Mortgage Corporation* case it was held that mortgagees will only gain priority over earlier unregistered mortgages if they 'substantively register' their mortgage charge. It will not suffice to merely register an 'ordinary notice' of the existence of the mortgage. Lenders who take a deposit of the land certificate do not 'substantively' register their mortgage and their only protection is usually to enter a 'notice' of their mortgage on the registered title at the land registry. Consequently, such lenders may find themselves bound by earlier mortgages even if those earlier mortgages have not been protected in any way. The reason given for this result in the *Mortgage Corporation* case was that if neither mortgage has been registered both mortgages will be deemed (by s. 106 of the Land Registration Act 1925) to take effect only in equity. Then the equitable rule as to priorities will apply, which is *qui prior est tempore potior est jure,* which roughly translates as 'the first in time has priority'. In the future, institutional lenders will no doubt be advised to incur the expense of substantive registration. While registration of a 'notice' is good protection against future mortgagees and purchasers, it is no protection against earlier mortgages affecting the registered title.